THE NAVAL HISTORY OF GREAT BRITAIN

VOLUME THE FIFTH

CAPT. SIR NESBIT WILLOUGHBY.

FROM AN ORIGINAL PICTURE BY BARBER.
IN THE POSSESSION OF LORD MIDDLETON.

THE
NAVAL HISTORY
OF
GREAT BRITAIN

FROM THE DECLARATION OF WAR BY FRANCE
IN 1793
TO THE ACCESSION OF GEORGE IV.

BY

WILLIAM JAMES

*A NEW EDITION, WITH ADDITIONS AND NOTES
BRINGING THE WORK DOWN TO 1827*

VÉRITÉ SANS PEUR

IN SIX VOLUMES
VOL. V.

London
MACMILLAN AND CO., Limited
NEW YORK: THE MACMILLAN COMPANY
1902

All rights reserved

Printed and bound by Antony Rowe Ltd, Eastbourne

CONTENTS.

VOL. V.

1809 (*in continuation*).

LIGHT SQUADRONS AND SINGLE SHIPS, 1—Onyx and Manly, ibid.—Capture of Iris and Hébé, 2—Cleopatra and Topaze, 3—Horatio and consorts with Junon, 4—Boats of Amphion at Melida, 9—Capture of the Var, ibid.—Proserpine with Pénélope and Pauline, 10—Boats of Arethusa at Lequito, 12—Amethyst and Niemen, 13—Capture of the d'Haupoult, 18—Intrepid with Furieuse and Félicité, 22—Capture of Félicité by Latona, 23—Bonne-Citoyenne and Furieuse, ibid.—Goldfinch and Mouche, 27—Boats of Spartan, Amphion, &c., off Pesaro, ibid.—Boats of Spartan and Mercury at Cesenatico, 29—Boats of Scout off Cape Croisette, and at Carri, 30—Topaze with Danaé and Flore, ibid.—Boats of Topaze at Demata, 31—Pomone and Lucien-Charles, 32—Cyane and Cérès, 33—Boats of Excellent and squadron at Duin, 35—Boats of Amphion at Cortelazzo, 36—Boats of Mercury at Rovigno and at Rotti, 37—Same at Barletta, 38—Boats of Melpomêne at Huilbo, ibid.—Boats of Tartar on coast of Courland, ibid.—Melpomêne and Danish gun-boats, 39—Boats of Bellerophon at Hango, ibid.—Boats of Implacable off Porcola, 40—Captain Forrest and Russian gun-boats at Fredericksham, 41—Boats of Lynx and Monkey off Dais head, 42—Diana and Zephyr, 43—Boats of Hazard and Pelorus at Sainte-Marie, 45—Boats of Thetis and consorts at the Hayes, ibid.—Capture of Nisus, 46—Also of Bearnais and Papillon, 47—Junon with Rénommée and consorts, ibid.—British Indiamen and French frigates, 54—Destruction of a nest of pirates, 67.

COLONIAL EXPEDITIONS, COAST OF AFRICA, ibid.—Capture of Sénégal, ibid.

WEST INDIES, 69—Capture of Martinique, ibid.

SOUTH AMERICA, 74—Capture of Cayenne, ibid.

1810.

BRITISH AND FRENCH FLEETS, 78—State of the British navy, ibid.—Sweden declares war, 79—Death of Lord Collingwood, ibid.—Captain Eyre at St. Maura, 80—Captain Blackwood off Toulon, 81—Captain Halliday off Toulon, 84.

LIGHT SQUADRONS AND SINGLE SHIPS, 86—Cherokee and French luggers, ibid.—Scorpion and Oreste, ibid.—Boats of Freija at Mahaut, 87—Thistle and Havik, 90—Rainbow and Avon with Néréide, 91—Boats of Christian VII. &c., in Basque roads, 95—Capture of Canonnière frigate, 97—Horatio and Nécessité, ibid.—Unicorn and Espérance, 98—Tribune and four Danish brigs, ibid.—Boats of Belvidera and Nemesis near Strudtland, 99—Queen Charlotte and Indomptable, ibid.—Boats of Surveillante at the Morbitran, 100 Also at the river Crache, 101—Boats of Caledonia and squadron in Basque roads, ibid.—Boats of Dreadnaught at Ushant, 102—Briseis and Sans-Souci, 103—Calliope and Comtesse d'Hambourg, 104—Orestes and Loup-Garou, ibid.—Boats of Quebec in the Vlie, 105—Diana and Niobe with Amazone and Eliza, 107—Phipps and Barbier-de-Séville, 108—Rosario and Mamelouck, 109—Entreprenante and four French privateers, 110—Rinaldo and Maraudeur, 111—Same with Vieille-Josephine and consorts, 112—Boats of Success at Castiglione, 113—Boats of Spartan and Success at Terreino, 114 —Spartan with Cérès and consorts, ibid.—Boats of Alceste at Agaye, 119— Boats of Amphion and Cerberus at Groa, 120—Captain Hoste and Commodore Dubourdieu, 122—Boats of Thames and consorts at Amanthe, 125 —Captain Hall at Barbate, 127—Boats of Blossom off Cape Sicie, 128— Captain Fane at Palamos, 129—Sylvia and armed prows, 130—British Indiamen and French frigates, 132—Captain Willoughby at Jacolet, 137— Capture of Isle Bourbon, 144—Capture of Isle de la Passe, 146—Captain Willoughby at Pointe du Diable, 149—Same at Isle de la Passe, 151—Captain Pym at Grand Port, 156—Boadicea with Vénus and Manche, 171— Africaine with Iphigénie and Astrée, 173—Ceylon and Vénus, 183.

COLONIAL EXPEDITIONS, WEST INDIES, 190—Capture of Guadaloupe, ibid.— Capture of St. Martin, 191.

EAST INDIES, 191—Capture of Amboyna, ibid.—Capture of Banda Neira, 195—Capture of the Isle of France, 205.

1811.

BRITISH AND FRENCH FLEETS, 206—State of the British Navy, ibid.—Sir Edward Pellew and M. Emeriau, 207.

LIGHT SQUADRONS AND SINGLE SHIPS, 211—Destruction of Amazone, ibid.— Scylla and Canonnier, 212—Diana and Semiramis in the Gironde, 213— Hawk and French convoy, 215—Barbadoes and Goshawk with French gun-brigs, 216—Rinaldo and Redpole with Boulogne flotilla, 217—Naiad and Boulogne flotilla, 218—Capture of the Ville-de-Lyon, 220—Boats of Quebec and consorts on coast of East Friesland, ibid.—Defence of Anholt, 222— Brevdrageren with Langland and consorts, 226—Manly with Loland and consorts, 229—Loss of the St. George, Defence, and Hero, 231—Boats of Active and Cerberus at Pescaro and Ortona, 232—Action off Lissa, 233— **Destruction of Giraffe and Nourrice**, 246—Belle-Poule and Alceste at

Parenza, 247—Alacrity and Abelle, 248—Guadaloupe with Tactique and Guêpe, 253—Boats of Unité at Port Hercule, 255—Boats of same and Cephalus on Roman coast, ibid.—Boats of Thames and Cephalus at Porto del Infreschi, ibid.—Boats of Active at Ragosniza, 256—Boats of Pilot at Strongoli, 257—Boats of Impérieuse at Possitano, 258—Boats of same and Thames at Palinuro, ibid.—Capture of the Corceyre, 260—Alceste and Active with Pauline and consorts, 261—Boats of Sabine at Sabiona, 266—Americans building new Frigates, 267—President and Philadelphia, 269—Dimensions of American Frigates, 271—Little Belt and President, 273—Action off Madagascar, 283.

COLONIAL EXPEDITIONS, EAST INDIES, 295—Capture of Java, 297.

1812.

BRITISH AND FRENCH FLEETS, 311—State of the British navy, ibid.—Russia declares war against France, ibid.—Escape of M. Allemand from Lorient, 312—Vice-admirals Emeriau and Sir Edward Pellew, 315.

LIGHT SQUADRONS AND SINGLE SHIPS, 316—Rosario and Griffon with French flotilla, 317—Recapture of the Appelles, 319—Destruction of the Arienne and Andromaque, 323—Sealark and Ville-de-Caen, 324—Dictator and consorts with Nayaden and consorts, 325—Boat of Briseis at Pillan, 327—Boats of Osprey near Heligoland, 328—Boats of Horatio on coast of Norway, ibid.—Attack and a French privateer, 329—Same and Danish gun-boats, 330—Boats of Medusa at Arcasson, 331—Narrow escape of the Magnificent, 333—Sir Home Popham on north coast of Spain, 335—Captain Ussher on south coast of Spain, 337—Capture of the Merinos, 338—Victorious and Rivoli, ibid.—Boats of Pilot and Thames at Policastro and Sapri, 341—Boats of America and Leviathan at Llanguelia, 342—Same at Alassio, 344—Swallow with Renard and Goéland, 345—Lieutenant Dwyer at Biendom, 347—Boats of Bacchante at Port Lemo, 349—Boats of Eagle at Cape Maistro, 350—Southampton and Améthyste, 351—Chase of the Belvidera, 355—Treatment of a British seaman at New York, 363—Minerva and Essex, 364—Alert and Essex, 365—Rattler and Essex, 367—Shannon and Essex, 368—Chase of the Constitution, 369—Guerrière and Constitution, 372—Frolic and Wasp, 389—Macedonian and United States, 394—President and Congress with Galatea, 407—Java and Constitution, 409—Laura and Diligent, 423.

1813.

BRITISH AND AMERICAN NAVIES, 425—State of the British navy, ibid.—The frigate-classes, ibid.—The sloop-classes, 433—The schooner-classes, 437—On building ships-of-war, 438.

APPENDIX 439
   Annual Abstracts 453
   Notes to Annual Abstracts 457

CONTENTS.

DIAGRAMS.

Action of the Amethyst and Niemen	15
,, Spartan with Ceres and consorts, commencement of action	116
,, Its termination	117

ACTION OFF LISSA.

Grounding of Favourite	235
Retreat of Corona, Danaé, &c.	237
Capture of Bellone and escape of Flore after surrender	239

ACTION OFF MADAGASCAR.

Its commencement	285
Squadrons becalmed	286
Action of the Guerrière and Constitution	379
,, Macedonian and United States	397
,, Java and Constitution	416

NAVAL HISTORY OF GREAT BRITAIN.

LIGHT SQUADRONS AND SINGLE SHIPS.

On the 1st of January, 1809, at daylight, the British brig-sloop Onyx, of eight 18-pounder carronades and two sixes, with 75 men and boys, Captain Charles Gill, cruising in latitude 53° 30′ north, longitude 3° east, discovered on her lee bow a sail standing to the southward. As soon as the Onyx had made the private signal, the stranger, which was the Dutch brig-sloop Manly, of 12 English 18-pounder carronades and four brass sixes (two of them stern-chasers), with 94 men and boys, Captain-lieutenant W. Heneyman, of the Dutch navy, hoisted her colours and hove to, as if prepared for battle. The British brig kept her wind until 8 A.M.; then, being perfectly ready, bore down and brought the Dutch brig to close action. The Manly made several attempts to rake the Onyx, but the superior manœuvring of the latter frustrated every attempt. At 10 h. 30 m. A.M., being much cut up in sails and rigging, and having most of her guns disabled by the close and well-directed fire of her antagonist, the Manly hauled down her colours, with the loss of five men killed and six wounded; while that on the part of the Onyx amounted to only three men wounded: a difference in execution very creditable to the latter's young ship's company, especially considering the difficulty of pointing the guns, in the turbulent state of the sea.

The slight superiority of force was on the side to render the parties about equally matched; and the officers and crew of the Onyx were entitled to great credit for the bravery, as well as skill, they displayed. It gives us pleasure to be able to add, that Captain Gill was immediately made a post captain, and that Lieutenant Edward William Garrett, first of the Onyx, became also promoted to the rank of commander. Having, previously to her capture by the Dutch in the river Ems, been the British gun-brig of the same name, the Manly was permitted to resume her station among her old class-mates in the British navy.

On the 2nd of January, at 11 A.M., being off the Welbank near the Texel, standing to the southward, the British 12-pounder 32-gun frigate Aimable, Captain Lord George Stuart, discovered a strange sail upon her weather-quarter, standing to the northward and eastward. Suspecting her to be an enemy, the Aimable wore round and made all sail; and, at 4 P.M. on the 3rd, after a chase of 24 hours, came alongside of the French ship-corvette Iris, of 22 carronades, 24-pounders, and two long 12 or 8 pounders, with a complement of 140 men, commanded by Captain Joseph-Jean Macquet. After a running fight of a few minutes, the Iris hauled down her colours.

To the credit of the French crew in the use of their guns, the Aimable had her mainmast shot in the head, mainyard shot away in the slings, mizenmast head, mizentopmast, and trysailmast shot away, and her rigging and sails greatly cut up. With all this damage, however, damage which very nearly caused the escape of the French ship, the Aimable had only one seaman and one marine slightly wounded. The loss on board the Iris amounted to two killed and eight wounded.

The Iris had sailed from Dunkerque on the 29th of December, with 640 casks of flour on board, bound to Martinique. She was a ship of 587 tons, launched at Dunkerque, October 12, 1806, and became added to the British navy by the name (an Iris being already in the service) of Rainbow. Her English armament was 20 carronades, 32-pounders, on the main deck, and six carronades, 18-pounders, and two long sixes on the quarter-deck and forecastle, total 28 guns: with a net complement of 173 men and boys.

On the 5th of January, at noon, latitude 39° 24' north, and longitude 11° 41' west, the British 38-gun frigate Loire, Captain Alexander Wilmot Schomberg, fell in with the French ship-corvette Hébé, of 18 carronades, 24-pounders, and two long twelves, with a crew of 160 men, commanded by Lieutenant Guillaume Botherel-Labretonnière, in the act of taking a ship and brig. On the Loire's approach, the Hébé bore up and made all sail, deserting her two prizes, and leaving the brig destitute of men. The Loire went immediately in chase, and at 8 P.M. got alongside of the French ship and brought her to close action. The

Hébé defended herself for about 20 minutes, and then hauled down her colours. Neither ship appears to have had a man hurt.

The Hébé was from Bordeaux bound to Santo-Domingo, with 600 barrels of flour. She measured 601 tons, and was afterwards added to the British navy by the name (a Hebe being already in the service) of Ganymede. The armament established upon her was 22 carronades, 32-pounders, on the main deck, and 10 carronades, 18-pounders, and two sixes, on the quarter-deck and forecastle, total 34 guns ; with a net complement of 173 men and boys.

On the 22nd of January, at 7 A.M., the British 18-gun ship-sloop Hazard, Captain Hugh Cameron, cruising off Guadaloupe, discovered in the south-west a ship and schooner standing in for the land. The schooner presently steered a different course, seemingly to induce the Hazard to follow her; but the British sloop, in a very gallant manner, bore up for the ship, which was the French 40-gun frigate Topaze, Captain Pierre-Nicolas Lahalle, from Brest since the early part of December, with 1,100 barrels of flour, bound to Cayenne ; but, having found that port blockaded by a "superior force," she was now on her way to Guadaloupe. At 9 A.M. the British 12-pounder 32-gun frigate Cleopatra, Captain Samuel John Pechell, hove in sight, in the south-east, and about the same time the 38-gun frigate Jason, Captain William Maude, made her appearance to the southward. Thus hemmed in, the Topaze had no alternative but to haul close in-shore ; which she accordingly did, and at 11 A.M. came to an anchor, with springs, under a small battery a little to the southward of Pointe-Noire.

Owing to light and baffling winds, the chasing ships made very slow progress, until about 2 h. 30 m. P.M.; when the regular sea breeze, or east-north-east wind, enabled the Cleopatra to begin working up towards the enemy. At about 4 h. 30 m. P.M. the Cleopatra got within 200 yards of the shore, and within half-musket shot of the Topaze. The latter immediately opened her fire ; and, as soon as she had anchored with springs upon her opponent's starboard bow, the Cleopatra did the same. In a short time, having had her outside spring shot away, the Topaze swang in-shore, with her head towards the Cleopatra ; who thereupon raked the French frigate with destructive effect, and so well maintained her position, that the Topaze could not, at any time afterwards, get more than half her broadside to bear. At the expiration of 40 minutes from the commencement of the firing, in which the battery on shore had, from the first, taken a part, the Jason and Hazard came up. While the Hazard cannonaded the battery, the Jason brought to on the starboard quarter of the Topaze, and opened a fire from her bow guns. Thus assailed, the French frigate had no chance of escape, and therefore, at 5 h. 20 m. P.M., hauled down her colours.

Neither the Jason nor the Hazard sustained any injury from the frigate or the battery; and the damages of the Cleopatra, on account of the secure position she had taken and the high firing of her antagonist, were chiefly confined to her rigging. The loss on board the Cleopatra, for the same reason, amounted to only two seamen killed and one wounded. The Topaze was tolerably struck in the hull, especially about the bows, and had, as acknowledged by her officers, 12 men killed and 14 wounded, out of a complement, including 100 soldiers, of about 430 men. One-third of these, when the frigates surrendered, took to the water; and several must have been drowned, or killed by the Jason's shot, in attempting to reach the shore. The Topaze, the same that, in July 1805, captured the Blanche,[1] was added to the British navy under the name of Alcmène, a Topaze being already in the service.

On the 8th of February, at 2 P.M., the British 16-gun brig-sloop Asp, Captain Robert F. Preston, and 14-gun brig-sloop Supérieure (with only, it appears, four of her carronades, 18-pounders, on board), Captain William Ferrie, cruising to the southward of the Virgin islands, discovered and chased a ship standing to the northward, with the wind at east-north-east. At 3 P.M. the leading brig, the Supérieure, having got into the latter's wake, tacked and stood directly for her. The ship, then about seven miles ahead, was the French 40-gun frigate Junon, Captain Jean-Baptiste-Augustin Rousseau, from the Saintes four days, bound to France. At 11 h. 30 m. P.M., when distant full four miles to windward of her consort, and about two astern of the Junon, the Supérieure fired a shot at the latter to bring her to; but the frigate, very naturally, disregarded the summons and pursued her route to the northward. In the course of the night the Asp dropped completely out of sight, and at daylight on the 9th the Supérieure and Junon were left to themselves At 8 A.M., just as the Virgin-Gorda bore from the Supérieure north-west by north distant five or six miles, the latter fired several shot at 'the frigate; who, at 10 A.M., hoisted French

[1] See vol. iv., p. 39.

colours, and fired two harmless broadsides at the brig, then about two miles off, on her lee-quarter. Even this did not check the ardour of Captain Ferrie. The Supérieure merely tacked to avoid a repetition of the salute, and then again pursued the French frigate; who, after bearing away to fire, hauled up again on the starboard tack, with the wind now at north-east by east. In the afternoon the 38-gun frigate, Latona, Captain Hugh Pigott, made her appearance to leeward, and joined in the chase.

On the 10th, at daylight, the Supérieure had the Junon on her starboard and weather-bow 12 miles off, and the Latona at about the same distance on her lee-quarter; all three vessels upon a wind, as before, steering about north by west. The brig soon shortened her distance from the Junon, but the Latona rather increased hers; and, from her great superiority of sailing over the latter, the Junon would no doubt have escaped, had not, at 10 h. 30 m. A.M., latitude 19° 50′ north, longitude 61° 30′ west, an enemy suddenly hove in sight upon her weather bow. This was the British 38-gun frigate Horatio, Captain George Scott, steering on the opposite or larboard tack south by east, and having astern of her, at the distance of about 15 miles, the 18-gun ship-sloop Driver, Captain Charles Claridge. At noon, having made out the Horatio to be an enemy's frigate, the Junon put right before the wind; but, in less than half an hour, perceiving the Latona standing across her path, hauled up again, and, having previously hoisted French colours, resumed her course to the northward, Captain Rousseau rightly considering that, if he could disable the weathermost frigate, he should, in all probability, be able to outsail the one that was to leeward.

At 36 minutes past noon the Horatio and Junon met on opposite tacks, and exchanged broadsides in passing. The Horatio then wore, with the intention of engaging her opponent to leeward; but the Junon wore almost at the same instant, and, having run a short distance to leeward, hauled up again on the starboard tack. In the meanwhile the Horatio, having come round more quickly, raked the Junon astern with her larboard broadside. The Horatio then ranged up alongside of her antagonist to windward; and the two frigates, running on upon the starboard tack, became closely and warmly engaged. At 0 h. 50 m. P.M. Lieutenant Manley Hall Dixon, first of the Horatio, was badly wounded by a musket-ball, which entered his left groin and passed through his thigh; and at 1 h. 10 m. P.M.

Captain Scott received a severe wound in the shoulder by a grape-shot. The command now devolved upon Lieutenant the Hon. George Douglas. At 1 h. 25 m. the Horatio had her main and mizentopmasts shot away, and at the same moment descried the Latona, at the distance of about eight miles upon her larboard and lee quarter, close hauled upon the starboard tack, standing towards her.

By 2 h. 12 m. P.M., besides the loss of her main and mizentopmasts, the Horatio had had her mainmast badly wounded, and foretopgallantmast shot away; also the foretopsail-tie and lifts, which brought the yard on the cap, and left her with only the foresail set. At this moment the Junon, having only her foretopsail-tie shot away, was enabled to range ahead out of gunshot. Now was the time for the Driver to have rendered assistance; but that sloop, although her signal to make more sail had been hoisted at 2 P.M., was still two miles distant on the Horatio's starboard-bow. The Supérieure, however, was near at hand, and raked the Junon, as the latter, with her three masts standing certainly, but with scarcely any rigging to support them, and with her sails all flying about and hull visibly shattered, put away nearly before the moderate breeze, which the previous heavy cannonade had then left blowing.

At 2 h. 24 m. P.M., Lieutenant Douglas hailed the Supérieure, and directed the brig to take the Horatio in tow, to enable her the more quickly to get again alongside of her antagonist. The Supérieure did as she had been ordered; but the Horatio, having set her foretopsail and hauled aft her main sheet, was presently going upwards of five knots with the wind on the quarter, and the brig cast her off. At 2 h. 40 m. P.M. the Driver fired her bow-chasers at the Junon, then nearly a mile distant from her. This sloop continuing to yaw about as if she was afraid to advance, the Horatio, at 2 h. 50 m. P.M. directed the Supérieure to make the Driver's signal to engage more closely.

Having, agreeably to his orders, hoisted this signal, and doubting, as it was not obeyed, whether it was rightly understood, Captain Ferrie resolved himself to show its practical meaning. Accordingly, at 3 h. 4 m. P.M., the Supérieure hauled across the French frigate's stern and gave her a broadside, in a very gallant style; but, having only two 18-pounders, not in so effectual a manner as the Driver might have done with her eight 24-pounders.

Finding that the force of example was in the present instance thrown away, the Horatio, at 3 h. 10 m. P.M., repeated the

Driver's signal to engage more closely, with two guns shotted. This produced some effect, for in five minutes the sloop set her foresail and steered towards the Junon, who was now firing at the Latona, as the latter was advancing to engage her. At 3 h. 25 m. P.M. the Latona, having arrived within pistol-shot, opened her broadside; and shortly afterwards the Driver, becoming more bold from having so efficient a consort, hauled across the French frigate's stern and discharged her broadside, receiving in return from the Junon's chase-guns a fire that cut away her foretopsail-tie and wounded one seaman. In five minutes after this, being closely pressed by the Latona, the Junon hauled up on the starboard tack, and had scarcely come to the wind, when her previously wounded main and mizenmasts, unable to resist the lateral pressure against them, fell over the side. The French frigate instantly struck her colours. This was at 3 h. 40 m. P.M., and in two minutes more the Junon's foremast fell over her bows. When that took place the Horatio was not above a mile and a half distant, with her starboard foretopmast and lower studding-sails set, rapidly approaching.

The Horatio, out of a crew on board of about 270 men and boys, had one midshipman (George Gunter) and six seamen killed, her captain, first-lieutenant (Manley Hall Dixon), boatswain (Andrew Lock), and 14 seamen badly, and one lieutenant of marines (Richard Blakeney), one master's mate (Robert King), and seven seamen and marines slightly wounded; and the Latona, one midshipman (John Hoope) and five seamen slightly wounded; making, with the Driver's one wounded, the total loss on the British side amount to seven killed and 33 wounded. From the number of shot-holes low down in her hull, the Junon was in a very leaky state; and her loss was very severe, amounting, out of a very fine crew of 323 men and boys, to 130 in killed and wounded, including among the mortally wounded her gallant commander.

As the Horatio and Junon each mounted 46 guns of nearly the same caliber, had they met singly, a fairer match could not have been desired; and, notwithstanding the skilful and resolute manner in which the Junon was manœuvred and fought, the relative damage and loss sustained by the two ships leaves it scarcely doubtful which combatant would have ultimately gained the victory. That the Junon, when at 2 h. 12 m. P.M., she made off from the Horatio, was in an unmanageable and defenceless state, may be inferred from her running to leeward directly into the fire of another enemy's ship: whereas, could she have hauled to the wind, her escape would have been certain, as the Horatio could set no after-sail to enable her to chase in that direction. Moreover, Lieutenant Jean-Léon Emeric, the French commanding officer, upon the removal of Captain Rousseau from the deck, declared that nearly all the injury done to the Junon, both in *matériel* and *personnel*, arose from the fire of the Horatio. When, also, the Latona's officer came on board to take possession, M. Emeric refused to deliver up his sword until the arrival of an officer from the Horatio—pointing to her; and Lieutenant John James Hough, third of that ship, presently afterwards came on board and received it. The case, in other respects, displays nothing very striking, unless it be the conduct of Captain Ferrie of the Supérieure, who, in his little vessel, so closely and perseveringly pursued the French frigate; and who, during the action between the Junon and the Horatio, did more with his four guns than the commander of another sloop that was present did with his 18, and those, too, of a heavier caliber.

The prize was nearly a new frigate, and of rather larger dimensions than the Horatio, who was herself one of the finest British-built frigates of the 18-pounder class. The Junon was carried to Halifax, Nova Scotia, and, as soon as repaired, was commissioned under the same name, as a cruising frigate in the British navy.

A contemporary, contrary to his usual practice, has been induced to give a somewhat detailed account of the action, which ended in the surrender of the Junon. Were it not for one circumstance, the source of his information might be gathered from the following paragraph : " This, we believe to be as accurate and impartial an account of the action as can be found. It differs a little from others, but we have merely placed Captain Pigott in his proper position, without taking away from the merits of Captain Scott and the Horatio."[1] We cannot suppose that any officer of the Latona would have made so gross a mistake respecting the " position " of that ship, as to say that she wore and " renewed the action on the larboard tack." We have now before us the log of every British ship that was present; and we may add, that those logs, coupled with private information of the highest authenticity, form the groundwork of our account of the Latona's proceedings. With respect to the Horatio's "throwing in stays under the stern of the Frenchman," it is sufficient to remind the reader, that the Horatio

[1] Brenton, vol. iv., p. 376.

engaged the Junon to windward. We leave it to Captain Brenton himself to reconcile the statement that the Junon, when she bore up, left "the Horatio a perfect wreck to windward," with that disclaiming any intention of "taking away from the merits of Captain Scott and the Horatio."

On the 8th of February the British 18-pounder 32-gun frigate Amphion, Captain William Hoste, cruising off Long island in the Adriatic, was joined by the British 18-gun brig-sloop Redwing, Captain Edward Augustus Down, with information that an armed brig and a trabacculo were lying in a small creek in the island of Melida. The frigate and sloop immediately made sail in that direction, and found the two vessels advantageously moored for defending the entrance of the creek; with a body of soldiers, which they had brought from Zara and were carrying to Ancona, drawn up behind some houses and walls.

A long 12-pounder on the shore, and the brig, which mounted six 10-pounder carronades, opened upon the Amphion and Redwing, as the latter were taking their position. The instant, however, that the British vessels brought their broadsides to bear, the French troops, 400 in number, as afterwards ascertained, fled in all directions, leaving the two vessels to their fate. The boats of the Amphion and Redwing, under the orders of Lieutenant Charles George Rodney Phillott, now landed and brought off three guns, and destroyed two warehouses of wine and oil. Nor, such was the panic spread among them by the cannon of the ships, did the French soldiers offer the least opposition to the British seamen and marines employed on this service.

On the 14th of February, in the morning, the British 38-gun frigate Belle-Poule, Captain James Brisbane, having been driven by a hard southerly gale about 12 leagues to the northward of the island of Corfu, discovered a suspicious vessel far distant on the lee bow. All sail was immediately made in pursuit; but, light and partial winds coming on, the Belle-Poule chased without success the whole day. Captain Brisbane, however, saw that it was the intention of the stranger, which was the French frigate-built storeship Var, of 22 long 8-pounders and four 24-pounder carronades, with a crew of 200 men, commanded by Captain Paul-François Paulin, to enter the gulf of Velona. The Belle-Poule, accordingly, steered in that direction.

On the 15th, at daybreak, the Var was discovered, moored with cables to the walls of the fortress of Velona, mounting 14 long 18 and 24 pounders; and, upon an eminence above the ship, and completely commanding the whole anchorage, was another strong fort. A breeze at length favouring her, the Belle-Poule, at 1 P.M., anchored in a position to take or destroy the Var, and at the same time to keep in check the formidable force prepared apparently to defend the French ship. The Belle-Poule immediately opened upon the latter an animated and well-directed fire; and, as the forts made no effort to protect her, the Var discharged a few random shot, which hurt no one, and then hauled down her colours. Before she could be taken possession of, her officers and the greater part of her crew escaped to the shore. The Var measured 777 tons, and was added to the British navy as a storeship under the name of Chichester.

At or about the commencement of the present year the British 18-pounder 32-gun frigate Proserpine, Captain Charles Otter, by the orders of Vice-admiral Thornborough, took her station off the road of Toulon, to watch the movements of the French fleet. The boldness of her approaches at length determined Vice-admiral Ganteaume to detach a force to chase her away. Accordingly, on the 27th of February, the two 40-gun frigates Pénélope, Captain Bernard Dubourdieu, and Pauline, Captain François-Gilles Montfort, weighed and sailed out to execute that service. They in a short time discovered the Proserpine, and the latter, as she was bound, retired before them; but, no sooner had the two frigates put about to return, than the Proserpine put about also, in chase of several small sail of coasting-vessels, running along-shore towards Marseille. Failing in cutting off the convoy, the Proserpine stood off for the night, and in a short time lay nearly becalmed.

The French admiral now formed an excellent plan for surrounding and capturing the British frigate. At 8 P.M. the Pénélope and Pauline got under way, and were quickly followed by the 40-gun frigate Pomone; also by the two fast-sailing 74-gun ships Ajax and Suffren, Captains Jean-Nicolas Petit and Auguste-François Louvel. The two first-named frigates worked to the westward, under the high land of Cape Sicie, upon short tacks, with variable winds. At about 1 A.M. on the 28th, the moon rose in the north-east; thereby casting the ships that were under the land in complete shade, and throwing a light upon objects in the offing. Thus favoured, the Pénélope and Pauline, at 2 A.M., discovered in the south-west by south the unsuspecting Proserpine, lying becalmed, with her head directed towards them. The two French frigates immediately bore up under all sail, before a freshening land-wind from the east-north-east. We will now take the account as given by the Proserpine herself.

At 4 A.M., Cape Sicie bearing north-east by north, distant 12 or 13 miles, the Proserpine discovered the two French frigates steering towards her from under the land. Having no doubt that they were enemies, Captain Otter, taking advantage of a light breeze which that moment sprang up from the east-south-east, wore on the larboard tack, and made all sail; just keeping near enough to the wind to permit the larboard topgallant studding-sails to draw. For the double purpose of being used as chasers, and of bringing the ship more by the stern to quicken her sailing, the two foremost 18-pounders were removed to the cabin. Before, however, they could be pointed through the ports, the two French frigates had arrived within gun-shot.

At about 4 h. 25 m. A.M., Captain Otter hailed the Pénélope, then approaching upon the larboard quarter. The French frigate answered by a single gun. Upon this the British crew were ordered to their quarters; and while the drum was rolling for that purpose, the Pénélope opened her broadside upon the Proserpine's larboard quarter. This was at 4 h. 30 m. A.M.; and almost at the same instant the Pauline commenced firing into the British frigate's starboard quarter. The fire was returned by the Proserpine, but not in so effective a manner as it might have been, the two guns, that had been brought into the cabin, disabling the two aftermost guns on the larboard side. The same untoward circumstance prevented any return to the raking fire kept up by the Pauline upon the Proserpine's stern and starboard quarter.

At 4 h. 40 m. A.M. the Pénélope ranged up alongside within pistol-shot of her opponent, and several broadsides were exchanged. The Pauline, in the meanwhile, preserved her station upon the Proserpine's starboard quarter, and continued to direct her fire chiefly at the latter's rigging and sails. By 5 h. 10 m. A.M. the Proserpine had her maintopsail-yard shot away, foremast half cut through nine or ten feet from the deck, main and mizen masts, mainyard, and foretopsail-yard badly wounded, and her stays, shrouds, braces, bowlines, and the whole of the running rigging destroyed: the Pénélope was also on her larboard bow, and the Pauline on her starboard quarter, each preparing to board. Being in this hopeless situation, the British frigate hauled down her colours.

The proper complement of the Proserpine was 251; but,

having manned some prizes, she had only 211 men and boys on board. Of these the Proserpine had one seaman killed, and 10 seamen and marines (including one mortally) wounded. As if ashamed of their very indifferent gunnery, the French officially declared, that the Proserpine's loss amounted to 11 killed and 15 wounded. But the guns on the British side appear to have been discharged with even less effect. For, according to the French accounts, neither the Pénélope nor the Pauline had a man killed or wounded; and the latter frigate suffered not at all, and the former very slightly, in the rigging and sails. "Notre bonheur est tel que, quoique nous avons combattu vergue à vergue et du nuit, la Pénélope et la Pauline n'ont pas eu un seul homme de tué, ni de blessé. La Pénélope a eu quelques avaries dans son gréement, et la Pauline, par la position habile qu'elle a su conserver, n'a nullement souffert."[1]

At daybreak, which was just as the two French frigates had taken possession of their prize, the two 74s were discovered about seven miles in the east-north-east, approaching under all sail; and shortly afterwards the Pomone made her appearance in the south-east. Captain Otter continued in France as a prisoner until the conclusion of the war. On the 30th of October, 1814, the captain and late officers and crew of the Proserpine were tried by a court-martial for the loss of their ship, and most honourably acquitted.

On the 15th of March, early in the morning, the British 38-gun frigate Arethusa, Captain Robert Mends, cruising off the north coast of Spain, detached her boats under the orders of Lieutenant Hugh Pearson and Lieutenant of marines Octavius Scott. At daylight these officers, with the seamen and marines under their command, landed, and destroyed upwards of 20 heavy guns mounted on the batteries at Lequito, defended by a detachment of French soldiers; a sergeant and 20 of whom, when the British forced the guard-house in the principal battery, threw down their arms and begged for quarter. These were made prisoners, but the rest of their comrades effected their escape by running. Notwithstanding a smart fire of musketry from the battery and guard-house as Lieutenant Pearson and his party advanced, this very gallant exploit was performed with so slight a loss as three men wounded. A small chaloupe, laden with brandy, was found in the harbour and brought away.

On the 16th, in the evening, having received information of two chasse-marées, laden with brandy for the French army in

[1] Moniteur, March 7, 1809.

Spain, being up the river Andero, the same party again landed, and found the vessels aground four miles up the river. The cargoes were destroyed: but the vessels having been forcibly taken from the Spaniards by the French, were restored to their owners.

On the 20th Lieutenant Elms Steele, with a party of seamen and marines, landed and destroyed the guns at Baigno, and captured a small vessel laden with merino wool, which had run in there for security, and was from San-Andero bound to Bayonne. In the mean time Lieutenant of marines John Fennele, accompanied by Mr. John Elliott the purser, and a boat's crew, ascended the mountain and destroyed the signal-posts. On the same evening, also, Lieutenant Pearson, with the officers and men who were with him at Lequito, took possession of the batteries of the town of Paissance, without opposition, and destroyed the guns; the small French force stationed at all the above places retiring as the British approached.

On the 5th of April, at 11 A.M., the Cordouan lighthouse bearing east by north, distant 42 leagues, the British 18-pounder 36-gun frigate Amethyst, still commanded by Captain Michael Seymour, standing about a point free on the larboard tack with the wind at east, and having in her company, within signal distance to the northward, or nearly astern, the 18-pounder 36-gun frigate Emerald, Captain Frederick Lewis Maitland, descried, in the east-south-east, a ship steering to the westward; and which, on discovering the two frigates, hauled up to the south-south-east. This was the French 40-gun frigate Niemen, Captain Jean-Henri-Joseph Dupotet, two days from Verdon road, with six months' provisions and a quantity of naval stores on board, bound to the Isle of France.

Both British ships made all sail in chase, and at noon the Niemen was about half-topsails down from the deck of the Amethyst. The chase continued all the afternoon; so little, however, to the advantage of the Amethyst, although a much better sailer than her consort, that at sunset the line of the Niemen's taffrail was all that could be seen from the lower part of the Amethyst's main rigging, bearing a point and a half on her weather or larboard bow. At 7 h. 20 m., which was just as it was getting dark, the Amethyst lost sight both of the Emerald that was astern, and the Niemen that was ahead of her.

Concluding that the French frigate, on getting rid of her

pursuers, would resume her course to the westward, Captain Seymour, at 9 P.M., bore up to south-west. At 9 h. 40 m. P.M., the wind then blowing in squalls from the east-north-east, the Amethyst discovered, on her weather-beam, the ship she was in search of; and who now, as rightly conjectured by Captain Seymour, was steering to the westward. The Amethyst lost no time in giving chase; and the Niemen, having only in view to execute her mission, wore and made all sail with the wind upon the larboard quarter, steering about south by west. At 11 h. 30 m. P.M., the Amethyst began firing her bow-chasers, and was fired at in return by the stern-guns of the Niemen. At 1 h. 15 m. A.M. on the 6th the Amethyst closed upon the Niemen's larboard quarter, and opened her starboard broadside. In return, the Niemen fired her guns on the larboard side, then wore round on the starboard tack, and steered to the north-west. As soon as she could wear and trim sail, the Amethyst hauled up after her opponent; and, as the rigging and sails of the Niemen had already received some damage, the Amethyst, at about 1 h. 45 m. A.M., ranged close alongside of her to wind-ward.

After an exchange of broadsides, the Amethyst, having passed ahead, bore round up, raked the Niemen, and then braced sharp up again on the same tack under the French frigate's lee-bow. At 2 h. 45 m. A.M. the Niemen fell on board the Amethyst, on her starboard beam and quarter; but, in a few minutes, the Amethyst shooting ahead, the Niemen got clear, and bore away south-west. At about 3 A.M. the Amethyst, having crossed over, got upon the larboard and weather beam of the Niemen. Scarcely had the mutual cannonade recommenced between the two ships in this position, ere the Niemen caught fire in her larboard hammock-netting. At 3 h. 15 m. A.M. the Niemen had her mizenmast and maintopmast shot away. The ship had also just caught fire in the maintop, and her mainyard was lowered half way down the mast. In this state the Niemen bestowed little or no return to the animated cannonade maintained by the Amethyst. At 3 h. 25 m. A.M., finding that her antagonist had ceased firing, the Amethyst ceased also, and bore up under her stern. At about 3 h. 30 m. A.M., as the Amethyst, with her mainyard square, was in the act of bringing to to leeward of the Niemen, the mainmast of the British ship, owing chiefly to the quantity of canvas that lay aback against it and the damaged state of the rigging, came down, carrying with it the mizenmast; and the wreck of the two masts fell over the lee quarter. Almost at the same moment the Niemen's mainmast, or what remained of it, came down by the board; and the 38-gun frigate Arethusa, Captain Robert Mends, just then announced to the Amethyst, by signal, her approach from the eastward.

The Amethyst meanwhile, in consequence of the great way upon the ship having caused the spread sails over the lee quarter to act as a back-water, disobeyed her helm, and wore with her stern abreast of the Niemen's starboard and lee beam. At 3 h. 45 m. P.M., while the Amethyst was in this unfortunate position, the Arethusa approached within gun-shot on the larboard quarter of the Niemen, who was then going nearly before the wind. The French ship thereupon hoisted a light, and fired one shot at the Arethusa and another at the Amethyst. The Arethusa then gave a small yaw and fired seven or eight of her foremost larboard guns at the Niemen. To this fire the French frigate made no return, but hauled down her light, and almost instantaneously raised and lowered it again as the signal of submission.

The following diagram will assist in explaining the different movements of the combatants :—

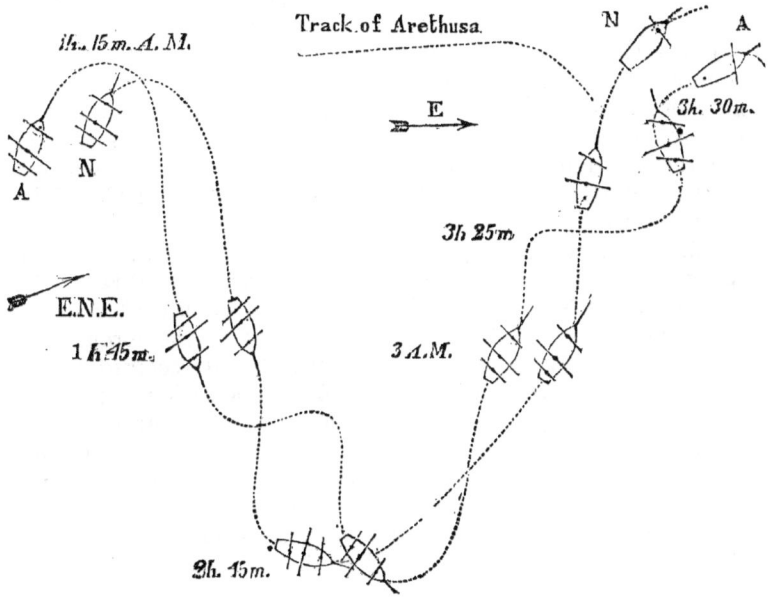

The guns of the Amethyst were precisely those which she mounted in her action with the Thétis; but in complement the frigate was short, having two lieutenants and 37 men absent; all, except one of the lieutenants (who had been appointed, but had not joined) away in prizes, the prisoners from which, 69 in number, were then on board. Of her 222 men and boys, the Amethyst had six seamen and two marines killed, and her first and second lieutenants of marines (Henry Waring and Samuel Prytherch), her boatswain (Mr. Lacey), 24 seamen, and 10 marines wounded.

The armament of the Niemen was the same as that of the Thétis, except that the former mounted two additional 36-pounder carronades, or 14 in all; making her total number of guns 46, two more than are stated in Captain Seymour's letter. The French frigate, whose hull was much cut up by shot, and whose remaining mast was in a tottering state, had on board as her complement, when the action commenced, 339 men and boys; of whom she lost 47 in killed, and 73 in wounded. The Arethusa, not having been fired at except by a single gun, sustained no loss or damage whatever. The same statement of comparative force, given in the action between the Amethyst and Thétis, will, without being more particular, suffice to show the relative force of the Amethyst and Niemen.

Every Englishman who is proud of the martial spirit of his country, must regret that a third party came to interrupt a meeting, which his own, although the numerically weaker side, was so near bringing to a favourable termination. A view of the relative damage and loss sustained by the two frigates, and of their relative means of further annoyance, as displayed by the vigorous fire of the one, and the slackened and still slackening fire of the other, cannot leave a doubt that, at the time the Arethusa made her appearance, the combat between the Amethyst and Niemen was virtually, if not formally, decided.

On the day succeeding that of the capture, the foremast of the Niemen, as a proof of the damage it had received in the action, fell over the side, and the Arethusa took the prize in tow. Being only nine months old, and a remarkably fine frigate, the Niemen became a great acquisition to the British navy; in which, under her French name, she classed the same as the Amethyst's former prize, the Thétis. Captain Seymour, soon after his return to port, was made a baronet of the United Kingdom; and the first-lieutenant of the Amethyst, Mr. William Hill, who, from the absence of two lieutenants, had a double share of duty to perform, was as deservedly promoted to the rank of commander.

That, as Captain Seymour in his official letter is careful to state, "the French captain defended his ship with great ability and resolution," the length of the action, the execution done to the Amethyst, and the circumstances under which the surrender took place, sufficiently testify. And yet the Moniteur of July 13, 1809, contains a letter purporting to be from M. Dupotet, which, if genuine (and there we have our doubts), does not speak much for the French captain's veracity. As may be conjectured, the effect produced by the fall of the Amethyst's main and mizen masts is taken due advantage of. "L'ennemi prit chasse vent arrière, ayant à la traîne ses deux mâts," says M. Dupotet; and he gravely adds :—" Au bout de quinze minutes mon premier lieutenant Valin me fit prévenir que l'ennemi était rendu, et qu'on criait de son bord de ne plus tirer. Je designai l'enseigne Kerangoué pour aller l'amariner; mais bientôt on vit venir une frégate qui venait au secours de celle-ci."

Knowing that Frenchmen, in many of their actions with the British at sea, have mistaken the cheers of triumph for the screams of despair, we pass over the statement that the people of the Amethyst called upon those of the Niemen to cease firing; but the assertion, that the mainmast of the Niemen fell after the Arethusa had opened her fire, is a deliberate falsehood, which can admit of no palliation. Fortunately for the cause of truth, it is disproved in an instant; for thus says the log of the Arethusa :—" At half-past 3, observed both ships going before the wind with only their foremasts standing. At 3h. 45m. commenced firing on the enemy." The assertion, that the foremast of the Amethyst was in a shattered and unsupported state is equally false, although that may have arisen from misinformation. The fact is, that the foremast was only struck by one grape-shot, and was not even fished after the action.

We designated the movement, forced upon the Amethyst by the fall of her masts and sails in the water, an unfortunate one. It was very much so. Less, however, in reference to the easily refuted misstatements of the captain of the Niemen, than, as we gather from the proceedings which afterwards took place in the admiralty prize-court, to the misconception that seems to have prevailed among the officers of the Arethusa. A little forethought in shortening sail, before the Amethyst bore up athwart the stern of her beaten antagonist, would have given quite a different tone to the letter of Captain Dupotet, if indeed any such letter had then been published; and would have left no grounds for a second British ship, by establishing a claim for head-money, to make it appear that she had any share in producing the surrender of an already silenced and defenceless French frigate.

It was formerly stated, that early on the morning of the 22nd of February, the day after Commodore Beresford was chased from off Lorient by the squadron from Brest, the three French frigates, Calypso, Cybèle, and Italienne, sailed from that port, and that they were not immediately followed by the three sail of the line at anchor in the road, because the tide did not suit.[1] In a few hours the depth of water became sufficient; and commodore Amable-Gilles Troude, with the three 74-gun ships Courageux, Polonais, and d'Haupoult, having under their convoy the two armed en flûte frigates, Furieuse and Félicité, laden with troops, flour, and military stores, for the island of Martinique, escaped from Lorient, unseen, or at all events unmolested, by any of the British ships cruising off the French coast.

On the 29th of March, having from some prizes he had made on the passage learnt that Martinique had surrendered to the British arms (an account of which will appear in its proper place), the French commodore entered the Saintes, to watch for an opportunity of getting across to Basse-terre, Guadaloupe. Scarcely, however, had the French ships anchored, than a superior British force arrived to blockade them. The line-of-battle portion of that force consisted of the

Gun-ship.			
98	Neptune	{	Rear-admiral (r.) Hon. Sir Alex. J. Cochrane, Bt.
			Captain Charles Dilkes.
74	{ York	,,	Robert Barton.
	Pompée	,,	William Charles Fahie.
	Captain	,,	James Athol Wood.
64	Polyphemus	,,	William Pryce Cumby.

The Saintes consist of two small islands, each about three leagues in circumference, exclusive of three or four still smaller ones, so arranged as to form a commodious road or harbour between the larger islands; the westernmost of which is called Terre d'en Bas, and the other Terre d'en Haut. They lie between Vieux Fort, near the southern extremity of Basse-terre, Guadaloupe, and Pointe des Ajoupas on the west side of Marie-Galante, about five leagues distant from the latter and two from

[1] See vol. iv., p. 393.

the former. The road or harbour of the Saintes, having three entrances in different directions, is not easily blockaded. Under these circumstances, it was thought advisable to land a body of troops, for the double purpose of driving the French ships to sea, and of reducing the Saintes islands, which had at all times afforded to the enemy's ships a capital shelter.

Accordingly, on the 12th of April, a small British squadron, under the orders of Captain Philip Beaver of the 40-gun frigate Acasta, accompanied by a fleet of transports, having on board from 2000 to 3000 men commanded by Major-general Frederic Maitland, sailed from Fort Royal bay, Martinique, and on the next day arrived off the Saintes. On the 14th the troops were landed with a very slight loss; and on the same afternoon possessed themselves, with some difficulty, of a mountain 800 feet high, called Morne-Russel, and which completely overlooked the ships in the harbour. Upon these two 8-inch howitzers were presently brought to bear with such effect, that at 8 P.M. the three line-of-battle ships began to get under way, and at 9 h. 30 m. P.M. sailed out through the windward passage; but, although favoured by an unusually dark, night not unseen by the British in-shore squadron of sloops and brigs, under the orders of Captain Hugh Cameron, of the 18-gun ship-sloop Hazard; and who immediately made the preconcerted signal to the admiral outside.

At this time the Neptune was off the south-west passage at some distance, and the Pompée about a mile and a half to the westward of Terre d'en Bas, or the Lower Sainte. In a very few minutes the Pompée discovered the three French ships bearing down under a press of canvas, followed by the Hazard and other vessels belonging to the in-shore squadron. At 10 P.M. the Pompée closed with the sternmost French ship, and endeavoured to stop her by the discharge of two broadsides; but, having a strong breeze in her favour, the latter continued her course to the west-south-west without returning a shot. At 10 h. 15 m. P.M. the 18-gun brig-sloop Recruit, Captain Charles Napier, got up and opened her fire at the enemy's sternmost ship. At 11 P.M. the Neptune joined in the chase, and at 33 minutes past midnight crossed so near to the same ship, that the latter fired into her and killed one and wounded four of her men.

On the 15th, at 4 A.M., the Recruit, by her superior sailing, again got near enough to discharge a broadside at the d'Haupoult, now the rearmost French ship; and the Pompée was very soon in a situation to open a distant fire from her bow-chasers; all three French ships as they steered in line abreast, returning the fire with their stern-chasers. At 10 h. 30 m. A.M. Captain Napier had his sergeant of marines wounded by a shot from one of the French ships; but the Recruit still persisted to harass them with her attacks. So annoying were those attacks, that at 10 h. 45 m. A.M. the d'Haupoult broached to and discharged her main and quarter-deck guns, cutting away two of the brig's fore-shrouds on the larboard side and doing other damage to her rigging, but fortunately, wounding no one. Even this did not intimidate Captain Napier; for, no sooner had the d'Haupoult resumed her course before the wind, than the Recruit ran across her stern, and poured in one or two broadsides, receiving in return a fire from the 74's stern-chasers. The Pompée also joined occasionally in the running fight; and thus the day passed. At 8 P.M. the French ships separated, the d'Haupoult altering her course to west-north-west, while her two consorts continued steering west-south-west. The Pompée immediately hauled up after the d'Haupoult, and was at this time about three miles to the eastward of the latter, full five miles to the east-north-east of the Courageux and Polonais, and about the same distance ahead of the Neptune; who, since the forenoon, had detached the Hazard and Supérieure, and was now in company with only the Hawk brig. At midnight, the Pompée could no longer see the two French ships in the west-south-west, but still kept sight of the d'Haupoult.

On the 16th, at daylight, the wind still from the eastward, the d'Haupoult was about three miles north-west half-west, and the Neptune about nine miles south-east half-east, of the Pompée. The Recruit, having dropped astern, on account probably of her damaged rigging, was not now in sight. In the course of the forenoon the British 38-gun frigate Latona, Captain Hugh Pigot, and 12-pounder 32-gun frigate Castor, Captain William Roberts, made their appearance in the north-east, and soon joined in the chase. At 5 P.M. the Neptune was no longer visible from the Pompée's mast-head; and the latter ship and the d'Haupoult sailed so nearly alike, that no apparent alteration had taken place in the distance between them since the preceding day. At 5 h. 30 m. P.M. the high land of Porto-Rico was seen from the Pompée, bearing north-north-east, about nine leagues distant. The night shut in extremely dark, and the ships, as they approached the land, were baffled with light and variable winds from the northward and westward. By midnight the Castor had got so far ahead as to be on the starboard bow of the Pompée, but the Latona had not been able to advance beyond the latter's starboard quarter.

On the 17th, at 2 h. 45 m. A.M., the Castor shortened sail; and at 3 A.M., when within little more than half a mile of the d'Haupoult's starboard quarter, commenced a fire with her larboard guns. In this way the action was maintained between an English 12-pounder frigate and a French 74 until 4 A.M.; when, owing to the latter having had frequently to yaw to bring her guns to bear, the Pompée got up. Passing between the Castor and her opponent, the Pompée engaged the d'Haupoult within musket-shot distance, gradually closing until 5 h. 15 m. A.M.; when the d'Haupoult ranged ahead, steering before the wind, and became again engaged with the Castor. Before many shot had been exchanged between these unequal antagonists, the Pompée, putting her helm a-port, fired her bow guns at, and was preparing with her broadside to rake, the d'Haupoult; when the French ship, now a complete wreck in rigging and sails, lowered her topsails, hove to, and hauled down her colours. This was a measure which could no longer have been delayed; for the opening daylight discovered the Neptune, York, and Captain, with the sloops Hazard, Ringdove, and Hawk, about nine miles to the eastward, and the Polyphemus, Ethalion frigate, and sloops Tweed and Recruit, within less than that distance to the westward; all, under a press of canvas, standing for the Pompée, Castor, and their prize, and whom the Latona was now also in the act of joining. Thus terminated a running fight, which had commenced to the southward of Vieux-Fort, Guadaloupe, at 10 P.M. on the 14th of April, and had ended within eight leagues north-east by north of Cape Roxo, Porto-Rico, at 5 h. 15 m. A.M. on the 17th.

The Pompée was nearly in as disabled a state, especially in rigging and sails, as the d'Haupoult herself, and had her gaff, mizenmast, mainyard, and bowsprit badly wounded, besides having received a number of shot in her hull. The Pompée's loss consisted of her boatswain (Edward Casey), seven seamen, and one marine killed, her captain, first-lieutenant (William Bone), one lieutenant of marines (Charles Edward Atkins), 22 seamen, and five private marines wounded. The damages of the Castor were comparatively trifling, and her loss amounted to only one seaman killed and six wounded. The loss of these two ships, added to that of the Neptune and Recruit already stated, makes the total loss on the British side 10 killed and

35 wounded. The hull of the d'Haupoult, as is usually the case against British opponents, had suffered more than the appearance of her sails and rigging indicated; and the French ship lost, out of a crew of 680 men and boys, between 80 and 90 in killed and wounded, including several officers.

In this case there was nothing that could cast the slightest imputation upon the French ship: the d'Haupoult retreated from a superior force, manœuvred skilfully, and, when at last overtaken, fought bravely. There were periods, probably, when Commodore Troude might have shortened sail and engaged to advantage; but, doubtless, he considered that, long before he could bring the contest to a favourable issue, Rear-admiral Cochrane and his squadron would be close at his heels; not merely to retake his prize (admitting the French commodore to have taken the Pompée), but to capture one or more of his ships, disabled as, in all likelihood, they would have been. The conduct of the Pompée was such as was expected of her, and the Castor gave proofs of a commendable zeal in closing with so powerful an antagonist; but what shall we say of the Recruit? Her behaviour was gallant in the extreme, and was well calculated to efface the stain which, not many weeks before, nor many degrees from the same spot, the Driver's conduct had, seemingly, put upon the sloop class.[1] Next to the pleasure o. recording acts of intrepidity like that performed by the Recruit, is the pleasure of being able to announce that they were appreciated in the quarter possessing the power to reward them. Sir Alexander Cochrane, with feelings highly honourable to him, appointed Captain Napier to the command of the d'Haupoult. The admiral did this on the spot, and then detached the York and Captain, with two frigates and a sloop of war, in quest of M. Troude; but who evaded all his pursuers and reached Europe in safety, anchoring, about the middle of May, in the road of Cherbourg. The d'Haupoult was a tolerably fine ship of 1871 tons, and, under the name of Abercromby, cruised for three or four years in the British service.

The two armées en flûte, Furieuse and Félicité, which we left at anchor in the road of the Saintes, did not get under way until 9 A.M. on the 15th: they then, accompanied by a brig-corvette, stood over for Guadaloupe, chased by the 64-gun ship Intrepid, Captain the Honourable Warwick Lake, one of the Acasta's squadron. At 10 A.M. the Intrepid commenced action with the two French ships, and also with the batteries on shore;

[1] See p. 6.

under the protection of which both her opponents soon obtained shelter, leaving the British ship with her masts, yards, rigging, and sails much wounded, and one boat cut from her quarter, chiefly by the heavy shot from Fort Matilda, but, as far as we can gather, with no loss of men.

On the night of the 14th of June these two French frigates, the Furieuse, armed with two long 18, and six long 8-pounders, and 12 carronades, 36-pounders, with a crew, including some military passengers, of about 200 men and boys, commanded by Lieutenant Gabriel-Etienne-Louis Le Marant-Kerdaniel, and the Félicité, armed with 14 long 12-pounders and a crew of 174 men and boys, and both frigates laden with a cargo of colonial produce, escaped from the road of Basse-terre, Guadaloupe, bound to France; but not unseen by some of the in-shore sloops and brigs of the blockading squadron, one of which, the gun-brig Haughty, Lieutenant John Mitchell, fired several shot at the two frigates. At daylight the whole British squadron went in chase; but, towards the afternoon, the only ships in sight of the enemy were the 38-gun frigate Latona, Captain Hugh Pigot, and 18-gun ship-sloop Cherub, Captain Thomas Tudor Tucker.

The chase of the two French frigates continued all the 15th and 16th and during a part of the 17th; when they separated. The Furieuse was pursued by the Cherub, and effected her escape; but the Félicité found all her efforts unavailing to get from the Latona; who, on the 18th, overtook and captured her with little or no opposition. The Félicité had belonged to the French 36-gun class, and measured about 900 tons; but, being old and nearly worn out, she was not considered eligible for the British navy. An agent from Christophe at St. Domingo purchased her, and, after being refitted, the Félicité sailed for Cape-François.

On the 5th of July, at 3 P.M., in latitude 43° 41' north, and longitude 34° west, the British ship-sloop Bonne-Citoyenne, of 18 carronades, 32-pounders, and two long nines, with a crew, including a few supernumeraries, of 127 men and boys, commanded by Captain William Mounsey, being on her way from Halifax, Nova Scotia, to Quebec, steering north-west by west, with the wind at south, descried, in the west-south-west, a large frigate, in the act of taking possession of an English merchant-ship. The Bonne-Citoyenne went immediately in chase of the ship-of-war, which was no other than the Furieuse, so far advanced on her way to Europe. On the sloop's approach, the

Furieuse abandoned the merchant-ship, and steered, under a press of sail, to the northward, followed by Captain Mounsey; who, from the French ship's inability to answer the private signal, had already discovered her to be an enemy. At sunset the two ships-of-war were about five miles apart, striving their utmost to get forward. During the night the Bonne-Citoyenne lost sight of the Furieuse, but, at 3 A.M. on the 6th, again descried her, at a great distance on the larboard quarter. The Bonne-Citoyenne immediately hauled up on that tack, with the wind now a point or two more easterly than it had been; and, by 4 A.M., got within nine or ten miles of the object of her pursuit.

At 9 h. 10 m. A.M. the Furieuse shortened sail, and hauled close upon a wind; as immediately afterwards did the Bonne-Citoyenne, in eager pursuit. In another ten minutes the French ship hove to; and in five minutes more the British ship got alongside and commenced the action, within pistol-shot distance. A smart cannonade was now mutually kept up; during which the Furieuse fired away more than 70 broadsides, and the Bonne-Citoyenne 129; the latter, alternately from the larboard and the starboard side, as she changed her position to avoid the necessity of slackening her fire from the carronades becoming overheated. This was, however, the case with three, which were dismounted and rendered useless early in the action. After the combat had lasted, in this way, for 6 hours and 50 minutes, and each ship had become greatly crippled in her masts and rigging; and after the Bonne-Citoyenne, in particular, had expended nearly the whole of her powder, Captain Mounsey gallantly took a position close athwart the bows of his antagonist, preparatory to boarding her with all hands. This bold demonstration decided the affair; and the Furieuse, at 6 h. 16 m. P.M., struck her colours.

The Bonne-Citoyenne had her fore and main topgallantmasts and mizentopmast shot away, her three lower masts badly wounded in several places, and nearly all the standing rigging, and every part of the running rigging, sails, boats, and booms, cut to pieces. With all this serious damage, the Bonne-Citoyenne's loss amounted to only one seaman killed, and four seamen and one marine badly wounded. The Furieuse was in a far more disabled condition. Her topmasts and all her yards, except the cross-jack and sprit-sail, were shot away, and her lower masts reduced to a tottering state: she had also 14 shot-holes between wind and water, and five feet water in the hold.

Her loss consisted of two quarter-masters, 27 seamen, and six soldiers killed, her commander, two lieutenants, three midshipmen, four gunner's mates, 19 seamen, one lieutenant of artillery, and seven soldiers, all dangerously wounded; total, 35 killed and 37 dangerously wounded. The slightly wounded probably amounted to 18 or 20 more.

According to the certificate of two of the surviving French officers, the Furieuse commenced the action with 195 men; but, admitting 35 to be the correct amount of the killed, the ship must have had 213 men, 178 being the number of prisoners that were received out of her. As there may have been a slight mistake in the number of killed, and especially as several of the soldiers consisted of invalids, we shall consider the Furieuse to have had no more than 200 men.

Comparative Force of the Combatants.

		Bonne-Citoyenne.	Furieuse.
Broadside-guns	No.	10	10
	lbs.	297	279
Crew	No.	127	200
Size	tons.	511	1085

Few cases occur wherein the usual figure-statement requires less to be left without remarks than the present case. The Furieuse presented herself, at first, in the size and formidable appearance of a full-armed 38 or 40 gun frigate. The Bonne-Citoyenne made sail in chase; and it was only upon a near approach that she could have discovered, that the 26 maindeck ports of the frigate were but partially filled with guns. After the action had commenced and the rigging of the Furieuse become injured, the frigate's size was rather a disadvantage: it rendered her unwieldy in comparison with the Bonne-Citoyenne; who, even when disabled in her rigging, could manœuvre much more quickly than her antagonist. With respect, also, to the mutual cannonade, the lowness of the sloop's, and the great height of the frigate's hull, gave a decided advantage to the Bonne-Citoyenne; and to that may be attributed, in a great degree, the comparative impunity with which the latter came out of the action.

In resolving to measure his strength with an antagonist of such apparently superior force, Captain Mounsey displayed a highly commendable zeal for the service; as, in conducting the six hours' engagement to its final, and to him glorious result, he did an equal degree of skill and intrepidity. On the other hand, when it is considered that the French commander and two of his lieutenants (perhaps the only two) lay dangerously wounded, that more than 70 of his people had been placed *hors de combat*, and his ship battered until she was totally unmanageable and scarcely seaworthy; that, when thus reduced, a body of British seamen, numerically equal, and, in the sickly state of a portion of the French troops, physically superior, to all his remaining hands, were ready to rush upon his decks: when all these circumstances are considered, few persons will think that the flag of the Furieuse could have been kept any longer flying.

It was not merely in gaining this victory, that the officers and men of the Bonne-Citoyenne displayed so large a portion of those qualities, by which British seamen have attained their admitted pre-eminence. Much remained to be done. Two crippled ships, one with five feet water in the hold, were to be carried from the middle of the Atlantic to a port of safety. The effective prisoners, too, were more than equal in number to those by whom, during so long a voyage, they were to be kept in subjection. It took the Bonne-Citoyenne until 1 h. 30 m. P.M. on the 7th, and that was by very great exertions, ere she could take her prize in tow and make sail for Halifax, Nova Scotia. On the 8th, at 9 h. 30 m. P.M., the main and mizen masts of the Furieuse, no longer able, in their shattered state, to withstand the motion of the sea, fell overboard; and thus was a ship of 500 tons, herself in a crippled condition, compelled to drag after her a dismasted ship of nearly 1100 tons. The Bonne-Citoyenne did so for 25 days, and anchored with her prize in Halifax. The season of the year, no doubt, was much in her favour: had it been winter, one ship, if not both, would in all probability have foundered.

The Furieuse was afterwards purchased for the use of the British navy, and became classed as a 36-gun frigate. When subsequently fitted for sea at Portsmouth, Captain Mounsey, who had been promoted to post-rank the moment his exploit reached the admiralty, was appointed to command her. Lieutenant Joseph Symes, first of the Bonne-Citoyenne at the capture of the Furieuse, gained also, what he justly merited, a step in his profession. Captain Mounsey, in his official letter, makes honourable mention of his second lieutenant, William Sandom, his master, Nathaniel Williamson, and his purser, John Nicholas C. Scott; also of two passengers on board the sloop, Mr. John Black and Mr. Angus M'Auley, who in the handsomest manner volunteered their services, and assisted at the guns, and wherever they could make themselves useful.

Steel's monthly Navy-list, until some correspondent caused the mistake to be partially corrected, made the Furieuse oi "50 guns," which exceeds by two the number Captain Mounsey states the ship to have been pierced for, by six the number she could have mounted without filling her chase-ports, and by as many as 30 the number she did actually mount when captured. The French were very sore at this exaggeration of the force of their frigate, but laid the blame in the wrong quarter. A publisher is seldom very scrupulous on these points; but a British officer, although liable to be charged with every printed misstatement magnifying his own action, is too honourable to countenance such barefaced cheatery.

On the 17th of May, at noon, latitude 44° 6' north, longitude 11° 20' west, the British 10-gun brig-sloop Goldfinch (eight 18-pounder carronades and two sixes, with 75 men and boys), Captain Fitzherbert George Skinner, standing close hauled on the larboard tack with the wind from the north-east by north, discovered and chased a ship directly to windward. This ship was the French corvette Mouche, of 16 long brass 8-pounders and 180 men and boys, commanded by Lieutenant de vaisseau Antoine Allègre; and, although of so decided a superiority of force, M. Allègre suffered himself to be chased all the afternoon and night, and until 3 A.M. on the 18th, when the Goldfinch gallantly brought the Mouche to action. The two vessels continued to engage on opposite tacks, but at too great a distance for the brig's carronades to produce their proper effect, until 7 A.M.; when the corvette, with the head of her foretopmast shot away, made off to windward, leaving the Goldfinch with the loss of three men killed and three severely wounded, and her masts, rigging, and sails a good deal cut up.

On the 21st, off the north coast of Spain, the Mouche fell in with the British hired armed lugger Black Joke, Lieutenant Moses Cannadey, and, after exchanging broadsides with her, stood away for the harbour of San-Andero. Here the Mouche, with a French gun-brig and schooner, was found and captured, on the 10th of June, by the British 38-gun frigates Amelia, Captain the Honourable Frederick Paul Irby, and Statira, Captain Charles Worsley Boys; who had arrived off that port to co-operate with the Spanish patriots under General Ballesteros in expelling the French from their territory.

On the 23rd of April, while the British 38-gun frigate Spartan,

Captain Jahleel Brenton, 18-pounder 32-gun frigate Amphion, Captain William Hoste, and 28-gun frigate Mercury, Captain the Honourable Henry Duncan, were cruising off the town of Pesaro, in the Gulf of Venice, a number of vessels were observed to be lying in the mole. Deeming it practicable to take possession of these, Captain Brenton anchored his three frigates, with springs on their cables, within half a mile of the town; and, having placed the boats of the squadron under the orders of Lieutenant George Wickens Willes, first of the Spartan, and formed them into two divisions, he directed the first division, composed of the launches with their carronades, and other boats carrying field-pieces, and commanded by Lieutenant Charles George Rodney Phillott, first of the Amphion, to take a station to the northward, and the second division, composed of rocket-boats, and commanded by Lieutenant William Augustus Baumgardt of the Spartan, to the southward, of the town.

As soon as these arrangements were made, Captain Brenton sent a flag of truce on shore, to demand the surrender of all the vessels; adding, that should any resistance be offered, the governor must be answerable for the consequences. At 11 h. 30 m. A.M. the officer returned to the Spartan, with a message from the commandant of Pesaro, stating that, in half an hour, the English commodore should have an answer. At the end of 35 minutes, observing no flag of truce flying on shore, but that troops were assembling in the streets and on the quays, and the inhabitants employed in dismantling the vessels, Captain Brenton hauled down the flag of truce, and fired one shot over the town to give warning to the women and children.

Shortly afterwards the three frigates and the gun and mortar boats, by signal from the Spartan, opened their fire upon the town. At 32 minutes past noon, observing several flags of truce hung out, Captain Brenton made the signal to cease firing. Lieutenant Willes then pulled into the harbour; where he was informed that the commandant had made his escape with all the military. Considering the place now as surrendered at discretion, Captain Brenton sent all the boats to bring out the vessels, and landed the marines under Lieutenant Thomas Moore, of that corps, to protect them. By 6 h. 30 m. P.M. 13 vessels, deeply laden, were brought off. Several others had been scuttled by the inhabitants and sunk, and some were aground. At 7 P.M. the castle at the entrance of the harbour was blown up, under the direction of Lieutenant Willes, and the British returned to their ships without a casualty. Nor was it known that any lives had been lost in the town, except one man, who, from not attending to the warning given him, was buried in the ruins of the castle.

On the 2nd of May the Spartan and Mercury (the Amphion having been detached) chased two vessels into the port of Cesenatico, the entrance of which is very narrow, and was defended by a battery of two 24-pounders and a castle. Observing that several other vessels were lying in the harbour, Captain Brenton determined to take possession of the whole of them. The coast is so shoal, that the two frigates had only four fathoms considerably out of gun-shot of the town. On this account the boats were detached ahead and on each bow, to lead in, with directions to make a signal when in three fathoms.

In this manner the two frigates, by noon, were enabled to anchor in a quarter three fathoms within grape-range of the battery. The latter was very soon silenced; and the boats under the orders of Lieutenant Willes, pushed in and took possession of it, turning the guns upon the castle and town, which were very soon deserted. The British captured on this occasion 12 vessels, some laden with corn for Venice, and others in ballast. The latter were filled with hemp and iron out of the magazines for those articles on the quay, and a vessel which had been scuttled was burnt. The castle and magazine were then blown up, the battery destroyed, and the guns spiked; and the British returned to their ships without having a single man wounded, although much exposed to the fire of the battery and of musketry. Nor was any damage done to the ships, although, in consequence of the zeal of Captain Duncan to get close to the enemy, the Mercury was for a short time aground.

On the 14th of June, in the morning, the British 18-gun brig-sloop Scout, Captain William Raitt, discovering a convoy of 14 or 15 sail of vessels, under the protection of two gun-boats, coming round Cape Croisette, made all sail in chase; but, about 1 P.M., it falling calm, and the convoy being a good deal dispersed, Captain Raitt despatched his boats under the orders of Lieutenant Henry Robert Battersby. On seeing this, seven sail pushed for a harbour about three leagues to the eastward of the cape, into which the boats proceeded under a heavy and well-directed fire of grape and musketry.

Lieutenant Battersby, with a part of his men, landed, and attacked the enemy, who were numerous among the rocks: he then stormed and carried the battery, mounting two 6-pounders in embrasures. These were spiked; and, the boats with Lieutenant John Farrant, Mr. John Batten, the master, and master's mate Granville Thompson, having in the mean time pulled up the harbour, the seven vessels were brought out; although, for their better security, they had been made fast with ropes from the shore to their mast-heads and keels. In the execution of this service, the British sustained a loss of one man killed and five wounded.

On the 14th of July, Lieutenant Battersby, at the head of a detachment of the Scott's seamen and marines, attacked a strong battery which commanded the port of Carri, between Marseille and the Rhone; carried the fort without any loss, spiked the guns, killed five of the enemy, and made seven prisoners. For his gallantry on this and other occasions, Lieutenant Battersby, in the succeeding September, was promoted to the rank of commander.

On the 12th of March, at 6 h. 30 m. A.M., the island of Anti Paxo in the Adriatic bearing about north distant six or seven leagues, the British 12-pounder 36-gun frigate Topaze, Captain Anselm John Griffiths, standing close-hauled on the starboard tack with a light breeze from the south-south-east in company with the 18-gun ship-sloop Kingfisher, Captain Ewell Tritton, discovered, and immediately bore up for, two strange frigates in the east-north-east. These were the French 40-gun frigates, Danaé and Flore. At 6 h. 40 m. A.M., mistaking, we suppose, the Kingfisher for a larger vessel than she was, the two frigates made all sail north by east. At 10 A.M. they were hull down from the Topaze in the east-north-east, and the Kingfisher was in the south-west between four and five miles off, under all sail in light airs, trying her utmost to close. At 11 A.M. the two frigates made sundry signals, and tacked off shore a little to the southward of Pargos. The Topaze then stood within three miles of the strangers, tacked, and hove to; the Kingfisher at this time eight or nine miles astern, still under all sail, and sweeping. The Danaé and Flore then wore and stood in shore again, Anti-Paxo at noon bearing from the Topaze west-north-west distant four or five miles.

At 20 minutes past noon the Topaze, with the wind now from north-north-west, wore and again made all sail after the two strangers, evidently frigates mounting from 44 to 48 guns each. At 1 P.M. the Danaé and Flore, who were now to windward, passed within hail of each other, and tacked off the main land. At 2 h. 10 m. P.M. they hoisted French colours, and one of them a broad pendant. In five minutes more the Topaze hoisted her colours and fired a shot at the headmost ship, which the latter returned: and the two frigates exchanged broadsides while passing on opposite tacks. The Topaze then stood on and engaged the sternmost frigate in a similar manner; and at 3 P.M. tacked from the main. The headmost French frigate at the same moment tacked off Paxo, and was presently followed in the manœuvre by her consort. At 3 h. 30 m. P.M. the Topaze and her two opponents engaged in crossing each other, the same as before; the Kingfisher at the distance of six or seven miles, and to leeward. At 4 h. 30 m. the Topaze and the two French frigates again commenced firing on opposite tacks, and continued engaging, at the distance of about a mile and a quarter, until nearly 5 P.M., when the Danaé and Flore tacked off Paxo out of gun-shot, and stood up the passage to Corfu under all sail; leaving to a single British frigate, with 12 pounders only, the credit of having obliged them to do so.

Shortly afterwards the Topaze bore up and closed the Kingfisher; without, as it appears, having sustained any loss in her action with her two very forbearing opponents, although one French 18-pound shot had gone through the gig, launch, yawl, and the quarter-deck bulwark. Our researches have not enabled us to give the names of the captains of these two French frigates; not, at least, with that degree of certainty which is requisite in a case circumstanced like the present. At all events it is evident that Captain Griffiths, in chasing and attacking two such opponents, evinced a considerabe share of gallantry.

On the 31st of May the Topaze, cruising off the coast of Albania, observed nine vessels lying at anchor in the road of Demata, situated behind the reef of rocks under the fortress of St. Maura. Finding that the ship could not with safety approach near enough to capture or destroy them, Captain Griffiths despatched upon that service the boats of the Topaze, under the orders of the first-lieutenant, Charles Hammond (whose right hand was nearly useless from a previous wound in cutting out vessels), assisted by the acting master George Garson, Lieutenants of marines Edward Smith Mercer and William Halsted, and master's mates Henry Packhurst Taylor and Robert Bisset Fenwick.

Being obliged to row along outside the reef, and having then to round it, the boats were necessarily exposed, within a musket-shot distance, to the galling fire of the enemy's whole force. Notwithstanding this formidable opposition, Lieutenant Hammond and his party gallantly pushed on; and, with so comparatively slight a loss as one marine killed and one seaman slightly wounded, boarded and brought out the whole nine vessels; among which were, one xebec of eight carriage guns and six swivels, with a crew of 55 men, one cutter of four, and one felucca of three guns, and two gun-boats of one gun each. After this act of gallantry performed by Lieutenant Hammond, and the severe wounds which his former services had cost him, we regret to find, by a reference to his name in the list, that he still bears the rank he did 20 years ago.

On the 13th of June, at 8 A.M., Cape Bon bearing south-west distant seven miles, the British 38-gun frigate Pomone, Captain Robert Barrie, captured, after a short chase, the Neapolitan privateer Lucien-Charles, a new bombard, mounting one long 12, and two long 6 pounders, with a crew of 53 men, commanded, of all things, by a French adjutant-general, and no less a man than the Chevalier Charles-Lucien Prevost de Boissi; who could also add, to his title of privateer's-man, that of " officier de la légion d'honneur."

On the 24th of June Rear-admiral Martin, with the 80-gun ship Canopus, Captain Charles Inglis, 74-gun ships Spartiate and Warrior, Captains Sir Francis Laforey, Bart., and John William Spranger, 22-gun ship Cyane, Captain Thomas Staines, and 18-gun brig-sloop Espoir, Captain Robert Mitford, with a numerous flotilla of British and Sicilian gun-boats, and a fleet of transports with troops, anchored to the northward of the islands of Ischia and Procida, in readiness to make an attack upon them. In the course of the evening, the rear-admiral detached the Cyane and Espoir, with 12 gun-boats, to take a station to the southward of those islands, for the purpose of preventing any reinforcements or supplies being thrown into them from the main.

On the 25th, at 8 A.M., when lying at anchor two miles south by east of the island of Procida, in company with the gun-boats, the Cyane and Espoir discovered a French frigate, a corvette, and several gun-boats, coming out of Pozzuoli bay. The British vessels, by signal from the Cyane, immediately got under way, and, having a light air from the north-east, stood to meet the enemy's vessels; with what chance of success, had one party been as daring as the other, some account of the force on each side will best explain. The Cyane mounted on her main deck 22 carronades, 32-pounders, and on her quarter-deck and forecastle eight carronades, 18-pounders, and two long sixes, total

32 guns; with a complement, if all were on board, of 175 men and boys. The Espoir mounted the usual armament of her class, 16 carronades, 32-pounders, and two sixes, with 120 men and boys. The French frigate Cérès appears to have been of the same class as the Franco-Venetian frigate Carrère, captured in 1801,[1] and consequently carried 18-pounders: her total number of guns was at least 42, some accounts say 44, and her complement was about 350 men. The corvette was the Fama, mounting 28 or 30 guns, including 24 long 8, or, according to some accounts, long 12 pounders, with a crew of 260 men. The gun-boats on each side were armed much in the same manner; each with a long 18 or 24 pounder.

At 8 h. 30 m. the Cyane and her consorts fired several broadsides at the French frigate and her consorts; which fire the latter returned, and then stood in for the land. At 9 h. 40 m. A.M. the firing ceased; and, on account of the distance at which it had been maintained, with no great effect on either side: the Cyane, however, had her maintopgallant-yard and some stays shot away. The British ship and brig continued all day cruising between Procida and the main, and at 9 P.M. re-anchored off the island. On the same evening Procida surrendered without opposition; as had Ischia in the morning, except a castle on the south-east point of the island, which made a demonstration of resistance, and did not capitulate till some days afterwards. On the night of the 25th, receiving intelligence that a flotilla of gun-boats was on its way from Gaeta to the bay of Naples, Rear-admiral Martin detached in that direction the few Sicilian gun-boats remaining with him.

On the 26th, at 6 h. 25 m. A.M., the Cyane, Espoir, and the British and Sicilian gun-boats in their company, having shortly before weighed, began engaging the French gun-boats, just as they were rounding the point of Baia. By his prompt and vigorous attack upon the gun-boats and batteries, Captain Staines checked the progress of the flotilla, and enabled the British and Sicilian gun-boats to bring their opponents to close action; whereby, before 10 A.M., 18 French gun-boats were taken and four destroyed. In this smart affair, the Cyane received 23 shot in the hull, had her masts, yards, rigging, and sails a good deal cut, and lost one seaman and one boy killed, one master's mate (David Jones) mortally, and six seamen slightly wounded. The Espoir appears to have escaped without any loss whatever.

[1] See vol iii., p. 78.

On the same afternoon, observing a flag of truce on a battery near Point Messino, Captain Staines detached the boats to the spot; and, after spiking four 36-pounders on the battery and destroying the carriages, the boats took off 15 deserters. At 7 P.M. the Cyane and Espoir, accompanied by 23 Sicilian gun-boats, stood into Pozzuoli bay, where the Cérès, Fama, and 12 gun-boats, were lying at anchor. Captain Staines continued working and sounding off the town of Pozzuoli; and at 8 A.M. on the 27th the Cyane found herself becalmed so near to the shore, that a battery of four guns opened upon her. At 10 A.M., the fire becoming troublesome, Captain Staines embarked in one of the gun-boats, and, leading them to the attack, soon silenced the battery. He then landed with a party of men, spiked four 36-pounders, destroyed the carriages, hove a 10-inch mortar into the sea, and returned to his ship without a casualty.

At 5 P.M., finding that the Cyane and Espoir lay becalmed in the offing, and considering the gun-boats in the bight of the bay was no obstacle, the French commodore weighed and put to sea with the Cérès, Fama, and 20 gun-boats, bound to Naples. At 5 h. 42 m. the Cyane made the Espoir's signal to prepare for battle and make all possible sail. At 6 h. 23 m. P.M. the Sicilian gun-boats began annoying the rear of the French gun-boats. At 6 h. 50 m., finding that the Espoir and Sicilian gun-boats were now too far astern to be of much service, and observing that the French frigate was nearly a mile and a half astern of the corvette, and about the same distance from the French gun-boats, the Cyane manned her sweeps and stood towards the Cérès, then not more than three miles from the mole of Naples.

At 7 h. 20 m. P.M. the Cyane succeeded in getting alongside of the French frigate, within half pistol-shot distance, and commenced the action with her. The Cérès, assisted occasionally by the corvette, the gun-boats, and the batteries of Naples, within gun-shot of which she had by this time arrived, returned the Cyane's fire. At 7 h. 30 m. the Cérès was observed to get a reinforcement of men from Naples. Notwithstanding this, at 7 h. 45 m., the frigate hauled down her colours, but re-hoisted them on getting a second reinforcement of men. At 8 h. 25 m. P.M. the fire of the Cérès slackened considerably. In two or three minutes more the frigate discontinued firing her main-deck guns; and at 8 h. 30 m. ceased firing altogether. But, as the Cyane, besides having expended all her powder, was at this time approaching fast towards the mole head of Naples, then scarcely a mile and a half distant, Mr. Joseph Miller, the master, upon whom, for the reasons that will shortly appear, the command had devolved, found himself unable to take advantage of the enemy's confusion.

This being the case, the Cyane hauled off, with all her sails completely riddled by the enemy's grape and langridge, her standing and running rigging cut to pieces, her fore and mizen masts badly wounded, 45 round shot in and through her sides, her chain-plates, and several port timbers destroyed, and four guns disabled from the drawing of the ring-bolts; also with a loss of one seaman and one marine killed, her captain and first-lieutenant, James Hall (both dangerously), second and only remaining lieutenant (John Ferrier), one midshipman (John Taylor), 11 seamen, four marines, and one boy wounded. The Espoir, who had some share in the latter part of this engagement, sent the gun-boats to the assistance of her crippled consort, and they towed her out of the bay. On account of her greatly disabled state, the Cyane was immediately sent to England to be refitted.

The wound of Captain Staines was indeed a severe one. He lost his left arm out of the socket at the shoulder, and was also wounded in the side. Lieutenant Hall's wounds were in the thigh and arms; and it gratifies us to observe that, in a few months after the very gallant service in which he had been engaged, he was promoted to the rank of commander. Of the proceedings of the Cyane altogether, in the vicinity of Procida, they are such as do honour to every officer and man who was on board of her; and, certainly, nobler behaviour than that which Captain Staines displayed on the occasion we have never had to record.

On the 28th of July, in the morning, the British 74-gun ship Excellent, Captain John West, being at an anchor off Triest, discovered an enemy's convoy standing along the northern shore towards that port. With the view of cutting off the vessels, Captain West got under way, and took up a position between them and their destined port. Seeing this, the convoy took shelter in Duin, a port four leagues to the north-west of Triest. Having in company with him the 18-gun ship-sloop Acorn, Captain Robert Clephane, and 16-gun brig-sloop Bustard, Captain John Duff Markland, Captain West deemed it practicable to get possession of this convoy; and accordingly, at 10 P.M., Captain Clephane, with the two sloops, and all the boats of the Excellent, under the orders of her first-lieutenant, Mr. John Harper, was detached to perform the service.

About midnight the boats covered by the Acorn and Bustard, who from her light draught of water led in, pushed through a heavy fire into the harbour; and, while Captain Robert Cummins, of the marines, landed with a small party to dislodge the enemy from the rugged precipices round the port, Lieutenant Harper and his detachment gallantly boarded and carried six Italian gun-boats, three of three long 24, and the remainder of three long 18 pounders; and which gun-boats, along with 10 laden trabaccolos, or coasters, were brought off with no greater loss to the British than the Bustard's master, Mr. Katly Robinson, and seven seamen and marines wounded, one of them mortally.

On the 24th of August the British 18-pounder 32-gun frigate Amphion, Captain William Hoste, reconnoitred the port of Cortelazzo, situated between Venice and Triest, and discovered lying there six Franco-Italian gun-boats, and convoy of merchant trabaccolos, moored in a strong position, under a battery of four 24-pounders, at the mouth of the river Piavie. Finding it impracticable, on account of the shallowness of the water, to enter the port with the frigate, Captain Hoste, having received from a fisherman a very correct account of the force and situation of the vessels and battery, resolved to send in his boats. To prevent any suspicion of design, he kept out of sight of land until the evening of the 26th; when, crowding all sail, the Amphion stood in shore, and at 1 A.M. on the 27th anchored off the entrance of the Piavie.

At 3 A.M. a detachment of 70 seamen and marines, commanded by Lieutenant Phillott, assisted by Lieutenant George Matthew Jones, and Lieutenant of marines Thomas Moore, landed about a mile to the southward of the battery; leaving Lieutenant William Slaughter, with the boats, to push for the river the instant the fort was carried. At 3 h. 15 m. A.M. the alarm was given; and at the same instant Lieutenant Phillott and his party attacked the fort. So vigorous was the assault, that, in 10 minutes, although surrounded by a ditch and a chevaux-de-frize, the fort was carried, and the concerted signal made for the boats to advance. The four 24-pounders on the battery were instantly turned upon the gun-boats, which were also attacked by a fire of musketry from Lieutenant Moore and his marines. Thus assailed, the gun-boats were boarded and carried, after a slight opposition, by the Amphion's boats under Lieutenant Slaughter.

Four of the gun-boats mounted one long 24-pounder each, and two of them, of a larger description, mounted each one long 24-pounder in the bow and one long 12-pounder in the stern, with four swivels along the gunwale and a crew of 36 men. Two trabaccolos with cargoes were taken, and five burnt. Having spiked the guns at the battery, and totally destroyed it, together with an adjacent barrack, Lieutenant Phillott and his detachment re-embarked at 1 P.M., with so slight a loss as one marine accidentally wounded by an explosion, and that not badly, after the battery and vessels had been captured.

In addition to the officers already named, there were present in this very gallant and important exploit, master's mates John Dalling and Thomas Boardman, midshipmen Joseph Gape, Charles Henry Ross, George Castle, Charles Henry Kempthorn, William Lee Rees, and Charles Bruce, and first-class volunteers, or boys, Thomas Edward Hoste, Francis George Farewell, and Robert Spearman; also surgeon's assistant Jonathan Angas. For his distinguished behaviour on this and on several previous occasions, Lieutenant Phillott was immediately promoted to the rank of commander.

On the 1st of April in the evening, the British 28-gun frigate Mercury, Captain the Honourable Henry Duncan, detached her boats, under the orders of Lieutenant Watkin Owen Pell, assisted by Lieutenant Robert James Gordon, Mr. Richard Hildyard the master, Lieutenant of marines James Whylock, Jeremiah Crawley the carpenter, George Anderson captain's clerk, midshipmen John Sterling, John Wilkes, William Parker, and Charles Adam, and Mr. Robert Williams acting surgeon, to cut out from the port of Rovigno, on the coast of Istria, two Franco-Italian gun-boats moored close to two heavy batteries.

After dark the boats pulled into the harbour, the entrance of which is not more than 100 yards wide; and, under a very heavy* fire of great guns and musketry, they boarded and carried, although fully prepared with boarding-nettings triced up to her mast-head, the gun-boat Léda, of one long 24-pounder and six large swivels, commanded by a French enseigne de vaisseau. The other gun-boat, similarly armed, was lying close to her, and would also have been captured; had not a fog unexpectedly come on, which completely deranged the plan of attack, and obliged the boats to tow the prize out under the additional fire of five guns, mounted upon an island that was to have been stormed by the marines. In this very gallant affair the British had one seaman killed, and Lieutenant Pell, who had previously lost a leg in the service, wounded severely in two places, and three seamen wounded slightly.

On the 15th of May the Mercury anchored within half gun

shot, in four fathoms, and cannonaded the town of Rotti, near Manfredonia. After pouring in a few broadsides, Captain Duncan sent in a boat's crew and a party of marines under Lieutenant Gordon, who landed and destroyed seven trabaccolos which had been hauled on shore, and returned to the ship with no other loss than himself severely wounded by an explosion of gunpowder while burning one of the vessels.

On the night of the 7th of September, the boats of the Mercury, under the orders of Lieutenant Pell, assisted by Lieutenant Gordon, Lieutenant Whylock of the marines, Mr. Sandell the gunner, and Mr. Anderson captain's clerk, each of whom commanded a boat, went into the harbour of Barletta near Manfredonia, and boarded and carried, in a very gallant style, the French national schooner Pugliése, mounting five 6, and two 18 pounders, with 31 men on board, commanded by an enseigne de vaisseau. Although the schooner fired as the boats approached, was moored with eight cables inside, almost touched the mole lined with musketry, and was within musket-shot of a castle mounting eight guns, and of two armed feluccas, from under the fire of which the Pugliése was towed without rudder or sails, so judiciously and promptly was the attack made by Lieutenant Pell, that not a man of his party was hurt.

On the 11th of May the British 38-gun frigate Melpomène, Captain Peter Parker, chased a Danish man-of-war cutter, of six guns, on shore at Huilbo, a harbour in Jutland. The Melpomène immediately anchored in 19 fathoms, and despatched her boats, under the orders of Lieutenants James Hanway Plumridge and George Rennie, to destroy the cutter. The boats, covered by the fire of the Melpomène, completely effected their object under a galling fire from the enemy, but not without loss, Lieutenant Rennie, two seamen, and three marines having been severely wounded.

On the 15th of May the British 18-pounder 32-gun frigate Tartar, Captain Joseph Baker, chased on shore near Felixberg, on the coast of Courland, a Danish sloop-privateer of four guns; the crew of which, 24 in number, landed with their muskets, and, being joined by some of the country people, posted themselves behind the sand-hills near the beach. Captain Baker immediately sent the Tartar's boats, under the orders of Lieutenants Thomas Sykes and Frederick Augustus Hargood Parker, to board the vessel and bring off or destroy her. The British boarded the privateer without loss, and, by turning her guns upon the beach, soon dislodged the party posted there. But the Danes, before they abandoned their vessel, had most dishonourably placed a lighted candle in a 12-pounder cartridge in the magazine, where lay several hundredweight of powder. Fortunately one of the Tartar's men discovered the light, and, with wonderful presence of mind, grasped the candle in his hand just as it had burnt within half an inch of the powder. Another minute, and all on board and alongside of the vessel would have been blown to destruction.

On the 23rd of May, at 10 h. 30 m. P.M., it being very dark, the British 38-gun frigate Melpomène, now commanded by Captain Frederick Warren, lying at single anchor in the Great Belt off Omoe island, nearly becalmed, discovered several large boats, standing towards her. The frigate immediately cleared for action, and at 11 P.M. commenced an engagement with about 20 sail of Danish gun-boats. Finding it impossible to bring her guns to bear with any effect while at anchor, and a light air of wind just then springing up, the Melpomène cut her cable, and made sail to close her opponents. In this way the action continued until 1 h. 15 m. A.M. on the 30th; when the gun-boats began to slacken their fire, and presently pulled away from the frigate with all their strength. The wind still continuing light, the Melpomène was unable to proceed in chase; and her individually small, but collectively formidable, antagonists got back to their port.

The long 18 and 24 pounders of the Danes had produced a very serious effect both upon the *matériel* and the *personnel* of the British frigate: her sails and rigging of every sort were cut to pieces; her mizenmast so badly wounded as to require to be fished; her bumpkin shot away, and her hull, both above and below water, greatly shattered. The loss on board the Melpomène amounted to four seamen and one marine killed, and 29 officers, seamen, and marines wounded. What loss was sustained on the part of the Danes we are unable to show; but it was probably of no very great amount, the darkness of the night concealing the gun-boats from view, and the calm state of the weather enabling them to take a position out of the reach of the frigate's broadside. Captain Warren, his officers, and crew behaved in the bravest manner; and, as a proof that their ship was really in the shattered state we have described, the Melpomène, on her return to England in two or three months afterwards, was put out of commission as a cruising frigate.

On the 19th of June the British 74-gun ship Bellerophon, Captain Samuel Warren, cruising off the coast of Swedish Finland in company with the Minotaur 74, Captain John Barrett was detached by the latter off Hangö. At sunset the Bellerophon discovered a lugger, apparently armed, and two other vessels, at anchor within the islands. Deeming it of importance to get hold of them, Captain Warren anchored, and detached the boats of the Bellerophon, under the orders of Lieutenant Robert Pilch, assisted by Lieutenants John Sheridan and George Bentham, Lieutenant of marines Alfred Octavius Carrington, and Mr. Mart the ship's carpenter, all volunteers. The party met no opposition in getting possession of the vessels; but, being found of no value, they were abandoned, especially as they lay within gun-shot of four strong batteries, not before observed, and of several gun-boats. It was now judged necessary, to prevent loss in returning, to dash at the nearest battery, which mounted four 24-pounders, and was garrisoned by 103 men. After an obstinate resistance, this battery was carried in the most gallant manner, the Russians retreating to some boats that lay on the opposite side of the island. The guns were spiked and the magazine destroyed, and the British got back to their ship with so comparatively slight a loss as five men wounded.

On the 7th of July, as a British squadron, composed of the 74-gun ships Implacable, Captain Thómas Byam Martin, and Bellerophon, Captain Samuel Warren, 38-gun frigate Melpomène, Captain Peter Parker, and 18-gun ship-sloop Prometheus, Captain Thomas Forrest, was cruising on the coast of Finland, a Russian flotilla of gun-boats and merchant-vessels was observed at anchor under Porcola Point. The gun-boats were eight in number, each armed with one long 24 and one long 30 pounder, and manned with 46 men. The position they had taken was of extraordinary strength, being betwixt two rocks, which served as a cover to their wings, and whence a destructive fire of grape could be poured upon any boats that should assail them. Notwithstanding this, it was resolved to attempt the capture or destruction of the flotilla; and Lieutenant Joseph Hawkey, first of the Implacable, was gratified with the command of the Enterprise, to consist of the boats of the four ships, 17 in number, containing about 270 officers and men. Among the officers employed were the following: Lieutenants William Houghton and Frederick Vernon, and Lieutenants of marines James Thomas Cracknell and James Clarke, of the Implacable; Lieutenants Charles Allen, John Sheridan, and John Skekel, and Lieutenants of marines George Kendall and Alfred Octavius Carrington, of the Bellerophon; Lieutenant George Rennie,

Lieutenant of marines Robert Gilbert, and midshipman John B. Mounteney, of the Melpomène; and Lieutenant James Stirling, of the Prometheus.

At 9 P.M. the boats proceeded to the attack, and, regardless of the heavy fire opened upon them in their advance, pushed on, not firing a musket until they touched the sides of the gun-boats; when the British seamen and marines boarded, sword in hand, and carried all before them. Of the eight gun-boats, six were captured, one was sunk, and one escaped; and the whole 12 merchant-vessels under their protection, and which were laden with powder and provisions for the Russian army, were also captured, together with a large armed ship. The latter was burnt, but the other vessels were brought safe out.

This truly gallant exploit was not accomplished without a serious loss. Lieutenant Hawkey, the commanding officer of the detachment, having taken one gun-boat, was killed by a grape-shot while in the act of boarding the second: and the last words of this gallant young man were:—" Huzza! push on, England for ever!" Captain Martin, in his letter to Vice-admiral Sir James Saumarez, thus eloquently touches upon the merits of Lieutenant Hawkey:—" No praise from my pen can do adequate justice to this lamented young man; as an officer, he was active, correct, and zealous, to the highest degree; the leader in every kind of enterprise, and regardless of danger, he delighted in whatever could tend to promote the glory of his country." The next officer, Lieutenant Charles Allen, of the Bellerophon, assumed the command of the party, and completed the business in the successful manner already described.

The whole of the loss on the British side amounted to two lieutenants (Messrs. Hawkey and Stirling), one midshipman (Mr. Mounteney), one second master (Benjamin Crandon), eight seamen, and five marines killed, and one boatswain (Matthew Vesey), 25 seamen, and 11 marines wounded. Among the loss acknowledged to have been sustained by the Russians were 63 killed. A great many of the Russian seamen escaped on shore, and several perished in the attempt; and, of the 127 prisoners taken, 51 were wounded.

On the 25th of July Captain Charles Dudley Pater, commanding a British squadron, composed of his own ship, the Princess Caroline 74, the Minotaur, of the same force, Captain John Barrett, 18-pounder 32-gun frigate Cerberus, Captain Henry Whitby, and 18-gun ship-sloop Prometheus, Captain Thomas Forrest, permitted the latter to lead the boats of the squadron, 17 in number, to the attack of four Russian gun-boats and an armed brig, lying at Fredericksham, near Apso roads, in the gulf of Finland. After dark the boats, commanded by Captain Forrest, who was assisted by, among other officers, Lieutenants James Bashford of the Princess Caroline, John James Callenan, and Lieutenants of marines William Wilkin, of the Minotaur, Lieutenants Robert Pettet and John Simpson, of the Cerberus, and Gawen Forster and Thomas Finnimore, of the Prometheus, pushed off from the squadron, and at 10 h. 30 m. P.M. commenced the attack. After a most desperate and sanguinary conflict, three of the gun-boats, mounting two long 18-pounders each, and having on board between them 137 men, besides an armed transport-brig, with 23 men, were captured and brought off.

Costly, indeed, were the prizes. The British loss amounted to one lieutenant (John James Callenan), one second-lieutenant of marines (William Wilkin), one midshipman (Gordon Carrington), and six seamen and marines killed; Captain Forrest himself, one lieutenant (Gawen Forster), three midshipmen (George Elvey, Thomas Milne, and John Chalmers), and 46 seamen and marines wounded. The Russians, on their side, acknowledged a loss of 28 killed and 59 wounded; making a total of 47 men killed and 110 wounded, in obtaining possession of three gun-boats. One of these gun-boats, No. 62, was so obstinately defended, that every man of her crew, 44 in number, was either killed or wounded before she surrendered: the killed alone amounted to 24. The result of this enterprise was a defeat to the Russians certainly, but under circumstances that reflected the brightest honour upon the character of their navy. For the gallantry he had shown on the occasion, Captain Forrest was promoted to post-rank.

On the 12th of August the British 18-gun ship-sloop Lynx, Captain John Willoughby Marshall, and gun-brig Monkey, Lieutenant Thomas Fitzgerald, being off Dais head on the Danish coast, discovered and chased a lugger, and on standing in-shore, discovered two others at an anchor. The latter got under way, and, with the one first seen, hoisted Danish colours, and re-anchored in line within the reef off Dais head. The water being too shoal to admit the Lynx to get within gun-shot of these luggers, Captain Marshall, at 4 P.M., detached the Monkey, accompanied by the boats of the Lynx under Lieutenant Edward Kelly, to make an attack upon them.

On the approach of the brig, the luggers, the largest of which mounted four guns and four howitzers and lay with springs on her cable, opened a fire upon her. The Monkey reserved her fire until she had anchored about half gun-shot from them; at which moment, owing to the intricacy of the navigation, the brig took the ground, but was presently got off without damage. The Monkey then opened her fire, and at the second broadside compelled the three luggers to cut their cables and run on shore. The Danes now attempted to scuttle their vessels; but, by the well-directed fire of the 18-pounder carronade mounted in the Lynx's launch, they were prevented from doing so, and the vessels were promptly boarded, and their guns turned upon their retreating crews. The British then proceeded to get the three luggers afloat, and by 5 A.M. on the 13th, brought them all out without the slightest casualty. This was peculiarly fortunate, as a cask of powder was discovered on board the largest lugger, close to the fire-place, where it had been put by the Danes with the evident intention of blowing up the vessel.

On the 10th of September, in the afternoon, the British gun-brig Diana, of 10 long 6-pounders and 45 men and boys, Lieutenant William Kempthorne, standing into the bay of Amarang on the north end of the Dutch island of Celebes, discovered the Dutch brig-of-war Zephyr, of 14 long Dutch 6-pounders and 45 men and boys, commanded by Captain-lieutenant Gillet Vander-Veld, lying at anchor close under a fort, with two cables fast to the shore. As the sea-breeze was blowing fresh into the bay, Lieutenant Kempthorne did not think it prudent to attack the brig in that position, but resolved to attempt cutting her out at night with the boats, when the wind would probably blow off the land.

The Diana, accordingly, beat about the bay, disguised as a merchant-brig; and, as soon as it became dark, Lieutenant Kempthorne detached the strength of his little crew to execute the hazardous service of cutting out the Dutch brig-of-war, keeping close after the boats with the Diana to be ready to give them support. After a fruitless search of two hours, the boats returned without having been able to find the brig. It immediately struck Lieutenant Kempthorne that, as the night was dark and hazy, and the land wind blew fresh, the Zephyr had made sail with the intention of sheltering herself under a strong fort in the bay of Monado at a short distance to the northward. The Diana immediately hoisted in her boats, and made all sail in that direction.

On the 11th, at daylight, the Dutch brig was discovered hull down ahead : but, although the Diana gained fast upon her, the Zephyr got under cover of the fort, when the British brig was still three miles off. As the sea-breeze had set in with great violence, and there was every appearance of a gale, the Dutch captain did not like to anchor on a lee shore. The Zephyr, accordingly, came to the wind and stood out towards the Diana. Lieutenant Kempthorne, with the view of drawing the Dutch brig beyond the reach of the fort, now practised every means to retard the Diana's sailing, so as to allow the Zephyr gradually to overtake her. However, when about nine miles from the fort, the Dutch brig wore and stood in again; and, deception being no longer available, the Diana wore and stood after her.

At 4 h. 30 m., just as the Zephyr had got within four miles of Monado fort, the land-breeze, which was unusually early, came off, and, taking the brig aback, compelled her to fill on the larboard tack. At the same time the Diana, still feeling the influence of the sea-breeze, came rapidly up, till she got within half gun-shot on her opponent's lee beam, when the British brig also filled on the larboard tack, with the land wind. The Diana immediately opened her fire, and the Zephyr returned it. In about 20 minutes, in order to get nearer to the fort, the latter wore round on the starboard tack. The Diana followed the manœuvre, and the two brigs renewed the engagement on the starboard tack. After the action had continued in this way about 40 minutes, the Zephyr, who had just had her gaff and maintopgallantmast shot away, encouraged by the appearance of five gun-boats sweeping off to her assistance, ran down within pistol-shot on the weather-beam of her opponent. Having shortly afterwards had both maintopsail sheets shot away, the Zephyr dropped nearly alongside of the Diana; whose crew were preparing to board, when, at about 5 h. 40 m. P.M., the Dutch brig hauled down her colours. The Diana instantly took her prize in tow; and, wearing, stood towards the gun-boats, who were then sweeping down in line upon her weather-beam, and closing fast. After receiving a few shot, however, from the Diana, the Dutch gun-boats put about and left the British brig in undisturbed possession of her prize.

Notwithstanding that this action had lasted altogether one hour and ten minutes, the Diana sustained no damage of the least consequence, and had not a man of her crew hurt. The Zephyr, on the other hand, was tolerably cut up in masts and rigging, and had her first-lieutenant and four men killed, and seven or eight men wounded. For the judgment as well as gallantry he had displayed, from his first descrying this Dutch brig to the moment at which he secured her as his prize, Lieutenant Kempthorne was promoted to the rank of commander.

On the 17th of October, at daylight, the British 18-gun ship-sloop Hazard, Captain Hugh Cameron, and 18-gun brig-sloop Pelorus, Captain Thomas Huskisson, cruising off Pointe-à-Pitre, island of Guadaloupe, observed a privateer-schooner moored under the battery of Sainte-Marie. Captain Cameron immediately despatched the boats, under the orders of Lieutenant James Robertson and Edward Flinn, first of each sloop, assisted by midshipmen John S. Brisbane and Hugh Hunter, and William Fergusson, boatswain of the Hazard, and Eleazer Scott, midshipman of the Pelorus, to capture or destroy the privateer; and the ship and brig stood in to cover them.

Although opposed, as they approached the shore, by a heavy fire of grape from the battery until it was silenced by the ships, and of grape and musketry from the privateer until they were nearly alongside, the boats pushed on, and gallantly boarded the vessel; the officers and crew of which, a minute or two before, had abandoned her and joined the long line of musketry on the beach. As the privateer, which mounted one long 18-pounder on a traversing carriage and two swivels, was moored to the shore with a chain from the mast-head and from each quarter, Lieutenant Robinson found it impracticable to get the vessel off. He and his party then proceeded to burn her; and, although opposed within 10 yards by musketry on the beach and two field-pieces, the British succeeded in blowing up the French privateer. This very gallant enterprise was not performed without a serious loss; six seamen and marines having been killed, and Lieutenant Flinn and Mr. Fergusson the Hazard's boatswain, much burnt at the explosion of the vessel, and seven seamen and marines wounded severely and slightly by the enemy's grape and musketry.

On the 12th of December, whilst the British 38-gun frigate Thetis, Captain George Miller, in company with the 16-gun brig-sloop, Pultusk, Captain William Elliott, 10-gun brig-sloop Achates, Captain Thomas Pinto, gun-brig Attentive, Lieutenant Robert Carr, and armed schooner Bacchus, Lieutenant Charles Deyman Jermy, was cruising off the north-west part of Guadaloupe, the French 16-gun brig-corvette Nisus, Capitaine de frégate Jacques-Gabriel La Netrel, was observed lying at an anchor in the harbour of Hayes, under the protection of a fort.

Captain Miller resolved to attempt cutting out this vessel, and for that purpose sent the boats of the Thetis, two sloops, and Bacchus, with the whole of their marines and a detachment of their seamen, under the order of Captain Elliott, assisted by Lieutenant Nathaniel Belchier, and by lieutenants of marines John Godfrey Ruell and Jervis Cooke.

The British landed in the evening without opposition, and proceeded, with considerable difficulty, through a thick wood and over a high hill, without any path or guide, till they reached the rear of the fort; which Captain Elliott and his party attacked and carried in the most gallant manner, forcing the garrison, represented to have amounted to 300 men, to retreat. Leaving Lieutenant Belchier to dismantle and destroy the battery, a service he effectually performed, Captain Elliott, supported by the squadron, but particularly by the Attentive, who entered a narrow harbour and maintained for upwards of six hours a close and vigorous cannonade, proceeded to attack, and very soon boarded and carried, the corvette. To add to the value of this service, it was executed with so slight a loss as one seaman and one marine of the party on shore, and two seamen on board the Attentive, wounded. The Pultusk had also a considerable share in the cannonade, and received into her larboard side amidships, a hot shot or carcass from the battery, which, although a foot under water, continued burning until a plug was driven into the hole.

The Nisus had sailed from Lorient on the 30th of October with a cargo of flour, had arrived at the Hayes on the 1st of December, and, when captured, was again ready for sea with a cargo of coffee. Being a fine brig of 337 tons, the Nisus was added to the British navy under the appropriate name of Gaudeloupe, or Gaudaloupe, as the name is spelt in the lists.

On the 14th the British 18-pounder 36-gun frigate Melampus, Captain Edward Hawker, cruising off Guadaloupe, after a chase of 28 hours, captured the French 16-gun brig-corvette Bearnais, of 109 men and boys, commanded by Lieutenant de vaisseau Louis-Charles-Gaspard Bonnefoy-de-Monthazin; who did not surrender till he had one man killed and several wounded, and had wounded two men on board the Melampus. The Bearnais was from Bayonne bound to Guadaloupe, with flour and warlike stores; and, being a brig exactly similar in size to the Nisus, was added to the British navy under the name of Curieux, the former brig-sloop of that name having recently been wrecked in the West Indies.

On the 17th, close in with the island of Sante-Cruiz, another French brig-corvette, of the same class as the Bearnais and Nisus, the Papillon, commanded by Capitaine de frégate Thomas-Joseph Lamourex de la Génetière, was captured after a 38 hours' chase, but without, as it appears, the slightest resistance, by the British 18-gun ship-sloop Rosamond, Captain Benjamin Walker. The Papillon mounted, like the rest of her class, 14 carronades, 24-pounders, and two sixes, with, including 30 troops, a crew of 110 men and boys; had been 33 days from Bordeaux, and was carrying a cargo of flour to Guadaloupe. Being a fine brig of 343 tons, and only two years old, the Papillon was added to the British navy under the same name.

On the 13th of December, at 1 P.M., latitude 17° 18' north, and longitude 57° west, as the British 38-gun frigate Junon, Captain John Shortland, in company with the 16-gun brig-sloop Observateur, Captain Frederick Augustus Wetherall, was lying to boarding an American ship, four large ships made their appearance to the northward. These were the French 40-gun frigates Renommée, Commodore Francois Roquebert, and Clorinde, Captain Jacques Saint-Cricq; having under their convoy the two armees en flûte and late 40-gun frigates Loire and Seine, commanded by Lieutenants de vaisseau Joseph Normand-Kergre and Bernard Vincent, mounting 20 guns each (iron 36-pounder carronades and long 18-pounders), and laden with troops and military stores for Guadaloupe; with which, on the 15th of the preceding month, they had sailed from Nantes.

The Junon and Observateur immediately made sail in chase, and at 4 P.M. discovered that the strangers were frigates. Soon afterwards, having cleared for action, the British frigate and brig hoisted their colours, and the Junon fired several guns to induce the strangers to show theirs. At 5 P.M., approaching near, the Junon made the private signal: on which the Renommée first, and then her consorts, hoisted Spanish colours, but showed no disposition to bring to. The British frigate, still bearing down, now hoisted the Spanish private signal, a blue pendant at the fore and a ball at the main; when, almost immediately, the Renommée hoisted a red flag with a white cross at the fore, which was the proper answer to the signal. Thus deceived, the Junon continued to approach the four French frigates; until, at 5 h. 30 m. P.M., the latter shortened sail and hauled their wind in line of battle on the larboard tack. The Junon immediately shortened sail also; and, when about a quarter of a mile to windward of the French squadron, the

Renommée, who was the leading frigate, hauled down the Spanish and hoisted French colours, and poured a destructive broadside into the starboard bow of the British frigate.

Finding, from the state of her rigging, that it was impossible to escape to windward, the Junon ran under the stern of the Renommée and raked her. The Observateur, about the same time, discharged her starboard broadside at the French frigate's bows, but at too great a distance for the brig's carronades to do execution. Meanwhile the Clorinde, the second astern to the Renommée, had hauled close to the wind, and now ran nearly foul of the Junon on her starboard side. In this position a spirited cannonade ensued for upwards of 10 minutes, to the apparent disadvantage of the Clorinde; when the Renommée, who, after having been raked by her opponent, had wore to avoid a repetition of the salute, ran foul of the Junon on her larboard side. As if these two French frigates were not sufficient to overpower the single British frigate, the Seine and Loire stationed themselves, one ahead, the other astern, of the Junon; and the troops on board of each, particularly of the Loire, who lay with her bowsprit over the British frigate's larboard quarter, kept up a most destructive fire of musketry, which nearly cleared the Junon's quarter-deck of both officers and men.

It was at about this time that Captain Shortland had his leg broken by a grape-shot, and was also badly wounded by splinters. The command of the ship, in consequence, devolved upon Lieutenant Samuel Bartlett Deecker. The Clorinde now attempted to board the Junon on the starboard quarter, but was most gallantly repulsed by a few men led on by Lieutenant John Green of the marines, who nobly fell in the struggle. The Renommée would probably have made a similar attempt on the opposite side; but the Junon, dropping her foresail, shot ahead, clear of her two opponents. The latter, however, were not slow in regaining their position, and, boarding the Junon simultaneously, one on each side, took possession of the British frigate, which had by this time fought her four opponents more than 45 minutes, the whole of the time, with two of them at least, yard-arm and yard-arm.

The Junon was cut to pieces in her hull and lower masts; and, out of her reduced crew of 224 men and boys, of whom 44 were Spaniards and Portuguese, she lost 20 officers and men killed and 40 wounded. The Observateur, who had hauled her wind as soon as she saw what was likely to be the fate of her consort, suffered neither damage nor loss. The Renommée, as acknowledged by Captain Roquebert, had, out of her 360 men and boys, 15 men killed and only three wounded; and the Clorinde, whose complement was the same, six killed and 15 wounded; total, 21 killed and 18 wounded. The two armées en flûte, each of which had on board, including 200 troops, about 400 men and boys, owing to their safe position during the engagement, escaped, it appears, without any loss whatever. In so shattered a state was the Junon at the time she surrendered, that her captors, despairing of getting their prize into port, although Guadaloupe, the island to which they were bound, was at no great distance to leeward, quickly removed the prisoners and set the ship on fire.

The Junon had on board her French guns, 46 in number,[1] and the Renommée and Clorinde were each armed exactly the same as she was. Commodore Roquebert is honourable enough to say of his antagonist, " Le capitaine anglais, a manœuvre sa frégate avec autant de courage que d'habileté; mais il lui était devenu impossible de nous échapper."[2] It is somewhat strange, however, that the French captain should refer to the Loire and Seine no otherwise than as, without naming them, "les transports que nous convoyons," and should not state that they took the slightest part in the action. We hope, for the sake of consistency in M. Roquebert, that the minister of marine, or the supervisor of official letters, has been the cause of so important an omission.

What is there in this action, that the account of it should have been denied a place in the usual depository of naval and military achievements, the London Gazette? Here is a British frigate defending herself against four ships, each of two of them her equal in guns, and greatly her superior in men, until she loses more than a fourth of her crew in killed and wounded, and inflicts upon her two principal antagonists a loss two-thirds as heavy as that which she suffers herself; thus combining, what is not always found united, even in a British ship, a high degree of gallantry with an equal share of practical skill. But the Junon's affair was a defeat. Was not the affair of the Blanche a defeat—a far less honourable defeat? Yet Captain Mudge was fortunate enough to get his long letter blazoned in the Gazette, and circulated all over the kingdom. As far as our humble efforts can prevail, justice shall yet be done to the officers and crew of the Junon; and these pages at least shall

---

[1] See p. 7.
[2] "Trois," Moniteur, February 3, 1810; probably a misprint for " vingt-trois.'

tell, of the brave defence maintained by that frigate against a force more than trebly superior to her own.

On the 15th, at 1 P.M., the Observateur arrived off Basse-terre, Guadaloupe; and, having telegraphed the 38-gun frigate Blonde, Captain Volant Vashon Ballard, that five French frigates (Captain Wetherall not having witnessed the destruction of the Junon) were within six hours' sail of her, stood on under a press of canvas towards Martinique. Captain Ballard, having then in his company the 38-gun frigate Thetis, Captain George Miller, and the 18-gun ship-sloops Hazard and Cygnet, Captains Hugh Cameron and Edward Dix, immediately made all sail for the channel between the Saintes and Guadaloupe, down which he expected the enemy would pass.

On the next day, the 16th, Captain Ballard was joined by the 18-gun brig-sloops Scorpion and Ringdove, Captains Francis Stanfell and William Dowers; and at 8 P.M. he detached the Hazard and Ringdove to reconnoitre Basse-terre. On the 17th, at 4 A.M., the Blonde and Thetis were joined by the 12-pounder 32-gun frigate Castor, Captain William Roberts, with important information. On the 15th, at 3 h. 30 m. P.M., the island of Désirade bearing south-south-east distant 11 miles, the Castor had re-captured the ship Ariel, of Liverpool, taken on the 4th by the Renommée, and her three consorts, and soon after-wards fell in with, and was chased by, the French frigates themselves; two of which, the Seine and Loire, being light rigged, were considered to be corvettes. The four ships after-wards lay to.

At daylight the Blonde and squadron, then nearly abreast of Basse-terre, descried two strange ships to the northward. These were the Loire and Seine, which, just as the Castor had lost sight of them, had separated from the Renommée and Clorinde, and were now making the best of their way to Basse-terre. The British ships instantly proceeded in chase; and at 8 A.M. the two French ships, finding themselves cut off from their port, steered along the coast to the north-west. At 10 A.M. they entered a cove named Anse la Barque, situated about three leagues to the north-west of Basse-terre. Here the two French ships anchored head and stern, with their broadsides to the sea, and under the protection of a battery on each point of the bay or cove.

At 2 h. 40 m. P.M. a battery on Pointe Lizard, a little to the southward of Anse la Barque, fired repeatedly at the British squadron, and presently sent a shot right through the hull of the Ringdove, who was then close in shore nearly becalmed. Captain Dowers immediately embarked with a party in his boats; at 2 h. 55 m. landed; at 3 P.M. stormed and carried the fort; at 3 h. 15 m. P.M. spiked the guns, destroyed the works, and blew up the magazine; and at 4 P.M. returned to the Ringdove without the slightest casualty. In the evening, being resolved to attack the French frigates and batteries, Captain Ballard sent the 12-gun schooner Elizabeth, Lieutenant Charles Finch, towards Anse la Barque, to try for an anchorage, and followed with the Blonde, to cover her from the enemy's fire. At 8 P.M. the Blonde opened a fire upon the battery, and was fired at in return. The schooner found anchorage, and she and the Blonde stood out without any material damage. On the same evening the 36-gun frigate Freija, Captain John Hayes, joined company from Martinique.

On the 18th, at 8 h. 30 m. A.M., a flag of truce came off from the shore; and at the same time the 74-gun ship Sceptre, Captain Samuel James Ballard, from Fort Royal, Martinique, joined company. Commodore Ballard instantly dismissed the flag of truce, and made preparations for an immediate attack upon the French frigates. The plan, as given out in orders, was for the Blonde to lead in, followed by the Thetis; which two frigates were to anchor abreast of and engage the two French frigates, while the Sceptre and Freija cannonaded the batteries. The Hazard, Cygnet, Ringdove, and Elizabeth, in the mean time, were to take the armed boats of the squadron in tow.

Owing to light airs and calms, the Blonde and Thetis found a great difficulty in nearing the shore. At 2 h. 25 m. P.M. one of the forts commenced firing on the British frigates. At 2 h. 40 m. the French frigates opened their fire, which the Blonde and Thetis returned. Having arrived within a quarter of a mile of the two French frigates, and within half pistol-shot of the fort, and not being able owing to the calm to get nearer, the Blonde anchored with springs and opened her starboard broadside. At 3 h. 20 m. P.M. her stream cable was shot away by the fort, which kept up a very annoying fire. The Thetis soon afterwards got near enough to anchor and open her fire. At 3 h. 30 m. the northernmost French frigate had all three masts shot away by the board. At 3 h. 35 m. she struck her colours. At the same moment the Blonde had her small bower cable shot away by the fort: she let go her best bower, and continued the engagement. At 3 h. 40 m. P.M., in consequence of one French frigate having struck, the Thetis slipped her bower cable and brought her broadside to bear on the fort. At 4 h. 20 m. the southernmost French frigate hauled down her colours; and at the same moment the other frigate was seen to be on fire. Having now compelled both French frigates to surrender, the Blonde and Thetis, at about 5 h. 10 m. P.M., cut their cables and made sail out of reach of the fort; which had latterly been keeping up a heavy fire of round, grape, and musketry. At 5 h. 20 m. P.M. the southernmost French frigate blew up with a tremendous explosion, and a part of the flaming wreck was seen to fall into the maintopmast cross-trees of the southernmost frigate, and to set her on fire.

Just about this time the boats of the squadron, under the orders of Captain Cameron, covered by the Sceptre, Freija, Hazard, Cygnet, and Ringdove, pushed off for the shore, and landed under a heavy fire. The British stormed and carried the fort, but not without a serious loss. Captain Cameron was wounded by a musket-ball while in the act of hauling down the French colours; and was killed by a grape-shot just as, having executed the service he had been sent upon, he was stepping into his boat to return to the Hazard. The gazette-account of the destruction of these two French armées en flûte and batteries is so very brief and imperfect, that we are not able to distinguish the loss sustained on board from that sustained on shore. The only ships named in the return of loss are the Blonde and Thetis. The Blonde, it appears, had her first-lieutenant (George Jenkins), one master's mate (Edward Freeman), four seamen, and two marines killed, her third-lieutenant (Cæsar William Richardson), one midshipman (Thomas Robotham), 10 seamen, and four marines wounded; and the Thetis, six seamen wounded; total, including Captain Cameron of the Hazard, nine killed and 22 wounded.

Among the persons landed out of the two French ships (the last of which blew up while the British were on shore) just previous to their being set on fire, was the gallant and dreadfully wounded captain of the Junon. Captain Shortland had suffered the amputation of his right leg above the knee, and of a finger: a grape-shot had also been extracted from his hand; and, had there been a probability of saving his life, other operations would have been necessary. His sufferings, when the Castor hove in sight, in being hastily removed from the captain's cabin to the gun-room, were extreme; and not less so were they, when with equal hurry he was removed from the French frigate to the shore at Anse la Barque, and then conveyed 13 miles in a scorching sun to the hospital. Human nature at length sank beneath this load of suffering; and on the 21st of January, after having been unable, during the five weeks and upwards that had elapsed since he was wounded, to sit up even in his bed, Captain Shortland expired. Although, as it would appear, shamefully inattentive to this brave British officer while living, the governor-general of Guadaloupe, General Enouf, paid to his mortal remains every possible respect. Captain Shortland was buried at Basse-terre with the highest military honours.

The capture of Guadaloupe, to be noticed hereafter, released Lieutenant Deecker and the other surviving officers and crew of the late Junon, that had been landed from the Loire and Seine; and on the 19th and 20th days of February, a court-martial was held upon them for the loss of their ship. In addition to a sentence of the most honourable acquittal, the court strongly recommended the Junon's late commanding officer for promotion. The recommendation, we are happy to say, was attended to; and on the 17th of the ensuing April, Lieutenant Deecker was rewarded with the commission of a commander. The late second and third lieutenants of the Junon, George Vernon Jackson and Henry Conn, had been taken on board the Renommée, of which ship and her consort we will now give some account.

After parting from the Loire and Seine on the evening of the 15th of December, off the north point of Guadaloupe, the Renommée and Clorinde bent their course back to Europe. On the 16th of January, in latitude 48° 50' north, longitude (from Greenwich) 12° 9' west, M. Roquebert was fallen in with by, as it appears to us, the British 38-gun frigate Virginie, Captain Edward Brace; who watched the Renommée and Clorinde during the day and until night concealed them from view: nor did the two French frigates evince any intention of molesting her. Thus avoiding by flight, even from an inferior force, all chance of being carried to a wrong destination, Commodore Roquebert, on the 23rd, anchored in the road of Brest.

We formerly mentioned that, on the 12th of November, 1808, the French 40-gun frigate Vénus, Commodore Jacques-Felix-Emmanuel Hamelin, sailed from Cherbourg for the East Indies. Some time previously, but exactly when we are uncertain, the 40-gun frigate Manche, Captain François-Désiré Breton, escaped from the same port, bound to the same distant station. Upon a similar destination sailed from the port of Nantes, the 40-gun frigate Bellone, Captain Victor-Guy Duperré; also from Flushing the 40-gun frigate Caroline; of whose captain's name we are uncertain, but we believe he died before, or very soon after, the frigate arrived at the Isle of France.

All four French frigates were at sea for the first time; and, by an extraordinary piece of good fortune, all reached their destination in safety. So intent, indeed, were the respective captains upon their voyage to a station which had already enriched three or four of their number, that, on their passage out, these frigates, we are certain, did not capture, and, we believe, did not chase or molest, a single British cruiser. In fact, when news reached England, that so many French frigates were still in the Indian seas committing depredations upon eastern commerce, no one appeared to know how or when they got there. We will now endeavour to give an account of their more important proceedings after they reached their appointed cruising-ground.

On the 2nd of May a small fleet of homeward-bound Indiamen quitted the Sand-heads of Bengal river, under the protection of the 18-gun ship-sloop Victor, Captain Edward Stopford. On the night of the 24th, in dark and squally weather, the Victor parted company; and on the 30th, after two ships had quitted the convoy from stress of weather, the following Indiamen remained in company: Streatham, Captain and senior officer John Dale; Europe, Captain William Gelston; and Lord Keith, Captain Peter Campbell. The Streatham and Europe were ships of 820 tons, and each mounted 20 medium 18-pounders on the main deck, and 10 carronades of the same caliber upon the quarter-deck, total 30 guns. The Streatham had a crew of 137 men, 60 of which were British and other European seamen, and the remainder, except four invalid soldiers, Chinese and Lascars; and the Europe, 72 British and other European seamen, and 56 Lascars, total 128. On board of each ship were also a few passengers. The Lord Keith was a ship of 600 tons, armed with 10 or 12 guns, and a crew of from 30 to 40 men.

On the 31st, at 5 h. 30 m. A.M., latitude 9° 15′ north, longitude 90° 30′ east, as the Streatham, Europe, and Lord Keith were steering south-south-east on the starboard tack, with the wind from south-west by south, a strange ship was seen about seven miles off in the south by west, standing to the north-west. The stranger was the French 40-gun frigate Caroline, now commanded by Lieutenant de vaisseau Jean-Baptiste-Henri Feretier. This frigate mounted, upon the quarter-deck and forecastle, eight iron 36-pounder carronades and 10 long 8-pounders; making her total number of guns 46, exclusive of 20 swivels carrying a one-pound ball, distributed along her gunwales and in her tops. Her crew consisted of 330 men and boys, all Europeans; besides, we believe, 50 or 60 troops taken on board at the Isle of France. The Caroline had sailed from Port Louis in the month of February, bound on a cruise in the Bay of Bengal. In the beginning of April the frigate arrived off the Sand-heads, cruised there about three weeks, capturing only one or two small vessels; and then, about three days before the India fleet sailed from the spot, steered for Carnicobar island to get a supply of water. While the Caroline was at these islands, the American ship Silenus, which had sailed from the Sand-heads under the protection, from pirates, of the Victor and her convoy, arrived there, and acquainted the French captain with the force, names, lading, and probable route of the Indiamen. Thus supplied with information, the Caroline made sail; and, in the course of a few days, M. Feretier was fortunate enough to find that, although the American captain had betrayed his protectors, he had not deceived him.

When first seen, the Caroline was taken for the Victor, but her size soon pointed out that she was a frigate. At a few minutes past 6 A.M., having previously made the private signal and got no answer, the Streatham made the signal to form the line; which was soon done, the Lord Keith leading, followed by the Streatham and Europe; but the two latter were at too great a distance apart. At 6 h. 30 m. A.M., having arrived abreast of the weather quarter of the Europe, the Caroline hoisted her colours and opened a fire upon that ship, which the Europe quickly returned. Between these two unequal antagonists, the action was maintained for nearly half an hour; at the end of which time the Indiaman had all her carronades and two of her main-deck guns dismounted, her foretopsail-yard cut in two, foremast badly wounded, rigging and sails cut to pieces, hull struck in several places, and two of her best men killed and one Lascar wounded. Having thus completely disabled the Europe, the Caroline ranged ahead, and, bearing up athwart the bows of her defenceless opponent, raked her. Captain Feretier then stood towards the lee-quarter of the Streatham, who had shortened sail to support the Europe, but had not been able to bring a gun to bear upon the French frigate.

At 7 A.M. the Caroline commenced action with the Streatham; and these two ships continued engaging until a few minutes before 8 A.M.: by which time the Caroline had reduced this antagonist to as disabled a state as her first, and had killed three, and wounded two, of the English sailors on board. Finding that all his carronades on the engaged side were dismounted, and that no inducements or threats could keep the Portuguese and Lascars to the main-deck guns, Captain Dale ordered the colours of the Streatham to be hauled down. The Caroline then wore from the latter, gave a broadside in passing to the Lord Keith, who, as well as the Europe, had fired occasionally at her while engaging the Streatham, and brought-to on the larboard quarter of the Europe; with whom she recommenced the action. After firing a short time in return, the Europe made sail to close the Streatham, and at 8 h. 20 m. A.M. learnt that she had struck. Finding this to be the case, and that the Lord Keith was well to windward, standing with all sail to the southward, Captain Gelston put before the wind. As soon as she had secured the Streatham the Caroline made sail in chase of the Europe; and at 10 A.M. the latter was obliged also to strike. The Lord Keith effected her escape, and arrived safe in England.

The loss on board the Caroline, according to the statement of her captain, amounted to only one killed, the ship's master, and M. Feretier and one or two men slightly wounded. The conduct of the French officers towards the passengers and crews of the captured Indiamen was, we are happy to be enabled to state, particularly kind and attentive. On account chiefly of the leaky state of the Europe, it took M. Feretier three days to refit his prizes: and, before the former ship could be made seaworthy, all her guns were obliged to be thrown overboard. The Caroline and her two richly laden prizes then set sail, and on the 22nd of July anchored in the bay of St. Paul, Isle Bourbon. While here, Captains Dale and Gelston addressed a joint letter of thanks to M. Feretier, for his good treatment of them and of his prisoners in general. To this letter M. Feretier returned a suitable reply; but in the reply, short as it is, he finds an opportunity of paying a compliment to the national character of his country. "Extrêmement sensible aux remercîmens que vous me faites, je suis aussi extrêmement content que l'évènement vous ait prouvé que, si le François sçait vaincre, il sçait aussi ce qu'il doit d'égards à de braves ennemis."

Some credit was undoubtedly due to the captain of the Caroline for his bold advance upon the three Indiamen, as well as for the skilful manner in which he attacked them. Had the Streatham, instead of only hauling up her foresail to wait for the Europe to close, tacked, and placed the French frigate between two fires, the Caroline would at all events have purchased her victory at a dearer rate. But having been allowed to conquer his opponents in detail, M. Feretier came out of the contest with almost entire impunity; and, on every consideration, the French lieutenant, who had thus ably filled a captain's post, deserved the reward bestowed upon him by General Decaen, the Governor at the Isle of France; which was a commission as capitaine de frégate. Nor must we omit to do justice to the two merchant captains, who certainly defended their ill-armed and worse-manned ships as long as was practicable; one of them, as we have seen, not surrendering his vessel until she was reduced to a sinking state.

On the 14th of August the British 18-gun ship-sloop Otter, Captain Nisbet Josiah Willoughby, cruising off Cape Brabant, Isle of France, discovered a brig and two fore-and-aft vessels at anchor under the protection of the batteries of Rivière-Noire. The brig had recently arrived from France with a cargo. One of the smaller vessels was a merchant-lugger, and the other a gun-boat attached to the French squadron on the station. Thinking it practicable, notwithstanding the immense strength of the batteries, to cut out these vessels by a *coup-de-main*, Captain Willoughby resolved to make the attempt that same night. In the mean time, to prevent suspicion, the Otter bore away for Bourbon until dark; then hauled up and worked back to the vicinity of Rivière-Noire. At 11 h. 30 m. P.M., when close enough in, Captain Willoughby pushed off in his gig, accompanied by Lieutenant John Burns in the launch, and midshipman William Weiss in the jolly-boat. The plan was, for the gig, supported by the two remaining boats, to carry the gun-vessel; the launch was then to secure the brig, and the jolly-boat the lugger.

Favoured by the darkness, the three boats got into the harbour unperceived; and having from the same cause, and the silence of the enemy, missed the gun-boat, the boats pulled alongside and captured the lugger. Having secured this vessel, Captain Willoughby detached the launch and jolly-boat to board the brig, and then proceeded with the gig in search of the gun-boat. Lieutenant Burns soon got alongside the brig, and found a body of soldiers drawn up on board to defend her. In the face of a heavy fire of musketry from these, the British boarded, and after a smart struggle on her decks, carried the vessel. The cable was then cut by one of the seamen left in the launch for that purpose; but not till he had been wounded in the head by the mate of the brig, and had killed him with a blow of his axe. Captain Willoughby having in the mean time approached so near to the innermost battery as to be hailed by one of the sentries, the alarm became general, and the batteries opened their fire.

Owing to her being firmly moored on the shore, and having her yards and topmasts down, there was no possibility of getting off the brig. Finding this to be the case, Captain Willoughby gave orders to take out the prisoners, all of whom had been secured in the hold, and burn the vessel. As, however, the prisoners, many of whom were wounded, could not in the emergency of the moment be removed, the brig was abandoned; and the three boats, taking the lugger in tow, carried her out, under a heavy fire from the batteries on both sides of the river. To enable them to distinguish their object in the dark, the Frenchmen on shore kept continually throwing up false fires of a superior description, which illuminated the whole river.

Under all these circumstances, it was rather surprising that no greater loss was sustained by Captain Willoughby and his party, than one man killed in the launch by a 24-pound shot which took his head off, and another wounded with the loss of his arm by a grape-shot; particularly as the lugger was much cut up in her rigging. The principal advantage derived from this attack was the evidence it afforded, of the feasibility of cutting out a vessel even from a place so strongly protected by nature and art as Rivière-Noire. And, had the gun-boat been found when the boats first entered, there cannot be a doubt that she would have shared the fate of the lugger. On clearing the entrance of the river, the lugger and the boats were met by the Otter's cutter, under Lieutenant Thomas Lamb Polden Laugharne; who on witnessing the heavy firing, had, with a commendable zeal, pushed off to render all the assistance in his power.

The harbour or bay of St. Paul at Isle Bourbon having long been the rendezvous of French cruisers on the Indian station, and, in particular, having, as has just appeared, afforded shelter to the Caroline and her two valuable prizes, Commodore Josias Rowley, of the 64-gun ship Raisonable, the commanding officer of the British force cruising off the isles of France and Bourbon, concerted with Lieutenant-colonel Henry S. Keating, commanding the troops at the adjacent small island of Rodriguez, recently taken possession of by the British, a plan for carrying, first, the batteries that defended, and then the shipping within, the road of St. Paul.

Accordingly, on the 16th of September, a detachment of 368 officers and men embarked at Fort Duncan, island of Rodriguez, on board the 12-pounder 36-gun frigate Néréide, Captain Robert Corbett, 18-gun ship-sloop Otter, Captain Nisbet Josiah

Willoughby, and the honourable Company's armed schooner Wasp, Lieutenant Watkins; and, on the evening of the 18th joined, off Port Louis, Isle of France, besides the Raisonable, the 18-pounder 36-gun frigate Sirius, Captain Samuel Pym, and 38-gun frigate Boadicea, Captain John Hatley. Early on the following morning 100 seamen from the Raisonable and Otter, and the marines of the squadron, 136 in number, forming, along with the troops, a total of 604 officers and men, were put on board the Néréide; Captain Corbett's perfect acquaintance with the coast rendering him the fittest person to undertake the important service of landing the detachment. Thus prepared, the squadron, in the evening, stood towards Bourbon, and early on the following morning, the 20th, arrived off the east end of the island.

On approaching the bay of St. Paul, the Néréide, to prevent suspicion, preceded the other ships; and, on the 21st, at 5 A.M., having anchored close to the beach, the frigate disembarked the troops, without causing any alarm, a little to the southward of Pointe du Galet, distant about seven miles from St. Paul. The troops and marines, commanded by Colonel Keating, and the detachment of seamen by Captain Willoughby, immediately commenced a forced march, with the view of crossing the causeways that extend over the lake, before the French could discover their approach. This important object the British fully accomplished; nor had the French time to form in any force until after Colonel Keating and his party had passed the strongest position.

By 7 A.M. the troops were in possession of the first and second batteries (Lambousière and la Centière), and immediately Captain Willoughby, with his detachment of seamen, turned the guns of those batteries upon the shipping; from whose fire, which was chiefly grape, and well directed, within pistol-shot of the shore, the troops suffered much. From the battery of la Centière, a detachment marched and took quiet possession of the third battery, or that of la Neuf; having previously defeated the islanders in a smart skirmish. The enemy having been reinforced from the hills, and having also received 110 troops of the line from the Caroline frigate, the guns of the first and second batteries were now spiked, and the seamen sent to man the battery of la Neuf; which soon opened its fire upon the Caroline and her consorts. The fourth and fifth batteries shared the fate of the others; and, by 8 h. 30 m. A.M., the town, batteries, magazines, eight field-pieces, 117 new and heavy guns of different calibers, and all the public stores, with several prisoners, were in the possession of Lieutenant-colonel Keating and the little army he commanded.

In the mean time the British squadron, having stood into the bay, had opened a heavy fire upon the French frigate, and the two Indiamen and other armed vessels in her company, as well as upon those batteries which, owing to their distance from the point of attack, were enabled to continue their fire. The British squadron then came to an anchor in the road, close off the town of St. Paul, and began taking measures to secure the Caroline and the rest of the French ships ; all of which, having cut their cables, had drifted on shore. The seamen of the squadron, however, soon succeeded in heaving the ships off, without any material injury.

Thus was effected, in the course of a few hours, by a British force of inconsiderable amount, the capture of the only safe anchorage at Isle Bourbon, together with its strong defences and shipping ; and that after a loss by no means so great as might have been expected. Of the naval detachment serving on shore, there were two seamen and five marines killed, one lieutennant (Edward Lloyd, Raisonable), two lieutenants of marines (Thomas Robert Pye, Boadicea, and Matthew Howden, Raisonable, the latter mortally), two seamen, 13 marines wounded, and one seaman missing ; and of the troops, eight killed, 40 wounded, and two missing: total 15 killed, 58 wounded, and three missing.

The captured ships were the Caroline French frigate, "Grappler," 14-gun brig, the honourable Company's late ships Streatham and Europe, and five or six smaller vessels. The British did not sustain any loss on board the squadron, and the ships were equally fortunate in respect to damage. The loss sustained by the French either afloat or on shore has not been enumerated. By evening the demolition of the different gun and mortar batteries and of the magazines was complete, and the whole of the troops, marines, and seamen returned on board their ships.

On the 22nd, in the evening, the appearance of a French force collecting upon the hills induced the lieutenant-colonel and commodore to reland the detachment of marines, accompanied by a few seamen, with orders to Captain Willoughby, who had again volunteered to take the command, to destroy the stores containing the public property. An extensive government store, containing all the raw silk which had been on board the Indiamen, and was valued at more than half a million sterling, was set on fire and destroyed. The remaining stores within reach were left untouched, merely because a doubt existed as to their being public property. This important service effected, the detachment re-embarked without the slightest casualty, although almost within gun-shot of a much superior force.

On the 23rd at daybreak, the troops, marines, and seamen were all in the boats ready again to land, under cover of the Néréide, when it was discovered that General Desbrusleys, the governor of Bourbon, had, in the course of the night, retreated across the island to St. Denis. The commandant of the town of St. Paul, Captain St. Michel, being now disposed to negotiate with the British, terms for the delivery of all public property in the town were drawn up and agreed to. General Desbrusleys having shot himself, through chagrin, as alleged, at the success of the British, a prolongation of the armistice was granted for five days. On the 28th the truce expired; and the British troops, marines, and seamen immediately began shipping the provisions, ordnance-stores, and small remainder of the cargoes of the captured Indiamen. Captains Dale and Gelston were then reinstated in the command of the Streatham and Europe; and with the aid of the British squadron, the ships were refitted for sea. This done, Commodore Rowley and his squadron made sail from the bay of St. Paul.

The Caroline, a tolerably fine frigate of 1078 tons, launched at Antwerp in August, 1806, was commissioned under the appropriate name (a Caroline being already in the service) of Bourbonaise, and Captain Corbett was appointed to command her. The vacancy in the Néréide was immediately filled up by giving post-rank to Captain Willoughby, who had so gallantly and so successfully exerted himself on the occasion; and of whom Lieutenant-colonel Keating and Captain Rowley, in their several despatches, speak in the highest terms.

The above, in substance, is as the account of the expedition of St. Paul's bay stands in our first edition; but a contemporary has given a somewhat different version of it. He names Captain Corbett as Captain Willoughby's assistant on shore, although the former never quitted the Néréide; and had he landed, would of course, from his superior rank, have assumed the command. The following paragraph also appears: "The Sirius (commanded, it appears, by 'Captain Corbet,' not Captain Pym) anchored with her stern within pistol-shot of the beach, and sustained the fire of the batteries, a frigate, two Indiamen, and a brig. She never returned a shot till both her anchors were let go; the British troops then rushed on; and in 20 minutes every French flag was struck. The grape-shot of the Sirius went over the most distant ships of the enemy; and so severe and well kept up was her fire, that both the French and English expressed their admiration."[1]

The principal part of this statement will be best answered by a short extract from the logs of two of the ships present at the attack. The Sirius herself says: "At 7 A.M. Néréide telegraphed Raisonable, 'troops on shore.' Observed a union-jack on one of the batteries. At 7 (h. 30 m. meant, it is believed) enemy opened a fire on the Néréide. At 8 Raisonable opened a fire on the French frigate. At 8, 10, Sirius fired several broadsides. Filled and made sail to windward. 8, 45, tacked and stood in shore. 9, 15, brought up with the stream and small bower, opened a raking fire on the Caroline, Indiamen, and battery. At 10 ceased firing, shipping and batteries in possession of the British troops." The Otter, by her log, says: "At 8, 45, observed all the batteries in our possession. 8, 50, observed Sirius make signal, 'Permission to anchor.' Affirmed by the Raisonable. 9, 14, observed Sirius anchor and open a raking fire on the frigate. 9, 20, the frigate hauled down her colours." Among other misinformation that appears to have reached Captain Brenton, is, that Captain Feretier, late of the Caroline, and not General Desbrusleys, committed suicide.

In the summer of the present year the French frigates Vénus and Manche, accompanied by the 14-gun corvette Créole, were cruising in the bay of Bengal. On the 26th of July, off the south end of the Great Nicobar island, the Vénus, then alone, captured the honourable Company's brig Orient, Captain Harman, bound with despatches from Madras to Prince of Wales island. Sending his prize to the isle of France, Commodore Hamelin cruised on the same station about a week longer, and then proceeded to Carnicobar island for water. He was there joined by the Manche and Créole. Having completed their water, the two frigates and corvette made sail for the Preparis isles, and then for Acheen-head.

The French commodore continued cruising, with very indifferent success, off the north-west coast of the island of Sumatra until the 10th of October; when he detached the Créole to seize the honourable Company's settlement of Tappanooly, on the small island of Punchongcacheel, close to the west side of Suma-

[1] Brenton, vol. iv., p. 398.

tra. On the 12th the Créole arrived off and took possession of the settlement. On the 21st the Vénus and Manche joined the Créole; and Commodore Hamelin immediately proceeded on the work of destruction. The few guns on the battery were disabled, the property, both public and private, confiscated, the buildings of every description set on fire, the cattle carried off, the horses maimed, and the plantations on the main destroyed. All the residents found at Tappanooly were brought on board the Vénus; but subsequently the female part of them were put on board a prize schooner, and allowed to proceed to Padang. According to a private letter from one of the sufferers, which appeared in the London papers of the day, the behaviour of Commodore Hamelin, to the female portion of his unhappy prisoners especially, was of the most disgraceful and revolting character. We shall not, however, enter into the particulars, but merely state, that on the 23rd of October the French squadron, having thus signalized itself, quitted Tappanooly, and steered for the bay of Bengal.

On the 18th of November, at daylight, latitude 6° 30' north, longitude 92° 45' east, the honourable Company's outward-bound ships Windham, Captain John Stewart, United Kingdom, Captain William Parker D'Esterre, and Charlton, Captain Charles Mortlock, while standing on the larboard tack with a light breeze from the westward, discovered in the east-south-east, about seven miles distant, three ships close hauled on the starboard tack. At 6 A.M. the strangers, which were no other than the Vénus, Manche, and Créole, tacked and stood towards the Indiamen.

The three latter were of the same size as the Streatham and Europe; and two of them, the Windham and Charlton, mounted the same guns on the main deck, with six medium 9-pounders on the quarter-deck. The United Kingdom mounted 20 medium 12-pounders on the main deck, and six 6-pounders on the quarter-deck. Each ship had a crew of 110 men, including Lascars; and between the three were distributed about 200 recruits going to join the Indian army. Opposed to two heavy French frigates and a corvette, the three Indiamen would have stood no chance; but, as it would have been equally impossible to escape, and particularly as one of the frigates, the Manche, was considerably detached and to windward of her two consorts, Commodore Stewart considered that a prompt and well-concerted attack upon her might succeed before she could be supported by the ships to leeward. He accordingly telegraphed his wishes to the

United Kingdom and Charlton, and they affirmed the signal. Upon this the Windham bore down under all sail, and was tardily followed by her two consorts.

At 8 A.M., having arrived well up with the weathermost French frigate, and finding that his two consorts still remained far astern, and were making no efforts to co-operate with him, Captain Stewart resolved singly to engage the French frigate, hoping to be afforded a chance of boarding her. His proposal was cheered by the ship's company and troops, and the Windham continued to advance towards the Manche. At 9 h. 30 m. A.M. the latter hoisted French colours and commenced a heavy fire, but the Windham continued to close without returning a shot. Seeing her determination, the French frigate evaded it by wearing round on the starboard tack. The Windham followed the frigate in the manœuvre and opened her fire; but Captain Stewart soon found that, while the shot of the Manche were flying over him, those of the Windham fell short. The latter now backed her maintopsail, and commenced a close action with the Manche; who, finding that the Windham's two consorts kept aloof from the battle, merely firing now and then a few distant and harmless shot, continued engaging the Windham till noon; when the French frigate wore and made sail to join the Vénus.

Seeing clearly that he should receive no effectual support from his consorts, and having already had three cadets and an ensign of foot killed, and two cadets wounded, and the ship's rigging and sails much cut, Captain Stewart, with the concurrence of his officers, made sail, in the hope of saving the Windham from the fate which a longer continuance in action would render unavoidable. While the Manche and the corvette attacked and captured the United Kingdom and Charlton, the Vénus made sail in pursuit of the Windham. Every attempt, by lightening herself and otherwise, was made by the latter to escape; but the superior sailing of the French frigate enabled her, not, however, until 10 h. 30 m. A.M. on the 22nd, and that after a smart running fight, to overtake and capture the Windham.

Having received on board the Vénus Captain Stewart and nearly the whole of his people, and placed a prize crew in the Windham, the French commodore made sail for the Isle of France. On the 6th of December the two ships fell in with the Manche and Créole, and their two prizes; but on the 19th, in thick bad weather, the Vénus parted as well from them as from the Windham. Steering now alone for the Isle of France, the Vénus on the 27th encountered a tremendous gale of wind or hurricane; in which the frigate lost all three of her topmasts, and, owing chiefly to the inattention of the officers and crew in keeping open the gun-room ports and not securing the hatchways, had seven and a half feet water in the hold.

In this extremity, when his crew had given up the ship as lost, and his officers had retired to their cabins to await the result, Captain Hamelin sent for Captain Stewart, and requested that he would endeavour, with the men of his late crew, to save the French frigate; but he, at the same time, wished him to give a pledge, that his men should not take possession of the frigate. Captain Stewart refused to give the pledge, but replied that M. Hamelin must take his chance of such an event taking place. Having caused all the arms to be removed, the French captain gave up the charge of his frigate to the British captain and crew, his prisoners. By great exertions on the part of the latter, the wreck of the frigate's topmasts, left by the Frenchmen hanging over her side, was cleared, and the water in the hold reduced to a very small quantity. In short, the Vénus was saved, and on the 31st anchored in Rivière-Noire, Isle of France, with scarcely a drop of water for the prisoners or crew, and no provisions except a small quantity of bad rice. In this state of things, it would have been impossible, even could the prisoners have retained possession of the ship, to have conducted her to a British port.

Captain Stewart and his people were marched across the country to Port Louis; where they arrived on the 1st of January, and on the next day the Manche arrived, in company with the United Kingdom and Charlton. The Windham, however, was not so fortunate. On the 29th of December, when close off the Isle of France, she was recaptured by the British 12-pounder 36-gun frigate Magicienne, Captain Lucius Curtis. The Windham was then sent to the Cape of Good Hope; where, shortly afterwards, Captain Stewart and his officers arrived in a cartel, and were allowed to rejoin their recovered ship.

On the 2nd of November, in the afternoon, off the Sand-heads in the Bay of Bengal, the British 18-gun ship-sloop Victor, still commanded by Captain Edward Stopford,[1] fell in with, and was chased by the French frigate Bellone. At about 10 P.M., after having had all her running-rigging cut to pieces, her mainmast

[1] See p. 54.

wounded in two, and her mizenmast in three places, and her foretopsail shot away, the Victor had no alternative but to haul down her colours. As the night was very dark, and the Victor lay very low in the water, her hull was comparatively uninjured, and her loss in consequence amounted to only two men wounded. Nor is it likely that her two 6-pounder chase-guns could have done any material injury to the Bellone.

Some newspapers stated, that Captain Stopford " determined to board the Bellone ;" and a contemporary historian has gone still further; by declaring that the captain " attempted to board his enemy,"[1] but failed. That no such attempt was made we are sure ; and, considering the immense disparity in size and force between the two vessels, one of which was nearly four times as large as the other, and had on board treble the number of men, we cannot believe that Captain Stopford had the least idea of undertaking so rash an enterprise.

On the 22nd, being still off the Sand-heads, the Bellone, with the Victor and another prize or two in company, fell in with the Portuguese frigate Minerva, Captain Pinto, of 52 guns, including 30 long 18-pounders on the main deck. At 4 P.M. an action commenced between these frigates ; and the French crew behaved so badly, notwithstanding they must have had the Victor to assist them, that, if the Portuguese crew had not been the most cowardly that ever manned a frigate, the Bellone would have been the prize of the Minerva. Instead of which, the Minerva became the prize of the Bellone, and was obtained at so trifling an expense as four or five wounded men and about twice as many cut ropes. As the striking of the colours remained with the officers, they, to their credit, did not surrender the ship until the fire of the Bellone had killed and wounded several persons on board of her. On the 2nd of January Captain Duperré, with his two men-of-war prizes in company, anchored in Port Louis.

Among the services performed by the British navy in this quarter of the globe during the year 1809, were several successful attacks made by the 12-pounder 36-gun frigate Chiffonne, Captain John Wainwright, and 18-pounder 36-gun frigate Caroline, Captain Charles Gordon, in company with the honourable Company's cruisers Mornington, Captain Jeakes, and Aurora, Nautilus, Prince of Wales, Fury, and Ariel, Lieutenants Conyers, Watkins, Allen, Davidson, and Salter, having on board a body of troops under Lieutenant-Colonel Smith, upon a nest of pirates

[1] Brenton, vol. iv., p. 400.

in the Persian Gulf, which had for a long time harassed the trade in that sea. On the 13th of November Ras-al-Khyma, the principal pirate-town, together with all the vessels in the port, upwards of 50 in number, including about 30 very large dows, and a considerable quantity of naval stores of every species, was set on fire and destroyed.

On the 17th twenty large pirate-vessels in the town of Linga shared the same fate, and on the 27th eleven others at the town of Luft; the sea-defences of both places being also completely destroyed. All this was not effected, however, without a desperate resistance on the part of the pirates; and, in consequence, the loss on the British side amounted to four men killed, one mortally, 15 severely, and 19 slightly wounded: a loss, nevertheless, of moderate amount, compared with the number of lives which these barbarians, had they been allowed to prosper in their gains, would very soon have sacrificed.

Colonial Expeditions.—Coast of Africa.

Much injury having been done to the African coasting-trade by small French privateers, fitted out at Sénégal, Captain Edward Henry Columbine, of the 12-pounder 32-gun frigate Solebay, the naval commanding officer at the settlement of Gorée, concerted with Major Charles William Maxwell, of the African Corps, the commandant of the garrison, a plan for the reduction of Sénégal. Accordingly, on the 4th of July, a detachment from the garrison of Gorée, amounting to 166 officers and men under the major's command, embarked on board the Agincourt transport; and the squadron, composed of the Solebay, the 18-gun brig-sloop Derwent, Captain Frederick Parker, and 12-gun brig Tigris, Lieutenant Robert Bones, the Agincourt, a flotilla of small armed vessels, consisting of the George government-schooner, and six sloops and schooners, collected for the purpose, and, in order to give the appearance of a greater force, one unarmed merchant-ship, two brigs, and one schooner, immediately weighed and set sail.

On the 17th, in the evening, the expedition, amounting to 14 sail of vessels, anchored off the bar of Sénégal; and on the 8th 160 of the African Corps, 120 seamen, and 50 marines, were got over the bar in 16 boats, through a very heavy surf. But, in surmounting this difficulty, the George was driven on shore and a schooner and a sloop were totally wrecked. Only one individual perished on the occasion; and that unfortunately was Captain Parker of the Derwent. It was now discovered that the French had collected their force, consisting of 160 regulars and about 240 militia and volunteers, at Babagué, a spot about five miles below the town of St. Louis and ten above the bar. Major Maxwell, with the detachment of troops and marines, numbering altogether about 210 men, landed without opposition on the left bank of the river, and immediately took up a position, with the intention of waiting until provisions could be passed from the shipping, and the schooner George could be got afloat.

On the 9th the French commandant marched out to attack the British, and Major Maxwell, supported by the boats, rapidly advanced to meet him. Finding the British stronger than he had expected, the former waited only to exchange a few shot with the troops and the boats, and then retreated so expeditiously, and with so perfect a knowledge of the country, that it was impossible to cut him off. The position to which the French had retired consisted of a formidable line of defence at Babagué, a battery on the south point of an island commanding the passage of the river. This post was further defended, at about a quarter of a mile in advance of the battery, by a chain secured to anchors on each shore, and floated all across the stream by large spars; and, at about a hundred yards in the rear of this boom, lay a flotilla of seven armed vessels and gunboats, mounting between them 31 guns.

On the 10th, in the evening, the sloop George was got afloat; and on the 11th the Solebay and Derwent, the latter now commanded by Captain Joseph Swabey Tetley, took up a position close to the narrow neck of land that divides the river from the sea, for the purpose of cannonading the fort of Babagué. This the two ships did with considerable effect; but, in the course of the ensuing night, the frigate, in shifting her birth, went on shore, and, although still in a position to annoy the enemy, became totally wrecked. Fortunately no lives were lost, and the crew managed to save a great proportion of the stores.

On the 12th, in the morning, the troops were re-embarked, and the flotilla proceeded up the river until within gun-shot of the fort at Babagué; when, just as everything was in readiness for a night attack, information arrived that the French commandant meant to capitulate. The attack was therefore postponed; and on the morning of the 13th it was discovered, that the French (probably the militia, who were disaffected) had broken the boom, and abandoned the vessels and the battery, leaving their colours flying upon both. Shortly afterwards a letter was brought from the commandant, offering to capitulate; and in the course of the day terms were agreed upon, surrendering the colony of Sénégal to the British arms.

This harassing and not unimportant service was effected with a loss to the British, besides that of Captain Parker of the Derwent, comparatively slight: one midshipman was drowned, one lieutenant of the troops died in the field from fatigue, and one man was wounded by the enemy's fire. The loss on the part of the French appears to have been also of trifling amount, not exceeding one man killed and two wounded.

West Indies.

The interception, in the summer of 1808, of some despatches from the colonial prefect of Martinique to the French minister of marine, exposing the wants of the island, and calling for a supply of provisions and troops, is thought to have directed the attention of the British government to the reduction of this valuable French colony. At all events, preparations for the attack began at Barbadoes as early as November; and the authorities at Martinique, as they themselves acknowledge, anticipated an attack towards the end of that month or the beginning of December. Matters were not, however, in perfect readiness until the latter end of January, when the following force was assembled:—

Gun-ship.		
98	Neptune	{ Rear-adm. (r.) Hon. Sir Alex. J. Cochrane, K.B. { Captain Charles Dilkes.
74	{ Pompée	{ Commodore George Cockburn. { Captain Edward Pelham Brenton.
	{ York	,, Robert Barton.
	{ Belleisle	,, William Charles Fahie.
	{ Captain	,, James Athol Wood.
64	Intrepid	,, Christ. John Williams Nesham.
44	Ulysses	,, Edward Woollcombe.

Frigates, Acasta, Penelope, Ethalion, Ulysses, Æolus, Circe, Cleopatra, and Eurydice; *ship-sloops*, Cherub, Gorée, Pelorus, Star, Stork; *brig-sloops*, Amaranthe, Eclair, Forrester, Frolic, Recruit, Wolverene; *gun-brigs*, Express, Haughty, and Swinger.

On the 30th of that month the expedition, consisting, as here named, of six sail of the line, one 44-gun ship, five frigates, one 22-gun ship, and 13 sloops and smaller vessels, forming a total of 28 sail of pendants, under the command of Rear-admiral the Honourable Sir Alexander Cochrane, having in charge a fleet of transports containing about 10,000 troops, commanded by Lieutenant-general Beckwith, arrived off the island of Martinique from Carlisle bay, whence it had sailed on the 28th. The land-force at this time at Martinique consisted of about 2400 effective regulars, and about an equal number of militia, or "national guards," a name, as it turned out, rather inappropriately given to them; and there were mounted upon Fort Desaix, the arsenal, Fort Royal, and the batteries on the coast, about 289 pieces of cannon. The naval force consisted of the French 40-gun frigate Amphitrite,[1] lying at Fort Royal, the 18-gun ship-corvette Diligente at St. Pierre's, and the late British brig-sloop Carnation at Marin. The governor-general of the island was Vice-admiral Villaret-Joyeuse, the opponent of Lord Howe on the 1st of June.

Early on the morning of the 30th, one division of the troops, nearly 3000 in number, commanded by Major-general Frederick Maitland, landed, without opposition, at Sainte-Luce, under the superintendence of Captain Fahie of the Belleisle; and a detachment of 600 men, under Major Henderson of the York Rangers, landed at Cape Salomon, also without opposition. The appearance of the former in Marin bay was the signal for the French to set fire to and destroy the Carnation. While these proceedings were going on upon the south-west or leeward coast of the island, a division of about 6500 men, commanded by Lieutenant-general Sir George Prevost, disembarked, under the direction of Captain Philip Beaver of the 40-gun frigate Acasta, at Baie Robert on the north-east or windward coast, still without experiencing any opposition. The fact is, that the French governor-general had committed the great mistake of sending to each of the two points at which the British had landed, Baie Robert and Pointe Sainte-Luce, two of the four battalions of militia on the island, unaccompanied by troops of the line. The consequence was, that the militia, or "gardes nationales," left the field to the enemy, and retired peaceably to their homes.

This traitorous conduct was partly the effect of a proclamation, addressed by the two British commanders-in-chief to the black or coloured population, of which, almost exclusively, the militia was composed. No copy of this proclamation accompanies the official letters; it is merely referred to in them. An enemy has an immense advantage, where the territory he is about to invade contains a slave population; but there is a homely proverb about persons with glass windows, &c., which might be

[1] See vol. iv., p. 380.

worth attending to by those who scruple not to resort to so barbarous, so unauthorized a mode of warfare, as that of inciting the slave, if not actually to murder, to betray his master.

The first meeting between the regular troops on each side was upon the heights of Desfourneaux and Surirey, on the 1st and 2nd of February; on each of which days the British forces, under the command nominally of Lieutenant-general Sir George Prevost, but really of Brigadier-general Hoghton,[1] were successful, but not without a loss amounting to 84 killed, 334 wounded, and 18 missing. The French, who, though decidedly inferior in numbers, were strongly posted, acknowledged a loss, in killed and wounded together, of 700 men. On the same night, or the succeeding morning, the French troops in this vicinity abandoned their advanced posts, and retired upon Fort Desaix. After the detachment of 600 York Rangers, under Major Henderson, had possessed themselves of the battery on Pointe Salomon, an attack was made upon Islet aux Ramiers, or Pigeon island; and, on the 4th of February, after being bombarded for 12 hours by 10 mortars and howitzers, five of which had been got to the top of a commanding height by the very great exertions of a detachment of seamen under Captain Cockburn of the Pompée, that important little spot surrendered. This post was acquired with a loss of only two seamen killed and one soldier wounded. Nor did the French garrison of 136 men, the retreat of whom had been cut off by the frigates Æolus and Cleopatra, Captains Lord William Fitzroy and Samuel John Pechell, and the brig-sloop Recruit, Captain Charles Napier, detached to the upper end of the bay, lose more than five killed and 11 wounded.

Sir Alexander immediately stood in with the squadron and anchored in Fort Royal bay; but, on the approach of the two frigates and sloop, the French had set fire to and destroyed the Amphitrite and the other vessels in the harbour. They had also abandoned all the forts in this quarter, at Case-Navire, and along the neighbouring coast, and shut themselves up in Fort Desaix. On the 5th, Major-general Maitland, who had marched

---

[1] That Sir George took no personal share in the battles that ensued, his own letters, on a careful perusal of them, sufficiently prove. For instance:—"I lost no time after this junction, and pushed forward" (not himself, but) " the Honourable Lieutenant-colonel Pakenham," &c. "This movement I supported" (not by leading his own division, but) " by the light-infantry battalion under Brigadier-general Hoghton," who, in fact, did all that was done. On another occasion Sir George writes:—"Having yesterday evening reconnoitred the enemy's advanced picket, I decided upon attempting the surprise of it in the course of the night, and gave directions accordingly to Major Pearson," &c.

from Sainte-Luce to Champin and La Croissades without the slightest opposition, pursued his march, and on the 8th arrived at Case-Navire, equally unmolested, thereby completing the investment of Fort Desaix on the western side. On the 9th, being garrisoned solely by militia, the town of St. Pierre and its dependencies, with the ship-corvette Diligente at anchor in the port, surrendered, on the first summons, to Lieutenant-colonel Barnes: and on the 10th the town of Fort Royal was occupied by the British troops.

From the 10th to the 19th the besiegers were occupied in constructing gun and mortar batteries, in landing cannon, mortars, and howitzers, with their ammunition and stores, in dragging them to the several points selected by the engineers, and in the completion of the works preparatory to a bombardment of Fort Desaix. On the 19th, at 4 h. 30 m. P.M., the British opened upon that fortress from six points, with 14 heavy pieces of cannon and 28 mortars and howitzers; and the bombardment continued without intermission until the 23rd at noon, when the French general sent a trumpeter with a letter proposing terms. These being considered inadmissible, the bombardment recommenced at 10 P.M., and continued until 9 A.M., on the 24th; when three white flags were discovered flying in the fortress. The British batteries immediately ceased; and in the course of the day, the French colony of Martinique surrendered by capitulation to the arms of Great Britain.

As far as appears in the Gazette, no loss was sustained by the British troops during the bombardment; but the seamen serving on shore under Captain Cockburn sustained a loss of five men and one boy killed, and the Amaranthe's boatswain and gunner (Thomas Wickland and John Thompson), one master's mate (James Scott), one midshipman (Thomas Mills), and the gunner (John Edevearn), of the Pompée, and 14 men wounded; total, six killed, 10 badly, and nine slightly wounded. The whole of the Amaranthe's loss, amounting to three killed, four badly, and two slightly wounded, arose from the accidental explosion of the laboratory tent in the rear of the great mortar battery on Tartanson. We must not part with the seamen without stating, that they were of the greatest use in the operations of the siege, particularly in dragging the heavy cannon up the heights.

The French acknowledge a loss in killed and wounded, by the bombardment alone, of 200 men: a loss which, had it not been for the timely surrender of the garrison, might have been much greater; for it appears that the shells of the besiegers had cracked and damaged in several places the roof of the magazine, and that the French troops were in momentary dread of an explosion. This, indeed, was the alleged, and it must be admitted to have been a very natural, cause of the proposal to capitulate. The court of inquiry which sat at Paris on the 6th of December, 1809, to investigate the causes of the surrender of the colony, strongly animadverted upon the neglect of not having previously removed the powder to the galleries of the fortress; and, for that and other causes, the governor-general, Vice-admiral Villaret-Joyeuse, together with some of the subordinate officers, was stripped of his rank and honours.

On the 8th of December, 1808, a small expedition, consisting of the British 20-gun ship Confiance, Captain James Lucas Yeo, the two Portuguese brigs Voader and Infante, and some smaller vessels, having on board about 550 Portuguese land-forces, under the command of Lieutenant-colonel Manoel Marques, and which had been fitted out at the Brazils, with the concurrence of Rear-admiral Sir William Sidney Smith, the British commander-in-chief on that station, took peaceable possession of the district of Oyapok in French Guyane, and on the 15th reduced that of Approuak. This success determined Captain Yeo and the Portuguese lieutenant-colonel to make a descent on the east side of the island of Cayenne; on which stands the town of the same name, the capital of the colony. The island is divided into two parts by an artificial river, or fossé, about 30 feet wide, named Crique fouillée: and is bounded on the north by the sea, on the south by the river "de tour de l'île," on the east by the river Mahuy, and on the west by that of Cayenne.

All the Portuguese troops, with 80 seamen and marines from the Confiance, and a party of marines from the Voader and Infante, having been embarked on board the small vessels, the latter, on the 6th of January, early in the morning, dropped into the mouth of the river Mahuy. In the evening Captain Yeo, with 10 canoes and about 250 men, proceeded to attack some forts that commanded the entrance of the river; having left the vessels that had on board the remainder of the troops in charge of Captain Salgado of the Voader, with directions to follow after dark, and, on being apprised by signal that the two forts were carried, to enter the river and disembark the men with all possible despatch. On the 7th, at 3 A.M., Captain Yeo reached Pointe Mahuy, with five canoes; the others, being heavy, could not keep up. The party then landed in a bay about half way between Fort Diamant and the battery named

Dégras de Cannes; but the surge was so high that all the boats soon went to pieces. Having ordered Major Joaquim Manoel Pinto, with a detachment of Portuguese troops, to proceed to the left, and take Dégras des Cannes, Captain Yeo, accompanied by Lieutenants William Howe Mulcaster and Samuel Blyth, and Lieutenant John Read of the marines, also Mr. Thomas Savory, the purser, William Taylor, the carpenter, George Forder and David Irwin, midshipmen, and a party of the Confiance's seamen and marines, marched to Fort Diamant. Both forts were promptly carried: the Diamant, mounting two long 24-pounders and one brass eight, with the loss of Lieutenant Read and one seaman and five marines badly wounded on Captain Yeo's side, and the commandant and three soldiers killed and four wounded, out of 50 men, on the part of the French; and the Dégras des Cannes, mounting two brass 8-pounders, without any lost to Major Pinto, but with two men killed on the part of the enemy, whose number at the commencement of the attack was 40.

The entrance of the river being thus in possession of the allied forces, the signal agreed upon was made, and by noon the whole of the remaining troops were safely disembarked. Information now arrived that General Victor Hugues had quitted Cayenne-town at the head of 1000 troops, to endeavour to retake the captured forts. The force of the allies being too small to be divided, and the distance between the forts being great, and they 12 miles only from Cayenne, Captain Yeo resolved to dismantle Fort Diamant, and collect his whole force at Dégras des Cannes. Leaving Lieutenant Mulcaster, with a party of the Confiance's men to do the needful at the Diamant, Captain Yeo, with the remaining troops and seamen, proceeded to Dégras des Cannes. On arriving here, Captain Yeo perceived two other batteries about a mile up the river on opposite sides: the one on the right bank, named Trio, situated upon an eminence commanding the Creek (Crique fouillée) leading to Cayenne; the other on the opposite side situated at the entrance of canal de Torcy, on the creek leading to the house and plantation of Victor Hugues, and evidently erected for no other purpose than its defence.

The Portuguese cutters, Lion and Vinganza, each armed with a few 4-pounders, were anchored abreast of the two forts, when a smart action commenced, and continued for an hour. Finding the superiority of the enemy's metal and position, and that many on board the vessels were falling from the incessant showers of grape-shot, Captain Yeo resolved to storm both the forts. Accordingly, while Mr. Savory, with a party of Portuguese troops, landed at the battery that defended the house of Victor Hugues, Captain Yeo, accompanied by Lieutenant Blyth and his gig's crew, also by a party of Portuguese troops, proceeded to attack Trio. Although both parties had to land at the very muzzles of the guns, the cool bravery of the assailants, in defiance of a continual fire of grape and musketry, soon carried both posts, each mounting two 8-pounders, and put to flight the 100 men divided between them.

Scarcely had this service been accomplished, when the French troops from the town of Cayenne attacked Colonel Marques at Dégras des Cannes. The allied forces being much dispersed, Captain Yeo, without waiting an instant, pushed off with the boats; and, arriving at the post, compelled the French, after a smart action of three hours, to retreat to Cayenne. At about the same time 250 men appeared before Fort Diamant; but, perceiving Lieutenant Mulcaster prepared to receive them, imagining his force to be much greater than it was, and learning what had been the fate of their general, they quickly followed his example. The strongest post yet remained to be taken, the general's private house; before which he had planted a field-piece and a swivel, with 100 of his best troops. On the 8th, in the morning, the allied forces proceeded to attack this post. As a preliminary measure, Captain Yeo tried the effect of a summons. The general's advanced guard allowed the gig with the flag of truce to approach within a boat's length, then fired two volleys at Lieutenant Mulcaster and his party, and quickly retreated. Upon this, Captain Yeo landed his men; but, considering that the outrage might have been committed without the knowledge of the French general, he again sent Lieutenant Mulcaster: at whom, this time, the field-piece was discharged. One of the general's slaves was next sent, and he returned with an answer that the communication must be in writing. At the same moment the general fired his field-piece as a signal to the troops, who lay in ambush in the wood to the right of the allied forces, and who now opened upon the latter a steady and well-directed fire; the field-piece also continuing to play upon them. Finding it impracticable to advance with his field-piece on account of fossés in the road, Captain Yeo proceeded without it; and his men, with the pike and bayonet, cheering as they rushed on, soon carried the general's gun and the general's house, Victor Hugues and his gallant troops flying through the back premises into the wood, as the British and Portuguese entered at the front.

Information now arriving, that about 400 of the enemy were about to take possession of Beauregard plain, an eminence which commands the several roads to and from Cayenne, the British and Portuguese commanders instantly marched thither with their whole force. On the 9th the allied troops reached the spot, and on the 10th Lieutenant Mulcaster and a Portuguese officer were sent into the town of Cayenne with a summons to the general. An armistice followed; and finally, on the 14th, the Portuguese troops, and the British seamen and marines, marched into Cayenne, and took possession of the town. The enemy's troops, amounting to 400, laid down their arms upon the parade, and were embarked on board the several vessels belonging to the expedition: at the same time the militia, amounting to 600, together with 200 blacks, both of whom had been incorporated with the regular troops, delivered in their arms.

Thus was acquired, by a force, the most effective if not the most numerous part of which was a British 20-gun ship's complement, the whole of the French settlement of Cayenne, extending along the coast to the eastward as far as the river Oyapok, where the Portuguese possessions begin, and along the western coast to the river Maroni, that separates the colony from the possessions of the Dutch. All this was effected at a comparatively trifling loss of men: the British had one killed (Lieutenant Read) and 23 wounded; the Portuguese, one killed and eight wounded; and the French, 16 killed and 20 wounded.

The previous achievements of Captain Yeo [1] had prepared us for a display of extraordinary zeal and courage, but we did not expect to find a naval officer so well qualified to fill the station of a general. From the 15th of December, the seamen and marines of the Confiance on shore had not slept in their beds; and, from the time they landed, on the 7th of January, until the surrender of the colony, they were without any cessation from fatigue. To add to their difficulties, the weather was constantly both boisterous and rainy, and the roads nearly impassable.

Even the Confiance, in the absence of her commander and full three-fourths of the crew, had the good fortune to accomplish, by her very appearance, what a ship of double her size and treble her force (her guns were only 18-pounder carronades), would have been proud of effecting by the fire of her artillery. For instance, on the 13th of January the French 40-

[1] See vol. iv., p. 33.

gun frigate Topaze, Captain Lahalle, appeared in the offing, with a reinforcement for the garrison; but Mr. George Yeo, the captain's brother and a mere lad, although his whole numerical force consisted of another young midshipman, Edward Bryant, 25 English seamen, and 20 negroes, managed, by his skilful manœuvres and the bold front he put on, to scare the French frigate from the coast, and to send her where, as we have already seen, she became a prize to two British frigates.[1]

[1] See p. 2.

BRITISH AND FRENCH FLEETS.

As the last Annual Abstract was remarkable for containing the greatest number of ships that ever did, or that probably ever will, belong to the British navy; so is the present,[1] for being the first that exhibits a declension in all its principal totals. In referring, as usual, to the prize and casualty lists of the year,[2] we have again to notice the heavy amount of loss sustained by the British navy. Yet care must be taken, that this is not absolutely, but relatively considered. A comparison of the three abstracts (Nos. 16, 17, and 18) containing the highest amount of loss, during the present war, with the three of the preceding war (Nos. 5, 9, and 10) similarly circumstanced, shows, that the aggregate loss in the former bore to the aggregate of its commissioned cruisers one tenth only more than was the case in the latter; an overplus of loss scarcely commensurate with the increased numbers and activity of the French marine during the years 1807, 1808, and 1809; particularly along the coasts, where far the greater proportion of the lost ships ended their days.

The number of commissioned officers and masters, belonging to the British navy at the commencement of the year 1810, was

Admirals	49
Vice-admirals	61
Rear-admirals	60
,, superannuated 34	
Post-captains	725
,, superannuated 27	
Commanders, or sloop-captains . . .	608
,, superannuated 47	
Lieutenants	3114
Masters	501

---

[1] See Appendix, Annual Abstract, No. 18.   [2] See Appendix, Nos. 1 and 2.

And the number of seamen and marines, voted for the service of the same year, was 145,000.[1]

Owing to the vigilance of the British blockading force, France was unable, during the whole of the present year, to get a fleet to sea. Napoleon, however, still went on increasing his navy. At Antwerp two new 80-gun ships, the Friedland and Tilsitt, were launched, and the keels of two three-deckers intended to carry 110 guns each, and to be named Hymen and Monarque, were laid upon the vacant slips. Towards the latter end of the summer 10 sail of the line evinced a disposition to put to sea from the Scheldt, but were restrained from making the attempt by a squadron of seven or eight sail of the line, under Rear-admiral Sir Richard John Strachan in the St. Domingo, cruising off Flushing.

Since the 6th of January, Sweden, owing to a change in her dynasty, had made peace with France; and on the 19th of November declared war against England. But Vice-admiral Sir James Saumarez, with five or six sail of the line, prevented either the Swedish or the Russian fleet from being in any degree troublesome.

Brest was this year a port of little consequence, containing in its road but three sail of the line, including one ship from Rochefort or Lorient, and about as many frigates. These were vigilantly watched by a British squadron outside; as were the few remaining ships of the line that lay in some of the minor French ports, along the Channel and Bay of Biscay frontiers.

At the commencement of the present year the command upon the Mediterranean station was still in the hands of Vice-admiral Lord Collingwood. But his lordship was in so infirm a state of health, that on the 5th of March he quitted Minorca in the Ville-de-Paris, bound to England for his recovery; leaving the fleet under the temporary command of Rear-admiral Martin, in the 80-gun ship Canopus. On the 7th of March, at 8 P.M., Lord Collingwood expired. The immediate cause of this distinguished officer's death was a stoppage in the pylorus or inferior aperture of the stomach: he had nearly attained his 60th year.

The French force in Toulon remained much the same as at the close of the preceding year; but we shall defer entering into particulars until we have given some account of a successful expedition in the Adriatic against the island of St. Maura, the ancient Leucadia; and which, with the neighbouring island of Corfu, was still occupied by a French garrison.

[1] See Appendix, No. 3.

On the 21st of March, early in the morning, the above expedition, consisting of the British 74-gun ship Magnificent, Captain George Eyre, 38-gun frigate Belle-Poule, Captain James Brisbane, and 16-gun brig-sloop Imogene, Captain William Stephens, three gun-boats, and five transports, having on board a body of troops under Brigadier-general Oswald, sailed from the island of Zante, and arrived the same evening off St. Maura. The Imogene and gun-boats anchored to cover the landing of the troops; and at daybreak on the 22nd the whole disembarked in the face of a slight resistance from some batteries. To the troops were added the marines of the Magnificent and Belle-Poule, and also of the Montagu 74, Captain Richard Hussey Moubray; which ship, having knocked off her rudder in working into the road of Zante, had for the present been left behind. Captains Eyre, Brisbane, and Stephens accompanied the troops in their march; and Captain Eyre was severely wounded in the head, and Captain Stephens in the foot, at the storming of the first redoubt: in the attack upon which the 38-gun frigate Leonidas, Captain Anselm John Griffiths, who had been detached to cruise to the northward of the island, lent her very effective co-operation.

On the 30th the Montagu, having re-hung her rudder, arrived at St. Maura. Immediately two of her lower-deck guns were landed, and 100 of her seamen joined themselves to the 150 previously landed from the Magnificent, who had also sent on shore 10 of her 18-pounders. On the 16th of April, after batteries had been opened against it for nine days, the fortress and island of St. Maura surrendered on capitulation. The loss of the British army, including the foreign troops serving with it, amounted to 16 officers and men killed, 86 wounded, and 17 missing, and of the British navy, to two seamen and six marines killed, and Captains Eyre and Stephens, one Captain of marines (William Havisand Snowe), one Lieutenant (Vernon Lamphier), one Lieutenant of marines (Arthur Morrison), six seamen, and 27 marines wounded; total, 24 killed, 127 wounded, and 17 missing. The French garrison amounted at the capitulation to 714 officers and men, exclusive of 17 sick and 69 wounded. The number of killed must also have been considerable. We now return to the Toulon fleet. Vice-admiral Ganteaume had been succeeded in the command of it by Vice-admiral Allemand. The Borée had got back to her port from Cette;[1] and the Robuste and Lion, her less fortunate consorts, were about to be replaced by three

---

[1] See vol. iv., p. 447.

new ships, the Wagram of 130, Sceptre of 80, and Trident of 74 guns. The first of these ships was launched on the 30th of June, and another three-decker was immediately laid down upon her slip. Exclusive of those three ships, the French fleet consisted of 13 sail of the line (one 130, two 120s, one 80, and nine 74s), besides eight or nine frigates and several large armed store-ships. Since early in the month of May Admiral Sir Charles Cotton had arrived on the station as the late Lord Collingwood's successor; and the force under the admiral's command, cruising off Toulon, consisted, in general, of 13 sail of the line, but frequently of less, with, as usual, a very small quota of frigates.

On the 15th of July a continuance of strong gales from the north-west obliged Sir Charles Cotton, with the main body of the fleet, to take shelter under Levant island, the easternmost of the Hyètes; and, while here, the violence of the wind drove the admiral as far to the eastward as Villa-Franca. In the mean time the port of Toulon was watched by a detached squadron, under the orders of Captain the Honourable Henry Blackwood, of the 74 gun-ship Warspite, consisting, besides that ship, of the 74s Ajax and Conqueror, Captains Robert Waller Otway and Edward Fellowes, the 18-pounder 36-gun frigate Euryalus, Captain the Honourable George Heneage Lawrence Dundas, and the 10-gun brig-sloop Shearwater, Captain Edward Reynolds Sibly

On the 17th, eight sail of the line and four frigates stood out of Toulon to exercise, and one of the 74s exchanged a few broadsides with the Euryalus, but without doing her any injury. Either on this or the preceding day a convoy of French coasters from the westward, under the protection of a frigate and corvette, was chased by Captain Blackwood's squadron into Bandol, a small harbour 10 or 12 miles to the westward of Toulon. On the 18th the Euryalus reconnoitred the French fleet, and discovered two line-of-battle ships and one frigate at anchor off Cape Sepet, 11 line-of-battle ships and seven frigates in the outer, and two line-of-battle ships and one frigate in the inner road; total, 15 sail of the line and nine frigates. Thirteen of these ships comprise all those named at pp. 68 and 69, except the Robuste and Lion: the two remaining ships were the Wagram of 130, and either the Sceptre of 80, or the Trident of 74 guns.

On the 20th, at 7 A.M., while the Shearwater lay close to the tongue of land that forms Cape Sepet, and the Euryalus more to the south-east, fronting the road of Toulon, six sail of the line (one three, and five two deckers) and four frigates, under a Vice-admiral, sailed out, with the apparent intention of releasing the frigate and her convoy at Bandol, as the latter, about the same time, got under way and stood to sea before a fine land wind. Just as Captain Sibly had made the signal of an enemy in the north-north-west, in which direction the Shearwater, since daylight, had been ordered to reconnoitre, the brig was recalled by the commodore; whose object, as he could not now prevent the junction of the frigate and convoy in Bandol, was to collect his own ships, and place them without the enemy, in the most eligible posture of defence in his power. Having, before she could reach her squadron, to cross the French van or advanced division, consisting of the 74-gun ship Ajax and 40 gun-frigate Amélie, the Shearwater became rather critically circumstanced; although it is doubtful whether, from her situation to windward, the Shearwater could have been molested by the French ships, had the brig been suffered to remain where she was. The Euryalus, who had also been ordered to close, was exposed to an equal degree of danger.

At 9 h. 15 m. A.M. the Shearwater received a broadside from the French Ajax, and presently two more broadsides, besides some straggling shot. The Amélie also fired two broadsides at the brig; but not a shot from either the 74 or the frigate struck her. The Euryalus, at whom a part of the fire was directed, came off equally untouched; and both the latter and the Shearwater effected their junction with Captain Blackwood; who, since 8 A.M., had brought to in line of battle, the Warspite leading, followed by the Conqueror and Ajax. The latter, being from her position in the line the nearest to her French namesake and the frigate, when they tacked to rejoin the main body, received also a portion of their fire. The Ajax, in the most gallant manner, tacked, and returned the fire with several broadsides. The Conqueror and Warspite, in succession, followed Captain Otway's ship in her manœuvre, and fired also a few distant shot; but no damage appears to have been done on either side, beyond the loss of the English Ajax's jib-boom by a shot, and some slight injury done to her rigging and sails. The French squadron, accompanied by the frigate and her convoy from Bandol, returned about noon to the anchorage of the fleet in Toulon road.

We are doubtful if we should have considered this transaction worthy of any notice, had not two letters on the subject appeared in the London Gazette: one from the British admiral on the station to the secretary of the admiralty; the other, and that a tolerably long letter, from the commodore of the reconnoitring squadron to the commander-in-chief. A third letter went also the round of the English newspapers; one from Sir Charles Cotton to Captain Blackwood, thanking him and those under his command for the service they had performed. According to these letters, particularly that of Captain Blackwood to his admiral, one French 130-gun ship, five French two-deckers, 80s and 74s, and four 40-gun frigates, were driven back into their port by three British 74s, a 36-gun frigate, and a 10-gun brig. Is there not an absurdity upon the face of this? Was no allowance to be made for the state of the wind? The account admits, that "the weather was light and variable," and that the wind "rather failed" the English ships; and the logs of all the latter plainly show, that at daylight the wind blew, even with them in the offing, at west-north-west, and at noon at south-west by west.

The French declare that the wind shifted to opposite points, and was directly against them when their leading ships gave over the chase; and they justly ridicule the idea of three sail of the line silencing the fire of six. An officer belonging to the Toulon fleet, under date of October 22, 1810, writes thus on the subject to the editor of the Moniteur:—"We have read in Nos. 282 and 288 of the Moniteur, article 'London,' containing extracts from the English papers, the inaccurate report of the English Captain Blackwood. He has raised the indignation of the whole fleet; every person on board which can attest, that only one 74, the Ajax, and the frigate Amélie, were able to approach the three enemy's ships, owing to the sudden fall of the wind, and its almost immediate change to a point directly ahead. The latter, therefore, had the sole power of attack; and yet, so far from advancing to a second action with the Ajax and Amélie, they retreated. The bravery of the seamen on board our fleet equals that of the English seamen; and the time may come when Captain Blackwood will have to give some other proof of his courage than that of which he has here boasted. It is false that the admiral's ship of 130 guns, fired a broadside at that captain, or at either of the others. Truly, had she been able to close them, they would soon have made the discovery. It requires, sir, the boastfulness of an Englishman, to wish to inspire a belief, that the fire of three English line-of-battle ships is able to silence the fire of six French, and compel them to fly."[1]

[1] See Appendix, No. 17, in vol. iv.

The writer, however, is incorrect in accusing Captain Blackwood of having stated that the French three-decker fired a broadside at any of his ships: that assertion appears in a letter addressed to a newspaper editor by "An officer of the Ajax," and is virtually contradicted by a subsequent paragraph in the same letter. Another extract from the English papers, referred to by the French officer, is a loose paragraph, stating that the Euryalus lost Lieutenant Williams and seven men killed, and 13 wounded. This statement, in which there is not a shadow of truth, is exultingly dwelt upon by the French officer, in a subsequent part of his letter, as a proof of the superiority of the fire of the French, not a man on their side having been hurt, over that of the English.

The most objectionable part of Captain Blackwood's letter is the boast of what his three 74s would have done, had the French three-decker, and the five two-deckers, one or two of which in all probability were 80-gun ships, been "bold" enough to engage him. "From the determined conduct of the squadron you did me the honour to place under my command," says the captain, "I am fully persuaded, had the ambition of the enemy permitted him to make a bolder attack, the result would have been still more honourable to his majesty's arms." Had Commodore Rodgers, or the equally renowned Captain David Porter, or even the French admiral himself, assisted by the Moniteur's embellishing powers, written in this style, no surprise would have been created. But what Englishman does not regret, that such boastful threats, from physical causes almost impossible to be realized, should have emanated from the pen of a British officer; and that British officer, one who had already so unequivocally distinguished himself?

It was not many weeks afterwards, ere a more decided display of British valour, although not a sentence respecting it is to be found in the London Gazette, occurred off the port of Toulon. In the early part of August three French store-ships, bound thither, were chased by the British in-shore squadron into the anchorage of Porqueroles, one of the Hyères, and were there watched by the 18-gun brig-sloop Philomel, Captain Gardiner Henry Guion. On the 26th, at daylight, the three store-ships, each of which was about equal in force to an English 28-gun frigate, weighed and pushed out; and one, covered by a division of the French fleet from the outer road, succeeded in getting round to Toulon. The remaining two, however, were obliged to put back and re-anchor. On the 30th these shifted their births to the entrance of the Petite-Passe, preparatory to a second attempt to reach the port of their destination. On the next morning, the 31st, at daylight, the Toulon fleet was seen in motion; and at 8 h. 30 m. A.M. the two store-ships were again under way. At 9 h. 30 m. A.M. the Philomel, still at her post, tacked, the wind a light breeze from the east-south-east, and at 10 h. 30 m. exchanged a few distant shot with the store-ships as they were coming round Pointe Escampebarion. In 10 minutes afterwards the 74-gun ship Repulse, Captain John Halliday, who was lying to on the larboard tack at some distance outside the brig, exchanged shots with the French advanced frigates. Meanwhile the two store-ships, favoured by the wind and protected by their friends, got safe into Toulon.

Having accomplished this object, the French squadron, under Rear-admiral Baudin in the 120-gun ship Majestueux, continued working out, in the hope, apparently, of capturing the Philomel, who now made all possible sail upon a wind to get clear of her foes. At noon the two headmost French frigates opened a fire upon the brig, which she returned with her two 6-pounders out of the stern-ports. At 0 h. 25 m. P.M. the Repulse also commenced firing her stern guns. At 0 h. 30 m. finding that the shot of the frigates were passing over the Philomel, the British 74 gallantly bore up, and, bringing to astern of the brig, opened so heavy and well-directed a fire upon the three headmost frigates, which were the Pomone, Pénélope, and Adrienne, that, in the course of a quarter of an hour, they wore and joined the line-of-battle ships; several of which were also, by this time, far advanced in the chase. These, soon afterwards, wore also; and, by 5 P.M., the whole were again at anchor in the road.

At the time this noble act was performed by the Repulse, the British fleet was out of sight to leeward, off Bandol, except the Warspite 74 and Alceste frigate, who were about nine miles distant in the same direction. Captains Blackwood and Murray Maxwell, and their respective officers and ship's companies, must have felt their hearts bound with delight at such a spectacle. Nor could the feelings of Captain Halliday and his ship's company have been other than of the most cheering kind; especially when Captain Guion, in a spirit of honourable gratitude, telegraphed the Repulse, "You REPULSED the enemy, and nobly saved us: grant me permission to return thanks."

Light Squadrons and Single Ships.

On the 10th of January the British 10-gun brig-sloop Cherokee (eight 18-pounder carronades and two sixes, with 75 men and boys), Captain Richard Arthur, reconnoitred the harbour of Dieppe, and perceived lying at anchor under the batteries, close together, and within 200 yards of the pier-head, seven French lugger-privateers. Notwithstanding the number and strong defensive position of these vessels, Captain Arthur resolved to attack them; and accordingly, at 1 A.M. on the 11th, the Cherokee, favoured by a southerly wind, stood in, and running between two of the luggers, gallantly laid one on board; which, after a fruitless attempt to board the Cherokee, was carried by the crew of the latter. The vessel proved to be the Aimable Nelly, a new lugger of 16 guns, 106 tons, and 60 men; of whom two were killed and eight wounded, three of them dangerously. The remaining six privateers kept up a smart fire of musketry; but the Cherokee, notwithstanding, succeeded in getting out her prize, with the loss of only two wounded, both in the hand, Lieutenant Vere Gabriel, and her boatswain, James Ralph. So daring and successful an act met its due reward, as is evident from the date of Captain Arthur's commission as a post-captain.

On the 11th of January Captain Volant Vashon Ballard, of the 38-gun frigate Blonde, commanding a British squadron, consisting, besides that frigate, of the sloops Scorpion, Cygnet, and Pultusk, Captains Francis Stanfell, Edward Dix, and John M'George, and gun-brig Attentive, Lieutenant Robert Carr, stationed off Basse-terre bay, island of Guadaloupe, directed the Scorpion to bring out a French brig-corvette at anchor near the shore. At 9 P.M., while standing in to execute this service, the Scorpion discovered the object of her attack, which was the French 16-gun brig-corvette Oreste, Lieutenant Jean-Baptiste-Anselme Mousnier, just clearing the north point of the bay. The British brig immediately made all sail in chase, but had very soon to use her sweeps on account of the fall of the wind. At 10 h. 30 m. P.M. the Scorpion began firing her bow-chasers, and at 11 P.M. brought the French brig to action. A sort of running fight, in which the Scorpion had occasionally to keep in check a battery on the shore, was maintained between the two brigs until 1 h. 30 m. A.M. on the 12th; when, being completely unrigged by her opponent's well-directed fire, the Oreste hauled down her colours. At this moment the barge of the Blonde arrived, and assisted in taking possession of the prize; who, could she have protracted the action many minutes longer, would have run herself on shore.

The Scorpion, whose guns were 16 carronades, 32-pounders, and two sixes, with a complement of 120 men and boys, received several shot in her hull, had her mainyard wounded in the slings, also her mainmast and gaff, and her sails and rigging much cut; but she escaped with no greater loss than four men wounded. The Oreste, whose guns were fourteen 24-pounder carronades and two sixes, with a complement of 110 men and boys, besides about 20 passengers, including a lieutenant-colonel and two other officers of the army, and the captains and some of the officers of the two French frigates Loire and Seine, recently destroyed at Anse la Barque, was damaged in the manner already stated, and lost two men killed, and her first and second captains and eight men wounded. Twelve officers and 79 men were received from her as prisoners, total 91; but the remaining survivors of the crew and passengers succeeded in reaching the shore in one of the brig's boats. Surrounded as the French brig was by an enemy's squadron, not the slightest imputation can attach to her officers and crew for surrendering. The Oreste, a fine brig of 312 tons, was afterwards added to the British navy by the name of Wellington.

On the 17th of January the 18-pounder[1] 36-gun frigate, Freija, Captain John Hayes, cruising off Englishman's Head, island of Guadaloupe, received intelligence from the log of a schooner captured by her, that there were three or four vessels at anchor in Baie Mahaut, a place of some strength situated on the north side of the neck of land connecting Basse-terre with Grande-terre. Captain Hayes came to the determination of attacking the forts that defended the harbour, with a division of boats from the little squadron then under his orders; and, as a preliminary step, the Freija made sail by herself to reconnoitre the spot. On the 21st, at noon, after a two days' search in a most intricate and dangerous navigation, the frigate discovered three vessels lying at anchor; but, owing to the distance, could only make out that one was a brig with topgallant-yards across and sails bent. The evening proving particularly fine, with little wind and smooth water, Captain Hayes resolved to send away the boats of the Freija alone, now quite out of signal-distance from any ship of her squadron.

[1] Of that class, but we believe the frigate carried Gover's 24s.

Accordingly, at 9 h. 15 m. P.M., four boats, containing 50 seamen and 30 marines, under the orders of Lieutenant David Hope, first of the Freìja, assisted by Lieutenant of marines John Shillibeer, master's mate A. G. Countess, and Mr. Samuel Bray, the gunner, pushed off from the frigate, and stood to the southward. At a few minutes past 11 P.M., after experiencing great difficulty in finding a passage, and meeting so many shoals that the headmost boat grounded eight or ten times, Lieutenant Hope detained a fisherman; from whom he learnt that a troop of regular cavalry and a company of native infantry had arrived at Baie Mahaut that evening from Pointe-à-Pitre. Undismayed by this information, the British hastened forward to the point of attack.

As soon as the boats arrived within gun-shot, a signal gun was fired, and then a discharge of grape from a battery at the north-east point, and from another at the head of the bay. The guns of the brig, found to be six in number, and all mounted on one side, also opened upon the boats; and they likewise received a fire of musketry from men concealed in the bushes that lay between one battery and the other. In the face of this very heavy fire, the boats pulled alongside the brig; and, as the British boarded her on one side, the Frenchmen fled from her on the other.

Leaving Mr. Bray, with a few hands, in charge of the brig, with directions to turn her guns upon the enemy, and cover the landing of the boats, Lieutenant Hope pushed for the shore; but the boats grounded at so great a distance, that the officers and men had to wade up to their middles to get to the beach. As the British advanced towards the first battery, the French retreated, and took post behind a brick breastwork, from over which they opened a fire of musketry. Pushing forward, the seamen and marines brought their broadswords and bayonets into play, and quickly drove the enemy from his position. The battery was found to consist of one 24-pounder, besides six howitzers which had been dragged to the beach to oppose the landing. The howitzers were now buried in the sand, the 24-pounder hove over the cliff, and the battery destroyed, as well as a magazine containing 20 barrels of powder. Lieutenant Hope and his party then pushed on, and stormed and carried the other battery mounting three 24-pounders. These the British immediately spiked, and set fire to and destroyed the carriages and guard-house. This battery was a very complete work, ditched all round, with a small bridge and a gateway entrance.

Having thus far succeeded in their perilous enterprise, Lieutenant Hope and his party returned to the brig; which they found fast in the mud, the crew, when they quitted her, having cut her cables. After great exertions, the seamen got the prize afloat. Near to the brig lay, fast aground in the mud, a large English-built ship, under repair, and inside of her a fine national schooner, pierced for 16 guns, but having only 12 on board. Finding it impracticable to float either of these vessels, Lieutenant Hope set fire to and destroyed them. This done, the British boats and the captured brig moved out of the bay, and in a very short time were close alongside the Freìja.

The whole of this very gallant and far from unimportant service was executed with so slight a loss to the British as two seamen severely wounded; one in going up to loose the brig's foretopsail, and the other in attacking the batteries. The loss on the part of the French could not be ascertained: two officers, one with two epaulets and supposed to be the commandant at the fort, were found dead, and some lay wounded. In his letter to Captain Hayes, giving an account of the service he had performed, Lieutenant Hope speaks in the highest terms of the officers and men under his command; and particularly notices the gallant manner in which Lieutenant Shillibeer led his marines to the charge: as well as the steady discipline of the latter, in keeping possession of the heights while the seamen were destroying the batteries.

Captain Hayes wrote to Vice-admiral Sir Alexander Cochrane, the commander-in-chief on the station, enclosing the letter of Lieutenant Hope; and Sir Alexander transmitted both letters to the secretary of the admiralty, with one from himself, in which, after dwelling upon the importance of the service, in reference to the intended attack upon the island at large, he says: "The conduct of Lieutenant Hope and his party, in driving so large a force before him, and surmounting so many difficulties in reaching the enemy's position, stamps their leader as a brave and meritorious officer; and he is deserving the notice of the lords commissioners of the admiralty." Not one of these letters, however, appeared in the London Gazette. Instead of them a sort of abstract was inserted in the following words: "The vice-admiral has transmitted a letter from Captain Hayes, of his majesty's ship Freìja, stating the destruction of the batteries at Bay Mahaut, in the island of Guadaloupe, and of a ship and national schooner at anchor there, and also the capture of an armed brig by the boats of the Freìja, under the direction of

Lieutenant David Hope, who appears to have displayed much gallantry in the performance of this service."

To epitomize official letters, so as to do justice to the cause and to the parties interested, is no easy task; and the admiralty clerk who made this very abstract has left it in some degree doubtful, whether the Freija did not destroy the batteries, ship, and schooner, and her boats capture the brig. At all events the service performed by Lieutenant Hope appeared of so little comparative merit, when thus, we suppose we must call it, "gazetted," that, although at that time not a very young lieutenant, he had to wait four or five years longer before he became a commander.

These abstracts of letters may possibly have originated in a press of official matter; but, then, how happens it that we occasionally see with them, in the columns of the Gazette, entire letters, announcing the capture of half a dozen insignificant chasse-marées, or of some privateer of trifling force, and that perhaps by a frigate? Nay, the space occupied by the letters of Sir Charles Cotton and Captain Blackwood, already adverted to,[1] would have contained at least two of the rejected letters, and have probably led to the promotion of two deserving officers.

To the naval annalist, these brief statements occasion great inconvenience; to him especially who feels bound to give a better excuse for the omission of the details of a well-conducted enterprise, than that the board of admiralty had not deemed them of sufficient importance to appear in the London Gazette. Unfortunately, too, the sources of information, which for their authenticity and minuteness we prefer to all others, fail us in the majority of those daring, and far from uninteresting cases, attacks by boats upon the enemy's armed vessels and shore batteries. The log seldom if ever states more, than that at such an hour the boats quitted the ship, and at such an hour returned: sometimes the loss in killed and wounded is inserted, and more rarely the name of the officer who commanded the party.

On the 10th of February, at 10 h. 30 m. A.M., latitude 25° 22' north, longitude 61° 27' west, the British 10-gun schooner Thistle (18-pounder carronades, with 50 men and boys), Lieutenant Peter Procter, steering north-east by north with the wind at south-east, discovered and chased a strange ship in the east-south-east. At 4 P.M., having by superiority of sailing neared the stranger considerably, the Thistle fired a gun and hoisted

[1] See p. 84.

her colours. The example was immediately followed by the ship, which was the Dutch corvette Havik, Lieutenant de vaisseau Jean Stéeling; a large India-built ship, pierced for 18 guns and mounting 10 (six long 4-pounders and four 2-pound swivels), with a complement of 52 men and boys, including the Batavian rear-admiral, Armand-Adrien Buyskes, late lieutenant-governor and commander-in-chief at Batavia, and his suite, bound from that port to New York, and partly laden with spices and indigo.

At 5 P.M., which made just seven hours and a half from the commencement of the chase, the Thistle got alongside the Havik, and firing across her bows, hailed her to bring to. The reply to this was a broadside. The action immediately commenced, and was maintained with mutual spirit. At 6 h. 15 m. P.M., the Havik attempted to run the schooner down; but the latter, hauling aft her sheets, adroitly avoided the bows of her huge opponent. The Thistle, three of whose carronades had been dismounted since the early part of the action, continued closely engaging the Havik until 6 h. 45 m. P.M.; when the latter made all sail and endeavoured to escape before the wind. This being the ship's best point of sailing, it was not until 7 h. 40 m. P.M. that the schooner got near enough to open her bow guns. Gradually advancing in the chase, the Thistle, at 8 h. 30 m. P.M., again arrived alongside. A second close engagement ensued, and continued until 9 h. 45 m.; when the Havik hauled down her colours and hailed that she had struck.

In this five hours' engagement and running fight, the Thistle had one marine killed, and her commander and six men wounded. On board the Havik one man also was killed, and the Dutch admiral and seven men badly wounded. The conduct of the Thistle in the affair was highly creditable to her commander, his officers, and crew. It was an act of some boldness for a schooner of 150 tons to attack a large warlike enemy's ship; nor was it less a proof of persevering courage for the Thistle, after three of her carronades had been dismounted, to continue the engagement for so long a time, and until she brought it to a successful issue. Lieutenant Procter, who is described by Vice-admiral Sir John Borlase Warren, the commander-in-chief on the Halifax station, as "an old officer of much merit," in four months afterwards, as we discover by a reference to the navy-list, was promoted to the rank of commander.

On the 12th or 13th of January the French 40-gun frigates, Néréide, Captain Jean-François Lemaresquier, and Astrée, Captain François-Désiré Breton, managed to effect their escape from the port of Cherbourg; the one laden with troops and supplies for the island of Guadaloupe, and the other with the same for the Isle of France. On the 9th of February, very early in the morning, the Néréide arrived off Basse-terre, and sent an officer and boat's crew on shore for a pilot. The boat did not return, for the colony had been three days in possession of the British; and the first peep of day discovered to the Néréide her perilous situation. From their anchorage off the west end of the Saintes, the following British vessels slipped their cables, and made all sail in chase :—

Gun-ship.
    74 Alfred . . . . Captain Joshua Rowley Watson.
Gun-frigate.
    38 { Blonde . . . . ,, Volant Vashon Ballard.
        { Thetis . . . . ,, George Miller.
    36 Melampus . . . ,, Edward Hawker.
    32 Castor . . . . ,, George Paris Monke.
Gun-brig-sloop.
    18 Scorpion . . . . ,, Francis Stanfell.

Shortly afterwards the Alfred shaped her course to the northward after a ship at anchor off Anse la Barque, supposed to be a second French frigate, but which proved to be the 18-gun ship-sloop Star, Captain William Paterson, who had also slipped on descrying the Néréide, but lay becalmed under the land. In the meanwhile the Blonde, Thetis, Melampus, Castor, and Scorpion, pursued the Néréide; who was under a crowd of canvas steering to the south-west, and at 8 A.M., the wind then a fresh breeze from the eastward, was but four miles ahead of the leading British ship, the Blonde. During the day's chase, the Néréide gained about two miles of the Blonde; when the latter, at 10 P.M., carried away her maintopmast and the yard with it, also her foretopsail-yard and fore and mizen topgallantmasts. The Blonde, in consequence, dropped astern; and the remaining ships continued the chase throughout the night, the Melampus leading. During the whole of the 10th the Néréide kept gaining by degrees on the Melampus; who at 8 P.M. lost sight of her squadron, and, at 10 h. 30 m. P.M., of the French frigate. In another hour the Melampus shortened sail, and hauled to the wind on the starboard tack, to rejoin her consorts.

Thus relieved of her pursuers, the Néréide steered a more northerly course, intending to make her voyage back by the windward passage, or that between the islands of St. Domingo and Cuba. On the 13th, at daylight, when within eight or ten leagues of Pointe Abacou upon the first-named island, another enemy made her appearance to windward. This was the British 22-gun ship Rainbow, Captain James Wooldridge. The latter hoisted the English and Spanish private signals, and, finding them not answered, bore up in chase and cleared for action. At 8 h. 30 m. A.M. the Néréide brought to to reconnoitre the ship which was so boldly approaching her, and must soon have discovered that she had but 10 ports and a bridle of a side on her main deck, three on her quarter-deck, and one on her forecastle, total 28 ports, just the number of guns the ship mounted.[1] Nor could the Rainbow's size have alarmed her, for the ship did not measure more than 587 tons. However, there was a something about the British ship that the Néréide did not like; and at 9 A.M. the latter bore up and made all sail. Captain Wooldridge followed; and at noon, Pointe Abacou then bearing north-north-west distant six or seven leagues, the Rainbow was within a mile and a half of a French frigate of more than double her force in guns, men, and size. The chase continued during the afternoon, without any perceptible advantage to either ship; and at 8 P.M. Captain Wooldridge, as his duty prescribed, let off several rockets, to apprise any friend who might be in sight of them, that the Rainbow was in pursuit of an enemy.

On the 14th, at 4 A.M., the Rainbow was within about a mile of the Néréide, and at 9 A.M. exchanged numbers with the 18-gun brig-sloop Avon (sixteen 32-pounder carronades and two sixes), Captain Henry Tillieux Fraser, then about six miles north-west by north of Cape Tiburon, and consequently to leeward of both ships. The Avon was soon under all sail in chase, standing across the enemy's course. At 1 h. 15 m. P.M. the Néréide fired her main deck stern-chasers at the Rainbow; and in 10 minutes the French captain cut away his stern-boat, in order that the quarter-deck chasers might also bear. A shot about this time carried away the Rainbow's larboard foretopmast studding-sail boom. At 2 h. 30 m. P.M. the French frigate, whose course had been north-west by west, hauled by degrees more to the southward, and at 3 h. 30 m. P.M. opened her broadside upon the Rainbow; who, hauling up also, in five minutes returned the fire. A warm action now ensued between this British 22-gun ship and French 40-gun frigate, until 4 P.M. when the Avon came up and raked the Néréide with a broadside. At 4 h. 5 m. P.M., leaving the Rainbow in a totally unmanage-

[1] See p. 2.

able state, the Néréide wore; as well to evade the raking fire of the Avon, as to punish her for her temerity. Between the British brig and French frigate an action now commenced, and continued until 5 P.M.; when, having reduced this opponent to even a worse state than her first one, the Néréide bore away under courses, topsails, stay-sails, and main and mizen topgallantsails.

The greater part of the Rainbow's standing and running rigging was cut to pieces, and her masts and yards were much wounded; but, owing to the high firing of her antagonist, her hull was not materially injured. It was this high firing that occasioned the loss of the Rainbow, out of a crew on board of 156 men and boys, to be so comparatively slight as 10 seamen and marines wounded. The Avon, in her rigging and sails, was as much disabled as her consort, and suffered more in her masts; which, along with her bowsprit, were completely crippled. The brig's hull, although much lower, and therefore more difficult to hit, than the Rainbow's, appears to have received the greater proportion of the Néréide's shot. Her upperworks were cut through; and several shot had entered between wind and water, causing her to have three feet water in the hold. The Avon had also two of her guns disabled, one man killed, another mortally wounded, and one acting lieutenant (Curtis Reid), one midshipman, and five men wounded severely.

What loss was sustained by the French frigate in this encounter, we have no means of ascertaining; and the only visible damage which the Néréide received, besides some cut rigging, was her foretopgallant-yard shot away. On ceasing her fire, the Néréide resumed her course to the north-west, and at 6 P.M. was out of sight of her two opponents; who, as soon as the Avon had joined the Rainbow, then about three miles distant in the south by east, made all the sail they could for Jamaica, and on the 16th anchored in the harbour of Port Royal. The Néréide, in all probability, conveyed to France the account of the fall of Guadaloupe before it was known in England. The Scorpion carried home the English despatches; but not having departed until after her return from the chase of the Néréide, did not arrive at Plymouth until the 13th of March.

One effect of the supremacy of the British navy was to compel France to make merchantmen and transports of her men-of-war: hence a frigate, despatched on a voyage to a colonial port, is ordered to chase nothing and speak nothing on her way. This may account for even two French frigates, as we have shown to have been the case, declining to engage one British frigate ; and, had the Néréide fallen in with the Rainbow and Avon before she reached Guadaloupe, might have explained why this French frigate ran from a British 22-gun ship and brig-sloop. But, having found that island shut against her, the Néréide would, one might suppose, resume her character of a ship-of-war, and endeavour to effect something that should do honour to a 40-gun frigate and confer a benefit, however slight in degree, upon the nation to which she belonged. Instead of this, acting as, after having knocked away his opponent's mainmast, he did on a former occasion,[1] Captain Lemaresquier waits merely until he has deprived his two inferior antagonists of the means of pursuit; then leaves them to repair their damages, and to boast, justly boast, of what their prowess had accomplished.

The conduct of the Rainbow and Avon, throughout this running fight, reflects the highest honour upon their respective officers and crews, as well as upon the flag under which they served; and the noble conduct of Captain Wooldridge, in his earnest pursuit, single-handed, of an enemy so much superior to the Rainbow, was just what might be expected from an officer who, on a former occasion, when commanding the Mediator fire-ship, behaved so gallantly. The prompt support which Captain Fraser afforded his friend, while it relieved the Rainbow from a destructive fire, brought upon himself and his little brig the whole weight of the French frigate's broadside; the serious effects of which we have already described. But, because the engagement produced no trophy as its result, the account of it did not appear in the London Gazette; and that having been the case, and no fresh opportunity offering for him to distinguish himself, Captain Fraser continued as a commander during the remainder of his life. He appears to have died in one of the latter months of the year 1816.

On the 10th of January, in the morning, while a small British squadron, under the orders of Captain Sir Joseph Sydney Yorke, of the 80-gun ship Christian VII. was lying in Basque roads, a convoy of French coasters were discovered, on their passage from Isle d'Aix to Rochelle. Immediately the boats of the Christian VII. and of the 38-gun frigate Armide, Captain Lucius Hardyman, were detached, under the orders of Lieutenant Gardener Henry Guion, to cut off the vessels. The boats soon drove the vessels on shore, within grape and musket range of the French battery. Notwithstanding their apparent security,

---

[1] See vol. iv., p. 372.

Lieutenant Guion and his party succeeded in capturing one chasse-marée, and in destroying a brig, a schooner, and two chasse-marées, all valuably laden; but which, owing to the fast ebbing of the tide, it was found impracticable to get afloat.

On the 20th, in the evening, another convoy of about 30 sail making their appearance in the Maumusson passage, and the van seeming inclined to push for Rochelle, the boats of the same two ships, still under the orders of Lieutenant Guion, were sent in chase. With their accustomed gallantry, the British attacked the convoy, which ran aground within a stone's throw of the batteries; when five of them, under a heavy fire of grape and musketry, were burnt, and a sixth was taken: the rest put back. The captured vessels were all chasse-marées, and were laden, as the former had been, with wine, brandy, soap, rosin, candles, pitch, oil, &c. In this affair one of the Armide's seamen was wounded, and two of the French seamen were killed.

On the 13th of February, three deeply-laden chasse-marées, part of a convoy of ten sail which had sailed on the preceding evening from the Charente in thick weather, blowing fresh from the west-south-west, having got on the reef that projects from the point of Chatelaillon between Aix and Rochelle, Sir Joseph Yorke detached, for the purpose of destroying them, three boats from the Christian VII., three from the Armide, and two from the 12-pounder 36-gun frigate Seine, Captain David Atkins, still under the orders of Lieutenant Guion.

As the eight boats of the British, manned and armed in the usual way, advanced towards the grounded chasse-marées, nine French boats, each carrying a 12-pounder carronade and six swivels, and rowing from 20 to 30 oars, pulled out to meet the former and prevent them from fulfilling their object. Lieutenant Guion made a feint of retreating, to decoy the French boats from their shore defences; and, having got to a proper distance, suddenly pulled round and stood towards them. The French immediately retreated; but the Christian VII.'s barge, in which was Lieutenant Guion, being a fleet boat, boldly advanced along the rear of the French line to their third boat. Finding, however, from circumstances, that the rearmost boat was the only one likely to be attacked with any prospect of success, Lieutenant Guion gallantly boarded and carried her, sword in hand. She had two men killed and three wounded, including her commanding officer, severely.

In the mean time Lieutenant Samuel Roberts, of the Armide,

had pursued two others of the French armed boats in the direction of the beach; and, by the steady fire which his men maintained upon them at a pistol-shot distance, they must have sustained a loss. The protectors of the chasse-marées being thus defeated, the British boats proceeded to execute the service for which they had been detached: they soon effectually destroyed the three chasse-marées on the reef, and got back to their ships without, as far as it appears, having a man hurt For the gallantry which he had displayed in these several spirited boat-attacks, Lieutenant Guion was deservedly promoted to the rank of commander.

On the 3rd of February, at daylight, the British 74-gun ship Valiant, Captain John Bligh, being close to Belle-Isle in light and baffling winds, discovered, about three miles off, and immediately chased, a strange frigate. This was the late famous French 40-gun frigate Canonnière, but now the French armed merchant-ship Confiance, Captain Jacques Peroud (the privateer Bellone's late captain), armed with only 14 guns, and laden with a cargo of colonial produce valued at 150,000*l.* sterling; with which, 93 days before, she had sailed from the Isle of France, having been lent by General Decaen to the merchants there, for the purpose of carrying home their produce, the frigate requiring more repairs to refit her as a cruiser than the colony could give her. At about noon, after a seven hours' chase, the wind suddenly took the Confiance by the head, and threw her round upon the Valiant's broadside. Her escape being now hopeless, the Confiance hauled down her colours: she had, it appears, been chased 14 times during the passage from Port Louis. Having been built since the year 1714, and wanting considerable repairs, the Confiance, although formerly a British frigate, was not restored to the service.

On the 21st of February, in the morning, latitude 33° 10' north, longitude 29° 30' west, the British 38-gun frigate Horatio, Captain George Scott, fell in with the French frigate-built store-ship Nécessité, mounting 26 guns of the same description as those carried by the Var and Salamandre, and having a crew of 186 men commanded by Lieutenant Bernard Bonnie, from Brest bound to the Isle of France with naval stores and provisions. After a long chase, and a running fight of one hour, during which she manifested some determination to defend herself, the Nécessité hauled down her colours. No loss appears to have been sustained on either side; and the Horatio escaped with only a slight injury to her masts and rigging.

On the 12th of April, close off the coast of France in the neighbourhood of the Isle of Ré, the British 18-pounder 32-gun frigate Unicorn, Captain Alexander Robert Kerr, fell in with and captured the late British 22-gun ship Laurel, at this time named Espérance, armed en flûte, and under the command of a Lieutenant de Vaisseau, from the Isle of France with a valuable cargo of colonial produce. The prize was afterwards restored to her rank in the British navy, but, a Laurel having since been added to it, under the name of Laurestinus.

On the 12th of May, at 1 h. 30 m. P.M., the British 18-pounder 36-gun frigate Tribune, Captain George Reynolds, cruising off the Naze of Norway, observed and chased two brigs under the land. At 2 P.M. the latter, now discovered to be Danish brigs-of-war, made all sail for the port of Mandal, and at 2 h. 30 m. hove to within the rocks. The Tribune immediately stood in, wore, and gave the two brigs a broadside, and then stood off again under easy sail. Several gun-boats now pulled out from behind the rocks, and presently two other large brigs came out and joined the two first seen. At 3 h. 15 m. P.M. the Danes began working out, as if intending to attack the frigate; who, at 3 h. 20 m., wore and stood in shore to meet them. At 3 h. 40 m. the Tribune hove to; whereupon the four Danish brigs, two of which mounted 20 guns, a third 18, and the remaining one 16 guns, tacked and stood towards the British frigate, formed in line of battle.

At 4 P.M. the Tribune filled on the starboard tack with light airs; and at 4 h. 30 m. wore round and discharged her larboard broadside at the four brigs then on the same tack to windward, distant rather less than half a mile. A smart engagement now ensued. Finding that the brigs were rather forereaching upon her, the Tribune set her courses, and maintained the cannonade with such effect, that at 6 h. 45 m. the Danish commodore, being in a very shattered state, ceased firing. This brig then made the signal to discontinue the action; and, followed by her three consorts, crowded sail to regain the port of Mandal. As quickly as possible afterwards, the Tribune tacked and made sail in chase; but, favoured by the weather-gage and the lightness of the wind, the brigs reached their port; out of which, as they approached, issued several gun-boats, to afford them protection.

This was rather a serious contest for the frigate. The Tribune had her fore and main stays and back stays, and maintopgallant-yard, shot away, fore and main topmasts and maintopsail-yard severely wounded, standing and running rigging and sails much cut, boats all rendered useless, and hull greatly shattered, with several shot between wind and water. Her loss amounted to four seamen, four marines, and one boy killed, and 15 seamen and marines wounded. The Danes at this time owned five or six brigs, two or three of the class and force of the Lougen; and some mounting not quite so many guns; but all, as it appears, carrying either long or medium 18-pounders, and consequently much more formidable vessels than their appearance indicated.

On the 22nd of July, in the evening, as the British 18-pounder 36-gun frigate Belvidera, Captain Richard Byron, and 28-gun frigate, Nemesis, Captain William Ferris, were standing close in-shore of Studtland, coast of Norway, Captain Byron sent his master, Mr. James M'Pherson, to sound round a deep bay. Perceiving three vessels at anchor, Mr. M'Pherson rowed up to reconnoitre them; when, late in the night, they opened a fire upon him, and proved to be three Danish gun-vessels; two of them, the Bolder and Thor, commanded by Lieutenants Dahlreup and Rasmusen, schooner-rigged, and mounting each two long 24-pounders and six 6-pounder howitzers with a crew of 45 men. The third gun-vessel was of a smaller class, and carried one long 24-pounder with 25 men.

On the morning of the 23rd Captain Byron detached upon the service of capturing or destroying these gun-vessels, the launch, barge, and two cutters of the Belvidera, also, the launch, pinnace, and yawl of the Nemesis: the four first boats under the orders of Lieutenants Samuel Nisbett, and William Henry Bruce, and Lieutenant of marines James Campbell; and the three last, of Lieutenants Thomas Hodgskins and Marmaduke Smith. The Danes opened a heavy fire upon the boats as they advanced, and received in return a fire from the carronades in the bows of the launches. In a very short time the two gun-schooners hauled down their colours and were taken possession of without the slightest loss, but the Danes on board of them had four men killed. The remaining gun-boat ran up a creek, and was there abandoned by her crew and burnt by the British.

On the 29th of August, at 3 P.M., the island of Alderney bearing south-south-west three or four leagues, the British hired armed cutter Queen Charlotte, of 76 tons, eight 4-pounders, and 27 men and boys, commanded by Mr. Joseph Thomas, a master in the royal navy, while proceeding towards the blockading squadron off Cherbourg, observed a large cutter, with an English white ensign and pendant, approaching from under the land in the south-east. At 3 h. 30 m. P.M. the stranger, whose true character had been suspected and caused suitable preparations to be made on board the Queen Charlotte, came close to the latter, luffed up, and, when in the act of changing her colours to French, received a well-directed broadside. The French cutter immediately sheered off, as if not expecting such a salute, but soon returned to the combat. A close action was now maintained, nearly the whole time within pistol-shot, until 5 P.M., when the French vessel ceased firing and hauled to the north-east; leaving the Queen Charlotte in no condition to follow, she having had her boatswain killed and 14 men wounded, including one mortally and several badly.

The French cutter was the late British revenue-cutter Swan, lengthened so as to measure 200 tons, and mounting 16 long 6-pounders, with a crew, as afterwards found on board of her, of 120 men. To have beaten off an antagonist so greatly superior in force, was a truly meritorious act on the part of Mr. Thomas and his brave associates. The Queen Charlotte, with more than half her crew in a wounded state, and with her rigging and sails very much cut, was obliged to put into St. Aubin's bay. Among the badly wounded was a passenger, Mr. P. A. Mulgrave, employed in arranging the telegraphic communication between the island of Jersey and the British squadron off Cherbourg. This gentleman, while in the act of firing his musket at the enemy, received a musket-ball through his hat, which carried away the outer angle of the socket of his left eye, and, passing through the centre of the upper eyelid, slightly grazed his nose. He, notwithstanding, refused to quit the deck, and continued to supply ammunition to those near him until the affair terminated.

On the 5th of September, in the morning, while the British 38-gun frigate Surveillante, Captain George Ralph Collier, and gun-brig Constant, Lieutenant John Stokes, were standing out of the Morbihan for the purpose of reconnoitring the Loire, a division of a French convoy was observed to take advantage of the frigate's departure and run from the Morbihan to the southward. The convoy was immediately chased, and a part of it driven back. One brig sought protection close under the rocks, and between the batteries of St. Guildas and St. Jacques. Captain Collier immediately despatched the boats of the Surveillante, under the orders of Lieutenant the Honourable James Arbuthnot, assisted by master's mate John Illingworth, and midshipmen John Kingdom, Digby Marsh, Edwyn Francis

Stanhope, William Crowder, John Watt, and Herbert Ashton, to attempt the capture or destruction of the brig.

Notwithstanding the protection afforded to the French brig by the batteries, and by the additional fire of a party of soldiers placed within the caverns and supported by field-pieces, Lieutenant Arbuthnot and Mr. Illingworth in the gig, assisted by the other boats, succeeded in carrying the vessel. The crew of the gig then cut her cables and hawsers, and the prize was brought out without the slightest loss on the part of the British. But Captain Collier handsomely acknowledges that this fortunate termination of the enterprise was mainly attributable to the "zeal and determination of Lieutenant Stokes, of the Constant, who, with admirable skill and judgment, pushed his brig in between the rocks and shoals of St. Guildas, and by a well-directed fire kept the enemy close within their holes and caves among the rocks." In performing this service, the Constant became necessarily exposed to showers of grape, but a few of those shot through her sails and bulwark comprised the extent of the injury she received.

On the 6th, late in the night, the Surveillante detached two boats, under the orders of master's mate John Illingworth, assisted by midshipmen John Kingdom and Hector Rose, to destroy a new battery of one long 24-pounder, and a guard-house having a small watch-tower attached to it, protecting the north side of, and the entrance into, the river Crache, in which lay at anchor several coasters. Although the day had dawned before the British reached the spot, they first decoyed the guard from the battery, and then drove them from the beach. Mr. Illingworth and his little party then pushed for, and made themselves master of, the battery and guard-house. After they had spiked the gun, a quantity of powder, carried on shore for the purpose, was so well disposed of, that in a few minutes the whole building was level with the ground and in flames. Having thus effectually executed the service upon which he had been detached, Mr. Illingworth returned to the frigate without the slightest casualty.

On the night of the 27th of September, the boats of the 120-gun ship Caledonia, Captain Sir Harry Neale, 74-gun ship Valiant, Captain Robert Dudley Oliver, and 38-gun frigate Armide, Captain Richard Dalling Dun, lying at anchor in Basque roads, were detached under the orders of Lieutenant Arthur Philip Hamilton, first of the Caledonia, to take or destroy three brigs lying under the protection of a strong battery at Pointe du Ché; and, as the enemy had been known to have strengthened his position with four field-pieces and a party of artillery stationed on a low point of the beach situated under the battery, as well as by a strong detachment of cavalry and infantry in the adjoining village of Angoulin, a body of 130 marines, commanded by Captains Thomas Sherman and Archibald M'Lachlan, Lieutenants John Coulter and John Couche, and Lieutenant Robert John Little, of the marine artillery, were added to the division of seamen from the three ships.

At about 2 h. 30 m. A.M. on the 28th, the marines were landed under Pointe du Ché; but, notwithstanding the near approach of the boats before they were discovered, the alarm was given by the brigs, and an ineffectual fire was immediately opened from the enemy's guns. Lieutenant Little pushed forward with the bayonet to the assault, supported by Captain M'Lachlan's division, and by a detachment under Lieutenants Coulter and Couche, and quickly carried the battery and spiked the guns. At the same time Captain Shearman, with his division of marines, took post on the main road by the sea side, with his front to the village, and one of the launches with an 18-pounder carronade on his right. In a few minutes a considerable body of men advanced from the village, but were checked in their approach by a warm fire from the marines and the launch. At this period the enemy had succeeded, under cover of the darkness, in bringing a field-piece to flank the line; but which the British picket immediately charged with the bayonet and took, putting the men stationed at it to flight. In the mean time the seamen had effected the capture of two of the brigs, and the destruction of the third.

The marines were then re-embarked without the loss of a man killed and only one private wounded, except Lieutenant Little at his first gallant charge. This officer, while struggling with a French soldier to get his musket from him, received the contents into his hand; which was so much shattered in consequence, as to render amputation necessary. The French had 14 men killed in defending the battery upon Pointe du Ché: what loss the party from the village sustained by the fire of Captain Shearman's division and the carronade in the launch could not be ascertained.

On the 7th of September the British 98-gun ship Dreadnaught, Captain Valentine Collard, bearing the flag of Rear-admiral Thomas Sotheby, while cruising off the coast of France, was informed by the 4-gun schooner Snapper, Lieutenant William Jenkins, that a ship was among the rocks on the west side of Ushant. The Dreadnaught made sail to the eastward, and about 6 P.M. on the 8th, on rounding the island, discovered the ship at anchor in a small creek, surrounded by rocks. Rear-admiral Sotheby determined to attempt cutting her out with his boats at daybreak on the following morning. To prevent suspicion, the Dreadnaught stood on until dark: she then bore up for the spot: and at 5 A.M. on the 9th, seven boats, well manned and armed, pushed off from her, under the orders of Lieutenant Thomas Pettman.

No sooner had the boats approached within gun-shot of the shore, than they were received by a heavy and destructive fire of musketry from a number of troops concealed among the rocks, and from two 4-pounder field-pieces on the beach. In the face of all this, the British pulled towards the ship, lying within half-pistol shot of the beach; and exhilarated by the sight of the French troops, that had been stationed on board to defend her, hurrying over the side in the greatest confusion, boarded and carried her. Now came the most serious part of the enterprise. A body of French soldiers, supposed to be 600 in number, stationed on a precipice nearly over their heads, opened on the British in the ship and in the boats a tremendous fire; a fire to which no return could be made, except occasionally by the 18-pounder carronade in the launch. The consequence was that, in recapturing this Spanish merchant-ship, the Maria-Antonia, from the French privateer who had taken her, and now lay an apparently unconcerned spectator in another creek at about a mile distance, the British sustained the serious loss of one master's mate (Henry B. Middleton), one midshipman (William Robinson), two seamen, and two marines killed, two lieutenants (Henry Elton and Stewart Blacker), two midshipmen (George Burt and Henry Dennis), 18 seamen, and nine marines wounded, and five seamen and one marine missing; total, six killed, 31 wounded, and six missing, or prisoners. Two of the boats had also drifted on shore during the action, and were taken possession of by the enemy.

On the 14th of October, at noon, the British 10-gun brig-sloop Briseis (eight 18-pounder carronades and two sixes, with 75 men and boys), acting-commander Lieutenant George Bentham, cruising about 80 miles west by south of Horn reef, in the North sea, fell in with the French privateer-schooner Sans-Souci, of Amsterdam, mounting ten 12-pounder carronades and four long 2-pounders, with a complement of 55 men, commanded by Jules

Jacobs. After an anxious chase of eight hours, the Briseis succeeded in bringing the schooner to action, which the latter maintained, in the most determined manner, for one hour; the two vessels touching each other the greater part of the time, and during which the privateer's men made three vain attempts to board the British brig. The Sans-Souci then struck her colours, with the loss of eight men killed and 19 wounded; and the Briseis sustained a loss of one master's mate (Alexander Gunn), her captain's clerk (James Davidson), and two seamen killed, and eight seamen and three marines badly wounded: a proof that the privateer was fought with skill as well as with resolution.

On the 25th of October, at 7 A.M., in latitude 54° 47' north, and longitude 2° 45' east, the British 10-gun brig-sloop Calliope (same force as Briseis), Captain John M'Kerlie, discovered a schooner in the south-east under easy sail standing towards her. As the vessel, evidently a privateer, appeared to take the Calliope for a merchant-brig, Captain M'Kerlie thought it prudent not to set any additional sail until the stranger found out her mistake. At 8 h. 30 m. A.M., when about three miles off, the privateer made the discovery, and instantly bore up and crowded sail to escape.

The Calliope was quickly in chase, and at 10 h. 30 m. A.M. began an occasional fire from her bow-chasers. At 11 A.M. she got near enough to fire musketry; but the Calliope could not bring her great guns to bear, as the schooner kept on her lee bow. At 11 h. 30 m. A.M. the brig got far enough advanced to open a fire of round and grape. At noon the schooner lost her mainmast by the board; and, in a minute or two afterwards, having had the sails and rigging on the foremast cut to pieces, her captain hailed that he struck. The prize proved to be the Comtesse d'Hambourg of 14 guns, eight of them 12-pounder carronades, and six described as 8-pounders, with a crew of 51 men. Of these, doubtless, several must have been killed and wounded; but the official account notices no other loss than that of the Calliope, which consisted of only three men wounded, two of them slightly.

On the 27th of October, at daylight, latitude 48° 30' north, longitude 8° 56' west, the British 16-gun brig-sloop Orestes, (14 carronades, 24-pounders, and two sixes, with 95 men and boys), Captain John Richard Lapenotiere, fell in with, and after an hour's chase overtook, the French brig-privateer Loup-Garou, of 16 guns (6-pounders probably), and 100 men and boys. After about half an hour's close action, the privateer hauled down her colours, with the loss of four men wounded, two of them dangerously. The Orestes suffered no damage of consequence, and had not a man of her crew hurt.

On the 8th of November, in the evening, as the British 12-pounder 32-gun frigate Quebec, Captain Charles Sibthorpe John Hawtayne, was running past the Vlie and Schelling, to resume her station before the Texel, a very fine French privateer-schooner was observed at anchor within the Vlie stroom. Lieutenant Stephen Popham, first of the frigate, immediately volunteered his services to make an attempt upon the vessel. The Quebec now brought to just without the sands and in sight of the enemy: and three boats, the first commanded by Lieutenant Popham, the second by Lieutenant Richard Augustus Yates, and the third by master's mate John M'Donald, pushed off. There were also present in the boats, Gilbert Duncan the captain's clerk, and Charles Ward "gentleman volunteer." The schooner to be attacked was the Jeune-Louise, of 14 guns (six 12, and eight 9-pounder carronades), and 35 out of a complement of 60 men, commanded by "Captain Galien Lafont, capitaine de vaisseau and a member of the legion of honour."

The three boats had to pull against a very strong tide, and they found the schooner closely surrounded by sands and fully prepared for the attack. At 9 h. 30 m. P.M., when within pistol-shot of the Jeune-Louise, the three boats grounded on the sand, and in that situation received three distinct broadsides of cannon and musketry. Notwithstanding this, Lieutenant Popham and his party extricated themselves, and boarded and carried the vessel, the French captain falling in a personal conflict with Lieutenant Yates. The British loss on the occasion amounted to one seaman killed, one wounded, and one drowned: one of the boats also was destroyed. The French had one seaman, besides the captain, killed, and one wounded.

A difficult part of the enterprise was still unaccomplished, to get out the schooner from among the sands and shoals by which she was surrounded. This was at length effected; and at daybreak on the 9th, after a long and anxious night passed by Captain Hawtayne and his officers, their fears were relieved by the sight of the schooner, with English colours over French, beating out of the enemy's harbour, through the intricate navigation of the passage. With respect to the alleged rank of the late captain of the Jeune-Louise, we think Lieutenant Popham must have been imposed upon by some of the prisoners; for we can find no such name as Galien Lafont, among the capitaines de vaisseau of the French navy: there was in 1810 a Mathias Lafond, "an officer of the legion of honour," but he was alive in 1812.

Some allusion has already been made to the immense works going on in the port of Cherbourg, by the orders of the French emperor. The principal improvement consisted of a basin capable of holding from 30 to 40 sail of the line with sufficient water at its entrance to float the largest ship when ready for sea. About 20 line-of-battle ships could also anchor in the roadstead, sheltered from every wind, as soon as the dike, then constructing at a vast expense, should be finished. From attacks of another sort the ships were also well defended, the three strong fortifications of Pelée, Fort Napoléon, and Querqueville completely commanding the road. No port belonging to France was so well calculated as Cherbourg, for carrying on offensive operations in the channel; not only from its centrical and projecting situation, but from the facility with which, with any wind in moderate weather, ships can sail in and out of it. Strong gales from north to north-west would, however, occasion a difficulty in getting out, on account of the heavy swell that such winds usually raise in the principal passage. But it is scarcely possible for one or two ships cruising outside to prevent vessels sailing in the night from Cherbourg, as strong tides, deep water, and a rocky bottom prevent the ships from anchoring; and they cannot, at all times, keep close enough in to see a vessel under the land. This accounts for the escape of so many French frigates from Cherbourg, until, on the arrival there in the summer of 1809 of the two French line-of-battle ships Courageux and Polonais,[1] the port became regularly blockaded.

In the autumn of the present year, the British force cruising off the port of Cherbourg consisted of the 74-gun ships Donegal, Captain Pulteney Malcolm, and Revenge, Captain the Honourable Charles Paget; with occasionally a frigate and a brig-sloop, to be ready to meet the new French 40-gun frigate Iphigénie, launched on the 10th of the preceding May, and a 16-gun brig-corvette, which now lay in company with the two line-of-battle ships, watching an opportunity to sail out. In the middle of October the Alcmène, a second 40-gun frigate from off the stocks in the arsenal, joined the Iphigénie, and was soon in equal readiness for a cruise. In the neighbouring port of

[1] See p. 22.

Havre, lay also two new 40-gun frigates, the Amazone, Captain Bernard-Louis Rousseau, and the Eliza, Captain Louis-Henri Freycinet-Saulce; hoping to elude the vigilance of the two British 38-gun frigates, Diana, Captain Charles Grant, and Niobe, Captain John Wentworth Loring, and, at all events, to get to Cherbourg, as the preferable port, although watched by a British force, for an escape to sea.

On the 12th of November, at 10 P.M., favoured by a strong north-east wind, the Amazone and Eliza sailed from Havre, and steered to the north-west. At half an hour after midnight, by which time the wind had shifted to north by east, the two French frigates and the Diana and Niobe gained a sight of each other, the two latter to-leeward and in-shore of the former. Captain Rousseau, doubtful probably of the force of the two ships in chase of him, continued his course, but could not, on account of the change in the wind, weather Cape Barfleur, nor, without some difficulty, the isles of St Marcouf. At 4 A.M. on the 13th the two French frigates tacked off shore. The Diana who lay on the starboard bow of the Amazone, the leading frigate, tacked also; while the Niobe, as she came up ahead of the Diana on the starboard tack, passed to-windward of the two frigates, and pushed on to endeavour to cut them off, particularly the Eliza, from the narrow passage at the west end of Marcouf. In the mean time the Diana had also tacked to the westward, and, passing close to-windward of the two French frigates, exchanged with them two ineffectual broadsides. The latter then bore up, and, being better acquainted with the navigation of the spot, succeeded in entering the passage of Marcouf; under the batteries of which island they anchored. At 11 A.M. the Amazone and Eliza weighed, and kept under sail between Marcouf and the main until 3 P.M.; when, observing that the Diana and Niobe had been drifted by the ebb-tide to the northward of Cape Barfleur, they steered for the road of Lahougue. Here the two French frigates anchored, under the protection of a strong battery.

On the 14th, in the morning, Captain Grant despatched the Niobe to Captain Malcolm of the Donegal, cruising off Cherbourg, with intelligence of the situation of the enemy's ships, and then made all sail to the anchorage of Lahougue. In the mean time, owing to a strong gale from the southward in the night, the Eliza had dragged her anchors, and had been obliged to strike her topmasts, and throw overboard a part of her stores and provisions, to save herself from being lost on the rocks. At

1 P.M. the Diana came to an anchor, and on the morning of the 15th, at the first of the flood, weighed and stood in to attack the Amazone; who, in her present position, appeared more assailable than her consort. But the Amazone quickly got under way, and proceeded close to the shoals of St. Vaast; where she again anchored between the batteries of Lahougue and Tatillon. Captain Grant, being resolved nevertheless to make the attack, stood in twice close alongside of the Amazone; but, having to sustain, not only the frigate's fire, but the fire of two powerful batteries, the Diana was compelled to abandon the attempt. Shortly afterwards the Donegal, Revenge, and Niobe arrived, and renewed the attack; the four ships successively opening their broadsides while going about. In this way they stood in three times, bringing their guns to bear only when head to wind. At 1 P.M., the British ships, having been drifted to leeward by the ebb-tide, desisted from the attack, and anchored out of gunshot. All four ships suffered more or less in masts, sails, rigging, and hull: the Diana had one man wounded, the Donegal three, and the Revenge seven, two of them mortally. On board the Amazone, the French acknowledged only one man killed and none wounded.

Having on board the Donegal some of Colonel Congreve's rockets, Captain Malcolm, the same evening, sent the boats, under the orders of Lieutenant Joseph Needham Tayler, to try their effect upon the two French frigates. Although, at daylight on the 16th, the latter was observed to be aground, and one, the Eliza, to heel considerably, neither frigate, according to the French accounts, sustained any injury from the rockets. Both frigates afterwards got afloat; and on the night of the 27th, just as Captains Malcolm and Grant were meditating to send in a fire-ship, the Amazone gave them the slip, and, before the dawn of day on the 28th, was safe at anchor in the port of Havre. The Eliza was watched with increased attention, and on the 6th of December was attacked by a bomb-vessel. This compelled the frigate to move further in; and she eventually got aground. Here the Eliza lay a wreck until the night of the 23rd, when the Diana sent her boats, under the command of Lieutenant Thomas Rowe, and effectually destroyed her.

On the 15th of November, at a little before midnight, the British 14-gun brig-sloop Phipps, Captain Christopher Bell, standing across from the Downs to the coast of France, fell in with and chased a French lugger-privateer; who led the Phipps close under Calais, and so near in-shore, that the brig was obliged, although firing grape-shot into the lugger, to discontinue the chase. Observing, while in chase of this lugger, two others lying to windward, Captain Bell considered that, by beating up in-shore of them, the Phipps might escape their notice until far enough to fetch them. This the Phipps did, and at 5 A.M, on the 16th, closed and commenced an action with one of the luggers. For a quarter of an hour the lugger maintained an incessant fire of musketry, and appeared determined to run on shore. As the only means of frustrating this design, especially as the brig was already in three and a half fathoms water, the Phipps ran alongside of her antagonist and poured in her broadside; under the smoke of which, Lieutenant Robert Tryon, assisted by master's mate Patrick Wright, and Mr. Peter Geddes the boatswain, at the head of a party of seamen, boarded, and in a few minutes carried, the lugger; which proved to be the Barbier-de-Séville, a perfectly new vessel, two days from Boulogne, mounting 16 guns, with 60 men, commanded by François Brunet.

The loss sustained by the Phipps amounted to one seaman killed, and Lieutenant Tryon, the gallant leader of the boarding party, dangerously wounded. But the loss on the part of the privateer was much more severe, she having had six men killed and 11 wounded, including among the latter every one of her officers except the second captain. The effect of the well-directed fire of the Phipps upon the hull of the Barbier-de-Séville was such, that the latter, soon after her capture, filled and sank, carrying down with her one of the seamen belonging to the British brig.

On the 10th of December, in the evening, the British 10-gun brig-sloop Rosario (same force as Briseis), Captain Booty Harvey, cruising off Dungeness, with the wind blowing hard from the westward, fell in with two large French lugger-privateers, whose intention was evidently to board her. Knowing their superiority of sailing, Captain Harvey, with the utmost gallantry and promptitude, ran the nearest lugger alongside: whereupon Lieutenant Thomas Daws, with a party of men, sprang on board, and in a few minutes succeeded in carrying her. The Rosario at the same time was engaged on the starboard side with the other lugger; but who, on seeing the fate of her companion, sheered off and effected her escape, owing principally to the loss of the Rosario's jib-boom in boarding the captured lugger, and her consequent inability to make sail to windward. The prize was the Mamelouck, of Boulogne, Captain Norbez Laurence, carrying 16 guns and 45 men; of whom seven were wounded. The loss on board the Rosario amounted to five men wounded, two of them severely.

On the 12th of December, at 8 A.M., the British cutter Entreprenante, mounting eight 4-pounders, with 33 men and boys, Lieutenant Peter Williams, while lying becalmed off the coast of Spain, about midway between Malaga and Almeria bay, observed four vessels at anchor under the castle of Faro. At 9 A.M., these vessels, which were French latteen-rigged privateers, one of six guns, including two long 18-pounders, and 75 men, another of five guns and 45 men, and the remaining two of two guns and 25 men each, weighed and swept out towards the cutter. At 10 h. 30 m. A.M. the privateers hoisted their colours, and opened their fire. At 11 A.M., which was as early as her lighter guns would reach, the Entreprenante commenced firing at the privateers; one of the two largest of which lay on her starboard bow, the other on her starboard quarter, and the two smaller ones right astern. The action was now maintained with spirit on both sides, at a pistol-shot distance, each party firing with round and grape shot, and the cutter with musketry also. At noon the Entreprenante had her topmast, peek-halljards and blocks, fore jeers, fore halliards, and jib-tie shot away; also two of her starboard guns disabled, by the stock of one and the carriage of the other being broken.

Seeing the cutter in this disabled state, the nearest of the two large privateers attempted to board; but her men were driven back by the British crew, who, with the two foremost guns and musketry, kept up an incessant fire. A second attempt was made to board, and a second time it was defeated, but with a loss to the cutter of one man killed and four wounded. The Entreprenante now manned her starboard sweeps, and, getting round, brought her larboard guns to bear. With two broadsides from these, she compelled three of her antagonists to sheer off. All the cutter's canister-shot and musket-balls were now expended; but at this moment two well-directed broadsides, doubled-shotted, carried away the foremast and bowsprit of the most formidable of the privateers. Grown desperate by a resistance so unexpected, the Frenchmen made a third attempt to board the British vessel, but met with no better success than before; although in their effort to repulse them, the Entreprenante had two of her larboard guns dismounted, and experienced some additional loss. The fire of the privateers now beginning to slacken, the cutter's people gave three cheers, and, with two guns double-shotted, poured a destructive raking fire into the vessel that was dismasted. This decided the business; and, at 2 h. 30 m. P.M., the two greatest sufferers by the contest were towed to the shore by boats. The Entreprenante continued sending her shot after her flying foes until 3 P.M., when they got beyond her reach. The castle of Faro at this time fired a few ineffectual shots at the British cutter.

Notwithstanding the length and severity of this action, and the more than double force opposed to the Entreprenante, the latter escaped with no greater loss than one man killed and 10 wounded. The loss on the part of her opponents could only be gathered from rumour, and that made it as many as 81 in killed and wounded; not an improbable amount, considering how numerously the privateers were manned, and how well the cutter plied her cannon and musketry. On his return to Gibraltar, Lieutenant Williams, and the officers and crew of the Entreprenante, received the public acknowledgment of the commanding officer on the station, Commodore Charles Vinicombe Penrose. Some other marks of favour were conferred upon the lieutenant; but the reward the most coveted, and, considering that a particle less of energy and perseverance might have lost the king's cutter, no one can say, a reward not fully merited, promotion, appears to have been withheld. We judge so, because, according to the admiralty navy-list, Lieutenant Williams was not made a commander until the 27th of August, 1814.

On the 7th of December, after dark, the British 10-gun brig-sloop Rinaldo (eight 18-pounder carronades and two sixes), Captain James Anderson, while cruising off Dover with the wind from the westward, discovered to windward, and immediately chased, two large armed luggers standing towards the English coast. The two French privateers, as they proved to be, the moment they saw the Rinaldo outside of them, endeavoured to pass her and effect their escape over to their own coast. One of them, the Maraudeur, of 14 guns and 85 men, after sustaining a running fight of several minutes' duration, attempted to cross the brig's bows; but the Rinaldo frustrated the manœuvre, by putting her helm hard a-port and running her jib-boom between the privateer's jib-stay and foremast.

By this evolution the two vessels were brought close alongside. The Frenchmen, being all upon deck, now attempted to board, but were repulsed by the Rinaldo's crew; who, in their turn, although only 65 in number, including several boys, boarded from the fore-chains, in the most gallant style, led by Lieutenant Edward Gascoigne Palmer, and soon cleared the privateer's decks and compelled her crew to call for quarter. This promptly decided and very spirited affair cost the Maraudeur her captain and four men wounded, two of them very severely; but no one was hurt belonging to the Rinaldo. While the latter was occupied in exchanging prisoners, the other lugger effected her escape into Calais. The prize was a fine fast-sailing vessel belonging to Boulogne, only 13 days off the stocks, pierced for 18 guns, and, as a lugger, of very large dimensions.

On the 17th of December, at 3 h. 30 m. P.M., while stretching out from St. Helens, on her way from Spithead to her station of Dover, the Rinaldo discovered four lugger-privateers in the offing, lying to, with all their sails lowered down. Knowing it would be useless to chase them, Captain Anderson altered his course and steered in-shore to the northward, with the view of decoying the privateers within the reach of his brig. To enable them to overtake her about dark, the Rinaldo trimmed her sails by, and kept in such a position as to prevent their making her out to be armed. The manœuvre succeeded, and the four luggers made all sail in chase of the British brig.

At 5 P.M., the Owers light bearing west-north-west distant half a mile, the two largest luggers came up under the Rinaldo's stern, and, hailing her in a very abusive manner to strike, poured in several volleys of small arms. The Rinaldo, being all prepared, allowed the privateers to come close upon her quarters, and then tacked, thus bringing a broadside to bear upon each of them: she then wore round on her heel, and poured a second broadside, within pistol-shot, into the larger of the two; who, having discovered her mistake, was endeavouring to escape by bearing up. This well-directed fire brought down the large lugger's masts and sails; and immediately the latter called for quarter, and requested boats to be sent, as she was sinking.

Just at this moment the second lugger, who had hauled her wind on receiving the first broadside, ran down upon the bow of the Rinaldo, apparently with the intention to board, keeping up, as she advanced, a constant fire of musketry. The brig immediately hauled off from the disabled privateer, and attacked the other, who, running within the light, lowered down her sails and called also for quarter. In wearing round and manning her boats, to assist the one, and take possession of the other lugger, the Rinaldo was carried by the calm and strong ebb-tide on board the Owers light-vessel, and became so entangled with the latter, that it was not deemed prudent to send away her boats; especially as, by this time, the two other luggers had come up and were beginning to fire into the brig.

While the Rinaldo was using every exertion to get clear, the second lugger that had struck ran up to the first one; and in a minute or two afterwards, finding that her consort was in the act of sinking, she made all sail to the French coast. The two remaining luggers made off about the same time, having received several shot from the Rinaldo as she lay alongside the light-vessel. It was afterwards ascertained that these four privateers, three of which mounted 14 guns, with 70 men each, belonged to Dieppe; and, from the Vieille-Josephine, of 16 guns, the one which sank, the captain and two men were all that were saved out of a crew of 80. The boom-mainsail and two topsails of the Rinaldo were completely riddled, and a number of musket-shot were found among the hammocks, but fortunately no one on board was hurt. In this little affair both seamanship and gallantry shone conspicuously; and Captain Anderson, and the officers and crew of the Rinaldo, were entitled to great credit for their performance.

On the 4th of April, at 1 P.M., the British 12-pounder 32-gun frigate Success, Captain John Ayscough, and 18-gun brig-sloop Espoir, Captain Robert Mitford, while running along the coast of Calabria, abreast of Castiglione, discovered three vessels on the beach and men loading them. Considering the destruction of these vessels an object worth attempting, Captain Ayscough despatched on that service the boats of the Success and Espoir, under the orders of Lieutenant George Rose Sartorius, third of the frigate, assisted by Lieutenant Robert Oliver, of the Espoir and master's mates George Lewis Coates and Richard Peace.

Just as the British had arrived within musket-shot of the shore, three of the boats struck on a sunken reef and swamped; whereby two of the Espoir's seamen were drowned, and the ammunition of all in the three boats was wetted and spoiled. The officers and men swam to the beach with their cutlasses in their mouths. At this moment a fire was opened upon them from two long 6-pounders and four wall-pieces; which, having been secreted behind the rocks, were not perceived till the boats grounded. Regardless of this, Lieutenant Sartorius and his party rushed on, and obliged the enemy to desert the guns and retreat to some adjacent houses; from the windows of which, until dislodged and driven to the mountains, the enemy maintained a fire of musketry. The British then spiked the two

6-pounders, and destroyed their carriages; and, having set fire to two laden vessels, already stove, and recovered their three swamped boats, the party returned on board with no greater additional loss than two marines wounded.

On the 25th of April, at 10 A.M., the British 38-gun frigate Spartan, Captain Jahleel Brenton, accompanied by the frigate Success, and brig-sloop Espoir, being off Monte Circello, discovered one ship, three barks, and several feluccas, at anchor under the castle of Terrecino. The two frigates and brig immediately made all sail; and on arriving off the town, Captain Brenton detached the boats of the squadron, under the orders of Lieutenant William Augustus Baumgardt of the Spartan, assisted by Lieutenant George Rose Sartorius of the Success, to endeavour to bring the vessels out.

At about 30 minutes past noon the boats pulled for the shore, covered by the ships; and Captain Mitford, with great energy and judgment, ran in with the Espoir and sounded under the batteries. Shortly afterwards the two British frigates and brig came to an anchor, and began cannonading the shore and the batteries. In the mean time Lieutenant Baumgardt, with the boats, pulled into the road, and, in the face of a heavy fire, gallantly boarded the ship; which mounted six guns, and was defended for some time by her crew. At length the latter abandoned her to the British; who also took possession of the three barks, and brought off their four prizes with no greater loss than one seaman killed and two wounded.

On the 1st of May, having detached the Espoir, Captain Brenton was cruising with the Spartan and Success; when, at 5 h. 40 m. P.M., the south-west point of the island of Ischia bearing south-east distant three miles, two ships, a brig, and a cutter were discovered in the bay of Naples. These were the French frigate Cérès and corvette Fama, the Cyane's old opponents,[1] with the armed brig Sparvière and cutter Achille. The two British frigates immediately bore up and crowded sail in pursuit, with the wind from the south-west; and at 7 P.M. the French squadron put about and made all sail for Naples, chased nearly into the mole by the Spartan and Success.

On the 2nd, at daylight, the Cérès and her consorts were seen at anchor. The two British frigates then stood out towards the entrance of the bay; and Captain Brenton, feeling satisfied that the French commodore would not put to sea while two British frigates were cruising off the port, detached the Suc-

[1] See p. 32.

cess that evening to the Spartan's rendezvous, from five to ten leagues south-west of the island of Capri. The Spartan then stood back into the bay with the intention, by daylight the next morning, of showing herself off the mole of Naples, in the hope to induce the French squadron to sail out and attack her. But Prince Murat had formed a bolder design than Captain Brenton gave him credit for. Having caused to be embarked in the frigate and corvette, 400 Swiss troops, and directed seven large gun-boats, with one long French 18-pounder each, to accompany the squadron, the prince ordered the commodore to get under way at daylight, and attack, and endeavour to board, the two British frigates, thus hovering about the bay and cutting off all commerce with the capital.

On the 3rd, at 4 h. 30 m. A.M., profiting by a light air which had just sprung up from the south-east, the Spartan stood into the bay of Naples on the starboard tack, under plain sails and rather off the wind. At 5 A.M., when about midway between Cape Misano and the island of Capri, the Spartan discovered the French squadron, distant six miles right ahead, standing out from the mole of Naples on the larboard tack. The force, thus advancing to attack a single British frigate, consisted of the Cérès, an 18-pounder frigate mounting 42 or 44 guns, with a crew of from 320 to 350 men, a large corvette, the Fama, mounting 28 guns, either 8 or 12 pounders, with a crew of more than 220 men, a brig, the Sparvière, mounting eight guns with 98 men, a cutter, the Achille, mounting ten guns with 80 men, and at least seven[1] gun-boats, of one long French 18-pounder and 40 men each. The Swiss troops, it appears, were in addition to the complements of the vessels: consequently, there were 95 guns, and about 1400 men, opposed to 46 guns and 258 men.

At 7 A.M. the Cérès, followed in line of battle by the Fama and Sparvière, hauled up, as if desirous to get to windward of the British frigate; but the Spartan frustrated that intention, by setting her courses and hauling up too. In a few minutes, finding his object defeated, the French commodore again steered with the wind a-beam: and at 7 h. 45 m. clewed up her courses; the Spartan immediately did the same. In this way the two parties were mutually approximating from opposite points of the compass.

At 7 h. 58 m. A.M., being within pistol-shot on the larboard or lee bow of the British frigate, the Cérès opened a fire from

---

[1] British official account says "eight;" French account, "six;" and Spartan's log "seven."

her larboard guns in quick succession. The Spartan "reserved her fire until every gun was covered by her opponent, and then returned a most destructive broadside, treble-shotted on the main deck. The carnage on board the Cérès was very great, particularly amongst the Swiss troops, which were drawn up in ranks, and extended from the cat-head to the taffrail, in readiness for boarding."[1] The Spartan then engaged in succession the Fama and Sparvière; and, as neither party was going at a faster rate through the water than from two to three knots an hour, the British frigate was enabled to discharge a broadside at each.

Since the commencement of the firing, the cutter and gunboats had hauled to the south-east. In order to cut off these from their consorts, the Spartan now kept her luff; and at 8 h. 13 m. A.M., having fired at the small-craft with her foremost starboard guns, the frigate hove in stays, and, as she came round, gave them the whole of her larboard guns: the starboard broadside having been recharged, was then fired at the Sparvièro and the two ships ahead of her. Now was the time for the Cérès to have supported the gun-boats, but the French commodore appears to have forgotten them altogether; for, instead of tacking to meet the Spartan, the Cérès wore and stood towards the batteries of Baia. This stage of the action will perhaps be better understood by a reference to the following diagram:—

As soon as she had come round on the larboard tack, the

[1] Brenton, vol. iv., p. 434.

Spartan kept her helm up, and wore in pursuit of the French frigate. But in a few minutes before 9 A.M. the breeze suddenly died away, and left the Spartan with her head exposed to the starboard broadside of the Cérès; having, also, on her larboard bow the corvette and brig, and sweeping up astern of her, the cutter and gun-boats. A heavy fire was now opened on the Spartan from every side, particularly on the stern and quarter from the long 18-pounders of the gun-boats. In a few minutes Captain Brenton, while standing on the capstan, the better to view his various opponents, received a grape-shot in the hip, and was obliged to be carried below. The command then devolved upon Lieutenant George Wickens Willes.

Scarcely had Captain Brenton been removed from the deck, ere a light breeze from the same quarter as before enabled the Spartan to take up a position on the starboard quarter of the French frigate and starboard bow of the corvette. The brig was at this time on the Spartan's larboard quarter or nearly astern, and the cutter and gun-boats on the frigate's stern and starboard quarter, making the best possible use of their advantage. The same breeze, that had enabled the Spartan to get into action was made use of by her two principal opponents to carry them out of it; and, owing to the disabled state of the Spartan's rigging, the Cérès and Fama, the latter hauling up to windward of her consort, succeeded in gaining the protection of the batteries of Baia. The Spartan then wore: and while with her starboard guns she severely raked the frigate and corvette, and cut away the latter's foretopmast, a single broadside from her larboard guns compelled the brig, with the loss of her maintopmast, to haul down her colours. This was at 10 A.M.; and the gun-boats presently afterwards came down, in a very gallant manner, and, by towing her away, rescued the crippled Fama from the fate of the Sparvière. The following diagram is meant to represent this, the termination of the contest:—

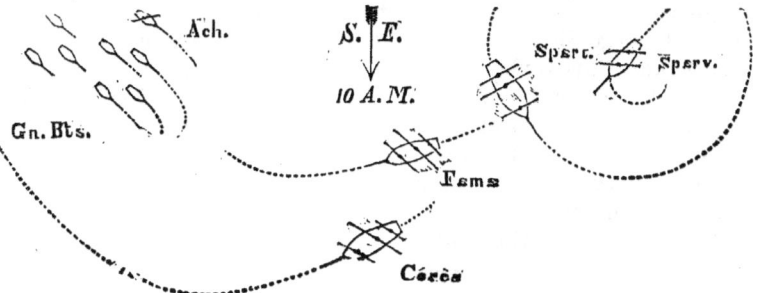

Although the proper complement of the Spartan was 281, having an officer and 18 men absent in a prize, and being four men short, the frigate commenced action with only 258 men and boys; exclusively of Captain George Hoste of the royal engineers, who was a passenger on board, and, during the attention of Captain Brenton and his first-lieutenant in manœuvring the ship, took charge of the quarter-deck guns. The loss on board the Spartan was tolerably severe, amounting to one master's mate (William Robson), six seamen, and three marines killed, her captain (severely), first-lieutenant (already named), 15 seamen and five marines wounded; total 10 killed and 22 wounded. This heavy loss was chiefly occasioned by the long 18-pounders of the gun-boats, while they lay upon the frigate's stern and quarter. The hull of the Spartan had, in consequence, been severely struck; and, although none of her masts were shot away, they were most of them wounded, and her rigging and sails cut to pieces.

The French acknowledged a loss of 30 officers and men killed and 90 wounded, exclusively of the loss on board the Sparvière; which, in killed, as 87 prisoners were all that were taken out of her, probably amounted to 11. Among the killed on board the Cérès, was the second captain; and the first captain is stated to have lost his arm. Some of the English accounts represented the loss on board the French squadron at 150 killed and 300 wounded. These round numbers, as our contemporary is also of opinion, are probably incorrect and exaggerated; "but," Captain Edward Brenton adds, "the slaughter, particularly on board the frigate, from her crowded decks, the close position, and the smoothness of the water, must have been very severe."[1]

In addition to the encomiums which he passes upon his first-lieutenant, and upon Captain Hoste of the engineers (brother to the captain of the Amphion), Captain Jahleel Brenton strongly recommends his two remaining lieutenants, William Augustus Baumgardt and Henry Bourne; also his master, Henry George Slenner, his two lieutenants of marines, Charles Fegan and Christopher Fottrell, and his purser, James Dunn, who took charge of a division of guns on the main deck, in the place of the officer already mentioned as absent in a prize. For the distinguished part which he took in the action, Lieutenant Willes, on the 2nd of June, was deservedly promoted to the rank of commander.

Soon after the action had ended in the manner we have stated,

[1] Brenton, vol. iv., p. 436.

the sea-breeze or south-west wind set in. The Spartan then, having repaired her principal damages, took her prize in tow, and stood in triumph directly across, and within about four miles of, the mole of Naples, to the great chagrin and mortification, as was afterwards understood, of Prince Murat; who had been the whole morning anxiously watching on the mole, to see his squadron tow in the British frigate. At this time the beaten French frigate and corvette had just dropped their anchors before the town. It would not do for the world, particularly for France, to know how the matter really stood. Hence the Moniteur is commanded to say: "Il est impossible de se battre avec plus de bravoure que ne l'a fait la flotille dans cette brillante affaire, &c." And then the Spartan herself is declared to have been " un vaisseau rasé, portant 50 bouches à feu, donc 30 canons de 24 et 20 caronades de 32."

On the 22nd of May the British 38-gun frigate Alceste, Captain Murray Maxwell, chased several French vessels into the bay of Agaye, or Agay, near the gulf of Fréjus. Finding that the two batteries, one on each side of the entrance, which protected the vessels, possessed by their height a great advantage over the ship, Captain Maxwell, in the evening, detached two strong parties to endeavour to carry them by storm. The party, under Lieutenant Andrew Wilson, first of the Alceste, that landed on the right of the bay, having to march through a very thick wood to get in the rear of the fort, was attacked in the midst of it by one of the enemy's pickets, whom the marines, under the command of Lieutenants Walter Griffith Lloyd and Richard Hawkey of that corps, without sustaining any loss, very soon dislodged: but the guide, taking advantage of the firing, made his escape, and Lieutenant Wilson was obliged to relinquish the enterprise and return on board. Meanwhile the other party, under Mr. Henry Bell, the master, reached undiscovered the rear of his fort, and attacked and carried it in the most spirited manner. As, however, the opposite battery had not been reduced, Mr. Bell was obliged to retire; but he did not do so until he had spiked the guns, two long 24-pounders, broken their carriages, destroyed the magazine, and thrown the shot into the sea. Having accomplished this, he and his men returned to their ship without a casualty.

Finding that the vessels would not quit their anchorage while the frigate lay off, Captain Maxwell, on the night of the 25th, sent the barge and yawl, one armed with a 12-pounder carronade, the other with a 4-pounder field-piece, under the command of Mr. Bell, accompanied by master's mate Thomas Day, and midshipman James Adair, with orders to lie in a little cove near the harbour's mouth, while the Alceste stood to some distance in the offing. The bait took; and on the morning of the 26th the French vessels sailed out quite boldly. To their astonishment, the two armed boats pulled in amongst them, and presently captured four feluccas, three of which were armed (one with six guns, and the two others with four each), drove two upon the rocks, and the rest back into the harbour. This the British effected, although exposed to a fire from the batteries, from some soldiers on the beach, and from two armed feluccas among the vessels that escaped. Mr. Adair, who, with two or three men, had been left in charge of the barge while Mr. Bell and Mr. Day were boarding the feluccas, made so good a use of the 12-pounder carronade, that the four prizes were brought off without the slightest hurt to a man of the party.

In the month of June, Captain William Hoste, of the 18-pounder 32-gun frigate Amphion, having under his orders the 38-gun frigate Active, Captain James Alexander Gordon, and 18-pounder 32-gun frigate Cerberus, Captain Henry Whitby, cruised in the gulf of Triest. On the 28th, in the morning, the boats of the Amphion chased a convoy of several vessels, reported to be laden with naval stores for the arsenal at Venice, into the harbour of Groa. The capture of the convoy, although, on account of the shoals, to be effected only by boats, being an object of considerable importance, Captain Hoste resolved to make the attempt without delay. In the evening the Amphion telegraphed the Active and Cerberus, to send their boats to her by 12 at night; but owing to her distance in the offing, the Active was not able to comply with the signal in time. Accordingly the boats of the Amphion and Cerberus, commanded by Lieutenant William Slaughter, second (first absent) of the Amphion, and assisted by Lieutenants Donat Henchy O'Brien of the same frigate, and James Dickinson of the Cerberus, Lieutenants of marines Thomas Moore of the Amphion, and Jeremiah Brattle of the Cerberus; also by master's mate Charles H. Ross, and midshipmen Joseph Gape, Thomas Edward Hoste, Charles Bruce, and Cornwallis Paley, schoolmaster James Leonard Few, and volunteer Samuel Jeffery, of the Amphion; and, belonging to the Cerberus, the gunner, John Johnson, and midshipmen John Miller, George Farrenden, Joseph Stoney, George Fowler, William Sherwood, Charles Mackey, and Lewis Rollier, pushed off, and before daylight on the morning of the 29th landed, without the firing of a musket, a little to the right of the town.

Advancing immediately to the attack of the town, above which the vessels lay moored, the British were met, about the dawn of day, by a body of troops and peasantry; who opened a very destructive fire, and obliged the former to retire to the shelter of some hillocks. Conceiving that their opponents were retreating to their boats, the French quitted their advantageous position, and charged with the bayonet. They were received with the bravery and steadiness so characteristic of British seamen and marines, and a lieutenant, a sergeant, and 38 privates of the 81st regiment of French infantry were made prisoners. Lieutenant Slaughter and his party now entered the town, and took possession of the vessels, 25 in number. At about 11 A.M. a detachment of the 5th regiment of French infantry, consisting of a lieutenant and 22 men, entered Groa from Maran, a village in the interior.

They were instantly attacked by the force that was nearest to them, consisting of a division of seamen and marines under Lieutenants Slaughter, Moore, and James Mears of the Active, whose boats had landed just as the men of the Amphion and Cerberus had achieved their exploit. The same intrepidity, which had insured success on that occasion, produced it on this; and the 22 French troops, with their officer, laid down their arms and surrendered. Every exertion was now made to get the convoy out of the river; but, it being almost low water, that object could not be effected before 7 P.M.; and then not without great labour and fatigue, the men having to shift the cargoes of the large vessels into smaller ones, in order to float the former over the bar. By 8 P.M., however, the whole detachment and the prizes reached the squadron, which had anchored about four miles from the town.

The loss on the part of the British, in performing this very gallant service, amounted to four marines killed, one lieutenant of marines (Brattle), three seamen, and four marines wounded; and the loss sustained by the French amounted to 10 killed, eight by bayonet wounds, a proof of the nature of the conflict, and eight wounded. Of the captured vessels, 11 were burnt in the river, because too large to pass the bar in the state of the tide, five were brought out and sent to Lissa with cargoes; as were also 14 or 15 small trading craft, laden with the cargoes of the burnt vessels.

The British official account is, as it ever ought to be where practicable, very precise in enumerating the force of the opposite party: we wish it had been equally so in stating the numerical amount of the attacking force. There is one part of Captain Hoste's letter which we should like to see oftener imitated. "No credit," he says, "can attach itself to me, sir, for the success of this enterprise; but I hope I may be allowed to point out those to whose gallant exertions it is owing." Captain Hoste then gives the christian as well as surnames of all the officers engaged; a plan that has enabled us, without that difficulty which we almost on every other occasion experience, to do the same.

In the autumn of the present year the French force cruising in the Adriatic was under the orders of Commodore Bernard Dubourdieu, and consisted of the two French 40-gun frigates Favorite (the commodore's ship, Captain Antoine-François-Zavier La Marre-la-Meillerie, and Uranie, Captain Pierre-Jean-Baptiste Margollé-Lanier, the Venetian 40-gun frigate Corona, Captain Paschaligo, and 32-gun frigates Bellona and Carolina, Captains Baralovich and Palicuccia, along with the brig-corvettes Jéna and Mercure. The duty of watching this squadron was intrusted to Captain Hoste, with his three frigates already named.

On the 29th of September the Franco-Venetian squadron sailed from Chiozzo, and arrived in a few days afterwards at Ancona; where, accompanied by a schooner and a gun-vessel, the squadron was descried, on the morning of the 6th of October, part under sail and part in the act of weighing, by Captain Hoste, who, having detached the Cerberus to Malta, had then with him only the Amphion and the Active. The wind was blowing a fine breeze from the south-east, and Ancona bore from the two British frigates south-south-west distant four leagues. At noon, having collected all his ships, Commodore Dubourdieu made sail in chase of the Amphion and Active; one division of three ships stretching out on the starboard tack, and the remainder of the squadron standing close hauled on the larboard tack, ready to take advantage of any change of wind. Captain Hoste stood towards the Franco-Venetian squadron, until he had distinctly made out its force. Finding the enemy's superiority to be such as it would be impossible to overcome, he then, at 1 P.M., tacked and stood to the north-east. Fearful either of an increasing gale, or of being drawn off the land, Commodore Dubourdieu, at 2 P.M., tacked and stood in towards the harbour of Ancona. Having seen this squadron of bold cruisers safe at anchor in their port, Captain Hoste steered for the island of Lissa ; and, arriving on the 9th, was so fortunate as to find the Cerberus, who had called there on her way to Malta.

On the 12th, having been joined by the 18-gun ship-sloop Acorn, Captain Robert Clephane, Captain Hoste put to sea, with his little squadron of three frigates and one sloop, and steered straight for Ancona, in quest of Commodore Dubourdieu, with his five frigates and two 16-gun brigs. A strong northerly wind, and then a calm of three days' continuance, made it the 20th before the Amphion and her consorts obtained a view of Ancona. M. Dubourdieu was not there. Concluding that he had gone to Corfu, Captain Hoste instantly put about, and crowded sail in that direction, intending to call off Lissa by the way. On the 21st, in the evening, when in sight of that island, the Active, looking out in the south-east, boarded a Sicilian privateer, that had been chased by the enemy, and had lost sight of him only six hours before off Vasto, steering under a press of sail to the south-south-east.

There was now just time before dark to recall the Cerberus, who had been despatched to Lissa for intelligence. The privateer's information confirming Captain Hoste in the opinion that M. Dubourdieu had gone to Corfu, particularly as the wind at this time was from the westward, the British squadron steered south by east all night, with almost a certainty of discovering the Franco-Venetian squadron at daylight between Pelagosi and St. Angelo. Daylight on the 22nd came, but no sail was in sight, except three fishermen off Pelagosi ; who, on being spoken, said they had left Lissa on the preceding day, but had seen nothing of the enemy. Little doubt now remained, that the enemy was still ahead of the British ; who, consequently, continued working to the south-east all that day and all the 23rd. On the 24th the squadron came in sight of Brindisi; and, as the wind was then blowing fresh from the south-east, the commodore thought it likely that M. Dubourdieu, finding the wind foul for Corfu, would stretch over to the Albanian coast, and perhaps rendezvous at Bocca de Cattaro ; where it was known that a convoy for Corfu were to assemble from Spalatro. Hearing no tidings of the enemy at Cattaro, and judging from the increased force of the south-east wind, that the French commodore was still to leeward, Captain Hoste retraced his steps to the northward. While this zealous and able officer is hastening towards Lissa, we will endeavour to trace the movements of the object of his anxiety

It was on the 18th of October that M. Dubourdieu, having on

board a battalion of the 3rd regiment of the line, sailed from Ancona. He then steered alongshore to the southward; and on the 21st, in the night, was informed by a fisherman, that the English squadron had gone to the southward upon a cruise. Having now little to fear, Commodore Dubourdieu crossed over from the coast of Apulia, and in the forenoon of the 22nd arrived off Port St. George, island of Lissa. Hoisting English colours, he entered the harbour with the Favourite, Bellona, and Corona; leaving the Uranie and the three remaining vessels to cruise in the offing, and give notice of the approach of any strangers. At 15 minutes past noon the three frigates anchored and debarked the troops. The commodore then, as he represents, took possession of 30 vessels, of which 10 were "superb" privateers, mounting altogether 100 guns, burnt 64, of which 43 were laden, and restored several other vessels to French, Illyrian, Italian, and Neapolitan subjects. The troops are stated to have taken the island without resistance, and to have made prisoners of the English "garrison," numbering 100. All this appears to have been the work of only six or seven hours; for the Franco-Venetian squadron, by dark the same evening, had re-embarked the troops and made sail out of the harbour: a sudden step for which we may presently be able to account.

The French commodore concludes his letter to Prince Murat by stating that the English squadron, composed of three frigates, one corvette, and "two brigs," avoided measuring strength with him, although his officers and crews were all extremely eager for the combat. "La division anglaise, composée de trois frégates, une corvette. et deux bricks, a évité de se mesurer avec nous. Je puis assurer à V. A. que les états-majors et équipages étaient dans les meilleures dispositions et fort désireux de se battre." He had previously described his own squadron, as consisting of "trois frégates, deux corvettes, et deux bricks." Thus representing, that the difference of force was only one "corvette;" a name applied, with singular propriety, to ships like the Bellona and Carolina, measuring 700 tons, and mounting 36 guns, including 24 long French 12-pounders on the main deck. The whole of this statement conveys a vile insinuation; and, if the paragraph, as it here stands, really formed part of the original letter, and was not superadded by the Moniteur, it leaves an indelible stain upon the character of M. Dubourdieu. With respect to the strong desire in the French officers and men to have a meeting with the British squadron, we may yet have to show how amply that desire was gratified.

We have given the Moniteur's version of the proceedings of Commodore Dubourdieu's squadron at Lissa: we will now state the circumstances as they really occurred. On the morning of the 26th Captain Hoste arrived off Port St. George; and his disappointment may be conceived on learning what had happened. The French commodore landed from 700 to 800 troops, and took possession of the port. A midshipman of the Amphion, who had been left in charge of some prizes, retired to the mountains with almost all the inhabitants and the crews of the privateers; and, when the enemy's troops disembarked, none but the constituted authorities remained in the town. In the afternoon the three fishermen, spoken by the squadron of Captain Hoste that same morning off Pelagosi, arrived in the harbour. The information they brought, of the British being so near, produced the utmost confusion on board the squadron that was "so desirous to meet them;" and, after destroying two British and three Sicilian privateers, Commodore Dubourdieu got under way, and departed with no other trophies of his exploit, than two detained vessels belonging to the British squadron and a privateer schooner. The precipitate retreat of a force, apparently so formidable, left upon the inhabitants of Lissa so unfavourable an impression of French naval prowess, that they almost all began to take up arms; and had the British squadron made its appearance off the island, the French would have found a resistance where they little expected it.

Without waiting to hear the details of what had taken place, Captain Hoste crowded sail to the north-west. But he was too late; for before the British squadron had even lost sight of the island of Lissa, the Franco-Venetian squadron was entering the harbour of Ancona: a harbour which we doubt if it ever would have entered, had the Active not fallen in with the Sicilian privateer. The arrival in the Adriatic of the 74-gun ship Montagu, Captain Richard Hussey Moubray, to take the command of the British squadron, and be ready for the new 74-gun ship Rivoli, expected soon to put to sea from the port of Venice, left M. Dubourdieu with a real excuse for remaining, during the rest of the year, quiet in Ancona.

On the 25th of July, at daybreak, as the British 12-pounder 32-gun frigate Thames, Captain Granville George Waldegrave, and 18-gun brig-sloop Pilot, Captain John Toup Nicolas, were standing along the coast of Naples, the 18-gun brig-sloop Weazle, Captain Henry Prescott, appeared off Amanthea, with the signal flying for an enemy's convoy, consisting, as afterwards discovered, of 32 transport-vessels from Naples, laden with stores and provisions for Murat's army at Scylla, and escorted by seven gun-boats, mounting one gun each, all long 18-pounders but two, which were brass 36-pounder carronades, four scampavias, or armed vessels, also of one gun each (8, 6, and 4 pounders), and an armed pinnace with swivels. Immediately on perceiving that the British ships were approaching towards them, the transports ran upon the beach under the town of Amanthea, where they were flanked by two batteries; while the gun-boats and other armed vessels, under the command of Capitaine de frégate Caraccioli, drew themselves up in a line for the protection of the former.

The weather being nearly calm, it was 2 P.M. before the frigate and the two brigs were enabled to form in a close line; when running along within grape-shot distance, they presently drove the Neapolitans from the vessels, and then anchored. Captain Prescott now set the example by pushing off with the Weazle's boats, having under him Lieutenant Thomas John James William Davis, Mr. George Cayme the master, and midshipman William Holmes and John Golding. The boats of the Thames, under Lieutenants Edward Collier and Francis Molesworth, midshipmen Matthew Liddon, Christopher Wyvill, John Veal, John Murray, the Honourable Trefusis Cornwall, and William Wilkinson, Mr. William Mullins the boatswain, and Mr. James Beckett the carpenter; and those of the Pilot, under Lieutenants Francis Charles Annesley and George Penruddock, Mr. Thomas Herbert the boatswain, and master's mate Thomas Leigh, promptly followed.

The marines of the Thames, under Lieutenant David M'Adam, were also landed, to cover the seamen while they were launching the vessels; the ships all the time firing on the batteries, and on every spot where musketry was collected to oppose the party on shore. The Neapolitans had not only thrown up an embankment outside the vessels, to prevent the British from getting them off, but also one within them, to afford shelter to the numerous troops collected; who, when driven from their entrenchments, still greatly annoyed the British from the walls of the town. At length every difficulty was surmounted; and by 6 P.M. all the vessels were brought off, except one transport laden with bread, too much shattered by shot to float, and one gun-boat, two armed vessels, and two transports, that could not be got off the beach, but all of which were destroyed.

This very gallant and important enterprise was accomplished

with so slight a loss on the part of the British, as one marine killed, and six seamen and marines wounded. The loss on the part of the Neapolitans nowhere appears; nor, indeed, can we discover that any account of the affair has been published. The Moniteur of August the 5th contains an article, under the head of "Scylla, le 20 Juillet," announcing the departure of Captain Caraccioli, with a division of gun-boats, to meet and protect this convoy; but, although accounts from the Neapolitan coast continued to arrive, no mention is made of the disaster that befel that convoy and those gun-boats.

In his letter to Rear-admiral Martin, giving an account of this affair, Captain Waldegrave, with a liberality and a modesty that do him great credit, thus expresses himself: "Gratified as I feel at an opportunity of testifying to the gallantry and zeal of Captains Prescott and Nicolas, and Lieutenant Collier, together with all the officers and crews of the ships (more particularly those in the boats), for their sakes I cannot help regretting it should not have fallen to their lot to have been under the command of one, whose testimony would have greater weight in insuring them that applause and reward to which such conduct so justly entitles them." For his gallantry in the command of the boats, Captain Prescott was promoted to post-rank, and his commission bears date on the day on which the service was executed.

On the night of the 28th of September, Captain Robert Hall, of the 14-gun brig-sloop Rambler, lying in Gibraltar bay, having been detached with some gun-boats in search of enemy's privateers to the westward, landed with 30 officers, seamen, and marines, after a pull of 20 hours at the sweeps, at a spot near the entrance of the river Barbate, or Barbet, about five miles to the north-west of Tarifa. Captain Hall and his party then crossed the sand-hills to get at a French privateer, lying about three miles up the river, protected by two 6-pounders, her own crew, and 30 French dragoons. After some sharp firing, the enemy retreated with the loss of five dragoons, seven horses, and two of the privateer's crew. The British then swam off to the privateer and carried her with no greater loss than one marine killed and one wounded. Among the officers present in this enterprise, we find the names of Lieutenant James Seagrove and Lieutenant of marines William Halsted.

Of all the official letters which we have had occasion to consult, this of Captain Hall's is the most difficult to understand. He speaks of landing with part of the crew of a gun-boat No. 14, "that of the Rambler and the marines and seamen of the Topaze, in all 30," and dates his letter on board "His majesty's sloop Rambler." We suppose, however, that both the Rambler and the Topaze, mentioned in the body of the letter, were gunboats. A little more explicitness would have enabled us to do justice to what appears to have been a very gallant exploit. Our contemporary seems also to have been led astray by the official letter. He says: "Captain Robert Hall, in the Rambler, a small brig of war, of 10 guns, took out of the river of Barbet, near Malaga, a French privateer, and some small vessels, with a degree of spirit and enterprise seldom exceeded."[1] No date is given but the year, and that is "1809." On this point the official letter is clear; as well as that one vessel only was taken, and that Barbet was "to the westward," and not as Malaga notoriously is, to the eastward, of the rock of Gibraltar.

On the 4th of November the 18-gun ship-sloop Blossom, Captain William Stewart, cruising off Cape Sicie, observed in the south-east and immediately chased a latteen xebec. At 4 P.M., when the ship had arrived within four miles of the xebec, it fell calm. Captain Stewart despatched the cutter, under master's mate Richard Hambly, to reconnoitre the vessel, strictly charging him not to risk the life of a man, should he find her armed and disposed to make obstinate resistance. Almost immediately afterwards the Blossom's yawl, manned with volunteers, and commanded by the first-lieutenant Samuel Davis, having under him midshipman John Marshall, joined the cutter; and the two boats pulled with all their strength to overtake the xebec.

At about 7 P.M., just as the boats had arrived within gunshot, the privateer, which was the César of Barcelona, of four guns and 59 men, opened a fire upon them; killing Lieutenant Davis and three seamen, and badly wounding (by a musket-ball through the collar-bone) Mr. Hambly and four men. With the 26 seamen and marines remaining, Mr. Marshall sprang on board of, and after a smart contest carried, the privateer; but not without the additional loss of five men wounded. The privateer had four men killed, and nine wounded; the greater part after boarding, as the seven marines divided between the two boats only fired twice before they and the seamen were on the xebec's decks. This was a very gallant exploit on the part of Mr. Marshall;[2] and, had it been properly represented, he cer-

[1] Brenton, vol. iv., p. 358.
[2] The author of the "Royal Naval Biography," occasionally quoted in these pages.

tainly would not have had to wait upwards of six years before he received a lieutenant's commission.

On the 13th of December, at 1 p.m., Captain Thomas Rogers, of the 74-gun ship Kent, having under his orders, off the southeast coast of Spain, the Ajax 74, Captain Robert Waller Otway, 40-gun frigate Cambrian, Captain Francis William Fane, and 18-gun sloops Sparrowhawk and Minstrel, Captain James Pringle and Colin Campbell, despatched the boats of the squadron, containing 350 seamen and 250 marines, with two field-pieces, under the command of Captain Fane, to capture or destroy an enemy's convoy in the mole of Palamos; consisting of one new national ketch mounting 14 guns, with 60 men, two xebecs of three guns and 30 men each, and eight merchant-vessels laden with provisions for Barcelona: the whole protected by two 24-pounders, one in a battery that stood over the mole, and the other, with a 13-inch mortar, in a battery on a very commanding height; besides, from the best information then received, about 250 soldiers in the town.

The boats, very soon after quitting the Kent, landed their men on the beach in the finest order, under cover of the Sparrowhawk and Minstrel, without harm, the French having posted themselves in the town; from which they also retired on the approach of the British, and the latter forthwith took quiet possession of the batteries and the vessels in the mole. The mortar was spiked, and the cannon thrown down the heights into the sea, the magazine blown up, and the whole of the vessels, except two which were brought out, burnt and destroyed; in short, the object of the enterprise was completely fulfilled, and that with the loss of only four or five men from occasional skirmishing. But, in withdrawing from a hill occupied by a part of the detachment, to keep the enemy in check until the batteries and vessels were destroyed, the British retired in some disorder, thereby encouraging the French soldiers, who had just received a reinforcement from St. Félice, to advance upon them. Instead of directing their retreat upon the beach, where the Sparrowhawk and Minstrel lay ready to cover their embarkation, the "brave but thoughtless and unfortunate men" passed through the town down to the mole. From the walls and houses, the French opened a severe fire upon the boats crowded with men, and in a dastardly manner fired upon and killed several who had been left on the mole and were endeavouring to swim to the boats.

The result was that, out of the 600 British officers and men who had landed, two officers, 19 seamen, and 12 marines were killed, 15 officers, 42 seamen, and 32 marines wounded, and two officers, 41 seamen, and 43 marines made prisoners; total, 33 killed, 89 wounded, and 87 (including one seaman that deserted) missing; comprising a full third of the party. Among the prisoners was Captain Fane himself, who, with characteristic firmness, remained on the mole to the last in the performance of his arduous duty. Because this was a defeat, we presume, not an officer is named in the official letter, or even in the returns of loss, except the commanding officer of the landed party, and Lieutenant George Godfrey, first of the Kent.

On the 6th of April, while the British cutter Sylvia, of ten 18-pounder carronades and 44, out of a complement of 50 men and boys, commanded by Lieutenaut Augustus Vere Drury, was proceeding through the Straits of Sunda, in the Indian ocean, an armed prow, of one long 6-pounder and 30 men, deceived by the cutter's insignificant appearance, swept out from under the isle of Cracatoa to attack her. The Sylvia soon drove on shore, captured, and destroyed the prow; bringing away her 6-pounder. On the 7th an armed prow, of large dimensions, carrying two 6-pounders, with 30 men, approached so close to the Sylvia, that, judging it necessary to deviate from his course and destroy this pirate also, Lieutenant Drury detached a boat, with an officer and a party of volunteers, to harass the prow. The latter now endeavoured to escape, but was prevented by the brisk fire of musketry kept up by the boat; which, after killing two and wounding one of the pirates, took possession of their vessel without the slightest loss.

On the 11th a large lugger-prow, armed with three 18-pounders and 72 men, weighed from under Cracatoa, and indicated an intention of trying if she could succeed in capturing the British cutter, now at an anchor. Lieutenant Drury placed on board the prize Sub-lieutenant John Christian Chesnaye and a party of volunteers, and sent her to attack the lugger. Mr. Chesnaye resolutely met the pirate, and compelled him to seek safety in flight. The intervention of a small island preventing the cutter from seeing the further progress of the action, Lieutenant Drury got under way with the Sylvia, and stood out to support his detached party. These were on the point of boarding the pirate, when the Sylvia arrived within gun-shot. The obstinate refusal of the enemy to yield compelled the cutter to open her fire; and, from its effects, the lugger presently sank with the greater part of her crew. In this last affair, the Sylvia had one man killed and seven men wounded.

On the 26th, at daybreak, while the Sylvia was cruising off Middleburgh island upon the coast of Java, three armed brigs, accompanied by two lug-sail vessels, were discerned in the vicinity of Edam island, hastening towards Batavia. The Sylvia instantly proceeded to attack the sternmost brig: and, after a sharp contest of 20 minutes' duration, captured the Dutch national brig Echo, of eight 6-pounders and 46 men, commanded by Lieutenant Christian Thaarup. This gallant little affair cost the Sylvia four men killed and three wounded, and the Dutch brig three killed and seven wounded.

The instant that a separation could be effected between the Sylvia and her prize, pursuit was given to the two headmost brigs. But these, aided by a favourable breeze and an intervening shoal, effected their escape to the batteries of Onroost; leaving the Sylvia to take possession of the two lug-rigged transports, mounting two long 9-pounders and defended by 60 men each, out 12 days from Sourabaya, laden with artillery equipage and valuable European goods. Considering that the Sylvia's originally small crew had been reduced by 12 men disabled by previous wounds, the whole of this business reflects the greatest credit upon Lieutenant Drury, Sub-lieutenant Chesnaye, and the few remaining officers and men on board the cutter.

The Sylvia was one of the 12 cutters built at Bermuda in the year 1805, of the pencil-cedar, and measured only 111 tons. We little expected, certainly, to find one of this small class of vessel cruising and distinguishing herself in the seas of Java. On the 2nd of May, Lieutenant Drury, as he well deserved, was promoted to the rank of commander; but Sub-lieutenant Chesnaye, although spoken of in the highest terms by his commander, does not appear to have been rewarded with the rank of a full lieutenant until nearly three years afterwards.

We last year left at Port Louis, in the Isle of France, the French 40-gun frigates Vénus, Commodore Jacques-Felix-Emmanuel Hamelin, Bellone, Captain Victor-Guy Duperré, and Manche, Captain François-Désiré Breton.[1] The late Portuguese frigate Minerva, or Minerve as now named, had since been fitted out, and the command of her given to the Bellone's late first-lieutenant, Pierre-François-Henry-Etienne Bouvet; a very active young officer, and who on the 1st of February was promoted to the rank of capitaine de frégate. There could have been no difficulty in manning this fine frigate, as the

[1] See p. 167.

Cannonière and Sémillante, on their departure for Europe as merchant-ships, had left behind the principal part of their crews. There was also, we regret to have to state, another source whence the French at the Isle of France derived a supply both of sailors and soldiers, but chiefly the latter. When any prisoners were brought in, every art was made use of to inveigle them into the French service. As the bulk of the prisoners consisted of detachments of soldiers taken out of the Indiamen, and as the majority of those were Irish Catholics, an assurance that France had not yet abandoned her intention of conquering Ireland and restoring the Catholic religion, was generally found a successful expedient; especially when coupled with threats of the most rigid confinement in case of refusal. Other deserters, no doubt, had not the excuse of the poor Hibernian to make. Nor were soldiers on this occasion the only traitors: between 20 and 30 of the late Laurel's crew entered with the enemy whom they had so resolutely fought.

On the 14th of March, taking advantage of the absence of the British blockading squadron from the station on account of the hurricane season, Captain Duperré, with the Bellone and Minerve frigates, and the recaptured ship-corvette Victor, now commanded by Captain Nicolas Morice, the same officer, with a step in his rank, who had commanded her when captured as the Jéna by the British frigate Modeste, in October, 1808, sailed from Port Louis on a cruise in the bay of Bengal. On the 1st of June, having taken and sent in two prizes, and there being no prospect of making any more this season, Commodore Duperré steered for the bay of St. Augustin, island of Madagascar, to repair his ships and refresh his crews. Having accomplished this object, the French commodore, in the latter end of the month, again sailed, and stood leisurely up the Mosambique channel, until he came in sight of the island of Mayotta, when an occurrence happened, which proved that his cruising-ground had been well chosen.

On the 3rd of July, at 6 A.M., or just as the day dawned, the island of Mayotta bearing east half north distant about 12 leagues, the three British outward-bound Indiamen Ceylon, Captain and senior officer Henry Meriton, Windham, Captain John Stewart, and Astell, Captain Robert Hay, steering their course to the northward, with a fresh breeze from the south-south-east, discovered about nine miles off in the north-north-east, under a press of sail, close hauled on the larboard tack, the Bellone, Minerve, and Victor. At 6 h. 30 m. A.M., agreeably to a signal from the commodore, the three Indiamen hauled their wind upon the larboard tack, under double-reefed topsails, courses, jib, and spanker. At 7 h. 30 m. A.M. the Ceylon made the private signal to the three strangers, then passing on the opposite tack at the distance of about four miles. No answer being returned, the British ships cleared for action. At 9 h. 30 m. A.M., in consequence of the Astell making a signal that she was over pressed, the Ceylon and Windham shortened sail.

Captain Meriton now telegraphed his two companions:—"As we cannot get away, I think we had better go under easy sail, and bring them to action before dark." The Astell answered, "Certainly." The Windham replied:—"If we make all sail and get into smooth water under the land, we can engage to more advantage." At 10 A.M. the three Indiamen, on account of the increasing power of the breeze, hove to and took in the third reef of their topsails; and even then the ships lay over so much, and the sea ran so high, that they could not keep open their lower-deck lee ports. At 11 h. 30 m. the Minerve tacked in the wake of the Indiamen and at the distance of about six miles from them; and shortly afterwards the Bellone, about four miles upon the lee beam, and the Victor about the same distance upon the weather quarter, also tacked. Perceiving the Minerve coming up astern very fast, Captain Meriton telegraphed:— "Form the line abreast, to bear on ships together, Ceylon in the centre." Accordingly the Windham, Ceylon, and Astell formed a close line in the order named, and awaited the coming up of the enemy; the two nearest ships of which, the Victor and Minerve, were fast approaching on the weather or starboard quarter.

At 2 h. 15 m. P.M. the Minerve, having arrived abreast of the British centre, and as well as the Victor who was ahead of her, hoisted French colours, fired one shot at the Windham, and then her whole larboard broadside into the Ceylon. The latter was at this time so close astern of her consort as almost to touch her; but the Astell was considerably to leeward and astern of the Ceylon. The corvette opening her fire, the action became general between the Minerve and Victor on one side, and the Windham, Ceylon, and Astell on the other. The Ceylon, however, from her situation directly a-beam of the frigate, certainly bore the brunt of the engagement. In a little while, finding the fire of the British too heavy for her, the corvette bore up and passed to leeward of the Astell. At 3 h. 40 m. P.M. Captain

Hay of the latter ship was severely wounded, and the command of the Astell devolved upon Mr. William Hawkey, the chief mate.

At 4 P.M. the Minerve shot ahead, and then bore down as if with the intention of boarding the Windham. This being a mode of attack to which the Indiamen, from the number of troops they had on board, were not much averse, the Windham made sail for the purpose of striking the French frigate on the larboard quarter, and the Ceylon and Astell closed their consort to co-operate with her in the manœuvre. But the Windham, having had her sails and rigging greatly damaged, did not possess way enough to accomplish the object, and the Minerve passed athwart her hawse at the distance of only a few yards. In the mean time all three Indiamen, by means of their troops, had maintained upon the Minerve an incessant and well-directed fire of musketry. Just as the latter got out of gun-shot, the Astell hauled sharp up, and, passing astern of the Windham, became the headmost and weathermost ship. At 4 h. 30 m. P.M., having passed obliquely down the British line, the Minerve wore, with the intention of cutting off the Windham, who was now the sternmost and leewardmost ship. No sooner, however, had the Minerve hauled to the wind on the starboard tack, than her main and mizen topmasts came down close to the caps.

A respite was thus afforded to the three Indiamen; but it was not of long duration, for at 6 P.M. the Bellone, followed by the Victor, commenced a heavy and destructive fire on the Windham. Passing on, the Bellone took up a position on the lee beam of the Ceylon, as the commodore's ship; directing her foremost guns at the Astell. Meanwhile the Victor kept up a smart, but, on account of the distance she maintained, not very effective fire on the lee quarter of the Windham. At 6 h. 30 m. P.M., while endeavouring to close the French frigate, in order to give full effect to his musketry, Captain Meriton received a severe grape-shot wound in the neck; and the command of the Ceylon, in consequence, devolved upon the chief mate, Mr. Thomas Widlock Oldham; who, in a minute or two afterwards, being himself severely wounded, was obliged to leave the deck in charge of the second mate, Mr. Tristram Fenning. At about 7 P.M., having had her masts, rigging, and sails badly wounded and cut, all her upper-deck, and five of her lower-deck guns disabled, and her hull so badly struck, that she made three feet water an hour; and having also sustained a serious loss in killed and wounded, the Ceylon bore up and ceased firing passing astern of the Bellone; who was still engaging the Windham, at this time close abreast of the Astell to leeward, and consequently sheltering the latter from the fire of the frigate. The Windham, it appears, hailed the Astell repeatedly, proposing a joint attempt to board the Bellone; but not understanding, we suppose, the purport of the hail, the Astell put out her lights and made sail, and received, just as she had passed clear of her consort, a heavy parting fire from the frigate.

At about 7 h. 20 m. P.M., being in the unmanageable state already described, the Ceylon hauled down her colours, and was taken possession of by a boat from the Minerve, then coming up on her starboard quarter. Shortly afterwards, in passing the Windham, the Ceylon hailed that she had struck. The Astell, just before she put out her lights, had received the same information, and had then her fore and main masts badly wounded, and her rigging and sails greatly disabled. The Windham, who by the Astell's departure was now left quite alone, finding that her damaged masts and the state of her rigging would not admit of her making sail, continued the action, chiefly for the purpose of favouring the escape of the Astell; when, at 7 h. 45 m. P.M., having had nine of her guns dismounted, and sustained a serious loss in killed and wounded, the Windham hauled down her colours, and was taken possession of by the Bellone. In the mean time the Victor had proceeded in chase of the Astell; but, owing to the time occupied in securing her two captured consorts and the extreme darkness of the night, the Astell effected her escape.

The Ceylon, Windham, and Astell were each 800-ton ships, and were armed nearly in the same ineffective manner. The force of the Windham has already appeared, and that will suffice for the force of either of her consorts. Commodore Duperré gave each of his prizes 30 guns; whereas 26, we know, were all the guns that the Windham mounted, and we believe the Ceylon and Astell mounted no more. Each Indiaman had on board a detachment of about 250 troops, exclusive of 100 Lascars, and from 12 to 20 British seamen. The Windham appears to have had only 12 British seamen and 160 effective soldiers: the remainder of the troops were probably sick.

We have now to show the loss on board each ship. The Ceylon had four seamen, one Lascar, and two soldiers killed, her captain, chief mate, seven seamen, one Lascar, one lieutenant-colonel and 10 soldiers of the 24th regiment (one mortally) wounded; total, six killed and 21 wounded. The Windham had one seaman, three soldiers, and two Lascars killed, seven soldiers, and two Lascars severely, and three of her officers and six others slightly wounded; total, six killed and 18 wounded. The Astell had four seamen and four soldiers killed, her captain, fifth mate, nine seamen, one Lascar, five cadets, and 20 soldiers wounded; total, eight killed and 37 wounded: making the aggregate loss on the British side amount to 20 killed and 76 wounded. The loss on the French side appears to have been as follows: Bellone, four killed and six wounded; Minerve, 17 killed and 29 wounded; Victor, one killed and three wounded: total, 22 killed and 38 wounded.

Great praise was undoubtedly due to the captains, officers, and crews of these three Indiamen, for their very gallant defence against a force so decidedly superior. Nor must we omit the officers in command of the troops and their men; who, we have no doubt, by their steady fire, inflicted a great proportion of the loss which the enemy sustained. The East India Company, to testify their approbation of the conduct of the crews of the three ships, presented each of the captains with the sum of 500*l.*, and bestowed a handsome remuneration upon the remaining officers and men.

The officers of the Astell certainly possessed a great advantage, in being able to publish their statement before the officers of the Ceylon and Windham could do so. As one proof of it, a contemporary says thus:—" The East India Company settled a pension of 460*l.* a year on Captain Hay, and presented 2000*l.* to the officers and crew, as a mark of approbation for their distinguished bravery. Andrew Peters, one of the seamen of the Astell, nailed the pendant to the maintopmast-head, and was killed as he descended the rigging. The lords commissioners of the admiralty, to testify their approbation of the defence of the Astell, granted to the ship's company a protection from impressment for three years."[1] But our reliance upon this statement is samewhat shaken by the glaring inaccuracies contained in the following passages :—" Du Perrée, in the Bellone, of 44-guns, with the Victor corvette, came up about 4 P.M. The Minerve was still a long way astern. The weight of the battle fell on the Ceylon and Astell."—" She (the Bellone) bore up, ran to leeward, and in the act of wearing, her topmasts fell." The loss of the Windham is also enumerated at only four men killed and four wounded. The colours of the Astell, it appears, were three times shot away. This may excuse M. Duperré for stating in

[1] Brenton, vol. iv., p. 463.

his official letter, that the Astell struck, but does not in the least justify the epithet, "indigne fuyard," which the French captain applies to her gallant, and, long before that time, disabled commander.

Early in the morning of the 4th, the French commodore made sail with the two captured Indiamen, and on the next day anchored in the bay of Johanna, in the island of that name. Here it took M. Duperré so long to refit his ships, particularly the prizes, the masts of which had all to be fished, that he was not able to sail again until the morning of the 17th. In three days, however, the French squadron and prizes made the high land at the back of Grand-Port, or Port Sud-Est in the Isle of France. At this critical moment we must leave M. Duperré, until we have given some account of the naval occurrences at the isles of France and Bourbon, during his four months' absence from the station.

In the latter end of March or beginning of April, a British naval force arrived off the Isle of France from the Cape, commanded by Captain Henry Lambert, of the 18-pounder 36-gun frigate Iphigenia, having under his orders the 50-gun ship Leopard, Captain James Johnstone, 12-pounder 36-gun frigate Magicienne, Captain Lucius Curtis, and one or two smaller vessels. The French force in Port Louis harbour consisted, at this time, of the two 40-gun frigates Vénus and Manche, and brig-corvette Entreprenant.

On or about the 24th of April the 12-pounder 36-gun frigate Néréide, Captain Nisbet Josiah Willoughby, from the Cape of Good Hope, which she had quitted on the 10th, joined Captain Lambert's squadron, and was immediately detached to cruise off the south-east coast of the island. On arriving abreast of the entrance of Rivière-Noire, a ship was discovered at anchor there, moored in such a manner between the powerful batteries of the place, that her stern was alone visible to the Néréide. She was evidently a ship-of-war, and was supposed to be a corvette. The Néréide in working up to the spot, discharged several broadsides at the French ship, and received in return a fire from the neighbouring batteries, but neither sustained, nor, it is believed, inflicted any injury. Instead of being a corvette, this ship was a fine French frigate of 1085 tons, the Astrée, already mentioned as having quitted Cherbourg in company with the Néréide, a frigate of the same force. Having been, as soon as he made the south-west point of the island, apprised by signal, that a British force was cruising off Port Louis, Captain Breton had put into

Rivière-Noire and moored the Astrée in the manner above stated.

On the 30th, while the British frigate Néréide was reconnoitring the coast of this part of the island, a large merchant-ship was discovered lying at the anchorage of Jacolet, within pistol-shot of two batteries, which commanded the entrance to the harbour. Notwithstanding these obstacles, having on board an excellent pilot, one of the black inhabitants of the Isle of France, Captain Willoughby resolved to attempt cutting the ship out. For this purpose he embarked in the boats at midnight, taking with him Lieutenants John Burns, Thomas Lamb Polden Laugharne, and Henry Collins Deacon, and Lieutenants of marines Thomas S. Cox and Thomas Henry William Desbrisay, together with 50 seamen and the same number of marines.

Having with much difficulty found and entered the narrow and intricate passage into the anchorage, Captain Willoughby had just reached the only feasible spot for effecting a landing, and even there the surf was half filling the boats, when the French national schooner Estafette, of four brass 4-pounders and 14 men, commanded by Enseigne de vaisseau Henri Chauvin, and lying at an anchor close abreast of the battery on the left, shouted, and gave the alarm. Both batteries, assisted by two field-pieces, immediately played upon the spot on which the British were landing; and, no sooner had the latter formed on the beach, than they became also exposed to a heavy fire of musketry. As every officer had already received his orders, the whole party was instantly upon the run, and in 10 minutes got possession of the nearest battery mounting two long 12-pounders.

Having spiked the guns, Captain Willoughby and his men marched towards the guard-house in the rear; which was protected by two 6-pounder field-pieces, 40 troops of the 18th regiment of the line, 26 artillerymen, and a strong detachment of militia. This party, while the seamen and marines were taking the battery, had attacked the small division of men left in charge of the boats, and had driven them and their boats into the centre of the harbour. The same party now opened a fire upon the British main body. This was the signal for the seamen and marines to charge. Captain Willoughby and his brave followers did so; and the French and colonial soldiers instantly gave way, flying with a speed which the British could not equal, and leaving not only their two field-pieces, but their commanding officer, Lieutenant Rockman, of the 18th regiment, who was made a prisoner while in the act of spiking the two field-pieces; and who, observes Captain Willoughby in his despatch, "deserved to command better soldiers."

Hitherto twilight had hid from view the force of the British, but full day now showed the Néréide's small band of volunteers to the enemy; whose strongest battery was still unsubdued, and to gain which it was necessary to pass the river le Galet, running at the foot of a high hill covered with wood, and defended by the commandant of the Savannah district, Colonel Etienne Colgard, with two long 12-pounders drawn from the battery on the right, and a strong body of militia. Owing to the recent heavy rains, the river had become so swollen and its stream so rapid, that the tallest man could scarcely wade across. The short, however, were helped over; and the whole party, more than half of whom were upon the swim, and all exposed to a heavy fire, succeeded in reaching the opposite bank, but not without the loss of the greater part of the ammunition. No sooner was the river crossed, than three cheers warned the enemy to prepare for the bayonet. On the gallant fellows rushed: and the hill, the two guns, and the battery, with its colours, were carried "in style;" and the commandant, Colonel Colgard, was taken prisoner. "Nor," says Captain Willoughby, with the candour of a brave man, "do I think an officer or man of the party except myself had an anxious thought for the result of this unequal affair."

Having spiked the guns and a mortar, burnt and destroyed their carriages, also the works and magazine, and embarked the two field-pieces, with a quantity of naval and military stores, Captain Willoughby was upon the point of returning to the Néréide, when the party which had been driven from the first battery appeared to have recovered from their panic, and, strongly reinforced by the militia and the bourgeois inhabitants of the island, were drawn up in battle array on the left. Knowing that this was the first hostile landing which had ever been effected upon the Isle of France; knowing, also, that its principal defence consisted in its militia, Captain Willoughby resolved to run some risk in letting the latter know what they were to expect if ever the island was attacked by a regular British force. He accordingly moved towards the assembled French militia and regulars; and these, on advancing within musket-shot, opened their fire. As a proof of his good generalship, Captain Willoughby resolved to get into the rear of his opponents in order to cut them off in the retreat, to which, ho knew, they would again resort. The captain and his party immediately turned into the interior, in an oblique direction to the islanders, who at first halted and remained upon their ground. But the moment the British, by moving in quick time, discovered their intention, the French militia, followed by the regulars, took to their heels, as had been conjectured, and, a second time, beat the British seamen and marines in fair running. On their way back to their boats, to reach which they had again to wade across the river Galet, the bold invaders burnt the signal-house and flagstaff, situated nearly a mile from the beach: a proof to what a distance the fugitives had led them. Having well sounded the harbour, Captain Willoughby took with him the French schooner, which the midshipman left in charge of the boats had secured just as she was sweeping to sea, and rejoined the Néréide in the offing. The ship, a fine vessel of 400 tons, proved to be an American: and, although she was detainable for a breach of blockade, Captain Willoughby did not capture her.

This very gallant, and, as we shall see, far from unimportant enterprise, was executed with so comparatively trifling a loss as one marine killed, Lieutenant Deacon (slightly), four seamen, and two marines wounded. The loss of the enemy could not be ascertained; nor was it exactly known what force the British had defeated. From information, corroborated by what fell from the French officers, a body of 600 troops could reinforce the batteries at the post, by signal, within an hour; and the signal for an enemy was flying during the whole four hours that the British remained on shore. Nor did the seamen or marines, much to the credit of themselves and their officers, commit the slightest injury to the houses or private property of the inhabitants.

As soon as the Néréide joined the squadron off Port Louis, Captain Lambert sent in a flag of truce, with the captured militia commandant, lieutenant of infantry, and enseigne de vaisseau, and received in exchange for them 39 British seamen and soldiers. This was an immediate good result of the enterprise at Jacolet. The benefits of a more permanent nature, arising from the exploit of Captain Willoughby, were, an instance of the practicability, hitherto doubted, of making a descent upon the Isle of France, and a proof that the principal part of the troops in the island consisted of militia; of whose prowess, also, as defenders of any spot of ground, some very conclusive evidence had been obtained.

Some time in the month of May, Captain Josias Rowley, late

of the 64-gun ship Raisonable, having by the orders of Vice-admiral William O'Brien Drury, the commander-in-chief at the Cape of Good Hope, superseded Captain John Hatley in the command of the 38-gun frigate Boadicea, arrived, with the latter frigate and the Sirius, off the Isle of France. The Raisonable in the mean time, being nearly worn out in the service, had sailed for England, commanded by Captain Hatley; and the Leopard having also quitted the Isle of France station for the Cape of Good Hope, the British force cruising off Port Louis consisted of frigates and sloops only, the Boadicea, Sirius, Iphigenia, Magicienne, Néréide, Otter, and a few others.

On the 15th of June, while Commodore Rowley, with the Boadicea and Néréide, was watering on Isle Platte, or Flat island, a small island close off the northern extremity of the Isle of France, preparatory to his departure for the Isle of Rodriguez, a very serious accident happened to the captain of the Néréide. Captain Willoughby was on shore exercising his men at small-arms, when a musket he was holding burst, and inflicted upon him a dreadful, and, as it was thought, mortal wound. His lower jaw on the right side was badly fractured, and his neck so lacerated, that the windpipe lay bare; and the surgeon feared, for several days, that it would slough away with the dressings, and of course end the life of the patient. For three weeks, Captain Willoughby could not speak. However, by the skilful attention of the surgeon, Mr. George Peter Martyn Young, and a temperate habit of body, but not until a painful exfoliation of the jaw had taken place, the wound healed. We formerly gave the name of Captain (then lieutenant) Willoughby among the wounded at the unfortunate business of the island of Prota, during the still more unfortunate proceedings in the neighbourhood of Constantinople. The wound Captain Willoughby then received was by two musket or pistol balls; one struck his left cheek, and injured the jaw on that side; the other entered his right nostril, and, from the upward position of his face at the moment, took a slanting direction towards the region of the brain. He lay, for half an hour, insensible on the ground, and was carried to the boats and the ship as one of whom no hopes were entertained. The surgeon introduced his probe several inches into the wound, and it was some time, we believe, before the bullet was extracted.

Having watered his two ships, and left the squadron off the Isle of France in the temporary charge of Captain Pym of the Sirius, Commodore Rowley made sail for the island of Rodriguez, a small uninhabited island situated about 100 leagues to the north-east of the Isle of France; and which had recently been taken possession of by Lieutenant-colonel Keating, as a sort of barrack for the troops with which it was in contemplation to attack Isle Bourbon. On the 24th the Boadicea and Néréide anchored at Rodriguez; and on the 3rd of July, having embarked as many of the European troops as they could stow, the two frigates sailed on their return, accompanied by 14 transports, having on board the remainder of the 3650 European and native troops, including 1850 of the latter, allotted for the expedition. On board the Boadicea were also, as passengers, Lieutenant-colonel Keating, the commanding officer of the troops, and Robert Townsend Farquhar, Esq., appointed to the government of the island as soon as it should be captured. The regular force on Bourbon at this time amounted to only 576 rank and file; but there was an organized militia force of 2717 men.

On the 6th, at 4 P.M., the expedition joined Captain Pym's squadron at the appointed rendezvous, about 50 miles to windward of Isle Bourbon; and the Sirius, Iphigenia, and Magicienne received on board from the transports all the remaining European and a portion of the native troops, together with as many of their boats as might be required for landing the men. This done, the five frigates and transports, early on the morning of the 7th, bore away for the different points of debarkation. The first brigade, under the command of Lieutenant-colonel Fraser, was to land at Grande-Chaloupe, a spot about six miles to the southward and westward of the town of St. Dénis, the capital of the island; while the second, third, and fourth brigades, under the respective commands of Lieutenant-colonel Keating, Campbell, and Drummond, were to land at Rivière des Pluies, about three miles to the eastward of the town. The first of these points was on the lee, the other on the weather side of the island.

While the main force drew the enemy's attention off Sainte-Marie, about two miles further to the eastward than Rivière des Pluies, Captain Pym, at 2 P.M., in the short space of about two hours and a half, effected the landing at Grande-Chaloupe, without opposition, of the whole of Colonel Fraser's brigade, consisting of 950 men, with some howitzers and the necessary ammunition. Owing to the able dispositions of Lieutenant John Wyatt Watling, second of the Sirius, who with a small detachment of seamen had charge of the beach, not an accident occurred to a single soldier, nor was any part of the ammunition injured. Lieutenant Watling, with his men, then kept possession, during the night, of a neighbouring height between the town of St. Paul and Colonel Fraser's rear; thereby preventing reinforcements being sent from St. Paul's to St. Dénis: he also drove in all the enemy's sharp-shooters, and took several cavalry horses.

The Boadicea, Iphigenia, Magicienne, and Néréide, when it was supposed that the first landing had been effected, pushed for an anchorage, and were followed by the transports as they arrived. The weather, which until now had been favourable, began to change. The beach on this side of the island, being steep and composed of large shingles, is generally of difficult access; but Captain Willoughby having reported it practicable, a landing was attempted under this officer's direction. Embarking on board the prize-schooner Estafette, Captain Willoughby (with the dressings still on his wound, and after a night's exposure in an open boat) succeeded, with a small detachment of seamen and about 150 troops, in effecting a landing; but not without having the schooner, which belonged to the Néréide's ship's company, dashed to pieces in the surf, together with several of the boats. Fortunately the only lives lost on the occasion were two soldiers, and two of the Néréide's seamen drowned. Lieutenant-colonel Keating considering it indispensable that a disembarkation should be effected on this most difficult side of the capital, a light transport brig, the Ulney, was run on shore as a breakwater; but the stern-cable parting, she formed only a momentary cover for a few boats: and it was found necessary, at the close of day, to relinquish, for the present, any further attempts to land at this point.

The small detachment on shore, having lost a great proportion of their arms, and had the whole of their ammunition spoiled, were now rather critically circumstanced; especially as, on account of the bad state of the weather, no boat could push off to communicate with the squadron. At length, a gallant young officer of the army, Lieutenant Foulstone, who was on board the Boadicea, volunteered to swim through the surf and convey to Lieutenant-colonel Macleod, the commanding officer of the detachment, Colonel Keating's orders. He did so; and the lieutenant-colonel took quiet possession of, and occupied for the night, the fort of Sainté Marie.

On the morning of the 8th, the beach still appearing unfavourable, the Boadicea, leaving behind the Iphigenia and transports, proceeded to Grande-Chaloupe; where, at about 11 A.M.,

Colonel Keating and the troops in the Boadicea disembarked. In the course of the day Captain Lambert succeeded in landing the troops from the Iphigenia and transports; but, in the mean time, after an outpost had been assaulted and carried by a detachment from Colonel Fraser's brigade, the French commanding officer on the island, Colonel St. Susaune, had requested a suspension of arms. This was agreed to, and at 6 P.M. the capitulation was signed, and Isle Bourbon became a British possession; that, too, with so slight a loss as one subaltern, one sergeant, and six rank and file killed, two rank and file and two seamen drowned, and one major (T. Edwards, of the 86th), seven subalterns, two sergeants, two drummers, 66 rank and file, and one seaman wounded; total, 22 killed and drowned, and 79 wounded. On the 9th Mr. Farquhar landed from the Boadicea, and, as had been previously arranged, assumed the government of the conquered island.

A part of the duty of the Sirius frigate was to take possession of the shipping in the bay of St. Paul. Observing a brig getting ready to sail, Captain Pym, at 11 P.M. on the 9th, despatched the barge under the orders of Lieutenant George R. Norman, to endeavour to bring the vessel out, or to cut her off should she attempt to escape. Finding, by boarding the other vessels in the bay, that the brig had sailed since 9 P.M., Lieutenant Norman pushed on, and, after a hard row of nearly 12 hours, overtook, boarded, and, with three men slightly wounded, carried in a most gallant manner, the Edward privateer, of Nantes, pierced for 16 guns, but with only four 12-pounders and 30 men on board; a fine brig of 245 tons, then on her way to the Isle of France with despatches from the government at home.

Immediately after the surrender of the Isle Bourbon, the Sirius returned to her station off the Isle of France; and, while standing along the south side, discovered a three-masted schooner making every exertion to haul herself on shore out of reach of the frigate. Captain Pym immediately despatched the cutter and pinnace of the Sirius, with 14 men in each, the former commanded by Lieutenant Norman, and the latter by Lieutenant John Wyatt Watling. The two boats hastened to the beach, and found the schooner fast aground, and under the protection of about 300 regulars and militia, with two field-pieces. Notwithstanding this, Lieutenant Norman and his little party succeeded, without sustaining any loss, in boarding and destroying the vessel, which was partly laden with supplies for the French army. While the service was executing, the tide had ebbed considerably; whereby the British, in their way back to their boats, were obliged to pass the whole posse militaire within half musket-shot. Unfortunately, too, the pinnace was aground; and, in the efforts to get her afloat, one seaman was killed and a midshipman badly wounded.

Soon after the boats had returned to the Sirius, the Iphigenia joined from Isle Bourbon; as, in a day or two afterwards, did the Néréide and the Staunch gun-brig. On board the Néréide were 12 Madras artillerymen under Lieutenant Aldwinkle, and 100 choice troops, consisting of 50 grenadiers of the 69th regiment under Lieutenant Needhall, and 50 of the 33rd, under Lieutenant Morlett, the whole commanded by Captain Todd of the 69th. This force had been placed on board the Néréide by Lieutenant-colonel Keating, in order to co-operate with Captain Willoughby, in an attack, in the first instance, upon Isle de la Passe, a small rocky island, situated upwards of four miles to the eastward of the town of Grand Port, or Port Sud-Est,[1] on the south-east side of the Isle of France; and the narrow and intricate channel to the harbour of which town, one face of the battery on the above small island completely commands.

The main object, in possessing this key to Grand Port, was to enable Captain Willoughby, by the aid of a black pilot serving with him in the Néréide, to enter the intricate channel to the harbour, and accompanied by an adequate force, to land in the vicinity of the town before the post could be strengthened from head-quarters; and then to distribute among the inhabitants copies of a proclamation addressed to them by Governor Farquhar of Isle Bourbon. This proclamation, like all others of the same kind, drew as frightful a picture of the present misery of the inhabitants as it did a flattering one of their future happiness, provided, when the British came to conquer their country, they offered no resistance. In short, as the principal strength of the island, after its forts were carried, consisted in its unembodied militia, the object was, by sapping their integrity, to render them comparatively powerless.

On the 10th of August, having left Captain Lambert, with the Iphigenia, off Port Louis, Captain Pym, with the Sirius, Néréide, and Staunch, arrived off Grand Port. On the same evening the boats of the two frigates, containing about 400 seamen, marines, and soldiers, under the command of Captain Willoughby, were taken in tow by the Staunch, who had on board the Néréide's black pilot, and proceeded to attack Isle de

[1] Called also Port Impérial.

la Passe. The night becoming very dark, and the weather extremely boisterous, so as to occasion several of the boats to run foul of each other and some to get stove, the pilot began to falter, and declared it was impossible to enter the channel under such disadvantageous circumstances. Captain Willoughby offered the man a thousand dollars, if he would persevere and carry the boats in; but the pilot persisted in his declaration of the impracticability of the undertaking, and the enterprise was given up. Daylight on the 11th discovered the boats scattered in all directions by the weather, but the frigates and gun-brig at length picked them up.

In order to lull the suspicions of the French as to any meditated attack upon Isle de la Passe, Captain Pym bore away with his small force round the south-west end of the island, and joined Captain Lambert of Port Louis. It was now arranged, to further the deception, that the two frigates should return off Isle de la Passe by different routes, the Sirius to beat up by the longest or eastern route, and the Néréide, accompanied by the Staunch, to proceed by the leeward or south-western route; and, as the Néréide sailed very badly, it was calculated that the two frigates would arrive off Grand Port nearly at the same time. Previously to the departure of the Sirius, two boats from the Iphigenia, under the command of Lieutenant Henry Ducie Chads, second of that ship, came on board to assist in the intended attack.

On the 13th, in the afternoon, the Sirius arrived off Isle de la Passe; but the Néréide and Staunch, having to beat up from the south-west end of the Isle of France, were still at a great distance to leeward. Fearing that the French might gain some intimation of his intention, and thus render the enterprise doubly hazardous, and perhaps impracticable, Captain Pym resolved to detach his own boats on the service; the more so, as the weather was unusually favourable, and as he had taken from the Néréide her black pilot. Accordingly, at 8 P.M., five boats, including the Iphigenia's two, containing between them 71 officers, seamen, and marines,[1] commanded by Lieutenant Norman, and assisted by Lieutenants Chads and Watling, and Lieutenants of marines James Cottell and William Bate, pushed off from the Sirius.

Of the nature of the fortifications upon Isle de la Passe we are not able to give so accurate a description as we could wish. The guns mounted upon the island consisted, we believe, of four

[1] We formerly said 110, but we are assured that the number in the text comprises all that embarked.

24, and nine 18-pounders, together with three 13-inch mortars and two howitzers. The landing-place was on the inner or north-west side of the island, and was defended by a chevaux-de-frise and the two howitzers. But, to get to this landing-place, it was necessary to pass a battery, on which most of the guns were mounted. The garrison on the island consisted, at this time, of two commissioned officers, and about 80 regular troops.

Fortunately for the British, just as the boats were approaching the principal battery, a black cloud obscured the moon, which had been shining very bright, and concealed them from view. Lieutenant Norman had previously directed Lieutenant Watling, who was in the launch of the Sirius, to lead, and cover the landing with her 18-pounder carronade. Lieutenant Norman, with the pinnace, kept close to the launch; and Lieutenant Chads, with the Iphigenia's cutter and the two remaining boats, was close astern of the launch and pinnace. Just as the boats, in this order, were approaching the landing-place, the enemy discovered them, and opened a fire, which killed two men and wounded three or four in the launch, and did nearly as much execution in the pinnace.

Dashing on, however, the boats gained the landing-place without further loss. Lieutenants Norman and Watling now attempted to scale the works, but failed in accomplishing their object. Lieutenant Norman was in the act of turning away to try another spot, when the sentinel over head shot him through the heart. The man was immediately shot by one of the launch's men, and the seamen, headed by Lieutenant Watling, quickly scaled the walls. A stout resistance followed; and it was not until the British had lost, in all, seven men killed and 18 wounded, that they succeeded in driving the French from the works. After rallying his men, Lieutenant Watling proceeded to attack the batteries on the south-east side, when he was met by Lieutenant Chads; who had landed at another point of the island, and, in the most gallant manner, had stormed and carried the works in that direction, without, as it appears, the loss of a man. The two lieutenants having united their forces, the French commandant offered no further opposition, but surrendered at discretion. This he did in such haste as to forget to destroy his signals, the whole of which fell into the hands of the conquerors.

We cannot understand how it happened, that the official account of this very dashing exploit did not find its way into the London Gazette. The following extract of a letter, from Commodore Rowley to Vice-admiral Bertie shows that the first-named officer forwarded Captain Pym's letter: "I had the honour to transmit to you, on the 31st of August, Captain Pym's report of a gallant and successful attack by his boats on the Isle de la Passe, and I beg to second his recommendation of Lieutenants Chads and Watling for their conduct on that occasion." As the names stand here, so was the seniority of these two lieutenants; and consequently, in our humble view, Lieutenant Chads took the command after the death of Lieutenant Norman. But here follows a paragraph in a document bearing the signature of Captain Pym: "I do further certify, that the conduct of the said Lieutenant Watling in the attack of l'Isle de Passe, under Lieutenant Norman of the Sirius, was truly gallant, and that after the latter was killed, by his (Lieutenant W.'s) side in the moment of victory, he took the command."

As far as respects the merits of these two young officers, the question is of no moment: each was equally gallant and equally successful; but still the responsibility, which in enterprises of this kind attaches to the commanding officer, confers upon him the paramount claim to reward. If Captain Pym in his official letter placed his lieutenant the first, the board of admiralty, knowing that Lieutenant Chads was nearly two years senior to Lieutenant Watling, may, on that sole account, have withheld the publication of Captain Pym's letter. Whatever was the cause, the non-appearance of the letter in the Gazette was truly unfortunate; as one of the two officers undoubtedly lost his promotion by it, and both were deprived of a strong public testimonial in their favour.

Considering it not unlikely that, from his long professional experience, the post captain, who is one of our contemporaries, would throw some light on the subject, we naturally turned to his pages. Our surprise may be judged, when we perused as follows: "Captain Pym, who had been stationed off the Isle of France, and particularly off Port Imperial, on the south-east or weather side of the island, conceived the possibility of more effectually preventing the ingress of the enemy's ships to the harbour, by occupying the Isle de la Passe, which completely commanded the narrows; he therefore stormed and carried it with the loss of 18 of his men killed and wounded."[1] Let us hasten to do Captain Pym the justice to declare our persuasion that he had no share in this misstatement, by reason that a very different version of the affair is given in the captain's biography,[2]

[1] Brenton, vol. iv., p. 465.   [2] Marshall, vol. ii., p. 717.

although, as in most of his other cases, Mr. Marshall appears to have had a direct communication with his officer.

On the 14th, in the morning, the Néréide and Staunch joined company; and on the 15th Captain Pym gave charge of Isle de la Passe to Captain Willoughby, and made sail to rejoin the Iphigenia off Port Louis. On the 16th, which appears to have been as soon as Captain Pym's order reached him, Captain Willoughby, having got back his pilot, entered the channel and anchored the Néréide and Staunch in a small bight of deep water just at the back of the island. He then placed, as a garrison upon Isle de la Passe, 50 of his grenadiers, with Captain Todd as the commandant, and immediately proceeded, in company with Lieutenant Davis of the Madras engineers, to reconnoitre the enemy's coast; where, like a second Lord Cochrane, Captain Willoughby soon began his bold and annoying attacks.

On the 17th, at 1 A.M., having embarked in the boats Lieutenants Morlett and Needhall, and 50 men of the 33rd and 69th regiments, Lieutenant Aldwinkle and 12 artillerymen from the Staunch, Lieutenant Davis of the Madras engineers, Lieutenants of marines Thomas Robert Pye and Thomas S. Cox and 50 of their corps, Lieutenant Henry Collins Deacon, and acting Lieutenant William Weiss, and 50 seamen, total 170 officers and men, Captain Willoughby proceeded to attack the fort on Pointe du Diable, commanding the small, or north-eastern passage into Grand Port. Before daylight the captain and his party landed at Canaille du Bois, and after a march of six miles reached the fort; which they immediately stormed and carried without the loss of a man, although, in defending their post, the French commanding officer and three men were killed, and three gunners taken prisoners.

Having, during a three hours' halt, spiked eight 24-pounders and two 13-inch mortars, burnt the carriages, blown up the magazine, and embarked a 13-inch brass mortar in a new prame well calculated for carrying troops or guns over flats, Captain Willoughby moved on to the old town of Grand Port, a distance of 12 miles, leaving in the houses and villages through which he and his men passed, the proclamations with which he had been intrusted. On the whole of their way along the coast, the party were attended by three boats, two belonging to the Néréide and one to the Staunch, fitted as gun-boats and commanded by Lieutenant Deacon; who so completely covered the road of march, that, except on one occasion, no enemy could show himself. On that occasion a strong party, under General Vandermaesen, the second in command on the island, attacked the British detachment, but were soon put to the rout with the loss of six men killed and wounded. Having, by sunset, succeeded in every object for which the landing had been undertaken, and gained from some of the most respectable inhabitants and well-wishers to the English the most satisfactory information, Captain Willoughby returned on board the Néréide.

On the 18th, in the morning, wishing to learn the effect of the proclamations delivered on the preceding day, Captain Willoughby again landed with the same force, taking the Staunch in with him, to support the detachment, and, if necessary, cover its retreat. Captain Willoughby pushed forward, and destroyed the signal-house, staff, &c., at Grande-Rivière, and perceived that the enemy had 700 or 800 men in or near the battery, but upon the opposite side of the river. He then returned to Pointe du Diable, and, after continuing there three hours, blowing up the remaining works, moved on to Canaille du Bois; whence the captain and his party embarked at sunset, leaving the Staunch at anchor near the spot. The gun-brig, however, soon afterwards weighed and proceeded to Port Louis.

During the whole of this march of nearly 22 miles in an enemy's territory, Captain Willoughby sustained no greater loss than Lieutenant Davis slightly, and one private of artillery badly wounded, and one sergeant of artillery missing, supposed to have deserted. This forbearance on the part of the islanders was in a great measure attributable, no doubt, to the orderly manner in which the British soldiers, marines, and seamen conducted themselves, and to the strict attention they paid to their commander's orders, to abstain from giving offence to the inhabitants by pilfering the slightest article of their property. Even the sugar and coffee, laid aside for exportation, and usually considered as legitimate objects of seizure, remained untouched; and the invaders, when they quitted the shore for their ship, left behind them a high character, not merely for gallantry, but for a rigid adherence to promises. The success of the enterprise, however, would have been very problematical, had not the commanding officer possessed qualities rarely found in one individual, an undaunted intrepidity blended with the utmost suavity of manners.

On the 19th and 20th Captain Willoughby again landed; and, as there were no more batteries in that quarter to attack and destroy, and no opposition was offered to him by either the regular troops in the vicinity, or by the inhabitants among whom, it may be said, he was sojourning, the trip on shore was considered in the light of a pleasant excursion, rather than a forced irruption into an enemy's territory; when, at about 10 A.M. on the last-named day, an event occurred which gave a complete change to the aspect of affairs, and placed the whole party, who had hitherto considered themselves so secure, in the utmost jeopardy.

This alarm was caused by the discovery of five ships, four of them large, away in the east-south-east or windward quarter, standing down under easy sail for the Isle de la Passe channel to Grand Port. Leaving his remaining boats to get up in the best manner they could, Captain Willoughby hastened away in his gig; and, after a hard pull of nearly five miles directly to windward, arrived, about noon, on board the Néréide. Considering that these ships, known to be French and suspected to be what they were, would, when united with the force in Port Louis, which the Iphigenia, on the 18th, had telegraphed as being ready for sea, be a decided overmatch for Captain Pym's three frigates, Captain Willoughby resolved to endeavour to entice the former into Grand Port. For this purpose a French ensign and pendant were immediately hoisted by the Néréide: and French colours almost as quickly appeared on the flagstaff at the island, with the signal, " L'ennemi croise au Coin de Mire." " The enemy is cruising off the Coin de Mire," a patch of rocks close off the northern extremity of the Isle of France. One of the French frigates then made the private signal, and was answered from Isle de la Passe. Upon which they severally announced themselves, by their numbers, as the Bellone, Minerve, Victor, and two prizes. The latter, as a reference to a few pages back will show, were the Windham and Ceylon.[1]

At 1 h. 30 m. P.M. the Victor, under her three topsails, led into the channel, and passing the sea-battery, arrived within pistol-shot of the Néréide, when the latter, at 1 h. 40 m. P.M., substituting the union jack for the French ensign, opened her fire with such effect, that the Victor hailed that she struck, and anchored on the Néréide's starboard and outer quarter. Captain Willoughby immediately sent Lieutenant John Burns and Lieutenant of marines Thomas Robert Pye, with a party of men, to take possession of the corvette. At 1 h. 45 m. P.M. the Minerve, followed by the Ceylon, both under their topsails, entered the channel, and were fired at ineffectually by the sea-battery of Isle de la Passe. While passing close to the Victor, after having ex-

[1] See p. 137.

changed broadsides with the Néréide, Captain Bouvet hailed Captain Morice, and ordered him to cut his cable, rehoist his colours, and follow. Although the Néréide's boat was then alongside of her, the Victor did as she had been ordered, and was quickly in the wake of the Ceylon steering towards Grand Port.

Unfortunately a very serious accident had happened at the island fort. While one of the men was in the act of hauling quickly down the French colours, in order to substitute the English, and begin firing at the enemy, the cotton texture of the former became ignited by a match lying near the flagstaff, and instantly caused the explosion of more than 100 cartridges; whereby three men were killed, and 12 severely burnt. Five of the sea-battery guns were also dismounted at the first fire; as was one of the four (two on open platforms), which protected the Néréide's anchorage. One of these, likewise, in the act of firing at the Minerve, mortally wounded a quartermaster in the boat of Lieutenant Burns, while on his way back from the unsuccessful attempt to secure the Victor.

The situation of the Néréide was now, as may be supposed, a very critical one; but the situation of her boats, with a great proportion of her crew on board, besides a party of soldiers and artillerymen, was still more critical. These were now pulling up the narrow channel, down which the Minerve and Ceylon were sailing, and their capture appeared inevitable. At this moment it was observed that the Bellone, instead of following the other ships through the channel, had hauled off on the larboard tack, as if intending, in company with the Windham, to seek another port. Although in a 12-pounder frigate, with a great part of her crew absent, Captain Willoughby thought himself a match for the Minerve, Victor, and prize Indiaman, especially if he took on board the troops from the island. At 2 h. 30 m. P.M., just as the soldiers were about to remove into the Néréide, and the latter had loosed her sails, and was preparing to slip, the Bellone, having left the Windham steering under a crowd of sail to the westward, bore up for the passage.

The plan of attacking the Minerve was now of course abandoned, and the Néréide began preparing to receive the Bellone. Just at this moment, to the surprise of all on board the Néréide, the boats were seen approaching, after having been passed, successively, by the Minerve, Ceylon, and Victor. It appears that the boats were so near to the Minerve, as to be obliged to lay in their oars, and that the French officers and men were assembled on the gangway, looking down upon them: nay, one boat actually struck against the frigate. But not a word was spoken by the frigate to the boats; nor, as may be supposed, by the boats to the frigate: an enigma in the former case, not to be explained, especially when it is considered how promptly and collectedly Captain Bouvet had just before hailed the Victor, and desired her to follow him. Had he given the same orders to the boats, they must have obeyed; otherwise, with the velocity with which they were sailing, the Ceylon and Victor could with ease have run them down. He did not do so; and the boats, and the 160 or 170 officers and men they contained, reached the Néréide in safety.

At about 2 h. 40 m. P.M. the Bellone let fall her topgallantsails; and, having exchanged a fire with the battery, hauled up a little for the Néréide, apparently to run her on board, but, as we conjecture, to be well to windward, in her passage down the channel, of a projecting part of the shoal. At all events the soldiers in the Néréide were drawn up in readiness upon her starboard gangway and forecastle, to repel any such attempt to board. But none was made; for Commodore Duperré, just as he was advancing upon the Néréide's starboard bow, kept more away. At 2 h. 45 m., when so close to each other that their yards almost touched, the Bellone and Néréide exchanged broadsides. By this fire the Néréide had her driver-boom shot away close to the jaws, her fore and mizen topgallant yards and main spring-stay shot away, some of her rigging cut, and her foremast badly wounded below the cat-harpins; but her loss amounted to no more than two seamen killed and one marine wounded. This slight damage and loss was attributed to the circumstance of a sudden gust of wind laying the French frigate over, just as she was in the act of firing. What damage or loss, if any, the Bellone, or either of the other French ships, sustained has not been recorded.

At 4 P.M. Captain Willoughby sent Lieutenant Deacon in the launch to Captain Pym, with a note, announcing the arrival of the French frigates, and offering, with one frigate besides the Néréide, to lead in and attack them. At 4 h. 30 m. P.M. the cutter, with Lieutenant Weiss, was sent upon the same errand, but at sunset returned, not having been able to pull ahead on account of the fresh breeze and rough sea. It may naturally be asked, why the Néréide, considering how exposed she lay to an attack by two heavy French frigates and other vessels, did not get under way herself and proceed to join the Sirius. The truth is, we believe, that Captain Willoughby, as he had been ordered to protect the newly-acquired post of Isle de la Passe, was resolved to do so as long as he was able.

The anchorage taken up by the French frigates being rather nearer than was safe or agreeable, Captain Willoughby ordered the artillery officer on the island to try the range of his mortars. This was done, and the first shell burst over the ships. Before many others could be thrown, Commodore Duperré either cut or slipped, and re-anchored at a greater distance off; but still in a situation to watch the motions of the Néréide, and make an attack upon her if deemed advisable.

At 9 A.M. on the 21st, to prove to Captain Duperré that the Victor had struck her colours, to impress upon him an idea of the confidence with which the Néréide maintained her position, and to reconnoitre and obtain a correct knowledge of that taken up by the French frigates, Captain Willoughby sent Lieutenant Burns, and Lieutenant of marines Pye, under a flag of truce, with a letter to the commodore, demanding the restoration of the Victor. Commodore Duperré replied that, before he could return an answer, he must send to the governor at Port Louis on the opposite side of the island, a distance of nearly 25 miles; and he desired Lieutenant Burns to come again at the same hour the next morning.

In full expectation that an attack would be made upon him by the squadron at anchor in Grand Port, Captain Willoughby and those under his orders used every means to strengthen their position and prevent surprise. There was no room on Isle de la Passe for any more guns; but a breastwork was thrown up, to prevent the approach of boats. The Néréide herself was fully prepared to effect quite as much as could be expected from her; and at night boats rowed guard between the frigate and the enemy. The only time, indeed, when any attack could be made, was with the land wind in the morning, just at the first peep of twilight. All eyes on board the Néréide, and at the island, were then directed to the north-west, and were only relieved when broad day burst forth, and the sea breeze was heard murmuring in the south-east.

At 9 A.M. on the 21st, the boat with the flag of truce again left the Néréide, and returned soon afterwards with such an answer as might have been expected: both the governor and the commodore were surprised at "so extraordinary a demand." Neither this demand, nor the circumstance which led to it, are touched upon in Captain Duperré's letter. He perhaps was ashamed to acknowledge, that the Victor had hauled down her colours; and yet of the fact there cannot be a doubt. We gather from the French commodore's letter, that, when he saw the British colours hoisted at Isle de la Passe, and a fire opened upon the corvette, he considered that the whole windward side of the Isle of France was in the possession of the English, and, hauling off, made a signal to do the same to the Minerve and Ceylon; but they had already entered the channel and could not put back. M. Duperré then resolved to force the passage, and ordered the Windham to follow the Bellone; but her prize-master either misunderstood the signal, or considered the risk too great, and bore away for Rivière-Noire. We will now detail occurrences there, in order to lead progressively to the important operations of which we shall soon have to give an account.

Early on the morning of the 21st, just as the Windham was about to enter Rivière-Noire, the Sirius, then cruising to the south-west of Port Louis, gained sight of her. Chase was instantly given: but the wind being off the land, the Sirius had no chance of cutting off the Indiaman from the formidable batteries at the mouth of the river. Not considering the vessel, in the twilight of the morning, to be of the force she really was, Lieutenant Watling volunteered to overtake and board her with the gig. He instantly pushed off with five seamen, and was followed by the jolly-boat with midshipman John Andrews and four men; but, owing to some strange mismanagement, not a weapon or fire-arm of any description was put into either boat.

Daybreak discovered a ship of 800 or 900 tons, armed apparently with from 30 to 34 guns, at the distance of at least three miles from the Sirius, and very near to the batteries of Rivière-Noire. Under these circumstances, Lieutenant Watling thought it best to wait for the jolly-boat. In the mean time the Sirius fired a broadside at the ship, but at so ineffectual a distance, that the shot nearly sank the gig. On the arrival of the jolly-boat, young Andrews and his four hands entered cheerfully into Lieutenant Watling's views, and the two boats hastened forward. The calm state of the weather soon enabled them to reach the ship; and the two officers and their brave little band, armed with the boats' stretchers only, fought their way up her side. Thus was the Windham, mounting 26 guns and manned by a lieutenant de vaisseau and at least 30 French sailors, captured by 11 unarmed British seamen, without the slightest loss; and that, too, within gun-shot of several formidable batteries.

As these batteries now began to fire at the ship, Lieutenant Watling was still in a very critical situation. At length, after having sustained the fire for 20 minutes, and had the Windham's standing and running rigging greatly cut, some of her masts and yards injured, and one Frenchman and two or three Lascars wounded, Lieutenant Watling brought off his valuable prize in safety. Of this very gallant exploit, we can find no official account, beyond a passage in a letter to the admiralty, from commissioner Shield at the Cape, stating that the Windham had been recaptured by the Sirius.

Captain Pym despatched the Windham to Commodore Rowley at St. Paul's bay; and, in consequence of the intelligence communicated by the prisoners and others on board of her, he sent the Magicienne, which had just joined, to bring the Iphigenia and Staunch to Isle de la Passe: whither the Sirius herself made all sail round the south side of the island. Captain Pym proceeded by this route to prevent suspicion; but it appears that General Decaen at Port Louis did suspect what was going on, and sent an express across to Grand Port. This it was that, in the course of the afternoon of the 21st, occasioned Commodore Duperré to remove his ships to a position close off the town of Grand Port. There he moored them, with springs on their cables, in the form of a crescent; stationing his van-ship, the Minerve, just behind a patch of coral, next to her the Ceylon, then the Bellone, and lastly the Victor, with her stern close to the reef that skirts the harbour.

The Sirius picked up the Néréide's boat with Lieutenant Deacon on board; and on the 22nd, at 11 h. 10 m. A.M., arrived off the island and exchanged numbers with the Néréide, still at anchor within it; and who immediately hoisted the signals: "Ready for action;" "Enemy of inferior force." Having, from the situation of the French squadron, decided on an immediate attack, Captain Pym made the signal for the master of the Néréide. Mr. Robert Lesby accordingly went on board the Sirius, to conduct her, as he supposed, to the anchorage at the back of the island. The Sirius now made all sail, with the usual east-south-east or trade wind, and bore up for the passage; and at 2 h. 40 m. P.M., agreeably to a signal to that effect from the Sirius, the Néréide got under way, and, under her staysails only, stood after her consort down the channel to Grand Port. At 4 P.M., having still the Néréide's master on board, but not her black pilot, who was the only person that knew the harbour, the Sirius unfortunately grounded upon a point of the shoal on the larboard side of the channel; and, having run down with her squaresails set, and consequently with a great deal of way upon her, the ship was forced a considerable distance on the bank. The Néréide immediately brought up, and Captain Willoughby went on board the Sirius, to assist in getting her afloat. Notwithstanding every exertion, this could not be effected until 8 h. 30 m. A.M. on the 23rd; after which the Sirius dropped anchor near the Néréide.

At 10 A.M. the Iphigenia and Magicienne were seen beating up for Isle de la Passe; and Captain Willoughby immediately sent his master, who had returned from the Sirius, to conduct them to the anchorage. At 2 h. 10 m. P.M. the two frigates anchored in company with the Néréide and Sirius. Although it was not until 4 P.M. that the decks of the latter could be cleared of the hawsers and ropes which had been used in heaving the ship off the bank, at 4 h. 40 m. P.M., by signal from the Sirius, the four frigates got under way; and, preceded by the Néréide with her black pilot on board, stood down the channel to Grand Port. The order of attack, as previously arranged, was for the Néréide to anchor between the Victor, the rearmost ship, and the Bellone, the Sirius, having 18-pounders, abreast of the Bellone, the Magicienne between the Ceylon and Minerve, and the Iphigenia, having also 18-pounders, upon the broadside of the latter ship.

The Néréide, still with staysails only, cleared the tortuous channel, and stood along the edge of the reef that skirts the harbour directly for the rearmost French ship. The Sirius, about a quarter of an hour or 20 minutes after she had weighed, keeping this time too much on the starboard hand, touched the ground. Very shoal water appearing ahead, the best bower anchor was let go; but the velocity of the ship was so great, as to run the cable out in spite of stoppers and every other effort to check her way. The small bower was then let go, but to no purpose, the ship continued to tear both cables out with great rapidity, and unfortunately, the helm having been put a-port, the ship struck on a coral rock, which, a minute or two before, must have been on her starboard bow. Just as the Sirius had taken the ground, the French ships began firing, and their shot passed over the Néréide.

With the Sirius as a beacon, the Magicienne and Iphigenia successively cleared the channel; but at 5 h. 15 m. P.M., while steering for her station, and of course wide of the track in which the Néréide with the only pilot in the squadron was steering, the Magicienne grounded on a bank, in such a position that only three of her foremost guns on each deck could bear upon the enemy; from whom she was then distant about 400 yards. Seeing what had befallen the Magicienne, the Iphigenia, who was close in her rear, dropped her stream-anchor, and came to by the stern in six fathoms; she then let go the best bower under foot, thereby bringing her starboard broadside to bear upon the Minerve; into whom, at a pistol-shot distance, the Iphigenia immediately poured a heavy and destructive fire. By this time the Néréide was also in hot action, and to her we must now attend.

Just as, regardless of the raking fire opened upon the Néréide in her approach, he was about to take up his allotted position on the bow of the Victor, Captain Willoughby saw what had befallen the Sirius; and, with characteristic gallantry, steered for, and in his 12-pounder frigate anchored upon, the beam of the Bellone, at the distance of less than 200 yards. Between these two ill-matched ships, at about 5 h. 15 m. P.M., a furious cannonade commenced, the Victor, from her slanting position on the Néréide's quarter, being also enabled to take an occasional part in it. At 6 h. 15 m. P.M., after having received an occasional fire from the bow-guns of the Magicienne and the quarter-guns of the Iphigenia, the Ceylon hauled down her colours; and Captain Lambert and one of his lieutenants immediately hailed the Magicienne, to send a boat to take possession. At that instant the Ceylon was seen with her topsails set, running on shore. At 6 h. 30 m. the Minerve, having had her cable shot away, made sail after the Ceylon. Both these ships grounded near the Bellone; but the Ceylon first ran foul of the latter, and compelled her to cut her cable and run also aground. The Bellone, however, lay in such a position, that her broadside still bore on the Néréide. Captain Lambert would have instantly cut his cable and run down in pursuit of the Minerve, had not a shoal intervened directly between the Iphigenia and the French squadron.

At a few minutes before 7 P.M. the Néréide's spring was shot away, and the ship immediately swang stern-on to the Bellone's broadside. A most severe raking fire followed. To avoid this, and bring her starboard broadside to bear, the Néréide cut her small bower cable, and, letting go the best, succeeded so far in her object. At about 10 P.M., or a little afterwards, a piece of grape or langridge from one of the Néréide's guns cut Captain Duperré on the head, and knocked him senseless upon the deck. As the fire of the Minerve was now completely masked by that of the Bellone, Captain Bouvet removed from the former on board the latter and took the command.

Since the early part of the action, Captain Willoughby had been severely wounded by a splinter on the left cheek, which had also torn his eye completely out of the socket. The first-lieutenant lay mortally, and the second most dangerously wounded: one marine officer, and the two officers of foot and one of artillery, and the greater part of the remaining crew and soldiers were either killed or disabled. Most of the quarter-deck, and several of the main-deck, guns were dismounted; and the hull of the ship was shattered in all directions and striking the ground astern. His ship being in this state, and five hours having elapsed since the commencement of the action without the arrival of a single boat from any one of the squadron, Captain Willoughby ordered the now feebly maintained fire of the Néréide to cease, and the few survivors of the crew to shelter themselves in the lower part of the vessel. He then sent acting Lieutenant William Weiss, with one of the two remaining boats, on board the Sirius, to acquaint Captain Pym with the defence-less state of the ship; leaving it to his judgment, as the senior officer, whether or not it was practicable to tow the Néréide beyond the reach of the enemy's shot, or to take out the wounded and set her on fire: an act that would have greatly endangered, and might have been the means of destroying, the Bellone herself, as well as the whole cluster of grounded ships, the situation of which cannot be better expressed than in the words of Captain Pym himself, "the whole of the enemy on shore in a heap."

At about 10 h. 45 m. P.M. a boat from the Sirius, with a lieutenant of that frigate, also Lieutenant Davis of the engineers and Mr. Weiss, who had left his boat behind, came on board the Néréide, with a kind message from Captain Pym, requesting Captain Willoughby to abandon his ship and come on board the Sirius. But, with a feeling that did him honour, Captain Willoughby refused to desert his few surviving officers and men, and sent back word that the Néréide had struck. Shortly afterwards a boat from the Iphigenia came on board, to know the reason that the Néréide had ceased firing. At 11 P.M. Captain Willoughby sent an officer in a boat to the Bellone, who still continued a very destructive fire, to say that the Néréide had struck; but, being in a sinking state from shot-holes, the boat returned without having reached the French ship. At about 30 minutes past midnight the mainmast of the Néréide went by the board. At 1 h. 30 m. A.M. on the 24th several of the Néréide's ropes caught fire, but the flames were quickly extinguished. At about 1 h. 50 m. A.M., after having been repeatedly hailed without effect by one or the other of the 20 French prisoners who were on board the Néréide, the Bellone discontinued her fire. The Iphigenia and Magicienne, a portion of whose fire had already dismounted the guns at the battery de la Reine, then ceased theirs; and all was silent.

At daylight the Bellone re-opened her fire upon the Néréide. To put a stop to this, French colours were lashed to the fore rigging; but still the French frigate continued her fire. It was now surmised, and very naturally too, that the cause of this persevering hostility was the union jack at the mizentopgallant-mast-head. That could not be hauled down; for, by one account, it had been nailed there, and, by another, which we hope is the more correct, the halliards had been shot away, as well as all the rigging and ropes by which the mast could be ascended. As the only alternative, the mizenmast was cut away, and the firing of the Bellone instantly ceased.

Captain Pym, speaking in his official letter of the loss on board the Néréide says: "Sorry am I to say, that the captain, every officer and man on board are killed or wounded." This information probably reached the Sirius by some of the men, about 15 in all, who took the opportunity, first of the Néréide's boat, and then of the boat of the Sirius, to escape the horrors of a French prison: they naturally would make the case appear as bad as possible to excuse, what might be considered, a desertion of their commander and comrades. But, even then, the expression is to be taken figuratively; being meant to except all who, from the duties of their station, and in a frigate they are no small number, were attending below. In the statement we formerly gave, as gleaned from the ship's muster-book, that the killed amounted to 35, we were decidedly wrong, and shall now proceed to show, upon such authorities as have since come to hand, that the killed amounted to nearly three times that amount.

The Néréide's established complement, deducting her three widow's men, was 251 men and boys: of this number, on quitting the Cape in the preceding April, she was 23 men short. In skirmishes with her boats, the ship had lost, in killed and invalided out of her, 10 men; and had away in a schooner tender a master's mate and 15 men. This left her with 202 officers, men, and boys of her proper crew. But the Néréide had since received, as her quota of prisoners obtained at Port Louis' in exchange for those she captured at Jacolet, 10 raw recruits going to India, and had also on board 69 officers and men of the 33rd and 69th regiments and Madras artillery; making a total of 281 in crew and supernumeraries on board the Néréide when she commenced her action with the Bellone.

Of those 281 men and boys, the Néréide had her first-lieutenant (John Burns), Lieutenants Morlett of the 33rd regiment, and Aldwinkle of the Madras artillery, one midshipman (George Timmins), and about 88 seamen, marines, and soldiers killed; her captain, second-lieutenant (Henry Collins Deacon), one lieutenant of marines (Thomas S. Cox), her master (William Lesby), Lieutenant Needhall of the 69th regiment, her boatswain (John Strong), one midshipman (Samuel Costerton), and at least 130 seamen, marines, and soldiers wounded; total, in killed and wounded together, about 230 out of 281. Nor will 130 be considered a large proportion of wounded to 92 killed, when it is known that, in consequence of the Néréide's upperworks being lined with fir, the splinters were uncommonly numerous. Captain Willoughby received his dreadful wound from a splinter, and Lieutenant Deacon was wounded by splinters in the throat, breast, legs, and arms.

The loss on board the only two remaining British ships that suffered any was of comparatively slight amount. The Iphigenia, out of a crew on board of about 255 men and boys, had five seamen killed, and her first-lieutenant (Robert Tom Blackler) and 12 seamen and marines wounded. The Magicienne, out of a complement the same as that established upon the Néréide, had eight seamen and marines killed and 20 wounded. A portion of the Magicienne's loss, as here enumerated, was, we believe, sustained on the 23rd. The Sirius, having, as it would appear, grounded out of range of shot, did not have a man of her crew hurt, nor, we believe, a rope of her rigging cut. We speak doubtfully of the situation of this frigate, owing to the statement in Captain Pym's letter in the Gazette, that the Sirius lay "within shot of all the enemy's forts and ships," and was only able to "return their fire with two guns." With an excellent French chart of the harbour before us, we find the situation of the Sirius, as marked out by one of her officers, to have been at least a mile and a quarter from the French van-ship; and, it will be recollected, the Minerve cut or slipped almost at the commencement of the action. With respect to the "forts," we know of none except the battery de la Reine, mounting three or four guns, and situated a little to the eastward of the town. We believe, however, that some works were afterwards thrown up, and a few guns mounted, to annoy the grounded British ships.

The loss on board the French ships, according to the official statement of Commodore Duperré, amounted to 37 killed, including two lieutenants of the Bellone and one of the Victor, and 112 wounded. Nearly the whole of this loss, we believe, was sustained by the Bellone; but we cannot help thinking it is underrated, chiefly because M. Duperré mentions the necessity he was under of receiving on board the Bellone fresh supplies of men from the Minerve, during the latter ship's state of inaction already adverted to. With the detachment acknowledged to have been received from the Manche and Entreprenant at Port Louis, the complement of the Bellone could scarcely have been fewer than 400 or 420 men, and none were wanted to attend to the sails. However, the admitted loss, considering that it must nearly all have been inflicted by the Néréide, was highly creditable to the skill and exertions of that ship's officers and crew.

At a few minutes past 4 A.M. Captain Lambert, having previously sent a boat to the Sirius for orders, was directed by Captain Pym, who had then considerable hopes of getting the Sirius afloat, to warp out of gun-shot. The Iphigenia immediately commenced warping by the stern with the stream and kedge anchors, and sent the end of her best bower cable on board the Magicienne, for her to endeavour to heave off by; thereby leaving herself with only one bower anchor and cable. At daylight, when the Bellone, as already mentioned, recommenced firing at the Néréide, the Magicienne renewed her fire at the French shipping and the shore; but the Iphigenia, being then in the act of warping, could not bring a gun to bear: indeed the Iphigenia, since soon after midnight, had been obliged to send to the Sirius for a supply of 18-pound shot.

Having before 7 A.M. warped the Iphigenia to the eastward of the shoal, which had on the preceding evening prevented him from closing with the Minerve after the latter had drifted from her station, Captain Lambert was extremely desirous to run down and endeavour to carry by boarding the Bellone and the other grounded French ships. Lieutenant Chads, with a message to this effect, and a proposal to take on board a portion of the crews of the Sirius and Magicienne, went immediately to Captain Pym; who returned for answer, that Captain Lambert must continue warping out, as he and his officers had still hopes of getting the Sirius afloat. The French shot continuing to hull the Iphigenia, Captain Lambert sent Lieutenant Edward Grimes to Captain Pym, to say that he should be obliged to recommence the action in his own defence. Shortly afterwards Lieutenant Watling came from the Sirius, with a note from Captain Pym, ordering Captain Lambert to warp out. The Iphigenia accordingly resumed her labours; and, as soon as she had hauled a little further off, the French directed the whole of their fire at the Magicienne. By 10 A.M. the Iphigenia had warped herself close to the Sirius; and these two frigates commenced a fire upon the French, who were endeavouring to remount the guns at the battery on shore.

Either because he was not willing to risk his boats while the British frigates still kept up their fire, or that his whole attention was taken up in preparations to resist an attack of the nature of that contemplated by the Iphigenia's gallant captain, the French commodore did not send to take possession of the Néréide until nearly 3 P.M. Lieutenant Albert-René Roussin went on board the Néréide for that purpose; and, having caused all the guns to be spiked, took with him the 20 Frenchmen who had been prisoners, and returned to the shore with every man of his party. This officer reported, that he found 100 dead or dying upon the Néréide's decks. "M. le Lieutenant de vaisseau Roussin," says Captain Duperré, "fut envoyé amariner la Néréide. Il la trouva dans un état impossible à décrire; 100 morts ou mourans étaient sur les ponts: son capitaine, M. Willoughby, était blessé." We must suppose that, in the course of the 17 hours which had elapsed since the discontinuance of the action by the Néréide, a portion of her killed had been thrown overboard. This account of M. Roussin, therefore, tends greatly to confirm the statement we have given of the Néréide's almost unexampled loss of men.

It being found utterly impracticable to get off the Magicienne, who lay with between eight and nine feet water in the hold, exposed to a heavy fire from the enemy, without the means of returning it except in a very partial manner, her officers and crew were ordered to remove into the Iphigenia, preparatory to her being set on fire. The Iphigenia, meanwhile, owing to the strength of the breeze, had been unable to get beyond the stern of the Sirius; where she accordingly brought up with her small bower in eight fathoms. The Iphigenia had previously lost her stream and kedge anchors; but she had since hauled on board the stream and bower anchors of the Sirius. At 7 h. 30 m. P.M. the Magicienne was set on fire by Captain Curtis and Lieutenant Robert Smith; and at 11 P.M. blew up with her colours flying.

On the 25th, at 4 A.M., the Iphigenia again began warping; and the French ships and a newly-erected battery on shore recommenced firing at her and the Sirius, which the latter returned with her forecastle guns. At 7 h. 30 m. a light air from the land enabled the Iphigenia to run completely out of gun-shot both of the ships and the shore. Every effort of her officers and crew to get the Sirius afloat proving utterly vain, Captain Pym came to the determination of destroying her. A great quantity of stores, including shot and cartridges, was now removed from the Sirius to the Iphigenia. At this moment a French man-of-war brig, of which we shall presently give some account, was observed in the offing, watching the motions of the two British frigates. At 9 A.M. the Sirius was set on fire, and her officers and men went on board the Iphigenia. Shortly afterwards, however, perceiving that the ship did not burn quickly, and that some French boats were stirring about the harbour, as if with the intention of boarding the Sirius and striking her colours, Captain Pym proceeded in the boats to dispute that point with them. Upon this, the French boats put back. Almost at the same moment the Sirius burst into flames, and at 11 A.M. blew up. The setting fire to this ship, while the sea-breeze was blowing fresh, caused great alarm to the French commodore; who sent again on board the Néréide, and made the unwounded prisoners on board wet her decks, to prevent any ill effects from the explosion. A similar precaution was used on board the Bellone and her two companions. By the direction of the French officer, who had come last on board the Néréide, her remaining dead were this day buried, and they amounted to 75; a tolerable proof that the account given in a preceding page of that ship's loss has not been overstated.

The Iphigenia continued during the afternoon to warp out; but, owing to the foulness of the ground and the consequent loss of one of her bower anchors, the frigate made very little progress. At 8 P.M. Lieutenant Watling, bearing Captain Pym's despatches to the commander-in-chief, departed in the pinnace with nine hands. The Entreprenant, the French brig, cruising off Isle de la Passe, chased the boat; but, by pulling in-shore among the breakers, Lieutenant Watling adroitly escaped from her, and arrived at St. Denis, Isle Bourbon, at 2 A.M. on the 27th. Meanwhile the Iphigenia continued her exertions to reach the anchorage under Isle de la Passe; which post Captain Pym, on giving up the command after the loss of his ship, had recommended Captain Lambert to support and protect.

On the 26th, at 4 A.M., the officers of the Iphigenia found that their ship had driven considerably during the night; also that the stock of the bower anchor was badly broken. The frigate now recommenced warping, but having fouled her stream-cable, was obliged to get out an 18-pounder to heave ahead by to clear it. At noon the Bellone was observed to have hove herself afloat. At sunset Captain Lambert despatched Lieutenant Robert Wauchope, with the barge of the late Magicienne, to endeavour to reach Bourbon; and at 8 h. 30 m. P.M. the Iphigenia came to with the bower and stream anchors, in 13 fathoms, at the distance of about three-quarters of a mile from Isle de la Passe.

On the 27th, at 8 A.M., while again warping and still making very slow progress, the Iphigenia discovered three strange frigates working up to Isle de la Passe. At noon the Entreprenant exchanged signals with them; and all the ships in Grand Port were seen to be afloat, the Bellone on the outside of them. The Iphigenia now cleared for action, and sent to the island as many men as left her with a crew of between 400 and 500, so as to be able to fight both sides of the ship at once. Unfortunately, however, there was not ammunition enough on board to maintain an action of any continuance with one side only, the ship having, in all, only 35 broadsides of 18-pound shot, and about 15 of grape and canister, for the main-deckers, and 30 broadsides of 32-pound shot, and about 20 of grape and canister, for the carronades. We will now endeavour to show how it happened that this second squadron of French frigates came thus to put an end to all hopes on the part of the Iphigenia.

This French squadron, consisting, besides the Entreprenant, of the three frigates Vénus, Astrée, and Manche, had sailed from Port Louis at midnight on the 21st, and was under the command of Commodore Hamelin, the senior French naval officer on the station. The sudden departure of these frigates was for the express purpose of relieving those in Grand Port, under M. Duperré. On the 23rd M. Hamelin, on his rout by the northern extremity of the island, fell in with and captured the English transport-ship Ranger, 24 days from the Cape, laden with nearly 300 tons of provisions for Commodore Rowley's squadron, and having on board a frigate's three topmasts, three topsail yards, and one lower yard; and consequently a prize of no inconsiderable value in this quarter of the world. An officer and 12 men were put on board, and the Ranger was despatched to Port Louis. Finding himself continually thwarted by head winds, M. Hamelin changed his route, and steered to pass to windward of the island. On the 25th, just as the three frigates had arrived abreast of Port Louis, the commodore received, by an aviso, intelligence of the successful issue of affairs at Grand Port, with orders to possess himself of the Iphigenia, as well as of the island that protected her.

On the 27th, at 1 P.M., the Vénus, Astrée, and Manche arrived and lay to off Isle de la Passe; and at 5 P.M. Commodore Hamelin summoned Captain Lambert to surrender at discretion both his frigate and the island. Captain Lambert refused to do this, but offered to surrender the island in its present state, provided the Iphigenia was allowed with the officers and men on board of her, and upon the island, to retire to any British port that should be pointed out. At sunset the Iphigenia got close to Isle de la Passe, but not in a good birth. As soon as it was dark Captain Lambert sent the launch to Bourbon under the command of Mr. John Jenkins, the late master of the Sirius.

On the 28th, at daylight, it was found that, owing to her insufficient tackle, the Iphigenia had drifted out into the middle of the passage. At 7 h. 30 m. A.M. a second flag of truce came from the frigates outside. By this the French commodore urged his previous demand, and promised that the officers and men in the frigate and on the island should be allowed their parole. At the moment that the flag of truce arrived from Commodore Hamelin, another was seen pulling from the harbour of Grand Port. At 9 A.M. this came on board, and proved to be a summons from Governor Decaen. To Commodore Hamelin, Captain Lambert replied, offering to surrender the Iphigenia and Isle de la Passe on the next day at 10 A.M., provided the French government would furnish, within a month, a conveyance for the crew of the frigate and the garrison of the island to the Cape of Good Hope or any other British possession. To the governor-general, Captain Lambert sent copies of his correspondence with Commodore Hamelin, and expressed a hope that his excellency would require no alteration in the terms proposed.

At 1 p.m. came a second letter from the governor-general. In this M. Decaen pledged the faith of his government that, within a month, he would send the crew of the Iphigenia, and the garrison of the little island under which she lay, either to the Cape of Good Hope or to England, on condition of not serving till regularly exchanged. A threat, we believe, accompanied this summons, to the effect that, if Captain Lambert did not accede to the terms proposed by General Decaen, the French frigates both without and within the harbour, would commence an attack upon the Iphigenia and Isle de la Passe; and, on carrying them, of which there could be no doubt, would put the crew and garrison to the sword. In this extremity, with only 16 tons of water to support upwards of 800 officers and men, including nearly 50 wounded and sick: surrounded by a force amounting, were she in the best state of equipment, to a fivefold superiority; and yet having scarcely ammunition enough left to maintain an action of half an hour with even an equal force, the Iphigenia had no alternative but to haul down her colours.

Thus, in a single enterprise, four frigates, two of them (Sirius and Iphigenia), very fine ones, were lost to the British navy; coupled, too, with a loss of life unusually and lamentably severe. Had the British ships, from previous acquaintance with the difficult navigation of the place, been enabled to take the stations severally assigned them, the enterprise, we have not a doubt, would have been crowned with success, and a very serious blow been inflicted upon the French naval power in these seas. While on this subject we must be allowed to express our opinion, little weight as it may have, that too much precipitation was used; that, had the attack, instead of taking place an hour or two before dark while the breeze was blowing fresh, been postponed till early next morning, when the water was smooth and the shoals easily distinguishable, the British commanding officer would have written his letter under very different feelings from those which must have possessed him, when writing the account of a defeat so complete, so calamitous, and so uncalled for, as that we have just detailed.

Commodore Duperré, as may indeed be expected, wrote a very triumphant letter on the occasion. After stating that, in consequence of the Minerve and Ceylon having had their cables cut and been forced on shore, the Bellone singly stood opposed to the enemy, he says: "This unexpected event gave him every advantage. Three of his frigates presented their broadsides to us; one only had touched forward and was unable to bring all her guns to bear." "Cet évènement inattendu lui promettait tous les avantages. Trois ses frégates nous présentaient le travers; une seule avait touché par l'avant et ne pouvait jouer de toute sa batterie." If ever Rear-admiral le Baron Duperré, as he now is, should honour these pages with a perusal, he will, we are sure, regret that he was induced to write so unfair an account of the victory which the shoals and rocks of Grand Port, rather than the prowess of French seamen, or the cannon of French ships, gained for him. A modern French writer, whose works bear a deservedly high character in this country as well as in his own, has travelled a little out of his road to commit a sad, and, we may be permitted to add, not a very liberal mistake, in reference to the action at Grand Port. He says: "The number of killed and wounded is greater on the part of the French, but the attribute of perseverance less on the part of the enemy." " Le nombre des morts et des blessés est plus grande du côté des Français; mais la constance est moins grande du côté des ennemis."[1] We wish M. Dupin, before he penned this passage, had had a few minutes' conversation with Rear-admiral Duperré. On that point, at all events, the baron would have done justice to a British officer, for whom, we are sure, he has the highest respect.

Unfortunately we are not permitted to dismiss this case, without an observation or two upon the English accounts of it. With respect to the official account, even did it contain more inaccuracies than it does, every allowance ought to be made for the peculiar circumstances under which Captain Pym wrote his letter. Few cases, it must be owned, have come forth officially in a more imperfect state; and yet no case, of which we are aware, more deeply affects the character of the British navy, than the defeat it sustained at Grand Port. Supposing that an historian, possessed of the *esprit de corps* for an additional stimulus, would make it a point of his ambition to elucidate a case, of which, to do justice to the parties, so much remained to be told, we turned to the pages of Captain Brenton. The following are among the one or two paragraphs that are new to us: "Captain Willoughby made the signal that he was ready for action, and that the enemy was inferior in force to the two British frigates, and the master of the Néréide assuring Captain Pym that he could lay him alongside the Bellone, an attack was immediately decided on." "No part of her (the Néréide) was

[1] Voyages dans la Grand Bretagne, par M. Charles Dupin, Force Navale, tome ii., p. 85.

sheltered; the shot of the enemy penetrated to the hold, and the bread-room, where a young midshipman was killed, as he lay bleeding from a previous wound. Captain Willoughby, having lost an eye and being otherwise severely hurt, was removed from the bread-room to the fore part of the hold, as less exposed to shot.[1]

The signal, "Ready for action," was made to counteract the effect of an indication to the contrary, by the appearance of a stage up the Néréide's foremast. The reason for hoisting the other signal, we cannot so readily explain; but that Captain Pym had previously made up his mind to attack the French squadron in Grand Port, is clear from the commencing words of his letter to Commodore Rowley: "By my last you were informed of my intention to attack the frigates, corvette, and Indiamen in this port." He says further, "At noon the Néréide made signal, 'Ready for action:' I then closed, and, from the situation of the enemy, decided on an immediate attack." How Mr. Lesby could undertake to act as "pilot" in a harbour which, according to our information, he never entered, we cannot conceive. The midshipman (Timmins) was wounded at his quarters on the main deck, and had his head shot off while sitting at the door of one of the cabins in the 'tween decks. Desperately wounded as Captain Willoughby was, the surgeon was justified, nay, he was bound to place him in any part of the ship where he thought he would be safe; but, from the concurring testimony of all the surviving officers of the Néréide, including Dr. Young himself, Captain Willoughby, after leaving the quarter-deck, was not in any other part of the ship than the cockpit and gun-room.

Captain Willoughby being now a prisoner, a council was held by the French governor, to determine whether or not he should be punished for having distributed proclamations among the inhabitants subversive of their allegiance. It was decided that, as the late captain of the Néréide, whatever may have been his previous liability, had been taken in honourable fight, he should be treated as a prisoner of war. His wounds not admitting of his removal, Captain Willoughby remained at Grand Port, and, we believe, was treated passably well. Not so with his brother officers. Captains Pym, Lambert, and Curtis, with their respective officers and men, were removed round to Port Louis, and were treated in the harshest manner. But, as men, they could not complain; for, several ladies, taken out of the captured In-

[1] Brenton, vol. iv., p. 469.

diamen, were thrown into the same prison and suffered the same privations. Where was General Decaen? Where was that "gallantry" of which Frenchmen are so apt to boast? What has M. Dupin, the advocate of French humanity, to say to this? Females made prisoners of war; nay, treated like criminals, and that by Frenchmen,—Frenchmen, who will not, even now, scruple to tell an Englishman, that their country is half a century more forward in civilization than his. Let us quit the sickening subject. We cannot, however, part with Commodore Hamelin, the hero of Tappanooly,[1] without stating that the officers and men under his orders plundered the British of almost everything, and added personal insult to the brave Captain Lambert.

In spite of the solemn pledge given by General Decaen, that the prisoners who capitulated to him on the 28th of August, should be sent home on parole or exchanged in the course of a month, they were found at the Isle of France upon its capture by the British in the succeeding December. Soon after this, to them and their fellow captives, most fortunate occurrence, Captains Pym, Lambert, Curtis, and Willoughby, and their several officers and men, were tried by court-martial on board the Illustrious 74, in Port Louis harbour, for the loss of their respective ships, and were most honourably acquitted. The sentence upon Captain Willoughby being rather of a special nature, we shall here give a copy of it. "The court is of opinion that the conduct of Captain Willoughby was injudicious in making the signal, 'Enemy of inferior force,' to the Sirius, she being the only ship in sight, and not justifiable, as the enemy evidently was superior. But the court is of opinion, that his Majesty's late ship Néréide was carried into battle in a most judicious, officer-like, and gallant manner; and the court cannot do otherwise than express its high admiration of the noble conduct of the captain, officers, and ship's company during the whole of the unequal contest; and is further of opinion that the Néréide was not surrendered to the enemy until she was disabled in every respect, so as to render all further resistance useless, and that no blame whatever attaches to them for the loss of the said ship." To this testimony in favour of the Néréide, we shall merely add, that the noble behaviour of her officers and crew threw such a halo of glory around the defeat at Grand Port, that, in public opinion at least, the loss of the four frigates was scarcely considered a misfortune.

[1] See p. 63.

The arrival of the Windham recaptured Indiaman in the bay of St. Paul, Isle Bourbon, on the evening of the 22nd of August, informed Commodore Rowley of Captain Pym's projected attack upon the French frigates in Grand Port. At this time, in consequence of a previous arrangement between Lieutenant-colonel Keating and the commodore, the flank-battalion of the 86th regiment was held in readiness to embark on board the Bombay transport, in order to establish a strong military post upon Isle Platte, or Flat island. With the view of co-operating more effectually with Captain Pym, the Boadicea took on board two of the flank companies and a detachment of artillery, and sailed the same evening; and the Bombay, with the remainder of the force, and a supply of provisions both for Isle de la Passe and Flat island, was directed to follow as expeditiously as possible. Owing to baffling winds, the progress of the Boadicea became very tedious; and on the 27th, in the morning, she picked up the Magicienne's barge, with Lieutenant Wauchope and 14 men, despatched by Captains Pym and Lambert, with letters (part of them duplicates of those brought by Lieutenant Watling), acquainting the commodore with the unfortunate issue of the attack upon the French squadron in Grand Port.

On the 29th, at daylight, the Boadicea made Isle de la Passe, and perceived two frigates lying to off the island. These were the Vénus and Manche; the former still engaged in receiving prisoners from the Iphigenia and Isle de la Passe. The Astrée had, the preceding evening, been detached to cruise between the Isles of France and Bourbon, but was seen to windward by the Boadicea, as the latter, with signals flying, approached the Iphigenia, under a hope that she was still in Captain Lambert's possession. When the Boadicea was nearly within gun-shot, the Vénus, making a signal to the Manche, that the admiral's motions were to be disregarded, crowded sail after the British frigate. The Boadicea thereupon tacked and stood off; and presently the Vénus made a signal to her consort to join in the chase. In a short time the two French frigates hauled off from the Boadicea; but, wishing to draw them down as far as possible from their station, in order to give the Bombay an opportunity to succour the Iphigenia, and to favour the escape of both, Commodore Rowley again stood towards the Vénus and Manche. On this the latter resumed the chase, and continued it until 8 h. 30 m. P.M. on the 30th, when the Boadicea reached in safety the road of St. Dénis, Isle Bourbon. On the 31st, in the morning, the Vénus and Manche made sail from before the road.

On the following day, the 1st of September, they chased ineffectually the British gun-brig Staunch, and late in the evening anchored in the harbour of Port Louis; where, had just previously arrived, the Astrée and Entreprenant.

Commodore Rowley, as soon as he had cast anchor, despatched an express across to the bay of St. Paul, with directions to Captain James Tomkinson, of the ship-sloop Otter, then dismantled for heaving down, to move, with his ship's company, on board the Windham, and join the Boadicea off the island; meaning, with this reinforcement, to proceed in search of the two French frigates. When the Boadicea arrived off St. Paul's, expecting to be joined by the Windham, the commodore learnt that Captain Tomkinson, considering that ship to be unfit for immediate service, had declined the command of her. In consequence of this, Captain Henry Lynne, of the Emma government transport, with a highly commendable zeal and indefatigable exertions, fitted that ship with the guns of the Windham, and presently joined the Boadicea off the road of St. Paul. The latter, accompanied by the Emma, immediately made sail towards the Isle of France; but, soon discovering that the transport could not keep company with the frigate, the commodore detached the Emma to cruise between Isle Ronde and Rodriguez in order to give notice to any friendly ships she might fall in with, of the comparative state of the British and French naval forces on the station. The Boadicea then proceeded alone off Isle de la Passe, and found the Iphigenia gone, but plainly saw four ships at anchor in Grand Port; the Bellone, with topgallant yards across and sails bent, and in apparent readiness for sea, the Minerve, with jury topmasts, and the Néréide with jury, main and mizen masts. Finding that nothing could be effected by a single frigate as matters then stood, the Boadicea put about, and on the 11th re-anchored in the road of St. Paul.

No sooner had the Vénus, Manche, Astrée, and Entreprenant arrived at Port Louis, than the governor-general of the Isle of France began taking measures to profit by the naval ascendancy which the French had so unexpectedly acquired in these seas. A squadron, to consist of the Iphigénie (late Iphigenia), Captain Bouvet, Astrée, Entreprenant, and Victor, was to be immediately formed, and placed under the orders of the former. Accordingly, on the 3rd of September, the Astrée and Entreprenant quitted Port Louis, to effect their junction with the Iphigénie and Victor off Isle de la Passe. On the 9th this object was effected; and in the afternoon Captain Bouvet detached the Victor round to Port Louis, to bring some articles of stores required for the Iphigénie. The latter frigate, with her two consorts, the Astrée and Entreprenant, then proceeded on a cruise off Isle Bourbon; where the Victor, as soon as she had executed her mission, was to join them.

On the same day the British 38-gun frigate Africaine, Captain Robert Corbett, on her way from England to Madras, touched at the island of Rodriguez to replenish her water; but, learning what had befallen his friends at the Isle of France, Captain Corbett changed his route, and hastened to join the squadron under Commodore Rowley. In the spring of the present year this frigate, commanded by Captain Richard Raggett, had returned to Plymouth from Annapolis; whither she had conveyed Mr. Jackson, the British ambassador to the United States. About the same time the 38-gun frigate Bourbonaise (late French Caroline), Captain Robert Corbett, anchored at Plymouth from the Cape of Good Hope. The admiralty, having determined to send the Africaine to the Isle of France station, wished to have the benefit of Captain Corbett's local experience, and therefore appointed him to supersede Captain Raggett in the command of that fine frigate.

On the arrival of Captain Corbett on board the Africaine, the ship's company manifested an alarming degree of discontent at the change of commanders, and proceeded to the extremity of declaring that they would not go to sea with Captain Corbett. Rear-admiral Sir Edward Buller, accompanied by Captains Thomas Wolley and George Cockburn, went on board the Africaine, by direction of the board of admiralty, to inquire of the ship's company, if they had any just cause of complaint against Captain Corbett. It now appeared that there was not a man on board the frigate, who had ever served under Captain Corbett, but that the crew were intimidated by his reported severity. It was explained to the men, how certain they were of being made very serious examples of, should they persist in so unreasonable an expectation, as that the admiralty would cancel the appointment of Captain Corbett; but that everything would be overlooked, if they received their captain without any further proof of disaffection.

By this prompt measure on the part of the admiralty, coupled with the temperate, but firm conduct of the officers charged with the performance of it, order was restored, and the men returned to their duty without its being found necessary to inflict the slightest punishment. In the month of June the Africaine sailed for the East Indies, and Captain Corbett was the bearer of despatches to the governor-general, containing orders for the immediate equipment of an expedition against the isles of France and Bourbon. The orders respecting the last-named island had, as we have seen, been successfully anticipated, some weeks before the Africaine arrived at Rodriguez. On the 11th of September, at daylight, the Africaine made the Isle of France ; and just as Isle Ronde bore north-north-east two miles, she discovered a schooner about four points on th larboard bow, standing on a wind to the southward. At 6 h. 15 m. A.M. the frigate hauled up in chase, stood close to the reef in Grande-Baie, and tacked ; in doing which she carried away her foretopmast. The schooner, which was the French aviso, No. 23, commanded by Enseigne François-Nicolas Massieur, from Port Louis, laden with stores for M. Duperré's squadron at Grand Port, then bore up off the land; but, after having proceeded about a quarter of a mile, the vessel hauled to the wind, stood in through a passage in the reef, and ran on shore in a small bay or creek of the Poudre-d'Or coast, within pistol-shot of the beach.

At 7 h. 3 m. A.M., being near the reef, the Africaine hove to and sent her jolly-boat, with master's mate Jenkin Jones and six men, to find the passage through which the aviso had run. The barge, under the command of Lieutenant Robert Forder, quickly followed the jolly-boat ; and the two boats pulled into the creek. It was now discovered that the rocks and beach were lined with soldiers, who immediately opened a heavy fire of musketry on the British. The fire was quickly returned by the marines, but with little or no effect, the French sheltering themselves behind the rocks. The barge grounded; but the jolly-boat, drawing less water, succeeded in boarding the schooner. Not finding on board anything which would serve to set her on fire, the party of seven endeavoured to stave the vessel by throwing her guns down the hatchway. This was scarcely done, when, having no other arms than their cutlasses, the British were compelled to relinquish the prize, with the loss of five (out of the six) men badly, and the master's mate slightly wounded. Meanwhile the barge, owing to her immovable state, had become a dead mark for the French soldiers ; and before she could extricate herself, two of her men were killed, one lieutenant of marines (James Jackson, the 2nd,—slightly), one midshipman (Henry Sewell,—severely), and eight men wounded ; making a total loss, in the two boats, of two men killed and 16 wounded; which was within six or eight of the whole party that had been sent upon this hazardous and—even had it fully succeeded—inadequate service. With the assistance afforded her from the shore, the aviso soon got afloat, and on the following day proceeded, without further molestation, to the port of her destination.

As soon as her two boats returned, which was not until 1 h. 30 m. P.M., the Africaine bore up for Isle Bourbon, and at 4 A.M. on the morning of the 12th made the island. At 6 A.M. the Africaine observed two ships in the offing of St. Denis, and at 7 A.M. learnt from a transport at anchor in the bay, that they were French, as well as a man-of-war brig now also seen to windward of the frigates. At 8 A.M. Captain Corbett went on shore; and the Africaine continued standing on and off the bay, where, as may be conjectured, the Iphigénie and Astrée telegraphed each other; and then the Entreprenant, the brig in company, made sail to the north-east and was soon out of sight. The Astrée and Iphigénie stood in upon the larboard tack, as if disposed to offer battle: whereupon Captain Corbett, who was employed in landing his badly wounded, that they might be sent to the hospital, hoisted a broad pendant and red ensign. The object of doing this was, by deceiving the French into a belief that the Africaine was their old acquaintance the Boadicea, to conceal the fact of any additional British force having arrived on the station.

At noon, or shortly afterwards, the Boadicea herself weighed from the bay of St. Paul, and accompanied by the 16-gun ship-sloop Otter, Captain James Tomkinson, and gun-brig Staunch, Lieutenant Benjamin Street, proceeded in chase of the two French frigates, also seen by them in the offing to windward. At 2 P.M. the Boadicea and her consorts rounded Pointe du Galet, having the wind well from the southward; while the Iphigénie and Astrée were under all sail on the starboard tack, with the wind, a common occurrence in the vicinity of Madagascar, fresh from the eastward. The instant she cleared the bay of St. Paul, the Boadicea was descried, and making her number, became at once recognised by the Africaine: from whom the French frigates at this time bore north distant eight miles. Commodore Rowley, when getting under way, had received an intimation from Lieutenant-colonel Keating, the lieutenant-governor of Isle Bourbon, that an English frigate, reported to be the Africaine, had arrived at St. Denis: he therefore knew that the frigate in sight was the Africaine. Captain Corbett now returned on board his frigate, attended by Major A. Barry of the Honourable Company's service, and Captain Elliott of the British regulars. At about the same time the frigate received from the shore a lieutenant and 25 soldiers of the 86th regiment, to replace her wounded, most of whom were able seamen.

The Africaine immediately made sail, close on a wind, upon the starboard tack, the same as that on which the French ships were standing. These, at about 3 P.M., had descried the Boadicea and her two consorts. The latter Captain Bouvet knew were the Otter and Staunch; but the Boadicea, on account of the ruse practised by the Africaine in the morning, he took to be the Windham, equipped as a ship-of-war. By 6 P.M. the Otter and Staunch had so dropped astern in the chase, as to be entirely out of sight of the Africaine; and about the same time the Boadicea, being headed by the east wind, took in her studding-sails and braced up. This brought her about eight miles on the Africaine's lee quarter. At 6 h. 20 m. P.M. the Africaine lost sight of the Boadicea; and in 10 minutes more the latter lost sight, in the opposite direction, of the Otter and Staunch. The weathermost French frigate, finding the Africaine approaching fast, bore up to join her consort; and at 7 h. 30 m. P.M. the Africaine was about two miles and a half on the weather quarter of the two frigates, with such a decided superiority in sailing, as to keep way with them under topsails and foresail, while they were carrying topgallantsails and courses.

Proceeding thus under easy sail, in order to allow the Boadicea time to get up, the Africaine, as soon as it grew dark, began firing rockets and burning blue-lights, to point out her situation to the Boadicea, between whom and the Africaine no signals, beyond the answering pendant of the latter to the Boadicea's number, had yet been exchanged. At 9 P.M. the Boadicea saw a flash in the south-east, and at 9 h. 30 m. P.M. observed the two French frigates and the Africaine burn blue-lights. At 1 h. 50 m. A.M. on the 13th, in the midst of a fresh squall, the French frigates bore up; and immediately the Africaine, fearing their intention might be to run or wear, bore up also, and manned her starboard guns. At 2 h. 10 m. A.M. the Astrée and Iphigénie again hauled to the wind on the same tack; and the Africaine, having hauled up likewise, found herself within less than musket-shot distance on the Astrée's weather-quarter. The Boadicea was now four or five miles distant on the lee-quarter of the Africaine; but having been thrown, by accident, into so good a position, and knowing that a run of two or three hours more would bring the French to Port Louis, Captain Corbett could not refrain from becoming the assailant.

Accordingly, at 2 h. 20 m. A.M., the Africaine fired her larboard guns, loaded with two round shot each, into the starboard and weather quarter of the Astrée, who immediately returned the fire. The second broadside from the Astrée mortally wounded Captain Corbett, a shot striking off his right foot above the ancle, and a blow from a splinter causing a compound fracture of the thigh of the same leg. The command of the Africaine now devolved upon Lieutenant Joseph Crew Tullidge; who was ordered by Captain Corbett, as he was removing below, to bring the enemy to close action. At 2 h. 30 m. A.M., having had her jib-boom and the weather clue of her foretopsail shot away, and fearing that her bowsprit had suffered, the Astrée ranged ahead clear of the Africaine's guns. On this the men at the Africaine's foremost main-deck guns began hurraing, and the remainder of the ship's company caught and repeated the cheer. The lightness of the breeze, which had been gradually falling since the firing commenced, would have deprived the Africaine of her former advantage in point of sailing, even had the Astrée's fire not cut away the greater part of her running rigging: hence the Africaine had scarcely steerage way through the water. The Iphigénie, meanwhile, had bore up, and now took a station on the lee quarter of her consort. The breeze freshening a little at this time, the Africaine made sail, and running alongside the Iphigénie to windward, recommenced the action, having the Astrée on her weather bow. A sudden fall in the wind enabled the latter ship to retain her position; and thus lay the Africaine, with one ship of equal force within half pistol-shot on her larboard beam, and another, of the same or a greater force, close on her starboard bow, raking her with a most destructive fire of round, grape, and langridge.

At 3 h. 30 m. A.M. the Africaine had her jib-boom and foretopmast shot away, and shortly afterwards her mizen topmast. Lieutenant Tullidge, by this time, had been severely wounded in four places, but could not be persuaded to go below. Lieutenant Forder, the next officer in seniority, had been shot through the breast with a musket-ball, and taken below; and at 4 P.M. the master had his head carried off by a round shot. Still the Africaine continued the action; but her fire gradually grew feebler, until about 4 h. 45 m. A.M., when it entirely ceased. The ship was now with her three lower masts reduced to a tottering state, her hull pierced in all directions, her quarter-deck nearly cleared of officers and men, and her main deck so thinned, that only six guns could be properly manned. Being in this disabled state, seeing also, from the calm state of the weather, no chance of relief from the Boadicea, whom the opening daylight discovered about four or five miles off, and having no hope of escape, nor means of further resistance, the Africaine, at a few minutes before 5 A.M., hauled down her colours. Although this was done, and every light extinguished, the French, contrary to the law of arms, continued, for nearly 15 minutes, to fire into the British frigate; whereby Captain Elliott of the army (by a grape-shot at the back of his head) and several men were killed.

The Africaine was armed like other frigates of her class, except in having two additional 9-pounders on her forecastle, making her total number of guns 48. Of her complement, including the detachment of soldiers, of 295 men and boys, the Africaine had her master (Samuel Parker), Captain Elliott of the army, 28 seamen, 14 private marines, and five soldiers killed, her captain (mortally), first and second lieutenants (Joseph Crew Tullidge and Robert Forder, severely), first-lieutenant of marines (James Jackson, this time[1] severely), two master's mates (John Theed and Jenkin Jones), two midshipmen (Charles Mercier and Robert Leech), one lieutenant of the army (Horne), 76 seamen, 12 private marines, and 17 soldiers (leaving only three out of the 25 in an effective state) wounded; total, 49 killed and 114 wounded. Captain Corbett had his leg amputated below the knee during the action, and died about six hours after the operation had been performed. Had he survived, he must have submitted to a second amputation above the compound fracture. The surgeon, although a skilful man, was himself a cripple, and very sickly; and, for want of sufficient assistance, had his attention too much distracted by the number of wounded officers and men that, in rapid succession, were brought to the cockpit.

The Astrée, when subsequently captured by the British, mounted 44 guns, similar to those carried at this time by other French frigates of her class; and she had, it appears, on commencing the action with the Africaine, a complement of 360 men and boys. The Iphigénie carried her English armament, consisting of 42 guns, similar to those of her class;[2] with a complement, as acknowledged, of 258 men and boys. The loss sustained by the French frigates, as stated in the letter of

[1] See p. 174.   [2] See vol. iv., p. 56.

Commodore Bouvet, amounted to nine men killed, and one officer and 32 men wounded, on board the Iphigénie, and one man killed and two wounded on board the Astrée; total, 10 killed and 35 wounded. The damages of the French frigates bore a proportion to their loss of men. The Astrée was very slightly injured in hull or spars. The Iphigénie had her masts, yards, and rigging more or less wounded and cut, but none of her masts so dangerously struck as to require renewing.

The twofold disparity against which this action was fought is as palpably conspicuous, as the valour that commenced, and the firmness that continued it; and yet the judgment of Captain Corbett, in not waiting the arrival of the Boadicea, has been questioned. Had the Africaine shortened sail for that purpose, there can be little doubt that the French frigates, who had clearly seen the Otter and Staunch in the morning, would have pursued their course to Port Louis. A near approach would soon have discovered to them, that the supposed Indiaman was a real frigate, and a large one too; and Commodore Bouvet, brave as he undoubtedly was, would, we think, have declined engaging two British frigates, a frigate-built sloop of war and an armed brig; and who could blame him? With respect to the conduct of the Africaine in commencing the action, it is not easy at all times to distinguish between discretion and shyness; and the very thought of such an imputation as the mildest of the two terms may convey is enough to fire the blood of any man who holds his gallantry sacred. Ten frigates, lost like the Africaine, weigh less, as a national misfortune, than one frigate given up without any, or even with an inadequate, resistance.

No sooner was the Africaine in possession of her captors, than her shot-lockers were ransacked to supply the Iphigénie, whose guns were of the same caliber; but only 50 round shot remained of the former's originally ample store. That they had been expended in the action is certain; but there is reason to believe that the Africaine's crew had been very little, if at all, exercised at the guns: consequently that, in nine times out of ten, the men might as well have fired blank cartridges as shot. A proof of this has already appeared in the trifling execution done to the two French frigates. That the Iphigénie, although mounting English guns, had stood in no actual need of shot for them, we infer, because not a complaint of the kind is discoverable in Captain Bouvet's account of the action. On the other hand, the French could have had but a very small quantity of English round shot left, and would naturally be anxious to procure as many of the Africaine's shot as they could, in order that the Iphigénie might be ready to defend herself in case of being attacked.

At a few minutes before the Africaine hauled down her flag, a breeze began to swell the sails of the Boadicea; and the latter, very soon after daylight, "passed within musket-shot of the enemy." It was now discovered that the Africaine was a prize to the two French frigates, and greatly disabled, while they apparently had suffered but little. At 6 A.M. the Boadicea tacked and stood to windward of the Iphigénie and Astrée, to look for the Otter and Staunch; whose very bad sailing was at this time particularly unfortunate. At 6 h. 10 m. A.M. the Africaine's foremast was seen to fall by the board; at 7 A.M. her mizenmast and maintopmast, and at 8 A.M. her mainmast. Her bowsprit, or the head of it, also, we believe, went; and thus was the Africaine a totally dismasted hulk.

We regret to find, that the only paragraph in Commodore Rowley's letter respecting the state of the Africaine's masts is the following: "Day dawned and showed us the result; the enemy appeared to have suffered little; the Africaine was in their possession, with no apparent loss but that of her mizentopmast." To this we cannot do better than oppose, in addition to the facts we have gleaned from the Boadicea's log, an extract from the official letter of Lieutenant Tullidge. "Of the Africaine's subsequent recapture by the Boadicea, their lordships must of course have been informed by Commodore Rowley. I must add, however, that her remaining masts and bowsprit fell over the side soon after our quitting her." But as Lieutenant Tullidge's letter, owing to the unfair and impolitic practice of suppressing the official details of a defeat, simply because it is a defeat, never appeared in the London Gazette, the contradiction, we fear, comes too late to produce much effect. In saying that the Africaine, when first seen by the Boadicea in the grey of the morning, had all three of her lower masts standing, Commodore Rowley was correct; but he omitted to mention, what all on board the Boadicea must have seen, or the entries would not have been in her log, that, within three hours afterwards, the Africaine was totally dismasted.

At 7 h. 30 m. A.M. the Boadicea discovered the Otter and Staunch to windward, and at 10 A.M. was joined by them. At 40 minutes past noon the Boadicea and her two companions bore up, with a fine breeze from the south-south-east, for the two French frigates and the wreck of the Africaine. At

1 h. 30 m. P.M. the Boadicea hauled up her foresail, and came to the wind on the larboard tack. At 3 h. 30 m. P.M. she and her consorts again bore up; and in ten minutes afterwards the Astrée, taking the Iphigénie in tow, abandoned the Africaine and made sail to windward. At 5 P.M., by which time the Boadicea had arrived close abreast of the Africaine, the latter fired two guns and hauled down the French colours.

The surprising spectacle was now seen of several of the Africaine's late crew swimming off from her to the Boadicea. Upon their arrival on board, the men expressed the utmost eagerness to renew the action with the two French frigates, under an officer whose mild system of discipline had been made known to them through the same channel as that by which they had formerly learnt the very opposite system pursued by the commander whom they were compelled to receive as the successor of Captain Raggett. If the act of the late Africaine's sailors, in swimming to the Boadicea, betrayed the nature of their feelings respecting Captain Corbett, it as decidedly showed, that, although their ship had been captured, their spirit was unsubdued.

On board the Africaine, at her recapture, were found about 70 of her wounded and 83 of her remaining crew, with the French prize-master and his nine men. At 9 P.M., the two French frigates still in sight working to windward, the Boadicea took the Africaine in tow; and, accompanied by the Otter and Staunch, proceeded towards the bay of St. Paul. On the 14th, at daylight, the Astrée and Iphigénie were again descried by the Boadicea and her crippled and two remaining consorts, and continued to be seen until 11 A.M.; when they disappeared, but were again discovered at 5 P.M., and remained in sight till dark. On the 15th, at noon, Commodore Rowley anchored in St. Paul's bay; but in the evening, weighed with the Boadicea, Otter, and Staunch, and made sail to the north-east. On the 16th, at daylight, the two French frigates were seen close off Castle St. Bernard. The latter then stood away to windward, and the British ships steered for the road of St. Dénis. On the 17th, at daylight, the two frigates were discovered to windward, in company with an armed brig. At 9 h. 40 m. the Iphigénie and Astrée bore up, as if with the intention of attacking, but more probably to reconnoitre the Boadicea and her two consorts, who were then waiting off St. Dénis for the return of a boat which Commodore Rowley had sent to the shore. At 11 h. 20 m. A.M. the French ships hove to, and shortly afterwards made sail to windward. At 2 P.M. Commodore Rowley put back toward

St. Paul's; at 6 p.m. lost sight of the two French frigates; and on the 18th, at 5 a.m., re-anchored in the bay. The armed brig, seen with the Iphigénie and Astrée, was the Honourable Company's cruiser Aurora, of 16 guns and 100 men, which they had just before captured. On the 22nd, in the morning, Captain Bouvet, with his two frigates and prize, anchored in the harbour of Port Louis. We shall by-and-by see, that the French commodore would have done better had he remained another day cruising off Isle Bourbon.

By way of excuse for the abandonment of his first prize on the approach of the Boadicea, accompanied by a sloop-of-war and a gun-brig, Commodore Bouvet thus expresses himself: "I thought it best not to wait for the enemy in the unrigged and dismantled state in which I found myself. I was therefore compelled, much to my regret, to abandon to him my prize, although but a hulk, filled with the dead and the dying." "Je jugeai à propos de ne pas attendre l'ennemi dans l'état de délâbrement et de dénuement où je me trouvais. Je fus aussi constraint, à mon grand regret, de lui abandonner ma prise, quoique ce ne fût qu'une carcasse chargée de morts et de mourans."

We are somewhat fearful of pressing too hard upon the French commodore, lest he should turn upon us and say, that, being crippled and deficient of ammunition, the Iphigénie could have made but a feeble resistance against the Otter and Staunch, while Commodore Rowley, with the Boadicea, might have gone in chase of the Astrée; and that admitting the latter to have escaped to windward, the Iphigénie, whose rate of sailing at best was but indifferent, would, now that her rigging was in disorder, undoubtedly have been recaptured. In justice to Captain Rowley, however, it becomes us to add, that he could have had no knowledge of the low state of the Iphigénie's ammunition; and, considering that the Boadicea was at this time the only British frigate upon the station, and that two French frigates, the Vénus and Manche, were cruising in the neighbourhood, it behoved the commodore to be particularly cautious in risking the loss of the small force left under his orders.

We, at a former page, attributed the little execution done by the Africaine to her two opponents, to the unskilfulness of her crew in gunnery. As one proof that the men had not been exercised at the guns, they frequently during the action threw the quoins aside, or put them in on their edges; in the one case elevating, in the other depressing, the guns beyond all mark. It is the general belief, we know, that the Africaine's crew were disaffected, on account of the ill treatment they had experienced from their captain. We regret to have to state, that the more our inquiries have been extended on that point, the more they have convinced us, that Captain Corbett was an excessively severe officer. We trace him in his career of cruelty, from the Seahorse to the Néréide, from the Néréide to the Bourbonnaise, and from her to the Africaine. If, in the Africaine, he flogged less than he did on board the Néréide, it was because the crew of the former, taken generally, were much better seamen than the crew of the latter.

There are many who will insist, that Captain Corbett's death-wound was inflicted by one of his own people. Had the wound been caused by a musket or pistol ball, a possibility might exist that such had been the case; but what becomes of the assertion, when the wound, and that the partial excision of a limb, was inflicted by a cannon ball? Others, and some of them officers of known veracity, have informed us that, unable to brook his defeat, Captain Corbett, during the temporary absence of an attendant, cut the bandages from his amputated limb, and suffered himself to bleed to death. A contemporary, in the statement, "Captain Corbett did not (we fear would not) survive his capture,"[1] appears to be of the same opinion. Still, looking to the source whence we derived it, we are disposed to consider our first information as the most correct, that the want of proper surgical aid, coupled with the existence of a compound fracture above the amputated limb, was the immediate cause of Captain Corbett's death.

On a subsequent day, April 23, 1811, the surviving officers and crew of the late Africaine were tried by a court-martial for the loss of their ship, and most honourably acquitted; and Lieutenant Tullidge was declared to have behaved "in the most gallant and determined manner, although he had received four severe wounds during the action." We are happy to add, that, on the 1st of the succeeding August, this brave and deserving officer was promoted to the rank of commander.

Returning to the proceedings of the year 1810 off the Isle of France, we have to state, that on the 17th of September, in the morning, the British 18-pounder 32-gun frigate Ceylon, Captain Charles Gordon, from Madras on her way to Isle Bourbon, arrived off Port Louis, in the expectation of falling in with the squadron under Commodore Rowley. After reconnoitring the harbour, and, on account of the many large ships within it,

[1] Brenton, vol. iv., p. 477.

estimating the French force of seven frigates and a large corvette, Captain Gordon bore up and made all sail on his course alongshore towards Isle Bourbon. Since 8 A.M., when off Canonnier point, the Ceylon had been descried from the signal-posts; and, although at first taken for an enemy's cruiser, was afterwards, chiefly on account of her having a poop, believed to be an Indiaman with troops on board. The French men-of-war at this time in Port Louis were the Vénus, Manche, and Victor, and at 1 h. 15 m. P.M. Commodore Hamelin weighed and put to sea with the Vénus and the corvette, in pursuit of the Ceylon, then nearly abreast of Morne-Brabant, at the south-western extremity of the island.

This will be the proper place to show how the parties, now on the eve of coming to blows, stood in point of relative force. Some time in the year 1805 the British government authorised the purchase in India, among other ships, of the Bombay, a frigate-built Indiaman of 672 tons. The ship was immediately put upon the establishment of a first-class 32-gun frigate, and armed with 24 long 18-pounders on the main deck, and two long nines and 14 carronades, 24-pounders, on the quarter-deck and forecastle, total 40 guns. In consequence of a 74 of the name of Bombay being laid down at Deptford, the name of the newly purchased frigate was changed to Ceylon. Her established complement appears to have been 235 men and boys. Of this number, the Ceylon, on quitting Madras, was 47 men short; but she there took on board 100 soldiers of the 69th and 86th regiments, a portion of whom were to serve as marines. So that, with Major-general Abercromby and six or seven other passengers, the Ceylon had on board a total of about 295 men and boys.

The Vénus was armed precisely as the Minerve[1] and other frigates of that class, and had a regular crew of 380 men and boys. The Victor was the same Jéna of which we have before spoken;[2] a mere shell of a vessel, not to be compared, in point of size or efficiency, with the 18-gun brig class, although carrying the same armament. At all events it is certain that, although, when fitted out in the British service, she was established with the old Victor's sixteen 32-pounder carronades and two sixes, yet Captain Morice, when he again commissioned her as a French corvette, landed two of her guns; thus leaving her with only 16, which were full as many as the ship could carry with ease to herself and security to her people.

[1] See vol. iv., p. 141. [2] See vol. iv., p. 366.

At 2 p.m. the Ceylon descried the Vénus and Victor in chase of her, and continued steering west by south, under all sail, with a fresh breeze at east-south-east. At dusk, observing that the headmost ship was considerably ahead of her consort, the Ceylon shortened sail, to allow the former to close; but at 10 p.m., discovering in the moonlight that the Vénus had reduced her sail, as if to await the coming up of her consort, the British frigate again made all sail to keep the two ships apart. The Vénus, as may be supposed, sailed much faster than the ci-devant Indiaman; and at 15 minutes past midnight, upon the near approach of the former, Captain Gordon, having previously made all clear, shortened sail to begin the action. In five minutes more the Vénus passed under the stern of the British frigate; and, after hailing and discharging two muskets, and receiving the fire of her stern-chasers, the former ranged up on the Ceylon's starboard quarter.

The mutual discovery now made, of the immense disparity in size and apparent force between the two ships, although it may not have disheartened the one, must have greatly animated the other. However, a severe conflict ensued, and continued until about 1 h. 15 m. a.m.; when, having by this time ascertained clearly enough, that her opponent was a ship-of-war, the Vénus wore round and dropped astern. The Ceylon was thus afforded an opportunity of repairing her damaged rigging, and of making sail to escape from an antagonist, who, although singly not what a British frigate would consider a decided overmatch, was deemed too powerful to be engaged when likely so soon to be aided by a consort, believed to be, at the least, of equal force.

The same superiority of sailing which had first enabled the Vénus to overtake the Ceylon brought her again alongside, and at 2 h. 15 m. a.m. the action recommenced. It was now maintained with such renewed vigour on both sides, that, by a little after 3 a.m., the Vénus had lost her mizenmast and her fore and main topmasts and gaff. The standing and running rigging of both frigates was also much cut, and the courses of the Ceylon were torn nearly to pieces by the fall of the topmasts. In this unmanageable state, the two frigates continued engaging until a few minutes past four, when the Vénus dropped about 450 yards to leeward, and fired only at intervals. At this time the Victor was seen from the Ceylon, coming down under a crowd of canvas. At about 4 h. 30 m. a.m., having passed close to windward of the Ceylon, the Victor placed herself athwart the latter ship's bows, as if intending to rake her. At this moment, being unable in her totally ungovernable state to evade a fire which, as coming from a ship supposed, even yet, to be a second Vénus in point of force, might have been very destructive, the Ceylon showed a light as a signal of having struck. At 5 h. 10 m. A.M. a lieutenant, with a party of men, came on board from the corvette and took possession of the prize: and Captain Gordon, his first and third lieutenants (George Henry Campbell and Edmund Malone), and Major-general Abercromby and the other army-officers, were taken on board the Vénus.

The loss of the Ceylon's topmasts has already been stated; her lower masts were also much injured; and her loss of men amounted to six seamen and four soldiers of the 69th regiment, acting as marines, killed, her captain, master (William Oliver, both severely), Captain Ross of the 69th regiment, her boatswain (Andrew Graham), 17 sailors, one marine, and nine soldiers wounded; total 10 killed and 31 wounded. The principal damage done to the Vénus consisted in the loss of her mizenmast and topmasts, as already described; but her loss of men, although in all probability full as severe as that on board the Ceylon, we are unable to state, owing to the silence of the published accounts, and the failure of our efforts to obtain the particulars from any private source.

It is generally an advantage to a well-disciplined ship to engage at night; because, in case of being assailed by a superiority of force, she may reduce the odds, nearly if not quite, to the level of her own powers, by a superiority of tactics. But the Ceylon would have done better had she fought her action by daylight; not owing to any lack of skill in her crew, as the damages of her antagonist testify, but because the obscurity of night caused her to overrate, far to overrate, the force of that antagonist's unengaged consort. Had the Victor been rigged with two masts instead of three, as, with one or two exceptions, all similarly armed vessels in the British navy at that time were, her real insignificance would have discovered itself even in the dark, and her approach been greeted with a broadside, which would probably have sent the Victor to the bottom, or, at all events, have disabled her from offering any effectual resistance. What resources would then have remained to the Ceylon, it is difficult to say; but, undoubtedly, she was in no worse state than the Vénus; and, had a suspension of the firing continued a few hours longer, the appearance of the British force, whose arrival we shall presently have to announce would have preserved the Ceylon's flag from falling, and would have prevented a French 16-gun corvette from claiming the honour of having summoned, successfully summoned, a British frigate to surrender.

At 7 h. 30 m. A.M. Commodore Rowley, whom with the Boadicea, Otter, and Staunch, we left at anchor in the road of St. Paul, first descried the two French ships and their prize, then abreast of St. Dénis, and about three leagues distant from the shore. At 7 h. 40 m. A.M., having received 50 volunteers from the Africaine, the Boadicea, accompanied by her two consorts, got under way and made sail in chase; and the Victor, who at 8 A.M. had discovered and signalled the British vessels as they cleared the bay, hastened to take the Ceylon in tow, and follow the Vénus, now using her best endeavours to get back to the Isle of France. Scarcely had the Victor made sail with the Ceylon, than the tow-rope broke; and it was not until nearly noon that the prize was again secured. The corvette, with the wind fresh from the east-south-east, again steered after the Vénus; who was standing on the starboard tack, under her foresail and mainsail, and a small sail upon the stump of her mizenmast. At 3 h. 30 m. P.M., being too small and light to tow the Ceylon with any effect, the Victor slipped or cast off the hawser; and, waiting only till he had taken his officer and men out of the prize, Captain Morice hauled up towards the Vénus. The latter wore to join her consort, and then came to on the larboard tack, with her head towards the Boadicea; while the Victor herself, as ordered by Commodore Hamelin, stood away to the eastward.

As soon as the Victor got out of gun-shot, the Ceylon rehoisted the colours which had been struck in the morning, and was again a British ship-of-war under the temporary command of Mr. Philip Fitz-Gibbon, the second lieutenant. At 4 h. 40 m. P.M. the Boadicea ran the Vénus alongside; and, after a 10 minutes' mutual cannonade, in which the Boadicea had her bowsprit badly struck and two men wounded, and the Vénus nine men killed and 15 wounded, the French frigate hauled down her colours. Soon after the Boadicea had taken her prize in tow, the Otter, by signal, rendered the same service to the Ceylon; and Captain Gordon, having by this time returned on board with his first and third lieutenants, resumed the command of his recovered frigate. The Victor being too far off to be pursued with any chance of overtaking her, Commodore Rowley returned with his prize and recapture to the bay of St. Paul.

In order to show what an important discrepancy occurs between the French and English official accounts of the capture of the Ceylon, we here subjoin an extract from each. Captain Morice says: "At this moment I discovered that the two vessels had lost their topmasts and one her mizenmast; each was at quarters,[1] and ready for action; the fire at length ceased, and I recognised the Vénus; I passed within pistol-shot of the enemy without being fired at; I wore round on the other tack, and again passed him at the same distance without receiving any fire; I closed the commodore, who ordered me to demand of this vessel whether or not she had surrendered; I immediately executed the service, and returned to the commodore with information that she had struck; I then lay to and sent a boat commanded by M. Ménager, enseigne de vaisseau, to take out the officers of this vessel, and convey them on board the Vénus; that order was executed. Daylight came; and I perceived that these vessels had fought with all sail set, from seeing a fore-topmast studding-sail hanging from the enemy's fore-yard-arm."[2]

Here follows an extract from the official letter of Captain Gordon: "At 5 A.M., the enemy's fore and main masts standing with the assistance of his foresail, enabled him to wear close under our stern, and take a raking position under our lee-quarter. His majesty's ship lying an unmanageable wreck, I directed the mizentopsail to be cut away, and endeavoured to set a fore staysail, in hopes of getting the ship before the wind, but without effect. The second ship having opened her fire with the great advantage the enemy had by having both his ships under command, enabled him to take and keep his raking position, and pour in a heavy and destructive fire, while his majesty's ship could only bring a few quarter guns to bear. In the shattered and disabled state of his majesty's ship, a retreat was impossible. The superiority of the enemy's heavy and destructive fire left me no hopes of success. Reduced to this distressed situation, feeling the firmest conviction that every energy and exertion was called forth, under the influence of the strongest impression I had discharged my duty and upheld the honour of his majesty's arms, feeling it a duty I owed to the officers and crew, who had nobly displayed that bravery which is so truly their characteristic, when I had lost all hopes of saving his majesty's ship, to prevent a useless effusion of blood,

[1] The lights in the ports would discover this.
[2] For the original extract, see Appendix, No. 4.

I was under the painful necessity of directing a light to be shown to the second ship that we had struck."

The following is an extract from the log of the Ceylon, authenticated in the customary manner: "At 4, enemy having dropped to leeward two cables lengths, his fire nearly done, saw his consort coming down under all sail. The ship at this period being entirely unmanageable, on the second ship crossing our bow, apparently to rake us, to prevent a further and unnecessary effusion of blood, struck our colours to enemy about ½ past 4. At 5, 10, a lieutenant and party of men came on board from the sloop-of-war Victor, of 18 guns." According, therefore, to the concurrent testimony of the French captain's account and the British ship's log, but in opposition to the British captain's public letter, the Ceylon struck to the Victor without being fired at by her. We must, however, in justice to Captain Gordon remark, that the expression, " enabled him to take and keep his raking position, and pour in a heavy and destructive fire," appears to refer to the Vénus, and the previous expression, "having opened her fire," to the Victor. A little more pains, in framing his letter, would have prevented this obscurity. With respect to the exact time of surrender, that is of little consequence; but the "showing of a light" proves that day had not quite broken, and consequently that it could not well have been after " 5 A.M."

Next to the loss of his frigate, the greatest misfortune that has befallen Captain Gordon, is the zeal with which a brother-officer of his, and a contemporary of ours, advocates his cause. "She (the Ceylon) mounted," not 40 but, " 30 guns."—" On the 17th of September, she arrived off Port Louis, and discovered seven sail of French frigates, and a corvette, lying in the harbour. The British squadron not being in sight, Captain Gordon made all sail for the island of Bourbon, pursued by two of the frigates, one of which brought him to close action, which was maintained for an hour and ten minutes. About midnight the enemy hauled off and dropped astern, but renewed the action at two in the morning, accompanied by the second frigate, who was very soon reduced to a mere wreck by the gallant fire of the Ceylon; and she fell astern with her mizenmast, and fore and main topmasts over the side. Unfortunately, the united fire of the two frigates shot away the topmasts of the Ceylon about the same time, and she became unmanageable. The action was still continued until five A.M., when one of the frigates, with her fore and main mast standing, took a raking position under the quarter of the British ship, where she kept up a fire, unchecked by any return from the Ceylon, whose gallant captain directed the mizentopsail to be cut away, to enable the ship to get before the wind. This resource failing, and everything having been done for the preservation of the ship, the colours were hauled down to superior force. The frigates were the Vénus, of 44 guns and 380 men, and the Victor (formerly English), of 16 guns and 120 men."[1]

A "frigate," indeed; such a frigate as Captain Brenton himself would have gladly met in the Merlin sloop;[2] such a frigate as he would have thought it a step to have been removed from into the Amaranthe brig;[3] such a frigate, in short, as the old 16-gun schooner Netley, with her non-recoil carronades, would have been ashamed to run from. As far as we can judge from the context, by the ship that, previously to midnight, sustained a close action of "an hour and ten minutes" with the Ceylon, is meant the Victor, "of 16 guns." If so, this is paying a high compliment to the French commander, and places in no very creditable light the conduct of his antagonist. Such, however, was evidently not the writer's intention; and it is perhaps not the least fortunate circumstance connected with Captain Brenton's narrative of operations in the vicinity of the Isles of France and Bourbon, that it is so confusedly put together, and contains so many contradictions and absurdities, as considerably to weaken its misleading powers.

The Boadicea's prize was a fine frigate of 1105 tons; and, to commemorate the gallant defence of the Néréide at Grand Port, Vice-admiral Bertie named the Vénus after her. For the capture of the Ceylon by the Vénus and her consort, Captain Gordon, his officers, and crew were tried by court-martial on board the Illustrious 74, belonging to the Cape station, and honourably acquitted.

Colonial Expeditions.— West Indies.

On the 27th of January a combined naval and military expedition, under the respective commands of Vice-admiral the Honourable Sir Alexander Cochrane, and Lieutenant-general Sir George Beckwith, anchored off the town of Gosier, island of Guadaloupe. On the 28th the troops landed without opposition: one division, commanded by Major-general Hislop, at the village of Sainte-Marie, under the direction of Commodore William Charles Fahie, of the 74-gun ship Abercrombie; and

---

[1] Brenton, vol. iv., p. 473. [2] See vol. iii., p. 202. [3] See vol. iv., p. 381.

the other division, commanded by Brigadier-general Harcourt, a league or two to the northward of Basse-terre, under the direction of Commodore Samuel James Ballard, of the 74-gun ship Sceptre. On the 3rd of February an engagement took place between Brigadier-general Harcourt's division, and a body of French troops on the ridge Beaupère St. Louis, and again in the evening between the British reserve under Brigadier-general Wale, in forcing the passage of the river de la Père. In both cases the British were successful; and on the following morning, the 4th, the French hoisted flags of truce in all their positions; on the 5th, the terms of capitulation were settled; and on the 6th the island of Guadaloupe surrendered to the British arms.

In justice to the governor, General Ernouf, and the French troops on the island, it must be stated, that a great proportion of the latter were sick: that the force opposed to them, even in the first instance, was an overwhelming one; and that, as in the case at Martinique in the preceding year, there was a defection among the colonial militia. The British army sustained a loss of 52 officers and privates killed, 250 wounded, and seven privates missing. The navy, not having been engaged, suffered no loss. That on the part of the French troops is represented to have been between 500 and 600 in killed and wounded.

Before the 22nd of the same month of February the same two commanders followed up their success, with obtaining the peaceable surrender of the Dutch islands at St. Martin, St. Eustatius, and Saba; thereby completing the reduction of all the French and Dutch colonies in the Antilles.

East Indies.

The British commander-in-chief on this station, Rear-admiral William O'Brien Drury, being resolved to endeavour to possess the principal settlement of the Dutch in the Molucca sea, entrusted the enterprise to Captain Edward Tucker, of the 38-gun frigate Dover, with directions to take under his orders the 44-gun frigate Cornwallis, Captain William Augustus Montagu, and 18-gun ship-sloop Samarang, Captain Richard Spencer. On the 9th of February, off the island of Amboyna, the first object of attack, the Dover and Samarang were joined by the Cornwallis; and the three ships, proceeding up the outer harbour of Amboyna, anchored, the same day in Lætitia bay with the view of examining the defences of the place. The principal was the castle of Victoria, and the batteries to the right and left of it, mounting altogether 215 pieces of cannon (of all calibers from 32 to half-pounders), with an extremely strong sea-face. A little further to the right of the fort, close on the beach, was the Wagoo battery, mounting nine guns, consisting of four 12, one 8, and two 6 pounder long guns, and one brass 32-pounder carronade; and, far out in the sea, built upon piles, was a battery mounting nine long 12-pounders and one brass 32-pounder carronade, both batteries with very thick parapets. There were also two batteries on the heights; one, named Wannetoo, mounted five 12, two 8, and two 6 pounders, and two $5\frac{1}{2}$ inch brass howitzers; the other, named Batto-Gautong, and situated about 1500 yards from the former, mounted four 12, and one 9 pounder. Both the last-named batteries commanded, as well the town of Amboyna, as the castle and anchorage of Victoria and the anchorage at Portuguese bay. The several forts were garrisoned by 130 European, and upwards of 1000 Javanese and Madurese troops; exclusively of 220 officers and seamen, many of whom were Europeans, late belonging to the three vessels sunk in the inner harbour, and exclusively, also, of the Dutch inhabitants and burghers.

On the 16th, in the morning, the plan of attack was arranged; and at 2 P.M., everything being in readiness, the Dover, Cornwallis, and Samarang weighed and stood across the bay, with the apparent intention of working out to sea. But the ships, by keeping their sails lifting, and other manœuvres, contrived to drift towards the spot fixed upon for a landing; the boats, all the while, remaining on the opposite side of the ships out of sight of the enemy. Upon a nearer approach, the three ships, by signal, bore up together, with a fine breeze; and, passing within a cable's length of the landing-place, slipped all the boats at the same moment, also by signal. The ships then opened their fire; and a smart cannonade was kept up between them and the different batteries on the shore.

The party in the boats, consisting of a detachment of 46 officers and privates from the Honourable Company's coast artillery, 130 officers and privates of the Madras European regiment, and 225 officers, seamen, and marines belonging to the ships, in all 401 men, under the command of Captain Major Henry Court of the first-named corps, landed without opposition. Immediately a division of 180 men, under the command of Captain Phillips of the Madras European regiment, marched to the attack of the battery at Wannetoo; which, after a determined opposition, was carried, with a loss to the garrison of two officers killed and one desperately wounded. Under the able direction of Lieutenant Duncan Stewart, of the artillery, who, although wounded, continued at his post, three of the Wannetoo guns were brought to bear upon the enemy in his retreat, and subsequently upon the position at Batto-Gautong; which had opened a fire upon the British, the instant the latter had taken possession of Wannetoo.

With the remaining force, Captain Court proceeded along the heights, to turn the enemy's position at Batto-Gautong. This division endured, with the greatest spirit and patience, a most fatiguing march; ascending and descending hills over which there were no roads, and many of which were so extremely steep that the men had to help themselves forward by the bushes. By a little after sunset, however, the British reached an eminence that commanded Batto-Gautong; whereupon the enemy, after spiking the guns, retreated, and the battery was entered without opposition.

After the cannonade between the ships and batteries had continued for two hours and a half, during which the former, having drifted very close in, had been exposed to a very heavy fire, partly with red-hot shot, the ships took advantage of a spirt of wind off the land, and anchored in Portuguese bay, now freed from further annoyance by the success of the party on shore. In the course of the night, 40 men were landed from the Samarang and two field-pieces from the Dover, under the direction of Captain Spencer; and the seamen succeeded in getting the guns up the heights, over a heavy and difficult ground. During the night, also, one 9, and two 12 pounders in the Batto-Gautong battery were unspiked, and on the following day brought to bear on Fort Victoria. The fire of the British from the two captured batteries caused the enemy to abandon the Wagoo and the water battery, and finally to capitulate for the surrender of Fort Victoria and of the whole island of Amboyna.

This important capture was effected with a loss to the British of only two privates of the Madras regiment, one marine, and one seaman killed, one lieutenant and one corporal of artillery, four privates of the Madras regiment, and four seamen wounded. We must not omit to state, also, that Lieutenant Jeffries, of the Dover, while serving on shore, received a concussion in the breast from a spent grape-shot, but remained at his post. The three Dutch national vessels that had been sunk in the inner harbour were the brig Mandarin, Captain Guasteranus, of

12 guns (afterwards weighed by the British), cutter, name unknown, Lieutenant Haum, of 12 guns, and San-Pan, Lieutenant Dukkert, of 10 guns.

The success of the British in this quarter led to the surrender in a few days afterwards of the valuable islands of Saparoua, Harouka, Nasso-Lant, Bouro, and Manippa, all without bloodshed or resistance. After sending all the Dutch officers and troops from Amboyna to Java, Captain Tucker proceeded in the Dover to the Dutch port of Gorontello, in the bay of Tommine, on the northern part of the island of Celebes; and, on or about the 16th of June, succeeded in persuading the sultan and his two sons, who represented the Dutch Company, to haul down the Dutch, and substitute the British colours: a ceremony complied with under every demonstration of attachment to the British government.

Having thus opened a large proportion of the Celebes to the English trade, Captain Tucker set sail for Manado; and, arriving there on the 21st, sent a flag of truce on shore, with a summons to the governor of Fort Amsterdam, on which and some adjacent batteries were mounted 50 pieces, of various, but chiefly very light calibers. The terms offered were immediately acceded to; and the Dutch garrison, numbering 113 officers and men, laid down their arms. Along with Manado fell its dependencies, the ports of Kemar, Le Copang, Amenang, and Tawangwoo.

On the 1st of March the Cornwallis chased a Dutch man-of-war brig into a small bay on the north side of the island of Amblaw, in the nighbourhood of Amboyna. As the wind was light and variable, and night approaching, Captain Montagu sent the yawl, cutter, and jolly-boat, under the command of Lieutenant Henry John Peachy, assisted by Mr. John Garland the master, and master's mate William Sanderson, to endeavour to bring the vessel out.

After a fatiguing pull during the whole night, the boats found themselves, at daylight, close to the vessel; which was the Dutch national brig Margaretta, mounting eight, but pierced for 11 guns, with a crew of 40 men. In the face of a heavy fire of grape and musketry, and of a brave defence by pikes and swords, Lieutenant Peachey and his party boarded and carried the brig, and that with so comparatively slight a loss as one man dangerously and four slightly wounded. The Dutch had one officer killed and 20 seamen wounded.

On the 10th of May the British 18-pounder 36-gun frigate

Caroline, Captain Christopher Cole, 38-gun frigate Piémontaise, Captain Charles Foote, 18-gun brig-sloop Barracouta, Captain Richard Kenah, and transport-brig, late Dutch prize, Mandarin, Lieutenant Archibald Buchanan, the two frigates having on board about 100 officers and men of the Madras European regiment, to be landed at Amboyna, and the transport a supply of specie and provisions for the same destination, set sail from Madras roads. Captain Cole had previously obtained from Rear-admiral Drury permission to make an attack upon some of the enemy's settlements that lay in his route to Amboyna; but that permission was accompanied by a friendly warning of the great strength of Banda, in reference especially to the small force then on board the frigates. On the 30th, after a very fine passage, the ships arrived at Pulo-Penang or Prince of Wales island, in the Straits of Malacca. Here, having made up his mind to attempt the reduction of the spice islands, and communicated his intentions to Captains Foote and Kenah, Captain Cole gained some slight information respecting Banda-Neira, the Dutch seat of government, but failed in obtaining what he most wanted, a plan of the island.

On the 10th of June, having been supplied by the Penang government with 20 artillerymen, two field-pieces, and 20 scaling-ladders, Captain Cole departed from the island, to make a passage into the Java sea against the south-east monsoon. On the 15th, when in the Straits of Sincapore, the ships fell in with the Samarang, and learnt from Captain Spencer, among other particulars, that the force at Banda, according to a return found at the capture of Amboyna, consisted of more than 700 regular troops. On the 25th the ships anchored, for a short time, under the north end of the island of Borneo, chiefly that the Piémontaise might repair her mainmast, which had been much damaged by lightning.

Apprehensive that Daendels, the Dutch captain-general of Java and the Moluccas, might succeed in throwing supplies and reinforcements into Banda before the arrival of the expedition, Captain Cole, the more quickly to get into the Soolo sea, entered the dangerous passage between Borneo and the small island of Malwali. The coral reefs were innumerable; and most of them just covered with water, and not easily seen until the sun had risen considerably above the horizon. By a good look-out and strict attention, the ships, in the course of 48 hours, had nearly cleared the shoals called by Dalrymple Felicia Proper, and the pilot had reported all danger as passed, when, right ahead, a ship was seen, wrecked on a coral reef just below the water's edge, and surrounded by piratical proäs, that fled as the frigates approached. Captain Cole went in his boat to examine the shoal and wreck, and found the deck of the ship streaming with fresh blood, and saw locks of human hair in several places; a sufficient indication that there had been a severe contest about the plunder.

The Piémontaise having in the meanwhile been ordered to proceed ahead with the Mandarin in tow, now made the signal for shoals in every direction between the north-east and south-east. This and the approach of night prevented any pursuit of the proäs; and Captain Cole on his return to the Caroline, found a much more important object to attend to. Indeed, nothing short of the greatest activity and perseverance, on the part of all three captains and their respective officers and crews, could have saved the ships. At 6 P.M. the small islands off the south-west end of Cagayan-Soolo were descried: and, as the only directions published for the Soolo sea mention the probability of a ship's being to the eastward of the shoals off the north-east coast of Borneo, when these islands are in sight, Captain Cole decided to run on, instead of anchoring till morning. The ships accordingly placed themselves under easy sail; and the Barracouta, leading, was followed by the others in her track. The night, which was rainy, dark, and squally, was passed by all the ships in sounding as quickly as the lead could be sent to the bottom, and in momentary expectation of the signal for danger. But the small island of Manbahenawan, close to them in the morning, gave a respite to the anxieties of every person on board; as it brought the assurance, that the greatest difficulties in the navigation had already been overcome.

On the 5th of July the ships anchored at Soolo; where they obtained a supply of water, fresh meat, and vegetables. While here, to give a more imposing appearance to the enterprise, the Barracouta was converted into a ship; an alteration that occupied her crew no longer than from daylight till breakfast time. On the 9th the ships quitted Soolo, and on the 10th entered the Pacific Ocean between the islands to the eastward of Soolo, and which are in sight of Basseelan. On the 21st, after a very favourable run, the ships gained a sight of the Cape of Good Hope (new) on the coast of New Guinea; and on the 23rd, late in the evening, having worked through Pitt's Straits against an adverse wind, entered the Java sea.

It took the ships nearly a fortnight to beat up to the island of

Goram, although distant only four degrees of latitude from Pitt's Straits; and on the 7th they communicated with the shore, but owing to the rapidity of the current and the strength of the monsoon, not without considerable difficulty. The rajah of the island now furnished Captain Cole with two Malay guides, who professed to have a knowledge of the roads and batteries of Banda-Neira; and the same evening the ships bore up for the Banda islands, which, with the prevailing wind, were only a 36 hours' sail from Goram.

The weather on the 8th was very fine, with a haze round the horizon, which favoured the approach of the ships; who were now under easy sail, to prevent as much as possible their being discovered. The final preparations for the attack were this day made; and at 2 P.M. the boats of the ships were hoisted out, and one day's provisions and 50 rounds of ball cartridge for each man put on board of them. At 5 P.M. the ships brought to. At 5 h. 30 m. the small island of Rosensgen became just visible through the haze; and at 6 P.M. Great Banda appeared at the distance of 10 or 11 leagues, towards the lee or eastern point of which the ships immediately bore up.

At 9 P.M. two shots were fired at the British from the island of Rosensgen; an unexpected occurrence, no intimation having been received that an outpost was stationed there. This circumstance, added to the fineness of the night and brightness of the moon, frustrated the plan of a surprise by the ships; and, against a place of such alleged strength as Banda-Neira, an attack in open day, by all the force which the little squadron could muster, promised very little success. At 2 h. 30 m. P.M. the ships again brought to, and at 10 P.M. the moon set. Soon afterwards the night became dark and squally. This sudden change in the weather suggested to Captain Cole the idea of a surprise by boats; for, although the Dutch had seen the ships, it was fairly inferred that they would not give the British credit for making, under all the circumstances of the case, so hazardous an attempt.

The excellent arrangements that had been adopted rendered signals unnecessary; and the ships closed near enough to each other to receive directions by the trumpet. Scarcely had the men rested half an hour with their arms by their sides, than they were summoned to the boats; and at a little before 11 P.M., the ships having then dropped within two cables length of the shore, about 400 officers and men, under the immediate command of Captain Cole, pushed off from the Caroline, shaping their course towards the east point of Great Banda. It is doubtful if there were quite so many as 400 men; for some of the soldiers intended to be of the party were left on board the Caroline for want of room in the boats, and the launch of the Piémontaise, in the dark and tempestuous weather which prevailed, went adrift with only half her allotted number.

The badness of the weather, and the increased darkness of the night, made it next to impossible for the boats to keep together; and, by 3 A.M. on the 9th, none of the party had assembled at the point of rendezvous, except Captains Cole and Kenah, in their respective gigs. About this time the three ships suddenly made their appearance within 100 yards of the two gigs: and Captain Cole, on going alongside the Piémontaise, had the satisfaction to learn from Captain Foote, that he had passed some of the boats at a short distance astern. Pulling in that direction, Captain Cole soon met a portion of his boats; and, receiving from the men in them the most animated assurances of support, he resolved to make the attack without waiting for the remainder of the party. This was a measure the more necessary, as the boats had still to pull three miles to the point of disembarkation; and that darkness, on which their success rested, was fast disappearing before the grey tints of the morning. The commencing twilight now discovered the shore of an island, known to be Banda-Neira; and the two large fires, blazing near the north point of it, indicated that the Dutch, as Captain Cole had judged would be the case, were collected there, in expectation that the attack, for which the two signal guns at Rosensgen had prepared them, would be made on the same spot on which Admiral Rainier's forces had formerly landed.

The group of islands, of which Banda-Neira is the capital, are 10 in number; six of which are named, Lontor, or Great Banda, Goonong-Api, Rosensgen, Pulo-Ay, and Pulo-Rhun. Banda-Neira is about two miles long and about three-quarters of a mile wide; it is extremely mountainous, and contains many excellent positions for repelling an invading force. At the time in question it possessed 10 sea-batteries, exclusive of Casteel-Belgica and Casteel-Nassau. The first of these castles, mounting 52 pieces of heavy cannon, commanded the other as well as all the sea-defences at that extremity of the island, and was deemed, by the Dutch at least, an impregnable fortress; and the whole number of guns mounted for the defence of the island was 138. The garrison of Banda-Neira, as we shall by-and-by satisfactorily show, amounted to 700 regular troops, and at least 800 militia—making a total of 1500 men. The party, now rapidly and silently advancing to surprise this force, consisted of 140 British seamen and marines, and about 40 soldiers of the Madras European regiment, under the command, as already stated, of Captain Cole, assisted by Captain Kenah, and by the following officers: Lieutenants Thomas Carew, Samuel Allen, George Pratt, Robert Walker, and Edmund Lyons, of the navy, Captain-lieutenant Nixon, Lieutenants Charles W. Yates, Philip Brown, and William Jones Daker, and ensign Charles Allen, of the Madras troops.

Just as a black cloud, attended by wind and rain, had thrown a temporary darkness over the island of Banda-Neira, the British boats grounded on a coral reef, situated within 100 yards of the shore, and, although unknown at the time, directly opposite to the battery of Voorzigtigheid, mounting 10 long 18-pounders. Such, however, was the violence of the storm, that the garrison at this battery remained in utter ignorance of what was going on so near to them: and the officers and men, leaping into the water, launched their boats over the reef. Shortly afterwards the British landed in a small sandy cove bordered with jungle; and the men were quickly formed as well as the pitchy darkness of the morning would admit. That done, Captain Kenah and Lieutenant Carew, at the head of a party of pikemen, advanced to take the battery in the rear. This service was so promptly and effectually executed, that the sentinel was killed, and an officer and 60 men made prisoners, without the firing of a pistol, although the enemy was at his guns with matches lighted. Captain Kenah had been directed to storm the next sea-battery, also mounting ten 18-pounders; but Captain Cole, being resolved to take the bull by the horns, or, in other words, to attempt carrying the castle of Belgica by a coup-de-main, recalled Captain Kenah and his party, and, leaving a small guard at the captured battery, pushed on, with the aid of one of his native guides, through a narrow path that skirted the town, towards the Dutch citadel, about half a mile distant.

The sound of the bugle was now spreading the alarm over the island; but, favoured by the storm that was raging over head, and making a rapid march, the British arrived within 100 yards of the citadel-ditch before they were discovered. An ineffectual fire of musketry was now opened from the ramparts. Regardless of this, the brave fellows rushed up the steep ascent; and, placing their scaling-ladders between the guns upon the outer pentagon, which, owing to the rain, burnt priming, were in an instant in possession of the lower works. The ladders were quickly hauled up and placed against the inner wall, but were found too short. This appeared to inspire the besieged with fresh courage, and three guns and several volleys of musketry were discharged; but the stormers soon found another way into the heart of the citadel. Just at this moment the gate was opened by the Dutch guard, to admit the Colonel-commandant, During, and three other officers, who lived in houses at the foot of the hill. At that gateway the British now made their rush. The Dutch colonel fell, covered with honourable wounds; and, after a slight skirmish, in which 10 others of the garrison shared the fate of their commanding officer, the British colours waved at the flagstaff of the castle of Belgica.

"With such examples," says Captain Cole, in allusion to his officers, " our brave fellows swept the ramparts like a whirlwind; and, in addition to the providential circumstance of the service being performed with scarcely a hurt or wound, I have the satisfaction of reporting, that there was no instance of irregularity arising from success." A part of the garrison, in the panic that prevailed, escaped over the walls; and the remainder, amounting to four officers and about 40 artillery-men,[1] surrendered themselves prisoners. Just as all this had been accomplished, "the day beamed on the British flag," and discovered to the new garrison of Belgica, the fort of Nassau, the town, and the different sea-defences, at their feet; but, as some drawback to the joy of the British at their extraordinary success, no ships were to be seen, nor even the boats containing the remainder of the landing-party. While a flag of truce is being despatched to the Dutch governor-general, we will pay some attention to the Caroline and her consorts, and also to the missing boats.

Immediately after the boats, containing Captain Cole and his party, had pushed off from the Caroline, the latter made a short stretch off; then tacked, and at 1 A.M. on the 9th, followed by the Piémontaise, rounded the east point of Great Banda, close to the shore, and entered the outer harbour, or that formed by the north-west side of Great Banda, by the islands of Goonong-Api and Neira, and by the two still smaller islands of Pulo-Ay and Pulo-Rhun to the eastward of the latter. The wind now became so baffling, and was attended with such heavy gusts, that the ships were frequently obliged to lower their topsails; not being able, in their short-manned state, to work the yards quick enough to keep them trimmed to the breeze. At 2 A.M. the

[1] The official account, by mistake, says two officers and 30 men.

Piémontaise hailed the Caroline, and informed Lieutenant John Gilmour, the officer in charge of her, that Captain Cole had hailed to say, that he and Captain Kenah had missed the boats at the rendezvous ;[1] and that, meaning to defer the attack till a more favourable opportunity, he wished the Caroline, who had a pilot on board, to lead in to an anchorage. Every exertion was now used to approach the land ; and the Caroline frequently got within her own length of it, but could not find bottom with the deepest line. Then a squall would pay her head right off, and in another moment she would be becalmed and ungovernable. At one time the Piémontaise, baffled in a similar manner, made stern-way at the rate of seven or eight knots an hour, and only avoided running foul of the Caroline by bearing up : the consequence of which was, that the Piémontaise lost as much ground in a few minutes as she had been all the night toiling to gain. As the Caroline, soon after daylight, approached Banda-Neira, several of the forts fired at her; but, not being able to spare any hands from working the sails, the frigate made no return. Fortunately for her, one shot only took effect ; nor did that do any greater damage than entering the quarter-deck bulwark and carrying away the midship spoke of the wheel. At 7 A.M. the Caroline descried the castle of Belgica ; and, about the same time, a well-directed shot from the latter silenced the sea-battery, which had annoyed her the most. It was now that a small English jack discovered itself above the Dutch colours ; and all on board the Caroline used increased exertions to reach the spot, where their gallant comrades had effected so much, and where they might yet have to effect more.

As the flag of truce had not yet returned from the governor, another was sent to say that, unless all hostility immediately ceased, Fort Nassau, at whose flagstaff the Dutch colours were still flying, would be stormed by the British, and the town laid in ashes by the cannon of Belgica. This decisive message produced the immediate and unconditional surrender of Banda-Neira and its dependencies ; and the Caroline, just before she anchored off the town, saw the Batavian flag lowered from Fort Nassau and the British hoisted in its stead. About the same time that the Caroline came to, some of the missing boats, after a night of great hardship and suffering, entered the harbour. The remainder of the boats had got on board the Piémontaise ; who, as well as the Barracouta and Mandarin, anchored a little before noon with the Caroline. In the course of this day 1500

[1] See p. 198.

regulars and militia, 400 of the former from the north point, laid down their arms on the glacis of Fort Nassau; a clear proof, coupled with the manifest strength of the defences, that the force of Banda-Neira had not been overrated.

Viewed in every light, the taking of the Banda isles was an achievement of no common order. Where are we to find, even in the annals of the British navy, more skill and perseverance than was employed in overcoming the difficulties of the navigation to the scene of conquest? Or where a greater share of address and valour than was displayed by Captain Cole and his 180 brave associates, more than three-fourths of them seamen and marines, in the crowning act of their bold exploit? Without seeking to discover shades of difference between two cases in their general features alike, we may point to the conquest of another Dutch colony: a conquest which, in the manner of its execution, spread as much renown over the British name in the western, as this was calculated to do in the eastern hemisphere; let no one, then, call up to his recollection Captain Brisbane and Curaçoa, without affording an equal place in his esteem to Captain Cole and Banda-Neira.

For the valuable and important conquest he had achieved, Captain Cole received the thanks of his commander-in-chief, of the governor-general of India in council, and of the lords of the admiralty; but we question if the sentiments contained in any one of the three letters, although forcibly expressed in all, went so straight to the heart as the contents of the letters addressed to Captain Cole by his shipmates and partners in glory. The first was from Captains Foote and Kenah, presenting a silver cup; the second from the lieutenants and other officers of the three ships, presenting a sword of a hundred guineas value; the third from the officers of the Honourable Company's troops engaged in the enterprise, presenting a sword of the same value; and the fourth from the crew of the Caroline, accompanied by a similar token of their admiration and esteem. These testimonials concur in vouching for one fact, which Captain Cole's modesty has induced him to refrain from stating, or even hinting at, in his official letter, the personal share he took in the conflict. The letter signed "The Caroline's" affords an unequivocal proof of another trait in their captain: it shows that he was as kind as he was brave.[1]

When we last quitted the neighbourhood of the Isle of France,

[1] For copies of the several letters see Marshall's "Royal Naval Biography," vol. ii. pp. 511, 512.

the French frigate Vénus, newly named Néréide, and the recaptured frigate Ceylon, had just been added to the force on the station under Commodore Rowley.[1] In a week or two afterwards that force was augmented by the arrival of several frigates; and it was at length determined, as soon as an expedition of sufficient strength could be assembled, to attempt the reduction of the Isle of France; in the principal port of which island, Port Louis, now lay the five French frigates, Bellone, Minerve, Manche, Astrée, and (late British) Iphigénie, also the Victor ship-corvette, brig-corvette Entreprenant and another of the same class, quite new, besides several French merchant-vessels. Two only of the frigates, the Astrée and Manche, were in a state of readiness for sea; and after the 19th of October these were blockaded by the three British frigates Boadicea, Nisus, and Néréide, under the command of Commodore Rowley of the former.

By the 21st of November all the different divisions of the expedition, except that expected from the Cape of Good Hope, had assembled off and at the anchorage of the island of Rodriguez; and it being considered, on account of the lateness of the season, unadvisable to wait for the arrival of the Cape division, the remaining divisions of the naval portion under the command of Vice-admiral Bertie, and the military under Major-general Abercromby, on the morning of the 22nd set sail for the Isle of France, but, owing to the light and baffling winds, did not, until the evening of the 28th, arrive in sight of the island.

The whole of the ships-of-war attached to the expedition, including a portion that blockaded Port Louis, consisted as follows:—

Gun-ship.
74 Illustrious . . . . Captain William Robert Broughton.

Gun-frigate.
44 Cornwallis . . . . ,, James Caulfield.
38 { Africaine . . . { Vice-admiral (r.) Albemarle Bertie. / Captain Charles Gordon, *acting*.
    Boadicea . . . . ,, Josias Rowley.
    Nisus . . . . . ,, Philip Beaver.
    Clorinde . . . . ,, Thomas Briggs.
    Menelaus . . . . ,, Peter Parker.
    Néréide . . . . ,, Robert Henderson, *acting*.
36 { Phœbe . . . . ,, James Hillyar.
    Doris . . . . . ,, William Jones Lye.

[1] See p. 190.

Gun-frigate.

32 { Cornelia . . . . Captain Henry Folkes Edgell.
Psyché . . . . ,, John Edgcumbe.
Ceylon . . . . ,, James Tomkinson, *acting*.

Sloops, Hesper, Captain William Paterson, Eclipse, Captain Henry Lynne, *acting*, Hecate, Captain George Rennie, *acting*, Actæon, Captain Ralph Viscount Neville; *gun-brig* Staunch, Lieutenant —— Craig, *acting*; *government-ship* Emma, Captain Benjamin Street, *acting*, and three smaller government vessels, and a great many transports. The number of troops accompanying the expedition appears to have been about 10,000.

On the 29th, in the morning, the men-of-war and transports, numbering altogether nearly 70 sail, anchored in Grande-Baie, situated about 12 miles to the north-eastward of Port Louis. The great obstacle to an attack upon the Isle of France had always been, the supposed impossibility to effect a landing, with any considerable force, owing to the reefs that surround the coast, as well as to find anchorage for a numerous fleet of transports. But these difficulties had been surmounted by the indefatigable exertions of Commodore Rowley; who, assisted by Lieutenant Street, then of the Staunch, Lieutenant Blackiston of the Madras engineers, and the masters of the Africaine and Boadicea, had sounded and minutely examined every part of the leeward side of the island. So that, in the course of the same day, the army, with its artillery, stores, and ammunition, the several detachments of marines serving in the squadron, and a large body of seamen under the orders of Captain William Augustus Montagu, disembarked without opposition or casualty. On the morning of the 30th there was a slight skirmishing between the adverse pickets; and on the 1st and 2nd of December an affair, rather more serious, took place between the British main body and a corps of the enemy, who with several field-pieces had taken a strong position, to check the advance of the invaders. The French, however, were soon overpowered by numbers, with the loss of their guns and several men killed and wounded. The loss on the part of the British, including that sustained on the 30th, amounted to 28 officers and men killed, 94 wounded, and 45 missing.

Immediately after the termination of this battle, General Decaen, who, in the slight support he received from the colonial militia, now learnt to appreciate the effects of the proclamations so industriously spread among them by Captain Willoughby in the spring, proposed terms of capitulation; and on the following morning, the 3rd, the articles were signed and ratifications exchanged, surrendering to the island of Great Britain. The garrison of the Isle of France consisted, it appears, of no more than 1300 regular troops, including, to their shame be it spoken, a corps of about 500 Irishmen, chiefly recruits taken out of the captured Indiamen. But the militia force amounted to upwards of 10,000 men; a number which General Decaen, no doubt, would have gladly exchanged for as many more regulars as he had under his command. Upon the numerous batteries of the Isle of France were mounted 209 pieces of heavy ordnance; the guns in excellent order, and the batteries completely equipped with shot, ammunition, and every other requisite for service. In Port Louis were the men-of-war already named; also the Charlton, Ceylon, and United Kingdom, late English Indiamen, and 24 French merchant-ships and brigs: two of the ships, the Althée and Ville-d'Auten, measured 1000 tons each.

Of the four captured 40-gun frigates, the Bellone, under the name of Junon, and the Astrée under that of Pomone, were all that were purchased for the use of the British navy. The Iphigenia was restored to her rank among the 18-pounder 36s; but the old battered Néréide, rendered so famous by the gallantry of her captain and crew, was in too bad a state to be removed from Grand Port, and was sold only to be broken up.

BRITISH AND FRENCH FLEETS.

The principal feature that distinguishes the present abstract[1] from the generality of those which have preceded it, is the insignificant total at the foot of the column of "Purchased enemy's national vessels."[2] This is to be attributed to the effectual manner in which the ports of France had been blockaded, rather than to any diminution of strength or spirit in the French navy. The latter, indeed, notwithstanding its reverses, had been, and was still, increasing in its numbers, as we shall presently have occasion to show. The decrease compartment of the abstract also exhibits a reduction, by as much as one-half, in the numerical, if not in the tonnage, amount of its first and more important column.[3]

The number of commissioned officers and masters belonging to the British navy at the commencement of the year 1811 was,

Admirals	65
Vice-admirals	60
Rear-admirals	56
,, superannuated 35.	
Post-captains	753
,, superannuated 29.	
Commanders, or sloop-captains	558
,, superannuated 50.	
Lieutenants	3071
Masters	544

And the number of seamen and marines, voted for the service of the same year, was 145,000.[4]

---

[1] See Appendix, Annual Abstract, No. 19
[2] See Appendix, No. 5.
[3] See Appendix, No. 6.
[4] Ibid., No. 7.

Such had been the unremitting exertions of the shipwrights in the arsenal at Antwerp, that, by the latter end of the summer, Vice-admiral Missiessy was at anchor at the mouth of the Scheldt, with a fleet of 15 sail of the line, one frigate, and nine brigs, waiting to elude the vigilance of Admiral Young; who, since the preceding May, had superseded Sir Richard Strachan in the chief command, and, with a corresponding fleet, was cruising outside. In addition to the above French force in this quarter, the Gorée squadron, consisting of three sail of the line, the Chatham of 80, Hollander of 74, and Tromp of 68 guns, had recently been buoyed over the flats and brought to Antwerp, where they were repairing. Upon the stocks at Antwerp, Terneuse, and Flushing, were from 12 to 15 ships of the line, five or six of them in a state of great forwardness. To protect the vast dépôt now formed and forming along the shores of the Scheldt, immense fortifications had been constructed, particularly at Flushing; the sea-front alone of which mounted 100 long 36-pounders and 60 (French) 12-inch mortars. The opposite or Cadzand shore had also had its fortifications greatly strengthened. In the Texel seven Franco-Batavian sail of the line were ready for sea. Proceeding southward, we find that, besides the two 74s at anchor in the road of Cherbourg, two were on the stocks in the arsenal; and that Lorient, Rochefort, and Toulon had all their building slips full.

The latter port, indeed, was dividing with Flushing the attention of the British. The road of Toulon, in the course of the present year, contained as many as 16 sail of the line, and nearly half as many frigates, including among the former four immense three-deckers. The command of this fine and powerful fleet had, since the preceding year, devolved upon Vice-admiral Emeriau, who had under him Rear-admirals Cosmao, Lhermite, and Baudin. During the first half of the year the British Mediterranean fleet remained under the command of Admiral Sir Charles Cotton; but the latter, returning to England to take the command of the Channel fleet, was succeeded off Toulon, on the 18th of July, by Vice-admiral Sir Edward Pellew, whose force consisted of the

Gun-ship.			
120	Caledonia	. .	Vice-admiral (r.) Sir Edward Pellew, Bart. Rear-admiral (b.) Israel Pellew. Captain Richard Harward.
	Hibernia	. . . .	Lieutenant William Holman, *acting*.
112	Ville-de-Paris	. .	Captain George Burlton.
100	Royal Sovereign	. .	,, John Harvey.

Gun-ship.		
98 Téméraire		{ Rear-admiral (r.) Francis Pickmore. { Captain Joseph Spear.
74 {	Rodney	{ Rear-admiral (b.) Th. Francis Freemantle. { Captain John Duff Markland.
	York	,, Robert Barton.
	Kent	,, Thomas Rogers.
	Conqueror	,, Edward Fellowes.
	Magnificent	,, George Eyre.
	Sultan	,, John West.
	Repulse	,, Richard Hussey Moubray.
	Bombay	,, William Cuming.
	Achille	,, Askew Paffard Hollis.
	Implacable	,, Joshua Rowley Watson.
	Leviathan	,, Patrick Campbell.

Frigates, Apollo, Impérieuse, and Franchise.

Early on the morning of the 19th of July the two French 40-gun frigates Amélie and Adrienne, on their return from Genoa with conscripts for the fleet, were endeavouring to enter Toulon by the Petite-Passe. Since daylight the semiphoric signals along the coast had apprised Vice-admiral Emeriau of the presence of these frigates: and, just as the British admiral, who was cruising off Cape Sicie with the above-named 16 sail of the line and three frigates, had made the signal for chase to the Conqueror and Sultan, the two in-shore line-of-battle ships, M. Emeriau weighed and sailed out of the road, with 13 sail of the line and the Incorruptible frigate, to cover the Amélie and Adrienne. At 11 h. 30 m. A.M. the Conqueror got near enough to open her fire upon the two frigates: and presently afterwards both the Conqueror and the Sultan exchanged a few distant broadsides with the French advanced division, consisting of the Ulm, Danube, Magnanime, and Breslau 74s. The two frigates very soon got completely under the protection of their fleet which then bore up and returned to Toulon road.

Neither of the two British ships appears to have been struck by a shot; but, according to M. Emeriau, the Ulm had some of her rigging cut by the fire of the British. As of course the Conqueror, who was the nearest in-shore, on finding herself getting within gun-shot of four French 74s, with a fleet of nine more line-of-battle ships close in their wake (M. Emeriau admits he sailed out with 13), shortened sail and tacked off to rejoin her fleet, the French admiral in his despatch, was enabled to say, "L'ennemi," meaning the British fleet, not the advanced 74, "ayant pris la bordée du large, j'ai fait retourner les vaisseaux au mouillage."

On the 7th of August the British fleet came to anchor in the bay of Hyères, out of gun-shot of the batteries, leaving a line-of-battle ship and two or three frigates, as a squadron of observation off Cape Sicie. This afforded to Vice-admiral Emeriau several opportunities to sail out with his fleet, and chase " the enemy " from off the port; but he invariably returned to his anchorage after effecting this important service: important, indeed, for the admiral wrote a despatch every time he weighed, and the minister of marine invariably published that despatch in the columns of the Moniteur.

On the 13th, while the British fleet was getting under way in very light winds, the Téméraire drifted near to the battery at Pointe des Mèdes. Instantly the battery opened a fire upon her; which was returned by the Téméraire, as well as by the Caledonia, who was also within gun-shot. By the aid of their boats, both ships got out of reach of the battery; but not until some shots had struck them, particularly the Téméraire, who had one of her main deck gun-carriages disabled, and her master, Mr. Robert Duncan, severely, and three seamen slightly wounded. A shot from her, or from the Caledonia, had also wounded two men in the French battery. The noise of the firing brought out M. Emeriau with 14 sail of the line, and furnished the Moniteur with another paragraph, to prove the fearlessness with which the French fleet could manœuvre within a league or two of its own port.

Almost every day that the British fleet remained at the Hyères, or cruised off Cape San-Sebastian, the French fleet, or a division of it, sailed out and in, to exercise the crews, the principal part of which were conscripts. On the 20th of November, when the only British force off Toulon were the two 38-gun frigates Volontaire, Captain the Honourable Granville George Waldegrave, and Perlen, acting Captain Joseph Swabey Tetley, and these had been blown to some distance from the coast, a fleet of 14 French ships of the line and several frigates sailed upon a cruise between the capes of Sicie and Sepet; intending to extend it a little beyond them, if wind and weather should permit, and if Sir Edward Pellew should approach no nearer than his present cruising-ground, off Cape San-Sebastian. The French admiral remained out all that night, and all the following day and night, without being crossed by a hostile sail.

At daylight on the 22nd, however, as the Volontaire and Perlen were lying to, at the distance of from two to three leagues west-south-west from Cape Sicie, the French advanced division, consisting of three line-of-battle ships and two frigates, made its appearance in the south-east. Both parties were soon under a crowd of sail. At 9 A.M. Captain Tetley exchanged several shot with a French frigate upon his lee-quarter; and, owing to the Perlen being able, from the peculiar construction of her afterbody (she was a Danish-built ship), to bring six guns, three on each deck, to bear upon what is usually termed the point of impunity, he so cut up the French frigate forward, that, at 10 A.M. the latter bore away out of gun-shot. The Trident 74 and Amélie frigate, in the mean time, had exchanged a few distant shot with the Volontaire. The French 74 and frigate then stood for the Perlen; at whom they began firing at 11 A.M., and upon whom they gained gradually in the chase. At noon Cape Sicie bore from the Perlen east-north-east 10 or 11 degrees. At 1 P.M., finding that the two ships were advancing rapidly upon her, the Perlen cut away the sheet, spare stream, and kedge anchors. At 2 h. 30 m. P.M. the Trident was on her lee, and the Amélie on her weather-quarter—both still keeping up a heavy fire, and the Perlen returning it. In another quarter of an hour, provoked at being fired at so effectually in a position from which she herself could bring no guns to bear, the Trident yawed and discharged her broadside. This of course occasioned the French 74 to drop astern; and, accompanied by the Amélie, the Trident stood for the Volontaire. In a little while, however, the two French ships, finding that the state of their rigging gave them no hope of success in the chase, altered their course, and bore away for Toulon.

The Perlen had her standing and running rigging and sails very much cut, and received two shot so low down, as to cause her to make nine inches of water per hour; but, fortunately, the frigate had none of her crew hurt. The Volontaire was not struck; although at one time two two-deckers, one with a rear-admiral's flag, fired several broadsides at her. Having thus chased away the only British force at this time off the coast, and which the magnifying optics of his reconnoitring captains made out to be "un vaisseau et une frégate," Vice-admiral Emeriau continued manœuvring about until the 26th; then re-anchored in the road of Toulon. On the same day Vice-admiral Sir Edward Pellew, with the British fleet, anchored off the south-east end of the island of Minorca.

The length of the French admiral's cruise required a few days' relaxation; and it was not, we believe, until the 9th of December, that the fleet again weighed from the road. On this day

M. Emeriau, having, as he states, been apprised by the signal-posts that a British fleet of 12 sail of the line was in the offing, put to sea with " 16 sail of the line and two frigates.". In a few hours, however, the French admiral returned into port; and this proved to be the last exploit of the Toulon fleet during the year 1811.

Is it not a little surprising that, out of upwards of 56 sail of the line in commission at the different ports of the French empire, namely, 18, including three Dutch ships, in the Scheldt, seven in the Texel, two in Cherbourg, two in Brest, four in Lorient, three in Rochefort, 16 in Toulon, and four at least in the ports of Genoa, Spezzia, Venice, and Naples, not one squadron, nay, not one line-of-battle ship, should have ventured out of sight of her own harbour? What prevented Vice-admiral Emeriau from going fairly to sea on the 20th of November? Where had the glory of the "great nation" hid itself? Where were the Duguay-Trouins, the De Grasses, and the Suffrens, when on the 6th of December, 1811, a French admiral, with 16 sail of the line, allowed himself to be driven back into port by a British admiral with 12? And yet, if report be true, Buonaparte had an object, a grand object, in view—no less than that of getting a powerful fleet to the East Indies, and thereby possessing himself of the immense territories belonging to Great Britain in that quarter of the globe.

Light Squadrons and Single Ships.

On the 24th of March, at daylight, Barfleur lighthouse bearing south by east distant 12 or 13 miles, the British 74-gun ship Berwick, Captain James Macnamara, observed a large sail directly between herself and the lighthouse, running along the shore. This was the French 40-gun frigate Amazone, Captain Bernard-Louis Rousseau, making another attempt to get from Havre to Cherbourg.[1] The 74 immediately gave chase, and compelled the frigate to haul in for a small rocky bay, about a mile to the westward of the lighthouse; where the Amazone anchored with the loss of her rudder. Thinking an attack by boats practicable when the tide suited, Captain Macnamara called in from the offing by signal the 38-gun frigate Amelia, Captain the Honourable Frederick Paul Irby, and the 16-gun brig-sloops Goshawk and Hawk, Captain James Lilburn and Henry Bourchier. At 8 A.M., the lee tide making strong, the

See p. 108.

Berwick, to avoid the rocks and shoals surrounding her, came to an anchor about two miles to the northward of the Amazone; as, upon their junction, did the Amelia, Hawk, and Goshawk.

At noon the 38-gun frigate Niobe, Captain Joshua Wentworth Loring, joined from the westward. At 4 P.M., the flood-tide making, and Captain Macnamara having relinquished the plan of attack by boats on account of the rapidity of the tides, the squadron got under way; and the Niobe, followed by the Amelia and Berwick in succession, stood in as close to the French frigate as the safety of the ships would admit. The latter being surrounded by rocks and shoals, their fire could only be bestowed in the act of wearing, and was consequently partial and of little effect. At 6 P.M. the British hauled off, with the loss of one man killed and one wounded on board the Amelia, and the standing and running rigging of all three ships much cut.

On the 25th, at daylight, Captain Macnamara stood in again with his squadron, for the purpose of renewing the attack; but the French captain rendered that step unnecessary, by setting fire to his ship; and the Amazone, a fine new frigate of the largest class, was soon burnt to the water's edge.

On the 8th of May, at 9 h. 30 m. A.M., the British 18-gun brig-sloop Scylla (sixteen 32-pounder carronades and two sixes), Captain Arthur Atcheson, being close in with the Isle of Bas, discovered to leeward, and immediately chased, the French gun-brig Canonnier, of 10 long 4-pounders, one 24-pounder carronade and four swivels, with 77 men, commanded by Enseigne de vaisseau Jean-Joseph-Benoit Schilds, having under her protection a convoy of five small vessels, which she had just sailed with from Péros and was conducting to Brest.

At 11 h. 30 m. A.M. the Scylla overtook, and commenced firing at, the Canonnier and her convoy. At 11 h. 45 m., being then within the Triagos and Portgalo rocks, off Morlaix, and finding that it was the intention of the French commander to run his vessel and convoy on shore, Captain Atcheson resolved to lay him on board. The Scylla, going at the time eight knots, accordingly did so; and in about three minutes her officers and crew carried the Canonnier, with a loss on their part of two seamen killed, and one midshipman (Thomas Liven) and one marine slightly wounded. As a proof that the French brig made a creditable resistance, she lost her commander, one midshipman, the boatswain, and three seamen killed, and one midshipman and 10 seamen wounded, five of them dangerously. One only of the convoy was secured, a sloop laden with grain: the remaining four got within the rocks and ran themselves on shore.

On the 24th of August, at 1 P.M., as the British 38-gun frigate Diana, Captain William Ferris, and 18-pounder 36-gun frigate Semiramis, Captain Charles Richardson, were standing towards the Cordouan lighthouse from Basque roads, five sail were descried inside of the shoals at the mouth of the river Gironde. Four of these were small merchant-vessels, which the fifth sail, the French (late British) gun-brig Teazer, mounting twelve 18-pounder carronades and two long 18-pounders, with 85 men, commanded by Lieutenant de vaisseau Jean-Alexandre Papineau, had escorted from Rochefort and was now taking to a place of security, on account of not being able, as represented, to weather Maumusson.

Aware that a direct attack upon these vessels, situated as they were amidst shoals and heavy batteries, would be attended with the sacrifice of many lives, Captain Ferris resolved to attempt accomplishing his object by stratagem. Accordingly, at 4 h. 30 m. P.M., having hoisted French colours, and the Diana a commodore's pendant and a French jack at the fore, the signal for a pilot, the two British frigates stood boldly in towards the mouth of the Gironde. The Teazer immediately hoisted her colours, and fired a gun to leeward, the signal for a friend. The two frigates promptly repeated the gun, and at 6 P.M. tacked. The battery at Pointe de la Coubre now fired a few shot; but Captain Papineau, as the Teazer ran past the battery, hailed the commandant, and informed him that the two frigates were the Pallas and Elbe from Rochefort. The battery, on this, ceased firing; and at 6 h. 30 m. P.M. a pilot-boat came alongside the Diana. The Frenchmen were soon handed out of her, and their boat secured astern. At 7 P.M., which was just as it got dark, the Diana and Semiramis anchored off Pointe de Grave, between the Cordouan and Royan; under the batteries of which latter place and of Verdon lay the Teazer, in company with the brig-corvette Pluvier, of 14 carronades, 24-pounders, and two sixes, commanded by the captain of the port, Capitaine de frégate Michael-Augustin Dubourg, and stationed there for the protection of the different convoys passing along that part of the coast.

The Teazer's convoy having anchored about four miles up the river, Captain Ferris, at 7 h. 30 m. P.M., despatched seven boats, to attempt cutting the vessels out; three from the Diana, under the orders of Lieutenants Francis Sparrow and George B. Roper, and master's mate William Holmes, and four from the Semiramis, under Lieutenants Thomas Gardner, Percy Grace, and Robert Nicholson, and master's mate Timothy Renou. The tide prevented the execution of this service until very late in the night; and at daylight on the 25th the boats and the captured vessels, five in number, were still up the river, at the mouth of which lay the two French men-of-war brigs. Captain Ferris now determined to attack the two brigs with the ships; and accordingly, at 6 A.M., the two frigates, using the same artifices as before, got under way and steered for Verdon road. As a proof that the deception fully succeeded, Captain Dubourg went on board the Diana in his boat, and did not discover his mistake until he had ascended the quarter-deck.

While the Semiramis stood towards the inner brig, the Pluvier, the Diana laid the outer one, the Teazer, close alongside, the frigate's lower yards carrying away the brig's two topgallantmasts. In an instant Lieutenant Robert White Parsons, first of the Diana, attended by Lieutenant Lewis Pryse Madden of the marines, Mr. Mark G. Noble the boatswain, and about 30 seamen and marines, sprang on board, and, without the loss of a man on either side, carried the brig. Lieutenant Parsons then caused the prisoners to be put below without the force of arms and consequent destruction of life; thereby evincing a humanity which did him much honour. One of the Diana's seamen was afterwards accidentally lost overboard.

The moment she discovered what had befallen the Teazer, and saw the Semiramis approaching to put the same plan in practice upon herself, the Pluvier, now commanded by Lieutenant de vaisseau Page St.-Vaast, cut her cables and made sail for the beach; where she grounded near to the battery of Royan. The Semiramis chased until she got into five fathoms water; then anchored with a spring, so as to bring her broadside to bear upon the brig and her bow guns upon the fort, within grape-shot distance of both. After a few minutes' engagement, and just as the boats were about to pull alongside the Pluvier to carry off her crew, numbering 136 officers and men, Lieutenant Gardner, with the barge, pinnace, and cutter, rejoined his ship from the service of capturing the convoy. These boats were immediately sent to attack the brig; and, after receiving the broadside of the Pluvier, Lieutenant Gardner boarded and carried her, with no greater loss, on the British side, than himself and two seamen wounded.

The prize being fast on shore, the ebb-tide running rapidly, and the Semiramis in only 25 feet water, Captain Richardson found it necessary to take out of the Pluvier the remainder of her crew and burn her; a service soon executed. The Semiramis then stood out to join the Diana, who had anchored in the Gironde out of gun-shot, in company with the Teazer and the five vessels late under her charge; one of which, the transport Mulet, mounted eight swivels, with a crew of 42 men, and was laden with ship-timber. At 1 h. 30 m. P.M. the Pluvier exploded; and thus was consummated an enterprise, planned with judgment, and executed with skill and gallantry.

After lying tolerably quiet for several years, the famous Boulogne flotilla began again, this autumn, to be seized with fits of restlessness. It consisted at this time of 16 prames, or ship-rigged gun-vessels, mounting 12 long 24-pounders, with 112 men each; 28 brigs, with false keels, mounting from three to eight long 24s, and occasionally a large mortar, with from 70 to 80 men each; eight schooners of 10 guns and 40 men each, and between 200 and 300 gun-boats, rigged chiefly as luggers, some with one, others with two, long 18 or 24 pounders and 26 men each.

On the 19th of August, at 2 P.M., the island of St. Marcouf bearing west by north distant six leagues, the British 16-gun brig-sloop Hawk, Captain Henry Bourchier, observed from the mast-head a convoy of French vessels steering for Barfleur. All sail was immediately made in chase; and, on her near approach, the Hawk discovered that the convoy was under the protection of three gun-brigs and two large luggers, the latter carrying from eight to 10 guns, and the former from 10 to 16, and apparently well armed. These five armed vessels immediately hauled out from their convoy, with the evident intention of giving battle to the British brig, and the latter hove to in readiness to receive them.

At 3 h. 30 m. P.M., Pointe Piercue bearing north-west half-west distant four miles, the action commenced within half pistol-shot, and continued with great spirit on both sides, until the Hawk succeeded in driving on shore two of the brigs and the two luggers, with 15 sail of their convoy. While in the act of wearing to prevent the third brig from raking her, the Hawk took the ground; whereby that brig and a few of her convoy, although they had previously struck, effected their escape. During an hour and a half that the Hawk was employed in lightening herself of booms, spars, anchors, and a few of her guns, she lay exposed to incessant discharges of artillery and musketry from the shore. Having got again afloat, the Hawk anchored to repair her damaged rigging; and Captain Bourchier took that opportunity of despatching his boats, under the orders of Lieutenant David Price, second of the brig (the first absent in a prize), assisted by John Smith the master, and Thomas Wheeler the gunner, to bring out or destroy as many of the vessels as practicable.

Lieutenant Price, under a galling fire of musketry from the beach, succeeded in bringing out the Héron, national brig, pierced for 16 guns, mounting when the attack commenced only 10 (and of these she had since, to lighten herself, thrown overboard four), together with three large transports, laden with ship-timber. The remainder of the grounded vessels were on their broadsides and completely bilged; but Lieutenant Price was prevented from burning them, owing to the strength of the tide against him. The loss sustained by the Hawk, in this her very gallant enterprise, amounted to one seaman killed and four wounded. Captain Bourchier, in his official letter, speaks very highly of Mr. Henry Campling, purser; "who," he says, "volunteered to command the marines and small-arm men, and from whose continued and well-conducted fire I attribute the loss of so few men." In these instances, where officers step out of their way to serve in posts of danger, we are particularly gratified in being able to record their names. For his gallantry on the occasion, Captain Bourchier was deservedly promoted to post-rank.

On the 6th of September, in consequence of information brought by some deserters from the French admiral's ship in Cherbourg, Captain Pulteney Malcolm, of the 74-gun ship Royal Oak, cruising off the port, detached the 28-gun frigate Barbadoes, Captain Edward Rushworth, and 16-gun brig-sloop Goshawk, Captain James Lilburn, to the eastward of Barfleur, for the purpose of intercepting some gun-brigs expected at Cherbourg from Boulogne. On the 7th the two British brigs fell in with seven French gun-brigs, mounting three long 24-pounders and a mortar each, and manned with 75 men. These the Barbadoes and Goshawk immediately attacked and chased into Calvados, driving one of them on shore.

On the 8th the 18-pounder 36-gun frigate Hotspur, Captain Josceline Percy, arrived off Calvados, to endeavour to destroy the French brigs. Having a pilot on board, who undertook to carry the frigate within pistol-shot of the enemy, Captain Percy stood in to the attack; and at 6 P.M., when within less than half gun-shot, the Hotspur grounded. Notwithstanding her situation, the frigate succeeded in sinking one gun-brig and driving two on shore, but lay fast for four hours, exposed all the while to a heavy fire from the vessels, a battery, and some field-pieces. The consequence was, that the Hotspur sustained a very serious loss; having two midshipmen (William Smith and Alexander Hay), two seamen, and one boy killed, and 19 seamen and three marines wounded. The ship also received considerable damage in her hull, masts, and rigging.

On the 3rd of September, at 11 A.M., while the two 10-gun brig-sloops Rinaldo, Captain James Anderson, and Redpole, Captain Colin Macdonald, were watching the main body of the French flotilla, moored along the coast of Boulogne bay, under the protection of the heavy batteries in that neighbourhood, four of the 12-gun prames, one bearing a commodore's broad pendant, four 4-gun brigs, and seven lugger-rigged gun-boats, of one gun each, got under way from the west end of the bay, with the flood-tide and a strong breeze from the east-north-east, apparently to shift their birth upon the eastern land. Hoping that a chance might offer, should these vessels venture a little way from the shore, of intercepting some of them, Captain Anderson, with his two brigs, hovered about them to windward. Observing, after a while, one of the prames and a brig astern of the others, the Rinaldo and Redpole made all sail in the expectation to cut one or the other of them off; but, seeing the British captain's intention, the French prame and brig also made sail, and succeeded in joining the others, who were lying to for them within the Basse bank.

At 1 P.M., having followed the prame and brig within the bank, the Rinaldo and Redpole commenced action with them and the rear of the flotilla. Having stood as close in-shore as they could, the prames, gun-brigs, and luggers tacked and stood out in two lines, pointing in the direction of the two British brigs, who were lying to receive them. After a little partial firing, the flotilla stood in again, followed and engaged by the Rinaldo and Redpole. This manoeuvre was repeated once or twice: and eventually the flotilla bore round up, and came to at their former anchorage, having done no greater injury to the two British brigs, than cutting away some of their rigging and making a few holes in their sails. Considering that the two British brigs mounted only 18-pounder carronades, and their antagonists long French 24-pounders, although we may wish for some further particulars of this action before we apply a term to the behaviour of the latter, we may safely say of the former, that they conducted themselves in the most gallant manner.

On the 20th of September, at noon, as the British 38-gun frigate Naiad, Captain Philip Carteret, was at anchor off Boulogne road, the French emperor, who was honouring the Boulognese with a visit, embarked in his barge, and, proceeding along the line of prames and gun-brigs, went on board the centre prame. The imperial flame immediately waved at the maintopgallantmast-head, and remained there for a short time; when, Napoleon departing, it was lowered down, and the flag of Rear-admiral Baste hoisted at the mizen. Several of the other vessels were honoured in a similar manner, and Buonaparte continued rowing about the road. All this was plainly seen from on board the Naiad. Whether the presence of this British frigate kindled the wrath of Napoleon, and he wished her away, or that he considered she would make an excellent target for his prames and brigs to exercise their guns at, certain it is, that he ordered a division of the flotilla to weigh and stand towards her. At 1 P.M., the wind at south-south-west, and a strong flood-tide setting to the north-east, Rear-admiral Baste, with seven prames, each armed and manned as already stated, got under way, and steered for the Naiad, then bearing from them nearly north.

As, in the state of the wind and tide, the Naiad by getting under way would only increase her distance from the prames, she remained at an anchor with springs on her cable. At 1 h. 40 m. P.M., the leading prame, having arrived just within gun-shot, opened her fire, and received the frigate's in return; then tacked and stood off. Each of the leading prame's six followers did the same; and at about 2 P.M. 10 brigs, mounting each four long 24-pounders, and a sloop fitted as a bomb-vessel, joined in the cannonade. At 3 h. 30 m. P.M., it being then slack water, the Naiad weighed and stood off on the larboard tack; partly to repair some trifling damage, but chiefly, by getting to windward, to be better able to close with the prames and brigs, and get within shore of some of them. At 4 h. 45 m. the flotilla stood in under the batteries to the eastward of Boulogne, and ceased firing. At 5 h. 30 m. the Naiad tacked and stood inshore, under all sail, in chase; but, about sunset, the wind fell, to a calm. Shortly afterwards the prames and gun-brigs came to anchor near Pointe la Crèche; and at 7 h. 30 m. P.M., the Naiad herself anchored in her former position without having a man hurt. Nor had she the smallest spar shot away, as some token to the French emperor, who, no doubt, was honouring the British frigate with his regards, that the long 24-pounders of his flotilla, having failed to drive the Naiad off the coast, had even struck her with any effect.

On the 21st, at 7 A.M., when the weather tide made, the seven prames, 10 brigs, and bomb-sloop, with several one-gun luggers got under way, and stood to the westward on the larboard tack, formed in two lines. The weathermost line consisted of three prames, the admiral's first, then a commodore's, and lastly a pendant prame; and the lee line, of four prames; the brigs and small craft taking stations as most convenient in the rear of either line. The British in-shore squadron consisted this morning, besides the Naiad, of the Rinaldo and Redpole, the 18-gun brig-sloop Castilian, Captain David Braimer, and the 8-gun cutter Viper, Lieutenant Edward A. D'Arcey. These four vessels, having during the night stood in upon the Basse bank at the westernmost part of the bay, near fort L'Heurt, had, when the prames weighed at 7 A.M., tacked and hove to, formed in line thus:—Rinaldo, Redpole, Castilian, Viper, with their heads to the west-north-west and colours hoisted, to await the approach of the enemy; the town of Boulogne bearing from the leading brig south-east by east distant five or six miles. At 8 h. 30 m. A.M. the Naiad, who had weighed when the prames did, joined the Rinaldo and her companions, and lay to on the same tack, slowly stretching off shore, in the hope of imperceptibly drawing the French from the protection of their formidable batteries.

At 9 h. 30 m. A.M., the rear-admiral's prame, which was the leading one of the weather line, tacked in-shore, and on coming round fired her broadside. The instant her helm was down, the British line, by signal from the Naiad, wore together and bore up in chase. The six remaining prames had wore at nearly the same instant as their admiral, and the whole were now crowding sail to regain the protection of the batteries. The Naiad hauled up for the prame of the French admiral; while the brigs, bearing away and passing the frigate, stood for the sternmost prame of the lee line. At 10 h. 20 m. A.M. the Naiad, having got nearly within pistol-shot between the two lines, opened her fire from both sides; and the Rinaldo and Redpole poured their broadsides into the sternmost prame of the lee line, the Ville-de-Lyon, commanded by Lieutenant de vaisseau Jean Barbaud, who had been gallantly endeavouring to succour his admiral. Finding it impossible to reach the latter owing to shoal water, the Naiad, being then on the starboard and weather bow of the Ville-de-Lyon, bore up, and, wearing round, boarded and carried her;

but not without an obstinate resistance on the part of the French officers and men, with a loss of between 30 and 40 of them in killed and wounded, including among the latter the prame's commander, Lieutenant Barbaud.

While the Naiad stood away with her prize in tow, the Rinaldo, Redpole, and Castilian continued engaging the remainder of the flotilla. The first two brigs succeeded in getting alongside the prame next in the line to the Ville-de-Lyon, and soon obliged her to haul up for the weather line. Being by this time fired upon by all the batteries, and having but three fathoms water under their bottoms, the three British brigs ceased firing and stood out to join the Naiad. The damages of the latter were very trifling; but her loss amounted to two seamen killed, one lieutenant of marines (William Morgan), one midshipman (James Dover), and 12 seamen wounded. The Castilian had her first-lieutenant, Charles Cobb, killed, and one seaman severely wounded; and the Redpole, her pilot wounded. The capture of this prame, out of the midst of the flotilla and almost under the guns of the batteries, must have wofully disappointed the spectators on shore, and have given rather an awkward finish to the morning's amusement of the French emperor and his generals.

On the 1st of August as a small British squadron, consisting of the 12-pounder 32-gun frigate Quebec, Captain Charles Sibthorpe John Hawtayne, 16-gun brig-sloop Raven, Captain George Gustavus Lennock, gun-brigs Exertion and Redbreast, Lieutenants James Murray and Sir George Morat Keith, Bart., and hired armed cutters Alert and Princess Augusta, was cruising off the coast between the Texel and the Elbe, information was received, that a division of gun-boats lay at an anchor within the island of Nordeney. The Quebec's first-lieutenant, Samuel Blyth, immediately volunteered, and was permitted to attempt, to cut them out.

Accordingly, 10 boats, containing 117 seamen and marines, including the following officers:—Lieutenants Samuel Blyth, of the Quebec, John O'Neale, Alert, Samuel Slout, Raven, and Charles Wolrige, Quebec, lieutenant of marines, Humphrey Moore, Quebec, sub-lieutenant Thomas Hare, Exertion, second master George Downey, Redbreast, carpenter Stephen Pickett, Raven, master's mates Robert Cook and John M'Donald, Quebec, midshipman Richard Millet, Raven, and mates James Muggridge (pilot to the expedition), Princess Augusta, and George Johnson, Alert, pushed off from the frigate, and shaped their course towards the coast of East Friesland. On the 2nd the boats entered the river Jahde, and captured a boat belonging to the imperial douaniers; whose peculiar duty it was to support the continental system, and to cut off all commercial intercourse with England. Passing through the intricate navigation called the Wadden, between the islands Wanger-oog, Spyker-oog, and Langer-oog, the British boats, on the same afternoon, came in sight of the enemy's gun-boats, four in number; each armed with one long 12, and two long 6 or 8 pounders and 25 men, including five soldiers, and commanded by a lieutenant de vaisseau in the French navy.

As soon as the British arrived within gun-shot, the gun-brigs opened upon them a fire of grape and canister. Lieutenant Blyth, in the Quebec's barge, pulling rapidly up, sprang upon the deck of the first gun-boat, and killed one man and wounded two in the struggle. Mr. Muggridge, who was also in the barge, was opposed, while boarding, by two soldiers, one of whom he shot dead; but the other wounded the young man in the throat with his bayonet; and had the latter not have fallen into the sea, he must have been killed. Mr. Muggridge eventually reached one of the boats. In a few minutes the British mastered the crew of the headmost boat, and, driving the hands below, turned the long 12-pounder upon the other three boats; which were so situated that they could not fire upon the captured vessel without destroying their own people. There was a quantity of cartridges lying on the deck, covered by a sail, and from these the British loaded the gun, but could find no lighted match. The gunner of the Quebec, having primed the 12-pounder from a French powder-horn, which from its peculiar construction scattered a part of the powder on the deck, discharged the piece by firing his pistol at the priming; when the flash, communicating to the loose powder on deck, and thence to the cartridges under the sail, caused an explosion that killed or wounded 19 persons, including Lieutenant Blyth himself, who was blown into the sea, but afterwards reached one of his boats. He had previously been wounded in the shoulder by a French soldier, and was burnt in his face, hand, and foot, by the explosion. This disaster, fatal as it was to the British on board the outermost gun-boat, did not save the other three from capture. In 10 minutes they were compelled to surrender, with the loss of two men killed and 10 wounded.

In the attack, the British lost two killed and nine wounded, including among the latter Lieutenants Blyth and Slout, and

Messrs. Millet and Muggridge. Lieutenant Slout had been dreadfully wounded by the second gun-boat's 12-pounder, which put two grape-shot through his thigh and one through his leg. The wounds in the thigh were so high up, that there was no chance of saving this young officer's life, but by taking off the leg at the hip-joint. To this painful and precarious operation Lieutenant Slout would not submit, and soon died from the effects of mortification. With respect to Mr. Muggridge, although, in case of being disabled, not belonging to the royal navy, he could expect no pension from the government, that gallant young seaman had volunteered his services; his wound, fortunately for him, was not dangerous. Of those blown up by the accident, three died the next day; and several were dreadfully scorched, including Lieutenant Moore of the marines. Having thus achieved their very gallant exploit, Lieutenant Blyth and his party, with their boats and prizes, returned to the little squadron off the island of Heligoland. As a reward for his behaviour on the occasion, Lieutenant Blyth was promoted to the rank of commander.

The small island of Anholt in the Cattegat, which, it will be recollected, was captured from the Danes in May, 1809,[1] became this year the scene of a very splendid exploit. The British garrison at present upon it consisted of 350 royal marines and 31 marine artillery; the marines under the command of Captain Robert Torrens of that corps, and the whole under Captain James Wilkes Maurice of the navy, the governor of the island, and the officer who, six years before, had so distinguished himself in his defence of the Diamond rock. The island of Anholt, in the languishing state of commerce occasioned by the rigorous edicts of Buonaparte, was found very useful to England as a dépôt and point of communication between her and the continent. Whether Napoleon instigated the Danes to aid his views by expelling the British from Anholt, or that the Danes themselves felt the laudable desire of recovering possession of an island which had formerly belonged to them, certain it is, that preparations for the attack began to be made in the summer of 1810. But, so long as the sea remained open, British cruisers continued to hover round the island; and the same hard weather, which at length drove the ships into more southern waters, shut up in their lakes and harbours the Danish gun-boats and transports.

The spring came, the ice melted, and the sea of Denmark

[3] See vol. iv., p. 431

and its vicinity again admitted the barks of the bold and adventurous to traverse its bosom. So early as on the 23rd of March a flotilla, consisting of 12 gun-boats, each mounting two long 24 or 18 pounders, and four brass howitzers, and manned with from 60 to 70 men, having under their protection 12 transport vessels, resembling the gun-boats in appearance, and containing between them, according to the Danish official account, about 1000 troops, including an organised body of 200 seamen, assembled in Gierrild bay. On the 24th the island was reconnoitred, or, in other words, was visited by an intelligent officer of the Danish navy, First-lieutenant Holstein, in the sacred character of a flag of truce. He soon ascertained that the garrison consisted of less than 400 men, that the lighthouse-fort was the only fortification of importance, and that the sole vessel-of-war cruising off the island was a small armed schooner. Nothing could be more satisfactory. Accordingly, on the 26th, the flotilla set sail from Gierrild bay; and on the 27th, at 4 A.M., in the midst of darkness and a heavy fog, the Danish troops disembarked, in perfect order, at a spot distant about four miles to the westward of Fort Yorke, the head-quarters of the garrison, and, being unseen, were of course unopposed.

Since the 10th of February, Governor Maurice had received an intimation of the intended attack upon his sovereignty, and had made use of every resource in his power to give a proper reception to the assailants. It was just before dawn on the 26th, that the out-pickets on the south side of the island made the signal for the flotilla's being in sight. The garrison was immediately under arms, and the brigade of four howitzers, covered by 200 rank and file, commanded by the governor in person, having with him Captain Torrens, major-commandant of the battalion, quitted the lines to oppose the landing; when Captain Maurice, having advanced to a ridge of sand-hills that runs nearly the whole length of the south side, to reconnoitre, discovered that the Danes had already landed and were then proceeding along the beach beneath him. As the two Danish wings out-flanked the British brigade, and, if the latter continued to advance, would get between the British and their works, Captain Maurice ordered a retreat. Before this could be effected, the corps of 200 Danish seamen, under Lieutenant Holstein, had gained the heights and were advancing with rapidity, cheering the retreat of the howitzers; when a heavy fire from the south-west angle of the Massareene battery obliged them to retire with precipitation to the beach, and soon afterwards to abandon a one-gun battery they had gained, and on which they had hoisted their colours. The Danes then took possession of two houses, and, on being driven from them by the fire of the Yorke and Massareene batteries, sheltered themselves behind the neighbouring sand-hills. Meanwhile the brigade of howitzers, and the British marines that covered them, had regained the works in good order, and without any loss.

As the day opened, the Danish flotilla was observed to have taken a position within point-blank shot of the works. A signal that the enemy had landed, and that the gun-boats had begun the cannonade, was immediately made to the British 18-pounder 32-gun frigate Tartar, Captain Joseph Baker, and 16-gun brig-sloop Sheldrake, Captain James Pattison Stewart, on the north side of the island, where they had only arrived the day before from England; and who, the instant they heard the firing, had got under way to attack the Danish gun-boats. Captain Maurice having signified, by telegraph, that the Sheldrake would be serviceable on the north side, the Tartar made the signal for the brig to remain behind, and stood on alone. The wind being from the westward, the Tartar had either to run 10 or 11 miles to leeward, to get round the reef extending from the east end of the island, or to beat up a still greater distance, in order to weather that branching off from its north-west part. Rightly considering that the knowledge of the frigate's being near the island, a circumstance of which the Danes were then ignorant, would make a considerable impression, Captain Baker resolved on going to leeward, round the shoal of Knoben, that being a course which would the sooner bring the Tartar in sight of the invaders.

Meanwhile the main division of the Danish army, under the orders of the commander-in-chief, Major Melstedt, had crossed the island and taken up a position on the northern shore, covered by hillocks of sand and inequality of ground. A detachment from this division, consisting, says the Danish official account, of 150 men, under Captain Reydez, advanced with uncommon bravery to the assault: but the discharges of grape and musketry from Forts Yorke and Massareene, which swept the plain and beach, obliged them to approach by degrees from sand-hill to sand-hill. The Danes rallied often and courageously, but were at length beaten back. Lieutenant Holstein's division, on the south side, had by this time succeeded in bringing up a field-piece, which enfiladed the Massareene battery. The apparent success of this induced Major Melstedt to order a general assault.

The Danish troops pushed boldly forward, and the Danish gunboats opened their fire; but the discharges of grape and musketry from the British batteries were irresistible. Major Melstedt was killed by a musket-ball when gallantly leading on his men; the next in command, Captain Reydez, had both his legs shot away by a cannon-ball; and another cannon-shot put an end to the life of the gallant Lieutenant Holstein. The incessant fire from the batteries had already strewed the plain with killed and wounded; and just at this moment, the Anholt schooner, a small armed vessel attached to the island, manned by volunteers and commanded by Lieutenant Henry Loraine Baker, anchored close to the northern shore, on the flank of the besiegers. The sand-hills being no longer a protection, and finding it impossible either to advance or retreat, the assailants hung out a flag of truce, and offered to surrender upon terms; but Governor Maurice would accept of nothing less than an unconditional surrender, and to that, after some deliberation, the Danes acceded.

The gun-boats on the south side, observing the approach of the Tartar, had in the meanwhile got under way and steered to the westward. Thus abandoned, and having no means of retreat, the Danes on this side also hung out a flag of truce. An officer from the works went to meet it, and must have smiled when he found the object of the truce was to call upon the British to surrender. However, the Danes very soon withdrew their claims, and consented themselves to surrender as prisoners of war; making, with those that had surrendered on the north side, a total of 520 officers and men, exclusive of 23 wounded. The remaining half of the assailants had fled towards the west end of the island, whither the gun-boats and transports had proceeded, in order to embark them. Captain Maurice, accompanied by Captain Torrens, immediately marched in that direction, with the brigade of howitzers and about 40 men, all that could be spared with reference to the safety of the prisoners; but the formidable appearance of the Danes preserved them from molestation, and they embarked without further loss. That previously sustained amounted to between 30 and 40 killed, including four principal officers and the wounded as already enumerated; and the loss on the British side amounted to two men killed and 30 wounded, including among the latter Captain Torrens, slightly.

Being enabled to sweep directly to windward, and from their light draught of water, to pass within the western reefs, the gun-boats were at the point of embarkation long before the Tartar could get near them; nor could the Sheldrake molest them, she being to leeward. Having re-embarked the remainder of the troops, the flotilla, at about 4 P.M., made sail in the direction of the Sheldrake, but shortly afterwards separated, eight of the gun-boats and nearly the whole of the transports steering for the coast of Jutland and the remaining four gun-boats and an armed transport running before the wind towards the coast of Sweden.

While the Tartar stood after the division standing for Jutland, the Sheldrake pursued that endeavouring to escape to Sweden. At 4 h. 30 m. P.M. the Sheldrake opened a heavy fire, and presently captured No. 9 gun-boat, mounting two long 18-pounders and four brass howitzers, with a lieutenant of the Danish navy and 64 men. Having removed the prisoners, the brig resumed the chase, and at 8 P.M. overtook, and after the exchange of a few shot captured, a large lugger No. 1, mounting two long 24-pounders and four brass howitzers, with a lieutenant and 60, out of a complement of 70 men. Another gun-boat, as declared by several of the Sheldrake's people, and acknowledged to be missing by the Danes, was sunk by the brig's shot. The Sheldrake, on her part, sustained no loss and very slight damage.

The division of which the Tartar was in chase, separated, and three of the transports steered for the island of Lessoe. These the frigate pursued, and succeeded in capturing two; one with 22 soldiers and a considerable quantity of ammunition on board, the other laden with provisions. Soon afterwards the shoal water to the southward of the island obliged the Tartar to haul off and discontinue the chase. Thus ended the Danish expedition to Anholt; an expedition, in the conduct of it, highly creditable to both parties; for, if the British gained honour by their victory, the Danes lost none by their defeat.

Captain Maurice, in his official letter, computes the whole Danish force employed in this expedition at 4000 men. The private letter of a British officer present at the attack reduces that amount to one-half. Our contemporary states the number at 1590 men;[1] and, although Captain Brenton gives the Danes more gun-boats and transports than, it appears, they had with them, we see no objection to his estimate of the aggregate number of troops and seamen.

On the 31st of July, in the evening, the British 10-gun cutter Algerine, Lieutenant John Aitkin Blow, and 12-gun brig Brev-

[1] Brenton, vol. iv., p. 505.

drageren, Lieutenant Thomas Barker Devon, lying off Long sound on the coast of Norway, discovered three brigs standing towards them from the shore. These were three Danish men-of-war, one brig the Langland, of 20 long 18-pounders, and, it is believed, two sixes out of the stern-ports, with 170 men; another the Lougen, already known to us,[1] and the third the Kiel, mounting two guns less than the latter, or 16 long 18-pounders, with about 159 men; total, 54 long Danish 18-pounders and 480 men. On the British side there were 10 carronades, 18-pounders, in the cutter, and the same, with two long 6-pounders, in the brig. The complement of each vessel was 60, but the Brevdrageren had only on board 47, men and boys.

Under these circumstances, Lieutenant Blow was justified in retreating; and accordingly the cutter and gun-brig, in the light airs then prevailing, used every exertion, by sweeping, to effect their escape. On the 1st of August, at 5 A.M., it was perceived that the three Danish brigs had gained considerably in the chase, the Langland being about four miles distant on the larboard and lee-beam of the two British vessels, and the Lougen and Kiel about two distant on the same quarter of their commodore, the Langland. Lieutenant Blow now sent a boat on board the gun-brig, and proposed to Lieutenant Devon, that the two vessels should bear down and cut off this brig. The proposal was cheerfully acceded to, and the Algerine and Brevdrageren began sweeping towards the Langland; but the latter, seeing their intention, bore away and closed her consorts. Their plan being thus frustrated, the cutter and gun-brig hauled up and resumed their efforts to escape.

This well-meant manœuvre, on the part of the Algerine and Brevdrageren, had brought them much nearer to the Danish brigs; and these, being now concentrated, resumed the chase with redoubled vigour. By 11 A.M. the Langland, with sails clewed up, and assisted by boats from her consorts, had again swept herself ahead of them. Again the Algerine and Brevdrageren, it now being quite calm, began sweeping towards her. On this occasion finding the Lougen at no great distance astern of him, the Danish commodore awaited the attack. At about noon the Langland began firing at the Algerine and Brevdrageren; and at a few minutes before 1 P.M., while the Brevdrageren was in close action with the Langland, and just as the Lougen had got upon the British brig's starboard

[1] See vol. iv., p. 317.

quarter, the Algerine suddenly ceased firing and swept herself out of the battle, making a signal to the Brevdrageren to do the same. Circumstanced as the gun-brig then was, with the Langland close on her larboard beam and the Lougen advancing rapidly on her starboard quarter, a compliance with the order was impracticable, unless the Brevdrageren hauled down her colours, and that Lieutenant Devon had no intention of doing. He therefore answered Lieutenant Blow's signal, by hoisting the recal. That was not attended to; and the Algerine, whose facility of moving by sweeps, both from the form of her hull and the increased number of her crew, far exceeded that of the Brevdrageren, was presently beyond the reach of active co-operation.

At 1 h. 30 m. P.M., when the Brevdrageren had received several shot between wind and water, and had had three of her guns disabled, a light air sprang up from the westward. Of this immediate advantage was taken by the British brig, whose sails, being already set, had only to be trimmed to the breeze; while the Langland still had hers clewed up. The promptitude of the Brevdrageren certainly saved her; for just as she had got one mile from the Langland, the breeze died away, and it was then only that the Danes, who had never ceased firing, began to sheet home their topsails to go in pursuit. The Langland continued to fire occasionally at the Brevdrageren; but, making a good use of her sweeps, and receiving a reinforcement of two additional sweeps and 10 men from the Algerine, the British brig kept gradually increasing her distance. When at about 5 P.M., the Lougen, having just got an air of wind, was advancing fast upon the Brevdrageren's starboard quarter, the Algerine hauled up and hove to, as if to cover her consort. This demonstration of resistance produced the desired effect, and the Lougen fell back. At sunset the Danes discontinued their fire, and at 9 P.M. gave up the chase of the two British vessels.

Although very much cut up in hull, masts, and rigging, the Brevdrageren escaped with so slight a loss as one man killed and three wounded. The Algerine had also one man killed, but suffered very little in other respects. The small crew of the gun-brig, as may be supposed, were nearly exhausted by their labour at the guns and at the sweeps; and great credit was undoubtedly due to the officers and men of the Brevdrageren for their gallantry and perseverance. "A very serious investigation," says our contemporary, " would have taken place on the conduct of the lieutenant of the Algerine, but before any complaint could reach the admiralty, he was dismissed from the command of his vessel for another breach of discipline."[1]

On the 2nd of September, at 1 h. 30 m. A.M., as the British brig-sloop Chanticleer, of eight 18-pounder carronades and two sixes, with 75 men and boys, Captain Richard Spear, and gun-brig Manly, mounting two more carronades than the Chanticleer, with 42 men and boys on board, Lieutenant Richard William Simmonds, were standing along the coast of Norway to the westward, three sail were descried by the Chanticleer, on her lee-bow. The sloop, who was considerably ahead of her consort, immediately bore away in chase; and, as the three strangers, which were the Danish 18-gun brigs (long 18-pounders, with 120 men each) Loland, Captain Holm, Alsen, First-lieutenant Lutkin, and Sampsoe, First-lieutenant Grothschilling, hauled up also in chase, the two parties were not long in meeting. At 2 h. 30 m. A.M. the Chanticleer closed and hailed the Sampsoe; who immediately replied by a broadside, and an action commenced between these two brigs. In a short time the Loland and Alsen, who had already opened their fire upon the Manly, wore round, and made sail to support their consort engaged with the Chanticleer. The latter, on observing this, wore under the stern of the Sampsoe, and made all sail on the larboard tack, followed by the three Danish brigs.

The Loland shortly afterwards hauled her wind for the Manly, then gallantly approaching on the starboard tack, to co-operate with her consort in repulsing the superior force which had so suddenly come upon them. At 4 A.M., having by her superior sailing got upon the larboard beam of the Manly, the Loland commenced firing at her; and these two brigs soon became warmly engaged. The action continued in this manner until 6 A.M.; when the Sampsoe and Alsen, having given over the chase of the Chanticleer, came up to the assistance of the Loland. The Sampsoe placed herself on the Manly's larboard bow; and the Alsen, taking the station of the Loland, who had tacked to get on her opponent's starboard quarter, lay on the Manly's starboard beam. Thus hemmed in, and having had her head-sails all shot away since the commencement of the action, her standing and running rigging cut to pieces, her remaining sails reduced to tatters, her two masts and bowsprit badly wounded, and four of her guns dismounted, the Manly hauled down her colours.

Although, as the Danish official account states, the Manly

[1] Brenton, vol. v., p. 329.

was much crippled, and there was no part of her hull but had more or less suffered, she came out of the action with so comparatively slight a loss as one seaman killed, and one seaman and two marines dangerously wounded. All three Danish brigs received some trifling damage in their sails and rigging; but the Loland alone is admitted to have sustained any loss, and that was only one man killed. The Danish Captain Holm, with a feeling that establishes him for a brave man, says in his letter to Rear-admiral Lutkin: "It must be confessed, that it reflects much honour on the commander of the Manly to have made such a resistance." And it is really a question, in our view of the subject, whether more honour was not gained by the loss of the Manly than by the escape of the Chanticleer. Lieutenant Simmonds, when subsequently tried for the loss of his brig, was not only most honourably acquitted, but received from the president of the court, Captain Richard Lee, when the latter returned him his sword, a very handsome eulogium on his conduct.

Before we quit the subject of Danish brigs-of-war, we will submit a remark or two upon the nature of their armament. From the concurrent testimony of all the British officers who have been engaged with them, the Langland, Lougen, Loland, and other Danish brigs of that class, carried "long 18-pounders;" and, if we are not mistaken, we have seen the same *caliber* of guns mentioned in some of the Danish official accounts. We strongly suspect, however, that the gun was not the "long 18-pounder," as usually understood by that term, but a sort of medium gun, not much longer nor much heavier than a Danish carronade of the same, or at all events of a 32-pound, caliber. Our opinion is founded upon the fact, that 18 long English 18-pounders, with their carriages, weigh about 856 cwt.; while 18 carronades, 32-pounders, with their slides and carriages, weigh but 415 cwt. The British brig that carries the latter measures about 382 tons, and therefore the Danish brig that could carry the former would measure at least 600 tons. Now the largest brig-of-war which the British have taken from the Danes was the Gluckstadt, and she maasured but 338 tons. Her force, as well as that of the seven or eight other Danish brigs taken with her, was officially stated to be 18 guns; but we doubt if any of these vessels had their guns on board. In this case the ports only (a practice that ought to be laid aside) would be reckoned; from which, in a single-decked vessel, a deduction of two is always to be made for the bridle or bow ports.

Hence the Gluckstadt and her companion, when fitted out in the British service, carried no more than 16 guns. The only Danish vessels taken on the same occasion capable of mounting 20 guns, were the Fylla and Little Belt, and they measured but 490 tons; less, by 20 or 30 tons, than the generality of French ships carrying the same number of guns. Upon the whole, we conclude, that the Lougen, and her consorts of the largest class, carried 18-pounders, about six feet in length and weighing from 26 to 28 cwt.; and that consequently, even at a moderate range, they were a full match for the largest class of British brig-sloops.

This year closed with a lamentable catastrophe, which befel a part of the British Baltic fleet, on its return to England for the winter months. On the 9th of November the British 98-gun ship St. George, Captain Daniel Oliver Guion, bearing the flag of Rear-admiral Robert Carthew Reynolds, accompanied by several other men-of-war of the Baltic fleet and a convoy of 120 merchant-vessels, sailed from Hano sound for England. On the 15th, when the fleet lay at anchor off the island of Zealand waiting for a fair wind, a violent storm arose, in which about 30 of the convoy perished, and the St. George drove on shore, but eventually got off with the loss of her three masts and rudder. The men-of-war, with the remainder of the convoy, then proceeded to Wingo sound; where the St. George was fitted with jury masts and a Pakenham's rudder, and the whole fleet got ready to depart with the first fair wind.

On the 17th of December the fleet, consisting of eight sail of the line, several frigates and smaller vessels-of-war, and about 100 merchant-vessels, sailed from Wingo sound; and as the St. George was, as we have seen, in a greatly disabled state, the 74-gun ships Cressy and Defence, Captains Charles Dudley Pater and David Atkins, were appointed to attend her. The fleet had just cleared the Sleeve, when a tremendous gale of wind came on, which blew successively from the west-north-west, the west, and south, and then shifted, with greater violence than ever, to the north-west. On the 24th, after combating with the gale for five days, the St. George and Defence were wrecked on the western coast of Jutland; and the whole of their united crews, except six men of the one, and 12 of the other, perished. The Cressy saved herself by wearing from the starboard tack, and standing to the southward; but Captain Atkins of the Defence could not be persuaded to quit the admiral without the signal to part company, and therefore shared his melancholy fate

On the 25th the 74-gun ship Hero, Captain James Newman Newman, who had sailed from Gottenburg on the 18th, met a similar fate on the Haak sand off the Texel, with the loss of all her crew except 12 men, that were washed on shore; making a total of nearly 2000 officers and men thus entombed in a watery grave. The 18-gun brig-sloop Grasshopper, Captain Henry Fanshawe, was in company, and struck also, but drove over the bank close in with Texel island. No alternative now remained but to surrender to the Dutch admiral; which the Grasshopper accordingly did.

On the 4th of February the British 18-pounder 32-gun frigate Cerberus, Captain Henry Whitby, and 38-gun frigate Active, Captain James Alexander Gordon, cruising off the north-east coast of Italy discovered four vessels lying at anchor in the port of "Peitichi" or Pescaro. It being nearly calm, Captain Whitby despatched Lieutenant George Haye of the Active, with the barge of each frigate, to endeavour to cut them out. Lieutenant Haye and his little party, although exposed to a heavy fire of musketry from the soldiers quartered at the place, succeeded, with the loss of only one man wounded, in capturing three of the vessels, and in destroying the fourth after removing her cargo. They were all merchant trabaccolos, last from Ancona.

On the 12th, in the morning, several vessels were discovered at anchor in the harbour of Ortona on the same coast; and, as the wind was light, Captain Whitby despatched the boats of the two frigates, under the orders of Lieutenant James Dickinson, first of the Cerberus, assisted by Lieutenant George Haye and George Cumpson, Lieutenant of marines Peter Mears, and master's mates James Gibson and James Rennie, to endeavour to bring out the vessels from the strong position in which they were moored. The harbour of Ortona is formed by a large pier, running out into the sea and connected with a range of hills leading to the town, which stands on the top of the highest, completely commanding the vessels in the harbour and in the road to it.

At 10 A.M., on the near approach of the boats, a fire of great guns and small arms was opened from an armed Venetian trabaccolo, not before observed, and from soldiers posted on the beach and hills. The British seamen and marines instantly gave three cheers, and, pushing on, carried all before them. Lieutenant Dickinson, in the gig of the Cerberus, supported by Mr. Rennie in the barge, boarded and almost instantly carried the armed trabaccolo, although she mounted six guns and was full of men. Lieutenant Dickinson then landed, with the marines under Lieutenant Mears and the small-arm men under Mr. Rennie; and this party had to climb up the rocks by their hands, with the prospect of falling down a precipice every step they took. At length the strong post was attained; and while the launches with their carronades kept the soldiers and inhabitants in check, Mr. Rennie planted the British colours at the very gates of the town. The seamen then secured the vessels in the harbour, which, besides the armed trabaccolo, were 10 in number, and all laden with wheat, oil, hemp, &c.; and the marines and division on shore burnt two large magazines, filled with all sorts of naval and military stores destined for the garrison of Corfu. Having, by 3 P.M., executed the whole of this important service, Lieutenant Dickinson and his party got back to their ships with so comparatively slight a loss as four men wounded.

We last year left in the harbour of Ancona, a Franco-Venetian squadron, under the orders of the French Commodore Dubourdieu; and who, it will be recollected, in his official letter published in the Moniteur, expressed regret that his squadron of five frigates and two 16-gun brigs should have been "avoided" by a British squadron of "three frigates, one corvette, and two brigs."[1] On the evening of the 11th of March M. Dubourdieu sailed from Ancona, with, besides his former ship, the Favourite, and three Venetian frigates Corona, Bellona, and Carolina,[2] the two French 40-gun frigates Danaé and Flore, the latter commanded by Captain Jean-Alexandre Péridier, but the name of the Danaé's we are unable to state. M. Dubourdieu had also with him the Venetian 16-gun brig-corvette Mercure, one 10-gun schooner, one 6-gun xebec, and two gun-boats, having on board from 400 to 500 troops, under Colonel Gifflenga of the Italian army, as a garrison for the island of Lissa, as soon as they should succeed in conquering it. Early·on the morning of the 13th this Franco-Venetian squadron, of four 40-gun frigates, two of a smaller class, brig-corvette and other vessels, arrived off the north point of Lissa, and there fell in with a British squadron, of three frigates and a 22-gun ship, under the orders of Captain William Hoste, the very officer who had commanded the squadron which M. Dubourdieu and his crews, as formerly mentioned, were so desirous to meet. Captain Hoste's three frigates were the Amphion, Cerberus, and Active, already so frequently named; and he had also with him the 22-gun ship Volage, Captain Phipps Hornby.

[1] See p. 124. [2] See p. 122.

At 30 A.M., when about a mile from the entrance of Port St. George, the Active, the weathermost ship of her squadron, close hauled on the larboard tack, with the wind a fine breeze from the north-north-west, discovered the Franco-Venetian squadron, lying to to-windward. After making the night-signal for an enemy, the Active bore up to join her consorts. At 4 A.M. the extremes of Lissa bore from the Amphion, who was then one mile off shore, from west by north to north by east. At daylight the force of M. Dubourdieu's squadron was made out, and the squadron of Captain Hoste carried all sail in chase. At 6 A.M. the Franco-Venetian squadron began bearing down to the attack in two divisions; the starboard or weather one consisting of the Favourite, Flore, Bellona, and Mercure, and the larboard or lee one of the Danaé, Corona, Carolina, and small craft.

The British ships immediately formed in line ahead, with, besides the customary red ensign at their respective peaks, union-jacks and ensigns, blue and red, at their foremast heads and at their different stays. Thus nobly decorated, the four ships continued working to windward to close the enemy. Just before the two squadrons got within gun-shot, aware of what would be the talismanic effect, at such a moment, of the name and example of his late friend and patron, Captain Hoste telegraphed, "REMEMBER NELSON!" The loud "hurrahs!" of the four ships' companies quickly responded to a signal, so admirably calculated to inspire the hearts of both officers and men with all the zeal, all the valour, and all the confidence, necessary to withstand a force of such apparently overwhelming superiority as that which, in the full expectation of achieving an easy victory, was now rapidly approaching.

At 9 A.M. the Amphion, then under top and topgallant-sails, on the starboard tack, with the Active, Volage, and Cerberus, in close order astern, so close indeed that the ships almost touched each other, opened her fire upon the Favourite, who was rather ahead of the Danaé, the leading ship of the larboard division. The Amphion and Active kept up so well-directed a fire upon the Favourite, and the line they formed was so close and compact, that M. Dubourdieu was completely frustrated in his gallant attempt to pass between those ships. The Favourite now evinced a disposition to board the Amphion upon the quarter, and the French crew seemed all ready on the forecastle to carry the plan into effect; when, just as the Favourite had approached within a few yards, a brass $5\frac{1}{2}$ inch howitzer upon the Amphion's quarter-deck, loaded with 750 musket-balls, was discharged at her larboard bow, and sweeping the French ship's forecastle, committed dreadful havoc among the crowd of boarders there assembled. Amidst them was observed, ready to lead on his men to the assault, the French commodore himself; and he, it appears, was among those who fell on the occasion.

As the British ships were moving at the rate of about three knots an hour, the course of each of the Franco-Venetian columns became more and more oblique, until the Danaé, Corona, and Carolina, especially the two former, brought their larboard guns to bear upon the Volage and Cerberus; which ships, although unable to cope with three such opponents, returned their fire with spirit. In the mean time, foiled in her endeavours either to board the Amphion, or to cut the line astern of her, and deterred by the Active's apparent superiority of force from wearing and coming to close action with her, the Favourite stood on engaging the Amphion, with the evident intention of rounding the latter ship's bows and placing the British squadron between two fires. At 9 h. 40 m. A.M., being within half a cable's length of the shore of Lissa, Captain Hoste threw out the signal for his ships to wear together. Just as the latter were in the act of obeying the signal, the Favourite made an effort to wear and get to leeward of the British line, but had scarcely put

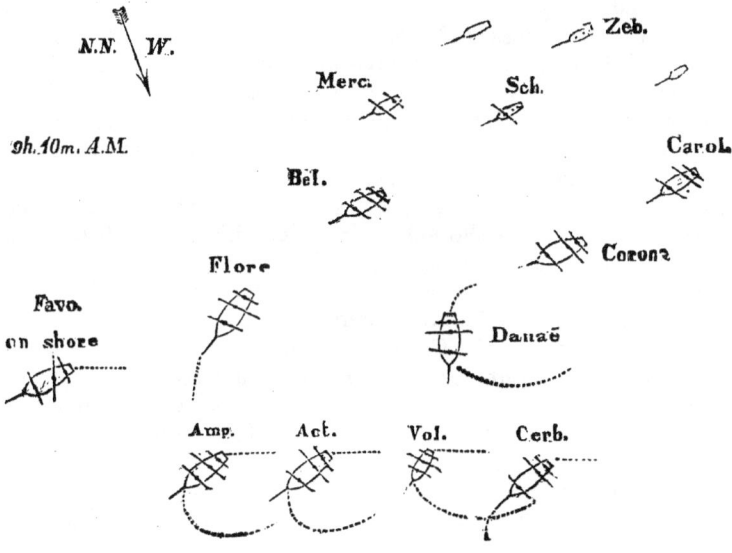

her helm up ere she struck on the rocks in the utmost confusion. This important circumstance of the battle, to produce which had been the object of Captain Hoste in standing so long upon the starboard tack, we have endeavoured to illustrate by the diagram on page 235.

While the Cerberus was in the act of wearing, her rudder became choked by a shot. This occasioned the Volage to get round before her, and that ship consequently took the lead on the larboard tack; on which board, being close to the wind, the four ships fell into a bow and quarter line. Sheltered as she had been in some degree by her leader, the Flore was in much better trim for performing any evolution; and, now that the British line had stood off from the land, Captain Péridier found no difficulty in passing under the stern of the Amphion. The Flore then opened her first fire, and immediately afterwards hauled up on the larboard tack upon the Amphion's lee-quarter. Almost at the same moment the Bellona hauled up on the Amphion's weather-quarter, and both ships opened upon her a heavy fire. (See the diagram on page 237.)

By this time the Danaé, carefully avoiding the Active's line of fire, had wore on the larboard tack, followed by the Corona and Carolina. Thinking to make an easy conquest of the Volage, the Danaé took up a station abreast of her. Thus honoured with occupying a frigate's post, the Volage bravely maintained a frigate's character, and poured in her 32-pound shot with steadiness and precision. Finding the unexpected weight of these, and soon discovering that they proceeded from carronades, the Danaé hauled off to a greater distance; where her long 18s could produce their full effect, but where carronades could not reach. The Volage was now obliged to increase the charge of powder for her carronades; and they, in consequence, broke their breechings and upset. So that, at last, the 6-pounder on the forecastle was the only gun which this gallant little ship had to oppose to the 14 long 18-pounders of her wary antagonist. While the Volage and Danaé were thus employed, the Cerberus and Corona were not looking inoffensively at each other. In a little time, however, the Cerberus, who was upwards of 90 men short of complement, became greatly shattered in hull, and nearly disabled in rigging, by the heavy and well-maintained fire of the Corona; with whom the Carolina co-operated only in a slight degree, that ship not appearing very ambitious of closing. At length the Active, who had been striving her utmost to get to the assistance of her two friends in the van, approached under a press of canvas. The moment they saw her coming up, the Danaé, Corona, and Carolina, made all sail to the eastward. The following diagram will serve to illustrate this period of the action; the date of which we may fix at from 10 to 10 h. 30 m. A.M. :—

Suffering greatly from the fire of the two ships that had placed themselves on her quarters, the Amphion gradually bore up to close her heaviest and most annoying opponent. Having passed so close ahead as almost to touch the Flore, the Amphion, at about 11 h. 15 m. A.M., came to the wind on the same tack as before, with her larboard broadside bearing directly on the French ship's starboard and lee bow.[1] So well-directed a fire was now opened upon the latter, that in about five minutes, the Flore ceased firing and struck her colours. Immediately after the Amphion had bore up, the Bellona did the same; and, placing herself across the former's stern, maintained a heavy and destructive fire. Although particularly careful not to fire into her late consort, some of the Bellona's shot appear to have struck the Flore, who had imperceptibly forereached upon the Amphion. Conceiving the shot to come from the Amphion, one of the officers of the Flore took the French ensign, halliards and all, and, holding them up in his hands over the taffrail, as if for the Amphion's people to witness the act, threw the whole into the sea.

After an ineffectual attempt, owing to the damaged state of her rigging and yard-tackle, to hoist out a boat to take possession of the Flore, the Amphion bore up to close and silence the Bellona. Having wore round on the starboard tack, and taken a position on the Bellona's weather bow, the Amphion poured

[1] See diagram at p. 239.

in one or two broadsides; and at a few minutes before noon compelled the Bellona to haul down the Venetian, as the Flore had the French colours. In the mean time the Mercure brig had also been firing occasionally at the Amphion; but an 18-pounder was at length brought to bear upon her, and the brig soon swept herself beyond the reach of either giving or receiving annoyance. Lieutenant Donat Henchy O'Brien, by Captain Hoste's orders, now went with two seamen in the punt, and took possession of the Bellona.

Having secured this prize, the Amphion wore round; and, making the signal for a general chase, brought to on the larboard tack, a little to leeward of the Cerberus and Volage, whose greatly disabled state had obliged them to bear up. The Amphion had now the mortification to see her first and most valuable prize, the Flore, out of gun-shot on her weather-bow, making sail for the island of Lessina; and towards whom the Danaé presently edged away, as if to encourage the Flore's commander in the dishonourable act: dishonourable indeed, for the French ship had lain for some time at the mercy of the Amphion. The Active, also, until she made sail after the Corona, might have sunk the Flore, and probably would have taken possession of her, but that it did not comport with Captain Gordon's spirit to stay by a beaten enemy while a fighting enemy remained to be subdued; above all, when a friend stood in need of his assistance. Had even the Cerberus or Volage been aware that the prize was not secured, either ship, as the Flore passed them, might have sent a boat and taken possession of her, having had her rigging and sails cut to pieces, and expecting her foremast every moment to fall, the Amphion was as much incapacitated from giving chase as the Cerberus and Volage.

The surrender of the Flore and Bellona, the escape of the former, and the closing of the Active with the Corona, we have attempted to show by the diagram in the next page.

Having her sails and rigging in a more perfect state than either the Cerberus or Corona, the Active soon passed to windward of the former, and at about 30 minutes past noon, when just in midchannel between Lissa and Spalmadon, received the fire of the Corona; a most galling fire, too, as the Active could not bring any number of her own guns to bear, without keeping off the wind, and of course losing way in the chase. At length, at about 1 h. 45 m. P.M., the Active closed the Corona to leeward. A spirited action now ensued between these two frigates, and continued until 2 h. 30 m. P.M., when the Corona surrendered.

after a resistance highly honourable to the Venetian flag; and which resistance she had protracted until almost within reach of the batteries of Lessina. The Carolina and Danaé, the latter of

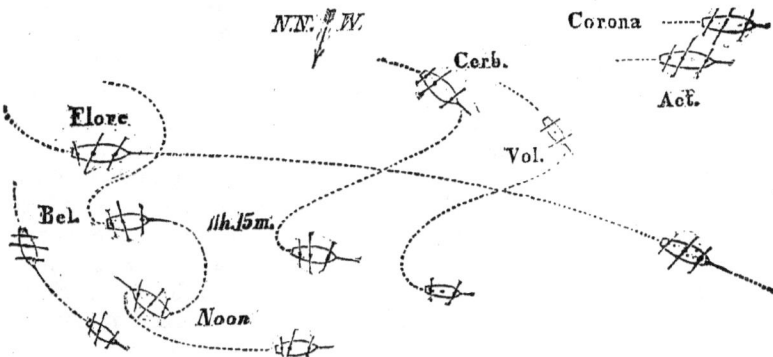

whom, had she supported the Corona, might perhaps have saved her from capture, were already in safety under the guns of those batteries, and just about to enter the road. The whole of the Venetian small-craft also effected their escape in different directions.

The Amphion had all her lower masts badly shot through, particularly her foremast as already stated, her larboard mainyardarm and mizentopmast shot away, and her sails and rigging much cut. Her loss, out of a complement of 251 men and boys, amounted to her boatswain (Richard Unshank), two midshipmen (John Robert Spearman and Charles Hayes), seven seamen, and five marines killed, her captain (in his right arm, and with some severe contusions, but he would not quit the deck till the action was over), one lieutenant (David Dunn, severely), one captain of marines (Thomas Moore), two midshipmen (Francis George Farewell and Thomas Edward Hoste), one captain's clerk (Frederick Lewis), two first-class volunteers (Charles Buthane and the Honourable William Waldegrave), 34 seamen, and four private marines wounded; total, 15 killed and 47 wounded. The Active, whose damages were comparatively slight, out of her complement of 300 men and boys, had four seamen killed, one lieutenant of marines (John Meares), 18 seamen, and five private marines wounded; total, exclusive of a subsequent loss, which will be noticed presently, four killed and 24 wounded. The Cerberus, although without a stick shot away except her mizentopsail-yard, was a good deal battered in the hull, as her loss will testify. Out of a complement the same originally as the Amphion's, but since reduced by absentees to about 160 men and boys, the Cerberus had her purser (Samuel Jeffery), one midshipman (Francis Surrage Davey), eight seamen, and three marines killed, one lieutenant (George Cumpston), 33 seamen (one mortally), and seven marines wounded; total, in the action, 13 killed and 41 wounded. The Volage had her mainyard shot away in the slings, and lost her foretopgallant-mast: she was also greatly damaged in sails, rigging, and masts. Her hull, on the larboard side especially, was completely riddled, and her loss of men was in proportion: in reference, indeed, to her complement, it was far more severe than that of any one of her consorts, except the Cerberus. Out of a crew of 175 men and boys, the Volage had one midshipman (John George), 10 seamen, and two private marines killed, one lieutenant of marines (William Stephens Knapman), 27 seamen, and four private marines wounded; total, 13 killed and 33 wounded: making the total loss of the British, in the action, 45 killed and 145 wounded.

Contrary to what is customary, the British official account makes not the slightest allusion to the loss sustained by the opposite party; a circumstance attributable, no doubt, to the difficulty of ascertaining it, and to the necessity of forwarding the despatch, in all possible haste, to Captain Eyre of the Magnificent, the British commanding officer in the Adriatic, in order that he might adopt measures to complete the capture or destruction of the enemy's squadron. Moreover, when he dictated the despatch, Captain Hoste was lying in his cot under severe sufferings from his wounds. Nor, minute as it is in other respects, does the French official account enumerate the killed and wounded on board the Favourite. We may gather, however, that, as 200 of her men were all that remained after the action, about the same number comprised the killed and badly wounded. Among the former were Commodore Dubourdieu and Captain Meillerie, the first-lieutenant and other of the principal officers; so that the command at last devolved upon Colonel Gifflenga, with an enseigne de vaisseau to direct the working of the ship.

The Corona had her rigging and sails cut to pieces, her masts all badly wounded, and her hull shattered in every direction; and appears, from subsequent inquiry, to have sustained a loss of upwards of 200, in killed and wounded together. The Bellona had 70 officers and men killed, and about the same number badly wounded, including Captain Duodo himself, who died of his wounds. This ship's masts and yards, at the close of the action, were all standing; but her hull, a mere shell in point of scantling, and at which principally the Amphion had directed her shot, was pierced through and through. The hull of the Flore was also the part in which she had suffered the most; and her loss of men, which was known to include her captain badly wounded, must have been tolerably severe.

At 4 P.M. the Favourite, having been set on fire by her surviving crew, blew up with a great explosion. Both the Corona and Bellona were very near sharing her fate, and placed in considerable jeopardy the lives of all that were on board of them. As soon as Lieutenant O'Brien arrived on board the Bellona to take possession, he interrogated the gunner as to the state of the magazine. The latter privately informed him, that Captain Duodo, at the commencement of the action, had ordered to be placed in a small bower-cable tier two or three barrels of gunpowder; intending, as soon as all hopes of further resistance were at an end, to set fire to the train, and, if not blow up the ship, to intimidate the British from taking possession, and thus enable the survivors of the crew to effect their escape. But Captain Duodo's wound came opportunely to prevent the fructuation of his diabolical design; and the officers of the Bellona themselves probably had, for their own safety, watched very narrowly the movements of their captain. Lieutenant O'Brien visited the cable-tier, saw the barrels of gunpowder, and, placing one of his men as sentry over them, proceeded to the cabin; where lay the mortally wounded projector, wholly unconscious of the discovery of his plot. Captain Duodo expressed his gratitude, in the strongest manner, for the attention paid by the British officer to a " beaten foe," but said not a word about the powder; nor were his dying moments disturbed with the slightest allusion to the circumstance.

The Corona was much nearer destruction. At 9 P.M., when in tow by the Active, the prize caught fire in the main top; and the whole of her mainmast, with his rigging, was presently in flames. The Active immediately cut herself clear, and the Corona continued burning until 11 h. 30 m. P.M.; when, owing to the prompt and energetic exertions of Lieutenants James Dickinson of the Cerberus, and George Haye of the Active, and their respective parties of seamen, the flames were got under, but not without the loss of the ship's mainmast, and, unfortunately, of some lives. Four seamen and one marine of the Active were drowned, and Lieutenant Haye was severely burnt; as were midshipman Siphus Goode and two seamen belonging to the Cerberus.

In reviewing the merits of the action, although we might easily show that, in point of force, the Amphion and Cerberus were both inferior, and the Active herself not more than equal, to any of the four 40-gun frigates on the opposite side, and that the Bellona and Carolina were either of them a decided overmatch for the Volage, we shall consider that the seven larger ships agreed with each other in force, and that the three smaller ones did the same. There were also, it will be recollected, one Venetian 16-gun brig, one armed schooner, one xebec, and two gun-boats, mounting altogether 36 guns, and perhaps equal, in the light winds that prevailed, to a second Bellona or Carolina, or, at all events, to a second Volage. The number of men in the British squadron appears to have been about 880, and the number in the Franco-Venetian squadron, at the lowest estimate, 2500. Hence the British had opposed to them a force in guns full one-third, and in men nearly two-thirds, greater than their own; and the whole of that force, as far as the number and appearance of the vessels could designate its amount, was plainly discovered, as the Amphion and her three consorts advanced to the attack. But the foe was met, the action fought, and the victory won; and fresh and unfaded will be the laurels which Captain Hoste and his gallant companions gained at Lissa.

The extraordinary circumstance, of a naval official account emanating from the pen of a colonel of infantry, would, of itself, justify a slight investigation of its contents; and really, if every officer, commanding a detachment of troops on board a French frigate, could make up so good a story as Colonel Alexandre Gifflenga, it would be well for the glory of the French navy that he, and not the captain of the ship, should transmit the particulars of the action. For instance, Colonel Gifflenga says: "At daylight we perceived the English division, consisting of a cut-down ship of the line and three frigates." The colonel then wishes to make it appear that, owing chiefly to the lightness of the breeze, the attacking ships went into action one by one. He proceeds: "At half-past ten, the masts of the Favourite having fallen, Ensign Villeneuve announced to me that he could no longer steer the ship. We at that moment struck upon the rocks off the island of Lissa. I ordered the people to be debarked: I took possession of several vessels, and caused the frigate to be blown up." " Je m'emparai de plusieurs bâtimens et je fis sauter la frégate." " The English, in the utmost distress," adds the colonel, " entered the port of St. George, after they had set fire to the Corona and one of their frigates: the cut-down line-of-battle ship, after being wholly dismasted, ran upon the rocks of the island, and in all probability was lost. The result of this action is the loss, on our part, of two frigates, and, on the part of the English, of one frigate and one cut-down ship of the line. It is the opinion of the sailors, that, if Captain Dubourdieu had kept his squadron together, we should have got possession of two English vessels, although the enemy had two cut-down ships of the line." To show that these extraordinary statements really form part of the colonel's letter, we subjoin the whole of the original passage:—"Les Anglais sont entrés dans le port de St. Georges dans le plus mauvais état, et après avoir mis le feu à la frégate la Couronne et à une de leur frégates : la vaisseau rasé, démâté de tous ces mâts, était échoué sur les roches de l'île. Il doit s'être perdu. Le résultat de ce combat est, pour nous, la perte de deux frégates qui ont péri, et pour les Anglais la perte d'une frégate et d'un vaisseau rasé. L'opinion de tous les marins est que, si le Capitaine Dubourdieu avait bien rallié sa division, nous prendrions deux bâtimens anglais, quoique l'ennemi eût deux vaisseaux rasés."

It is not a little extraordinary that Colonel Gifflenga's "vaisseau rasé," was at this time within five or six of being the smallest ship of the numerous class of British 38-gun frigates; but she was larger, undoubtedly, than either of the two 32-gun frigates associated with her. The Active measured 1058, the Amphion 914, the Cerberus 816, and the Volage 529 tons. Yet the Active was a smaller ship than the Corona, which measured 1094 tons, and than either the Favourite, Danaé, or Flore; not one of which, we believe, measured less than the Corona. Why, therefore, the Active should have been so avoided during the battle, and so magnified in force after it was over, we cannot conceive. The fire on board the Corona accounts, in some degree, for what is stated respecting that ship; and had any one of the British ships merely touched the ground, there would have been a pretext for the colonel's assertion on that head; but no accident of the kind occurred. In stating, at the commencement of his letter, that the British had one "cut-down ship of the line," and at the end of it, that they had two, the writer reminds us of that prince of braggarts Falstaff and his men of buckram.

Leaving the letter of Colonel Alexander Gifflenga to the contempt it merits, we shall make a few admissions, which, even in the opinion of a reasonable Frenchman or Italian, will outweigh all the colonel's rodomontade. Commodore Dubourdieu advanced to the attack in a brave and masterly manner; and had the Favourite escaped being driven on shore, a much more serious task, in the nature of things, would have devolved upon Captain Hoste. Captain Péridier also deserves credit, for the gallant manner in which he seconded the views of his unfortunate chief; and, as the captain was badly wounded and below at the time the Flore struck to the Amphion, we should be disposed to exculpate him from the dishonourable act of making sail after his ship had so unequivocally surrendered. Of the Danaé's captain, we are unable to state the name ; and perhaps it is better for him that we are so. With respect to the Corona's captain, no officer, to whatever navy he may belong, could have fought his ship better. The Corona, it will be recollected, was not subdued by one opponent : she had two frigates upon her in succession ; and both, the first in particular, felt the effects of her steady and well-directed fire. By his gallant behaviour in the action, and his frank and manly deportment afterwards, Captain Paschaligo not only afforded a bright example to the little navy of Venice, and ennobled an already noble name, but gained for himself the hearts of those into whose temporary custody he had fallen.

After the destruction of the Favourite, the 200 survivors of her late crew retired to Lissa: in which port lay two prizes to the Active, in charge of two of her midshipmen, James Lew and Robert Kingston. These enterprising young men, assisted by some privateer's men, actually summoned the 200 French seamen and troops to surrender. As a contrast to this very gallant behaviour, a Sicilian privateer-brig, of 14 guns, commanded by Clemento Fama, lying in the port, hauled down her colours to a one-gun Venetian schooner : and that in the face of the British squadron. This was "Fama" indeed ! The Active's two midshipmen, with the true Gordon spirit, went on board and took charge of the brig, beat off the schooner, and prevented her from destroying the British and Sicilian vessels in the bay.

On the 15th Captain Hoste sent a letter by a flag of truce to Captain Péridier of the Flore, at anchor in the road of Lessina, demanding restitution of the frigate in the same state as when she struck to the Amphion. This letter was replied to by the captain of the Danaé; who, in consequence of the wounds of M. Péridier, had assumed the command of the Franco-Venetian squadron. He declared that the Flore did not strike her colours,

CAPT^N SIR WILLIAM HOSTE, BAR^T

FROM AN ORIGINAL PICTURE IN THE POSSESSION OF LADY HOSTE.

but had them shot away, and requested Captain Hoste, if he had anything further to say, to address himself to the French government. This letter was neither signed nor dated; and Captain Hoste sent it back, repeating his demand to have the Flore restored to him. Thus ended the business. The Danaé, Flore, and Carolina remained at Lessina about a week, and then proceeded to Ragusa.

The Corona was a remarkably fine frigate, built early in the preceding year at Venice, and became added to the 38-gun class of the British navy by the name of Dædalus. The Bellona, a ship of 692 tons, was purchased for a troop-ship, and named Dover. Each of the four captains present at the Lissa action received a medal: and the first-lieutenants of the ships, David Dunn of the Amphion, James Dickinson of the Cerberus, William Henderson of the Active, and William Wolrige of the Volage, were each promoted to the rank of commander.

If only to add another to the many proofs which the world has witnessed, that the boldest heart in deeds of arms is generally the most alive to the softer impulses of humanity, we subjoin an extract from a letter of condolence addressed by Captain Hoste to a near relative of John Robert Spearman, one of the two young midshipmen killed on board the Amphion. "It is impossible I can describe to you the exemplary conduct of the poor lad I am now writing to you about. If it is any consolation to his friends to learn how he behaved, tell them that, even in those days when all strove to emulate, he distinguished himself amongst his shipmates in the post where honour or danger was in view. And I assure you, not only am I deprived of a most excellent youngster, and one whom I dearly esteemed, but his country, as far as his youth may speak for him, has lost one of its brightest hopes: indeed, he is deeply lamented by all."

On or about the 25th of March the two French 40-gun frigates Amélie and Adrienne, accompanied by the 20-gun storeship Dromadaire, laden with 15,000 shot and shells of various sizes, and 90 tons of gunpowder, escaped out of Toulon, bound to the island of Corfu. On the 26th, Admiral Sir Charles Cotton detached the 74-gun ship Ajax, Captain Robert Waller Otway, and the 18-pounder 36-gun frigate Unité, Captain Edwin Henry Chamberlayne, to the eastward in pursuit. On arriving off Corsica, Captain Otway sent the Unité round Cape Corse, and with the Ajax pushed through the straits of Bonifacio.

On the 30th, when off the isle of Elba, the Unité fell in with and was chased by the three French ships; who, on hauling off from her, steered for the Piombino passage, and were left working through it. On the same evening the Ajax joined company, and the two British ships proceeded in chase under all sail. On the 31st, at daylight, Captain Otway discovered the objects of his pursuit to windward. Owing to the short distance they were from the land, the Amélie and Adrienne effected their escape into Porto-Ferrajo; but the Dromadaire was overtaken and captured. She was a fine ship of 800 tons, and had a complement of 150 men, commanded by a lieutenant de vaisseau. The two French frigates afterwards got into Genoa; and thence reached Toulon in the succeeding July, as already mentioned.[1]

In the latter part of the month of April the two armed store-ships Giraffe and Nourrice, each mounting from 20 to 30 guns, the first with 140, the other with 160 men, having in their company a merchant-ship, also armed, and laden, as they also were, with ship-timber for the dockyard at Toulon, lay at anchor in the bay of Sagone, island of Corsica, under the protection of a battery, mounting four guns and one mortar, and of a martello tower above the battery, mounting one gun. On the 30th, in the evening, the British 38-gun frigate Pomone, Captain Robert Barrie, the frigate Unité, and the 18-gun brig-sloop Scout, Captain Alexander Renton Sharpe, arrived off the coast, with the intention of attacking these ships. The French commodore well imagining what was meditated against his ships, moored them within a stone's throw of the battery, each with two cables on shore, so as to present their broadsides to the narrow entrance of the bay. As an additional defence, the Nourrice landed her quarter-deck guns; and about 200 regular troops, along with her marines and those of the Giraffe, were posted on the neighbouring heights.

All these preparations were seen from the British ships on the morning of the 1st of May, and only rendered those on board of them the more anxious to commence operations. Notwithstanding the strong position of the three French ships, the crews of the two British frigates and brig came forward in the most noble manner, and volunteered their services to land, or, as it was quite calm, to attack the enemy by boats. Neither of these methods being considered practicable, Captain Barrie resolved, as soon as a breeze sprang up, to make the attack by the ships. Finding, by 5 h. 30 m. P.M., that the calm still continued, and fearing that any longer delay would enable the French to increase their force, the Pomone, Unité, and Scout, in the most

[1] See p. 208.

animated manner, were towed by their respective companies, in the face of a heavy raking fire, into a position within range of grape; when, at 6 P.M. the British ships opened their broadsides. The mutual cannonade lasted, without any intermission, until 7 h. 30 m. P.M.; when the Giraffe, bearing a commodore's pendant, and then the Nourrice, was observed to be on fire. Afterwards the brands from the Nourrice set fire to the merchantman, and in 10 minutes all three ships were completely in a blaze. The Pomone and her consorts now quickly towed themselves out of danger from the explosions; the first of which, that of the Giraffe, took place at 8 h. 50 m. P.M., and that of the Nourrice a few minutes afterwards. Some of the timbers of the latter, falling on the tower, entirely demolished it, and the sparks set fire to the battery below, which also exploded.

The object of the attack having thus completely succeeded, the three British vessels stood out to sea, to repair their damages; which, except as to the Pomone, who, having had to choose her station, became of course exposed to the brunt of the action, were not very material. The Pomone had two seamen killed, and 10 seamen (four dangerously), seven marines (one dangerously), and two boys wounded; the Unité, one midshipman (Richard Goodridge), one seaman, and one marine slightly wounded; and the Scout, her first-lieutenant (William Neame), severely, and her boatswain (James Stewart) and one seaman slightly wounded; total, on board the three British ships, two killed and 25 wounded. The loss on the part of the French could not be ascertained, but, in all probability, was very severe.

On the 4th of May, at 10 A.M., the British 38-gun frigates Belle-Poule, Captain James Brisbane, and Alceste, Captain Murray Maxwell, being off the coast of Istria, discovered and chased a French man-of-war brig, of 18 guns, which shortly afterwards hauled into the small harbour of Parenza. Having received intelligence that a vessel of that description was expected at Ragusa, with supplies for the French frigates Danaé and Flore, which had escaped from Captain Hoste off Lissa, Captain Brisbane resolved to attempt the capture or destruction of the French brig. Although there was only 15 feet of water in the harbour, and therefore no passage for the frigates, it was ascertained that the brig could be cannonaded with effect where she was then lying. Accordingly the Belle-Poule, followed closely by the Alceste, stood in within a cable's length of the rocks at the entrance of the harbour, and opened an animated fire, as well upon the brig as upon a battery under which she lay; and, after an hour's cannonade, compelled the brig to haul on shore under the town out of gun-shot. In this attack the two frigates had been frequently hulled, but sustained no other damage than could be immediately repaired, and no greater loss than the Belle-Poule one, and the Alceste two, seamen slightly wounded.

All further efforts on the part of the ships being useless, the Belle-Poule and Alceste, after the close of the day, anchored about five miles from the shore; and Captain Brisbane determined to take possession of an island that lay in the mouth of the harbour, and was within musket-shot of the town. Accordingly at 11 P.M., the boats of the two frigates, containing 200 seamen and the whole of the marines (about 100 in number), under the orders of the Belle-Poule's senior Lieutenant John M'Curdy, assisted by Lieutenants Richard Ball Boardman, Edward A. Chartres, and Alexander Morrison, and Midshipmen Hamilton Blair, Charles Matthew Chapman, Edward Finlay, Henry Maxwell, John Hall, and Arthur Grose, of the Belle-Poule, and Lieutenants John Collman Hickman and Richard Lloyd, Mr. Howard Moore the master, and Messrs. James Adair, Charles Croker, and Thomas Redding, midshipmen of the Alceste, proceeded and took quiet possession of the island. By 5 A.M., on the 5th, with incessant labour and the most extraordinary exertions, a defence was thrown up, and a battery of four pieces, two howitzers and two 9-pounders, mounted on a commanding position. A field-piece was also placed at some distance on the left, to divide the attention of the enemy; who, aware of the operations of the British, had been busily employed during the night in planting guns in various parts of the harbour. Soon after 5 A.M. the French opened a cross fire from four different positions, which was immediately returned; and the mutual cannonade continued, with great vigour, during five hours. At the end of that time, the French brig being cut to pieces and sunk, and of course the object of making the attack accomplished, the British re-embarked with their guns and ammunition; after having sustained a loss of four men, the gunner and one seaman of the Belle-Poule, and two marines of the Alceste, killed, and one man slightly wounded; making the total loss to the British on the occasion four killed and four wounded.

On the 26th of May, at daybreak, the British 18-gun brig-sloop Alacrity (sixteen 32-pounder carronades and two sixes), Captain Nesbit Palmer, cruising off Cape St. André, island of

Corsica, with the wind a moderate breeze from the eastward, discovered about six miles to leeward, and immediately chased, a large man-of-war brig, which proved to be the French brig-corvette Abeille, of 24-pounder carronades, commanded by acting-Lieutenant de vaisseau Ange-René-Armand De Mackau. Observing that the vessel approaching was a brig, Lieutenant De Mackau knew at once the extent of her force; and accordingly shortened sail, hoisted his colours, and fired a gun of defiance. By manœuvring skilfully, the Abeille managed to pour into the Alacrity one or two raking fires. The French brig now tried for the weather-gage, and having obtained it, passed and engaged her opponent on the opposite tack, then bore up, and running close under the Alacrity's stern, raked her. The Abeille afterwards hauled up on the same (the larboard) tack as the Alacrity, and engaged her to leeward, keeping just upon the British brig's quarter: so that, while her own guns were playing havoc upon the decks of her antagonist, the Alacrity had scarcely a gun which she could bring to bear. In a vessel whose tiller works on deck, the quarter is much more decidedly the "point of impunity," than in a vessel whose tiller works below. For instance, in the Alacrity and brigs of her class, the space between the aftermost port and the stern is upwards of 11 feet, to allow room for the sweep of the tiller, consequently, the whole of the space, one-ninth part of the length of the deck, is without a gun.

The damage of the Alacrity's rigging soon obliged her to drop astern, and thereby afforded her the opportunity of bestowing a few shot in return for the many she had received; but the Abeille quickly freed herself from the effect of those by ranging ahead, and placing herself upon the Alacrity's starboard bow, the latter, feeling sensibly the ill effects of this diagonal fire, threw all back, and endeavoured to pass astern of her antagonist; but the Abeille saw the well-meant manœuvre, and at once frustrated it by bearing up. The two brigs continued thus engaged, side by side, for a few minutes longer; when the Alacrity, having had her sails and rigging cut to pieces, fell off, with her stern completely exposed to the Abeille's broadside. In this defenceless state the British brig remained, until, having had all her officers killed or driven from the deck but the boatswain, she was compelled to haul down her colours. This took place about three-quarters of an hour after the commencement of the action.

The Alacrity, out of a crew on board of 100 men and boys

including 13 of the latter, had her first and only lieutenant (Thomas Gwynne Rees) and four seamen killed, her captain (slightly), master (David Laing), one and her only master's mate (Mr. Warren, mortally), surgeon (William Turner, slightly, while dressing the wounded), boatswain (severely), and eight seamen and marines, wounded. Lieutenant De Mackau, in his letter, as given in the Moniteur, enumerates 15 killed and 20 wounded; but the account, as we have stated it, may be depended upon as correct. The Abeille, whose crew amounted to at least 130 men and boys, lost, according to the acknowledgment of her officers, seven seamen and marines killed and 12 wounded. Neither brig, as far as it appears, had any mast shot away; although both, particularly the Alacrity, had received damage in them as well as in the rigging, sails, and hull.

Here were two brigs, when the action began, about equally matched, and when it ended, nearly equal sufferers in point of numerical loss: a circumstance that renders the termination of it, by the capture of one of them, so much the more extraordinary. It was, however, in numbers merely, that the loss came so near to an equality; as the Alacrity's almost unparalleled loss of officers has already in part shown, and as the further explanation, which our duty calls upon us to give, will completely establish. Out of her full net complement of 120 men and boys, the Alacrity sailed upon her last cruise with only 101 men and 13 boys. Falling in with and detaining a Greek ship, rather largely manned, Captain Palmer sent on board his second-lieutenant, Mr. Alexander Martin, a skilful and zealous officer, and 13 able seamen, with orders to carry the ship to Malta. This was in the beginning of May. Thus left with all her boys, and with very little more than four-fifths of her men, the Alacrity encountered the Abeille in the manner already stated. In the early part of the action, Captain Palmer received a lacerated wound in his hand and fingers, and went below, and remained below. The command, in consequence, devolved upon Lieutenant Rees, and a more efficient officer could not be found. Presently Lieutenant Rees had his leg badly shot, and was borne to a carronade-slide. There he sat, persisting in not being carried below, and animating the men by every means in his power, until a second shot laid him dead on the deck. His place was filled by Mr. Laing, the master. While he was in command, the master's mate, Mr. Warren, received his mortal wound; and at length Mr. Laing got wounded also, by a contusion in the upper part of the thigh, and he went below.

The men on the quarter-deck now called out, that there was no officer to command them. Instantly James Flaxman, the boatswain, stepped aft, who, although he had received a painful wound in the left arm by a nail, and been knocked into the waist by a splinter, was again at his post on the forecastle cheering the people. Here, again, all might have gone on well, in spite of the disheartening effect produced upon the crew by the absence of their finger-wounded captain. Although his hand had been dressed, the latter was so stomach-sick, or so sick somewhere else, that he remained below; and, whether it was that a shot, which about this time wounded the surgeon in the cockpit alarmed the captain in the cabin, or that the latter began to compassionate others, as well as himself, Captain Palmer sent up orders to strike the colours. No sooner was the order announced on the quarter-deck than, snatching up a pistol from off the binnacle, the boatswain swore he would blow out the brains of the first man who attempted to execute it. The threat had its effect, and the ensign of the Alacrity continued to wave at her gaff-end. In a very short time, however, while the intrepid Flaxman was standing near the main hatchway, exhorting the crew to act like British seamen, the gunner, who ranked above the boatswain, and seems to have caught the captain's infection, hauled down the brig's colours.

It was as fortunate for the memory of the Alacrity's late commander, as, in reference to the merits of this action, it was unfortunate for the cause of truth, that he died a month afterwards of a locked jaw brought on by his originally insignificant wound. Every person does not know that, in warm climates, a comparatively slight cut between the thumb and forefinger will frequently produce locked jaw; and therefore the undisputed fact, that Captain Palmer "died of his wounds," not only exonerated him, in public opinion, from all blame, but stamped his character with a quality to which, as is now evident, he had not a pretension. Let those who maintain that the dead are not to be ill spoken of, answer the question, whether the good of the individual should not give way to the good of the many? Whether, in short, it is not more consonant to justice to show that a certain mishap or calamity arose from the defection of one man, than leave it to be inferred that 100 men failed in their duty?

But there were gems in the British character that, had the Alacrity not met the Abeille, and had the captain of the former not behaved as he did, would perhaps for ever have lain hid

Lieutenant Rees, for instance, might never have had an opportunity of displaying the trait of heroism which caused his death; nor James Flaxman, the boatswain, the undaunted spirit that animated him, and which at least delayed, although it could not prevent, the surrender of the British brig. Satisfied we are that, if the details of every British naval defeat were fully made public, instead of, as is usually the case, suppressed or but partially given, sufficient glory would be elicited to counteract the disgrace, which the unexplained result of the action is, in almost every case, calculated to produce.

Before we dismiss the action of the Alacrity and Abeille, let us do justice to the officers and crew of the latter. They did their duty like brave men and good seamen; and, as an additional proof that they were brave men, treated their prisoners with attention and kindness. With respect to the Abeille's commander, he obtained the promotion to which his gallantry so justly entitled him: he was immediately confirmed in his appointment of a lieutenant de vaisseau, and made a member of the legion of honour. On the 7th of February, 1812, Lieutenant De Mackau was made a capitaine de frégate; soon afterwards a baron of the French empire: and on the 1st of September, 1819, a capitaine de vaisseau.

On the 30th of May, 1814, on board the Gladiator at Portsmouth, a court-martial sat on the surviving officers and crew of the Alacrity. The court acquitted them of all blame, and attributed the brig's loss to so many of her officers having been killed or wounded, and to the "captain's not returning on deck after having had his wound dressed by the surgeon." The court also greatly eulogized the conduct of James Flaxman, the boatswain; and he afterwards, we believe, filled a similar station on board a line-of-battle ship.

The French official account states the force of the Alacrity at "20 carronades, 32-pounders." For this there was some ground, the brig having really mounted two small brass guns, 2 or 3 pounders, abaft. But there were no shot for them; they were the captain's playthings, and served occasionally to exercise the crew in the necessary art of polishing. Of this oversight, or whatever it may have been, in Captain De Mackau, we feel the less disposed to complain, because he fairly states the force of his own brig at "20 carronades, 24-pounders." A French writer, whose works are of deservedly high repute in this country, has selected about four cases out of the mass to be found in these pages, in order to show, that "French valour can triumph over British bravery," "la vaillance française pouvait triompher de la bravoure britannique."[1] Far be it from us to discourage the laudable endeavours of M. Dupin to re-animate the drooping navy of his country: we heartily wish he may succeed, because we are convinced that unless the French navy thrives, the British navy will droop. By the French the British can afford to be beaten occasionally; and, had the British been oftener defeated during the six years that preceded, they would, we are sure, have been oftener successful in the three years that followed, the 18th of June, 1812.

However, not to lose sight of M. Dupin, let us remark that, in stating the broadside-force of the Alacrity at 127 "kilogrammes," and that of the Abeille at 109, he proves the inaccuracy of his information respecting the mounted force of the two vessels. M. Dupin may correct his error by reducing the following into French weights: Alacrity, broadside-force 262 lb., Abeille, same, 260 lb. In stating that the French brig Renard was of the same force as the Abeille, M. Dupin is also wrong, owing probably to his being unacquainted, that the Abeille was not a regular-built French corvette, but a large American brig, purchased at some port in the Mediterranean and fitted out by the admiral at Toulon as a cruiser. The very circumstance of her having mounted, before carronades were so much in use in the French navy, 18 long 8-pounders and two brass 36-pounder carronades,[2] shows that the Abeille must have been a brig of very large dimensions, especially when it is considered that the Alacrity's class, averaging 383 tons, was originally designed to carry 18 long 6-pounders.

On the 27th of June, at 11 h. 30 m. A.M., the British brig-sloop Guadeloupe, of 14 carronades, 24-pounders, and two sixes, with 102 men and boys, Captain Joseph Swabey Tetley, being off Cape Cerus at the north-eastern extremity of Spain, with the wind a fresh breeze from south-south-east, discovered and chased two strange sail in the north; which afterwards proved to be the French brig-corvette Tactique, of 16 carronades, 24-pounders, and two long 8-pounders, with at least 150 men and boys, and the armed xebec Guêpe, of two long 18-pounders and six 18 or 12 pounder carronades, with 65 or 70 men and boys. At about 15 minutes past noon the brig and xebec tacked and stood inshore; and in another quarter of an hour all three vessels hoisted their colours.

At 0 h. 40 m. P.M. the Guadeloupe, who had previously

[1] Dupin, Force Navale, tome ii., p. 85.   [2] See vol. iv., p. 142.

shortened sail, received the Tactique's starboard broadside, then, passing under the latter's stern, returned it with interest, and immediately afterwards lay her opponent close alongside to leeward. A spirited action now ensued, in which the xebec took a safe, but at the same time very effective part, by raking the Guadeloupe astern. At 1 h. 30 m. P.M. the Tactique made an attempt to board the British brig, but was repulsed with considerable slaughter. The French brig then passed the stern of the Guadeloupe: on which the latter bore up to close and renew the action. About this time two batteries near the town of Saint-André, one of four, the other of nine guns, opened a distant fire upon the Guadeloupe. Shortly afterwards the two brigs again came to close action, and continued engaged until 2 h. 15 m. P.M.; when the Tactique, having had quite enough of fighting, bore up, set her topgallant-sails, and stood in-shore under the batteries, whither the Guêpe had just before fled for shelter. The Guadeloupe, from whom the town of Vendré at this time bore south-west by south distant not more than two miles, gave the French brig a parting broadside from her larboard guns, then hauled to the wind and stood off-shore.

The Guadeloupe was a good deal cut in her sails and rigging but not materially damaged in her hull: her loss amounted to one man killed, her first-lieutenant and nine men severely, and two or three others slightly wounded. Although the Tactique did not appear to have had any of her spars shot away, the damages in her hull may be gathered from the extent of her loss, as it was afterwards reported to the British. The account received by the Guadeloupe's officers made the Tactique's loss 11 men killed and 48 wounded, including 16 of the number mortally. Even admitting the amount to be somewhat overstated, enough remains to show, that the Guadeloupe performed her part in a very gallant and efficient manner, evidently beating off, without reckoning the xebec, a French brig superior in force to herself; and which brig the Guadeloupe would in all probability have captured, had the action been fought at a greater distance from the shore, where the Tactique had no batteries to fly to for protection. It has already appeared that Captain Tetley, in a month or two after this action, commanded a British frigate, and behaved with great judgment and firmness.[1] On the 7th of the succeeding January, as the lists inform us, he was confirmed in his post-rank.

On the 4th of July, at daylight, the British 18-pounder

[1] See p. 209.

36-gun frigate Unité, Captain Edwin Henry Chamberlayne, being off Port Hercule on the Roman coast, despatched, to cut out an armed brig at anchor there, a part of her boats, under the orders of Lieutenant Joseph William Crabb, accompanied by Lieutenant of marines George Victor, master's mates Michael Dwyer and Henry Collins, and midshipman Duncan Hutchinson. On approaching the coast, the boats were vigorously attacked by the brig, which was the St. François de Paule, mounting four 6-pounders, four 3-pounders, and a quantity of small-arms, protected by a battery of two 8-pounders on the beach. Very light and variable winds preventing the ships from closing to co-operate, Captain Chamberlayne detached the launch under Lieutenant John M'Dougal, to support the other boats; but ere she could reach them, Lieutenant Crabb and his party, without the slightest loss, had driven the crew from the brig, and were bringing her out, in a very handsome manner, under showers of grape from the battery. At 7 A.M. the prize, which was partly laden with ship-timber, joined the Unité; and, although the brig was materially damaged in her hull, masts, and rigging, no person on board was hurt by the fire of the battery.

At 9 A.M. the 18-gun brig-sloop Cephalus, Captain Augustus William James Clifford, joined company; and the British frigate and sloop stood along the coast. At 5 P.M. several vessels were discovered at anchor between Civita-Vecchia and the mouth of the Tiber. Captain Clifford, in a most handsome manner, offered to lead into the anchorage, and to head the boats in any enterprise which to Captain Chamberlayne might appear practicable. The Cephalus then, by the latter's directions, stood in, and, pointing out the soundings by signal, came to an anchor under the fire of a battery of four 8 and 6 pounders; by a grape-shot from one of which, Mr. Isaac Simon, the brig's master, was slightly wounded. The Unité shortly afterwards anchored in four fathoms, and the French were quickly driven from their guns at the battery. The boats of the Unité, commanded by the same officers who had distinguished themselves in the morning, then joined the boats of the Cephalus, under Captain Clifford; and the whole went in and brought out, without the slightest loss, although exposed to a smart fire of musketry from their crews, and from a party of soldiers drawn up on a height above them, three merchant-vessels. The remainder of those at anchor in the road proved to be fishing-vessels.

On the 21st of July, at 5 P.M., the British 12-pounder 32-gun frigate Thames, Captain Charles Napier, joined the Cephalus off

Porto del Infreschi, into which port the latter had the day before compelled a French convoy of 26 sail to run for shelter. The Cephalus, followed by the Thames, then stood in and anchored: and the two opened a heavy cannonade upon 11 French gun-boats and a felucca, mounting between them six long 18-pounders, two 12-pounder carronades, three brass and two iron 6-pounders, and manned with 280 men; moored across the port, for the protection of 15 merchant-vessels, and of 36 spars for the line-of-battle ship and frigate building at Naples.

The fire of the gun-boats, as well as of a round tower, and of a body of musketry on the adjacent hills, was soon silenced; and while the boats, under Captain Clifford, took possession of the vessels-of-war and merchantmen, the marines, under Lieutenant David M'Adams, landed, and stormed and carried the round tower, making an officer and 80 men prisoners. Within two hours from their anchoring, the Thames and Cephalus were again under way, with all their prizes in company, and all the spars alongside, except two which could not be got off. Nor did this dashing and important enterprise cost the life of a man; the whole loss sustained amounting to the boatswain (Hood Douglas) and three seamen of the Cephalus wounded.

On the 27th of July the British 38-gun frigate Active, Captain James Alexander Gordon, anchored off the town of Ragosniza on the island of that name in the Adriatic, and despatched her boats, with the small-arm men and marines, under the orders of Lieutenant James Henderson, assisted by Lieutenants George Haye, who, though an invalid, very handsomely volunteered, and Robert Gibson, Lieutenant of marines Peter Mears, master's mate Charles Friend, and midshipmen Henry Lew, Redmond Moriarty, Norwich Duff, William Simpkins, Joseph Camelleri, Nathaniel Barwell, Charles Bentham, George Moore, William Wood, and William Todd Robinson, to attack a convoy of 28 vessels, laden with grain for the garrison of Ragusa, which had run up above the island and taken shelter in a creek on the main.

The creek being very narrow at its entrance, and protected by three gun-boats, as well as by a force of armed men on each point, reported to amount in the whole to 300, Lieutenant Henderson, accompanied by Lieutenants Haye and Mears and Mr. Friend, and the small-arm men and marines, landed on the right, in order to take possession of a hill that appeared to command the creek; leaving Lieutenant Gibson to push for the gun-boats, the moment a concerted signal should be made from the top of the hill. After dislodging several soldiers, who fired upon them during their ascent, Lieutenant Henderson and his party gained the summit, and found themselves immediately above the gun-boats and convoy. Having made the preconcerted signal, Lieutenant Henderson descended the hill, exposed to the fire of one of the gun-boats and several soldiers; but the attack had been so well planned, and was so nobly executed, that the boats under Lieutenant Gibson boarded the gun-vessels immediately after Lieutenant Henderson's men had fired two volleys into them. Being attacked so warmly, the crews of the gun-boats, except three men and several others that were wounded, jumped overboard and got on shore just as the frigate's boats came alongside. The guns in the vessels were immediately turned towards the flying enemy; and the British, without experiencing any further resistance, took possession of the whole convoy. Ten of the latter were burnt by the captors, and the remaining 18 vessels, along with the three gun-boats, were brought safely out; nor was there the usual drawback of a serious loss to lessen the value of the exploit, four men only having been wounded in the British boats.

On the 26th of May, in the morning, the British 18-gun brig-sloop Pilot, Captain John Toup Nicolas, observing four settees on the beach almost immediately under the town of Strongoli, near the entrance of the gulf of Taranto, despatched her boats to bring them off, under the orders of Lieutenants Alexander Campbell and Francis Charles Annesley, Mr. Roger Langland the master, master's mate Henry Pierson Simpson, midshipman John Barnes (the second), and Mr. Scotten the carpenter. The Pilot herself at the same time anchored off the spot, but, on account of the shoal water, not so close as was desirable.

In spite of an opposition from 75 gens-d'armes, all dragoons, and 30 regular foot-soldiers, sent from Cotrone, and above 40 of the civic militia, Lieutenant Campbell and his party effected a landing; and after dislodging the enemy from an advantageous position behind a bank and in a tower within half musket-shot of the beach, launched three of the vessels, and destroyed the fourth, because unable from shot-holes to float. The whole of the service was executed with no greater loss than one marine slightly wounded.

On the 6th of September, early in the morning, the Pilot, cruising off the town of Castellan in the same neighbourhood, observed an armed ketch secured to the walls of the castle of that name. The brig immediately anchored close to the town; and, having by her guns driven away the troops there collected for the protection of the ketch, Captain Nicolas despatched the boats, under the orders of Lieutenant Campbell, to bring out the vessel. This officer and his party gallantly landed under the ruins of the castle, and after some opposition, advanced to the town; whence the few troops remaining there precipitately fled. Finding the ketch bilged, he threw her guns overboard and set her on fire. The seamen then, while the marines took post at the castle, loaded their boats with a quantity of corn and flax, and returned on board the sloop by 4 P.M. without having sustained the slightest loss.

On the 11th of October, in the morning, the British 38-gun frigate Impérieuse, Captain the Hon. Henry Duncan, being off Possitano in the gulf of Salerno, discovered three gun-vessels, of one long 18-pounder and 30 men each, moored under the wall of a strong fort. At 11 A.M. the Impérieuse anchored within range of grape, and in a few minutes sank one of the gun-boats and silenced the fire of the fort; but a shot from the latter had previously cut away the frigate's foretopsail-yard. The fort being walled all round, the ship could not dislodge the soldiers and crews of the gun-vessels, who had sheltered themselves within it; and yet that measure became necessary, before possession could be taken of the two remaining gun-boats. Captain Duncan therefore despatched the boats of the Impérieuse, under the orders of Lieutenant Eaton Travers, first of the frigate, assisted by Lieutenant of marines Philip Pipon. These two gallant officers, at the head of a detachment of seamen and the whole of the marines, forced their way into the battery, under a heavy fire of musketry from more than treble their numbers; all of whom, except about 30 men left behind, with 50 stand of arms, the British compelled to fly in every direction. The guns mounted on the battery, which were 24-pounders, were then thrown over the cliff, the magazines destroyed, and the two gun-vessels brought off: nor was any greater loss sustained, in executing the whole of this dashing exploit, than one marine killed and two wounded. The Impérieuse, however, had had her rigging damaged, and, as already stated, her foretopsail yard shot away, by the commencing fire of the battery.

In a few days afterwards the Impérieuse was joined by the 12-pounder 32-gun frigate Thames, Captain Charles Napier; and on the 19th the two frigates anchored close to the shore near

Palinuro on the coast of Calabria. The boats, commanded by Lieutenant Travers, then landed under cover of the fire of the ships, and launched and brought off, without the slightest casualty, 10 armed polacres laden with oil, although the vessels for their better security, were banked up with sand, and were defended by a large detachment of Neapolitan troops.

On the 21st the Impérieuse and Thames discovered 10 Neapolitan gun-boats lying in the port of Palinuro, together with a number of merchant-vessels, also a quantity of spars hauled up on the beach, intended for the equipment of the Neapolitan navy. From the strength and situation of the harbour, Captain Duncan did not consider that he had a sufficient force to make the attack with a prospect of complete success. He therefore sent the Thames to Sicily, to request Lieutenant-general Maitland to lend him a detachment of soldiers. On the 28th the Thames returned, with 250 of the 62nd regiment under Major Darby; but, as this was just at the commencement of a south-west gale, no operation could for the present be carried on.

On the 1st of November, in the evening, the time proving favourable, the troops under Major Darby, together with the marines of both frigates under Lieutenant Pipon, and a detachment of seamen under Lieutenant Travers, the whole commanded by Captain Napier, were disembarked from the Thames at the back of the harbour. The British immediately ascended and carried the height in a very gallant style, under a heavy fire from the French, who had assembled in force to oppose them, and who, soon after dark, endeavoured to retake their position; but one well-directed volley obliged the enemy to retire. The Impérieuse, meanwhile, had been endeavouring to occupy the attention of the gun-boats and battery in front; but the light and baffling winds prevented the frigate, during the evening, from getting nearer than long range.

On the 2nd, in the morning, finding that nothing could be done on the land side against the battery and a strong tower that protected the vessels on the beach, and within pistol-shot of which the gun-boats were moored, Captain Duncan ordered the Thames to close, and Captain Napier to return to her from the shore. This done, the two frigates bore up at the commencement of the sea-breeze, and, running along the line of gun-boats within half musket-shot, sank two and obliged the remainder almost instantly to surrender. The Impérieuse and Thames then anchoring close to the fort, silenced it in 15 minutes, and in 15 minutes more compelled the garrison to haul down the colours. The fort was instantly taken possession of by Lieutenant Travers: who, on seeing the ships stand in, had most gallantly pushed down the hill with a party of seamen and marines, and was waiting almost under the walls of the fort, ready to take advantage of any superiority the ships might gain over it.

The guns at the fort, 24-pounders, being thrown into the sea, and the gun-boats secured, the crews of both frigates proceeded to launch the vessels and the spars. This could not be accomplished until the afternoon of the 3rd; when the troops, who had all this time remained in undisturbed possession of the heights, were re-embarked, and the marines withdrawn from the tower. The tower was then completely blown up, together with two batteries, and also a signal-tower on the hill. The two ships, accompanied by their prizes, consisting of six gun-boats of one long 18-pounder each, 22 feluccas laden with oil, cotton, &c., and 20 large spars brought off from the beach, put to sea with the land breeze. Four other gun-vessels, one with two long 18-pounders, were also destroyed; but this very dashing service was not executed without loss, Lieutenant Kay of the 62nd regiment and four men being killed, and Lieutenant Pipon of the marines and 10 men wounded. The commanding officer of the gun-boats was Captain Caraccioli, and the troops and armed peasantry, estimated at 700 men, were commanded by General Pignatelli Cercaro. Although Lieutenant Travers was an older lieutenant than many who were at that time commanders, and although Vice-admiral Sir Edward Pellew, the Mediterranean commander-in-chief, requested the attention of the lords of the admiralty to " the distinguished services " which he had on that and on former occasions performed, Lieutenant Travers, as we observe by the list, was not made a commander until the 15th of June, 1814.

On the 27th of November, at 9 A.M., Fano in the Adriatic bearing south-east distant four leagues, the British 74-gun ship Eagle, Captain Charles Rowley, discovered and immediately chased three vessels in the north-west quarter. These were the French 40-gun frigate Uranie, the armed en flûte frigate Corceyre, and brig-corvette Scemplone, from Triest on the 13th, bound to Corfu. In the course of a short time the brig separated from her two companions; and the Eagle continued in pursuit of the latter down the north-east coast of Italy until about 7 h. 30 m. P.M.; when, having lost her fore topmast by an overpress of sail, and been otherwise crippled by the 74's fire, the Corceyre hauled down her colours.

Owing to the extreme darkness of the night and the necessity, in the disabled state of the prize and the strength and direction of the wind, for the Eagle to stay by the Corceyre to prevent her going on shore near Brindisi, the Uranie effected her escape, as was supposed, into that port. The Corceyre is represented to have been pierced for 40 guns, and to have mounted 26 long 18-pounders on the main deck and two 6-pounders on the quarterdeck, with a crew of 170 seamen and 130 soldiers; of whom she had three men killed and six or seven wounded, including her commander, Lieutenant de vaisseau " Longlade." The Corceyre was laden with 300 tons of wheat, and a quantity of military and other stores.

On the 28th of November, at 7 A.M., while the British 38-gun frigates Alceste and Active, Captains Murray Maxwell and James Alexander Gordon, 18-pounder 36-gun frigate Unité, Captain Edwin Henry Chamberlayne, and 20-gun ship Acorn, Captain George Miller Bligh, were lying in Port St. George, island of Lissa, the telegraph on Whitby hill announced three suspicious sail south. Captain Maxwell, the senior officer in the port, immediately unmoored the squadron and prepared to go in pursuit of what was supposed to be a French squadron from Triest bound to Corfu, consisting of the 40-gun frigates Danae and Flore and 32-gun frigate Carolina, the fugitives from Captain Hoste in the preceding March. As a strong French force was at this time assembled at Scisina, for the avowed purpose of making an attack upon Lissa, Captain Maxwell could not leave the island without providing for its defence. Accordingly a lieutenant, midshipman, and about 30 seamen, from the Alceste and Active were embarked on board three prize gun-boats lying in the port; and the whole of the marines belonging to the Alceste, Active, and, we believe, Unité, were landed as a garrison for the two batteries erected on Hoste island at the entrance of the harbour. Leaving, then, the direction of affairs to Captain Bligh of the Acorn, Captain Maxwell, with the Alceste, Active, and Unité began warping out of the harbour against a fresh east-north-east wind; and by 7 P.M., after very great exertions on the part of their officers and crews, the three British frigates were at sea.

At 9 h. 30 m., when close off the south end of Lissa a strange vessel to windward fired two guns, and the Unité boarded her. She proved to be a neutral, on board of which Lieutenant John M'Dougal, of the Unité, had taken his passage to Malta. On that same morning, about 40 miles to the southward, this vessel had discovered three French frigates. Lieutenant M'Dougal instantly obliged the master of the neutral to put back, in order that the squadron might be informed of the circumstance, and the vessel was on her return to Lissa when thus fallen in with by the squadron. With the cheering prospect in view, Lieutenant M'Dougal resumed his station on board the Unité; and the three British frigates were soon under all the sail they could carry, against the fresh wind that now blew from the east-south-east.

On the 29th, at 9 h. 20 m. A.M., the island of Augusta in sight, the Active made the signal for three strange sail in the east-north-east. At 10 A.M. the strangers were made out to be frigates, and were in fact, not the three French ships already named, but the 40-gun frigates Pauline, Commodore François-Gilles Monfort, aine, and Pomone, Captain Claude-Charles-Marie Ducamp-Rosamel, and the frigate-built storeship Persanne, of 26 guns, Captain Joseph-André Satie, from Corfu since the 16th, going to join the French squadron at Triest; for which, and for the batteries of the place, they had on board a quantity of iron and brass ordnance. At first the three French frigates formed in line on the larboard tack, and stood towards the British ships; but, on making out the latter to be an enemy's squadron, M. Monfort bore up to north-west, and set studding-sails, followed, under an equal press of canvas, by the Alceste and her two companions.

At about 11 A.M., finding that she could not keep way with the Pauline and Pomone, the Persanne separated from them and stood to the north-east. The Active now steered for the Persanne, but was immediately recalled, and the Unité detached after her. In the mean time the Alceste and Active continued in pursuit of the Pauline and Pomone, and, especially the Alceste, were rather gaining upon them. At 11 h. 50 m. A.M. Captain Maxwell telegraphed the Active, "Remember the battle of Lissa." At 30 minutes past noon, just as the rocky island of Pelagosa bore from the Alceste south-west distant five leagues, the Persanne was seen to fire her stern chase-guns at the Unité, and to receive in return a fire from the latter's bow-chasers.

At 1 h. 20 m. P.M., the Alceste, then running above nine knots an hour with the wind on the larboard quarter, fired a shot from her foremost gun on the starboard side directly into the larboard quarter of the Pomone; who immediately hoisted a French ensign and pendant, and fired a single shot, which splintered the Alceste's maintopgallantmast. The Pauline, who was close ahead of the Pomone, also hoisted her colours, with a commodore's broad pendant. At 1 h. 24 m., being still under a crowd of sail to get to the French commodore, the Alceste opened her broadside upon the Pomone, and received a fire in return. At 1 h. 40 m., when directly a-beam of the Pomone, with every prospect of quickly reaching the Pauline, who had taken in her royals to keep nearer to her consort, the Alceste received a shot from the Pomone, which carried away her maintopmast just above the cap. As the wreck, with the topgallant and royal studding-sails, fell over on the starboard side, and the Alceste in consequence dropped a little astern, "cheers of 'Vive l'empereur!'" says Captain Maxwell, "resounded from both ships: they thought the day their own, not aware of what a second I had in my gallant friend Captain Gordon, who pushed the Active up under every sail."

At about 2 p.m., having gained a station on the starboard or lee-quarter of the Pomone, the Active brought that frigate to close action. At about 2 h. 20 m. p.m., resetting his royals, the French commodore braced up, and presently tacked and stood for the weather-beam of the Alceste. At 2 h. 30 m. the latter and the Pauline became closely engaged. At about 3 h. 5 m. p.m., seeing that the Pomone stood no chance with the Active, and observing, probably, the British 18-gun ship-sloop Kingfisher, Captain Ewell Tritton, approaching in the distance, the French commodore set all sail and stood to the westward. Shortly afterwards the Active, although with all three topsails to the mast, unavoidably shot ahead of her antagonist, and a suspension of the firing ensued. At about 3 h. 40 m. p.m., just as the Alceste had arrived up and opened a fire from her starboard broadside, the main and mizen masts of the Pomone came down by the board; and almost immediately afterwards the French frigate hoisted a union-jack as the signal of his having struck. Neither of the two British frigates being now in a condition to make sail in pursuit, the Pauline effected her escape.

The Alceste, whose crew, after deducting those left on shore at Lissa, amounted to only 218 men and boys, had one midshipman (Charles Nourse) and six seamen killed, one lieutenant (Andrew Wilson), 11 seamen, and one marine wounded. The Active, who had about the same number of men absent as her consort, lost one midshipman (George Osborne), five seamen, and two marines killed, her captain (leg amputated), two lieutenants (William Bateman Dashwood, arm amputated, and George Haye), 21 seamen (one mortally), and three marines wounded. It was about the middle of the action that Captain Gordon received his wound: he was standing on a shot-bag and leaning on the capstan, giving his orders in his usual collected manner, when a 36-pound shot came in through a port-hole, grazed the carriage of a carronade, took off a seamen's leg, and struck the captain on the knee-joint; carrying all off as if it had been done with a knife, and leaving the leg hanging by the tendons. Although, of course, he instantly fell, Captain Gordon did not become insensible, but calmly directed the first-lieutenant, Mr. Dashwood, to fight the ship; and, as he was being carried below, told the second-lieutenant, Mr. Haye, who commanded on the main deck, to do his best, should any mischance befal his senior officer. Shortly afterwards Lieutenant Dashwood had his right arm shot away; and Lieutenant Haye, taking the command, fought the Active, although himself wounded, until her opponent's colours came down.

The damaged state of the Pomone at her surrender clearly proved that her colours had not come down until all further resistance was vain. Her main and mizen masts fell, as we have stated, during the action, and her foremast very soon shared their fate. The hull of the Pomone was so shattered by the Active's quick and well-directed fire, that the ship had five feet water in the hold; and her loss, out of a crew of 332 men and boys, amounted, as acknowledged by her officers, to 50 in killed and wounded, including Captain Rosamel himself by a grape-shot in the mouth. With respect to the damage or loss of the Pauline, nothing can be stated with certainty; but it was afterwards understood, that she entered Ancona in a very disabled state from her sufferings in the action.

Here were two pairs of combatants, as equally matched, all circumstances considered, as could well have been brought together; and here was an action gallantly fought, we were going to say, on both sides. As, however, the French commodore certainly abandoned the action before the fall of his consort's masts had given the British a superiority, we feel disposed to concur in opinion with Captain Rosamel, that his commodore shamefully deserted him; and that, at one time, there was every probability, that a spirited co-operation on the part of the Pauline would have enabled both French frigates to have effected their escape.

The best voucher an officer can obtain of his good conduct in action is the testimony of his enemy; but, unfortunately, it is not every heart that can cherish such a sentiment, nor every understanding that can perceive how much it redounds to true glory, to give to that sentiment free and unrestrained utterance. Captain Rosamel, however, had the happiness to fall into the hands of an officer who both felt and publicly expressed what was due from one brave enemy to another. Captain Maxwell thus expresses himself on the subject: "Captain Rosamel fought his ship with a skill and bravery that has obtained for him the respect and esteem of his opponents." That this act of justice emanated solely from principle, may be gathered from the following well-attested anecdote. According to the etiquette of the service, Captain Maxwell, as senior officer of the two British frigates, became entitled to the sword of the French captain; indeed, the French captain would deliver his sword to no one else; but no sooner did Captain Maxwell receive it, than, considering the Pomone to be the fair trophy of the Active, he sent, or rather took, the sword to Captain Gordon, as his by right of conquest.

It was about noon when the Unité so far closed in the wake of the Persanne, whose end-on appearance indicated that she also was a frigate, as to exchange bow and stern chasers; but the variable state of the wind, which shifted from south to east, and the continuance of the Persanne in a course that kept the Unité directly astern, made it nearly 4 p.m. before the latter got close enough to open a part of her broadside. As soon as this was done, the Persanne fired a broadside in return, and hauled down her colours.

The masts, yards, sails, and rigging of the Unité were more or less cut by the galling stern-fire to which she had been exposed; but her loss was restricted to one seaman severely wounded. The Persanne was also tolerably damaged aloft; and, out of her 190 men in complement, had two killed and four wounded. Animated by the same spirit of fairness which, as we have shown, characterised his commodore, Captain Chamberlayne says in his official letter, that Captain Satie's "masterly manœuvres and persevering resistance, for nearly four hours, reflect great credit on him."

The Pomone was one of the largest class of French frigates, and had in her hold 42 iron guns, chiefly 18-pounders, and nine brass guns, besides 220 iron wheels for gun-carriages. The Persanne, whose 26 guns were 8-pounders, was a ship of 860 tons, and had in her hold 130 iron 24-pounders, and 20 brass 9-pounders. The Pauline, in all probability, had on board a quantity of the same description of warlike stores. The Pomone was built by the citizens of Genoa at the commencement of the war of 1803, and presented to Jérôme Buonaparte on his being appointed a capitaine de frégate.[1] Like most of these presented ships, the Pomone had been rather hastily run up, and, on being brought to England in September, 1812, was found defective and taken to pieces. The Persanne was not a ship calculated for the British navy: she was therefore sold to the Bey of Tunis.

Lieutenant Wilson, first of the Alceste, was promoted to the rank of commander on the 17th of September, 1812. The second-lieutenant was James Montagu, and the acting third-lieutenant, James Adair. Lieutenants Dashwood and Haye, first and second of the Active, were made commanders on the 19th of May, 1812. The officer, acting as third-lieutenant of the Active, was Redmond Moriarty. The first-lieutenant of the Unité was Joseph William Crabb, already named in these pages; and who, to our great surprise, still appears with no higher rank than he held when the Unité captured the Persanne. Captain Chamberlayne, therefore, had some reason for dwelling upon the "extreme disappointment" it was to his officers, on finding, when the latter ship surrendered, that they had been opposed to a vessel of inferior force.

On the 26th of May, in the evening, the 16-gun brig-sloop Sabine, Captain George Price, cruising on the Cadiz station, detached her boats, five in number, under the orders of Lieutenant William Usherwood, assisted by Lieutenant Patrick Finucane, and Mr. Thomas Settle the master, also by some of the warrant-officers and midshipmen (we wish Captain Price had enabled us to give their names), to attempt cutting out five French privateers at anchor in the port of Sabiona. They were small fast-sailing vessels, of two 4-pounders and 25 men each, and had been very destructive to the commerce on that part of the coast.

The boats entered the port; and, although the privateers were moored under a battery, the attack had been planned with so much judgment, and was executed with so much promptitude and gallantry, that each British boat succeeded in capturing a privateer, and that without the slightest loss. Two of the privateers were afterwards dragged on shore, by means of a hawser made fast to the lower gudgeon; and, in repulsing the French soldiers and crews with the cutlass, one British marine was wounded by a musket-ball. The three remaining privateers were brought safe off. Although the crews of the five privateers considerably out-numbered the whole complement of the Sabine,

[1] See vol. iv., p. 11.

and although Captain Price describes his first-lieutenant, who headed the party that performed the exploit, as "an excellent officer," the name of William Usherwood still appears among the lieutenants belonging to the British navy.

As we are now entering upon the first exploit of one of the far-famed American 44-gun frigates, we conceive it will be useful to examine, a little more minutely than we have done, the force and qualifications of a class of ship, little known in Europe, until the President brought herself into notice in the manner we shall presently have to relate.

In our account of the action between the Constellation and Insurgente, we mentioned that, in March, 1794, when a rupture was expected with the regency of Algiers, the government of the United States ordered the construction of four frigates of 44, and two of 36 guns; and we stated that one class was to mount 56 guns, including 30 long 24-pounders on the main deck, and the other 48 guns, including 28 long 18-pounders.[1] But we are inclined to think that this was not the armament originally intended for these ships; and our opinion is founded on the following facts. Soon after the passing of the Act of Congress of the 27th of March, 1794, the differences with Algiers were amicably settled; but in the course of the same year, feeling an interest in the success of republican France, the United States pushed their complaints against England to an extremity bordering on war. Now the Algerines possessed no stronger vessels than frigates, and those not of the first class; but England could send to sea a fleet of line-of-battle ships. It was this, we believe, that occasioned the American president to direct, as by a clause in the act he was empowered to do, that, instead of the four 44 and two 36 gun frigates, two 74-gun ships, and one frigate of 44 guns, should be constructed.

An English shipwright, Mr. Joshua Humphreys, resident at Philadelphia, was required to give in an estimate of the cost of building a 74-gun ship, to measure 1620 tons American, which, as we shall by-and-by show, is about 1750 tons English. He did so, and computed the expense, without reckoning the guns, at 342,000 dollars. Upon this estimate, as it appears, the timbers were prepared for two 74s; one to be built at Philadelphia and named United States, the other at Boston, and named Constitution. The 44-gun frigate was to be built at Baltimore, and to be named Constellation. Scarcely, however, had the keels of any of these ships been laid down, ere Mr. Jay's treaty

[1] See vol. ii., p. 362.

restored the amicable relations between England and America, and occasioned a stop to be put to their construction.

As the most eligible mode of converting the timbers prepared for the two 74s, it was resolved that, although begun as line-of-battle ships, they should be finished as frigates. This was to be done by contracting the breadth of the frame about three feet and a half, and discontinuing the topside at the clamps of the quarter-deck and forecastle. As these enormous "frigates," although intended to mount 62 guns, were to rate only 44, it was decided that the frigate originally intended to class as a 44 should bear the designation of a 36. The United States was launched on the 10th of May, 1797, and cost, exclusive of her ordnance, 299,336 dollars; and the Constitution was launched on the 31st of October, in the same year, and cost 302,718 dollars. This, in either case, was not much below the original estimate, even had the ships been completed as 74s, and shows what a slight change had been effected in their construction. The Constellation was built under the personal direction of Commodore Truxton, who first commissioned her, and was launched on the 7th of September, 1797. Owing partly to the dearness of materials, and, partly, we believe, to some expensive alterations in her construction, the Constellation cost the enormous sum of 314,000 dollars.

When, in the spring of the year 1798, the expense of building these frigates, two of "44," and one of "36 guns," came to be submitted to congress, some explanation was required; and on the 1st of April the secretary at war delivered in a report, of which the following is an extract:—"It appears that the first estimate rendered to congress was for frigates of the common size and dimensions, rated at 36 and 44 guns, and that the appropriations for the armament were founded upon this estimate. It also appears that, when their size and dimensions came to be maturely considered, due reference being had to the ships they might have to contend with, it was deemed proper so to alter their dimensions without changing their rates as to extend their sphere of utility as much as possible. It was expected, from this alteration, that they would possess, in an eminent degree, the advantage of sailing; that, separately, they would be superior to any single European frigate of the usual dimensions; that, if assailed by numbers, they would be always able to lead ahead; that they could never be obliged to go into action but on their own terms, except in a calm: and that, in heavy weather, they would be capable of engaging double-decked ships. These are the principal advantages contemplated from the change made in their dimensions. Should they be realized, they will more than compensate for having materially swelled the body of expenditures."

In the course of the year 1798, two more 44-gun frigates were built; one the President, at New York, the other, the Philadelphia, at Philadelphia. Of the latter we know very little, on account of her loss already mentioned;[1] but of the former we are enabled to furnish some far from unimportant particulars. Being constructed of timbers prepared for them alone, these frigates were more handsomely moulded than their two predecessors. The President, indeed, was considered to be the most beautiful and the best sailing of all the American frigates; and, being lower in the water than either the United States or Constitution, was a much more deceiving ship. Her scantling is represented not to have been so stout as theirs; which may have been one reason that she cost only 220,910 dollars, while they cost, as we have seen, 300,000.

With respect to the materials of which the ships were constructed and the pains taken in building them, we can but repeat our former remarks on the same subject. Everything that was new in the navies of England and France was tried, and, if approved, adopted, no matter, it falling so light from the paucity of individuals, at what expense. There were no contractors, to make a hard bargain pay, by deteriorating the quality of the article; no deputies, ten deep, each to get a picking out of the job. The executive government agreed directly with the artisan; and not a plank was shifted, nor a long-bolt driven, without the scrutinising eye of one of the captains or commodores; of him, perhaps, who expected at no distant day, to risk his life and honour on board the very ship whose equipment he was superintending.

As the number and nature of a ship's guns depend, in a very great degree, upon her size and scantling, we must endeavour to convey an idea of the dimensions of the American 44-gun frigate, before we enter upon the subject of her armament. The United States, Constitution, and President measure within a few fractions of a ton the same; namely, from 1444 to 1445 tons American. We say "tons American," because although the American standard of weight and measures, the pound and the foot, for instance, is the same as the English, the mode of casting the tonnage of a ship is widely different. This will appear evi-

[1] See vol. iii., p. 300.

dent when it is known, that the American frigate President, according to the official register in the office at Washington, measured 1444 tons and a fraction;[1] whereas, when subsequently measured at Portsmouth dockyard, she was found to be 1533 tons and a fraction.

The President's "keel for tonnage," as given in an American publication, is 145 feet; but the English mode of casting the tonnage makes it 146 feet $7\tfrac{3}{4}$ inches. In both cases, it is a mere calculation, intended to allow for the rake or inclination of the ship's stem and stern. The first multiplicator of the Americans is the breadth across the frame, or moulded breadth, by them usually called the breadth of beam, but the first multiplicator of the British is the extreme breadth, or that produced by adding to the moulded breadth double the assumed thickness (in ships of the higher classes five inches) of the plank on the bottom. The second multiplicator of each is the respective half-breadths. The American divisor is 95; the British 94. Thus:

	Ft. in.		Ft. in.		Tons.
Am. method	145 0	×43 6	= 6308	×21 9 = 137198 ÷ 95 =	1444 18-95ths
Brit. ditto	146 $7\tfrac{3}{4}$	×44 4	= 6502	×22 2 = 143044 ÷ 94 =	1533 25-94ths

As it is not generally known, even among the most experienced naval officers of either nation, that any difference exists in the mode of measuring British and American ships-of-war, the reduction in the alleged tonnage of the latter greatly facilitates the deception, eulogized for its "advantages" by the American government, and to the influence of which upon the European world the American flag owes so much of its glory.

If we consider, that it is only to add about four feet to the extreme breadth of the President, to make her a larger ship than the generality of British 74s, and that her yards are as square, and her masts as stout as theirs, some idea may be formed of the size and formidable appearance of the American 44-gun frigate. In point of scantling, also, that which is acknowledged to be the lightest built of these frigates is at least equal to a British 74 of the largest class. This is proved by taking the thickness of the topsides at the midship main deck, and foremost quarter-deck, port-sill. In the President, the main deck port-sill measures 1 ft. 8 in., and, in any British 74 of 1800 tons, 1 ft. 7 in.; and, while in the latter the quarter-deck port-sill measures only 1 ft. 1 in., it measures in the former 1 ft. 5 inches.

Now for the armament of these 44-gun frigates. Having had ocular proof of the manner in which the President was fitted,

---

[1] Clark's Naval History of the United States, vol. ii., p. 240.

we shall take her for our guide. This beautiful ship has, or rather had, for she has long since been taken to pieces, 15 ports and a bridle of a side on the main deck, eight of a side on the quarter-deck, and four of a side, without reckoning the chase-port, on the forecastle. This gave the ship 54 ports for broadside guns; but she had the means of mounting 62 broadside guns. For instance, instead of her gangway, or passage from the forecastle to the quarter-deck, being of the usual width of four or five feet, it was ten feet. This deviation from the common plan was to allow room for the carriage and slide of a 42-pounder carronade; and a novel and very ingenious method was adopted to obviate the necessity of uniting the quarter-deck and forecastle barricades, or bulwarks, and consequently of destroying that single-decked appearance which, for the purpose of deception, it was necessary to maintain. Between the two barricades the same open or untimbered space remained, as is seen in any other frigate; but the stanchions for supporting the hammock-cloths were of extraordinary stoutness, and so arranged along the gangway as to form ports for four guns. The breechings were to pass round the iron stanchions, chocks were fitted to the deck to receive the carriages, and the guns could be as effectively mounted as any in the ship.

We formerly doubted[1] if these eight gangway guns were put on board the President or either of her class-mates; but it has been asserted by British officers, who visited some of the large American frigates during the war with Tripoli, that they at that time mounted guns along the whole extent of their spar-decks. If so, the ships probably landed them upon the return of peace with the Barbary states. The ships were then found to work so much better, that it was decided, we believe, not to supply these eight singularly constructed ports with guns, but merely to add two carronades to the 54 guns, which the ship could mount in the regular way. This was done by fitting the gangway or entrance port to receive a carronade; making nine of a side on the quarter-deck. So that the American 44-gun frigate mounted, with her 30 long 24-pounders on the main deck, 18 carronades, 42-pounders, on the quarter-deck, and 6 carronades, 42-pounders, and two long 24-pounders on the forecastle; total 56 guns. This is the number invariably assigned as the force of each of the three "44-gun frigates" in Mr. Clark's American Naval History.[2]

The main-deck guns of the United States were English sea-

---

[1] The fact is confessed by Fenimore Cooper.

[2] Clark's 'Naval History of the United States,' vol. i. p. 171, and vol. ii. p. 22.

service guns, measuring nine feet and a half in length, and weighing about 50 cwt. Those of the Constitution were English land-service, or battery-guns, in length 10 feet, and in weight about 54 cwt.; but the guns of the President were of American manufacture, measuring eight and a half feet, and weighing only 48½ cwt. We may here mention that, although the four masked or gangway ports were left vacant, a case might occur, in which they would be of essential benefit. For instance, suppose the ship to be attacked in port, and to be moored in such a manner as to be only assailable on her outer side: she could easily transfer from the opposite side four of her carronades, and thus present a broadside force of 32, or, admitting that some inconvenience would arise from the closeness of the aftermost of those four guns to the temporary gun in the gangway port, of 31, heavy guns.

For the purpose of showing that, if the President and her two formidable class-mates had been equipped with the whole of the 62 guns which they were constructed to carry, they would have required no addition to their established complement of men, we will state a few facts relative to the composition of American crews. When, in the year 1794, the Americans began arming against the Algerines, the following were ordered to be the proportions, in which the different ratings or classes of a crew of 370 men were to bear to each other; officers and petty officers 66, able seamen 150, ordinary seamen 100, marines 54. Here, be it observed, are wanted two ratings, either of which usually forms no inconsiderable proportion of a British crew, landmen and boys. In later years, however, a few boys or lads were admitted; and, estimating the crew of an American 44-gun frigate at 475 men and boys, we may venture to give the following as its organization: officers and petty officers 80, able seamen 180, ordinary seamen 145, marines 65, boys 5. But, in reality, the distinction between the able and the ordinary seaman was merely nominal, the fastidiousness of the American government requiring the latter to be nearly equal in qualifications to the former. Nor was it enough to be a practised seaman: the volunteer must also, in age, stature, and bodily vigour, be able to stand the test of the strictest scrutiny.

While, therefore, the officers, or the greater part of them, were native Americans, the petty officers consisted, almost wholly, of the first order of British seamen; of whom, also, the bulk of the crew was composed. Owing to the absence of any restraint similar to that imposed by the game-laws of England, the American peasant is a sportsman from his infancy. Hence, the marines consisted of native Americans; not only as being the best marksmen, especially with the rifle, but because the British marine corps, to its credit, afforded very few deserters. It may now be understood what is meant, when it is stated, that an American ship-of-war is manned with a picked crew.

Having now, as we trust, clearly shown that those who called the American 44-gun frigate a "line-of-battle ship in disguise," did not commit the gross mistake with which they were charged, we shall offer a word or two on the subject of the American 36-gun frigate. Even here was a frigate more than equal to any French or English frigate of the largest class, carrying long 18-pounders; and, be it remembered, in the year 1811, France did not own any, and England only three frigates (Cornwallis, Indefatigable, and Endymion), that carried long 24-pounders. Upon a certain occasion, which will soon pass in order of detail, the Americans loudly proclaimed, that the Chesapeake was the very worst frigate they possessed. The Chesapeake was a 36-gun frigate, and, as we have elsewhere shown, had the ports for mounting on her two broadsides 54 guns.[1] For a short time, we believe, the ship did mount that number of guns, with a crew of about 440 men. Besides the Constellation and Chesapeake, built in 1797, there were the Congress and New York, built in 1799. Had the Americans possessed no stronger frigates than the heaviest of these, Europeans would not have been so surfeited with tales of American naval prowess.

On the 10th of May, 1811, the United States 44-gun frigate President, Captain Charles Ludlow, bearing the broad pendant of Commodore John Rodgers, with sails unbent, and the principal part of her officers on shore, lay moored off Annapolis in the Chesapeake; when, at 3 P.M., the commodore came unexpectedly on board, and immediately all hands went to work bending sails and getting the ship ready for sea. The surgeon, too, began preparing his plasters and splinters, and rubbing up his instruments of amputation; rather an extraordinary occupation on board a neutral frigate. All this bustle and preparation was not, however, without an object. On the 1st of the month, in the forenoon, the British 38-gun frigate Guerrière, Captain Samuel John Pechell, cruising off Sandy-Hook, boarded the American brig Spitfire, from Portland bound to New York, and impressed out of her a man named John Deguyo, a passenger

[1] See vol. iv. p. 253.

and a native citizen of the United States. The Guerrière had also impressed, or did shortly afterwards impress, from vessels that she boarded off the coast, two other native American citizens, Gideon Caprian and Joshua Leeds. That John Deguyo was a native American, or, at all events, that he was not a British subject, is clear from the circumstance, that on the 12th of June the Guerrière discharged him into the British 18-gun ship-sloop Gorée, Captain Henry Dilkes Byng; and, on the 30th, the latter put him on board an American ship for a passage to the United States. Caprian was also discharged, but not Leeds, because he had entered.

The Spitfire arrived at New York on the same day, or the day after, Deguyo had been pressed out of her; and the occurrence, within five or six days at the furthest, must have been known at Washington. The written orders to Commodore Rodgers were probably, as Mr. Secretary Munroe asserts, "to protect the coast and commerce of the United States;" but the officers who arrived from Washington on the 11th of May, to join their ship, must have brought some verbal orders of a more particular nature; for one of the President's officers, in a letter to a friend, says: "By the officers who came from Washington we learn, that we are sent in pursuit of the British frigate, who had impressed a passenger from a brig." This British frigate was reported to be the Guerrière; and the American officer anticipates, with a refusal on the part of her commander to deliver up the man, an engagement between the President and a British frigate "exactly her force."

On the 12th of May, at daylight, the President got under way, and began working down the bay. On the 13th the commodore spoke a brig, which had the preceding day seen a ship, supposed to be the Guerrière, off Cape Henry. But, if the date and place are correct, it could not have been the Guerrière; as, at noon on the 12th, she was nearly abreast of Cape Roman, South Carolina. An extra quantity of shot and wads were now got on deck, and the ship was cleared for action. In the evening the wind shifted to a fair quarter, and the President ran before it. On the 14th the American frigate was off Cape Henry; but no British frigate was there. The commodore now stood slowly to the north-east, expecting every moment to discover the object of his pursuit. The 15th passed without any occurrence; but on the 16th, at about 25 minutes past meridian, Cape Henry bearing south-west distant 14 or 15 leagues, the wind a moderate breeze from the northward, the President, from her mast-head discovered a vessel in the east quarter, standing towards her under a press of sail.

The vessel thus descried was the British ship-sloop Little Belt, Captain Arthur Batt Bingham, mounting 18 carronades, 32-pounders, and two nines, with 121 men and boys, on her return to the southward from off Sandy-Hook; where she had been seeking the Guerrière, for whom she bore despatches from the commander-in-chief at Bermuda, Rear-admiral Sawyer. The Little Belt had discovered the President since about noon, and considering her suspicious, had hauled up on the starboard tack in chase. Captain Bingham, in his letter, says, it was "eleven" when he descried the President; the Little Belt's log says "half past." Even the latest of these times would, according to the letter of Commodore Rodgers, make it 40 minutes after the Little Belt had descried the President before the latter discovered her: a circumstance not very probable; although it does appear, that the American ship did not keep the best look-out; otherwise, when first seen by the President, the Little Belt would have been steering south, instead of towards the President, or north by west, a deviation from her course caused solely by the latter's appearance. We have therefore, as on other occasions, paid less attention to the absolute, than to the relative time.

At 1 h. 30 m. P.M. each ship, the two then about 10 miles apart, supposed the other to be a vessel-of-war. The President thereupon hoisted her ensign and commodore's pendant, and edged away, as if to meet the Little Belt. The latter, about the same time, made her number, and afterwards the customary signal (No. 275), calling upon the stranger, if a British ship-of-war, to show hers. The non-compliance with this signal indicating that the President was, what by her colours she appeared to be, an American frigate, the Little Belt, at 1 h. 45 m. P.M., hoisted her colours, wore, and resumed her course to the southward under all sail. "Being," as Commodore Rodgers says, "desirous of speaking her, and of ascertaining what she was," the President crowded sail in chase. Observing this, the Little Belt made the private signal. Finding it unanswered, Captain Bingham felt assured that the stranger, notwithstanding her persisting to chase, was an American frigate, and therefore, hauling down both ensign and signal, continued his course round Cape Hatteras.

Although the wind, since 1 P.M., had been gradually falling, the superior sailing of the President brought her, by

6 h. 30 m. P.M., so near to the Little Belt, that Captain Bingham, wishing before dark to remove all remaining doubts on either side, shortened sail, rehoisted his colours, and hove to on the larboard tack.

To avoid being taken by surprise, the Little Belt double-shotted her guns, and got all clear for action. The President, by the manner of her approach, appearing as if she intended to take a raking position, the Little Belt, to frustrate that design, wore three times. This brought the latter upon the starboard tack; and at a few minutes past 8 P.M., when the two ships were about 90 yards apart, Captain Bingham hailed the President in the customary manner, but received no answer, probably because he was not heard. The President still advancing, as if desirous to pass astern of the Little Belt, the latter wore a fourth time, and came to on the larboard tack. The President now hauled her foresail up, and also hove to on the larboard tack, distant about 80 yards from the sloop's weather-beam. Captain Bingham, standing on the gun abaft the larboard gangway, hailed, "Ship a-hoy!" "Ship a-hoy!" was repeated from the neutral frigate. "What ship is that?" asked Captain Bingham. "What ship is that?" repeated Commodore Rodgers. At this instant a gun was fired, let us for the present say, by each ship; and, let us also say, that both guns went off by accident.

Each ship believing the other to have fired first, and that intentionally, and neither being disposed to brook the slightest insult, the two began a furious engagement; which lasted, including an intermission of a few minutes, about half an hour.[1] The Little Belt, owing to the loss of her after-sail and the damaged state of her rigging, having fallen off, so that no gun would bear, ceased firing; and the President, finding that to be the case, did the same. Shortly afterwards Commodore Rodgers, hailing the Little Belt, learnt, what he and his officers must have known before, that she was a British ship, but did not, it appears, hear her name; and, to a question, desiring to know if his antagonist had struck, was answered by Captain Bingham in the negative. The latter then asked the name of the American frigate; but the same cause, the increased freshness of the wind, that had prevented the commodore from hearing the whole of the answer to his question, kept Captain Bingham in ignorance of the name, though not of the nation, of the ship by which the Little Belt had been so battered and ill-used.

[1] Captain Bingham says "three-quarters;" some of the American officers, "a quarter of an hour or twenty minutes."

The damages of the Little Belt were indeed, as might be expected, of a very serious description. The greater part of her standing and the whole of her running rigging were cut to pieces: not a brace nor a bowline was left. Her masts and yards were all badly wounded, and her gaff was shot away. Her upperworks were completely riddled, and her hull in general much struck: several shot were sticking in her side, and some had entered between wind and water. Nothing, we conceive, but the lowness of her hull in the water, and the consequent difficulty of hitting it, prevented the sloop from being sunk. The loss on board the Little Belt bore a proportion to her damage: she had one midshipman (Samuel Woodward), seven seamen, and one marine killed, two seamen mortally, her acting master (James M'Queen), seven seamen, one boy, and two marines severely, and her boatswain (James Franklin), five seamen, two boys, and two marines slightly wounded; total, 11 killed and mortally wounded, and 21 wounded severely and slightly. The President appears to have had her sails and rigging slightly injured, and to have received one 32-pound shot in her foremast and another in her mainmast: her loss is also represented not to have exceeded one boy wounded.

After the action the President wore, and, running a short distance to leeward of the Little Belt, came to the starboard tack, to repair her trifling damages. This done, the frigate filled and lay to on different tacks, in order to wait until daylight should afford the commodore a clear view of what his prowess had effected. The Little Belt brought to on the larboard tack, and commenced her more serious occupation of repairing damages and stopping leaks. During the night the sloop's topgallantmasts were got on deck, and the cut rigging partially repaired.

At daylight on the 17th the President, now about nine miles to windward, bore up under topsails and foresail, and, to all appearance, ready to renew the action. At 8 A.M. the American frigate passed within hail, and the commodore said: "Ship a-hoy! I'll send a boat on board, if you please, sir."—"Very well, sir," was Captain Bingham's reply. The boat came, under the command of the First-lieutenant John Orde Creighton, with a message from the commodore, to the effect, that he lamented much "the unfortunate affair," and that, had he known the British ship's force was so inferior, he would not have fired into her. On being asked why he had fired at all, the lieutenant replied, that the Little Belt had fired first. This was most positively denied on the part of Captain Bingham. Lieutenant Creighton, in the name of the commodore, then offered every assistance, and suggested that Captain Bingham had better put into one of the ports of the United States. This the latter declined. The boat returned. The President made sail to the westward, and the Little Belt, as soon as she was able, to the northward. On the 23rd the latter was joined by the Gorée, Captain Byng, and on the 28th the two vessels anchored in Halifax harbour.

In discussing the merits of the action between the Little Belt and the President, we shall consider it in the double light of an attack by a neutral upon a belligerent, and an engagement between an American frigate and a British sloop-of-war. We shall begin by freely admitting, that the act of the Guerrière, in pressing a native American citizen out of an American coaster, in the very mouth of an American port, was an act unjustifiable, unnecessary, and impolitic; and that this wanton encroachment upon neutral rights, coupled with many others which had been practised along the same coast, was a sufficient ground for the government of the United States to take every measure, short of actual war, for protecting their commerce and citizens from a repetition of such acts of violence.

Well, the American frigate sails forth, in diplomatic language, "to protect the coast and commerce of the United States," but, in reality, to speak the British frigate Guerrière, to demand from her the American citizen whom she had impressed, and, in case of refusal, to endeavour to take that American citizen by force of arms. We must suppose that a refusal was anticipated; or why were such preparations made? why such quantities of ammunition brought upon deck; and why did the commodore, as the President was descending the bay, so significantly question his people as to their readiness for action?

A ship is descried, a man-of-war, "from the symmetry of her upper sails" and her making signals,[1] she is supposed to be the British frigate Guerrière, and that supposition is confirmed in the mind of the captain of the President, from her proximity to the coast, and every person on board is so fully engrossed with the idea of that frigate, as to be incapable of bestowing a thought upon any other. Chase is given. The ships approximate, so that the upper part of the Little Belt's stern shows itself to those on board the President.[2] Still the delusion continues. As evening approaches, the British sloop discovers her broadside

[1] Official letter of Commodore Rodgers.   [2] Ibid.

"Nevertheless," says the commodore, "her appearance indicated that she was a frigate." Had the Little Belt been a deep-waisted or frigate-built ship, such a mistake might have happened; but she was a low flush vessel, similar in size, number of ports, and general appearance, to the American sloop Hornet. The ships mutually approach within hailing distance. Captain Bingham hails, let us admit, without being heard. Commodore Rodgers hails, and is hailed back. "Having," he says, "asked the first question, I of course considered myself entitled, by the common rules of politeness, to the first answer: after a pause of 15 or 20 seconds, I reiterated my first inquiry of 'What ship is that?'"

Let us also pause; and, leaving "the rules of politeness" to serve the commodore on some other occasion, examine upon what more stable ground he claims the privilege of being first answered. The President was a neutral, the Little Belt a belligerent ship: one was at peace with all the world, the other at war with the greater part of it. The belligerent vessel has an unquestionable right to conceal her condition, to wear false colours, give a false answer, or no answer at all; in short, to practise every artifice to deceive or mislead her supposed enemy; and she is to take every ship she meets as an enemy, until the contrary be shown. A neutral vessel, on the other hand, armed or unarmed, has no motive, and therefore no right, to practise deception: she is bound to observe common civility, if not "politeness," to every ship she meets; and, when questioned as to her name or national character, is bound to give it with frankness, because she has nothing to dread from the most ample disclosure of her situation. Hence Commodore Rodgers, waving the law of politeness, should have conformed to the law of nations, and have answered Captain Bingham's hail, although under the impression that he himself had asked the first question. But, in truth, the American frigate at this moment was, to all intents and purposes, a ship-of-war: she was not only armed, but prepared, for battle, and was resolved to have a battle with the ship, the little ship, that now so opportunely lay under her guns.

From the numerous contradictions and cross swearings that have grown out of this case, it has hitherto been a disputed point who fired the first shot. Having, however, learnt by experience, not to place implicit reliance in all that an American says or swears, we shall not let the subject pass without such a scrutiny as may satisfy the minds of some, although it may not remove the doubts of all. The principal officers examined upon oath, at the court of inquiry held upon Commodore Rodgers, were the acting captain, three out of the five lieutenants, two officers of marines, the master, and the chaplain. Captain Ludlow is "uncertain which fired the first gun, but the second gun was from the President." The first-lieutenant believes the first shot was fired from the Little Belt. The second-lieutenant is sure it was; and so swears the junior lieutenant. Both officers of marines and the master depose to the same effect. The chaplain thinks the gun came from the Little Belt, as he felt no jar in the President. With respect to the second gun, or that admitted to have been fired by the President, the lieutenant of marines swears it went off "in six seconds," and the master "in three or four seconds," after the first, or Little Belt's gun.

So that the two guns were fired within, taking the lowest estimate, three seconds of each other. Might not the guns have been fired at the same instant? In short, might there not have been one gun, and one gun only fired? If so, that must have been the President's gun, because one of her guns is admitted to have gone off by accident; while the most positive denial exists as to the occurrence of any accident of the kind on board the Little Belt. Moreover the captain, two lieutenants, master, and surgeon of the latter have solemnly declared, that the first gun was fired from the President. In this they are borne out by two British seamen, who, in company, as they say, with nearly 300 more, were on board the President during the action; and who, fearing a rupture with their native country, deserted from the frigate soon after she arrived at New York, and proceeded to Halifax, Nova Scotia. One of these men, William Burnet, swears that he was stationed at the second division of guns on the main deck; that, while the commodore was hailing the second time, a gun in his division went off, he thinks by accident; and he was then looking at the Little Belt through one of the ports, and is positive that she did not fire. The other man, John Russell, corroborates his shipmate's testimony, and adds, that a man got entangled in the lanyard of the lock and thus occasioned the gun to go off. Burnet swears also, that Lieutenant Belding, who commanded in his division, knew and declared that the President fired the first shot, and, just before dark, saw with his glass, and observed to him, that the Little Belt's colours were British. Burnet states likewise, that the ship was a small ship. It is therefore easy to conjecture why Lieutenant Belding was not summoned to give his evidence at the court of inquiry: perhaps the other absent lieutenant might have been equally unfit for a witness in the commodore's cause.

Not a doubt, therefore, remains upon our mind that the first gun was fired, unintentionally we admit, by the American frigate; and, had the British sloop immediately opened her fire in return, being satisfied at the time that it was a neutral man-of-war she was engaging, we should have no hesitation in saying, that Captain Bingham acted with precipitation: that he ought to have repeated his hail, or sent an officer on board, to demand an explanation. As it was, however, both parties appear to have given a simultaneous vent to their fury; one, as Lieutenant Creighton swears Captain Bingham informed him, on the supposition that he was defending himself against an avowed enemy; the other, according to the American version of the proceeding, with the intention of chastising the insolence of a pretended friend.

In awarding this "chastisement" Commodore Rodgers tells us, he was governed by "motives of humanity and a determination not to spill a drop of blood unnecessarily;" and yet his own captain swears, that the commodore's orders were "to fire low and with two round shot." His subordinate officers and men, emulous to please, fired low enough, and loaded their guns, not only with round and grape shot, but with "every scrap of iron that could possibly be collected." The consequences of this humane and magnanimous conduct on the part of, in the words of an American editor, "one of the largest 44s that ever floated," against a ship that was considerably less than one-third of her size, and not one-fourth equal to her in point of force, have already been detailed.

True it is, that one of the President's officers has sworn, that he "thought the Belt a heavy frigate until next day," and another, that he "took her for a frigate of 36 or 38 guns." The commodore, too, confesses himself to have been similarly deceived. What must have been the astonishment of all these swearers, when "the next day" discovered their late antagonist to be a ship scarcely exceeding in length the space between the President's bows and her gangway ladder, and whose topmast heads ranged very little higher than their ship's lower yard-arms! That such a mistake should have happened seems unaccountable; especially when there was light enough for Captain Ludlow to see that his opponent's "gaff was down, and her maintopsail-yard on the cap," and when the distance between the two ships is admitted not to have exceeded 70 or 80 yards. However, the American commodore, in all he said was believed, and for all he had done was commended, in the quarter to which alone, beside his conscience, and that probably was not an over-squeamish one, he considered himself responsible. On the other hand, the captain, officers, and men of the Little Belt, for the spirit and firmness they had manifested throughout the whole of the unequal contest, which, according to our contemporary, "it was the great misfortune of Captain Bingham" to be engaged in,[1] were greeted with applause by every generous mind, some in America not excepted; and on the 7th of February, 1812, as a proof that the lords of the admiralty were far from displeased with his conduct, Captain Bingham was promoted to post-rank.

On the 2nd of February, at 5 P.M., the three French 40-gun frigates Renommée, Commodore François Roquebert, and Clorinde and Néréide, Captains Jacques Saint-Cricq and Jean-François Lemaresquier, sailed from Brest, each having on board 200 troops and a supply of munitions of war, bound, in the first instance, to the Isle of France; the capture of which in the preceding December was of course unknown, although as a contingency provided against, by the port of Batavia's being named for the succedaneous destination. Bad weather nearly separated the frigates the first night; and a continuance of contrary winds occasioned the squadron to be 18 days going the first 200 leagues of the voyage. On the 24th of February, by some Lisbon newspapers found on board a Portuguese ship, the French commodore gained intelligence, that an attack was intended, and had perhaps already been made, upon the island to which he was first destined. The favourable change in the wind was taken immediate advantage of, and all sail crowded upon the three ships. On the 13th of March the frigates crossed the line; on the 18th of April, in latitude 38°, doubled the Cape of Good Hope; and on the 6th of May, at 11 P.M., being the 93rd day since their departure from Brest, arrived within five miles of Isle de la Passe, situated, as already known, at the entrance of Grand Port, or Port-Sud-Est. Soon after midnight a boat from each frigate was despatched to the shore, to gain intelligence.

The night was calm, and yet not a musket could be heard. This encouraged the hope, that the island was still in French possession. Daylight on the 7th arrived, and the colours hoisted

[1] Brenton, vol. iv., p. 555.

at the fort upon Isle de la Passe were French; but they were unaccompanied by the private signals. This gave the first serious alarm to Commodore Roquebert and his companions. At sunrise five sail successively hove in sight to leeward: and about the same time was observed, at Isle de la Passe and along the coast, the signal of three French frigates being to windward; a signal fully understood by the latter, as being made according to the code in use at the island previously to its surrender.

Two of the five sail thus seen were unarmed vessels, probably coasters; but the remaining three were the British 18-pounder 36-gun frigates Phœbe and Galatea, Captain James Hillyar and Woodley Losack, and 18-gun brig-sloop Racehorse, Captain James de Rippe, part of a squadron which had been ordered by Rear-admiral the Honourable Robert Stopford, the commander-in-chief on the Cape station, to cruise off the Isle of France, to endeavour to intercept these very frigates, and two others, in all probability, the new 40-gun frigates Nymphe and Méduse, from Nantes, of whose expected arrival intelligence had been received. The British ships were presently under all sail upon a wind in chase; the Galatea's gig, with the intelligence, having previously been despatched to Captain Charles Marsh Schomberg, of the 18-pounder 36-gun frigate Astrea, lying in Port Louis.

In the course of the forenoon the Renommée's boat returned on board, with information of what had befallen the colony; the details of which were communicated by two negroes whom the boat had brought off. The boats of the Clorinde and Néréide appear to have been captured. The three French frigates now tacked and stood to the eastward, followed by the two British frigates and brig-sloop. At 3 P.M. the French hoisted their colours, and the British soon afterwards did the same. At sunset the French squadron bore south-east of the British, distant about three leagues, the wind a moderate breeze from the same quarter.

On the 8th, at 4 A.M., the distance between the two hostile squadrons was distinguished to six or seven miles; and at 8 A.M. the French frigates bore up, and, with a light air of wind, stood towards the Phœbe and Galatea. These, with the Racehorse, shortly afterwards wore and steered to the westward, in the direction of Isle Ronde, then distant five or six leagues. Wishing, with the odds against him, to have a commanding breeze to manœuvre with, and expecting every moment to be joined by the Astrea from Port Louis, Captain Hillyar rather avoided than sought an engagement; and towards evening, when the two squadrons were scarcely five miles apart, Commodore Roquebert, considering it, as he states, unsafe to follow the British ships into the current that runs between Isle Ronde and Isle Serpent, discontinued the chase and hauled up to the eastward.

On the 9th, at daylight, the two squadrons regained a distant sight of each other; but, the Phœbe and Galatea bearing up about noon to join the Astrea, the French ships disappeared. The three British frigates then steered for Port Louis, and on the 12th came to an anchor off the harbour. It appears that, at one period, while the two squadrons, before the junction of the Astrea, were in the presence of each other, the ship's company of the Galatea went aft and requested their captain to bring the enemy to action. In order to concert with his senior officer upon that or some other subject, Captain Losack went on board the Phœbe; and, on his return, the crew of the Galatea, supposing their wishes were about to be gratified, gave him three cheers.

Commodore Roquebert reduced the crews of his ships to two-thirds allowance of provisions, and resolved to attempt a surprise upon some post on the windward side of Isle Bourbon. Having, by the 11th, passed 20 leagues to windward of the Isle of France, the three French frigates bore up for Isle Bourbon, and on the same night made the land. The boats of the squadron, having on board a division of the troops, attempted to disembark at a post that was known to be weakly manned, but were prevented by the heavy surf. Thus disappointed, the French commodore stood across to the coast of Madagascar, to endeavour to obtain a supply of provisions. On the 19th the ships made the Isle of Prunes, and the same evening surprised the small settlement of Tamatave, in Madagascar: the garrison of which consisted of about 100 officers and men of the 22nd regiment, and except a small proportion, were sick with the endemial fever of the country. This settlement had been taken from the French on the 12th of the preceding February, by the above detachment of British troops, sent thither by Mr. Farquhar, the governor of the Isle of France, in the 18-gun brig-sloop Eclipse, Captain William Jones Lye.

On the 20th, at daybreak, Captain Schomberg, with his three frigates and brig-sloop, and who, very judiciously, had sailed from Port Louis on the 14th direct for this spot, discovered himself to M. Roquebert; then, with his three frigates, close to the land near Foul point, and directly to windward of the former. The British ships immediately made all sail in chase, with a light breeze from off the land, or from the west by north; but the French ships continued lying to, to await the return of two of their boats from Tamatave. The Renommée's boat at length came off; and at noon the French commodore formed his three frigates in line of battle, placing the Renommée in the centre, the Clorinde ahead, and the Néréide astern. The British, in the meanwhile, were closing their opponents as fast as the light and variable winds would permit, formed in the following order; Astrea, Phœbe, Galatea, in line ahead, and the Racehorse nearly abreast of the Phœbe or centre-ship, to leeward.

At 3 h. 50 m. P.M. the French frigates, being on the larboard tack, wore together, and, after keeping away for a short time, hauled up again on the same tack. The British ships were now approaching on the opposite or starboard tack; and, as soon as the Astrea, who was considerably ahead of her second astern, had arrived abreast of the Renommée, the latter opened her fire at long range. At a few minutes before 4 P.M. the Astrea returned this fire; as did also the Phœbe and Galatea, as they advanced in succession. Thus:—

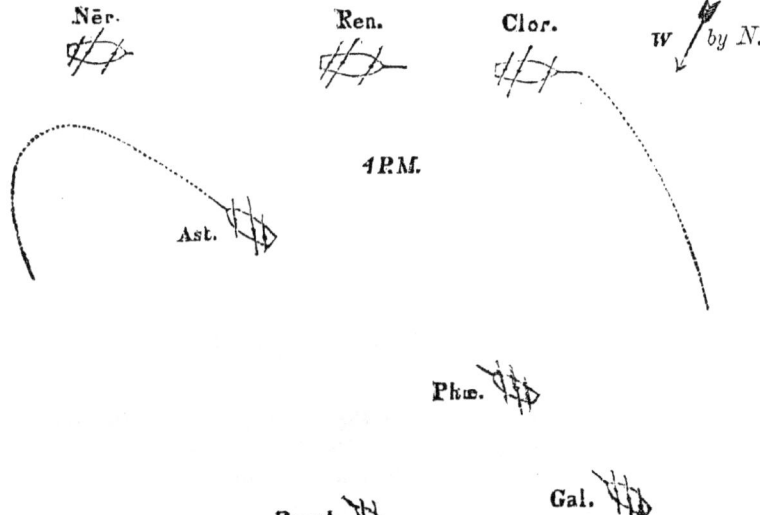

Having passed out of gun-shot astern of the Néréide, the Astrea prepared to tack and renew the action; but, as was to have been expected, so near to the land, particularly Madagascar, the cannonade produced an almost instantaneous calm to leeward. Having, in consequence, missed stays, the Astrea attempted to wear, and had scarcely accomplished that, ere there was an entire cessation of the breeze. From their weatherly position, the French ships of course felt its influence the longest; and the breeze did not quite leave them until the Clorinde and Renommée had bore up and stationed themselves, in a most destructive position, across the starboard quarters and sterns of the Phœbe and Galatea. Now was the time for the Racehorse, with her facility of sweeping, to have distinguished herself, by taking a position close athwart the hawse of the Néréide, between whom and the Astrea a distant and partial carronade was maintained. The Racehorse did begin sweeping, but stopped to engage long before her shot could reach the French frigate: and, in consequence, the Astrea made the brig's signal to engage more closely; and, as it was never answered, kept it flying. Owing to the leeward position of the Galatea, and the efforts of the Phœbe, by backing her sails, to support her consort, these two ships lay nearly abreast of each other, in the manner represented in the following diagram:—

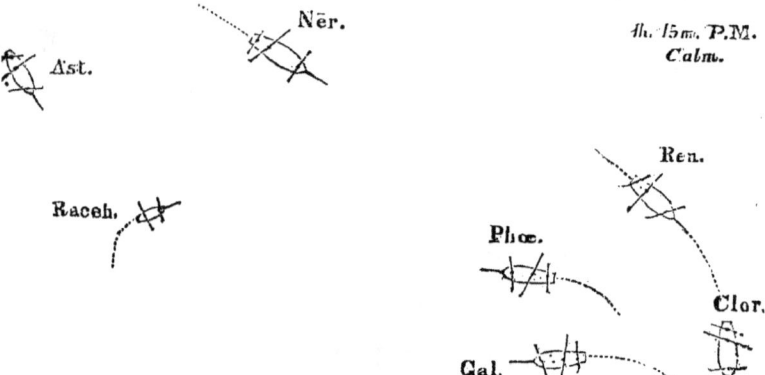

On the starboard quarter of the Phœbe lay the Renommée, and on her starboard bow the Néréide; who had just cleared herself from the Astrea and Racehorse, then upwards of a mile and a half ahead of their two consorts, and like them in an ungovernable state for the want of wind. At 6 h. 30 m. P.M. a light air from the south-east enabled the Phœbe, who had hitherto been able only to bring her bow guns to bear on the

Néréide and her quarter ones on the Renommée, as the swell hove her off and brought her to, to close the Néréide in a raking position; and whom, at the end of 25 minutes, the Phœbe completely silenced, but was then obliged to quit, as the Renommée and Clorinde were fast approaching to the support of their nearly overpowered consort.

These two frigates, in the mean time, having kept their broadside to bear by the aid of their boats, had terribly battered the Galatea. The cutter of the latter having been cut adrift by a shot while towing astern, the jolly-boat was got ready to tow the ship's head round; but a shot sunk her just as the tow-rope was being handed on board, and scarcely were the tackles got up to hoist out a third boat, when a shot carried away the foreyard tackle. Some seamen now got sweeps out of the head; and at length the Galatea was enabled to open her broadside upon her two antagonists, particularly upon the Renommée, who received the greater portion of her fire. About this time, as already mentioned, a light breeze sprang up; and, while the Renommée and Clorinde made sail to support the Néréide, the Galatea, with her masts much wounded, and her hull greatly shattered, hauled towards the Astrea and Racehorse, and at 8 p.m. ceased firing. At 8 h. 30 m. p.m., just as the Galatea, under a press of sail, was passing to leeward of the Astrea, and Captain Losack had hailed Captain Schomberg, to say that his ship had suffered considerably, the Galatea's foretopmast fell over the larboard bow, and the mizentopmast upon the mainyard. Having at this time three feet 10 inches water in the hold, her foremast, mainyard, maintopmast, and bowsprit badly wounded, and her rigging of every sort cut to pieces, the Galatea hailed the Racehorse for assistance, and Captain De Rippe sent on board a midshipman and 10 men. Captain Losack then made the night-signal of distress to the commodore. The Astrea immediately closed the Galatea; and, hailing, was informed, that the latter was in too disabled a state to put her head towards the enemy and renew the action.

The Astrea then wore round on the larboard tack; and Captain Schomberg ordered the Racehorse to follow him closely, as he intended to renew the action as soon as the Phœbe was in a state to give her support. This frigate was promptly reported ready; and at about 8 h. 25 m. p.m. the Astrea, Phœbe, and Racehorse bore up towards the enemy, whose lights were then visible in the west-north-west. It appears that, after the Renommée and Clorinde had obliged the Phœbe to quit the

Néréide, the latter, on account of her disabled state, was ordered by the commodore to make for the land; while the Renommée, followed by her remaining consort, hauled up in line of battle to renew the engagement. Shortly afterwards the Clorinde lost a man overboard, and, in bringing to to pick him up, necessarily dropped astern of her leader. Captain Roquebert, however, in the most gallant manner, stood on his course, and at 9 h. 50 m. P.M. came to close action with the Astrea, whom, with a heavy fire of round, grape, and musketry, the Renommée attempted to lay athwart hawse; but, aware of the numerical superiority of her opponent, the Astrea avoided coming in contact. After an animated cannonade of about 25 minutes, during which the Phœbe fired a few raking shot at the Renommée, and the Racehorse discharged a whole broadside directly between the masts of the Astrea, and set her mainsail on fire, the French ship made tne signal of surrender. Captain Hillyar now ordered the Racehorse to take possession of the Renommée; but the brig, just at this moment losing her foretopmast from a wound it had received, was unable to do so. Captain Schomberg then sent on board the prize, in a sinking boat, Lieutenant Charles Royer,[1] Lieutenant of marines John Drury, and five seamen; and the Astrea and Phœbe made all sail after the Clorinde, who had shamefully kept aloof during her commodore's gallant action, and was now under a press of canvas on the larboard tack, endeavouring to effect her escape.

Captain Schomberg says: "Another frigate, on closing, struck, and made the signal also; but, on a shot being fired at her from her late commodore, she was observed trying to escape;" and, in another place, "The ship that struck and escaped was La Clorinde." Nothing of this appears in the French accounts. On the contrary, the complaint there is, that the Clorinde avoided closing. If we are of opinion that the French ship did not surrender, it is not because the French captain has said so, but because we cannot discover that the Clorinde was so pressed as to render such a step necessary. That will be more apparent when we come to state her loss. Moreover it was dark; and our experience in investigating accounts has taught us, that mistakes of the kind are frequently made, even where the action is fought in broad daylight. The chase of the Clorinde was continued until 2 A.M. on the 21st; when, finding that, on account of the perfect state of her rigging and sails, the Clorinde gained considerably on the Astrea and Phœbe, the two latter wore, to

[1] Called Rogers in the Gazette letter.

cover the captured ship, and form a junction with the Galatea. At this moment the foretopmast of the Phœbe, from the wounds it had received, fell over the side.

The principal damages of the Astrea were in her sails and rigging, and they were not material. Out of her complement (admitting all to have been on board, which we rather think was not the case), of 271 men and boys, she had two seamen killed, her first-lieutenant (John Baldwin), 11 seamen, three marines, and one boy wounded; total, two killed and 16 wounded. The Phœbe, besides the loss of her foretopmast, had her three masts and bowsprit badly wounded, her sails and rigging much cut, and her hull struck in several places; and her loss, out of a complement the same as the Astrea's, consisted of seven seamen killed, one midshipman (John Wilkey, severely), 21 seamen (one mortally and nine severely), and two marines wounded; total, seven killed and 24 wounded. The disabled state of the Galatea's masts and rigging has already been described. The ship had 55 shot-holes in her hull, 29 on the starboard and 26 on the larboard side; and her stern was also much shattered. Her loss, out of a complement the same as that of either of her consorts, was her first-lieutenant of marines (Hugh Peregrine), eight seamen, and five private marines killed, her captain with a lacerated wound by a splinter, but his name does not appear in the official return, second-lieutenant of marines (Henry Lewis), 14 seamen (two mortally), five private marines, severely, and her first-lieutenant (Thomas Bevis), two midshipmen (Henry Williams and Alexander Henning), 17 seamen, four private marines, and three boys slightly wounded; total, 16 killed and 46 wounded. The Racehorse, notwithstanding that some chance shot had knocked away her foretopmast, appears to have escaped without any loss.

With respect to the French ships, the Renommée, according to the French official account, sustained a loss, out of a complement, including troops, of 470 officers and men, of 93 killed and wounded. Among the former, was her gallant captain, M. Roquebert, and among the severely wounded, Colonel Barrois, the senior officer of the troops; also her first-lieutenant, Louis-Auguste Defredot-Duplanty, who only went below to have his wound dressed, and fought the ship in the bravest manner. The Néréide, upon the same authority, had her captain and 24 seamen, marines, and soldiers killed, and 32 wounded; and the Clorinde, occasioned probably by the fire of the Galatea when the latter got her broadside to bear, had one man killed and six wounded. The British official account states the killed and wounded of the Renommée at 145, and that of the Néréide at 130.

The relative force of the parties in this contest requires a few observations. The three British frigates were all of the same class, and of nearly the same size, the Astrea measuring 956, the Phœbe 926, and the Galatea 945 tons. The forecastle and quarter-deck establishment of the Astrea and Galatea was, 14 carronades, 32-pounders, and two long nines, making the total number of guns 42. The Phœbe appears to have mounted two more nines, making her number of guns 44. The complements have already been enumerated. With respect to the Renommée, Néréide, and Clorinde, they were not quite so formidable as some of the French frigates which have been named in these pages. When it is known that the French 36-pounder carronade weighs seven per cent. more than the English 42, it will be readily conceived, that 10 or 12 of the former were too much for the quarter-deck of a French frigate of 1080 or 1100 tons; especially, in the usual contracted state of that deck and the comparative flimsiness of its barricade. It appears, therefore, that in the year 1810 the establishment of the French 40-gun frigate was altered, from twelve 36-pounder carronades and four or six eights, to fourteen 24-pounder carronades and two eights; and even the French 24-pounder carronade weighs within about 120 pounds of the English 32, and so nearly agrees with the latter in size, as to be easily taken for a carronade of that caliber. According to this statement of the guns on each side, the broadside force of either the Astrea or Galatea was 467 lb., and that of any one of the three French frigates 463 lb. The complements of either of the latter, even without the troops, far out-numbered that of either of the three British frigates. In point of size, two French frigates had also the advantage; the Renommée measuring 1073, the Clorinde 1083, and the Néréide 1114 tons.

The difference in guns, men, and size, therefore, between a British 18-pounder 36 and a French 40 gun frigate, rendered the parties in this action, notwithstanding the presence of the brig, who, it is clear, might have been in Port Louis harbour, about equally matched; that is, making due allowance for the side which possessed the inferiority in number of men. Had the Renommée not have been somewhat roughly handled by the Galatea, and had the Clorinde, when the Renommée was attacked by the Astrea and Phœbe, given to the former the support that was in her power, the French commodore's ship, in all probability, would have effected her escape; and that without the slightest disparagement to the Astrea. The resolute conduct of the Néréide, in not surrendering to the Phœbe after having sustained so heavy a loss in killed and wounded, redeems, in some degree, the previous shyness, on two occasions, of Captain Lemaresquier;[1] unless we are to consider that, as he fell in the action, the credit of not striking the colours is due to the next officer in command, Lieutenant François Ponée. With respect to the Clorinde, the behaviour of her captain on the present, perfectly agrees with his behaviour on a former occasion. M. Saint.-Cricq abandoned his commodore in March, 1806;[2] he does the same in May, 1811: then his heels could not save him; now they do save him. Upon the whole, if some glory was lost to the French navy by the misconduct of the Clorinde, more was gained to it by the acknowledged good conduct of the Renommée and Néréide.

On the 21st, at daylight, the Astrea, Phœbe, and Racehorse discovered the Renommée and Galatea to windward; and their bearings, as taken on board the Racehorse, were, Galatea, south-west by south, Renommée south-west by west. A very singular circumstance appears to have prevented the Galatea from joining her three consorts to leeward. It will be remembered, that only two officers and five men were sent to take possession of the Renommée, who had then a crew of nearly 400 effective officers and men. In this state of things, the surprise is, that the French did not retake their ship. It appears that the crew wished to do so; but that Colonel Barrois who, according to the etiquette of the French service, was now the commanding officer, acting upon a principle of honour which some of the French naval captains would do well to imitate, refused to give his sanction to the proceeding. Hence Lieutenant Royer and his few hands remained throughout the night in quiet possession of the prize; but were not permitted when daylight came, to hoist the English over the French flag, nor to make any signal, either to the Galatea, who was to windward, or to the Astrea and her consorts, who were at a great distance to leeward of them. Not knowing, of course, that the Renommée had been captured, and getting no answer to his signals from this ship for the reason already stated, nor from the Astrea and Phœbe because of their great distance off, Captain Losack doubted if it was not the French squadron of

[1] See vol. iv. p. 372; and vol. v. p. 95.   [2] See vol. iv., p. 134.

which he was in sight; and, while the Renommée bore up to join the Astrea and Phœbe, the Galatea made the best of her way to Port Louis.

Having taken out the prisoners from the Renommée, and placed on board a proper prize-crew, Captain Schomberg now first learnt the situation of Tamatave. The damaged state of the Phœbe not admitting her to beat up quickly against the wind and current, Captain Schomberg despatched the Racehorse in advance, to summon the French garrison to surrender. On the evening of the 24th the brig rejoined the Astrea, with the intelligence of the arrival of the Néréide at Tamatave. As this was the nearest port in which he could get his ship repaired, Lieutenant Ponée had proceeded straight thither, and immediately moored the Néréide in the most advantageous manner for resisting the attack which he hourly expected to be made.

The Astrea, Phœbe, and Racehorse immediately made sail for Tamatave, but were prevented by a strong gale from getting a sight of the French frigate, until the afternoon of the 25th; when, no one in the British squadron possessing any local knowledge of the spot, and it being considered impracticable to sound the passage between the reefs without being exposed to the fire of the frigate and a battery of 10 or 12 guns, Captain Schomberg sent Captain De Rippe, with a flag of truce at his brig's mast-head, and a summons of surrender to the French commanding officer. In that summons the latter is informed, that the "Renommée and Clorinde have struck after a brave defence." The inference here intended is pretty clear, and a ruse may be allowed in such cases; but an officer should be cautious how he signs his name to a document bearing upon the face of it what may afterwards subject his veracity to be called in question.

Lieutenant Ponée, like a brave man, refused to surrender unconditionally; but proposed to deliver up the frigate and fort to the British, on condition that he, his officers, and ship's company, and the troops in garrison on shore, should be sent to France, without being considered as prisoners of war. The terms were agreed to; and on the 26th the fort of Tamatave and its dependencies, the frigate and a vessel or two in the port, were taken possession of by Captain Schomberg; who, having first, as a precautionary measure on account of the number of prisoners in the two frigates, caused the guns on the battery to be spiked, went into Tamatave with his squadron.

Having thus disposed of two of M. Roquebert's three frigates, we will endeavour to show what became of the other. Captain Saint-Cricq made so good a use of the entire state of the Clorinde's rigging and sails, that by daylight on the 21st he had run completely out of sight of both friends and foes. After ruminating awhile on his "melancholy" situation, the French captain bent his course towards the Seychelle islands: under one of which he anchored, and on the 7th of June set sail on his return to France. On the 26th the Clorinde reached the island of Diego-Garcia; and, having obtained some cocoas and a supply of wood and water, sailed thence on the 28th, and on the 1st of August rounded the Cape of Good Hope. Between the 23rd of August and 16th of September, Captain Saint-Cricq fell in with several English and American provision-laden merchant-vessels, and from among them supplied the principal part of his wants.

On the 24th, when close to the port of her destination, the Clorinde was very near sharing the fate of her late consorts. At daylight she was discovered and chased by the British 80-gun ship Tonnant, Captain Sir John Gore; who ineffectually endeavoured to cut her off from entering the passage du Raz. At noon the Tonnant fired a shot at the Clorinde; and at about 1 h. 30 m. P.M., when the Saintes islands bore north-east by north four miles, discharged her broadside. The British 80 continued the chase, in a fresh gale at north-west and heavy sea, and passed though the Raz. At 2 P.M., when running, under a press of sail, between the Vieille rock and Pointe Carnarvan and coming up fast with the frigate, the Tonnant lost her maintopmast and fore and mizen topgallantmasts by the violence of the wind.

The latter nevertheless opened a smart fire upon the Clorinde, then within little more than pistol-shot distance; but the frigate, having judiciously reduced her sails when the squall came on, now possessed them all in a perfect state, and soon outran her pursuer. After receiving a few harmless shot from the battery on Pointe Trépassée, the Tonnant gave over the chase; and at 5 P.M. the Clorinde anchored in the road of Brest.

It unfortunately happened, that the action off Madagascar was not allowed to pass without a charge, an implied charge, at all events, of misconduct on the British side. Having previously stated, in his official letter, Captain Losack's report of the disabled state of his ship, Captain Schomberg says: "I am, however, called upon by my feelings, and a sense of duty, to bear testimony to the meritorious conduct of the officers and ships' companies of his majesty's ships Phœbe and Astrea." Not a maravedi, in the way of praise, is bestowed upon the Galatea or Racehorse Admitting the brig to have been a little shy, what had the frigate done, to deserve such treatment? The Galatea was certainly more struck in her hull than either of her two consorts, and had lost two of her topmasts, when they had every topgallantmast standing. The Galatea had also lost nearly four times as many men in killed and wounded as the Astrea, and a third more than the Astrea and Phœbe united. We can hardly suppose that Captain Schomberg expected the Galatea, in such a state of disability, to renew the action, but merely wished her to put her head the right way. That was not done, although we see no reason, judging from the Galatea's previous conduct, to doubt that the attempt was made. It was this apparent omission, coupled with the circumstance of hoisting, in the presence of the enemy, a signal of distress, when not reduced to the emergency of being actually sinking or on fire, that called down upon the Galatea's captain, officers, and crew, the severe punishment inflicted by Captain Schomberg.

Although the account of this action, given by our contemporary, partakes largely of the inaccuracies that pervade all his accounts of proceedings in the vicinity of the isles of France and Bourbon, Captain Brenton has, we are assured, stated one fact correctly:—"Captain Losack, on his return to England, demanded a court-martial, which the lords commissioners of the admiralty, judging no doubt from the log-books, did not think proper to grant, and informed Captain Losack, that they were satisfied with his conduct."[1] But in a case like this, in which the courage of a naval officer is publicly impugned, the approbation, if it amounts to that, of the lords commissioners of the admiralty is of very little value: the opinion of the profession at large, that by which alone the character of the officer is to stand or fall, is not moved a jot by it. We think, with submission, that the board of admiralty should not have refused Captain Losack's application. A court-martial would have completely settled the point; and, admitting that the captain, as the director of the movements of the ship, was the responsible party, why did not the first-lieutenant, on behalf of the remaining officers and crew of the Galatea, as was done in the instance of

[1] Brenton, vol. iv. p. 561.

the Uranie,[1] apply to have Captain Losack brought to trial? In a case like this, no effort should be spared to get redress; and, had redress been zealously and pertinaciously sought by Captain Losack, we cannot think but that he would have eventually obtained it.

It was not during many months that the captain of the Clorinde was allowed to enjoy the ease and comfort, the good cheer and safe quarters, of a home-port. On the 13th and five succeeding days of March, 1812, Captain Saint-Cricq was tried by a court-martial, for not having done all in his power in the action in which the Renommée had been captured; for having separated from his commodore in the heat of the battle, when he ought to have closed him, &c.; and for having omitted to proceed to Java, as prescribed by his instructions dated December 22, 1810, in case of inability to enter the Isle of France. Upon these charges the French captain was found guilty, and sentenced to be dismissed the service, degraded from the legion of honour, and imprisoned for three years.

The Néréide and Renommée, being both new frigates, and the first a particularly fine one, were added to the class of British 38s; the Néréide, under the name of Madagascar, and the Renommée, under that of Java. Lieutenants John Baldwin and George Scott, first of the Astrea and Phœbe, were each deservedly promoted to the rank of commander; but Lieutenant Thomas Bevis, the first of the Galatea, and who was wounded in the action, still remains a lieutenant. This, surely, is an extension of the blasting effects of the charge against the Galatea never contemplated by its author.

Colonial Expeditions.—East Indies.

On the 18th of April, the expedition destined for the conquest of the Dutch island of Java having, under the personal directions of Captain Christopher Cole of the 36-gun frigate Caroline, by the express orders of Vice-admiral Drury issued during the illness that terminated his life, completed its preparations, the first division of the troops, commanded by Colonel Robert Rollo Gillespie, sailed from Madras roads under the convoy of the Caroline, and on the 18th of May anchored in the harbour of Penang or Prince of Wales island, the first point of rendezvous. On the 21st the second division of the troops, commanded

---

[1] See vol. iv., p. 262.

by Major-general Wetherall, and escorted by the British 38-gun frigate Phaëton, Captain Fleetwood Broughton Reynolds Pellew, arrived also, having quitted Madras about six days after the Caroline. On the 24th the Caroline and Phaëton, with their respective charges, sailed from Penang, and on the 1st of June arrived at Malacca, the second rendezvous. Here the expedition was joined by a division of troops from Bengal, and by Lieutenant-general Sir Samuel Auchmuty, and Commodore William Robert Broughton of the Illustrious 74, the military and naval commanders-in-chief. The whole of the troops thus assembled, including 1200 too sick to proceed, amounted to 11,960 officers and men, of whom very nearly half, or 5344, were Europeans.

On the 11th of June the fleet, leaving behind the 1200 sick, sailed from Malacca, and in a few days entered the straits of Sincapore. Having cleared these, and passed Timbalan and a number of other islands, the expedition arrived on the 3rd of July at the High Islands, which had been appointed the third rendezvous. On the 10th the fleet quitted the High Islands, and on the 20th reached Point Sambar, at the extremity of the south-west coast of the island of Borneo, the fourth and last point of rendezvous. Quitting Sambar on the following day, the 21st, the fleet arrived on the 30th off Boompies island, which lies nearly abreast of Indramayo river on the Java coast. Here the two commanders-in-chief waited awhile, in expectation of being joined by some frigates with intelligence.

We will take this opportunity of narrating two or three creditable little affairs that occurred on the Java coast, while the expedition was on its way from Madras and waiting off Boompies island. On the 23rd of May, at daylight, thé British 12-pounder 32-gun frigate Sir Francis Drake, Captain George Harris, being about 13 miles to the north-east of the port of Rembang, island of Java, on her way to Sourabaya, discovered, lying at anchor about three miles nearer to the shore, a flotilla of Dutch gun-vessels, consisting of 14, nine of them felucca, and the remaining four prow, rigged On seeing the frigate, the gun-vessels weighed and stood for Rembang, but were so closely pressed, that by 7 A.M. three or four broadsides brought five of the feluccas to an anchor under the Drake's guns, and they were immediately taken possession of. The others, finding themselves cut off from their port, furled sails, and pulled up in the wind's eye directly for the shore.

Shoaling his water considerably, Captain Harris despatched

Lieutenants James Bradley and Edward Brown Addis, Lieutenant of marines George Loch, Midshipmen George Greaves, John Horton, and Matthew Phibbs, also Lieutenant Knowles, Mr. Gillman, and 12 privates of the 14th regiment of foot, in four six-oared cutters and a gig, to board the gun-vessels; the Drake keeping under way, and working to windward, to cover the boats. By 8 A.M., notwithstanding a sharp fire of grape from several pieces of ordnance, Lieutenant Bradley and his party, without the loss of a man, made prizes of the remaining nine vessels, the crews of which leaped overboard or fled to the shore in their boats just as the British were ready to spring on board. The gun-boats had only been launched 15 days, and were large vessels measuring 80 feet overall, and 17 broad; fitted to carry a 7-inch howitzer and a 24-pounder carronade aft, and to pull 30 oars. Only one of the vessels, however, was found with her guns on board; and it was supposed, either that the crews had thrown the guns overboard, or that the vessels were proceeding to Sourabaya to be fully armed and equipped.

The small British squadron cruising off Batavia was under the orders of Captain George Sayer, of the 18-pounder 36-gun frigate Leda. Since Sir Edward Pellew had proved that Batavia and Sourabaya were assailable anchorages, the harbour of Marrack, situated about 74 miles to the westward of Batavia, was the only spot to which the French frigates, daily expected with troops, could run for safety. The anchorage was defended by a strong fort, standing upon a promontory, and mounting 54 pieces of cannon, 18, 24, and 32 pounders, with a garrison of 180 soldiers. Captain Sayer resolved to make a night-attack upon this fort with the boats of the Leda and of the 74-gun ship Minden, Captain Edward Wallis Hoare. The force, with which the attempt was to be made, was to consist of 200 seamen and marines and 250 troops, the latter to be embarked in the flat-boats which the two ships had on board; and Lieutenant Edmund Lyons, of the Minden, who had previously reconnoitred the fort, was, at his particular request, to lead the party. A few hours before the boats were to push off from the Minden, intelligence reached Captain Hoare, of the arrival of a battalion of Dutch troops at the barracks situated about half a mile in the rear of the fort. Under these circumstances, the attack was deemed too hazardous, and the Leda's boats returned to their ship.

On the 25th of July, Captain Hoare, by Captain Sayer's

direction, detached Lieutenant Lyons with the Minden's launch and cutter, containing 19 prisoners, with orders to land them at Batavia; and, while there and on his return down the coast, to gain all the information possible as to the movements in that part of Java. On the 27th, Lieutenant Lyons landed his prisoners at Batavia; and, from a conversation which he held with an intelligent resident, was fully persuaded that the Dutch had no intimation of the expedition being near Java, and did not expect to be attacked during the present monsoon. Conceiving that an attack at the north-western extremity of Java would draw the Dutch troops in that direction, and thereby operate a favourable diversion, Lieutenant Lyons, on the morning of the 29th, determined to make a midnight attack upon Fort Marrack. This would appear, indeed, a rash undertaking for two boats' crews of 35 officers and men, especially when a force of 450 men had been thought inadequate to the service; but Lieutenant Lyons was one of the officers who, about a twelvemonth before, had accompanied Captain Cole in the storming of Belgica: he therefore made light of difficulties, which to many, and those brave men too, would have seemed insurmountable.

Having made, during the day, every necessary arrangement, Lieutenant Lyons, at sunset, placed his two boats behind a point, which sheltered them from the view of the enemy's sentinels. At half an hour past midnight, the moon sinking in the horizon, the boats proceeded to the attack, and, on opening the point, were challenged by the sentinels, who almost at the same instant fired their pieces; a proof that all hopes of a surprise had vanished. Still resolved, Lieutenant Lyons ran the boats aground, in a heavy surf, under the embrasures of the lower tier of guns; and he and his gallant fellows, placing the ladders, sprang up them in an instant. Some of the first that gained the walls killed three soldiers, who were in the act of putting matches to the guns; and in a few minutes the British found themselves in complete possession of the lower battery. Lieutenant Lyons now formed his men; his 34 men; and, leading them on, stormed and carried the upper battery. On reaching the summit of the hill, the little band of British perceived the Dutch garrison drawn up to receive them. The sailors fired, then rushed to the charge; Lieutenant Lyons calling out, that he had 400 men, and would give no quarter. On hearing this, the Dutchmen fled in a panic through the postern gateway at the rear of the fort.

At 1 A.M. on the 30th the Dutch opened a fire on the fort

from a small battery in the rear, also from two gun-boats at anchor in the harbour. This fire was returned by a few guns : and, in the meanwhile, the remainder of the small party of British were employed in disabling the other guns, and in destroying as much as practicable of the battery. The first shot, fired at Fort Marrack from the battery in the rear, had struck the top of the postern or gateway through which the garrison had retreated; the second shot went through the gate; and the third shot, taking the same direction, convinced Lieutenant Lyons that the Dutch had previously ascertained the range. The situation of the British was now critical and alarming, as the barracks in which was a whole battalion of Dutch troops was only half a mile distant, and the drums were heard beating to arms. At this moment midshipman William Langton, the second British officer in command, and who had greatly distinguished himself in the assault, suggested to Lieutenant Lyons to open the gate, and allow the shot to pass harmlessly through. This was done, and in the course of half an hour the enemy directed his shot considerably to the right of the gate; which left no doubt that the troops were advancing to the attack. Two 24-pounders, loaded almost to the muzzles with musket-balls, were now placed near the entrance of the gateway. This was hardly done when the enemy's column was seen advancing; and, lest the guns should be fired too soon, Lieutenant Lyons held one match and Mr. Langton the other. The head of the enemy's column, on arriving within about 10 yards of the gate, perceived that it was open. The Dutch troops immediately shouted, cheered, and rushed on. At that instant the two guns went off, and the gate was shut. The foremost of the assailants were mowed down by the murderous discharge ; and those behind, seeing the gate shut, fled pêle-mêle down the hill, leaving the handful of British withinside to destroy the fort at their leisure.

This service was completed by dawn of day, and the last shot fired from the last gun that was spiked had sunk one of the two gun-boats. Lieutenant Lyons now deemed it prudent to retire. He did not do so, however, without leaving the British flag flying on the fort; and which flag had been hoisted under a heavy fire, in the most gallant manner, by midshipman Charles Henry Franks, a lad only 15 years of age. On coming to their boats, the British found the barge bilged, and beat up so high in the surf as to leave no prospect of getting her afloat. The whole 35, including Mr. Langton, slightly wounded with a bayonet, and three seamen also slightly wounded, embarked in the cutter, carrying with them the Dutch colours. Thus to see them carried off as a trophy by a single boat's crew, an undeniable proof of the few men by whom the fort had been carried, must have been to the Dutch a truly mortifying sight.

But for one circumstance, we should probably have had to state that, for having thus accomplished, with 35 men, that which had been deemed too hazardous to undertake with 450, Lieutenant Lyons was immediately promoted to the rank of commander. The bar was, that he had acted without orders. Captain Hoare called upon Lieutenant Lyons to state his reason for making an attack, "the success of which," says the former in his letter to Commodore Broughton, "so very far surpasses all my idea of possibility with so small a force, that comment from me would be superfluous." "I have only to add, that his conduct on every former occasion, since he has been under my command, has merited my warmest approbation and esteem." Commodore Broughton, we believe, considered the undertaking as a rash one, and would not forward the account to the admiralty; but the commodore's successor on the station, Rear-admiral Stopford, was of a very different opinion, as is evident from his reply to a letter of Captain Sayer's, requesting that Lieutenant Lyons, in the expedition of which we shall presently give an account, might act as his aide-de-camp at the batteries of Batavia. "I beg," says the rear-admiral, "you will tell Mr. Lyons from me, that I consider myself fortunate and happy in procuring the services of an officer who so eminently distinguished himself by his gallant and successful attack on Fort Marrack, and I fully approve of his remaining with you."

During the night of the 30th the 18-gun brig-sloop Procris, Captain Robert Maunsell, in obedience to orders from Captain Sayer, stood in and anchored near the mouth of Indramayo river, and at daylight on the 31st discovered lying there six gun-boats, each armed with two guns, a brass 32-pounder carronade forward, and a long 18-pounder aft, and a crew of 60 men, protecting a convoy of 40 or 50 prows. The brig immediately weighed, and ran into a quarter less than three fathoms water, but was then scarcely within gun-shot. Finding that the fire of the Procris made very little impression upon the gun-boats, and considering it an object of importance to attempt their destruction, Captain Maunsell proceeded to the attack in his boats; embarking in them, in addition to their respective crews, Lieutenants Henry J. Heyland and Oliver Brush, and 40 privates of the 14th and 89th regiments, detachments from which happened to be on board his vessel.

Although opposed by a heavy fire of grape and musketry, the British boats succeeded in boarding and carrying five of the Dutch gun-boats; the crews of which, after throwing their spears at the assailants, leaped overboard. The sixth gun-boat would have shared the same fate, but caught fire and blew up before the British could get alongside of her. This exploit was performed without any loss of life on the British side, and with no greater loss in wounded than one master's mate (William Randall), seven seamen, one boy, and two soldiers. Captain Maunsell speaks in the highest terms, as well of the troops and their officers, as of his first-lieutenant George Majoribanks, and the three master's mates George Cunningham, William Randall, and Charles Davies.

Having waited until the 2nd of August without being joined by the expected ships, the expedition set sail, but had not proceeded far before the frigates hove in sight; and Colonel Mackenzie, the officer who had been deputed to reconnoitre the Java coast, reported, as the most eligible spot for the disembarkation of the army, the village of Chillingching, about 12 miles to the eastward of Batavia. The commander-in-chief concurring, the fleet proceeded in that direction; on the 3rd, in the evening, made Cape Carawang; and on the 4th, early in the morning, ran in for the mouth of Marandi river. Here the ships anchored during the interval between the land and sea breezes; and, weighing on the return of the latter, again stood in, and, before 2 P.M., were at anchor abreast of Chillingching.

So complete had been the arrangements, and so well chosen was the spot, that before dark the whole of the effective portion of the British infantry, amounting to upwards of 8000 men, of whom, as already stated, about half were Europeans, landed, without loss or opposition. covered on the left by the 36-gun frigate Leda, Captain Sayer, who, being well acquainted with the coast, ran close in, and on the right by the frigates Caroline, Modeste, and Bucephalus, also the ship and brig sloops and Honourable Company's cruisers attached to the expedition. "The rapid approach of the fleet had prevented the enemy from ascertaining the intended place of landing in time to send a force thither to guard it: this being noticed by Captain Cole, he made the signal from the Caroline for the advance of the army to land immediately, then hoisted out his boats. tripped his anchor, and dropped the Caroline nearer to the shore. No time was occupied in arranging the order of the boats, they being ordered to shove off when manned and filled with troops. His example being followed by Captains Elliot and Pelley, and the boats of the other men-of-war being sent to assist in conveying the troops, about 8000 soldiers, with their guns, ammunition, and provisions, were landed in safety by half-past six o'clock. Soon after dark the British advanced guard had a skirmish with the enemy's patroles, who, but for Captain Cole's alacrity and promptitude in making the above signal, without waiting to complete the arrangement of boats, &c., as usual in such cases, would have taken post in a wood at the back of the beach, and might have occasioned great loss to the invading army."[1]

General Daendels, the late governor-general of Java, had recently been superseded by General Jansens; and the latter, who had only been apprised of the intended attack since the 1st or 2nd of the month, was now with his army, amounting to between 8000 and 10,000 effective troops, native and European, shut up in the stronghold of Meester-Cornelis, an intrenched camp, situated about nine miles from the city of Batavia, and defended by two rivers, one on the east, the other on the west, with a number of redoubts and batteries guarding each pass. The circumference of these fortified lines was nearly five miles, and there were mounted in different parts of it 280 pieces of cannon.

On the 6th the Leda and small cruisers proceeded off the entrance of the river Anjole, or Antziol, distant about two miles from the capital; and the fleet anchored off Tonjong-Prioch; where, in the course of the day, the advance of the British army, under the command of Colonel Gillespie, took post. On the 7th, in the night, the advance crossed the river Anjole on a bridge of flat boats, prepared by the navy, under the direction of Captains Sayer, Maunsell, and Reynolds. On the 8th, in the morning, a flag of truce was sent into the city of Batavia, and a deputation came out from the inhabitants, requesting to surrender at discretion, and put themselves under the protection of the British. The lieutenant-general and commodore having agreed to respect private property, the advance under Colonel Gillespie took immediate possession of the city; and the men-of-war and transports removed to the anchorage before it.

On the 9th Rear-admiral the Honourable Robert Stopford

[1] Marshall, vol. ii., p. 515.

joined the expedition, and superseded Commodore Broughton in the command of the fleet, which now consisted of the

Gun-ship.

74	Scipion	{	Rear-admiral (r.) the Hon. Rt. Stopford. Captain James Johnson.
	Illustrious	{	Commodore Will. Rob. Broughton. Captain Rob. Worgan Geo. Festing.
	Minden	,,	Edward Wallis Hoare.
64	Lion	,,	Henry Heathcote.

Gun-frigate.

44	Akbar	,,	Henry Drury.
38	Nisus	,,	Philip Beaver.
	Présidente	,,	Samuel Warren.
	Hussar	,,	James Coutts Crawford.
	Phaëton	,,	Fleetw. Broughton R. Pellew.
36	Leda	,,	George Sayer.
	Caroline	,,	Christopher Cole.
	Modeste	,,	Hon. George Elliot.
	Phœbe	,,	James Hillyar.
	Bucephalus	,,	Charles Pelly.
	Doris	,,	William Jones Lye.
32	Cornelia	,,	Henry Folkes Edgell.
	Psyche	,,	John Edgcumbe.
	Sir Francis Drake	,,	George Harris.
Slps.	Procris	,,	Robert Maunsell.
	Barracouta	,,	William Fitzwilliam Owen.
	Hesper	,,	Barrington Reynolds.
	Harpy	,,	Henderson Bain.
	Hecate	,,	Henry John Peachey.
	Dasher	,,	Benedictus Marwood Kelly.
	Samarang	,,	Joseph Drury.

Company's cruisers, Malabar (Commodore John Hayes), Aurora, Mornington, Nautilus, Vestal, Ariel, Thetis, and Psyche; making, with the transports and captured gun-boats, a total of nearly a hundred sail.

On the 10th a smart skirmish took place between the advanced division of each army; which ended in the defeat of the Dutch, and in the occupation by the British of the important post of Weltervreeden, distant about six miles from the city on the road to Cornelis. Preparations were now made to attack General Jansens in his intrenched camp at the latter place, distant about a league beyond Weltervreeden. On the 20th, in the night, the British army broke ground within 600 yards of the enemy's works; and on the evening of the 21st the batteries, mounting 20 long 18-pounders, together with eight howitzers and mortars, were nearly completed. To assist in erecting and fighting these batteries, 500 seamen had been landed from the squadron, under the orders of Captain Sayer, assisted by Captains Festing, Maunsell, Reynolds, and Edward Stopford: the latter a volunteer from on board the Scipion, where he was waiting to join his ship the Otter. A detachment of marines, under Captain Richard Bunce of that corps, had also been disembarked from the ships, to increase the strength of Sir Samuel's army, already considerably reduced by sickness.

On the 22nd, early in the morning, the Dutch made a sortie, attacked the works of the British, and gained a momentary possession of one of the batteries; but the former were at length repulsed and driven within their lines. Being thus foiled, the Dutch began to open from their redoubts a tremendous fire. Thirty-four heavy guns, 18, 24, and 32 pounders, bore upon the British front, and kept up an incessant and very destructive cannonade. On the 23rd neither party fired; but on the 24th a severe cannonade began on both sides, and continued throughout that and the following day, with much mutual slaughter, and to the evident disadvantage of the Dutch, many of their guns being dismounted and their front line of defence much damaged. In this state of things, an assault was resolved upon, and that truly gallant officer Colonel Gillespie was entrusted with the command of the principal attack. At midnight on the 25th the troops moved off, and, after a most desperate struggle, in which the British seamen and marines bore a distinguished part, carried all before them. Nearly 5000 troops, including three general officers, 34 field-officers, 70 captains, and 150 subaltern officers, were taken prisoners, more than 1000 were found dead about the works, and many others must have fallen in the pursuit.

General Jansens made his escape with difficulty during the action, and reached Buitenzorg, a distance of 30 miles, accompanied by a few cavalry, the sole remains of his army. The Dutch commander-in-chief quitted Buitenzorg, a little while before the British cavalry entered the town, and fled to the eastward. The loss to the British army including the natives attached to it, from the 4th to the 27th of August inclusive, amounted, according to the official returns, to 141 killed, 733 wounded, and 13 missing; and the loss to the British navy, between the same dates, amounted to 11 seamen and four marines killed, Captain Stopford (right arm carried off by a cannon-shot) one lieutenant (Francis Noble), two lieutenants of marines, (Henry Elliot and John Stepney Haswell), two master's mates (John Dewdney Worthy and Robert Graham Dunlop), 29 seamen and 20 marines wounded, and three seamen missing;

making the total loss of the two services, up to the 27th of August, 156 killed, 788 wounded, and 16 missing.

The two new French 40-gun frigates Nymphe and Méduse, which, under the orders of Commodore Joseph-François Raoul, of the former, had escaped from Nantes in the spring of the year, were at this time lying in the harbour of Sourabaya. Rear-admiral Stopford, on the day after his arrival in Batavia road, despatched four frigates, the Akbar, Phaëton, Bucephalus, and Sir Francis Drake, to look after these French frigates, and watch the different entrances by which they might effect their escape. On the 30th of August the Akbar, who had been in company with the Bucephalus at an anchor off the east end of Java, weighed and sailed to the westward.

On the 3rd of September, at 3 P.M., the two French frigates, having received on board several of General Jansen's aides-de-camp, and others of the principal fugitives from Cornelis, weighed and began warping themselves into the outer road. The Bucephalus saw the manœuvre, and instantly weighed and made sail close to the enemy. On the 4th, at daylight, the Barracouta joined the former, and at 10 A.M. the British frigate and brig wore and stood towards the two French frigates; who, during the night, had warped themselves considerably ahead, and were now under sail working out of the harbour, with the wind a moderate breeze at north-east. The Bucephalus and Barracouta immediately proceeded in chase; and at midnight the two French frigates bore from the first, who was far ahead of her consort, north-west half-west distant three or four miles. By daylight on the 5th the Bucephalus was ahead of the Barracouta six or seven miles, and the French frigates on the former's lee bow, the weather nearly calm. At 5 h. 30 m. A.M. a breeze sprang up from the eastward; and at sunset the French frigates bore north-east by north distant seven or eight miles. During the 6th, 7th, and 8th nearly the same distance was preserved between the two French frigates and the one British frigate, which, accompanied by a brig sloop-of-war, was so earnestly pursuing them; but, at midnight, notwithstanding all her efforts to keep up, the Barracouta dropped entirely out of sight of her consort.

The Bucephalus, now entirely alone, persevered in the chase during the whole of the 9th, 10th, and 11th, and at 6 A.M. on the 12th saw the island of Great Pulo-Laut, bearing east-south-east, and her enemy south, distant about four leagues, with the weather-gage in his favour. At 9 A.M. the two French frigates bore down, with the apparent intention of embaying the British frigate between Borneo and Paulo-Laut; but the Bucephalus wore and bore up, in order to keep off shore. The Nymphe now signalled the Méduse; and shortly afterwards the two frigates wore, and made all sail in line abreast after the Bucephalus, then within four miles of them, steering west by north, and soon under an equal press of sail with her pursuers. By noon the Nymphe had got ahead of her consort, and was gaining on the Bucephalus, now steering about west by south. At 1 P.M. the latter commenced firing her stern-chasers; and shortly afterwards the Nymphe returned the fire with her bow-chasers, yawing occasionally, as she advanced on the British frigate's larboard quarter, to get her foremost main-deck guns to bear. This yawing necessarily checking her progress, the Nymphe dropped a little astern. At 2 h. 30 m. P.M. the Méduse got up on the starboard or lee quarter of the Bucephalus, and after receiving a few of the latter's shot, yawed also, and fired her broadside. By this time the Nymphe had hauled to windward, on the larboard quarter of the Bucephalus, out of gun-shot; and, the Méduse dropping also out of gun-shot on the opposite quarter, the British frigate ceased firing. At 4 P.M. two shoals were discovered right ahead of the Bucephalus. Confiding in his skill and experience, Captain Pelly passed between the shoals, in the hope of decoying both or one of the French frigates upon them; but they, seeing the danger in time, shortened sail and tacked to the north-east, and at dark were lost sight of; at daylight on the 13th the island of Arentes bore from the Bucephalus south-south-west: and at 11 A.M. the two French frigates were again seen at a great distance in the north-east, but shortly afterwards wholly disappeared.

The Bucephalus had not a man hurt, and sustained very slight damage in her rigging, sails, masts, or hull. To what extent her shot had injured the Nymphe and Méduse is not known; but it was evident that the rigging and sails of the Nymphe had in some degree suffered. Admitting that these frigates were justified in using the utmost despatch to get away from the Java coast, and from the fleet that was hovering near it, what had they to dread on reaching the coast of Borneo? It is true that Commodore Raoul then chased in his turn; but he desisted from pursuit on the first appearance of danger from shoal water, and abandoned a British frigate which, obstinately defended as she undoubtedly would have been, must have ultimately been his prize.

The conduct of Captain Pelly, on the other hand, was in the highest degree praiseworthy: he was induced to chase an enemy more than doubly superior to himself, in the hope of being able to separate one French frigate from the other, or of falling in with a consort, with whose assistance he might have a fair prospect of conquering the two; and his perseverance in chasing, and success in keeping sight of, two French frigates, during so many days and nights, afforded a decided proof both of his gallantry and his seamanship. Of the Nymphe and Méduse, we have nothing further to state, than that they made their long voyage in safety, and arrived at Brest on the 22nd of December.

While these two French frigates were meditating an escape from the channel formed by the west end of the small island of Madura, the two British frigates Sir Francis Drake and Phaëton lay unconsciously at anchor off the east end, close under the isle of Pondock. They were not, however, lying inactive, as the following details will show. On the 29th of August, Captain Harris, the senior officer, having resolved to attack the fort of Samanap, the capital of the island, sent the Dasher sloop round the south end of Pulo 'I Lanjong, to gain an anchorage as near as possible to the fort, and in the evening, accompanied by Captain Pellew, proceeded with the boats of the two frigates, in two divisions. On the 30th, at daylight, the boats sailed through the channel formed by the east end of Madura and Pulo 'I Lanjong, and by 30 minutes past midnight effected a landing, without discovery, at a pier-head about three miles from the fort.

At 1 h. 30 m. A.M. on the 31st, two columns, composed each of 60 bayonets and 20 pikemen, flanked by a 12, 4, and 2 pounder field-piece, having in reserve the marines of the Hussar, began their march, in the utmost order, towards the fort. Silence among the men was so rigidly observed, that, notwithstanding the governor had intimation of the Dasher's having weighed and being seen entering the harbour, and that the British boats had been seen standing in for the town, the Dutch garrison at the fort did not discover the approach of the storming-party until the outer gate, which had been left open, was passed. The gallantry of the rush at the inner gate prevented the Dutch from securing it, and only allowed time for two or three guns at the south-west bastion to be fired. The assault was as sudden as it was resolute; and by 3 h. 30 m. A.M., after a ten minutes' feeble struggle with 300 or 400 Madura pikemen, who with their chief were made prisoners on the ramparts, the British became masters of the fort of Samanap, a regular fortification, mounting sixteen 6-pounders.

On the appearance of daylight, observing French colours flying on a flagstaff at the east end of the town, and perceiving the natives begin to assemble in numbers, Captain Harris despatched Captain Pellew, at the head of a column of 100 bayonets and one field-piece, with a flag of truce to the governor, calling upon him to surrender in ten minutes, and promising that private property should be respected. To this was received an answer, requiring Captain Harris to evacuate the fort; and Captain Pellew sent intelligence, by midshipman John William Oldmixon, described as an intelligent young officer, that the Dutch force appeared to be about 2000 men, protected by four field-pieces in front, and posted on a bridge, possessing every advantage of situation, the troops of an enemy having to advance along an even and straight road for a quarter of a mile before they could force the bridge.

Not at all daunted by this alleged superiority of force, Captain Harris sent orders to Captain Pellew, to advance when the first gun was fired from a column that the former would lead out of the fort, and with which he meant to turn the enemy's left wing. Accordingly, with 70 small-arm, and 20 pikemen, supported by a 4-pounder field-piece (leaving in the fort, as a reserve, 40 or 50 men), Captain Harris proceeded to put his bold plan into execution, and soon had the satisfaction to observe the Dutch governor, whose force, as acknowledged by himself, consisted of 300 muskets, 60 artillerymen, and 1500 to 2000 pikemen, armed each with a long pike, a pistol, and a crees, draw off two field-pieces and break his line, in order to oppose the small but resolute column advancing against his left. Both British columns discharged their volleys nearly at the same time, and, for nearly five minutes, a sharp fire was given and returned; but as Captains Harris and Pellew and their respective parties advanced nearer, the Dutch gave way, and an animated charge by the British left them masters of the field, the colours, and the guns. The governor and the other Dutch inhabitants were made prisoners; and Captain Harris accepted a flag of truce from the rajah of Samanap, who was present, on condition that none of the inhabitants of the district should again arm themselves against the British.

This very gallant exploit was not achieved without a loss on the part of the latter of three men killed and 28 wounded; and the loss on the opposite side, although it could not be ascertained, was known to be severe, including among the killed the commander-in-chief of the native troops, second in rank to the rajah, and his two sons. This success was followed up by the total overthrow of the French authority in Madura and the adjacent isles. The spirited conduct of Captain Harris, in bringing matters to such a close, proves that his own element is not that alone in which a naval officer, possessing zeal, activity, and judgment, may be enabled to distinguish himself.

Among the wounded in storming the town of Samanap, was Lieutenant Roch of the Sir Francis Drake's marines, who was speared twice by two natives, while resolutely endeavouring to wrest the colours out of the hands of a French officer. During the time that Captain Pellew, by the direction of Captain Harris, was negotiating with the governor of Madura, Lieutenant Roch, with a column of marines, destroyed, in the face of the enemy, a fort at the mouth of the river, which leads, as we suppose, to Samanap, mounting twelve 9-pounders.

In order to intercept the retreat of General Jansens from Cornelis to the eastward, Rear-admiral Stopford, on the 31st of August, detached the Nisus, Présidente, and Phœbe frigates, and Hesper sloop, to Cheribon, a seaport about 35 leagues to the eastward of Batavia. On the 3rd of September, at dark, the three frigates anchored off the port; and at daylight on the 4th Captain Beaver, having despatched Captain Warren with a flag of truce to summon the French commandant of the fort to surrender, weighed with the frigates, and anchored as near the fort as the depth of water would admit; when, instantly, the French colours were hauled down and the British hoisted in their stead. The marines of the three frigates, amounting, including a party belonging to the Lion 64, to 180, immediately landed, and took possession of the fort. Just at that moment General Jamelle, the commander-in-chief of the French troops, who had arrived at the landroosts from Buitenzorg, was, while changing horses to proceed to the eastward, taken prisoner by Captain Warren, with the aid of his gig's crew; as were also an aide-de-camp of General Jansens and a lieutenant of infantry.

Hearing from the French general, that 350 infantry and 350 cavalry were hourly expected to arrive at Cheribon from Buitenzorg, Captain Beaver landed 150 seamen to garrison and defend the fort; leaving the marines to act offensively against the enemy in the field, should occasion require it, and placing three launches, with carronades, in the river, to enfilade the two chief approaches to it. On the 5th, in the morning, the Hesper, who had been delayed by bad sailing, joined the Nisus, Présidente, and Phœbe. On the two following days a quantity of treasure and valuable stores, and several prisoners, were brought from Carang-Sambang, a place about 35 miles in the interior, by a detachment of seamen and marines sent thither for the purpose. On the 11th, by 1 A.M., all the seamen and marines that had been landed were re-embarked, having made about 700 prisoners, including 237 Europeans; and at 4 A.M. the Nisus and Phœbe weighed and steered for Taggal, a port about 20 or 25 leagues further to the eastward. On the 12th the Phœbe arrived off the harbour; and landing some sepoys and a detachment of seamen and marines, Captain Hillyar took quiet possession of the fort and public stores.

While the British navy was thus effectually lending its aid, by subduing and taking possession of the different sea-defences of this valuable colony, the commander-in-chief of the British army was pressing close upon General Jansens; so close that, on the 16th of September, the latter, then at the fort of Salatiga, about 30 miles to the southward of Samarang, which is 343 miles east from Batavia, proposed to capitulate; and on the 18th the island of Java and its dependencies were surrendered to the British arms.

BRITISH AND FRENCH FLEETS.

The abstract, showing the state of the British navy at the commencement of the present year,[1] so nearly resembles the last, as to call for no additional remarks.[2]

The number of commissioned officers and masters, belonging to the British navy at the beginning of the year 1812, was:—

Admirals	62
Vice-admirals	65
Rear-admirals	60
,, superannuated 31	
Post-captains	777
,, superannuated 32	
Commanders, or sloop-captains	566
,, superannuated 50	
Lieutenants	3163
Masters	567

And the number of seamen and marines, voted for the service of the same year, was 145,000.[3]

With respect to the fleets of the powers at war, another inactive year passed; and yet France continued adding to her already powerful navy new line-of-battle ships and frigates. On the 19th of March, Russia declared war against France; and on the 18th of July a treaty of peace was signed at Orebo between Russia, Sweden, and Great Britain. The Scheldt fleet, of from 16 to 20 sail of the line and eight or nine frigates and smaller vessels, evinced, several times, an inclination to put to sea, but was too narrowly watched by the indefatigable officer that cruised off Flushing, Vice-admiral Sir Richard John Strachan. Towards the end of the year, however, a want of men, owing to the frequent draughts made to supply the army, contributed to

---

[1] See Appendix, Annual Abstract, No. 20.   [2] See Appendix, Nos. 8 and 9.
[3] Ibid., No. 10.

keep the French fleet stationary. A squadron of seven, and latterly of nine, sail of the line in the Texel threatened also to sail out, but was restrained from the attempt, by the dread of encountering the British force stationed off that port. At Amsterdam, in the beginning of October, the keels of two 74-gun ships, the Audacieux and Polyphème, were ordered to be laid down, to commemorate the entry of Buonaparte into Moscow; but, before probably a timber belonging to either ship was set up, the French emperor's forced exit from the Russian capital had also taken place.

The French squadron at anchor in the port of Lorient, consisted of five line-of-battle ships, one only of which, the Vétéran, had ever been at sea. This ship had, but when we are unable to state, managed to effect her escape from the neighbouring port of Concarneau, where she had been so long blockaded. In the months of February and March, four of those ships, the Eylau, of 80, and the Guilemar, Marengo, and Vétéran, of 74 guns, with two ship-corvettes, under the command of Vice-admiral Allemand, lay watching an opportunity to elude the vigilance of a British squadron, of the same numerical force, under Captain Sir John Gore, of the 80-gun ship Tonnant, having with him the 74-gun ships Northumberland, Colossus, and Bulwark, Captains the Hon. Henry Hotham, Thomas Alexander, and Thomas Browne. On the 9th of March, early in the afternoon, leaving her three consorts lying to off the island of Hedic, the Tonnant made sail and worked up through the Taigneuse passage against a fresh north-east wind, in order to reconnoitre the port of Lorient. At 6 P.M. Sir John discovered that M. Allemand had effected his escape; and at 8 P.M., the Tonnant anchored for the night off the south-east point o Groix. At daybreak on the 10th the Tonnant weighed and made sail towards Lorient; and at 8 A.M. clearly observed that there was no ship-of-war in the port, except a two-decker, with topgallantmasts pointed and rigged, fitting at the arsenal. Having now ascertained, beyond all doubt, that the French admiral had sailed, Sir John bore up to join his squadron, then just visible in the south-south-west.

M. Allemand had, in fact, put to sea on the night of the 8th; and, but for his extraordinary good fortune, might, as we shall presently see, have terminated his cruise in Portsmouth or Plymouth, instead of in Brest, whither it appears he was bound. On the 9th, at 1 P.M., when about seven leagues to the southward of the Penmarks, these four French sail of the line and two corvettes were discovered by the British 38-gun frigate Diana, Captain William Ferris, but were lost sight of in the evening. On the 10th, however, at 9 A.M., when close hauled on the starboard tack with the wind at north-east, the Diana regained a sight of the French squadron, then on her weather-bow, 12 or 13 miles distant, steering the same course as herself, north by west. The frigate continued sailing parallel with the French ships, to watch their manœuvres, until 3 P.M.; when the 74-gun ship Pompée, Captain Sir James Athol Wood, joined company to leeward. At 4 P.M. Captain Ferris hove to to communicate with his superior officer; and, at 4 h. 30 m. P.M., the British 74 and frigate filled and made all sail on the starboard tack. Shortly afterwards the Diana, who still kept to windward of the Pompée, observed two vessels on her weather-beam, to windward of the French squadron; the ships of which immediately bore up, under all sail, evidently to avoid them.

These two vessels were the British 74-gun ships Tremendous, Captain Robert Campbell, and Poictiers, Captain John Poer Beresford, chasing the French squadron, which they had discovered since daylight, when cruising six or seven leagues west-south-west of Ushant. At 11 A.M. Captain Campbell had detached the Poictiers in chase of a ship to the eastward, which proved to be the British 18-gun ship-sloop Myrtle, Captain Clement Sneyd; and whom Captain Beresford, on joining him at 1 P.M., sent to warn an English convoy, then seen in the north-east, standing to the westward, of the presence of an enemy's squadron. At 4 P.M., the Poictiers having rejoined the Tremendous, the two 74s resumed the chase of M. Allemand, and were descried by the Diana in the manner we have just related.

As the French ships, when they bore up to avoid the Tremendous and Poictiers, steered in a direction to cross the bows of the Diana and Pompée, the two latter, at 6 h. 15 m. P.M., tacked to the south-east. Soon afterwards the Diana lost sight of the Pompée in the south-south-east, and about the same time observed and answered the night-signal for an enemy made by her two friends to windward. The Pompée also observed the flashes of guns and rockets, which were the signals made by the Tremendous and Poictiers; but it does not appear that she answered them. Towards midnight the wind shifted to the north-north-west; and, at about 30 minutes past midnight, the Pompée suddenly discovered two ships in chase of her in the south-east. The British 74 immediately bore up and made all sail, altering her course frequently to avoid her pursuers; one of whom got near enough to fire three or four shot at her. On this the Pompée started 80 tons of water, and then gained so rapidly upon the two supposed enemy's ships, that at daylight on the 11th they were no longer to be seen. In the course of the forenoon of that day the Diana, and in the evening the Bulwark and Colossus joined company with the Pompée; as, on the following, did the Tonnant, Tremendous, and Poictiers. The two latter had lost sight of the French ships at dark on the 10th; but, having again discovered them at daylight on the 11th, had chased them until 2 P.M.; when, foggy weather coming on, the Tremendous and Poictiers shortened sail and hauled to the wind on the larboard tack.

Thus left to himself, M. Allemand cruised about at his leisure, and on the 15th of March, in latitude 47° 39' north, longitude 10° 20' west, fell in with and chased the British 12-pounder 36-gun frigate Nijaden, Captain Farmery Predam Epworth; but the frigate, although frequently fired at by the French van-ship, and a good deal damaged in her sails and rigging, managed to effect her escape. Captain Epworth, also, by his signals, prevented the Northampton, Monarch, and Euphrates, homeward-bound Indiamen, from becoming prizes to the French admiral; towards whom they were unsuspiciously steering until apprised of their danger by the Nijaden. After making a few inconsiderable prizes, the French squadron bent its course towards Brest, and on the evening of the 29th anchored in the road; a matter of just boast to M. Allemand, as two or three British squadrons, besides the one he had escaped from, were anxiously looking out for him.

The account we have given of the escape of the French admiral from the Pompée, Tremendous, and Poictiers, although the only account to be seen in print, is far from being so full and clear as it might have been made, could we have gained a sight of the minutes of the court of inquiry which, it appears, was held at Portsmouth on the subject. We turned to the biography of Sir James Athol Wood in the work of Mr. Marshall; but, although 13 closely-printed pages are devoted to an account of the rear-admiral's professional life, not a line is spared to throw some light on the proceedings of the Pompée in the spring of 1812.

In the latter part of the present year the Ocean, and four of the six two-deckers which, with her, had so nearly been destroyed by the British in 1809, were again in the road of Isle d'Aix, watching an opportunity to proceed to Brest; whither the Courageux and Polonais, in the port of Cherbourg, were also waiting to get; and where Buonaparte wanted once more to assemble a respectable fleet. The French port, which at this time, owing to the powerful fleet at anchor within it, was a much more important station than Brest, now claims our attention.

The British Mediterranean fleet still continued its listless task of watching a superior, though, excepting a little demonstration now and then off the port, inactive enemy. On the 3rd of January, 14 sail of the line, four frigates, and several corvettes, under Rear-admirals Lhermite, Baudin, Violette, and Duperre, weighed from Toulon road, sailed out, and sailed in. Once or twice also during the month of May, this manœuvre was repeated, under Vice-admiral Emeriau himself; but the French admiral took care to sail out only when the wind was quite in his favour, and Sir Edward Pellew, if in sight at all, at a great distance to leeward.

On one occasion, however, a few shot were exchanged, and a British frigate was rather critically circumstanced. On the 28th of May, at 7 h. 30 m. A.M., the 38-gun frigate Menelaus, Captain Sir Peter Parker, Bart., being on the look-out off Cape Sicie, discovered a French frigate and brig in Hyères bay, standing under all sail, with the wind at east-south-east, for the Petite-Passe. The Menelaus immediately made sail to cut off the two vessels from entering Toulon; whereupon the latter, which were the 40-gun frigate Pauline and 16-gun brig Ecureuil, from the Adriatic, shortened sail to the topsails, and hauled upon a wind, to wait for the protection of their fleet, which had just then weighed from the road, to the number of 11 sail of the line and six frigates. As soon as they observed that the fleet was sufficiently advanced to cover them, the Pauline and Ecureuil bore up and steered for Toulon. The Menelaus, nevertheless, boldly stood on; and at 9 h. 30 m. A.M., when close under Pointe Ecampebarion, the batteries of which had already opened upon her, commenced firing at the French frigate and brig, within musket-shot distance. In less than half an hour a shot from one of the batteries cut the foretopmast of the Menelaus almost in two, and obliged her to wear and stand out. By this time the two advanced line-of-battle ships of the French fleet were nearly in the wake of the British frigate, and the British inshore squadron of four sail of the line, consisting of the Repulse, Centaur, Malta, and Kent, under Rear-admiral Hallowell, was hull-down to leeward. But, by extraordinary good management, notwithstanding that her foretopmast was only held together by fishes of capstan bars, and that her rigging and sails were greatly damaged, the Menelaus got clear off without losing a man.

On the 15th of August the 74-gun ship Ville-de-Marseille, and on the 6th of December the 130-gun ship Montebello, were launched at Toulon; thus making the French force in the port 18 sail of the line, including five three-deckers. At Genoa there was the new 74-gun ship Agamemnon; besides the 40-gun frigates Galatée, launched May 3, and Driade, launched October 7; and at Naples, the Capri 74. There were, also, at these two ports and at Spezzia, three or four sail of the line on the stocks.

Venice was now becoming an important naval dépôt. On the 6th of September, 1810, a fine 74-gun ship, the Rivoli, was launched at the arsenal at Malamacca, about five miles distant from the city, and was floated over the bar that crosses the passage at about midway, by means of a camel, or water-tight box, the same as is used at Amsterdam and St. Petersburg. This ship put to sea, for the first time, in February of the present year; but it was only, as we shall presently show, to fall into the hands of a British ship of the same force. In the latter end of 1811 or beginning of 1812 two other 74s were launched at Malamacca; the Mont-St.-Bernardo and Regenitore. The first was commissioned under French colours, and in July bore the flag of Rear-admiral Duperré; the other under Venetian colours, and was commanded by Captain Paschaligo, the gallant captain of the Corona in the action off Lissa. On the 2nd of August the Castiglioni 74 was launched, and, as soon as she could be fitted, was commissioned by the late captain of the Danaé, whose frigate had recently been burnt by accident in the port of Venice. The Castiglioni afterwards received the flag of Rear-admiral Duperré. On the 15th the Reali-Italiani 74, and Piane frigate were launched; but the 74 was only completed as high up as her main deck. There were eight other two-deckers on the stocks, two of which were in a forward state; but a scarcity of timber, owing to the poverty of the local government, greatly retarded the progress of the workmen.

Light Squadrons and Single Ships.

On the 27th of March, at 8 h. 30 m. A.M., the town of Dieppe bearing south-west distant four or five miles, the British brig-sloop Rosario, of eight 18-pounder carronades and two long sixes, Captain Bootey Harvey, observed a flotilla of 12 brigs and one lugger standing alongshore. This was the 14th division of the Boulogne flotilla, commanded by Capitaine de vaisseau Louis-Pierre-François-Ricard-Barthelemi Saizieu. Each brig mounted three long 24-pounders and an 8-inch brass howitzer, with a complement of 50 men. The commodore had sailed from Boulogne at 10 P.M. on the 26th, and was bound to Cherbourg. As the Rosario made sail to cut off the leewardmost of these 12 brigs, the whole, by signal from the commodore, formed in line, and severally engaged the British brig while passing on the opposite tack; and when the Rosario luffed up to cut off the sternmost brig, the remaining 11 and the lugger bore down to support their friend and close with the daring enemy.

Finding them thus determined to support each other, and the Rosario's small force not justifying the risk of being laid on board by several such opponents at once, Captain Harvey, with the signal flying for an enemy, bore up to a brig which he then observed in the offing. The moment the latter, which was the brig-sloop Griffon, of fourteen 24-pounder carronades and two sixes, Captain George Trollope, answered the signal, the Rosario again hauled to the wind, and at 40 minutes past noon recommenced harassing the rear of the flotilla, then endeavouring, under all sail, to get into Dieppe. The Rosario tacked and wore occasionally, in order to close, receiving each time the fire of the whole line. At 1 h. 30 m. P.M., being far enough to windward, the Rosario most gallantly ran into the body of the French flotilla, and, by cutting away the running rigging of the two nearest brigs, drove them on board of each other: she then, backing her maintopsail, engaged them within musket-shot, until they were clear, and afterwards stood on and engaged a third brig; who, losing her mainmast and foretopmast by the board, dropped her anchor. Passing her, the Rosario drove the next brig in line on shore. Two more brigs of the flotilla yet remained to leeward. Bearing up for these, the Rosario, at that time not more than three-quarters of a mile from the shore, ran the nearest brig on board, and quickly carried her.

So far the Rosario had acted alone, the Griffon, with all her exertions, not having yet arrived within gun-shot. While, however, the Rosario was bearing away with her prize, clear of the batteries, Captain Harvey passed and hailed his friend, directing him to chase the remaining brig of the two which the Rosario had last attacked with so much success. The Griffon immediately proceeded on the service, and drove the French brig on shore near St. Aubin, under a very heavy fire from the batteries. Seeing no probability of the Griffon's being able to destroy the brig, Captain Harvey, who was occupied in removing his prisoners and repairing the running-rigging of the Rosario, signalled the Griffon to attack the remaining nine brigs of the flotilla in the south-east, then anchoring close in-shore. In obedience to this signal, the Griffon ran in-shore of one of the brigs at anchor near the centre, and, in the most gallant manner, boarded and carried her. Captain Trollope then cut the cables of his prize, and stood out with her, in the face of a heavy fire from the batteries, and from the remaining eight French brigs.

Finding as the Griffon passed him, that she was too much disabled in her rigging immediately to renew the attack, yet determined, although his prisoners already equalled his sloop's company, to have another of the brigs, Captain Harvey ran on board the brig which the Rosario, by her fire, had previously dismasted; and which, unknown to him at the time, on account of the darkness of the evening, had just been abandoned by her crew. While, with their three prizes, the Rosario and Griffon stood out to the offing, leaving two other brigs on shore, the French commodore, with the seven remaining brigs of his flotilla, got under way and entered Dieppe. In this truly gallant exploit, no other loss appears to have been sustained on the British side than one midshipman, Jonathan Widdicomb Dyer, who conducted himself most nobly, and four men wounded, on board the Rosario. It is pleasant to be able to state, that merit met its reward: Captain Harvey was made post, and Mr. Dyer a lieutenant, on the same day, the 31st of March.

On the 3rd of May, in the afternoon, receiving a telegraphic communication from the 18-gun brig-sloop Castilian, Captain David Braimer, at Dungeness, that the 16-gun brig-sloop Skylark, Captain James Boxer, and 14-gun brig-sloop Apelles, Captain Frederick Hoffman, were on shore to the westward of Boulogne, Captain Alexander Cunningham, of the 10-gun brig-sloop Bermuda, accompanied by the Rinaldo of the same force, Captain Sir William George Parker, got under way and hastened towards the French coast, in the hope to be able to render assistance to the two brigs, particularly the Apelles, whose fate was more uncertain than that of her consorts.

On the 4th, at daybreak, the Rinaldo discovered and chased the Apelles, which had just been got afloat by the French, from a spot about five miles to the eastward of Etaples, and was now steering alongshore under jury-sails. At 9 A.M. the Bermuda and Rinaldo closed with the brig, and, after a few broadsides, drove her on shore under a battery about two miles nearer to Etaples. As the tide was falling, Captain Cunningham discontinued the attack, in consequence of the advantage which the French would have in placing their field-pieces and small-arm men close to the Apelles at low-water mark. Before the tide served to renew the attack, Captain Cunningham was joined by the Castilian, also by the 14-gun brig-sloop Phipps, Captain Thomas Wells.

At 2 h. 30 m. P.M. the Bermuda, followed in line of battle by the other brigs, stood in close under the battery; each sloop, as she got abreast of the Apelles, pouring in her broadside. By these vigorous means, the French troops who were on board the Apelles were driven out of her. The boats of the squadron, as had been previously arranged, under the orders of Lieutenant Thomas Saunders, first of the Bermuda, then pushed for, and, covered by the fire of the sloops, boarded the grounded brig; and, although for a considerable time exposed to a galling fire of shot and shells from the battery and from a collection of field-pieces on the beach, Lieutenant Saunders and his party, by 4 P.M., succeeded in getting the Apelles afloat and restoring her to the service. Notwithstanding the unremitting fire kept up from the shore, not a man either in the brigs or in the boats was hurt on the occasion.

Four of the French soldiers, not having time to escape, were taken in the Apelles; as well as the whole of her late crew, except Captain Hoffman and 19 men. The officers and crew of the Skylark, after having set their vessel on fire, also arrived in safety on board the little squadron. For his zeal and promptitude in executing this service, Captain Cunningham was shortly afterwards promoted to post-rank.

On the 9th of January the two French 40-gun frigates Arienne and Andromaque, and 16-gun brig-corvette Mamelouck, under the orders of Commodore Martin Le Foretier, sailed from Nantes upon a cruise. On the 15th, at noon, in latitude 44° 10′ north, longitude 14° 14′ west, they fell in with the British 24-pounder 40-gun frigate Endymion, Captain Sir William Bolton. In about an hour afterwards the latter, who was to leeward, exchanged numbers with the 50-gun ship Leopard, Captain William Henry Dillon, having under her protection a convoy from Lisbon. At 2 P.M. the Endymion, one of the fastest sailing ships in the British navy, tacked after the two French frigates and brig, and at 4 P.M. was joined in the chase by the Leopard; who had previously signalled her convoy to make the best of their way into port. At 4 h. 30 m. P.M. the French vessels were observed to be under easy sail, as if in no dread of being overtaken. At 5 P.M. the Endymion ran the Leopard out of sight, and at 8 P.M. the French squadron ran her out of sight.

Having thus effected their escape, the French frigates very soon commenced their depredations upon commerce; plundering and destroying, not only English merchant-vessels, but those of Spain, Portugal, and the United States of America. Intelligence of all this reaching the board of admiralty, the commander-in-chief of the Channel fleet, Admiral Lord Keith, then resident at Plymouth, was directed to order the officer in command off the port of Brest, to detach a force to endeavour to intercept these French frigates on their return to France.

The vessel, which Rear-admiral Sir Harry Neale selected to cruise off the port of Lorient for the purpose in view, was the 74-gun ship Northumberland, Captain the Hon. Henry Hotham; and certainly an officer possessed of more zeal, ability, and local as well as general experience, could not have been chosen. On the 19th of May the Northumberland parted company from the Boyne and squadron off Ushant, and made sail for her destination. On the 22nd, at 10 A.M., the north-west point of Isle Groix bearing north distant 10 miles, and the wind a very light breeze from west by north, the Northumberland discovered the three objects of her search in the north-west, crowding all sail before the wind for Lorient. Captain Hotham endeavoured to cut off the French squadron to windward of the island, and signalled the British 12-gun brig Growler, Lieutenant John Weeks, then about seven miles in the south-west, to chase; but, finding it impossible to accomplish that object, the Northumberland pushed, under all sail, round the south-east end of Groix, and, hauling to the wind close to leeward of the island, was enabled to fetch to windward of the harbour of Lorient before the French squadron could reach it.

Seeing himself thus cut off from his port, M. Le Foretier, at 2 h. 30 m. P.M., signalled his consorts to pass within hail, and then hauled up on the larboard tack to windward of Pointe Talcet. Meanwhile the Northumberland, eager to close, continued beating to windward between Groix and the continent,

1812.]   DESTRUCTION OF THE ARIENNE AND ANDROMAQUE.   321

exposed to the batteries on each side, when unavoidably standing within their reach. At 2 h. 49 m. P.M., the wind considerably fresher that it had been, and blowing about west-north-west, the Arienne, Andromaque, and Mamelouck, formed in close line ahead, bore up, under every sail, with the bold intention, favoured by the wind and covered by the numerous batteries along that part of the coast, to pass between the Northumberland and the shore.

The British 74 immediately stood in as close as she could to Pointe de Pierre-Laye, and there, with her head to the shore and maintopsail shivering, took her station, ready to meet the frigates; but these hauled so very close round the point, following the direction of the coast to the eastward of it, that Captain Hotham, being ignorant of the depth of water so near the shore, did not think it practicable, consistent with the safety of the Northumberland, whose draught of water was nearly 25 feet, to lay the leading frigate aboard, as had been his intention. The Northumberland therefore bore up, and, steering parallel to the French squadron, at the distance of about 400 yards, opened her broadside; receiving in return, as well from the two frigates as from three batteries on the coast, a very animated and well-directed fire.

Captain Hotham's object now being to prevent the French frigates from hauling outside the dry rock Graul, the Northumberland had not only to steer sufficiently near to that rock, to leave her opponents no room to pass between it and her, but to avoid running on it herself: a most difficult and anxious duty, the clouds of smoke, as they drifted ahead of the ship, totally obscuring the rock from view. However, by the care and attention of Mr. Hugh Stewart, the master, of the Northumberland passed the rock, within the distance of her own length, on the south-west side, in a quarter less than seven fathoms water; and the two French frigates and brig, as their only alternative, were obliged to steer inside of it. Here there was not water enough to float them; and at 3 h. 45 m. P.M. the two frigates, and in five minutes afterwards the brig, grounded, under every sail, upon the ridge of rocks extending from the Graul to the shore.

The Arienne lay nearest to the main land; the Mamelouck in a transverse direction upon that frigate's starboard bow, and the Andromaque ahead of, and considerably without, both her consorts. Having, in the course of a 21 minutes' cannonade, had her sails and rigging considerably damaged, the Northumberland now left the two frigates and brig to the effects of the falling tide, it being then one-quarter ebb, and hauled off to repair her rigging and shift her foretopsail, which had been rendered entirely useless.

At 4 h. 22 m. P.M., having repaired her principal damages, the Northumberland tacked, and began working up, against a fresh west-north-west wind, to engage the enemy again, and avoid falling to leeward of the Graul. At 4 h. 48 m. the Mamelouck cut away her mainmasts by the board; and just then the Growler was seen rounding the south-east end of Groix under a press of sail. At 5 P.M. the Growler joined, and opened an occasional fire upon the grounded vessels, all of which had by this time fallen over upon the larboard side, or that nearest the shore. At 5 h. 23 m. P.M. the mainmast of the Arienne went by the board. At 5 h. 28 m. P.M. the Northumberland anchored in six and a half fathoms water, Pointe de Pierre-Laye bearing north-west half-north, the citadel of Port Louis north-west three-quarters north, and the Graul rock north half-east 400 yards distant; having, by means of a spring, brought her broadside to bear, at point-blank range, upon the two French frigates and brig, lying in the position already described, with her copper exposed to view.

At 5 h. 34 m. P.M. the Northumberland opened her starboard broadside, receiving in return a fire from three or four guns of the Andromaque, and a heavy fire from three batteries on the main; but of which batteries one only, in the judicious station Captain Hotham had chosen, was able to reach the ship. At 5 h. 55 m. the Andromaque caught fire in the fore top. At 6 P.M. the flames were spreading fast: her foretopmast then fell, and several boats began pulling from the ship to the shore. At 6 h. 45 m. the main and mizen masts of the Andromaque went by the board. Having kept up a deliberate and careful fire until 6 h. 49 m. P.M., which was near the time of low water, and observing the visible effects of it to be, that the crews had quitted their vessels, that the bottoms of the latter were pierced through with shot so low down as to insure their filling on the rising tide, and that the hull of the Andromaque was already in flames. the Northumberland got under way, and stood out of gun-shot of the nearest battery.

The fire from this single battery had done the Northumberland as much injury in the hull, as all the fire to which, in running along the coast engaging the ships and batteries, she had previously been exposed. Her loss, in consequence, amounted to four seamen and one marine killed, one lieutenant (William Fletcher), three petty officers, 19 seamen, and five marines wounded; of whom four were wounded dangerously and 10 severely. The Growler, who, when the Northumberland ceased firing, had stood in and opened her fire upon the Arienne and Mamelouck, to prevent their crews from returning on board, suffered neither damage nor loss.

At about 8 p.m. the Andromaque blew up, with an awful explosion, leaving no remains of her visible. At 8 h. 10 m. p.m. the Northumberland anchored out of reach of the batteries on both sides, although a battery on the isle of Groix continued throwing shells. At about 9 p.m. a seaman belonging to a Portuguese vessel, which had been taken by the French squadron, having jumped overboard from the Andromaque just before she blew up, swam on board the Northumberland. At 10 p.m. the Arienne was seen to be on fire; and at 11 h. 30 m. p.m. the flames burst forth from the ports and other parts of the hull with unextinguishable fury. The Mamelouck was at this time on her beam ends, with her bottom completely riddled. Nothing further remaining to be done, the Northumberland, at about 30 minutes past midnight, got under way, with a light air from the northward, and accompanied by the Growler, stood out to sea. Being retarded in her progress by the calm state of the weather, the Northumberland, at 2 h. 30 m. a.m. on the 23rd, witnessed the explosion of the Arienne; and, before the day was over, a third fire and explosion announced that the Mamelouck had ended her career in a similar manner.

A fine French two-decker, with sails bent and topgallant-yards across, in the harbour of Lorient, lay a mortified spectator of this gallant achievement, by which two French 40-gun frigates and a 16-gun brig were driven on shore and destroyed, under the fire of at least one heavy French battery, by a British 74 and gun-brig. Mortified, indeed; for, in the state of the wind, the commanding officer of the port could do no more than send boats to assist in removing the crews of the wrecks. With upwards of 900 men, including soldiers, on board, what was to hinder these two frigates and brig, when all hopes of escape by running had vanished, from boarding a ship, having a crew of about 600 men? Even had the attempt failed, it is not probable that more than one frigate would have been captured: the other, in the confusion, with the brig, might have reached Lorient; and certainly the loss of men would not have been by any means so great as was sustained by the grounded vessels, both from the fire of the Northumberland and Growler, and from the hurried endeavours of the panic-struck to reach the shore.

The two French frigates and brig, thus effectually destroyed, had themselves destroyed 36 vessels of different nations, and had taken the most valuable part of their cargoes on board. The frigates, in consequence, were very deep; but, had they drawn no more than their usual water, they still could not have passed clear, as it is evident from the brig grounding so close to them. We are happy to be able to state, that Lieutenant Weeks of the Growler, and Lieutenant John Banks, first of the Northumberland, were each promoted to the rank of commander for the part they had performed in Captain Hotham's exploit.

On the 3rd of July, in the afternoon, the British 16-gun brig-sloop Raven, Captain George Gustavus Lennock, while hauling over the Droograan, observed 14 brigs, of the French flotilla out of the Scheldt, exercised to leeward of the Weiling. Thinking it practicable to cut off some of them, Captain Lennock stood into the Weiling, and at 6 h. 15 m. P.M. began firing occasionally at the flotilla in passing. The wind blowing strong on the shore, the superior sailing and working of the Raven enabled her to overtake seven of the brigs; four of which she compelled to anchor close to the surf under the batteries. The remaining three the Raven drove on shore; and at daylight the next morning they were still lying on the beach, apparently bilged, with the sea beating over them. Only one shot struck the Raven, and that did not hurt any one. This dashing little service was performed in sight of the French fleet lying at Flushing; and it must have greatly mortified the French admiral and his captains to see 14 of his brigs, armed each with three or four long 24-pounders, unable, or rather unwilling, to prevent three of their number from being driven on shore by a single British brig, mounting fourteen 24-pounder carronades.

On the 21st of July, as the British schooner Sealark, of ten 12-pounder carronades and 60 men and boys, Lieutenant Thomas Warrand, was cruising off the Start, a signal was made from the shore of an enemy in the south-east quarter. The Sealark immediately made all sail in the direction pointed out, and after a three hours' run discovered a large lugger, under English colours, chasing and firing at two ships, apparently West-Indiamen, standing up Channel. As soon as the lugger, which was the Ville-de-Caen, of St. Maloes, mounting 16 long 4 or 6 pounders, with a crew of 75 men, commanded by M. Cochet, discovered that the schooner approaching her was a cruiser, she quitted the merchantmen and altered her course to starboard, under all possible sail. Finding the Sealark gaining on her, the lugger shortened sail, and wore repeatedly to get to windward of the schooner.

Fearing the lugger might succeed and thereby effect her escape, Lieutenant Warrand gallantly ran the Ville-de-Caen on board, between her fore and main chains. A close and furious engagement now commenced, both with great guns and musketry, the privateer's men using a profusion of hand-grenades to set the schooner on fire: instead of which, however, the lugger set herself on fire. Seeing this, Mr. James Beaver, the Sealark's acting-master, at the head of a few men, sprang on board, and almost instantly carried the Ville-de-Caen, after an action nearly the whole time sides touching, of one hour and 30 minutes.

The Sealark had her captain's clerk (John Purnel), five seamen, and one marine killed, her commander, one midshipman (Alexander Gunn), 17 seamen, and three marines wounded: a very serious loss, it must be owned, especially as several of the wounds were dangerous. The loss on the part of the Ville-de-Caen amounted to her captain and 14 men found dead on her deck, and 16 wounded, most of them severely. The gallantry of this little action obtained for the Sealark's commander that reward, the prospect of which is a never-failing stimulant to deeds of valour, promotion. The case of Captain Palmer of the Alacrity[1] may seem to militate against this principle; but, if we are rightly informed, and we see no reason to doubt our authority, he had his post-captain's appointment in his pocket when he began the action with the Abeille.

On the 6th of July, in the evening, as the British 64-gun ship Dictator, Captain James Patterson Stewart, accompanied by the brig-sloops Calypso, 18, Captain Henry Weir, and Podargus, 14, Captain William Robilliard, and gun-brig Flamer, Lieutenant Thomas England, was off Mardoe on the Norway coast, the mast-heads of several vessels were seen over the rocks, known to be a Danish squadron, consisting of the new 40-gun frigate Nayaden, carrying 24-pounders on the main deck, and 48 guns in all, and the 18-gun brigs Laaland, Samsoe, and Kiel. Having a man on board the Podargus acquainted with the place, Captain Robilliard volunteered to lead in after the enemy; but the Podargus unfortunately took the ground, just as she had

[1] See p. 251.

entered the passage. Leaving the Flamer to attend her, Captain Stewart stood on with the 64 and the remaining brig. By 7 h. 30 m. P.M. the two vessels, the Calypso leading, had arrived within a mile of the Danish frigate and her consorts, then running under a press of sail, inside the rocks. Shortly afterwards the engagement began between the Danish squadron and several gun-boats on one side, and the Dictator and Calypso, which latter, having grounded for a short time, was now astern of her consort, on the other. At 9 h. 30 m. P.M., after having run 12 miles through a passage, in some places scarcely wide enough to admit the Dictator's studding-sail booms to be out, Captain Stewart had the satisfaction to run his ship with her bow upon the shore, and her broadside bearing, within hailing distance, upon the Danish frigate and three brigs, all of whom had anchored close together, with springs on their cables, in the small creek of Lyngoe.

The Calypso closely followed the Dictator; and such was the well-directed fire opened from the two British vessels, especially from the 64, that the Nayaden, according to the British official account, was "literally battered to atoms," the three brigs compelled to haul down their colours, and such of the gun-boats as were not sunk to seek their safety in flight. Scarcely had the action ended, and the Dictator got afloat, than the gun-boats rallied; but the latter were so warmly attacked by the Calypso, that they soon ceased their annoyance. Meanwhile the Podargus and Flamer, which latter had also grounded, were warmly engaged with the shore-batteries and another division of gun-boats. At length, by the indefatigable exertions of their respective officers and crews, both the Podargus and Flamer got afloat, very much cut up. At 3 A.M. on the 7th the Dictator, Calypso, and the two prize-brigs, the Laaland, commanded by Lieutenant James Wilkie of the Dictator, and the Kiel, by Lieutenant Benjamin Hooper of the Calypso, in attempting to get through the passages, were assailed by a division of gun-boats from behind the rocks, so situated that not a gun could be brought to bear upon them from either vessel. In this attack, both prize-brigs, already complete wrecks, grounded; and, notwithstanding every exertion on the part of the lieutenants and men placed in them, they were obliged to be abandoned: that, too, without being set on fire, owing to the wounded men of their crews remaining on board.

In this very bold and well-conducted enterprise, the British sustained a loss as follows: Dictator, three seamen, one marine, and one boy killed, one midshipman (John Sackett Hooper), one captain's clerk (Thomas Farmer), 16 seamen, two boys, and four marines wounded; Podargus, her purser (George Garratt), one first-class volunteer (Thomas Robilliard), and six seamen and one marine wounded; Calypso, one seaman and two marines killed, one seaman wounded, and two missing; and Flamer, one seaman killed, and one midshipman (James Powell) wounded; total, nine killed, 35 wounded, and two missing. The Danes acknowledged a loss, in killed and wounded together, of 300 officers and men. For their gallant conduct on this occasion, Captain Weir was immediately, and Captain Robilliard in the ensuing December, promoted to post-rank, and the Dictator's first-lieutenant, William Buchanan, was made a commander.

On the 19th of June the British 10-gun brig-sloop Briseis, Captain John Ross, by the orders of Rear-admiral Thomas Byam Martin, stood into Pillau roads in the Baltic, to communicate with the British merchant-ship Urania, and found that she was in possession of the French troops, and that they intended to destroy her if the Briseis approached. Captain Ross accordingly tacked and stood off, and at midnight detached the pinnace, under the command of Lieutenant Thomas Jones, the 2nd, with midshipman William Palmer and 18 men, to endeavour to recapture the ship.

The instant she got within gun-shot of the ship, the pinnace was fired at by the French on board, who had six carriage-guns and four swivels mounted. But every obstacle was overcome by the gallantry of Lieutenant Jones and his small party; who gave three cheers, boarded over the small-craft that were alongside, and drove the French troops off the decks into their boats which were on the opposite side. The cable was then cut, and the Urania was brought out, together with a French scout that had been employed in unlading her. In executing this dashing service, the British had one seaman killed, and Mr. Palmer and one seaman slightly wounded.

On the 16th of July Captain Timothy Clinch, of the 18-gun ship-sloop Osprey, cruising in company with the 10-gun brig-sloops Britomart and Leveret, Captains William Buckly Hunt and George Wickens Willes, detached a boat from each, under the respective commands of Lieutenants William Henry Dixon of the Britomart, William Malone (2) of the Osprey, and Francis Darby Romney of the Leveret, in chase of a French lugger privateer about nine leagues to the north-west of the island of Heligoland.

At 1 h. 30 m. P.M., when the three boats were about five leagues off, the lugger came to an anchor; but, shortly afterwards, on perceiving the boats, she got under way and made sail. Lieutenant Dixon then cheered the boats, and sailed on until 3 h. 30 m. P.M.; when the Britomart's boat, being ahead, opened her fire, at about musket-shot distance, and received from the lugger, after she had hoisted French colours, a fire in return which wounded one man. The Osprey's boat then closed: but Lieutenant Dixon considered the lugger too powerful to be attempted without the aid of the Leveret's boat, then about half a mile distant. As soon as the latter came abreast of the two remaining boats, it was arranged that the Britomart's boat should attack the larboard, the Leveret's the starboard side, and the Osprey's the stern, of the French lugger.

The British then cheered and prepared for boarding. At this moment the oars of the Leveret's boat got foul of the Britomart's boat, and occasioned the former to drop astern. Lieutenants Dixon and Malone now grappled the lugger's stern, and, after a 10 minutes' obstinate struggle, made good their boarding. But it was not until after a 10 minutes' further resistance on the lugger's deck, that her colours were hauled down. Even then the French crew continued firing pistols up the hatchway, and wounded one or two of the British. These at length silenced the enemy's fire, and hoisted the English ensign. The lugger proved to be the Eole, of Dunkerque, pierced for 14 guns, but having only six mounted, with a crew on board of 31 officers and men. In this very spirited enterprise the British sustained a loss, in the two boats that made the attack, of two seamen killed, Lieutenant Dixon (slightly) and 11 men wounded.

On the 1st of August, as the British 38-gun frigate Horatio, Captain Lord George Stuart, was in latitude 70° 40' north, running down the coast of Norway, a small sail was seen from the mast-head close in with the land; and which, just before she disappeared among the rocks, was discovered to be an armed cutter. Considering it an object of some importance to attempt the destruction of the enemy's cruisers in this quarter, Lord George despatched the barge and three cutters of the Horatio, with about 80 officers and men, commanded by Lieutenant Abraham Mills Hawkins, assisted by Lieutenant Thomas James Poole Masters, and Lieutenant of marines George Syder, to execute the service. Gaining information on shore, that the cutter had gone to a village on an arm of the sea about 35 miles distant over land, Lieutenant Hawkins detached one of the cutters, under master's mate James Crisp, to disperse some small-arm men collected on the shore, and, with the remaining three boats, proceeded for the creek in which the Danish cutter lay.

On the 2nd, at 8 A.M., Lieutenant Hawkins discovered the vessel, which was the Danish cutter No. 97, of four 6-pounders and 22 men, lying at anchor in company with the Danish schooner No. 114, of six 6-pounders and 30 men, commanded by Lieutenant Buderhorf of the Danish navy, the commodore, and an American ship of 400 tons their prize. On the approach of the British boats, the Danish vessels presented their broadsides with springs on their cables, and were moored in a capital defensive position. The British, nevertheless, advanced to the attack, and at 9 A.M. received the fire of the Danes; whom, however, Lieutenant Hawkins and his party, assisted towards the end by Mr. Crisp's boat, completely subdued, after a most sanguinary combat.

The British lost in this affair Lieutenant Syder, seven seamen, and one marine killed, Lieutenants Hawkins and Masters, assistant surgeon James Larans (mortally), the boatswain (William Hughes), one midshipman (Thomas Fowler, severely), nine seamen (one mortally), and two marines wounded; total, nine killed and 16 wounded. The loss on the Danish side was also very severe; amounting to 10 killed and 13 wounded, including the commander of the schooner and the cutter severely, and some other officers. Both the British and the Danes fought in the bravest manner, and between them sustained a loss, for which their prizes were a poor compensation. As a reward for his gallantry, Lieutenant Hawkins was made a commander in the ensuing December.

On the 4th of July, at 6 P.M., Calais cliff bearing south by east distant four miles, the British gun-brig Attack, Lieutenant Richard William Simmonds, observed a transport-galliot, a sloop, and a privateer come out of Calais harbour and endeavour to run alongshore. Knowing that the least manifestation of a pursuit would induce the vessels to put back or run themselves on shore, Lieutenant Simmonds made sail to windward, in the hope to decoy the vessels far enough from the French coast to enable him to cut them off. Having proceeded to a sufficient distance, the Attack detached the gig, with six men, commanded by Mr. Couney, the second master.

At midnight, when within half gun-shot of the French shore, the gig discovered the galliot in tow of the privateer. Undaunted by the inequality of force, and regardless of a galling fire of musketry, Mr. Councy boarded the transport on one side, as a detachment from the privateer did on the other; but, as soon as Mr. Couney had killed one of their men, the Frenchmen retreated to their vessel and sheered off, leaving the seven British in possession of the prize. The situation of Mr. Couney and his six men was extremely critical even after he had recaptured the galliot; for, independent of the fire of the privateer's musketry, the vessel was exposed to a continued fire of round and grape from the French batteries; nor could the Attack, on account of the calm state of the weather, approach to co-operate with her gig's crew in this very gallant little exploit. Fortunately neither Mr. Couney, nor one of his six men, was hurt on the occasion.

On the 16th of August, at 11 p.m., Foreness in the Cattegat bearing west-north-west distant six or seven miles, the Attack observed two vessels approaching supposed to be gun-vessels. The brig immediately cleared for action, and in about 20 minutes, when nearly becalmed, was attacked by a division of Danish gun-boats, supposed, in the darkness that prevailed, to be 10 or 12 in number. The engagement continued until 1 h. 40 m. A.M. on the 19th, when the gun-boats ceased firing. A light breeze springing up, the Attack set all sail and got out her sweeps, in the hope to be able to join the Wrangler gun-brig, Lieutenant John Campbell Crawford, whom another division of gun-boats had also been attacking. But, owing to a strong south-east current and a total cessation of the breeze, Lieutenant Simmons could not succeed. Shortly afterwards the Wrangler entirely disappeared.

The Attack had already had her main-boom shot away, her foremast and bowsprit badly wounded, two guns dismounted, a great number of shot-holes between wind and water, and her sails and rigging cut to pieces. At 2 h. 10 m. A.M., while the British gun-brig, with only 49 men on board, was employed in refitting herself, 14 Danish gun-vessels, each armed with two long 24-pounders and two howitzers, and with from 65 to 70 men, besides four large row-boats carrying swivels and howitzers, formed in a crescent, within pistol-shot, upon her larboard beam, bow and quarter, and commenced a heavy fire of round, grape, and grenades. The Attack immediately returned the fire, and continued defending herself until 3 h. 20 m. A.M.; when, being a complete wreck, and in a sinking state, the British brig hauled down her colours, with two seamen killed, and 12 wounded. The

Danes were honourable enough to pay a high compliment to Lieutenant Simmonds for his gallant defence of the Attack; and at the court-martial subsequently held upon him and his officers for the loss of their brig, the most honourable acquittal was pronounced.

On the 4th of June, in the night, Captain the Honourable Duncombe Pleydell Bouverie, of the 18-pounder 32-gun frigate Medusa, sent the boats of the frigate, under the orders of Lieutenant Josiah Thompson, to cut out the French storeship Dorade, of 14 guns and 86 men, commanded by a lieutenant de vaisseau, lying at an anchor in the harbour of Arcasson. In spite of the rapidity of the tide and the intricacy of the navigation, and although discovered and hailed before they arrived within musket-shot, the boats succeeded in getting alongside the ship. The Frenchmen were found at their quarters, and perfectly prepared to defend their vessel; but nothing could resist the impetuosity of Lieutenant Thompson and his men, who rushed on board and carried the Dorade after a desperate struggle in which the whole of her crew, except 23 men, were either killed or compelled to jump overboard: among the latter was the French commander, severely wounded.

The ship had on board a full cargo of ship-timber, and had been since April 1811, watching an opportunity to escape. At daylight on the 5th the prize was got under way; but, after proceeding about a league down the harbour, the ship grounded on a sandbank. As the tide was then running out with great violence, Lieutenant Thompson was obliged, after taking out the wounded of her crew, to set the Dorade on fire; and the ship soon afterwards blew up. This done, the boats returned to the Medusa, having sustained, in performing their gallant exploit, no greater loss than five men wounded.

Here is another of the abstracted cases. How justly proud might every lieutenant, master's mate, and midshipman have been who assisted in capturing the Dorade; and yet not one is named except the officer who commanded the party. "Captain Bouverie," says the abstract, "highly commends the conduct of Lieutenant Thompson and the other officers and men employed on this occasion." To "the other officers," this recommendation could be of no avail, as they were not named; not at least in the Gazette, the only record preserved. And, even had they been named, what could they expect, when their commanding officer, he who so gallantly led them up the side of the enemy's ship, bears still the same rank he bore then?

The manner in which the British 74-gun ship Magnificent, Captain John Hayes, on the night of the 16th of December in the present year, was saved in a gale of wind on the coast of France is so extraordinary, and at the same time so creditable to the nautical skill and presence of mind of her captain, and to the expertness, alacrity, and good discipline of British seamen, that we shall be doing, not merely an act of justice to the officers and crew of the Magnificent, but a service to the whole profession, by giving all the publicity in our power to an account of the circumstance, which has already appeared in a popular periodical work devoted to naval subjects:—" The ship was anchored in the evening between the reef of Chasseron, and the reef of Isle de Ré, nearly mid-channel, in 16 fathoms water, in the entrance to Basque road; the courses reefed, and topgallant-yards down. At 8 o'clock, the weather appearing suspicious, and the wind beginning to blow, the topgallantmasts were got down on deck : at half-past, it came on squally, and the ship was veered to a cable and a half. At 9 she was found to be driving, and in only 11 fathoms water; the small bower was instantly let go, which brought her up in 10 fathoms. Yards and topmasts were immediately struck, as close down as they could be got. The moon was not to be seen, yet it was not a dark night : it just gave sufficient light to show us our dangerous situation; the sea breaking on the reef with great violence, about a quarter of a mile astern, and on the starboard quarter. As soon as the topmasts were down, orders were given to heave in upon the best bower, which appeared to be slack, as though the anchor had broken. Three-quarters of a cable were got in, when the stock appearing to catch a rock, it held fast: service of course was put in the wake of the hawse, and the cable secured. The inner cable of the best bower was unspliced, and bent to the spare anchor; and a leads-man was kept in the chains to heave the lead, the same as though the ship had been under way, in addition to the deep-sea lead, attended at the gangway by a quarter-master, when it was discovered by the man in the chains that there was a large rock under the ship's bottom, of three fathoms in height: in fact, the ground was covered with rocks, and the ship in the midst of them, with the wind at west-south-west blowing a gale, with small rain and a heavy sea In this state we remained, with people stationed with axes to the sheet and spare anchors, till daylight, when the man at the deep-sea lead declared the ship to be driving. The spare anchor was directly cut away, and the range taken out; when the ship brought up again, and when the ebb-tide made, she took the whole cable service, and rode with the best and small bowers ahead, and the spare anchor broad on the starboard bow. The gale appeared to increase; the sea was high; and, as it broke sometimes outside the ship, it proved she was in the midst of rocks, and that the cables could not remain long without being cut. The wind at this period was west, and St. Marie church bore east, and the distance where the ship would have gone to pieces, about one cable's length; the shoalest part of the reef about two cables, lying in a south-south-east and north-north-west direction. The wind now came to west by north; but to counteract this favourable change, it was a lee tide, and a heavy sea setting right on the reef, and neither officers nor men thought it possible, in any way, to cast her clear of the reef, and to make sail, more particularly as the yards and topmasts were down. The captain, however, gave orders to sway the fore-yard two-thirds up; and while that was doing, to get a hawser for a spring to cast the ship by from the starboard quarter to the spare cable; while this was doing, the spare cable parted, and we had only the sheet anchor at the bows; but, as she did not drive, that was not let go. The main-yard was now swayed outside the topmast, two-thirds up the same; as the fore-yard and the spring brought on the small bower cable, people were sent on the yards to stop each yard-arm of the topsails and courses with four or five spun-yarn stops, tied in a single bow, and to cast off and make up all the gaskets: the people were then called down, except one man to each stop, who received very particular orders to be quick in obeying the commands given them, and to be extremely cautious not to let a sail fall, unless that sail was particularly named: if particular attention were not paid to this order the ship would be lost. The yards were all braced sharp up for casting from the reef, and making sail on the starboard tack. The tacks and sheets, topsail sheets, and main and mizenstaysail-halyards were manned, and the spring brought to the capstan and hove in. The captain now told the people, that they were going to work for life or death; if they were attentive to his orders, and executed them properly, the ship would be saved: if not, the whole of them would be drowned in five minutes. Things being in this state of preparation, a little more of the spring was hove in; the quarter-masters at the wheel and bow received their instructions. The cables were ordered to be cut, which was instantly done; but the heavy sea on the larboard bow would not let her cast that way. The probability of this had happily been foreseen. The spring broke, and her head paid round in towards the reef. The oldest seaman in the ship at that moment thought all lost. The captain, however, gave his orders very distinctly to put the helm hard a-starboard, to sheet home the fore-topsail,[1] and haul on board the fore-tack, and aft fore-sheet, keep all the other sails fast, square the main and mizen topsail-yards, and cross-jack yard, keep the main-yard as it was. The moment the wind came abaft the beam, he ordered the mizentopsail to be sheeted home, and then the helm to be put hard a-port—when the wind came nearly aft—haul on board the main-tack, aft main-sheet, sheet home the maintopsail, and brace the cross-jack yard sharp up. When this was done (the whole of which took only two minutes to perform), the ship absolutely flew round from the reef, like a thing scared at the frightful spectacle. The quarter-master was ordered to keep her south, and the captain declared aloud, 'The ship is safe.' The gaff was down, to prevent its holding wind, and the try-sail was bent ready for hoisting, had it been wanted. The main and mizen staysails were also ready, but were not wanted. The foretopmast-staysail was hoisted before the cables were cut: thus was the ship got round in less than her own length; but, in that short distance, she altered the soundings five fathoms. And now, for the first time, I believe, was seen a ship at sea under reefed courses, and close reefed topsails, with yards and topmasts struck. The sails all stood remarkably well; and by this novel method, was saved a beautiful ship of the line, and 550 souls. I cannot find any man or officer who ever saw a ship in the state before; yet all seemed surprised that they should never before have thought of it. Indeed it has ever been the prevailing opinion (perhaps for want of giving the subject proper consideration), that a ship with yards and topmasts struck was completely disabled from making sail, except with staysails."[2]

The British squadron, stationed off the north coast of Spain, to co-operate with the loyal Spaniards and guerillas in expelling the French from their country, was commanded by Captain Sir Home Popham of the 74-gun ship Venerable; who had under his orders, among some other vessels whose names do not appear, the 38-gun frigates Surveillante and Rhin, Captains Sir George Ralph Collier and Charles Malcolm, 18-pounder

---

[1] The yards were all braced up for the starboard tack; consequently, when she cast the other way, the foresail and fore-topsail were set as flat a-back as they could be; and they were not altered in bringing her to her course; the way she was managed it was not necessary.

[2] See Naval Chronicle, vol. xxix., p. 21.

32-gun frigate Medusa, Captain the Honourable Duncombe Pleydell Bouverie, and 10-gun brig-sloop Lyra, Captain Robert Bloye.

In the middle of the month of June a small body of French troops held possession of a hill-fort at Lequertio, mounting three 18-pounders, and calculated to resist infantry, and another body, of about 200, was posted in a fortified convent within the town, the walls of which were impervious to anything less than an 18-pounder. The convent might have been destroyed by the ships; but as the town would have materially suffered, and as the guns of the Venerable made no visible impression on the fort, it was determined to erect a battery on a hill opposite to the latter, which the enemy considered as quite inaccessible to cannon and in that confidence rested his security.

Accordingly, on the forenoon of the 20th, a gun was landed, chiefly by the exertions of Lieutenant James Groves of the Venerable, notwithstanding the sea was breaking with such violence against the rocks at the foot of the hill, that it was doubtful whether a boat could get near enough for that purpose. The gun was then hove up a short distance by a moveable capstan; but this operation was so tedious, that it was at length dragged to the summit of the hill by 36 pair of bullocks, 400 guerillas, and 100 seamen headed by Captain Bouverie. The gun was immediately mounted; and at 4 P.M. fired its first shot. It was afterwards so admirably served, that at sunset a practicable breach was made in the wall of the fort, and the guerillas volunteered to storm it. The first party was repulsed, but the second party gained possession without any considerable loss: several of the French troops escaped on the opposite side and got into the convent. In the course of the evening, the sea abating a little, a landing was made on the island of San-Nicolas, although with some difficulty, by Lieutenant Dowell O'Reilly of the Surveillante; a detachment of marines from that frigate, the Medusa, and Rhin also landed, with a carronade from each ship. Captain Malcolm now took command of the island, and Captain Sir George Collier of the Venerable's battery on the hill. On the 21st, at daybreak, a 24-pounder was brought to the east side of the town within 200 yards of the convent, and another was in the act of being landed on San-Nicolas to bombard it in that direction, when the French commandant beat a parley and surrendered, with the remainder of his troops, amounting to 290.

The squadron afterwards proceeded along the coast to the

westward, and destroyed the batteries at Bermeo, Plencia, Algorta, Bagona, el Campillo las Queras, and Xebiles. On the 6th of July the Venerable arrived off Castro; and on the 7th the French were driven out of the town by the fire of the squadron. On the 8th a party landed and took possession of the castle of Castro. On the 10th the squadron proceeded off Puerta Galletta, to co-operate in an attack upon it with the Spanish troops under General Longa; but, the enemy being found stronger than the Spaniards had expected, the attack was abandoned. During the morning, Captain Bloye landed with a party of marines, and knocked the trunnions off the guns in the Bagona battery; he also destroyed one gun mounted on a height.

On the 18th, early in the morning, one 24-pounder under Lieutenant Groves, and a howitzer under Lieutenant Thomas Lewis Lawrence, of the marine artillery, were landed from the Venerable near Guetaria, and mounted on a hill to the westward of the town, under the directions of Captain Malcolm; while Captain Bouverie landed a medium 24-pounder and a 12-pounder carronade from the Medusa, and, after many difficulties, mounted these two guns on the top of a hill to the eastward. At noon the Venerable opened her fire and continued it until sunset; when the guns of the enemy opposed to those of the Venerable were silenced, and the Medusa's two guns were got in readiness to open the next morning. During the night, however, intelligence was received of the approach of between 2000 and 3000 French troops. In consequence of some delay on the part of the Spaniards, Captain Bouverie had to destroy his two guns: after which he and his party re-embarked. Captain Malcolm met with so much detention, that he was obliged to leave in the hands of the enemy a midshipman and 29 men.

On the 30th of July and on the 1st of August a combined attack was made on the town of Santander and the castle of Ano, by the detachment of marines serving on board the squadron, placed under the orders of Captain Willoughby Thomas Lake, of the 74-gun ship Magnificent, and Captain Sir George Collier, and acting in conjunction with the guerillas under General Pórlier. The castle was taken possession of by the marines; but, the garrison of Santander having received reinforcements which made it stronger than had been expected, General Porlier was unable to advance upon the place; and the marines, who had pushed on to co-operate in the attack, were obliged to fall back upon the castle, with some loss. Captains Lake and Sir George Collier were among the wounded; as was also Captain of marines Christopher Noble, who was taken prisoner. On the 3rd the French evacuated the town of Santander, and a detachment of marines from the British frigates in the harbour immediately took possession of it.

In the month of May the British force stationed off the coast of Grenada, to assist the Spanish patriots, consisted of the 20-gun ships Hyacinth and Termagant, Captains Thomas Ussher and Hamilton, and gun-brig Basilisk, Lieutenant George French. In consequence of the destruction, by the Hyacinth, on the 20th, of the castle at Nersa, the guerillas, on the 25th, came down from the mountains and entered the town; and Captains Ussher and Hamilton went on shore and waited upon the guerilla leader. By him they learnt that the French had retreated to Almunecar, a town about seven miles to the eastward; and that they had a force of about 300 men, against whom the guerillas meant immediately to march.

In order to co-operate effectually with them, Captain Ussher, at 4 P.M. on the 26th, bore up for Almunecar; and anchoring his two ships and brig within point-blank range, silenced the castle in less than an hour. The guerillas not advancing as was expected, Captain Hamilton, at 8 P.M., went in his gig back to Nersa, and returned at 4 A.M. on the 27th, with information that the guerillas were waiting for an expected reinforcement. At 7 A.M. the French troops, having during the night mounted a howitzer in a breach made by the ships in the covered way to the castle, re-opened their fire; but, by 10 A.M., the castle was again silenced, and the French were driven with great loss into the town, where they fortified themselves in the church and houses. Desirous of sparing the unfortunate inhabitants, Captain Ussher ceased firing; and at 2 P.M., after having destroyed a privateer, of two guns and 30 or 40 men, at anchor under the castle, weighed and ran down to Nersa, for the purpose of concerting plans with the guerillas.

Having arrived at Nersa, Captain Ussher embarked 200 guerilla infantry on board his little squadron, and stood back with them towards Almunecar, having directed his cavalry to hasten through the mountain. The delay occasioned by a calm acquainted the French troops with the combined movement; and, joining a corps of 200 men at Notril, the whole detachment retreated upon Grenada. On arriving at his anchorage before the castle, Captain Ussher detached Lieutenant Francis Brockell Spilsbury and a guerilla officer, with directions to hoist the respective flags on the castle, and then to demolish the works.

After considerable difficulty, owing to the strength of the works, the service was effectually executed.

On the 13th of February, at daybreak, the British 38-gun frigate Apollo, Captain Bridges Watkinson Taylor, while rounding Cape Corse, fell in with and chased the French frigate-built store-ship Mérinos ; pierced for 36, but mounting only 20 guns, long 8-pounders, with a crew of 126 men, commanded by Capitaine de frégate Honoré-Cyprien Courdouan, in company with a ship-corvette. After the Apollo had closed from to-leeward, and killed six and wounded 20 of the crew of the Mérinos, that ship hauled down her colours. Notwithstanding the signals for assistance made to her from the Mérinos, the corvette, with the help of boats from the island of Corsica, effected her escape. Although, in consequence of the calm state of the weather and her proximity to the shore, the Apollo was exposed, during four hours, to a fire from a battery on the cape and another on the islet of Giraglia, she did not have a man hurt.

On the 16th of February the British 74-gun ship Victorious, Captain John Talbot, accompanied by the 18-gun brig-sloop Weasel, Captain John William Andrew, arrived off Venice, to watch the motions of the new French 74-gun ship Rivoli,[1] Commodore Jean-Baptiste Barré, and two or three brigs-of-war, lying ready for sea in that port. Foggy weather made it the 21st, before Captain Talbot was enabled to reconnoitre the port. On that day, at 2 h. 30 m. P.M. the Victorious descried a brig in the east-north-east, and at 3 P.M., in the same direction, a large ship, with two more brigs, and two settees. The ship was the Rivoli herself; the three brigs were the Jéna and Mercure of 16, and the Mamelouck of eight guns; and the two settees were gun-boats ; all about 12 hours from Venice, bound to the port of Pola in Istria, and at this time steering in line of battle ; the two gun-boats and one brig ahead, then the Rivoli, and astern of her the two remaining brigs. The British 74 and brig were presently under all sail in chase, and soon began to gain upon the French squadron.

At 2 h. 30 m. A.M. on the 22nd, perceiving that one of the two brigs in the rear had dropped astern, and that the Rivoli had shortened sail to allow her to close, Captain Talbot hailed the Weasel, and directed Captain Andrew to pass the Victorious if possible, and bring the sternmost brig to action. Captain Andrew was so prompt in obeying the order, that at 4 h. 15 m. A.M. the Weasel overtook the Mercure, and engaged her within

---

[1] See p. 316.

half pistol-shot. After the action between these two brigs had lasted about 20 minutes, the brig that had been in company with the Mercure, the Jéna, shortened sail, and engaged the Weasel distantly on her bow. Thus opposed, the latter still continued a close and well-directed fire upon the Mercure until another 20 minutes had elapsed; at the end of which the French brig blew up. In an instant the Weasel lowered down her boats, but only succeeded in saving three men, and those much bruised. In the meanwhile, taking advantage of the darkness of the morning and the damaged state of the Weasel's rigging, the Jéna had made off, and soon disappeared. At daylight, however, the British brig regained a sight of both French brigs, one a short distance astern of the other; and, having by this time refitted herself, she crowded sail in pursuit, sweeping occasionally, owing to the lightness of the breeze; but the Jéna and Mamelouck outsailed the Weazel, and kept gradually increasing their distance.

At 4 h. 30 m. A.M., just a quarter of an hour after the Weasel had begun her engagement with the Mercure, the Victorious, having a light air of wind on her larboard-beam, arrived within half pistol-shot of, and opened her starboard guns upon, the Rivoli; who immediately returned the fire from her larboard broadside, and continued, with courses clewed up, but royals set, standing on towards the gulf of Triest. A furious engagement now ensued between these two line-of-battle ships, interrupted only when, for a few minutes together, the fog or the smoke hid them from each other's view. In the early part of the action, Captain Talbot received a contusion from a splinter, that nearly deprived him of his sight, and the command of the ship devolved upon Lieutenant Thomas Ladd Peake, who emulated his wounded chief in bravery and judgment. After the mutual cannonade had thus continued for three hours, and the Rivoli, from the superior fire of the Victorious, had become unmanageable and reduced to such a resistance as two quarter-deck guns only could offer, Lieutenant Peake, by signal, recalled the Weasel, to have the benefit of her assistance, in case either ship, the Victorious herself being in a disabled state, and both ships at this time in seven fathoms water off the point of Groa, should happen to get aground. Having bore up in obedience to the signal, the Weasel stood across the bows of the Rivoli; and, at 8 A.M., when within musket-shot distance, poured in her broadside. This the brig, wearing or tacking as necessary, repeated twice. Meanwhile the Victorious maintained a steady cannonade, and at 8 h. 45 m. A.M. shot away the Rivoli's mizenmast. In another quarter of an hour the French 74 fired a lee gun, and hailed the Victorious that she had struck. Point Legnian then bore from the latter north-north-west distant seven miles.

The Victorious had her rigging cut to pieces, gaff and spanker-boom shot away, her three topmasts and mainmast badly wounded, her boats all destroyed, except a small punt belonging to the ward-room officers, and her hull struck in several places. Out of her actual crew of 506 men and boys (60 of the men sick, but only a few absent from their quarters), she had one lieutenant of marines (Thomas H. Griffiths), and 25 seamen and marines killed, her captain (slightly), one lieutenant of marines (Robert S. Ashbridge, mortally), two master's mates, (William H. Gibbons and George Henry Ayton), two midshipmen (Henry Bolton and Joseph Ray), and 93 seamen and marines wounded; total, 27 killed and 99 wounded. The Weasel had the good fortune not to have a man hurt, either in her forty minutes' engagement with the Mercure, or her very spirited, and in all probability, not ineffective cannonade of the Rivoli.

According to the letter of Captain Talbot, the Rivoli had on board 862 men; but the French officers have deposed to only 810, including 59 men late belonging to the French frigate Flore wrecked near Venice. Out of her (taking the smallest amount) 810 in crew and supernumeraries, the Rivoli lost 400 men in killed and wounded, including her second captain and the greater part of her officers. Not only had her mizenmast been shot away, but her fore and main masts were so badly wounded, that they fell over her side in a few days after the action. In her hull the Rivoli was dreadfully shattered; as, indeed, the severity of her loss would indicate.

The Victorious was a 74 of the 18-pounder class, and was consequently armed on her first and second decks in the manner represented at N or O in the first Annual Abstract. On her quarter-deck and forecastle, the Victorious appears to have mounted 18 carronades, 32-pounders, and two long 18-pounders, and on her poop six 18-pounder carronades; total 82 guns. The Rivoli, on her first and second decks, was armed exactly the same as the French 74 in the little table at p. 59 of the first volume, and appears to have mounted on her quarter-deck and forecastle 12 long 8-pounders and eight iron carronades, 36-pounders; total 80 guns, all of French caliber.

Comparative Force of the Combatants.

		Victorious.	Rivoli.
Broadside-guns	No.	41	40
	lbs.	1060	1085
Crew	No.	506	810
Size	tons.	1724	1804

This may be considered as at least an equal match; for the slight overplus that appears in the right-hand set of figures is amply compensated by the ineffective state of the Rivoli's crew. These had but just quitted port for the first time since they had assembled; and yet they fought their ship most bravely, as the length of the action, coupled with their severe loss, testifies, and far from unskilfully, as the loss sustained by their antagonist clearly demonstrates. The Rivoli's commander had the good fortune to be captured by an officer who could fully appreciate merit in an enemy; and accordingly Captain Talbot, in his official letter, expresses himself thus:—" I feel great satisfaction in saying, that the conduct of Commodore Barré, during the whole of the action, convinced me I had to deal with a most gallant and brave man, and in the manœuvring of his ship a most experienced and skilful officer. He did not surrender his ship until nearly two hours after she was rendered unmanageable, and had 400 killed or wounded," &c.

Placed under the charge of Lieutenants Edward Whyte and John Townshend Coffin, the Rivoli was conducted by the Victorious to Port St. George, island of Lissa; where both ships arrived on the 1st of March. The Rivoli was afterwards added to the British navy, and Captain Talbot, at a subsequent day, was knighted for his gallantry in capturing her. Lieutenant Peake also received the promotion which was due to him upon the occasion; and, in the month of September, Captain Andrew, of the Weasel, obtained his reward in a post-captain's commission.

On the 16th of April the British 18-gun brig-sloop Pilot, Captain John Toup Nicolas, observing nine coasting-vessels hauled up on the beach under the town of Policastro near Cape Palinuro, anchored close to the shore, and opened her fire, in order to drive away any armed force collected for their protection. Captain Nicolas then detached the boats, with a party of seamen and the marines, under the orders of Lieutenant Alexander Campbell, assisted by acting master Roger Langlands. Through the gallantry of these officers and their men in keeping in check a body of about 80 of the enemy, the whole of the nine vessels were launched and brought off without a casualty, and that in the short space of four hours. On the 28th the Pilot fell in with and harassed a large convoy laden with timber protected by 14 gun-boats and several scampavies; but, from its being perfectly calm, they effected their escape.

On the 14th of May the 12-pounder 32-gun frigate Thames, accompanied by the Pilot, attacked the port of Sapri, defended by a strong battery and tower, mounting two 32-pounders, and garrisoned by an officer and 38 men. After being battered for two hours within pistol-shot, the garrison surrendered at discretion; "but," says Captain Napier, "in consequence of their gallant defence, I allowed them to march out with the honours of war, but not to serve against us in this expedition." The British found 28 vessels laden with oil, some of them nearly a quarter of a mile in the country; all of which were launched and the battery blown up before sunset. Captain Napier speaks in the highest terms of Mr. Langlands, who, by his able disposition of the Pilot's marines placed under his command (no officer of that corps being on board the brig), kept upwards of 200 armed peasantry in check, and had only one man wounded. In a month or two afterwards, Mr. Langlands was promoted to the rank of lieutenant.

On the 29th of April, Captain Patrick Campbell, of the 74-gun ship Leviathan, detached the boats of that ship and of the 38-gun frigate Undaunted, Captain Richard Thomas, under Lieutenant Alexander Dobbs, to attack a French privateer and several merchant-vessels in the port of Agay. Lieutenant Dobbs, without any loss, boarded and carried the privateer, a brig of 14 guns and 80 men, lying aground, but could not get her afloat. Four of the merchant-vessels were brought off; but, during the endeavours to get off the privateer, two men were killed and four wounded by the fire of the enemy on the shore; who also succeeded in extinguishing the fire which had been put to the brig.

On the same day the boats of the Undaunted, with those of the 38-gun frigate Volontaire, Captain Charles Bullen, and 18-gun ship-sloop Blossom, Captain William Stewart, placed under the orders of Lieutenant John Eagar of the Undaunted, attacked a French convoy of 26 vessels at anchor near the mouth of the Rhone, brought out seven, burnt 12, including a national schooner of four guns and 74 men, and left two stranded on the beach. This spirited and important service was performed without any loss, the boats having been ably covered and protected by the fire of the Blossom.

On the 9th of May the British 74-gun ships America and Leviathan, Captains Josias Rowley and Patrick Campbell, and 18-gun brig-sloop Eclair, Captain John Bellamy, fell in with a French convoy of 18 deeply laden vessels, which took shelter under the town and batteries of Languelia. The two captains concurring in opinion as to the practicability of bringing out or destroying the vessels by getting possession of the batteries, the marines of both ships, about 250 in number, were, at daybreak on the 10th, landed to execute the service, under the orders of Captains Henry Rea of the America, and John Owen of the Leviathan, assisted by Lieutenants John Nearne, William Beddeck Cock, Paul Kyffin Carden, and John George Hill. Unfortunately the landing was not effected without an accident of a very serious nature. The yawl of the America was sunk by a chance shot from the only gun that could bear on the boats; and, before assistance could be afforded, 10 marines and one seaman were drowned.

A party, under Captain Owen, was detached to carry a battery of five 24 and 18 pounders to the eastward; which he performed in a very spirited and judicious manner, the French officer who commanded falling in the attack. The main body of the marines, in the mean time, rapidly advancing through a severe fire of grape, carried the battery adjoining the town of Languelia, consisting of four 24 and 18 pounders and one mortar, although protected by a strong body of the enemy posted in the wood and in several contiguous buildings; upon the latter of which the guns of the battery were immediately turned with much effect.

The French troops were now driven from the houses lining the beach by the fire of the Eclair, who had swept in for the purpose. The boats of the squadron, under Lieutenant William Richardson, assisted by Lieutenants Bouchier Molesworth and Robert Moodie of the America, and Alexander Dobbs and Richard Hambly of the Leviathan, also by master's mate John Harvey, and several other young officers not named in the despatch, then proceeded to bring out the vessels. These were secured by various contrivances to the houses and beach, and the sails and rudders of most of them removed on shore. After considerable exertions, 16 laden settees were towed off, another was burnt in the harbour by the boats, and a second, making the 18th, was too much damaged by shot to be got afloat. The marines of the squadron were re-embarked in the most perfect order, under cover of the fire of the Eclair, the only vessel enabled by the light and baffling winds to get close enough to act. This was accomplished without molestation from the French troops on the spot, although a strong party was advancing from the town of Alassio to reinforce them.

Exclusive of the heavy loss sustained at the onset of this dashing enterprise, one sergeant of marines, three privates, and one seaman were killed, and 18 marines and two seamen wounded; total killed and drowned 16, wounded 20.

Another French convoy, of 18 square and lateen-rigged vessels, having assembled at Languelia and Alassio, Captain Campbell of the Leviathan, having under his orders the Impérieuse, Captain Duncan, 18-pounder 36-gun frigate Curaçoa, Captain John Tower, and brig-sloop Eclair, detached the marines under Captain Owen, who, covered by the fire of the Eclair, effected a landing between the two towns. Scarcely had the marines formed on the beach ere they were attacked by treble their number; but nothing could withstand the bravery of the officers and men, who dashed at the French troops with the bayonet, and drove them from two batteries into the town, killing many and making 14 prisoners.

After spiking the guns, consisting of nine and a mortar, and destroying the carriages, the marines embarked; but, although the three ships had anchored within less than musket-shot of the two towns, and the Eclair had kept on her sweeps, going where she could be of most effect, and although the launches and other boats, under the command of Lieutenant Dobbs, had with their carronades maintained a heavy fire, the French troops could not be expelled from the houses so as to enable the boats, without a very great risk, to bring off any of the vessels; which were made fast to the shore in all manner of ways, and had their sails unbent and rudders unshipped. The loss already incurred was sufficiently severe, amounting to one seaman and three marines killed, and Lieutenant William Walpole, one seaman, and nine marines wounded.

On the 11th of June the French brig-corvette Renard, of fourteen 24-pounder carronades and two long sixes, commanded by Lieutenant de vaisseau Charles Baudin des Ardennes, and schooner Goéland, of twelve 18-pounder carronades and two sixes, commanded by Enseigne de vaisseau Belin, along with some gun-boats, and a convoy of 14 vessels laden with naval stores for Toulon, sailed from the port of Genoa. On the 15th M. Baudin and his charge were driven for shelter under the island of Sainte-Marguerite by a British squadron, consisting of the America 74, Curaçoa frigate, and brig-sloop Swallow, of sixteen 32-pounder carronades and two long sixes, Captain Reynolds Sibly. While the 74 and frigate kept in the offing on account of the shoal water, the Swallow, by signal, stood in to reconnoitre the convoy. On the 16th, at daybreak, the vessels of the latter were observed to be getting under way; and the Renard and Goéland, having a light breeze in-shore, soon made all sail in chase of the Swallow, who lay nearly becalmed. At about 6 A.M., however, finding that the Swallow was benefiting by a light breeze which had just sprung up from the south-west, the French brig and schooner hauled their wind, tacked, and used every exertion, by sweeps and boats, to effect their escape. Having at last accomplished their object, they and their convoy stood towards the bay of Fréjus.

Captain Sibly had now very small hopes of bringing on an action; when, at a few minutes past noon, on the breeze freshening, the Renard and Goéland, having received on board from Fréjus a number of volunteers, with a detachment of soldiers, again stood off on the starboard tack, the schooner keeping a little to windward of her consort. The Swallow being at this time ahead on the opposite tack, the two parties neared each other fast. At 1 P.M., finding she could weather the Renard, the Swallow closed, and, passing her to windward within 30 yards, gave and received a broadside. Captain Sibly then wore close under the French brig's stern, in the hope of keeping her head off shore; but, having had her own head-braces shot away, the Swallow was not able to lie so close to the wind as her captain intended. The Renard consequently got round on the larboard tack, and in that position was furiously cannonaded by the Swallow to leeward. The Goéland, meanwhile, had taken an annoying position out of the reach, except occasionally, of the British brig's guns. After the Swallow had sustained, during 40 minutes, the close and determined attacks of her two opponents, the larger of whom made several attempts to board, the proximity of the shore, and the strength of the batteries that lined it, compelled Captain Sibly to haul off and rejoin his commodore in the offing. The Renard and Goéland then stood on under all the sail they could set, and were presently at anchor with their convoy in the bay of Grimaud.

The Swallow was much cut up in sails, rigging, masts, and hull; and, of a crew of 109 out of 120 men and boys, lost six seamen and marines killed, and 17 wounded, including the purser, Mr. Eugene Ryan, who had gallantly volunteered to serve on deck. The Renard was much injured in her masts and most severely shattered in her hull; especially on the starboard side. Her loss, out of the 94 men that constituted, as it appears, her regular crew, was 14 men killed and 28 wounded; including among the latter her gallant commander, who was struck by a splinter upon the stump of the arm which some years before he had honourably lost. The total number of persons on board the Renard at the commencement of the action, consisting partly of troops as already mentioned, is represented to have been 180. The loss sustained by the Goéland, whose crew is stated to have consisted of 113 men, does not appear in M. Baudin's letter; and yet, as the schooner, at one time in particular, was exposed to a close and well-directed fire from five of the Swallow's carronades, loaded each with 64 pounds of double cannister and 32 of musket-balls, making 96 pounds in all, a considerable slaughter must have ensued.

That this was an affair very creditable to Captain Sibly, the officers, and crew of the Swallow, cannot admit a doubt; and that the latter would have made a prize of the Renard, had she not run for protection to the batteries, is, from a review of all the circumstances, equally clear. And yet some dozens of cases have been passed over, to celebrate this as an action glorious in the extreme for the navy of France. "The Renard," says a well-known French writer on English subjects, "of the same force as the Abeille, escorting a convoy in the gulf of Genoa, meets the Swallow, of the same force as the Alacrity. A frigate and an English ship of the line are in view; it matters not: the Swallow must fly, or be taken, before she can be succoured. A furious combat ensues between the two brigs, and the Swallow avoids her inevitable capture, only by flying for protection, under all sail, to the two large vessels, who are also crowding all sail to save her."[1] This is M. Dupin; who reads English, and writes liberally, except when national self-love interposes to screen truth.

On the 10th of August the British 20-gun ship Minstrel, Captain John Strutt Peyton, and 18-gun brig-sloop Philomel, Captain Charles Shaw, observed three small French privateers in the port of Biendom, near Alicant; where they were protected by a castle mounting 24 guns. As a further security, two of the vessels were hauled on shore, and a battery formed with six of their guns, which were manned with their united crews, amounting to 80 men, chiefly Genoese. Under these circumstances, the British ship and brig could only blockade the pri-

[1] For the original passage, see Appendix, No. 11.

vateers; and, to do this more effectually, a boat was sent from one or the other of them every night, to row guard near the shore.

On the 12th of August a boat, with Midshipman (or rather Lieutenant, for he had been promoted since the 21st of the preceding March, but had not yet received his appointment) Michael Dwyer and seven seamen, departed from the Minstrel upon this service. Considering, that if he could take the battery on the beach, he might succeed in capturing the privateers, the midshipman questioned the Spaniards, who came off in boats from the town; and they all agreed in the relation that the French had retreated, leaving but 30 men in the battery and 20 in the castle. Relying upon the tried courage and steadiness of his seven men, Mr. Dwyer resolved, notwithstanding the numbers of the enemy, to attempt carrying the battery by surprise. With this view, at 9 h. 30 m. P.M., he and his little party landed at a spot about three miles westward of the town; but scarcely had they done so than they were challenged by a French sentinel. The midshipman, with much presence of mind, answered in Spanish that they were peasants. The British were suffered to advance, and, arriving at the battery on the beach, attacked it without hesitation. After a smart struggle, the garrison, consisting not of 20, but of 80 Genoese, abandoned the battery to Mr. Dwyer and his seven men.

The British were a few minutes only in possession before they were surrounded by 200 French soldiers. Against these Mr Dwyer and his seven men defended themselves until one of the latter was killed, the midshipman shot through the shoulder, and a seaman through the eye, and all their ammunition expended. The moment the firing ceased, the French rushed upon the garrison with their bayonets. Mr. Dwyer was too weak, from loss of blood, to sustain a hand-to-hand fight; and, after he had been stabbed in 17 places, and all the men except one severely wounded, the French recovered possession of the battery. The gallant fellow who was wounded in the eye, on recovering from the stupefaction caused by the wound in his head, deliberately took his handkerchief from his neck, and, binding it over the wound, said, "Though I have lost one eye, I have still one left, and I'll fight till I lose that too."

The admiration of Captain Foubert and his troops, a detachment from the 117th regiment of voltigeurs, at the invincible courage of the little band of British, was unbounded; and when the latter, in their wounded state, were conveyed to the head-quarters of General Goudin, the French commanding officer in this quarter, the same benevolence and solicitude were shown to them by him and his suite. The general sent an invitation to Captain Peyton to visit him on shore, and receive in person as well his brave boat's crew as the congratulations of the general and the other French officers on having such men under his command. Captain Peyton accepted the invitation, dined with the French general, and received back his midshipman and six out of his seven men. Thus is it ever, that the brave sympathize with the brave; and he who gallantly does his duty, meets far from the most inestimable part of his reward, in the admiration which he elicits from the breast of his enemy.

On the 11th of August, the Menelaus, Captain Sir Peter Parker, observed several small vessels and a large brig running alongshore; on perceiving the frigate, they hauled up for Port St. Stefano, in the bay of Orbitello. Reconnoitring the harbour, a battery of two guns, one of four guns, a tower with one, and a citadel of 14 guns were seen; and although so well defended, and within half musket-shot of the shore and batteries, Sir Peter Parker resolved to cut them out. He stood out to sea that his preparations for the attack might not be noticed by the enemy, as well as to lead them to suppose that, discouraged by the strength of the place, he had given up the intention of attack. At dark he again stood in for the bay, in the hope, by storming the town, of carrying the vessels. The service being of a most desperate nature, to which, in the event of failure, an imputation of rashness might possibly attach, Sir Peter resolved to head the attack himself. The boats left the Menelaus at 11 P.M., but failed in their endeavours to reach the port, and returned under a heavy fire from the citadel and batteries. Foiled, but not discouraged, he deferred his attack until the night of the 13th, when he again left the ship with two gigs, two cutters, a launch with an 18-pound carronade, carrying 130 seamen and 40 marines. The force opposed to the above was 400 men, who manned the batteries, and many inhabitants of the town who had armed to repel the intruders. The plan suggested was that Lieutenants Beynon and Wilcocks, of the marines, were to storm the batteries, while Sir Peter Parker pushed on and secured the vessels. They approached the shore under a heavy fire; the marines landed in spite of all opposition, charged up a hill and drove before them about 90 of the enemy into the four-gun battery, which was instantly stormed and taken; the guns were spiked, and the marines re-embarked. Sir Peter in the mean time, boarded and carried the brig, and scuttled and destroyed the other vessels; the brig was brought out, although she was close under the guns of the citadel, and moored to the shore by six cables, with the loss of one midshipman (Thomas Munro) killed, and five seamen wounded.

On the 29th of September, in the evening, having received information that the French had laden six vessels with shells at Valencia for Peniscola, Captain Peyton despatched the boats of the Minstrel, under Lieutenant George Thomas, assisted by midshipmen William Lewis, B. S. Oliver, and Charles Thomas Smith, to endeavour to bring them out; keeping the ship close in shore to cover and protect the boats. Although the vessels were moored head and stern to the beach, between two batteries of two 24-pounders and two mortars, with a strong garrison in the Grao, and had their sails unbent and rudders unshipped, Lieutenant Thomas and his party gallantly succeeded in bringing out four of them. A fifth was also in the possession of the British; but, owing to the wind suddenly shifting round to the south-east with a heavy squall, this vessel grounded, and was retaken with three men in her. With that exception, the loss sustained by the British amounted to only one seaman severely wounded.

On the 31st of August, as the British 38-gun frigate Bacchante, Captain William Hoste, lay at anchor off Rovigno on the south-west coast of Istria, information arrived, that several vessels, laden with ship-timber for the Venetian government, were at Port Lemo. Captain Hoste, on the same evening, despatched the Bacchante's boats, five in number, containing 62 officers and men, under First-lieutenant Donat Henchy O'Brien, assisted by Lieutenant Frank Gostling, Lieutenant of marines William Haig, master's mate George Powell, and Midshipmen James Leonard Few, and Thomas William Langton.

Having captured two merchant-vessels at the entrance of the port, Lieutenant O'Brien received information that the vessels which he was going to cut out lay under the protection of a French xebec of three guns and two gun-boats. Notwithstanding this unexpected force, he left his two prizes in charge of Mr. Langton and six seamen, and, with the remaining 55 men, dashed on to the attack. The skill and gallantry of the commanding officer and his party carried all before them; and the British captured, without the loss of a man, as well the timber-vessels, seven in number, as the French xebec Tisiphone, of one 6 and two 3 pounders and 28 men, a gun-boat of one 8 and two

3 pounders and 24 men, and another of one 8-pounder and 20 men, intended for the protection of the trade on the coast of Istria, from Pola to Triest.

On the 3rd September, off the mouth of the river Mignone near Civita Vecchia, the Menelaus, Captain Sir Peter Parker, perceived a large letter-of-marque at anchor, pierced for 14 guns and protected by two strong batteries. As soon as it was dark, two boats were despatched, the crew of which succeeded in boarding and bringing out the St. Juan, and, notwithstanding the heavy fire, not a man was killed or wounded. The following day the Menelaus drove three sloops-of-war into Port Hercule, and on the 5th, at the mouth of the lake of Orbitello, Sir Peter cut out, in the most gallant and masterly style, under a very heavy fire, a large French ship, strongly defended by a tower, having previously anchored the Menelaus under the fire of the latter. In this last occasion the Menelaus lost one seaman killed, and Sir Peter Parker was wounded by a splinter which struck him on the breast.

On the 18th of September, at daybreak, cruising off the coast of Apulia, the Bacchante discovered and chased an enemy's convoy between the islands of Tremitti and Vasto, standing alongshore to the north-west. Baffling winds and calm weather preventing the frigate from closing, Captain Hoste despatched his boats, six in number, containing 72 officers and men, under the command, as before, of his first-lieutenant, assisted by Lieutenant Silas Thomson Hood, second of the Bacchante, instead of Lieutenant Gostling. On the approach of the boats, the 18 merchant-vessels anchored, and hauled themselves aground, leaving outside for their protection eight armed vessels, each mounting one long 12-pounder, three of them with three swivels each and 16 men, the remainder with 12 men; making in all, eight long 12-pounders, six swivels, and 104 men. Besides these, there were the crews of the merchant-vessels, who, having disembarked, lined a thick wood, well adapted for bush-fighting and completely commanding the coast.

In this situation, the convoy and vessels-of-war confidently awaited the British boats; but the officers and men in these, led on as they were, were not to be so daunted. Pushing through a heavy fire of grape and musketry, the seamen rushed like lions to the attack, boarding and carrying the vessels, and driving their crews over the sides in every direction; while the marines, headed by their intrepid leader, Lieutenant Haig, landing, forced the fugitives from the wood, and secured the possession of the whole convoy and the armed vessels protecting it. To enhance the valour of this second exploit of Lieutenant O'Brien and his brave associates, it was achieved with so trifling a loss on their part as two seamen wounded and those not dangerously.

On the 16th of September, in the evening, the British 74-gun ship Eagle, Captain Charles Rowley, having anchored off Cape Maistro, near Ancona, the latter despatched Lieutenant Augustus Cannon, with the three barges, to intercept the enemy's coasting-trade. On the morning of the 17th, Lieutenant Cannon perceived a convoy of 23 sail, protected by two gun-boats standing towards Goro. As the barges intrepidly advanced, the convoy, each vessel of which was armed with a 6 or an 8 pounder, drew up in line of battle, under cover of a 4-gun battery and the beach lined with armed people, having also the two gun-boats advanced in front.

The British, in the most gallant manner, and notwithstanding that their boats, owing to the shallowness of the channel, grounded frequently in their advance, attacked and carried the largest gun-boat; and then, turning her guns upon the second gun-boat, captured her and all the convoy but two, which effected their escape. Not being able to man all his prizes, Lieutenant Benjamin Morton Festing, who had succeeded to the command in consequence of Lieutenant Cannon having been mortally wounded, burnt six and brought out the remaining 17, including the two gun-boats. Besides Lieutenant Cannon mortally wounded, and who died on the 22nd, there was one seaman killed, another mortally, and three slightly wounded. Lieutenant Festing, it appears, still holds the same rank that he did, when he succeeded to the command in this successful and truly gallant exploit.

On the 2nd of February, as the British 12-pounder 32-gun frigate Southampton, Captain Sir James Lucas Yeo, was lying in the harbour of Port-au-Prince, the captain of Petion's dominions in the island of St. Domingo, intelligence arrived that a large frigate, a corvette, and a brig-of-war, belonging neither to Petion nor to his rival chief Christophe, but to a third party, formed out of revolters from both, were cruising on the south side of the adjacent island of Guanaboa. Although bound by his instructions to respect the flags of Petion and Christophe, Sir James had received no orders to acknowledge any other Haytian flag; he considered also that, if the squadron was allowed to quit the bight of Leogane, the commanding officer would be less scrupulous about the national character, than about the lading of the merchant-vessels he might fall in with; in short, that M. Gaspard, well known as an experienced privateer's man, might feel it to be to his interest to turn pirate.

Those, who communicated the information respecting this frigate pointed out, in reference to the Southampton, her superior force, particularly in men, of whom the number was stated to be upwards of 600. Far from deterring such a man as Sir James Lucas Yeo, all this stimulated him the more to execute a service which, hazardous as it might be, a sense of duty taught him was necessary; and accordingly, in the night, the Southampton weighed her anchor, and proceeded in quest of this formidable frigate and her two consorts.

Some account of the force of the two frigates may here be introduced. The Southampton was at this time the most ancient cruiser belonging to the British navy, having been built since the year 1757.[1] The Améthyste was the late French frigate Félicité, captured in June, 1809, when armed en flûte, by the British frigate Latona.[2] She was deemed unfit for the British navy, and was sold, as already stated, to an agent of Christophe's, to whose little navy she was afterwards attached. Treachery, or something of the kind, subsequently removed her into the possession of M. Borgellat, who had assumed the command of the department of the south in St. Domingo, upon the death of the revolter Rigaud. The frigate's name was then changed from Améthyste to Heureuse-Réunion; but, in all the accounts respecting her, she is called Améthyste. The Southampton mounted 38 guns, including ten 24-pounder carronades and two sixes; and the Améthyste, 44 guns, consisting of 18 long French 12 and eight long 18 pounders on the main deck, and four long 12-pounders and 14 carronades, 24-pounders, on the quarter-deck and forecastle.

On the 3rd, at 6 A.M., having arrived off the south side of Guanoboa, the Southampton fell in with the Améthyste, the corvette, and the brig. On hailing the Améthyste, Sir James was answered, "From Aux-Cayes." He then sent on board to request the captain of the frigate to wait upon him with his papers. Captain Gaspard declined doing this; but sent his first-lieutenant with a paper, purporting to be an order to cruise, and signed, "Borgellat, general-in-chief of the South of Hayti." Knowing of no authority that this M. Borgellat had to send armed vessels to sea, Sir James replied, that he felt it to

---

[1] See vol. i., p. 31.   [2] See p. 23.

be his duty to conduct the frigate and the two vessels in her company to Port Royal, Jamaica, that the British commander-in-chief on the station might determine upon the validity of M. Borgellat's claim; and he gave the captain of the Améthyste five minutes to consider the message. A lieutenant of the Southampton accompanied the lieutenant of the Améthyste back to his ship, in order to wait the time; but, before three minutes had elapsed, Captain Gaspard acquainted the former, that he would rather sink than comply with the demand: he requested however, that, if the British captain really meant to enforce his demand, he would fire a gun ahead of the frigate.

As the boat of the Southampton pulled round her stern towards the opposite gangway, the unsuccessful result of the mission was communicated. Off went the bow gun; and in another instant, then just 6 h. 30 m. A.M., the second and remaining guns upon the Southampton's broadside followed in rapid succession. The fire was returned; the action proceeded; and, aware of what was the chief arm of her strength, the Améthyste made several efforts to board; but the Southampton, by her superiority in manœuvring, frustrated every attempt. It had always been an essential point in Sir James Yeo's system of discipline to practise his men at gunnery; and they now gave unequivocal proofs of the proficiency to which they had attained. Before the cannonade had lasted half an hour, the main and mizen masts of the Améthyste had fallen; and her hull soon became riddled from stem to stern. Still the desperate crew continued a feeble and irregular fire. The two consorts of the Améthyste, in the mean time, had made sail, and were running for shelter under the batteries of Maraguana. At 7 h. 45 m. A.M., desirous to put an end to what now could hardly be called a contest, Sir James Yeo hailed to know if the Améthyste, whose colours had long been shot away, had surrendered. Some one on board replied in the affirmative; and the Southampton ceased her fire. Scarcely had she done so, ere the foremast and bowsprit of the Améthyste went by the board.

A proof of the inexperience of the crew of the latter, and of the confusion into which they had been thrown by the smart and destructive fire of their antagonist, may be seen in the Southampton's loss; which, out of a crew of 212 men and boys, amounted to only one seaman killed, and a midshipman and nine seamen and marines wounded. On the other hand, the Améthyste, out of a crew of 700 men (Frenchmen, Americans, Haytians, a motley group of almost every nation), had 105 killed and 120 wounded, including among the latter her captain, M. Gaspard. The whole of the surviving crew, except about 20 men, were landed at Maraguana, Petite-Goäve, and Porte-au-Prince; and the frigate, under jury-masts, fitted to her while she lay in Port-au-Prince, proceeded, in company with the Southampton, to Port Royal, Jamaica. On a subsequent day the Améthyste was restored to Christophe; and the conduct of Sir James Yeo, in all he had done, was approved by his commander-in-chief.

When the belligerents of Europe, opposed to England, had their commerce swept from the ocean by the armed ships of the latter; when there was every probability that Buonaparte would soon be compelled to curb his ambitious temper and restore to Europe the blessings of peace, neutral America stepped forward, and hired herself to be the carrier between the colony and the parent state. The consequence in a little time was, that although not a single merchant-vessel belonging to France or to Holland crossed the Atlantic or doubled the Cape of Good Hope, the products of the western and the eastern world sold cheaper in their markets than they did in those of England, who sent her ships wheresoever she pleased. Thus relieved, France pushed on the war with vigour, and neutral America prospered by fanning the flames. This moral and religious people actually grew rich and great, commercially great at least, out of that which depopulated Europe, which robbed the wife of her husband, and the child of its father.

Every citizen of every town in the United States, to which a creek leads that can float a canoe, becomes henceforward a "merchant;" and the grower of wheat or tobacco sends his son to the counting-house, that he may be initiated in the profitable art of falsifying ships' papers and covering belligerent property. Here the young American learns to bolt custom-house oaths by the dozen, and to condemn a lie only when clumsily told, or when timorously or inadequately applied. After a few years of probation, he is sent on board a vessel as mate or supercargo; and, in due time, besides fabricating fraudulent papers and swearing to their genuineness, he learns (using a homely phrase) to humbug British officers, and to decoy, and make American citizens of, British seamen. The merchant's hope of gain, in these trips to and from the port of one belligerent, resting mainly on a quick passage and a careful avoidance of the cruisers belonging to the other, the American vessel is constructed and fitted in the best manner for sailing; and, having no convoying ship-of-war to show him the way, the American master becomes, of necessity, a practical navigator of the first order.

When England, at length, began her attempts to check this intercourse between her enemy and neutral America, neutral America grumbled, and, resorting to new subterfuges, went on. Other restrictions followed. Then came loud complaints, mixed with threats. Napoleon, next, began to feel the effects of England's restrictive system. Her proclamation, issued on the 16th of May, 1806, declaring the ports of France from the Elbe to Brest in a state of blockade, provoked the French emperor, on the 21st of the succeeding November, to fulminate from Berlin his sweeping decree; declaring the British islands in a state of blockade; ordering all British letters, subjects, and property to be seized; prohibiting all trade in British produce and manufactures; and pronouncing all neutral vessels, that had touched in England, or in any of her colonies, liable to confiscation.

This was, at once, an extinguisher upon all neutral nations; it was tantamount to a declaration of war against neutral America; but neutral America blamed, not her dear France, but England. There can be no doubt that, in retaliation for such a violation of all public law, England would have been justified in laying waste the French coast with fire and sword; but she contented herself with issuing, on the 7th of January, 1807, an order in council, directing that no vessel should be permitted to trade from one port to another, in the possession of France or her allies. Finding that this order did not produce the expected effect, England, on the 11th of November in the same year, issued another; in which, imitating France in her extravagant tone, she declared all the ports of her enemies, both in Europe and the colonies, in a state of blockade. This was followed by the Milan decree of December 17, 1807; by which every vessel that should have submitted to be searched by an English ship, or paid any tax to the English government, was declared to be denationalised, and to have become British property, and therefore lawful prize; and every ship sailing from England or her colonies, or from any other country occupied by her troops, was also to be made lawful prize; but, says the arch framer, "these measures shall cease to have any effect, with respect to all nations, who shall have the firmness to compel the English government to respect their flag."

The object of this proviso was too palpable to be misunderstood. Accordingly, after a few years of growling and snarling, when, owing to the vigour of the British arms by sea and land, not a colony remained to France or her allies in either hemisphere; when, the neutral trade being extinct, American ships were rotting at their moorings, and the untrodden wharfs of New York and Philadelphia becoming choked with grass and weeds, America boldly cast off her neutral disguise, and resolved, in the language of the noble race she had displaced, to "take up the hatchet" and go to war. With whom? was the next point to be considered. This, like everything else in the United States, was to be settled by a calculation of profit and loss. France had numerous allies; England scarcely any. France had no contiguous territory; England had the Canadas ready to be marched into at a moment's notice. France had no commerce: England had richly laden merchantmen traversing every sea. England, therefore, it was, against whom the deadly blows of America were to be levelled.

On the 14th of April, at a secret sitting of Congress, an act passed, laying an embargo on all ships and vessels of the United States, during the space of 90 days; for the purpose, no doubt, of lessening the number of vessels that would be at the mercy of England when war was formally declared. By the end of May most of the fastest sailing ships, brigs, and schooners in the American merchant service were fitted or fitting as privateers; and many lay ready to sail forth, the instant the tocsin of war should be sounded. They had not to wait long. The president's message to congress of the 1st of June was the preparative; and an act of congress, which passed on the 18th, declaring the "actual existence of war between the United Kingdom of Great Britain and Ireland and the United States of America" struck the blow.

Although New York is 240 miles from Washington, the American seat of government, Commodore Rodgers received his instructions in sufficient time to get under way from the harbour of the first-named city on the morning of the 21st, with the President and United States frigates, the latter commanded by Commodore Stephen Decatur, the 18-pounder 36-gun frigate Congress, Captain John Smith, 18-gun brig-sloop Hornet, Captain James Lawrence, and 16-gun brig-sloop Argus, Captain Arthur Sinclair; and, by evening, the American squadron was clear of Sandy Hook lighthouse.

The first object of Commodore Rodgers was to get possession of a fleet of about 100 sail of homeward-bound Jamaica-men, known to be not far from the coast, under the protection of so comparatively small a force as the British 18-pounder 36-gun frigate Thalia, Captain James G. Vashon, and 18-gun brig-sloop Reindeer, Captain William Manners. This fleet had sailed from Negril bay, Jamaica, on the 20th of May, under the additional convoy, as far as Cape Antonio, of the 64-gun ship Polyphemus, Captain Cornelius Quinton, and had passed Havana on the 4th of June. On the 23rd, at 3 A.M., the commodore spoke an American brig, bound from Madeira to New York, and was informed by her that, four days before, in latitude 36°, longitude 67°, she had passed the Jamaica fleet, steering to the eastward In that direction the American commodore immediately steered.

At 6 A.M., Nantucket shoal bearing north-east distant 35 miles, and the wind blowing moderately from the west-northwest, a large sail was descried in the north-east, standing directly for the American squadron. This was the British 18-pounder 36-gun frigate Belvidera, Captain Richard Byron; who, until her discovery, a few minutes before, of the strangers approaching her, had been lying to, waiting to intercept the French privateer-schooner Marengo, hourly expected from New London. At 6 h. 30 m., just as the Belvidera, having arrived within six miles, had made out the three largest ships to be frigates, they and the sloops, by signal from the commodore, hauled to the wind on the starboard tack in chase. The British frigate immediately tacked from the strangers; and at 8 h. 15 m. A.M., finding the private signal not answered, Captain Byron made all sail, keeping away to about north-east by east. At 11 A.M. the wind began to decrease and draw more to the westward. At 11 h. 30 m. the Belvidera hoisted her colours; and immediately afterwards the American squadron did the same, the two commodores also displaying their broad pendants.

Having now ascertained that the squadron approaching belonged to a "friendly power," Captain Byron would probably have shortened sail, to allow the American van-ship to close; but a New York pilot-boat had a few days before spoken the Belvidera, and informed her of what was likely to happen. Coupling this with the persevering efforts of the American commodore in the chase, Captain Byron no longer doubted the hostility of his intentions. The Belvidera, as a matter of course, had cleared for action and loaded her guns, and had shifted to her stern ports two long 18-pounders on the main deck and two 32-pounder carronades on the quarter-deck; but, although the cartridges of the guns were pricked, the priming was not laid on. This was done by Captain Byron's express orders, to prevent the possibility of any such charge being brought against the Belvidera, as had been made so much of in the case of the Little Belt.

The wind, which since 2 P.M. had veered to west-south-west, and was therefore nearly aft in the course the ships were steering (about north-east), began gradually to fall. This of course favoured the ships astern: and at 4 h. 20 m. P.M., being the van-ship of her squadron and distant about 600 yards astern, or rather, about half a point on the larboard and weather-quarter of the Belvidera, the President opened a fire from her bow guns. The first three shot all took effect in the British ship's hull: one struck the rudder-coat, and the others entered the counter and transom, but hurt no one, the men being above at quarters. A fourth shot struck the muzzle of the larboard chase 18-pounder, and, breaking into several pieces, killed one seaman, wounded mortally another, severely two others, and slightly a lieutenant (William Henry Bruce), in the act of pointing the gun, and two seamen standing near him. In five minutes after the President had commenced her fire, the Belvidera returned it from her stern-chasers. At 4 h. 30 m. P.M. one of the President's 24-pounders burst: by which accident 16 persons were killed and wounded, including among the latter the commodore himself severely in the leg; and the main and forecastle decks near the gun were so much shattered, as to prevent the use, for a considerable time, of a chase-gun on that side.

After having, owing to the accident, suspended firing for 10 minutes, the President put her helm a-starboard and discharged her starboard main deck guns; the shot from which (all single) did considerable injury to the rigging and sails of the Belvidera, but scarcely touched her hull. The most serious accident, which now befel the Belvidera, was the frequent breaking of the long-bolts, breeching-hooks, and breechings, of the long guns and carronades; by a blow from one of which latter Captain Byron received a severe contusion in the inside of his thigh, a little above the knee. Nothing, however, could exceed the alacrity of the crew, as well in refixing and securing the guns, as in splicing and knotting the damaged rigging. In the meanwhile the captain and his senior-lieutenant, John Sykes, personally superintended the pointing of the quarter-deck chase-carronades; while the 18-pounders in the cabin were equally well served under the direction of Lieutenants Bruce and the Hon. George Pryce Campbell. This was a duty of some importance, as it was upon the nicety of the aim that their hopes of escape in a great degree rested.

At 5 p.m. being much annoyed by the steady stern-fire of the British frigate, the President again put her helm a-starboard, and fired her main-deck guns, at the distance, now, of rather less than 400 yards: she then renewed her course in the Belvidera's wake, receiving, as before, an animated fire from the latter's stern-chasers. Notwithstanding that the Belvidera had by this time had several of her backstays, main shrouds, and studding-sail halliards shot away, and her cross-jack yard badly wounded, the crew, under the direction of Mr. James Kerr, the master, repaired the one and fished the other; so that the ship had lost very little of her advantage in the chase.

At 5 h. 20 m. p.m. the President again endeavoured to free herself from the galling stern-fire of her persevering opponent (who, from her two cabin 18-pounders, fired upwards of 300 round shot), by luffing up athwart the Belvidera's stern and discharging two broadsides; neither of which, however, produced much effect. About this time the Belvidera gave a broad yaw to starboard, with the intention of firing her broadside; but, the President quickly answering her helm, no guns would bear with effect, and none were discharged. Yet Commodore Rodgers, in his journal declares, that the Belvidera's "four aftermost guns were fired, without bearing within 25 or 30 degrees of the President."

Finding that the President was now getting so near, that she had it at her option to run alongside and bring on a close action, the Belvidera, at 6 h. 25 m. p.m., cut away one bower, one stream, and two sheet anchors; and, in five minutes more, the latter got so far ahead of the President, owing chiefly to her yawing about instead of steering a direct course, that the American frigate ceased her fire. This apparently shy conduct on the part of the President, coupled with the damaged state of her rigging and sails, enabled the Congress to get abreast of her; and at 6 h. 30 m. p.m. that frigate opened her fire, but, finding her shot fall short, almost immediately desisted. In the mean time the Belvidera, for the same reason, had ceased her fire; and, to get clear of this second opponent, started 14 tons of water, and threw overboard her yawl, barge, gig, and jolly-boat. The good effect of this was soon visible; and the British crew now devoted their principal attention to fishing their ship's maintopmast, which was badly wounded. By 8 p.m. the Belvidera was two miles ahead of the American van-ship. At 11 p.m. Captain

Byron altered his course from north-east to east-south-east, and set her starboard studding-sails. At 11 h. 25 m. P.M. the President, who was still the leading frigate of her squadron, and now about three miles astern of the Belvidera, shortened sail and at midnight lay to, in company with the Congress, to await the coming up of her remaining friends.

The force of the President has already been fully described. The Belvidera measured 946 tons, and was armed precisely according to the establishment of her class, with 42 guns, including 14 carronades, 32-pounders, and two long nines. The Congress was a remarkably fine ship, about the size of the British frigate Cambrian, or from 1150 to 1170 tons; and carried the same armament as the Chesapeake when she was attacked by the Leopard,[1] with four 32-pounder carronades in addition, making 50 guns in all. Some accounts give the Congress 52 guns. Her complement was 440, with scarcely a boy among them.

The principal damages of both ships have already been stated. The Belvidera's loss, besides that sustained at the commencement of the attack, amounted, out of 230 men and boys of her complement, to 17 wounded; making her total loss two killed and 22 wounded, the greater part slightly. According to the American official account, the President lost, altogether, two midshipmen and one marine killed, the commodore, one lieutenant, one lieutenant of marines, three midshipmen, and 12 seamen wounded, one mortally, and several severely; making her total loss in killed and wounded 22, of which number six had suffered by the Belvidera's fire. This was paying rather dear for the day's amusement; but the 15 hours' dance, which the Belvidera had led the commodore, did him more injury than her guns or his own: it lost him the Jamaica fleet, by carrying his squadron too far to the northward. At daylight on the 23rd, when the commodore began chasing the Belvidera, the American squadron was in latitude 39° 26' north, longitude 71° 10' west; and at noon on that day the Jamaica fleet was in latitude 39° 35', longitude 61° 38'.

Having repaired the most material of her damages, the Belvidera steered towards Halifax, and on the 27th anchored in the harbour, in company with two or three American merchant-vessels, which, on receiving so unequivocal a proof that war had been declared by the United States, Captain Byron had ventured to detain; but all of which Rear-admiral Sawyer restored, con-

[1] See vol. iv., p. 253.

sidering that the affair, after all, might have originated in some mistake of the American commodore's. On the evening of the same day on which the Belvidera anchored in Halifax, the Mackerel schooner was despatched to England with the intelligence, and arrived in Portsmouth on the 25th of July.

It took the President a full day to repair her damages. That done, the American squadron proceeded in quest of the Jamaica fleet. On the 1st of July, a little to the eastward of the bank of Newfoundland, the squadron fell in with a fleet, not of ships, but of cocoa-nut shells, orange-peel, &c.;[1] and the commodore and his officers promised themselves a West India dessert to their next day's dinner. They longed in vain; and, after being thus tantalized from the 1st to the 13th, they steered for Madeira, and thence for the Azores. To increase the misfortunes of the cruise, the scurvy broke out among the men, and conferred additional value upon the limes that were known to be in such profusion on board the Jamaica ships. The squadron captured six or seven small merchantmen, and recaptured one American vessel; but, although he chased the British 38-gun frigate Statira, Captain Hassard Stackpoole, for several hours, Commodore Rodgers returned to Boston without one national trophy to signalize his maiden cruise. He arrived there on the 29th of August; just six days after the Thalia, having brought home her charge in safety, had anchored in the Downs.

One of the two great blows against England, the subjugation of the Canadas and the capture of a West India fleet of more than 100 sail, contemplated by Mr. Madison, was thus warded off; and to the judgment and promptitude of Captain Byron on his first falling in with the American squadron, to the skill of the Belvidera's officers and crew in pointing their guns and working their ship, and to their bravery and perseverance in defending her during a long and arduous chase, while engaged with a force so greatly superior, is the nation indebted for the little mischief done to British commerce by a formidable American squadron, possessing the singular advantage of having its hostile intentions unknown.

Had the President, when she fell in with the Belvidera, been cruising alone, we can readily imagine, judging from what took place in the Little Belt's case, that Commodore Rodgers would have magnified the British frigate into a line-of-battle ship, and have done his utmost to avoid her; but we are quite at a loss,

---

[1] Official letter of Commodore Rodgers.

we confess, to account for the commodore's irresolution in not closing with the Belvidera, when he had a squadron of friends close at his heels. It was that irresolution which produced those many yawings and traverses in the President's course; and it was those yawings and traverses that, coupled with the masterly manner in which the Belvidera was handled, saved her from being captured. Meaning, some have thought, to compliment, others to *quiz*, his political opponent, the democratic commodore, Captain Isaac Hull of the Constitution, a stanch federalist, says to the secretary of the American navy: " I am confident, could the commodore have got alongside the Belvidera, she would have been his in less than *one hour*."

A contemporary informs us, that Lieutenant Sykes "was promoted to the rank of commander, as a compliment, not only to his captain and himself, but to the officers and ship's crew, which certainly would not have been done, had there been any want of discipline observable in the ship."[1] With respect to the Belvidera's first-lieutenant, Captain Brenton had been misinformed. Lieutenant Sykes was not made a commander until the 2nd of November, 1814; and, as he had then been a lieutenant more than 19 years, he was entitled to the promotion upwards of two years before, even had he not distinguished himself in the Belvidera, and been recommended to the admiralty by her captain as "an excellent officer." Our contemporary's mysterious allusion about "want of discipline" we do not understand.

It was intended that the frigate Essex lying at New York should form part of the squadron of Commodore Rodgers, but she could not be got ready in time. The Essex was the smallest frigate belonging to the United States, measuring only 867 tons. Her armament consisted almost wholly of 32-pounder carronades: she mounted 24, with two long 12-pounders on the main deck, and 16, with four long 12-pounders on the quarter-deck and forecastle; total 46 guns. The rate of the Essex in the American navy-list was of "32 guns;" and her complement, as subsequently acknowledged by Captain David Porter, who so long commanded her, was 328 men. The usual addition of, " and boys," as applied to the crew of an American ship, would convey a very erroneous impression; therefore we do not use it. But, to those acquainted with the usual composition of the crews of British ships-of-war, it will appear the most extraor-

[1] Brenton, vol. v., p. 47.

dinary circumstance, that, out of those 328 men, Captain Porter himself should have declared (and for which the American government must have been not a little displeased), in his famous "Journal of a Cruise," there were but 11 landsmen. This is a most important fact, and deserves to be held in remembrance by all who desire to judge fairly in those encounters between British and American ships, of which we shall soon have to give some account.

Having the authority of a respectable eye-witness for the accuracy of as much of the following account as relates to the proceedings on shore, we feel bound to give it insertion; if but to show the importance that was attached to the retention of British seamen on board the American ships-of-war, as well as the barbarous means to which an American officer could resort, to punish a native of England for refusing to become a traitor to his country. A New York newspaper, of June 27, 1812, contains the following as the substance of the formal deposition of the victim of Captain Porter's unmanly treatment. "The deposition states, that John Erving was born in Newcastle-upon-Tyne, England; that he has resided within the United States since 1800, and has never been naturalized; that, on the 14th of October, 1811, he entered on board the Essex, and joined her at Norfolk; that Captain Porter, on the 25th of June, 1812, caused all hands to be piped on deck, to take the oath of allegiance to the United States, and gave them to understand, that any man who did not choose to do so should be discharged; that, when deponent heard his name called, he told the captain, that being a British subject he must refuse taking the oath; on whch the captain spoke to the petty officers, and told them they must pass sentence upon him; that they then put him into the petty launch, which lay alongside the frigate, and there poured a bucket of tar over him, and then laid on a quantity of feathers, having first stripped him naked from the waist: that they then rowed him ashore, stern foremost, and landed him. That he wandered about, from street to street, in this condition, until Mr. Ford took him into his shop, to save him from the crowd then beginning to gather; that he stayed there until the police magistrate took him away, and put him into the city prison for protection, where he was cleansed and clothed. None of the citizens molested or insulted him. He says he had a protection, which he bought of a man in Salem, of the same name and description with himself, for four shillings and sixpence, which he got renewed at the Custom-house, Norfolk. He says he gave, as an additional reason to the captain, why he did not choose to fight against his country, that, if he should be taken prisoner, he would certainly be hung."

This, having been copied into other papers, met the eye of Captain Sir James Lucas Yeo, of the 12-pounder 32-gun frigate Southampton, then attached to the Jamaica station. Persons, acquainted with that officer, can judge of his feelings upon reading an account of the ill-treatment of a British sailor. Some expression, marking his abhorrence of the act and his contempt for the author, did very likely escape Sir James; and that, in the hearing of one or more of the American prisoners then on board the Southampton. Through this channel, which was none of the purest, the words probably became what they appeared in a Philadelphia newspaper, the "Democratic Press," of the 18th of September, 1812, a sort of challenge, couched in vulgar terms, from the Southampton to the Essex. It has been thought that Mr. Binns himself was at the bottom of it, to give his friend (but not countryman) Captain Porter an opportunity of blustering himself into more creditable notice, than the affair of John Erving was calculated to gain for him. At all events, a formal acceptance, by Captain Porter, of the alleged challenge, went the round of the American newspapers.

Although, according to the best of our inquiries on the subject, no such message was sent by Sir James Yeo, the Southampton cruised, for several weeks along the southern coast of the United States, in the hope of falling in with the Essex, the nature of whose armament Sir James fully knew. The Southampton had 212 men and boys, and in reference to the quality of her crew, was well manned. All that her captain and his officers wanted was the weather-gage, to enable the Southampton to choose her distance and bring her long 12s into fair competition with her opponent's short 32s; or else to afford the British seamen an opportunity of getting on board the American ship early in the action, and of deciding the contest by their favourite mode, a hand-to-hand struggle.

It was on the 3rd of July that the Essex sailed from New York. On the 11th at 2 A.M., in latitude, by her reckoning, 33°, longitude 60°, the Essex fell in with a small convoy of seven British transports, going from Barbadoes to Quebec, under the protection of the British 12-pounder 32-gun frigate Minerva (same force as Southampton), Captain Richard Hawkins, and succeeded in cutting off the rearmost vessel, a brig

No. 299, having on board 197 soldiers. At 4 A.M., observing a strange ship very close to one of the brigs of her convoy, the Minerva wore to reconnoitre the intruder. Finding, however, after a while, that, by continuing in chase of the American frigate and her newly-made prize, he would run the risk of losing the remaining six vessels of his convoy, Captain Hawkins left the brig (captured, by the Minerva's reckoning, in latitude 34° 3' north, longitude 66° 39' west) in the quiet possession of the Essex, and resumed his course towards Quebec.

Captain Porter was discreet, as well as shrewd enough to chuckle at this: and, disarming and paroling the soldiers, and ransoming the vessel, he allowed the latter to proceed with the intelligence of the outrage she had suffered. He of course obtained from his prize the name of the convoying frigate, whose protection was of so much use to her, and by the first opportunity wrote home an account of his exploit; concluding with the, as applied to a British ship, most galling words: "We endeavoured to bring the frigate to action, but did not succeed." This letter appeared in several English as well as American newspapers, but we can find no explanation of the circumstance out of which it originated. Had Captain Porter really "endeavoured" to bring the Minerva to action, we do not see what could have prevented the Essex, with her decided superiority of sailing, from getting alongside of her. But no such thought, we are sure, entered the head of Captain Porter. This will be clear to all, as we proceed in our analysis of that gentleman's claim, or claims rather, for they are numerous, to wear the laurel.

On the 13th of August, but in what spot off the American coast nowhere appears, the Essex fell in with the British 16-gun ship-sloop Alert, Captain Thomas Lamb Poulden Laugharne. The ship, thus raised to the dignity of a sloop-of-war, had, eight years before, carried coals from Newcastle to London. In the year 1804 twelve of these craft were purchased for men-of-war; and the Oxford collier became the Alert sloop, fitted with 18-pounder carronades, the highest caliber she would bear. Had she been a little smaller, and rigged with two masts instead of three, the Alert would have been a gun-brig; but her unfortunate mizenmast exalted her above scores of vessels, any one of whom, among the two classes next below her in our abstracts, except perhaps the Alacrity, would have gloried in having such a ship to contend with: nay, some of the Alacrity's fine class would not have declined a combat with two such opponents. By the end of the year of 1811, ten of these choice men-of-war had either been broken up, or converted to peaceable harbour-ships. But there were two that yet remained; and, as if it was supposed that they in reality possessed the qualities of which their names were significant, the Avenger and Alert sailed for the station of North America, the very month before the United States declared war against Great Britain.

When the American frigate Essex, as we have stated, fell in with the Alert, the latter was in search of the Hornet; such another sloop-of-war as the Little Belt or Bonne-Citoyenne, and who of course would, or at least ought to, have captured both the Alert and Avenger, had she encountered them together. Either mistaking the Essex for what she was not, or aiming at a still higher flight than the Hornet, the Alert bore down upon the former's weather-quarter, and opened her puny fire. In a quarter of an hour, the ci-devant collier had seven feet water in her hold, three of her men wounded, and her colours down, and had neither hurt a man or done any other injury, on board the Essex.

The conspicuous gallantry of Captain Laugharne entitled him to a better ship than the Alert, a better first-lieutenant than Andrew Duncan, who gave him no support, and a better crew than his officers and men, who except Johanson Clering the master, and William Haggarty the purser, went aft to request their captain to strike the colours. Captain Porter disarmed his fine prize, and sent her with the prisoners, 86 in number, as a cartel, to St. John's, Newfoundland; where, on the 8th of October, Captain Laugharne and his officers and men were tried for the loss of their ship. The captain, master, and purser, were most honourably acquitted; the first-lieutenant was dismissed the service; and the remaining officers and crew obtained, with their acquittal, the marked disapprobation of the court. On her return to a port in the United States, being found unfit for a cruiser, the Alert was laid up in ordinary, but, after the lapse of some months, was fitted as a storeship. The moment, however, that her sails were unfurled, her creeping, collier-like pace betrayed her origin, and sent back the Alert to New York, to grace the harbour as a block-ship, and to be pointed out to the citizens as one of the national trophies of war.

As Captain Porter was a great favourite at the city of Washington, Mr. Clark, who was patronized by all the great men there, could do no less than insert in his book any little tale which the former might wish to see recorded in the naval history of his country. "On the 30th of August," says one of those tales, "the Essex, being in latitude 36° north, longitude 62° west, a British frigate was discovered standing towards her, under press of sail. Porter stood for her under easy sail, with his ship prepared for action; and, apprehensive that she might not find the Essex during the night, he hoisted a light. At 9, the British vessel made a signal: it consisted of two flashes and a blue light. She was then, apparently, about four miles distant. Porter stood for the point where she was seen until midnight, when, perceiving nothing of her, he concluded it would be best to heave to for her until morning, concluding she had done the same; but, to his great surprise, and the mortification of his officers and crew, she was no longer in sight. Captain Porter thought it to be not unlikely, that this vessel was the Acasta, of 50 guns, sent out, accompanied by the Ringdove, of 22, to cruise for the Essex."[1]

It did not perhaps occur to Mr. Clark, that ships usually carry log-books, in which are entered every day's proceedings with the latitude, longitude, &c.; and that these can be referred to, in case the false assertions of any historian, or paragraph-writer, or American captain, may be worth the trouble of disproving. Considering what a formidable man Captain Porter was, nothing less than the Acasta "of 50 guns," and Ringdove, "of 22," could be sent out to cruise for the Essex. Unfortunately for the fame of the captain of the Essex, on the 30th of August, 1812, the day mentioned, the Acasta was cruising in the latitude of 43° north, longitude 65° 16′ west; and the Ringdove, whose force, by-the-by, was only 18 guns, was lying at an anchor in a harbour of the island of St. Thomas. It was certainly very modest of Captain Porter, to "think it not unlikely," that one of the finest 18-pounder frigates in the British navy, accompanied too by a sloop-of-war, would be sent out to "cruise for the Essex." The fact is, the ship, which Captain Porter fell in with, was the 18-gun sloop Rattler, Captain Alexander Gordon; and who, we believe, not considering himself a match for the American frigate, rather avoided than sought an engagement with her.

On the 4th of September, at noon, in latitude 39° 11′ north, longitude 70° 22′, the Essex, then having under her convoy the

[1] Clark's Naval History of the United States, vol. i. p. 180.

American merchant-ship Minerva, fell in with "two ships-of-war," as Captain Porter declared them to be,[1] were the British 38-gun frigate Shannon, Captain Philip Bowes Vere Broke, and the merchant-ship Planter, which she had just recaptured from the Americans. The Shannon, as may be supposed, was soon under all sail in chase; but in a little time the wind, which had been blowing right aft, headed the ship flat aback. With the wind thus suddenly changed in her favour, the Essex, keeping the Minerva close astern of her, bore down, as if to bring the Shannon to action; but at 4 h. 30 m. P.M., just as she had got within about ten miles of the British frigate, the Essex suddenly hauled up, and, after making some private signals, crowded sail to get away; leaving the poor merchant-ship, whom she had thus led into danger, to shift for herself.

The Shannon continued chasing to windward, under a press of canvas, until dark; when, losing sight of the Essex, the former tacked and seized the merchant-ship. Captain Broke intended to burn the vessel directly, that the Essex might see the flames, and perhaps bear down to revenge the indignity offered to the American flag; but the night becoming dark and squally, Captain Broke would not risk his boats in removing the crew. Consequently the Minerva, in ballast only, was not burnt until the following morning; and by that time the Essex had made so good a use of her sails, that she was no longer to be seen by the Shannon. This was the last exploit Captain Porter performed in this his first cruise; and three days afterwards, namely, on the 7th of September, the Essex, "covered with glory," anchored in Delaware bay.

On the 28th of June, which was the day after the Belvidera had arrived at Halifax with the account of the unexpected attack made upon her by an American squadron, Vice-admiral Sawyer despatched the 18-gun brig-sloop Colibri, Captain John Thompson, as a flag of truce to New York, to obtain an explanation of the matter. On the 9th of July the Colibri anchored off Sandy Hook, and on the 12th weighed and sailed on her return; having on board, besides a copy of the declaration of war, the British ambassador, Mr. Foster, and consul, Colonel Barclay. On the day previous to the arrival of the Colibri at Sandy Hook, the British 4-gun schooner Whiting, Lieutenant Lewis Maxey, from Plymouth, with despatches for the American government, arrived in Hampton roads, ignorant of the war.

[1] Clark's Naval History of the United States, vol. i., p. 180

As Lieutenant Maxey was proceeding on shore in his boat, the American privateer-schooner Dash, Captain Garroway, bound on a cruise, got possession of him, and then ran alongside the Whiting; and, having upwards of 80 men in crew, captured her without opposition. The despatches had previously been sunk. The Whiting was only 75 tons, and mounted four carronades, 12-pounders, with a complement of 18 men and boys. Of these, a third were absent in the boat; and those in the schooner had not the least suspicion of being in an enemy's waters. The Dash mounted one heavy long gun upon a pivot carriage. This, and a suppression of the principal circumstances, enabled the American writers to state, with some degree of exultation, " The British schooner mounts four guns, the Dash only one." The Whiting was afterwards restored, but was captured on her way to England by the French privateer-brig Diligent.

On the 17th the Colibri returned to Halifax; but, having in the mean time received positive intelligence that the United States had declared war, Rear-admiral Sawyer had, since the 5th, despatched to cruise off the American coast, under the orders of Captain Broke, all the effective ships which were then in the harbour, consisting of the Shannon and Belvidera, the 64-gun ship Africa, Captain John Bastard, and the 18-pounder 32-gun frigate Æolus, Captain Lord James Townsend. On the 9th, in latitude 41°, longitude 66° or nearly abreast of Nantucket island, the* squadron was joined by the 38-gun frigate Guerrière, Captain James Richard Dacres, then on her way to Halifax to refit.

When it is known, that the Guerrière had nearly expended, not only her water and provisions, but her boatswain's and carpenter's stores—that her gunner's stores were also deficient—that what remained of her powder, from damp and long keeping, was greatly reduced in strength—that her bowsprit was badly sprung, her mainmast, from having been struck by lightning, in a tottering state, and her hull, from age and length of service, scarcely seaworthy—no one will deny that this rencounter with a squadron, the commodore of which had orders to supply her with three months' provisions and take her under his command, was rather unfortunate; in fact, such was the state of general decay in which the Guerrière at this time was, that, had the frigate gone into Portsmouth or Plymouth, she would, in all probability, have been disarmed and broken up.

On the 14th, when arrived off Sandy Hook, Captain Broke

received the first intelligence of the squadron of Commodore Rodgers having put to sea; and, as may be supposed, a sharp look-out began immediately to be kept by each of the British ships. On the 16th, at 3 P.M., when the British squadron was abreast of Barnegat, about four leagues off shore, a strange sail was seen, and immediately chased, in the south by east or windward quarter, standing to the north-east. This sail was the United States 44-gun frigate Constitution, Captain Isaac Hull, from Chesapeake bay since the 12th, bound to New York. The chase continued throughout the afternoon and evening, in light winds; and at 10 P.M. the Guerrière, who since dusk had lost sight of her consorts to leeward, found the Constitution standing towards her, making signals. These two frigates continued to near each other, and at 3 h. 30 m. A.M. on the 17th were only half a mile apart; when, observing on his lee beam two other frigates, the Belvidera and Æolus, and astern of them three more vessels, the Shannon, Africa, and a schooner, none of whom answered or appeared to understand his signals, Captain Dacres concluded that they were the squadron of Commodore Rodgers, and tacked. The consequence of this mistake was, that at daylight the Guerrière and Constitution were nearly two miles instead of only half a mile from each other.

At daylight it was quite calm. The Constitution, while she steered, kept her head to the southward. At this time the Belvidera was about four miles on her lee-quarter, or bearing about north-east by north; the Guerrière at some distance astern of the Belvidera; the Shannon upon the latter's weather-quarter, or about west-north-west, distant two miles; and the Æolus at no great distance from the Shannon. The Africa was considerably astern of these two ships, and gradually losing ground in the chase. At 5 h. 30 m. A.M., the Constitution no longer steering, the boats were sent ahead to tow the ship's head to the southward. At the same time a 24-pounder was hoisted up from the main deck; and that and the forecastle 24-pounder were got aft to be used, along with the quarter-deck 24-pounder, as stern-chasers. The taffrail was then cut away, to give the three guns room, and two more 24-pounders were pointed through the stern ports on the main deck. At about 5 h. 45 m. the Belvidera and other British ships began towing with their boats. At 6 A.M. the Constitution got her head to the southward, and set topgallant studding-sails and staysails. At 7 A.M., having a few minutes before sounded in 26 fathoms, Captain Hull, at the suggestion of Lieutenant Charles Morris, first of the ship, got out a kedge, and began warping ahead. At 7 h. 30 m. the Constitution hoisted her colours, and fired one shot at the Belvidera.

At 9 A.M. a light air sprang up from the south-south-east, and the ships all trimmed sails on the larboard tack. The Belvidera gaining, the Constitution started a portion of her water, and threw overboard some of her booms. At 10 h. 30 m. the breeze freshened; but, in a few minutes, again subsided to nearly a calm. Observing the benefit that the Constitution had derived from warping, Captain Byron did the same; "bending all his hawsers to one another, and working two kedge anchors at the same time, by paying the warp through one hawse-hole as it was run in through another opposite."[1] The effect of this was such, that the Belvidera, by 2 P.M., got near enough to exchange bow and stern chasers with the Constitution, but without effect on either side. At 3 P.M., a light breeze having sprung up, the Constitution rather gained, and the firing ceased. During the afternoon and night the chase continued, to the gradual advantage of the American frigate.

On the 18th, at daylight, the Constitution bore from the Belvidera south-west distant four miles, and the Shannon bore from the latter north-east distant six miles. At 4 h. A.M. the Belvidera tacked to the eastward, with a light air from the south by east; and at 4 h. 20 m. the Constitution did the same. At 9 A.M. an American merchant-ship was seen bearing down towards the squadron; upon which the Belvidera, by way of a decoy, hoisted American colours. To counteract the effect of this ruse, the Constitution hoisted English colours, and the merchant-vessel hauled off and escaped capture. At 4 P.M., owing to the permanency of the breeze, the Constitution was seven miles ahead, and at daylight on the 19th had attained double that distance. The British squadron persevered until about 8 h. 30 m. A.M.; then gave up the chase, and stood to the northward and eastward; latitude at noon the same day 38° north, and longitude 71° 20' west.

On the 29th of July, in latitude 40° 44', longitude 62° 41', Captain Broke fell in with the expected homeward-bound Jamaica fleet, consisting of about 60 sail, under convoy of the 38-gun frigate Thetis, Captain William Henry Byam; and on the 6th of August, having escorted it over the banks of Newfoundland, to about latitude 43° 20', longitude 50°, he stood back towards the American coast. On this or the following

[1] Marshall, vol. ii., p. 627.

day the Guerrière parted company for Halifax, to obtain that refit which could now no longer be postponed. Indeed, the ship was in a far less effective state than when she had joined the squadron, having sent away in prizes her third-lieutenant (John Pullman), second-lieutenant of marines, three midshipmen, and 24 of her best seamen; thus leaving herself with only 250 men and 19 boys.

On the 19th of August, at 2 A.M., latitude, by her reckoning, 40° 20' north, longitude 55° west, standing by the wind on the starboard tack under easy sail, with her head about west-southwest, the Guerrière discovered a sail on her weather-beam. This was the Constitution; who, after her escape from the Guerrière and her consorts on the morning of the 19th of July, finding herself cut off from New York, had proceeded to Boston; where she arrived on the 26th. On the 2nd of August, Captain Hull again set sail, and stood to the eastward, in the hope of falling in with the British 38-gun frigate Spartan, Captain Edward Pelham Brenton, reported to be cruising in that direction. Having run along the coast as far as the bay of Fundy without discovering the object of her pursuit, the Constitution proceeded off Halifax and Cape Sable, and then steered to the eastward in the direction of Newfoundland. Passing close to the isle of Sable, the American frigate took a station off the gulf of St. Lawrence, near Cape Race, for the purpose of intercepting vessels bound to, or from Quebec and New Brunswick. On the 15th, Captain Hull captured, and on account of their small value burnt, two merchant-brigs and a bark; and on the 17th recaptured from the British ship-sloop Avenger, the American brig Adeline, on board of which he placed a prize-master and six or seven men, to take her to Boston. Having received intelligence that the squadron which, by a display of so much skill and perseverance, the Constitution had already once evaded, was off the Grand Bank, Captain Hull changed his cruising-ground, and stood to the southward. On the 18th, at midnight, an American privateer gave information that she had the day before seen a British ship-of-war to the southward. The Constitution immediately made sail in that direction; and, in the course of a few hours, Captain Hull found he had not been misinformed.

The Guerrière, when she arrived on the North-American station, was armed the same as the other frigates of her class, with 46 guns, including 16 carronades, 32-pounders, and two long nines on her quarter-deck and forecastle. Like most

French ships, the Guerrière sailed very much by the head; and, to assist in giving her that trim, as well as to obviate the inconvenience of a round-house which intervened between the foremost and bridle ports on each side, and prevented the gun stationed at the former port from being shifted to the latter when required to be used in chase, two additional 18-pounders, as standing bow-chase guns, were taken on board at Halifax; thus giving the Guerrière 48 guns, including 30 long 18-pounders on the main deck. The mere fact, that, for any use they could be in either broadside, these bow guns might as well have been in the hold, is not the principal point cleared up by the explanation. Those who are aware, that no frigate in the British navy, except the Acasta and Lavinia, and none at all belonging to the French navy, mounts as her establishment 30 long 18-pounders on the main deck, would have a right to consider the Guerrière as a frigate of a superior class and description; and so, for that very reason, is she still generally considered, as well on this as on the opposite side of the Atlantic. We are surprised that neither of our contemporaries, both of whom have given proofs that the first edition of this work has been occasionally consulted by them, has thought it worth his while to point out so important a peculiarity in the Guerrière's armament.[1]

We have already, at some length, shown how particular the Americans were in manning their ships; and how easy, having so few ships to man, it was to supply them with picked crews. For many years previous to the war, America had been decoying the men from British ships, by every artful stratagem. No ship that anchored in her waters could send a boat on shore without having the crew assailed by a recruiting party from some American frigate fitting in the vicinity. Many British seamen had also entered on board American merchant-vessels; and the numerous non-intercourse and embargo bills, in existence at different periods during the four years preceding the war, threw many merchant sailors out of employment. So that the captains of the American frigates, when preparing for active warfare, had to pick their complements from a numerous body of seamen. Highly to the credit of the naval administration of the United States, the crews of their ships were taught the practical rules of gunnery; and ten shot, with the necessary powder, were allowed to be expended in play, to make one hit in earnest.

[1] Brenton, vol. v., p. 52. Marshall, vol. ii., p. 974. note.

Very distinct from the American seamen, so called, were the American marines. They were chiefly made up of natives of the country; and a deserter from the British would here have been no acquisition. In the United States, every man may hunt or shoot among the wild animals of the forest. The young peasant, or back-woodman, carries a rifled-barrel gun, the moment he can lift one to his shoulder; and woe to the duck or deer that attempts to pass him, within fair range of his piece. To collect these expert marksmen, when of a proper age, officers were sent into the western parts of the Union; and, to embody and finish drilling them, a marine-barrack was established near Washington: from which dépôt the American ships were regularly supplied.

With respect to a British ship-of-war, her case was widely different. Although the captain was eased of much of his trouble, by having, in proportion to the size and mounted force of his ship, a considerably smaller crew to collect, by having about one-twentieth part of that crew to form of boys and widows' men, or men of straw, and by being permitted to enter a large proportion of landsmen, a rating unknown on board an American ship-of-war; still was the small remainder most difficult to be procured, even with all the latitude allowed in respect to age, size, and nautical experience. Sometimes when a captain, by dint of extraordinary exertions, had provided himself with a crew, such as a man-of-war's crew ought to be, the admiral on the station to which he belonged would pronounce the ship "too well manned," and order a proportion of her best men to be draughted on board the flag-ship at her moorings, to learn to be idle and worthless: sending, in lieu of them, a parcel of jail-birds and raw hands, to make those among whom they were going nearly as bad as themselves.

There was another point in which the generality of British crews, as compared with any one American crew, were miserably deficient; skill in the art of gunnery. While the American seamen were constantly firing at marks, the British seamen, except in particular cases, scarcely did so once in a year; and some ships could be named, on board of which not a shot had been fired in this way for upwards of three years. Nor was the fault wholly the captain's: the instructions, under which he was bound to act, forbade him to use, during the first six months after the ship had received her armament, more shots per month than amounted to a third in number of her upper-deck guns; and, after those six months had expired, he was to use only half the quantity. Considering by this, either that the lords of the admiralty discouraged firing at marks as a lavish expenditure of powder and shot, or that the limits they had thus set to the exercise of that branch of naval discipline destroyed its practical utility, many captains never put a shot in the guns until an enemy appeared: they employed the leisure time of the men in handling the sails, and in decorating the ship. Others, again, caring little about an order that placed their professional characters in jeopardy, exercised the crew repeatedly in firing at marks; leaving the gunner to account, in the best manner he could, for the deficiency in his stores. As the generality of French crews were equally inexperienced with their British opponents, the unskilfulness of the latter in gunnery was not felt or remarked: we shall now have to adduce some instances, in quick succession, that will clearly show how much the British navy at length suffered by having relaxed in its attention to that most essential point in the business of war, the proper use of the weapons by which it was to be waged.

That our opinion on this subject is in perfect accordance with what was the opinion of a British officer of the first rank and distinction, will appear by the following quotation from the work of a contemporary:—" The Earl of St. Vincent," says Captain Brenton, " in a letter to the author in 1813, thus expresses himself, ' I hear the exercise of the great gun is laid aside, and is succeeded by a foolish frippery and useless ornament.' How far this may have been the case," proceeds Captain B., " in the Mediterranean, or East or West Indies, with ships of the line, we shall not say; but certainly on the coast of North America it was not so, the ships on that station being kept constantly in exercise under the daily expectation of a war."[1] Notwithstanding this to us wholly unexpected dissent on the part of Captain Brenton from an opinion given by Earl St. Vincent, we shall consider the latter to be the highest authority on the subject; especially as the former, in including the Mediterranean among the stations on which ships of the line were neglected to be exercised, has overlooked the very strict and commendable attention paid to that important branch of discipline by Vice-admiral Sir Edward Pellew.

We have already given the best account which the imperfect state of the American records has enabled us to give of the construction, size, and established armament of the three American 44-gun frigates. We have now to notice a slight alteration, that

[1] Brenton, vol. v., p. 44.

was afterwards made in the armament of the Constitution. In the summer of 1811, when that frigate was fitting for sea at Norfolk, Virginia, Captain Hull considered that her upper-works would not strain so much as they had been found to do if her 42-pounder carronades were exchanged for 32s. This he got effected; and on or about the 31st of July the Constitution sailed for Cherbourg, with those guns and a reduced crew of 380 men on board. On the 6th or 7th of September the Constitution reached her destination, and in a month or two afterwards returned to her anchorage at Norfolk.

Having discovered that 380 men, even in peaceable times, were not enough for so large and heavily-rigged a ship as the Constitution, Captain Hull, during his stay in the Chesapeake, enlisted as many more as restored his complement to 476. But, finding probably that the removal of six tons from the Constitution's upper battery afforded the ship great relief in a heavy sea, Captain Hull did not take back his 42-pounders. He contrived, however, to reduce the inequality of force by opening a port in the centre of the gangway for one of the two 24-pounders on the upper-deck; or rather, as to be precise we should designate them, the two English long 18-pounders (battery-guns, we believe), bored to carry a 24-pound shot. We formerly noticed the extraordinary size and weight of the Constitution's main-deck 24-pounders. It appears that the guns were mounted on very high carriages, which the height of the deck, represented to be nearly eight feet, rendered no inconvenience. The height of the President's midship main-deck port-sill from the water's edge was eight feet eight inches, and she is described as the lowest ship of the three. This goes far to reconcile the statement we have often heard made, that the Constitution's main deck battery was upwards of 10 feet from the water; a height which, at a long distance, gave her a decided advantage in the range.

It is a remarkable fact, that no one act of the little navy of the United States had been at all calculated to gain the respect of the British. First was seen the Chesapeake allowing herself to be beaten, with impunity, by a British ship only nominally superior to her. Then the huge frigate President attacks, and fights for upwards of half an hour, the British sloop Little Belt. And, even since the war, the same President, at the head of a squadron, makes a bungling business of chasing the Belvidera. While, therefore, a feeling towards America, bordering on contempt, had unhappily possessed the mind of the British naval officer, rendering him more than usually careless and opiniative.

the American naval officer, having been taught to regard his new foe with a portion of dread, sailed forth to meet him with the whole of his energies roused. A moment's reflection taught him, that the honour of his country was now in his hands; and what in the breast of man could be a stronger incitement to extraordinary exertions? Thus situated were the navies of the two countries, when, with damaged masts, a reduced complement, and in absolute need of that thorough refit for which she was then, after a very long cruise, speeding to Halifax, the Guerrière encountered the Constitution, 17 days only from port, manned with a full complement, and in all respects fitted for war.

It was, as we have already stated, about 2 P.M. that the Guerrière, standing by the wind on the starboard tack, under topsails, foresail, jib, and spanker, with the wind blowing fresh from the north-west, discovered the Constitution bearing down towards her. At 3 P.M. each ship made out the other to be an enemy's man-of-war; and at 3 h. 30 m. each discovered, with tolerable precision, the force that was about to be opposed to her. At 4 h. 30 m. P.M. the Guerrière laid her maintopsail to the mast, to enable the Constitution the more quickly to close. The latter, then about three miles distant, shortened sail to double-reefed topsails, and went to quarters. At 4 h. 45 m. P.M. the Guerrière hoisted one English ensign at the peak, another at the mizentopgallantmast-head, and a union-jack at the fore; and, at 4 h. 50 m. P.M.,[1] opened her starboard broadside at the Constitution. The Guerrière then filled, wore, and, on coming round on the larboard tack, fired her larboard guns, "her shot," says Captain Hull, "falling short;" a proof, either that the Guerrière's people knew not the range of their guns, or that the powder they were using was of an inferior quality: both causes, indeed, might have co-operated in producing the discreditable result.

At 5 h. 5 m. P.M., having run up one American ensign at the peak, lashed another to the larboard mizen rigging, and hoisted a third flag at the foretopgallantmast-head, the Constitution opened her fire; and, it is believed, none of her shot fell short. To avoid being raked, the Guerrière wore three or four times; and continued discharging her alternate broadsides, with about as little effect, owing to her constant change of position and the necessary alteration in the level of her guns, as when her shot fell short. After the Constitution had amused herself in this

[1] In noticing the time, we shall generally, as on former occasions, take the mean of the two statements.

way for half an hour, she set her maintopgallantsail, and in five minutes, or at about 5 h. 45 m. P.M.,[1] brought the Guerrière to close action on the larboard[2] beam; both ships steering with the wind on the larboard quarter. At 6 h. 5 m. P.M. a 24-pound shot struck the Guerrière's mizenmast and carried it away by the board. It fell over the starboard quarter, knocked a large hole in the counter, and, by dragging in the water, brought the ship up in the wind, although her helm was kept hard a-port. By this accident to her opponent, who had then sustained only a very slight loss, the Constitution would have ranged ahead; but, bearing up, she quickly placed herself in an admirable position on the Guerrière's larboard bow. Now the American riflemen in the Constitution's tops had an opportunity of co-operating with their friends on deck; and a sweeping and most destructive fire of great guns and small-arms was opened upon the British frigate, whose bow-guns were all she could bring to bear in return.

At 6 h. 15 m. P.M. the two ships fell on board each other, the Guerrière's bowsprit getting foul of the Constitution's starboard mizen rigging. The crew of the latter now prepared to board the Guerrière; but, in addition to the impracticability of the attempt owing to the motion of the ships, a slight pause was created by the fall of some of the American leaders: a shot from a British marine brought down the first-lieutenant of marines while leading forward his party; another well-directed musket-shot passed through the body of the first-lieutenant of the ship while at the head of the boarding seamen; and a third shot entered the shoulder of the master, as he was standing near Lieutenant Morris. The riflemen in the Constitution's tops, in the mean time, continued their unerring fire. Among those who suffered on the occasion was Captain Dacres himself, by a ball fired from the enemy's mizentop, which inflicted a severe wound in his back, while he was standing on the starboard forecastle hammocks, animating his crew. Although suffering greatly, he would not quit the deck. At about the same moment the master was shot through the knee, and a master's mate (Samuel Grant) was wounded very severely. In a few minutes the two ships got clear. Having disentangled her bowsprit from her opponent's mizen rigging, the Guerrière now came to a little, and was enabled to bring a few of her foremost guns on the starboard side to bear. Some of the wads from these set fire to the Constitution's cabin, but the flames were soon extinguished. The

---

[1] See diagram at p. 379. [2] "Starboard," by mistake, in the Gazette account

Guerrière's "bowsprit, at that moment striking the taffrail of the Constitution, slacked the fore-stay of the Guerrière, and, the fore-shrouds on the larboard or weather side being mostly shot away, the mast fell over on the starboard side, crossing the main-stay: the sudden jerk carried the mainmast along with it, leaving the Guerrière a defenceless wreck, rolling her main-deck guns in the water."[1]

At about 6 h. 23 m.[2] the Constitution ranged ahead: and the Guerrière soon began clearing away the wreck of her masts, to be ready to renew the action. Just, however, as she had succeeded in doing so, her spritsail-yard, upon which she had set a sail to endeavour to get before the wind, was carried away. The Guerrière now lay an unmanageable hulk in the trough of the sea, rolling her main-deck guns under water: to secure which required increased efforts, the rotten state of the breechings, as well as of the timber-heads through which the long-bolts passed, having caused many of them to break loose. While the British frigate was in this state, the Constitution, at 6 h. 45 m. P.M., having rove new braces, wore round and took a position within pistol-shot on her starboard quarter. It being utterly in vain to contend any longer, the Guerrière fired a lee-gun, and hauled down the union-jack from the stump of her mizenmast. The following diagram will show the progress of this action, from the time the two ships closed to the moment of the Guerrière's surrender.

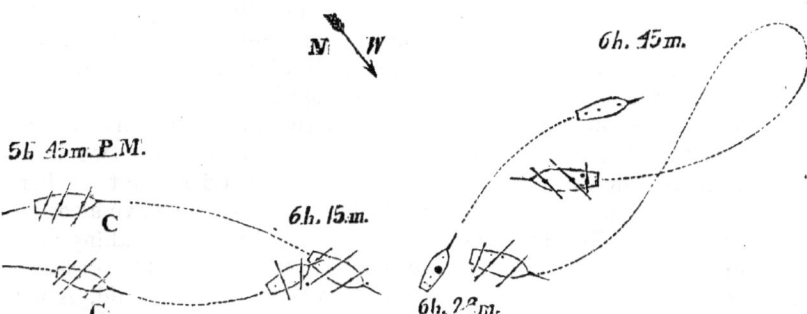

Much to his credit, the moment the Constitution hoisted her colours, Captain Dacres ordered seven Americans, that belonged to his reduced crew, to go below: one accidentally remained at his gun, the remainder went where they had been ordered. This just left 244 men and 19 boys. Out of this number,

[1] Brenton, vol. v., p. 51.   [2] See diagram.

the Guerrière had her second-lieutenant (Henry Ready), 11 seamen, and three marines killed, her captain (severely), first-lieutenant (Bartholomew Kent, slightly), master (Robert Scott), two master's mates (Samuel Grant and William John Snow), one midshipman (James Enslie), 43 seamen, 13 marines, and one boy wounded; total, 15 killed and 63 wounded, six of the latter mortally, 39 severely, and 18 slightly. Out of her 468 men and boys, the Constitution, according to Captain Hull's statement, had one lieutenant of marines (William S. Bush) and six seamen killed, her first-lieutenant (Charles Morris, dangerously), master (John C. Alwyn, slightly), four seamen (three of them dangerously), and one marine wounded; total, seven killed and seven wounded. But several of the Guerrière's officers counted 13 wounded; of whom three died after amputation. An equal number of killed and wounded, as stated in the American return, scarcely ever occurs, except in cases of explosion. In the British service, every wounded man, although merely scratched, reports himself to the surgeon, that he may get his smart-money, a pecuniary allowance so named. No such regulation exists in the American service; consequently the return of loss sustained in action by an American ship, as far as respects the wounded at least, is made subservient to the views of the commander and his government.

Although Captain Hull does not give his prize any guns at all, no other American account gives the Guerrière less than 49 guns. It is true that, besides the 48 guns already specified, the ship had an 18-pounder launch carronade, mounted upon the usual elevating carriage for firing at the tops; but the priming-iron, when put into the touch-hole just before the action commenced, broke short off and spiked the gun. In this state it was found by the captors. Consequently, as the two bow 18-pounders were equally useless, the Guerrière, out of her 49 guns, could employ in broadside only 23. We have already shown that the American 44-gun frigate, without making any use of her concealed gangway ports, could present 28 carriage-guns in broadside; but the Constitution could and did, as we now verily believe, present one gun more.[1] Of the fact of one of her two upper-deck 24-pounders being stationed on the forecastle and the other on the quarter-deck, we have not a doubt, from the following entry in the log of the Constitution when she was pursued by the British off New York, and was about to open a fire from her stern-chasers,—" Got the forecastle gun aft." But

[1] See p, 376.

the disparity in her action with the Guerrière is sufficiently great without adding this gun to the Constitution's broadside: we shall therefore, as in common cases, take no more than half the mounted number.

As it would be not only unjust, but absurd, to compare together the totals of two crews of men and boys, in a case where each opponent uses the latter in so very different a proportion as the British and the Americans, we shall, making an ample allowance for those in the American crew, exclude the boys altogether from the estimate.

This action affords a strong practical proof of the advantages possessed by a large and lofty ship. While the main deck of the Guerrière was all afloat with the roughness of the sea, the Constitution's main deck was perfectly dry. If that was the case before the fall of the Guerrière's masts had destroyed her stability, what must it have been afterwards? It is this consideration that renders the tonnage so important an item in any statement of comparative force. The relative scantling is another essential point, for which the one-third disparity in size between these figures will partly allow. By an unfortunate typographical (as we take it) error, Captain Brenton represents the Constitution as " an American frigate of the same force as the President, though inferior (superior?) as to scantling."[1] Now, the extraordinary thickness and solidity of the Constitution's sides had long obtained her, among the people who best knew her, the name of "Old Ironsides." We have already shown that the President, an acknowledged lighter ship, possessed stouter sides than a British 74: we may therefore consider, that the topsides of the Constitution were at least equal in thickness to the topsides of a British 80.

With respect to the advantages of stout scantling, we are willing to take the opinion of the Americans themselves. A letter from Mr. Paul Hamilton, the secretary of the American navy, written a few months after the Guerrière's capture, and addressed to the "Chairman of the Naval Committee of the House of Representatives," contains the following paragraph: "A 76 is built of heavier timber, is intrinsically much stronger than a frigate in all her works, and can sustain battering much longer, and with less injury. A shot which would sink a frigate might be received by a 76 with but little injury: it might pass between wind and water through a frigate, when it would stick in the frame of a 76." Nor is this merely the

[1] Brenton, vol. v., p. 49.

opinion of Mr. Secretary Hamilton: it is the result of "a very valuable communication received from Charles Stewart, Esq., a captain in the navy of the United States, an officer of great observation, distinguished talents, and very extensive professional experience; in whose opinion," adds Mr. H., "I believe all the most enlightened officers in our service concur." By a singular coincidence, too, subjoined to this highly-complimented officer's communication to Mr. Hamilton, are the signatures of Captain Hull and his first-lieutenant to a brief but comprehensive sentence of approval: "We agree with Captain Stewart in the above statement in all its parts."[1]

We have before remarked upon the great care and expense bestowed by the Americans in equipping their few ships-of-war. As one important instance may be adduced, the substitution of fine sheet-lead for cartridges, instead of flannel or paper. This gives a decided advantage in action, an advantage almost equal to one gun in three; for, as a sheet-lead cartridge will hardly ever leave a particle of itself behind, there is no necessity to sponge the gun, and very seldom any to worm it: operations that, with paper or flannel cartridges, must be attended to every time the gun is fired. The advantage of quick firing no one can dispute, any more than, from the explanation just given, the facility with which it can be practised by means of the sheet-lead cartridge. The principal objection against the use of this kind of cartridge in the British navy is its expense; another may be, that it causes the powder to get damp. The last objection is obviated by filling no more cartridges than will serve for present use; and, should more be wanted, the Americans have always spare hands enough to fill them.

Although, in the American accounts of actions, no other description of cannon-shot is ever named as used on board their ships than "round and grape," it is now so well known as scarcely to need repetition, that the Americans were greatly indebted for their success over the British to a practice of discharging, in the first two or three broadsides, chain, bar, and every other species of dismantling shot, in order to cut away the enemy's rigging, and facilitate the fall of his masts. As an additional means of clearing the decks of British ships of the (seldom over numerous) men upon them, the carronades, when close action commenced, were filled with jagged pieces of iron and copper, rusty nails, and other "langridge" of that description. Of the riflemen in the tops we have already spoken; but

[1] Clark's Naval History, vol. ii., pp. 236, 246.

even the remaining musketry-men of the crew were provided in a novel and murderous manner: every cartridge they fired contained three or four buck-shot, it being rightly judged, that a buck-shot, well placed, would send a man from his quarters as well as the heaviest ball in use. We mention these circumstances not to dwell for a moment upon their unfairness, but merely to show the extraordinary means to which the Americans resorted, for the purpose of enabling them to cope with the British at sea. Now, then, for the

Comparative Force of the Combatants.

			Guerrière.	Constitution.
Broadside-guns	. . . .	No	24	28
		lbs	517	768
Crew (men only)	. . .	No.	244	460
Size		tons.	1092	1533

Even this statement, with the one-third disparity in guns, and nearly two-fold disparity in men, which it exhibits, will not convey a clear idea of the real inequality of force that existed between the Guerrière and Constitution, without allowance is made for the ineffective state in which the former commenced the action. There is one circumstance, also, which has greatly contributed to mislead the judgment of the public in deciding upon the merits of this and its succeeding fellow-actions: a belief, grounded on the official accounts, that British frigates of the Guerrière's class had frequently captured French frigates carrying 24-pounders on the main deck. But, in truth, the Forte is the only 24-pounder French frigate captured by a British 38-gun frigate; and the Forte, in point of force and readiness for action, was not to be compared with the Constitution.[1] That even French 18-pounder frigates were not, in common cases, captured by British frigates of the same class, without some hard fighting, and a good deal of blood spilt on both sides, these pages afford many proofs. Upon the whole, therefore, no reasonable man can now be surprised at the result of the action between the Guerrière and Constitution. Nor was there in the conduct of the Guerrière, throughout the engagement, anything that could militate, in the slightest degree, against the long-maintained character of British seamen. With respect to Captain Dacres, he evinced a great share of personal bravery on the trying occasion; and we confess ourselves to have been among the number of those who did not recollect

[1] See vol. ii., p. 261.

that, although the Guerrière had made herself very obnoxious to the Americans, it was before Captain Dacres was appointed to her.

The chief cause of quarrel between the Americans and the Guerrière undoubtedly arose while Captain Pechell commanded her; but still it was the same ship, or, to those who doubted that fact, a ship of the same name, which Captain Hull had captured. Most desirable, therefore, would the Guerrière have been as a trophy; but the shattered state of her hull precluded the possibility of getting the ship into port. At daylight, on the day succeeding the action, the American prize-master hailed the Constitution, to say that the Guerrière had four feet water in the hold, and was in a sinking condition. Quickly the prisoners were removed out of her; and at 3 h. 30 m. P.M., having been set on fire by Captain Hull's order, the Guerrière blew up.

Having by the evening repaired her principal damages, including a few wounds in each of her three masts, the Constitution made sail from the spot of her achievement, and on the 30th anchored in the harbour of Boston. As may well be conceived, Captain Hull and his officers and crew were greeted with applause by their native and adopted countrymen. He and they also received, at a subsequent day, the thanks of the government, accompanied by a present of 50,000 dollars.

It is a singular fact, that in the letter published in the "National Intelligencer," as that transmitted by Captain Hull to his government, not a word appears respecting the force of the ship which the Constitution had captured. Captain Hull's letter is in this respect an anomaly of the kind. Perhaps, as the American newspapers had frequently stated, that the Constitution mounted 56 guns, and as dead ships, like dead men, "tell no tales," Captain Hull thought it better to leave his friends and countrymen to form their opinion, relative to the force and size of his prize, out of the following sentence: "So fine a ship as the Guerrière, commanded by an able and experienced officer." If Captain Hull did practise this ruse (and the men of Connecticut are proverbially shrewd), the effect, as we shall presently see, must almost have exceeded his hopes.

When the British says to an American officer,—"Our frigates and yours are not a match," the latter very properly replies: "You did not think so once." But what does this amount to? Admitting that the force of the American 44-gun frigate was fully known before the Guerrière's action, but which was only

GUERRIERE AND CONSTITUTION.

partially the case; and admitting that the British 38-gun frigate was considered able to fight her, all that can be said is, that many, who once thought otherwise, are now convinced, that an American and a British ship, in relative force as three to two, are not equally matched. The facts are the same: it is the opinion only that has changed. Man the Constitution with 470 Turks or Algerines; and even then she would hardly be pronounced, now that her force is known, a match for the Guerrière. The truth is, the name "frigate" had imposed upon the public; and to that, and that only, must be attributed the angry repinings of many of the British journalists at the capture of the Guerrière. They, sitting safe at their desks, would have sent her and every soul on board to the bottom, with colours flying, because her antagonist was a "frigate;" whereas, had the Constitution been called "a 50-gun ship," a defence only half as honourable as the Guerrière's would have gained for her officers and crew universal applause.

Captain Hull, and the officers and men of the Constitution, deserve much credit for what they did do; first, for attacking a British frigate at all, and next, for conquering one a third inferior in force. It was not for them to reject the reward presented by the "Senate and House of Representatives of the United States," because it expressed to be, for capturing a frigate (now for the effect of Captain Hull's "fine ship Guerrière"), "mounting 54 carriage-guns," instead of, with two standing bow-chasers and a boat-carronade included, 49. Smiling in their sleeves at the credulity of the donors, the captain and his people, without disputing the terms, pocketed the dollars. But is a writer, who stands pledged to deal impartially between nation and nation, to forbear exposing this trickery, because it may suit the Americans to invent any falsehoods, no matter how barefaced, to foist a valiant character upon themselves?

The author of the American "Naval History," Mr. Clark, remarks thus upon the Guerrière's capture: "It has manifested the genuine worth of the American tar, and that the vigorous co-operation of the country is all he requires, to enable him to meet, even under disadvantageous circumstances, and to derive glory from the encounter, with the naval heroes of a nation which has so long ruled the waves."[1] But was it really "American tars" that conquered the Guerrière? Let us investigate, as far as we are able, this loudly-asserted claim. Our contemporary says, "It appeared in evidence on the court-martial,

[1] Clark's Naval History of the United States, vol. i. p. 174.

that there were many Englishmen on board the Constitution, and these were leading men, or captains of guns. The officers of the Guerrière knew some of them personally, and one man in particular, who had been captain of the forecastle in the Eurydice, a British frigate, then recently come from England. Another was in the Achille at Trafalgar; and the third-lieutenant of the Constitution, whose name was Reed, was an Irishman. It was said, and we have no reason to doubt the fact, that there were 200 British seamen on board the Constitution when she began the action."[1] One fellow, who after the action was sitting under the half-deck busily employed in making buck-shot cartridges to mangle his honourable countrymen, had served under Mr. Kent, the first-lieutenant. He now went by a new name; but, on seeing his old commanding-officer standing before him, a glow of shame overspread his countenance.

In the latter end of the year 1816 a work issued from the Washington press, entitled, "A Register of Officers and Agents, Civil, Military, and Naval, in the Service of the United States, &c. Prepared at the Department of State, by a resolution of Congress." Affixed to the list of names in this official document, is one column headed "State or Country where Born." Turning to this column in the "Navy Department," we find that, out of the 32 captains, one only, "Thomas Tingey," has "England" marked as his birthplace. There was another, we know; but he had died about a twelvemonth before, Captain Smith of the Congress. Three blanks occur; and we consider it rather creditable to Captains "John Shaw," "Daniel T. Patterson," and "John Orde Creighton," that they were ashamed to tell where they were born. Of the 22 masters commandant, one only appears to have been born out of the United States, and that is "George C. Read," of "Ireland;" the same, no doubt, mentioned by Captain Brenton, as the third-lieutenant of the Constitution in August, 1812. Of the 160 lieutenants, there appear to be only five born out of the United States; of which five, "Walter Stewart," "William Finch," and "Benjamin Page, jun.," are stated to be of "England," and "James Ramage," of "Ireland." To 17 names, all English and Irish, appears no birthplace. We shall pass over the surgeons, their mates, the pursers, chaplains, and midshipmen; among whom we find, besides a few blanks, only eight of England and Ireland. As we descend in the list, the blanks in the column of "Country where born" increase surprisingly. Now, as the native Ameri-

[1] Brenton, vol. v., p. 54.

can seaman usually carries about him his certificate of citizenship; and, as scarcely any man is to be found who, if he can speak at all, cannot answer the question, "Where were you born?" we must consider that the birthplace is purposely omitted, because, being a native of Great Britain or Ireland, and probably a deserter from the British navy, the fellow is ashamed or afraid to avow it. Hence, out of the 83 sailing-masters, we find eight born in England, Scotland, Ireland, and Bermuda, and 15 without any birthplace assigned to them. Among the 20 boatswains, one is stated to have been born in England, four in the United States, and the rest nowhere. Of the 25 gunners, three appear to have been born in the United States, one in Germany, another in Portugal, and the remaining four-fifths in some nameless country. Of the 18 carpenters, 11 sail-makers, and four master's mates, 33 in all, five only have been able or willing to enable the Washington state-clerk to fill up the important blanks.

Can any one, after the analysis we have given of this curious American state-document, entertain a doubt that, during the late war between Great Britain and the United States, one third in number, and nearly one-half in point of effectiveness, of the seamen that fought in the ships of the latter were bred on the soil, and educated in the ships of the former? This may appear very discreditable to British seamen, considered as a body; but it should be recollected, that the total of the seamen belonging to the American ships-of-war formed only a small portion of those employed in the British navy. Moreover, a large proportion of the deserters and renegades that entered the service of the United States, were Irish Roman Catholics. It is for this reason that an American captain can sometimes assert, with no great degree of untruth, that he has a few "Englishmen" among his crew.

There were, it appears, on board the Constitution, so many men whom the crew of the Guerrière considered as their countrymen, so many who felt, as well they might feel, some degree of compunction at their fallen state, that Captain Hull was afraid the two bodies united would overpower him and his Americans, and carry the Constitution to Halifax. He very naturally, and very properly, we think, "kept his prisoners manacled and chained to the deck during the night, and the greater part of the day."[1] One reason for doing this, might be to render more alluring the offer of liberty made to those who would turn traitors,

[1] Brenton, vol. v., p. 54.

Being perfectly aware, that all the British whom they could persuade to enter, would fight in the most desperate manner rather than be taken and turned over to their certain and merited fate, Captain Hull and his officers, as well while the Constitution was steering for Boston, as after she had arrived there, used every art to inveigle the late Guerrière's crew to enlist in the American service. Eight Englishmen, however, were all that remained in the United States; and only two of those entered on board the Constitution.

On the 2nd of the succeeding October, a court-martial assembled on board the Africa 64, Halifax harbour, to try the captain, officers, and late crew of the Guerrière; when, as may be anticipated from the details already given, the following sentence of acquittal was pronounced:—" Having attended to the whole of the evidence, and also to the defence of Captain Dacres, the court agreed, that the surrender of the Guerrière was proper in order to preserve the lives of her valuable remaining crew; and that her being in that lamentable situation was from the accident of her masts going, which was occasioned more by their defective state than from the fire of the enemy, though so greatly superior in guns and men. The court do, therefore, unanimously and honourably acquit the said Captain Dacres, the officers and crew, of his majesty's late ship the Guerrière, and they are hereby honourably acquitted accordingly. The court, at the same time, feel themselves called upon to express the high sense they entertain of the conduct of the ship's company in general, when prisoners, but more particularly of those who withstood the attempts made to shake their loyalty, by offering them high bribes to enter into the land and sea-service of the enemy, and they will represent their merit to the commander-in-chief."

In his official letter, dated at Boston, September 7, Captain Dacres compliments Captain Hull and his officers, for their treatment of his men, " the greatest care being taken to prevent them losing the smallest trifle." But, considering perhaps that, in an enemy's country, it would be unwise to commit complaints or the chance of leading to further oppression, Captain Dacres remained silent about the attempts to inveigle his crew, until he addressed the members of his court-martial at Halifax. The concluding passage of that address is in the following words: " Notwithstanding the unlucky issue of this affair, such confidence have I in the exertions of the officers and men who belonged to the Guerrière; and I am so well aware that the success of my opponent was owing to fortune, that it is my earnest wish, and would be the happiest period of my life, to be once more opposed to the Constitution, with them under my command, in a frigate of similar force to the Guerrière."

That the captain of the Guerrière should have expressed such an opinion on such an occasion is allowable enough; but we are surprised to find that opinion seconded by the captain of the Spartan, a frigate of the same force as the Guerrière, a frigate which the Constitution herself had just come from seeking when she fell in with the latter. "Thus far," says Captain Brenton, "the two ships had fought with an equal chance of success, when the day was decided by one of those accidents to which ships-of-war are ever liable, and which can be rarely guarded against."[1] He then describes the fall of the Guerrière's mizen-mast. We are stopped, however, in the comments we were going to make, by observing, at the conclusion of the account of the Guerrière's capture, the following paragraph, whether in confirmation or contradiction of the former passage, let others decide: "The inference is erroneous (that our navy was declining and our officers and men deficient in their duty), founded on a supposition, that, if two ships happen to be called frigates, the lesser one, being manned and commanded by Englishmen, ought to take the greater, though a ship very nearly double her force, in size, guns, and men: we need scarcely enter into any argument to prove the fallacy of such an expectation."[2]

On the 12th of September the British 18-gun brig-sloop Frolic, Captain Thomas Whinyates, quitted the bay of Honduras, with about 14 sail of merchantmen under convoy, for England. On arriving off Havana, the master of a Guernsey ship informed Captain Whinyates of the war with America, and of the Guerrière's capture. Having been five years in the West Indies, and being very sickly in her crew, the Frolic was by no means in a fit state to encounter an enemy's vessel of a similar class to herself. However, there was no alternative; and the brig proceeded on her voyage along the coast of the United States.

On the night of the 16th of October, in latitude 36° north, longitude 64° west, a violent gale of wind came on, which separated the Frolic from her convoy, carried away her main-yard, sprung the maintopmast, and tore both topsails to pieces. By dark on the evening of the 17th, six of the missing ships had joined; and on the 18th, at daybreak, while the Frolic, in a very turbulent sea, was repairing her damages, a sail hove in sight to

---

[1] Brenton, vol. v., p. 50. [2] Ibid., p. 54.

windward, which was at first taken for one of the convoy. But the near approach of the stranger, and her not answering signals, soon marked her for an enemy: whereupon, removing her main yard from off the casks and lashing it to the deck, the Frolic hauled to the wind under her boom mainsail, and (her foretopmast having been sprung previously to the gale) a close-reefed foretopsail, in order to let her convoy pass sufficiently ahead to be out of danger.

At a few minutes before 11 A.M., apprehensive that the strange ship-of-war might pursue the merchantmen instead of himself, Captain Whinyates hoisted Spanish colours as a decoy; having two days before passed a convoy under the protection of a Spanish armed brig, and which convoy, it was imagined that the strange vessel might also have seen. The latter, which was the United States 18-gun ship-sloop Wasp, Captain Jacob Jones, five days only from the Delaware, immediately hoisted her colours, and bore down for the Frolic, then awaiting her approach on the larboard tack. On arriving within 60 yards of the Frolic, the Wasp hailed: whereupon, quickly exchanging her colours to British, the brig opened a fire of great guns and musketry. This was instantly returned by the Wasp; and, as the latter dropped nearer to her antagonist, the action became close and spirited. In less than five minutes after she had commenced firing, the Frolic shot away the Wasp's maintopmast; and, in two or three minutes more, the latter's gaff and mizentopgallant-mast also came down. The sea was so rough, that the muzzles of the guns of both vessels were frequently under water. Still the cannonade continued, with mutual spirit; the Americans firing, as the engaged side of their ship was going down, the British, when their engaged side was rising. The consequence was, that almost every shot fired by the Wasp took effect in her opponent's hull; while most of the Frolic's shot passed among the rigging or over the masts of the Wasp.

Being in a very light state from a deficiency of stores, and being unable, on account of the sprung state of her topmasts and the want of a main-yard, to steady herself by carrying sail, the Frolic laboured much more than the Wasp, and experienced, in consequence, greater difficulty in pointing her guns with precision. In a minute or two after the Wasp's maintopmast had come down, the Frolic's gaff head-braces were shot away Having now no sail whatever upon the mainmast, the brig had lost the means of preventing the Wasp from taking a position on her larboard-bow. A *ship* would not have been so circumstanced, even had she lost her mizenmast by the board; as she could still have set a trysail upon her mainmast.

Thus, in less than 10 minutes after the action had commenced, chiefly by her previous inability to carry sail, the Frolic lay an unmanageable hulk upon the water, exposed to the whole raking fire of her antagonist, without the possibility of returning it with more than one of her bow-guns. The Wasp continued pouring in broadside after broadside, until, believing that he had so thinned the deck of the British brig, that no opposition could be offered, Captain Jones determined to board and end the contest. The Wasp accordingly wore, and, running down upon the Frolic, soon brought the latter's jib-boom between her fore and main rigging, and two of her own carronades in a direction with the bow-ports of her defenceless antagonist. Having so fine an opportunity of further diminishing the strength of his opponent, Captain Jones would not board until a raking fire was poured in: it was poured in, and swept the whole range of the Frolic's deck.

A British seaman belonging to the Wasp, named Jack Lang, was now about to spring on the brig's bowsprit and put a stop to the carnage; but Captain Jones, observing that some one yet lived on the Frolic's deck, pulled him back, and ordered another broadside to be fired. At length, when the action altogether had lasted 43 minutes, and when the American ship had had nearly the whole firing to herself for 33 minutes, the officers and men of the Wasp, led by Lieutenant George William Rodgers, boarded the Frolic. The Americans, according to their account, did not see a single man alive upon the Frolic's deck, except the seaman at the wheel and three officers. Two of those officers were Captain Whinyates and his second-lieutenant, Frederick Boughton Wintle; both so severely wounded as to be unable to stand without supporting themselves. Contrary to the American statement, however, 17 of the Frolic's men were also on deck. The remainder of the survivors were below, attending to the wounded, and performing other necessary duties. Lieutenant James Biddle, first of the Wasp, had now the honour of striking the Frolic's colours, as they were lashed to the main rigging.

The Frolic was of course much shattered in her hull; and her two masts, from the wounds they had received, fell over the side in a few minutes after her surrender. Out of her 92 men (including one passenger, an invalided soldier) and 18 boys, the Frolic had 15 seamen and marines killed, her commander, two lieutenants (Charles M'Kay, mortally, and Mr. Wintle), master (John Stephens, mortally), and 43 seamen and marines wounded. The Wasp received a few shot in her hull, one near her magazine; and her three lower masts were wounded, but, owing chiefly to the goodness of the sticks, none of them fell. The American sloop began the action with a crew of 138, one of whom was a lad of 17 or 18 years of age, the remainder young and able-bodied seamen, with, as subsequently proved, many British among them ; and even the midshipmen, of whom the Wasp had 12 or 13, while the Frolic had but one, and he a boy, were full-grown men, chiefly masters and mates of American merchantmen. Out of this fine crew, the Wasp had eight killed, and about the same number wounded.

The Frolic was armed like every other vessel of her class, with 16 carronades, 32-pounders, and two long sixes. The brig had also the established 12-pounder carronade for her launch, mounted on the usual elevating carriage; and she had likewise on board a second 12-pounder carronade, taken out of some prize probably, but it was dismounted and lashed upon the forecastle. As the boat carronade, when used at all in action, can only be fired *en barbette*, we shall not consider it as worthy a place among the broadside guns. The Wasp mounted 16 carronades, 32-pounders, and two brass long 12-pounders, exclusively of two brass 4-pounders, one of which was usually mounted in the fore, and the other in the maintop; but, in consequence of the gale, they had been brought on deck. Although, strictly speaking, there was not a single boy belonging to the Wasp, we shall allow three. The following, therefore, will be the

Comparative Force of the Combatants.

		Frolic.	Wasp.
Broadside-guns	No.	9	9
	lbs.	262	268
Crew (men only[1])	No.	92	135
Size	tons	384	434

With her masts entire, and a healthy instead of a debilitated crew, the Frolic would have encountered a tolerably equal opponent. As the matter stood, her officers and men deserve great credit for maintaining a resistance so long after their vessel had become unmanageable and defenceless. Surely there was nothing in the result of this action that could cast the slightest

[1] See p. 382.

slur upon the British naval character; and yet, with the wonted exaggerations of American officers, the latter made it, as we shall see presently, a victory over a superior force.

Captain Jones, however, was not allowed to carry his trophy, his "22-gun sloop-of-war," into port; for, in the course of a few hours after the action, the British 74-gun ship Poictiers, Captain John Poer Beresford, heaving in sight, captured one vessel and recaptured the other. With a just appreciation of the merits of Captain Whinyates, Captain Beresford continued him in the command of the Frolic. At the court-martial which was subsequently held upon the captain, officers, and crew of the Frolic, for the loss of their vessel, they were, as a matter of course, most honourably acquitted. Captain Whinyates, although he was unacquainted with the circumstance, had been made a post-captain since the 12th of the preceding August.

A word or two upon the American official account of this action. Captain Jacob Jones describes the vessel he captured, as "the British sloop-of-war Frolic, of 22 guns, 16 of them 32-pound carronades, and four 12-pounders on the main deck, and two 12-pounders, carronades on the topgallant forecastle; making her," says Captain Jacob Jones, "superior in force to us by four 12-pounders." Unfortunately for Captain Jacob Jones, Lieutenant Biddle, without his privity, wrote a letter to his father in Philadelphia, in these words: "The Frolic was superior in force to us: she mounted eighteen 32 lb. carronades, and two long nines. The Wasp, you know, has only 16 carronades." Mr. Biddle being a man of some note, got his son's letter into the Philadelphia papers as quickly as Mr. Paul Hamilton, the secretary of the American navy, could get the letter of Captain Jacob Jones into the "National Intelligencer." Here was a business! Comments are unnecessary. Suffice it that neither letter contained a word relative to the disabled state of the Frolic when the action commenced; and that the Congress of the United States, willing believers in a matter so flattering to their self-love, voted 25,000 dollars, and their thanks, to Captain Jacob Jones, the officers, and crew of the Wasp; also a gold medal to Captain Jones, and silver medals to each of the officers, in testimony of their high sense of the gallantry displayed by them in the capture of the British sloop-of-war Frolic, of "superior force."

On the 8th of October the American Commodore Rodgers, with the same three frigates he commanded before,[1] accom-

[1] See p. 356.

panied by the brig-sloop Argus, Captain Arthur Sinclair, sailed from Boston upon his second cruise against British men-of-war and merchantmen. On the 10th, at 8 A.M., when in latitude 41° north, longitude 65° west, steering to the westward, with a light northerly wind, the squadron discovered ahead the British 38-gun frigate Nymphe, Captain Farmery Predam Epworth. The Nymphe hauled on the starboard tack in chase: and at noon, finding the private signal not answered, Captain Epworth made out the three ships and brig to be American cruisers. At 4 h. 30 m. P.M. the Nymphe boarded a Swedish brig from the island of St. Bartholomew to New York; and which, at 8 P.M., was boarded by the American squadron. With the intelligence thus gained, Commodore Rodgers proceeded in chase; but in the course of an hour, lost sight of the British frigate.

On the 12th of October the frigate United States parted company; and we shall at present follow her fortunes. On the 25th, soon after daylight, in latitude 29° north, longitude 29° 30' west, this American 44, being close hauled on the larboard tack with the wind blowing fresh from the south-south-east, descried on her weather-bow, at the distance of about 12 miles, the British 38-gun frigate Macedonian, Captain John Surman Carden. The Macedonian immediately set her foretopmast and topgallant studding-sails, and bore away in chase, steering a course for the weather-bow of the stranger.

While the tracks of the two ships are thus gradually approximating, we will give an account of the force of each. In addition to her 28 main-deck long 18-pounders, the Macedonian mounted on the quarter-deck and forecastle 16 carronades, 32-pounders, fitted with their chocks outside (a new, but as far as we can learn, not much approved principle), the two long 12-pounders, and two brass long French 8-pounders (the captain's private property), total 48 guns, exclusive of the usual 18-pounder launch carronade. The crew of the Macedonian at this time consisted of 262 men and 35 boys. To account for this extraordinary proportion of boys, we must state that, shortly before the Macedonian sailed on her last cruise, 12 supernumerary boys were put on board, by way, possibly, of " strengthening" her crew. With respect to the quality of the 35 boys, very few of them, it appears, were worth ship-room. It has already been shown, that the established armament of the United States was 56 guns, long 24-pounders, and 42-pounder carronades.[1] Subsequently the ship appears to have landed two of her 42s,

[1] See p. 271.

and to have received on board, in lieu of them, a travelling 18-pounder carronade; making her carriage-guns, in all, 55. She also mounted a brass howitzer in each top. With respect to crew, the United States victualled 477 men and one lad or boy.

At about 7 h. 30 m. A.M. the two ships were not above three miles apart. Having by this time hoisted her ensign and broad pendant, the United States was known to be one of the American 44s; but, having on board one of Commodore Rodgers's spy-glasses, Commodore Decatur mistook the Macedonian for a much larger ship, a sail-of-the-line probably. The United States accordingly wore round on the starboard tack, keeping a point or two off the wind. Having sailed from Portsmouth as long ago as the 29th of September, Captain Carden, although he knew of the war, had received no information of the Guerrière's capture. The Macedonian had since been at Madeira, where she had heard that the American frigate Essex was cruising; but, even had the force of the United States in guns and men been at this time fully known, such was the confidence of victory on board the Macedonian, that every officer, man, and boy, except perhaps the eight foreigners, who requested and were allowed to go below, was in the highest spirits.

As, from sailing better than the United States, the Macedonian gradually advanced more fully into view, the American officers seem to have fallen into the opposite mistake. They now believed the Macedonian to be a 32-gun frigate; and, with the determination to attack her, the United States, at 8 h. 30 m. A.M., wore round the larboard tack, and hauled sharp up. This brought the two ships, at 8 h. 45 m., into the relative positions marked in the diagram at p. 397. Knowing that the greatest force of his ship lay in her quarter, and the smallest force of the enemy's ship in her bows, the first-lieutenant of the Macedonian wished that the latter should continue her course, so as to pass ahead of the United States, in the manner represented by the strong line in the diagram. But Captain Carden having decided to keep the weather-gage, the Macedonian hauled close to the wind. At 9 A.M., when abreast of the United States on the opposite tack, the Macedonian received her passing fire; but it did not produce the slightest effect, the principal part of the shot falling short of, and the rest going over her.

The rubicon being now passed, the Macedonian wore in pursuit; and, owing to her superiority of sailing already noticed, reached, at about 9 h. 20 m. A.M., a position on the larboard quarter of the American frigate. Here a broadside was exchanged: by that discharged from the Macedonian, the mizentopgallantmast of her opponent was shot away, and, by that from the United States, the Macedonian lost her gaff-halliards and mizen-topmast, the latter falling into the maintop. "This," as a contemporary well observes, "produced an equality in the rate of sailing, and the United States kept her enemy in one position on the quarter in a running fight."[1] The United States steered about two points off the wind, and, by her diagonal fire, soon cut away the chock of, and dismounted, every carronade upon the starboard side of her opponent's quarter-deck and forecastle, besides shattering the Macedonian's hull, and disabling a great portion of her crew. Having by this means reduced his antagonist to the use of her main-deck battery only, and increased the disparity that previously existed to more than double, Commodore Decatur, at about 10 h. 15 m. A.M., laid his maintopsail to the mast, and allowed the Macedonian, now that it was too late, to come to close action.

By a few minutes past 11 A.M. the Macedonian had had her mizenmast shot away by the board, and which had fallen over the starboard or engaged quarter, her fore and maintopmast shot away by the caps, and her main-yard in the slings, her lower-masts badly wounded, rigging of every sort destroyed, a small portion only of the foresail left to the yard, and two guns on the main battery, and all on the upper but two, disabled. The ship had also received upwards of 100 shot in her hull, several of them between wind and water; and had all her boats, except the jolly-boat towing astern, destroyed, and more than a third of her crew killed and wounded. Owing, likewise, to the heavy sea and her dismasted state, the Macedonian rolled her main deck guns under water; while the United States, having no sail that she could not set but her mizen-topgallantsail, remained perfectly steady.

In this defenceless state, the men of the Macedonian still possessed the spirit of British seamen; and at 11 h. 10 m., when the United States was making sail, to get from under the lee of her opponent, and the British frigate, as a last resource, had put her helm a-weather, with the intention of laying the American frigate on board, "every man was on deck," says Lieutenant (now Captain) Hope "several who had lost an arm, and the universal cheer was, 'Let us conquer or die!'"[2]

[1] Brenton, vol. v., p. 59. See also diagram at p. 397.   [2] Marshall, vol. ii., p. 1018.

Fortunately, considering the unnecessary carnage that must have ensued, the fore-brace was at that moment shot away, and the yard, swinging round, threw the ship up in the wind. The United States then stood athwart the bows of the Macedonian, without firing a shot; having, it appears, expended all her cartridges. This circumstance, being unknown on board the Macedonian, led to a very erroneous impression; and the crew continued to cheer after an enemy, who, until the United States hove to out of gun-shot, they supposed was making off. As soon as she had refilled her cartridges and refitted her rigging, the United States tacked, and at about noon stationed herself in a raking position across the stern of her defenceless antagonist;

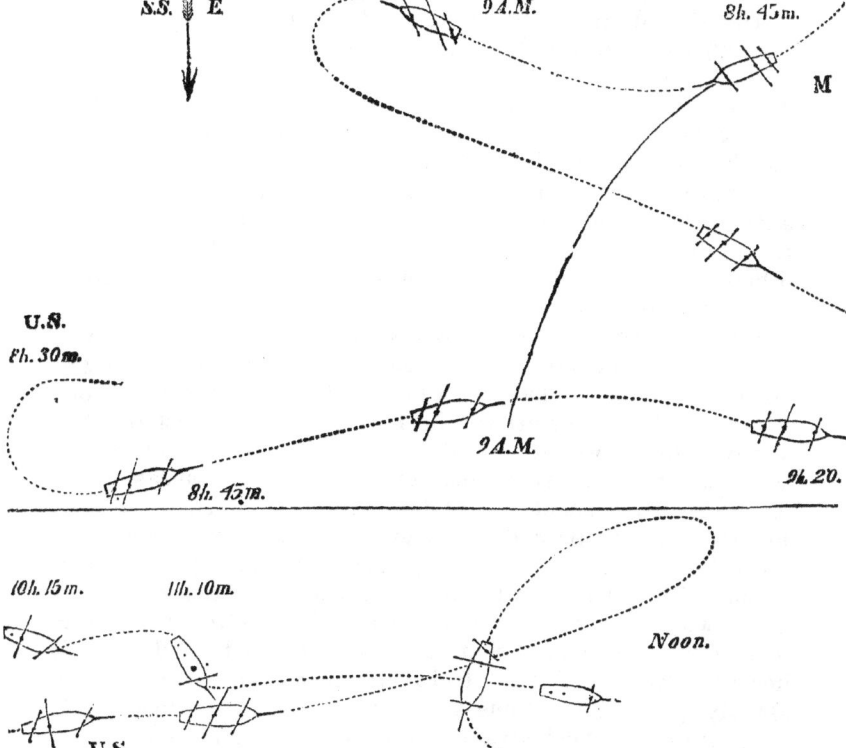

who, having no means of making a further resistance, struck her colours.

The above diagram is intended to represent the movements

of the two ships, from the time that the Macedonian hauled up to pass to windward of the United States, to the termination of the contest.

Of her 254 men (deducting the eight foreigners who refused to fight) and 35 boys, the Macedonian had her boatswain (James Holmes), one master's mate (Thomas James Nankivee), her schoolmaster (Dennis Colwell), 23 seamen, two boys, and eight marines killed, her first-lieutenant (David Hope, severely), third-lieutenant (John Bulford, slightly), one master's mate (Henry Roebuck), one midshipman (George Greenway), one first-class volunteer (Francis Baker), 50 seamen (two mortally), four boys (two with each a leg amputated), and nine marines wounded; total, 36 killed and 68 wounded.

The United States is represented, by her captain and his officers, to have had her masts and rigging not materially injured, and to have received only nine shot in her hull. "It is remarkable," adds one of her officers, "that, during an action of one hour and a half, and a fire which I believe was never equalled by any single deck, not an accident occurred, nor a rope-yarn of our gun-tackle strained." Her loss, from the same authority, amounted to no more than five seamen killed, Lieutenant John Musser Funk and one seaman mortally, and five others badly wounded. The slightly wounded, as in all other American cases, are omitted.

With respect to the damage sustained by the United States, although Commodore Decatur makes very light of it, Captain Carden represents, that the United States "was pumped out every watch till her arrival in port, from the effect of shot received under water, and that two 18-pounders had passed through her mainmast in a horizontal line."[1] The masts of the American 44, it should be stated, are as stout as those of a British 74-gun ship; and, to render them still more secure from the effects of shot, four large quarter-fishes are girthed upon them. Although none of her masts, except her mizen-topgallant-mast, were shot away, the rigging of the United States was much cut. The reason that the American frigate had to refill her cartridges, all of which had been expended in the action, has already appeared;[2] and one of her officers, in a letter to a friend, exhibits the practical advantages of sheet-lead cartridges in the statement, that, during the time the Macedonian was firing 36 broadsides, the United States fired 70. But an allowance must here be made for the inability of the Macedonian, during a third

[1] Marshall, vol., ii., p. 1012.   [2] See p. 382.

at least of the action, to bring more than a few of her bow-guns to bear.

We shall, as in the case of the Guerrière, exclude from the broadside force the Macedonian's boat-carronade. We might be justified in doing the same with the two French 8-pounders: for, it appears, they "were only fired once, the solder, by which pieces of metal for securing the locks had been affixed to them, having run the first discharge, and filled the touch-holes."[1] With respect to the United States, we shall exclude her topguns, although, during the time the close action lasted, they were used incessantly and with considerable effect, the shot from them frequently passing through the Macedonian's decks as she rolled; but the travelling carronade, having a port expressly fitted for its reception,[2] we shall estimate as a part of the broadside force, and consider to have been an 18-pounder, although we are doubtful if it was not a 24. Captain Carden appears to think that he has underrated the crew of the United States, and that the number, instead of being 478, as expressed in his official letter, ought to be 509, "the officers' names not being entered in her victualling-book."[1] We differ from him on this point, and shall abide by his official statement; allowing four boys, although one only was seen, and he was at least 17 years of age.

Upon the authority of a statement made by Captain Carden, Mr. Marshall has represented the size of the United States to be "1670 tons," as "taken from the register of New York dockyard."[1] In the first place, there was no national dockyard at New York, until long after the United States was launched. Secondly, that frigate, as we have already shown, was built at Philadelphia. Thirdly, 1670 tons, American measurement, which the statement must mean, if it means anything, would be equal to 1800 English; thus swelling the American 44-gun frigate to a most extravagant size indeed. In direct opposition to this, a British officer of distinction was informed by an officer belonging to the United States, at a time when there was no motive to deceive, that that frigate measured between 1400 and 1500 tons; which, allowing for the difference already pointed out between British and American tonnage, nearly agrees with our account. Had the note subjoined by Mr. Marshall, in support of the accuracy of the "1670" set forth in his text, run thus, we think it would come near to the truth: "Taken from the columns of the New York Daily Advertiser;" for we re-

[1] Marshall, vol. ii., p. 1013.   [2] See p. 271.

collect seeing some statement of the kind in a New York paper, but then it was in the form of an extract from an English paper, and was merely given at length, in order that the American editor might expose its absurdity.

Mr. Marshall has also inserted the following passage respecting the scantling of the United States:—"The United States was superior to any ship of her class in the American navy. Her sides, on the cells of her main-deck ports, were of the same scantling as our 74-gun ships on their lower-deck port-cells, composed of live-oak; and her sides such a mass of this wood, that carronade grape would scarcely penetrate them. She was termed the 'Waggon of the American navy,' from her thick scantling having been originally intended for a larger-class ship; and her masts were precisely of the same dimensions as those of our then second-class 74s."[1] Into this subject we have already fully entered; but we believe the nickname of Waggon was given to the United States on account of her being in comparison with her two class-mates, a slow sailer; and we well remember asking an American the reason of her being so named, and receiving for a reply, "Because she was built by an Englishman." In further proof that the United States was built of larger scantling than the President, Commodore Chauncey as we stated more than nine years ago, in a conversation respecting the capture of the President, held with some British naval officers since the peace, declared, that he would much rather fight a battle in the frigate United States, because her sides were stouter than those of the President, and she would, he thought, stand a longer battering.

Comparative Force of the Combatants.

		Macedonian.	United States.
Broadside-guns	No.	24	28
	lbs.	528	864
Crew (men only)	No.	254	474
Size	tons	1081	1533

A greater disparity in broadside weight of metal, than even in the Guerrière's case: what then must have been the disparity when the Macedonian's carronades had become disabled? There was, however, in this case, no deteriorated powder to weaken the effect of the remaining guns; and yet the shot from them made very little impression upon the hull or masts of the United States. This state of impunity, as well as much of the opposite

---

[1] Marshall, vol. ii., p. 1012.

effect produced on board the British frigate, was attributable, after the first opportunity of closing had been missed by the Macedonian, to the Parthian or retreating mode of fighting adopted by her antagonist. Had the United States brought to in a bold, and, considering her great superiority of force, becoming manner, the action would have been sooner decided, and the disparity between the two ships, in point of execution, not have been so great. No imputation rests upon the Macedonian's crew, for, to the very last, they behaved well; nor could the gallantry of the first-lieutenant, David Hope, be well exceeded; he was severely wounded in the leg at the commencement, and more severely still in the head towards the close of the battle, and then taken below, but was soon again on deck, filling his post as became a brave officer.

The crew of the United States were the finest set of men ever seen collected on ship-board. Had Captain Decatur and his five lieutenants been below in the hold, there were officers enough among the ship's company to have brought the action to the same successful issue. As it was, however, the American captain and the American officers gained all the credit, and pocketed the principal part of the cash; while the poor silly Britons, whose prompt attention to the sails, and steady perseverance at the guns, had contributed so mainly to the victory, slunk away in the back-ground, disowned by those whom they had so effectually served, and scorned and scouted by those against whom they had so traitorously fought.

That a very great proportion of the crew of the United States were British seamen, will have been assumed from our previous statements on the subject. That such was the fact was proved, by several of the Macedonian's men recognising old shipmates. One of the officers' servants, a young lad from London, named William Hearne, actually found among the hostile crew his own brother! This hardened traitor, after reviling the British, and applauding the American service, used the influence of seniority, in trying to persuade his brother to enter the latter. The honourable youth, with tears in his eyes, replied: "If you are a d—d rascal, that's no reason I should be one." It appears, likewise, that one of the Macedonian's quartermasters had served his time with many of the crew of the United States, out of the ports of Sunderland, Shields, and Newcastle. The great proportion of British seamen among the crew of the American frigate accounted for so many of her guns being named after British ships, and some of the most celebrated British naval victories. "Captain Carden," says Mr. Marshall, "observing 'Victory,' painted on the ship's side over one port, and 'Nelson' over another, asked Commodore Decatur the reason of so strange an anomaly; he answered, 'The men belonging to those guns served many years with Lord Nelson, and in the Victory. The crew of the gun named Nelson were once bargemen to that great chief, and they claim the privilege of using his illustrious name in the way you have seen.' The commodore also publicly declared to Captain Carden, that there was not a seaman in his ship, who had not served from five to 12 years in a British man-of-war."[1] After reading this, we naturally take up the "Register," which has already been so useful to us, to see of what state Commodore Decatur was a native: we find, as we expected, that he did not come so far north as Captain Hull, having been born in Maryland, Virginia.

"The manner," says Mr. M., "in which Captain Carden was received by his generous enemy after the surrender of the Macedonian, is worthy of mention. On presenting his sword to Commodore Decatur, the latter started back, declared he never could take the sword of a man who had so nobly defended the honour of it, requested the hand of that gallant officer, whom it had been his fortune in war to subdue, and added that, though he could not claim any merit for capturing a ship so inferior, he felt assured Captain Carden would gain much, by his persevering and truly gallant defence. The commodore subsequently gave up all the British officers' private property, extending his generosity to even a quantity of wine, which they had purchased at Madeira for their friends in England."[2] That Commodore Decatur should have held out his hand to Captain Carden, will not be considered surprising, when we state that, not many months before, the two officers had met as friends in Chesapeake bay; nor will it appear extraordinary that, on seeing his old acquaintance, the former should have "started back," especially when he recollected the opinion which Captain Carden, in some friendly disputation about the relative force of their two frigates, had given, respecting the comparative effectiveness of 18 and 24 pounders. Commodore Decatur's treatment of the Macedonian's late officers, and his behaviour about the wine, was certainly very creditable to him: we may perhaps come to something presently, which will be, in the language of the law, a good set-off.

With the profusion of stores of every sort which was to be

[1] Marshall, vol. ii., p. 1019. Ibid. p. 1014.

found on board the American frigate, with so many able seamen that could be spared from her numerous crew, and with all the advantages that a fortnight's calm weather gave him, it took the whole of that time to place his prize in a seaworthy state; a clear proof how much the Macedonian had been shattered. That service accomplished, the two frigates, the Macedonian, under the command of Lieutenant William Henry Allen, late first of the United States, made sail towards the coast of America. Owing to adverse and baffling winds, the ships were until noon on the 4th of December ere they came in sight of New London lighthouse, on their way through the Sound to New York. Singular indeed was it, that these two frigates, one so crippled in her masts, should have been, during a passage of more than five weeks, not merely unmolested, but, as far as we know, unseen by a single British cruiser. On her arrival at New York, the Macedonian was of course purchased by the American government, and, being nearly a new ship (built in 1810), became a great acquisition to the republican navy, in which, under the same name, she was rated as a 36-gun frigate, and was the smallest ship of her class.

It was not enough for the lieutenants, petty-officers, and seamen of the frigate United States, to try the effect of their eloquence upon the late crew of the Macedonian; Commodore Decatur must use his personal endeavours to inveigle them into the service of their country's enemy. On arriving off New London, as if the shrewd-inspiring air of Connecticut had already begun to exert its influence, the commodore sent the British officers on shore on their parole; meaning to carry the Macedonian's late crew with him to New York. These he threatened to put in the prison-ship there, if they did not immediately enlist. Fortunately for the poor fellows, some delay arose in the two ships moving from before New London; and, in the mean time, the British officers on shore became acquainted with the very honourable scheme of an American officer, "who," says Captain Brenton, "was an ornament to his country."[1] The officers remonstrated with the commodore on the subject, and returned on board. The consequence was, that the seven or eight foreigners, who were fiddlers and trumpeters on board the Macedonian, and three or four others of her late crew represented as Americans, were all that entered the American service.

In his letter to the secretary of the American navy, Captain

[1] Brenton, vol. v., p. 61.

Decatur gives his prize, "49 carriage-guns;" thus officially reckoning, for the first time, we believe, a boat-carronade found on board a captured frigate. He describes the Macedonian to be of the "largest class." What then must the United States be, that was nearly half as large again? He says: "The enemy, being to windward, had the advantage of engaging us at his own distance, which was so great, that for the first half-hour we did not use our carronades, and at no time was he within the complete effect of our musketry and grape; to this circumstance, and a heavy swell, which was on at the time, I ascribe the unusual length of the action." In answer to this, Captain Carden says, that one of the first shot that struck the Macedonian was a 42-pounder, which killed the sergeant of marines.[1] "The damage," says the commodore, "sustained by this ship was not such to render her return into port necessary; and, had I not deemed it important that we should see our prize in, should have continued our cruise."

Not a word is there in Commodore Decatur's letter to lead the public to suppose, that he had captured a ship of "inferior force."[2] What he may have said in private was one thing; what he was magnanimous enough to tell to the world is another. His end was answered. The national legislature of the United States voted their thanks to Commodore Decatur, his officers and crew; also a gold medal to the commodore, and silver medals to each of the officers, in honour of "the brilliant victory gained by the frigate United States over the British frigate Macedonian." A special committee also determined, that the Macedonian was quite equal to the United States; and, an Act of Congress of the 28th of June, 1798, having provided that, "if a vessel of superior, or equal force, shall be captured by a public-armed vessel of the United States, the forfeiture shall accrue wholly to the captors," the amount of the Macedonian's valuation, 200,000 dollars, was paid over to Commodore Decatur, his officers, and crew.

In March, 1813, Captain Carden, his officers, and surviving crew arrived from the United States at the island of Bermuda, and on the 27th of the succeeding May were tried for the loss of their ship. The following was the sentence pronounced: "Having most strictly investigated every circumstance, and examined the different officers and ship's company; and having very deliberately and maturely weighed and considered the whole and every part thereof, the court is of opinion, that,

---

[1] Marshall, vol. ii., p. 1013.   [2] See p. 402.

previous to the commencement of the action, from an overanxiety to keep the weather-gage, an opportunity was lost of closing with the enemy; and that, owing to this circumstance, the Macedonian was unable to bring the United States to close action until she had received material damage. But, as it does not appear that this omission originated in the most distant wish to keep back from the engagement, the court is of opinion that Captain John Surman Carden, his officers, and ship's company, in every instance throughout the action, behaved with the firmest and most determined courage, resolution, and coolness; and that the colours of the Macedonian were not struck until she was unable to make further resistance. The court does therefore most honourably acquit Captain John Surman Carden, the officers, and company of his majesty's late ship Macedonian, and Captain Carden, his officers, and company are hereby most honourably acquitted accordingly. The court cannot dismiss Captain Carden, without expressing their admiration of the uniform testimony which has been borne to his gallantry and good conduct throughout the action, nor Lieutenant David Hope, the senior lieutenant, the other officers and company, without expressing the highest approbation of the support given by him and them to the captain, and of their courage and steadiness during the contest with an enemy of very superior force; a circumstance that, whilst it reflects high honour on them, does no less credit and honour to the discipline of his majesty's late ship Macedonian. The court also feels it a gratifying duty to express its admiration of the fidelity to their allegiance and attachment to their king and country, which the remaining crew appear to have manifested, in resisting the various insidious and repeated temptations which the enemy held out to them to seduce them from their duty, and which cannot fail to be duly appreciated."

Of all the cases recorded in these pages, none are so difficult to render intelligible as those in which British ships are defeated; first, because there is seldom any official letter, and next, because there is never any log to refer to for particulars. It is true that, in each of the three frigate cases with America, an official letter was allowed to appear in the London Gazette; but, of all three (including, with the letter of Captain Dacres, his address to his court-martial), the letter of Captain Carden is the most barren of details. It happens, also, that the letter of Commodore Decatur, and the other American accounts of this action, are equally brief and unsatisfactory. Thus limited in means, we drew up and published our first account nearly nine years ago. It now appears, for the first time, that we overrated the Macedonian's force by giving her 18 carronades, 32-pounders, instead of 16, with two long twelves; making a difference in the broadside-force of just 21 lbs. This very important oversight, and the strictures we were induced to pass upon what we supposed to be the unskilfulness of the Macedonian's crew, have given rise to a very intemperate letter. The mistake about the guns is too trivial to notice; but we readily acknowledge, that we were wrong in supposing that the crew of the Macedonian were unpractised or inexpert gunners: we have shown, we trust pretty clearly, what it was that occasioned their powder and shot to be so wastefully employed. The very first clause in the sentence of the court-martial fortunately bears us out in our statement; and we certainly feel much indebted to Captain Carden, as well for the opportunity he has afforded us of amending our former account in that important particular, as for the stimulus he has given us to seek and obtain some additional facts connected with the action between the Macedonian and United States.

We have, as will be seen, borrowed a few paragraphs relating to this action from each of our two contemporaries, the post-captain and the lieutenant. The latter, whether he intends to bestow his praise or his censure, always alludes to us in a becoming manner, by name; but the former usually prefers the indirect and, he will excuse us for adding, American fashion of leaving his meaning to be "guessed" by the epithet he applies. Accordingly, Captain Brenton says: "It need scarcely be noticed, that Captain Carden has been accused by a very incompetent judge of running down to bring his enemy to action, in a heedless and confident manner. He ran into action as his brother officers had done, and will do again, to fight his enemy and decide the day as quickly as possible; how could Captain Carden have closed sooner, &c." "His conduct has therefore been most cruelly misrepresented." "A court-martial acquitted him, his officers, and crew, of all blame for the loss of the ship."[1] If we add a very fine compliment to Commodore Decatur, and an account of his death, which took place 10 or 12 years afterwards, we have nearly all that is comprised in Captain Brenton's account of the Macedonian's capture. Not a word is there to show on which tack the ships fought; when they began, or when they ended the action, or how long it continued.

[1] Brenton, vol. v., p. 60

Commodore Rodgers and his two frigates and brig-sloop now demand our attention. The Argus parted company on the same day as the United States. On the 15th, when near the great bank of Newfoundland, the President and Congress fell in with and captured the Jamaica homeward-bound packet Swallow, with a considerable quantity of specie on board. On the 31st, at 9 A.M., latitude 32°, longitude 30°, they fell in with the British 36-gun frigate Galatea, Captain Woodley Losack, having under her charge two South Sea whalers, the Argo and Berkeley, with which she had sailed from the island of Ascension on the 3rd. At this time both parties were standing on the starboard tack, the Galatea, with the Berkeley in tow, to windward. Casting off her tow, the Galatea bore down to reconnoitre; and at 10 A.M., discovering that the two strangers were enemies, she made the signal to her convoy to make the best of their way into port. Having arrived within about four miles upon the weather-beam of the President, who, with the Congress in close line astern of her, was still on the starboard tack hastening to get to windward, the Galatea hauled up on the same tack. The two American frigates now displayed their colours, and the commodore hoisted his broad pendant. Fortunately for the Galatea, Captain Losack had heard of the war three days before from the outward-bound Indiaman Inglis.

At about noon the President tacked, as if to get into the wake of the Galatea; who began to be apprehensive that she should be placed between her two enemies, and was only relieved when she observed the Congress tack in succession. Shortly afterwards the Galatea herself tacked, and did so again upon the American ships tacking towards her. The Galatea now edged away, to get upon her best point of sailing; and just at this moment the Argo having bore up, in the vain hope of crossing the hawse of the American frigates and escaping to leeward, was intercepted by them. After the two frigates had lain to a long time, and witnessed, with apparent unconcern, the gradual departure of the Galatea, the President filled and made sail, but in such a manner as clearly indicated, that the commodore did not like to proceed in chase of the sister-ship of the Belvidera, unaccompanied by his consort. The President set her topmast studding-sails, then her topgallant, and lastly her lower studding-sails, and, as soon as it became dark, took all in and hauled to the wind. The Galatea of course escaped, although, being 93 men short of complement, she could scarcely have resisted with any effect, an attack by the smaller of the two American frigates.

From the 1st to the 30th of November the President and Congress did not see a sail. They subsequently cruised between Bermuda and the Capes of Virginia, and on the 31st of December anchored in the harbour of Boston; having, in the course of their 84 days' unsuccessful cruise, been as far to the eastward as longitude 22° west, and to the southward as latitude 17° north. Soon after the arrival of these frigates at Boston, 25 of the crew of the Congress went on the quarter-deck to deliver themselves up as Englishmen. Captain Smith, who though an Englishman by birth, was an American by education, cunningly answered, "Very well, ; you shall go in the first cartel to Halifax, and be put on board the guardship there." The men replied, "Oh, no, we don't wish to be sent to a man-of-war, as we are nearly all deserters from the king's service, but we wish for our discharge to go on shore." This the American captain refused, saying, "If you are Englishmen, you shall be sent to an English man-of-war." They added: "Rather than be punished for our desertion, we will remain where we are." They consequently all took the oath of allegiance to America, except five, who, having never been in a British ship-of-war, departed with some prisoners which the two frigates had made in their cruise. Had those 20 men succeeded in obtaining their discharge, so as to have gone ashore and got to England in the best manner they could, it was understood that nearly 100 more on board the Congress would have immediately followed their example.

Aware of the injury that would accrue to British commerce by the presence of an enemy's squadron in the South Seas, the American government ordered Commodore William Bainbridge, in the absence of Captain Hull, who wished to attend to his private affairs, to proceed thither with the Constitution, and the Hornet, Captain James Lawrence; calling off St. Salvador, on the coast of Brazil, for the Essex, Captain Porter, who had been directed to join them at that rendezvous. On the 27th of October the Essex sailed from the Delaware; and on the 30th the Constitution and Hornet sailed from Boston. Towards the latter end of December Commodore Bainbridge arrived off St. Salvador; and, not finding the Essex at the rendezvous, sent the Hornet into the port to make inquiries respecting her. On the 29th of December, at 2 P.M., latitude 13° 6' south, longitude 30' west, while lying to about 10 leagues off the coast, waiting to be joined by the Hornet, then seen approaching from the coast, the Constitution descried in the offing the British 38-gun frigate Java, Captain Henry Lambert, having in tow the American merchant-ship William, which she had recently captured.

A little of the previous history of the Java may render more intelligible the details that are to follow. On the 17th of August, in the present year, the late French frigate Renommée,[1] under the name of Java, was commissioned at Portsmouth by Captain Lambert, in order to carry out to Bombay the newly-appointed governor, Lieutenant-general Hislop and suite, together with a supply of stores, particularly of copper, for the Cornwallis 74, and Chameleon and Icarus 10-gun-sloops, building at Bombay. There was no difficulty in commissioning the ship, in calking her sides and decks, in fitting up her accommodations, in putting on board her 46 guns, or her stores for the voyage, or for the new ships building; but there was a difficulty in providing her with a crew. Officers, and a few petty-officers, were soon obtained. The ship's 50 marines also came on board; and, although 18 of the number were raw recruits, they were upon the whole a good set of men. Then came about 60 Irishmen who had never smelt salt water, except in crossing from their own shores to England. As a fine addition to a crew that, in less than a month after the ship sailed, might have to fight an American frigate similar to that which had taken the Guerrière, a draught of 50 disaffected wretches came on board from the 18-gun ship-sloop Coquette, lying at Spithead. Pressgangs and the prison-ships furnished others not much better. As to boys, the established number, 23, was easily filled up; and, at at length, 292, out of a complement of 300 men and boys, were got together.

Feeling as every brave officer must feel, Captain Lambert remonstrated about the inefficiency of his ship's company; but he was told that a voyage to the East Indies and back would make a good crew. It was in vain to urge the matter further; and, as some slight amendment to the Java's crew, eight seamen were allowed to volunteer from the Rodney 74. Thus, out of a complement of 300 men and boys, the whole number of petty-officers and men, exclusively of those of the former that walked the quarter-deck, who had ever been present in an action, amounted to fewer than 50. Here was a ship's company! As several officers and men were to come on board as passengers, some hopes were entertained that these might compensate for

[1] See p. 295.

the worthlessness of the crew ; but of the 86 supernumeraries, a very large proportion turned out to be Marine-society boys.

Manned in this way, with a total of 397 persons of every description, the Java, on the 12th of November, set sail from Spithead, having in charge two outward-bound Indiamen. On the 12th of December the Java captured the American ship William, and placed on board a master's mate and 19 men, (the latter of some experience, undoubtedly, or they would have been of no use there,) with orders to keep company. On the 24th, being rather short of water, and being unable without much difficulty, to get at what remained in the hold, on account of some articles of stores that lay over the casks, Captain Lambert determined to put into St. Salvador. With this object in view, the Java altered her course; but the two Bombay ships, not wishing to go so far out of their way, parted company, and proceeded alone on their voyage.

Hitherto, owing to the necessity, in a newly-fitted ship, of setting up the rigging—to the length of time, that a crew so inexperienced as the Java's would expend in the operation—to the number of other extra duties required on board a fighting ship so loaded and lumbered as the Java—and, particularly, to a succession of gales of wind since the day of departure, the men had only been exercised occasionally at training the guns. But, as the ship was now approaching a coast, where there was a a probability of falling in with an enemy's frigate, French or American, Captain Lambert, on the 28th, ordered the crew to be exercised at firing the guns. Accordingly, for the first time since she had become a British frigate, the Java, on that evening, discharged six broadsides of blank cartridges. With the majority of the crew, of course, those six broadsides were the first they had ever assisted in firing. What a crew to go into action, not with an American frigate a third superior, but with a French frigate barely their equal! Previously to his departure from Portsmouth, Captain Lambert had actually declared to some of his friends, that, owing solely to the ineffective state of his crew, he did not consider himself equal to any French frigate he might meet.

Having no private brass guns, like the Macedonian, and no pair of long 18-pounders forward to bring down her head like the Guerrière, the Java mounted no more, including 16 carronades, 32-pounders, and two long nines, than her 46 guns and a boat carronade. Since her action with the Guerrière, either because the ship was beginning to hog, or for some unexplained reason, the Constitution had disarmed herself of two of her 32-pounder carronades, and taken on board one 18-pounder carronade fitted on a travelling-carriage; and for which, as has already been shown, she had more than one pair of spare ports.

Casting off the William, with directions to her to proceed to St. Salvador, the Java, soon after 8 A.M., with the wind blowing moderately from the north-east, bore up in chase of the Constitution, then in the south-south-west, standing on the larboard tack. At 10 A.M. the Java made the private signals, English, Spanish, and Portuguese, in succession; none of which were answered. At 10 h. 45 m. the Constitution tacked to the northward and westward, and stood for the Java; whom Commodore Bainbridge took for his expected consort the Essex. At noon, when about four miles distant, the Constitution hoisted the private signal. Having kept it flying 10 minutes, and finding it not answered, the Constitution wore from the Java, as the American account states, to avoid being raked; and, again setting her mainsail and royals, kept away about two points free, in order as Commodore Bainbridge says, to draw the Java from her consort the William merchantman, then standing in for the land, and supposed probably to be another ship-of-war.

Hauling up, the Java steered a course parallel to that of the Constitution, and gained upon her considerably; but, the breeze freshening, the Java, who was then going ten knots, lay over so much, that she was obliged to take in her royals. At about 1 h. 30 m. P.M. the Constitution, who found no inconvenience from carrying her royals, hoisted a commodore's pendant at the main, one American ensign at the mizen-peak and another at the maintopgallantmast-head, also an American jack at the fore. At 1 h. 40 m., by which time the Java had closed her within two miles, the American frigate shortened sail to top and topgallant-sails, jib, and spanker, and luffed up to the wind. The British frigate now hoisted her colours, consisting of an ensign at the mizen-peak, one union-jack at the mizentopgallantmast-head, and another lashed to the main-rigging: and, putting herself under top and topgallant sails, jib, and spanker, the Java stood for the Constitution, then bearing about three points on her lee-bow

At 2 h. 10 m. P.M., when by her slanting course the Java had approached within half a mile of the Constitution, the latter opened a fire from her larboard guns; the shot from which, as a proof of their good direction, splashed the water against the

Java's starboard side. Not being so close as he wished, Captain Lambert stood on until within pistol-shot on the Constitution's weather or larboard bow; when, at 2 h. 20 m. P.M., having received a second broadside, which, because the guns were now elevated too much, as before they had been too little, passed over her, the Java returned a broadside in return. Almost every shot of this broadside took effect. The Constitution had her wheel knocked away, besides receiving other damage, and lost four men killed and several wounded.

Dreading a repetition of this warm salute, the American frigate, having fired her third broadside without much effect, wore in the smoke to get further to leeward. As soon as she discovered that her wary antagonist was running before the wind, the Java made sail after her; and at 2 h. 25 m. P.M.,[1] the Constitution, and then the Java, having come round on the starboard tack, the two frigates again exchanged broadsides. Again the Constitution wore to get away. The Java wore also; and at 2 h. 25 m., passing slowly under the latter's stern, with her larboard main yard-arm over the Constitution's taffrail, which, owing to the height of her lower battery from the water and her being nearly eight feet between deck, was nearly as high as that of the 74-gun ship Plantagenet,[2] the British frigate might have raked the American frigate in a most destructive manner.[3] But, either panic-struck at the sight of so large and formidable a ship, or unable, from sheer ignorance, to appreciate the value of the opportunity thus afforded them of reducing the strength of their antagonist, the Java's crew did not fire a gun, except the 9-pounder on the forecastle; and that was pointed and discharged by Lieutenant James Saunders, one of the supernumerary officers. The Constitution had now the weather-gage; but this did not suit her long-shot tactics: the American frigate therefore made sail free on the larboard tack, followed by the British frigate; who, at 2 h. 40 m. luffing up, crossed again, but in an oblique manner, the Constitution's stern, and fired, this time, two or three of her foremast starboard guns.

At 2 h. 43 m. P.M., feeling ashamed of thus avoiding an antagonist so much inferior in size and force to himself, or impelled by his officers, some of whom, perhaps, hinted at the powerless state of the Java's battery, as recently witnessed, Commodore Bainbridge, as he tells us in his journal, "determined to close with the enemy notwithstanding his raking." The Constitution

---

[1] See diagram at p. 416.
[2] Built, as well as the Courageux, without a poop.
[3] See diagram.

accordingly hauled on board her fore and main tacks, and luffed up for her opponent. On arriving abreast of the Java, who had stood on upon the larboard tack, and now lay close to windward, the Constitution shortened sail and engaged her. At 2 h. 52 m. P.M., having shot away the head of the Java's bowsprit,[1] the American frigate repeated her favourite manœuvre of wearing; and, owing to the smoke, was not perceived until nearly round on the starboard tack. Having now neither jib nor foretopmast-staysail, the Java, as the quickest mode to get round in pursuit, hove in stays, hoping to do so in time to avoid being raked; but, from the operation of the same cause that had brought her so readily to the wind, the want of head-sail, the ship paid off very slowly. At 2 h. 55 m.,[2] luffing sharp up, the Constitution set the Java's men a good example, by discharging, within the distance of about 400 yards, a heavy, but, as it happened, not a very destructive fire into the British frigate's stern. This salute the Java, as she fell off, returned with her larboard guns. Immediately on receiving their fire, the Constitution wore round on the larboard tack, and was followed by the Java; who, as quickly as she could, ranged up alongside to windward, as yet, not much the worse for her 40 minutes' engagement with an antagonist, that ought, in the time, to have knocked her to pieces.

At 2 h. 58 m. P.M., being again abreast of each other, and within pistol-shot distance, the two frigates mutually engaged: so much, however, to the disadvantage of the Java, that, in the course of ten minutes, her rigging was cut to pieces, and her fore and main masts badly wounded, her master carried below wounded, and several other officers and men killed or wounded. In this state, Captain Lambert determined on boarding, as the only chance of success left. With such intent, the Java, at 3 h. 8 m. P.M., bore up, and would have laid the Constitution on board at her larboard main-chains, had not the foremast at that instant fallen, and which, by its weight and the direction of its fall, crushed the forecastle, and encumbered the principal part of the main deck. The remains of the Java's bowsprit, passing over the Constitution's stern, caught in her starboard mizen rigging, and brought the ship up in the wind, whereby the opportunity to rake, as well as to board, was lost.

The Java now lay at the mercy of her antagonist; who, at

---

[1] The American account says the jib-boom had just before got foul of the Constitution's mizen rigging, but this fact does not appear in the English account.
[2] See diagram.

3 h. 15 m. P.M.,[1] wearing across her bows, raked her with a very heavy fire, and shot away her maintopmast; the wreck of which and of the foremast rendered useless the greater part of the starboard guns. Running past her unmanageable, and now nearly defenceless, opponent to leeward, the Constitution at 3 h. 20 m. P.M., luffed up and raked her on the starboard quarter; then wore round on the larboard tack, and, resuming her position, fired her larboard broadside with most destructive effect. At 3 h. 30 m. P.M.,[2] Captain Lambert fell, mortally wounded in the left breast by a musket-ball from the Constitution's maintop, and was carried below. The command of the Java then devolved upon Lieutenant Henry Ducie Chads; who, although he had been painfully, but not dangerously, wounded since the commencement of the action, still remained on deck, animating the surviving officers and crew by his noble example.

At 3 h. 50 m. P.M. the Java had her gaff and spanker-boom shot away, and at 4 h. 5 m. her mizenmast. All this while, the Constitution lay on the Java's starboard-quarter, pouring in a tremendous fire of round, grape, and musketry. The Constitution, from the damaged state of her rigging, ranging ahead, and the Java, from the fall of her mizenmast, falling off a little, the two frigates again became opposed broadside to broadside. Whether inspirited by the intrepid conduct of the Rodney's eight seamen and a few others (who almost fought the main deck), or recovered from their panic by knowing that the chief of the slaughter had hitherto fallen among their comrades on the deck above, the men at the Java's 18-pounders began blazing away with the utmost animation; blazing, indeed, for, the wreck lying over the guns on that side, almost every discharge set the ship on fire. Having effectually done her work, the Constitution, at 4 h. 25 m. P.M.,[3] made sail ahead out of gun-shot, to repair her damages: leaving the Java a perfect wreck, with her mainmast only standing, and that tottering, her main-yard gone in the slings, and the muzzles of her guns dipping in the water from the heavy rolling of the ship in consequence of her dismasted state. Mistaking the cause of the Constitution's running from them, or becoming more attached to their new occupation by the few hours' practice which they had had, the tyro ship's company of the Java cheered the American frigate, and called to her to come back.

While, with far more care than appeared to be requisite, considering that the loss of her maintopsail-yard, with some cut

[1] See diagram. [2] Ibid. [3] Ibid.

rigging, was the only visible injury she had sustained, the Constitution lay at a distance on the Java's weather and larboard bow, getting ready to give the finishing blow to this, by her means chiefly, protracted contest, the Java, with one union jack lashed to the stump of her mizenmast, and another, where, notwithstanding the assertion of Commodore Bainbridge, that it was down when he shot ahead, it had remained during all the action, in her main rigging, was busied in clearing away the wreck of her masts and putting herself in a state to renew the action, as soon as her antagonist, with whom the option lay, should re-advance to the attack. The Java's first endeavours were to get before the wind: with this view, a sail was set from the stump of the foremast to the bowsprit; and, as the weather mainyard-arm still remained aloft, the main tack was got forward. A topgallantmast was also got from the booms, and begun to be rigged as a jury foremast, with a lower studding-sail for a jury foresail; when, owing to the continued heavy rolling of the ship, the mainmast was obliged to be cut away, to prevent its falling in-board. This was at 4 h. 40 m. P.M.; and in half an hour after that service had been executed, the Constitution wore and stood for the hulk of the Java; whose crew, with very creditable alacrity, had reloaded her guns with round and grape, and seemed, notwithstanding their almost hopeless state, far from dispirited.

At 5 h. 45 m. P.M., full three hours and a half from the commencement of the action, the Constitution placed herself in a very effectual raking position, close athwart the bows of her defenceless antagonist. Having, besides the loss of her masts and bowsprit as already mentioned, had six of her quarter-deck, four of her forecastle, and several of her main deck, guns disabled, the latter chiefly from the wreck lying over them, all her boats shot to pieces, her hull shattered, and one pump shot away, and having also much water in the hold, the British frigate, as a measure that could now no longer be delayed, lowered her colours from the stump of the mizenmast; and at 6 P.M. the Java was taken possession of by the Constitution.

The following diagram is meant to illustrate the numerous evolutions in this action, from 15 minutes after its commencement at 2 h. 10 m., to the Java's surrender at 5 h. 45 m. P.M. Some of the dates will be found slightly to disagree with those specified either in the British or the American official accounts. This has been done to bring the two accounts nearer together, but great care has been taken in marking the relative time, which is by far the more material consideration. The remarks formerly made respecting the impracticability of giving the proper elongation to the tracks, or dotted lines, apply to this diagram, to the second or lower compartment of it especially.

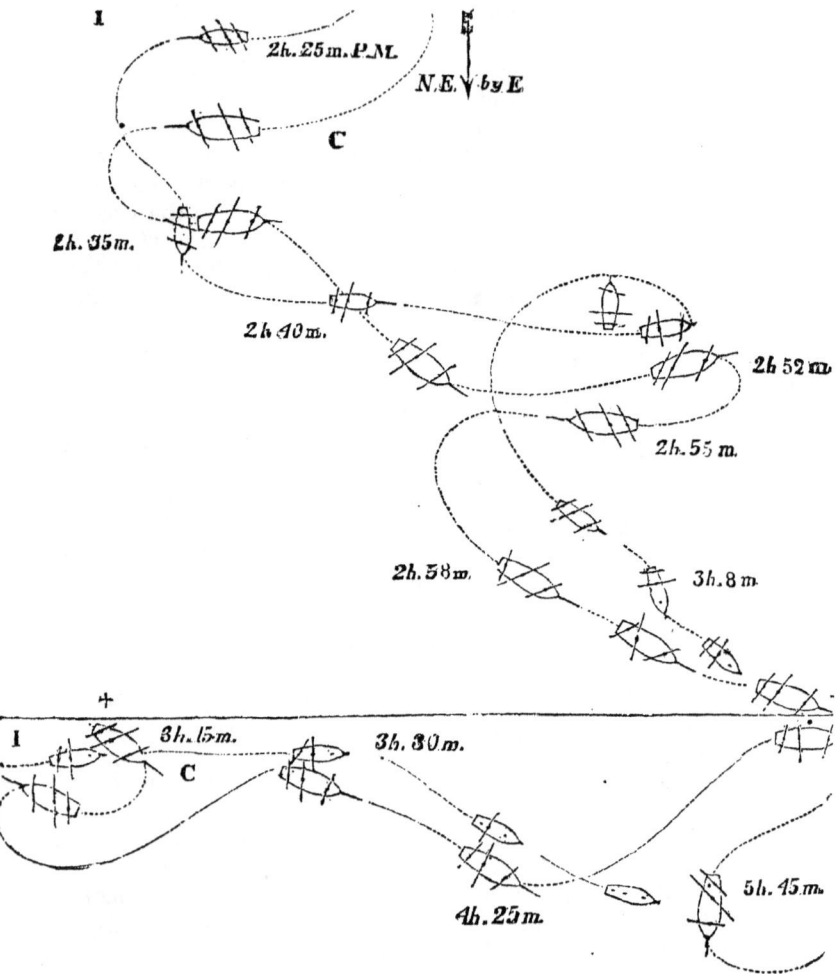

Out of her crew, supernumeraries included, of 354 men and 23 boys, the Java had three master's mates (Charles Jones, Thomas Hammond, and William Gascoigne), two midshipmen

(William Salmond and Edward Keele), one supernumerary clerk (Thomas Joseph Matthias), 12 seamen, and four marines killed, her captain (mortally), first-lieutenant (already named), master (Batty Robinson), second-lieutenant of marines (David Davies), boatswain (James Humble, severely), four of her midshipmen, 55 seamen (one mortally), four boys and 21 marines (with the killed, just half the number on board) wounded; and, of her supernumeraries, one commander (John Marshall), one lieutenant (James Saunders), Captain Wood, aide-de-camp to General Hislop, one master's mate (William Brown), and nine seamen also wounded: total, 22 killed and 102 wounded; two mortally, five dangerously, 52 severely, and 43 slightly.

The midshipman Keele was not killed outright, but died the day following. He was only thirteen years of age, and it was the first time he had ever been to sea. He had his leg amputated, and anxiously inquired soon after the action was over, if the ship had struck. Seeing a ship's colour spread over him, the gallant youth grew uneasy, until he was convinced it was an English flag. The following is the account, which Mr. Humble, the boatswain, gave of himself at the court-martial:—"I was down about an hour, when I got my arm put a little to rights by a tourniquet being put on it—nothing else; my hand was carried away, and my arm wounded about the elbow. I put my arm into the bosom of my shirt, and went up again, when I saw the enemy ahead of us, repairing his damages. I had my orders from Lieutenant Chads, before the action began, to cheer up the boarders with my pipe, that they might make a clean spring in boarding."

The Constitution received several shot in her hull, and also in her masts, particularly her fore and mizen masts; but these, the mainmast especially, were far too stout even to require fishing in consequence. Out of her eight boats, it is acknowledged that the ship, when the action ended, had only one left in a state to take the water; a tolerable proof that her damages were by no means so trifling as was afterwards represented by the Americans. From the same cause, the loss on board the Constitution, although stated by Commodore Bainbridge at only nine killed and 25 wounded, must have been quite as much as the British official account makes it: 10 men killed, her fifth-lieutenant, Mr. John C. Aylwin (the same who was wounded as master in the Guerrière's action), and four men mortally wounded, the commodore wounded slightly, and about 42 others, most of them severely Having none of her men absent in prizes, the

Constitution had on board her full complement, besides two or three supernumeraries; making 477 men and three (as we shall say, although one only, a lad of 17, was seen) boys. By adding about 100 men to the Guerrière's crew, the "Comparative force" in her action will suffice to refer to on the present occasion.[1]

The Constitution captured the Java certainly, but in so discreditable a manner, that, had the latter been manned with a well-trained crew of 320 men, no doubt remains in our mind, and we have considered the subject seriously, that, notwithstanding her vast superiority of force, the American frigate must either have succumbed or have fled. Indeed, if American report be worth attending to, Captain Bainbridge, once during the heat of the action, had an idea of resorting to the latter alternative; but his First-lieutenant, Mr. Parker (a native of Great Britain, we have been informed[2]), succeeded in dissuading him from the measure.

If, on coming on board the Constitution, the surviving British officers were surprised at the immense force, both in *matériel* and *personnel* to which they had so long been opposed, the American officers, on boarding the Java, were mortified at seeing the little screwed-up ship (her sides tumbled in so, that she appeared, at the gangways, scarcely wider than the Hornet), which had given them so much trouble to take. The thing, however, was done: and it only remained, by arts which none know better than Americans how to practise, to swell the victory into one of the grandest triumphs that any nation, except America, had hitherto gained.

Lieutenant Parker, the prize-master of the Java, having reported to the commodore her disabled condition, received orders, as soon as he had removed the prisoners and their baggage, to set the ship on fire. This tedious service, with only one boat to perform it, being at length accomplished, the Java, on the forenoon of the 31st, was set on fire; and the Constitution retired to a distance to avoid the effects of the explosion. Now occurred a curious scene on board the Constitution. The Java was burning without the customary emblem of her newly-acquired national character. Not finding, as he had expected, an American flag among the Java's signals, and deeming it unnecessary, owing to the present distance between the ships, to send for one, Lieutenant Parker left the Java burning without any colours at all. Scarcely had Commodore Bainbridge recovered

---

[1] See p. 383.   [2] His name does not appear in the "Register" of 1816.

from the rage into which this, in point of national etiquette, very serious event had thrown him, than one of the two or three deserters, that had already entered on board the Constitution, informed him, that the Java had an immense quantity of specie in her hold. After a while some of the late officers of the Java, pitying the acuteness of his feelings, assured the American captain that the cases contained neither gold nor silver, but copper.

At about 3 P.M. the Java exploded; and that evening the Constitution, having quite refitted herself, made sail for St. Salvador. Although entirely dismasted, the Java was not in such a damaged state in the lower part of her hull, but that the crew of a British frigate would have refitted her sufficiently for the voyage to America. But why did not Commodore Bainbridge take her with him into that port? He carried thither, as a prize, the English schooner Eleanor; and the Hornet went in there with her recapture, the William. There is a mystery about the destruction of the Java which we cannot penetrate. Shortly after the Constitution had made sail from the scene of her exploit, her consort the Hornet hove in sight. Another British frigate to a certainty! Here was a scene of bustle and confusion. The swearing and blustering of officers, and the free-and-easy nonchalance of the men, almost made the British officers smile notwithstanding their recent misfortunes. At length the Hornet approached near enough to be recognised, and some degree of order was restored.

The manner in which the Java's men were treated by the American officers reflects upon the latter the highest disgrace. The moment the prisoners were brought on board the Constitution, they were handcuffed. Admitting that to have been justifiable as a measure of precaution, what right had the poor fellows to be pillaged of almost everything they possessed? True, Lieutenant-general Hislop got back his valuable service of plate, and the other British officers were treated civilly. Who would not rather that the governor's plate, at this very time, was spread out upon Commodore Bainbridge's sideboard, than that British seamen, fighting bravely in their country's cause, should be put in fetters, and robbed of their little all? What is all this mighty generosity but a political juggle, a tub thrown to the whale? Mr. Madison says to his officers, "Never mind making a display of your generosity, where you know it will be proclaimed to the world. If you lose anything by it, I'll take care Congress shall recompense you twofold. Such conduct, on the

part of an American officer of rank, will greatly tend to discredit
the British statements as to any other acts of yours not so
proper to be made public, and will serve, besides, as an im-
perishable record of the national magnanimity and honour."
One object the Constitution's officers missed by their cruelty.
Three only of the Java's men would enter with them: the
remainder treated with contempt their reiterated promises of
high pay, rich land, and liberty. Partly as a compliment for
restoring his plate, and partly to induce Commodore Bainbridge not to put into effect his threatened intention of re-
taining Lieutenant Chads as a hostage for the due observance
of the terms on which the other officers and men were paroled,
Lieutenant-general Hislop presented the former with an elegant
sword.

On the 3rd of January, in the morning, the Constitution and
Hornet arrived at St. Salvador; where lay the William, recaptured by the latter. On that same day the commodore disembarked the prisoners received out of the Java, 355 in number,
and Captain Lawrence landed the 20 officers and men whom he
had found on board the William; making a total, out of the
original crew of the Java, of 375, or with the 22 killed, of 397,
men and boys. The death of Captain Lambert and of one seaman, and the delivery up, to the governor of St. Salvador, of
nine Portuguese seamen, reduced the number of prisoners out of
the two prizes to 364. But the number paroled by Commodore
Bainbridge is officially reported by himself at 361. How is this?
Why the commodore states that he allowed "three passengers,
private characters, to land without any restraint." But who
were these "three passengers, private characters," so gene-
rously exempted from parole? No others, it would seem, than
the three sailors of the Java, who had been fools enough to
enter the American service. To deduct them from the amount
of prisoners received would be making the Java's complement
appear three men short of what by a proper arrangement of
the figures it could be proved to have been. To confess the
fact, would never do; therefore the whole of the Java's passengers—naval, military, and civil—were paroled as "officers,
petty officers, seamen, marines, and boys," and the hiatus made
by the three traitors was cleverly filled up with three nominal
"passengers, private characters, whom the commodore did not
consider prisoners-of-war, and permitted to land without any
restraint;" and of whom, of course, no further account was
taken. So that, as Commodore Bainbridge officially declared,

the Java "certainly" had 60 killed; and, as he took no notice whatever of the recaptured ship William, his 361 paroled and 12 unparoled prisoners showed, in the clearest manner, that the Java, when the action commenced, had 433 men. But the commodore merely gives his prize "upwards of 400 men." What greater proof, then, can there be of Commodore Bainbridge's modesty, as well as of his scrupulous regard not to overstep the bounds of truth?

On the 4th the young and gallant Captain Lambert breathed his last, and on the 5th was buried with military honours in Fort St. Pedro, attended by the governor of St. Salvador, the Condé Dos Arcos, and the Portuguese in general, but not (will it be believed?) by either Commodore Bainbridge or Captain Lawrence, or by any of their respective officers. But the commodore afterwards made some amends for a piece of disrespect so marked and public, by writing the following private note to Lieutenant-general Hislop. "Commodore Bainbridge has learned, with real sorrow, the death of Captain Lambert. Though a political enemy, he could not but greatly respect him for the brave defence he made with his ship; and Commodore Bainbridge takes this occasion to observe, in justice to Lieutenant Chads, who fought the Java after Captain Lambert was wounded, that he did everything for the defence of that ship that a brave and skilful officer could do, and that further resistance would have been a wanton effusion of human blood."

On the 6th, requiring more repairs than she could obtain in any foreign port, the Constitution got under way from St. Salvador, and breaking up her cruise to the Pacific, bent her course towards home; leaving the Hornet to blockade in the port the British sloop-of-war Bonne-Citoyenne. We shall by-and-by set this matter right, confining our attention at present to the Constitution; who, without any further event of consequence, anchored, on the evening of the 15th of February, 1813, in the harbour of Boston. The reception given to Commodore Bainbridge, his officers, and crew may readily be conceived; as well as the exaggerated accounts that were published of his victory. We shall merely state, that the Congress of the United States voted 50,000 dollars and their thanks to the captain, officers and crew of the Constitution; also a gold medal to Commodore Bainbridge, and silver medals to each of his officers, with suitable devices.

At this moment our eyes light upon a passage in a book before us, giving an account of the reception of Commodore Bainbridge by the citizens of Boston, and we cannot resist the temptation of placing it before the British public. "On the following Thursday (that succeeding the frigate's arrival), Commodore Bainbridge landed at the long wharf from the frigate Constitution, amidst acclamations and roaring of cannon from the shore. All the way from the end of the pier to the Exchange coffee-house was decorated with colours and streamers. In State-street they were strung across from the opposite buildings, while the windows and balconies of the houses were filled with ladies, and the tops of the houses were covered with spectators, and an immense crowd filled the streets, so as to render it difficult for the military escort to march. The commodore was distinguished by his noble figure, and his walking uncovered. On his right hand was the veteran Commodore Rodgers, and on his left Brigadier-general Welles; then followed the brave Captain Hull, Colonel Blake, and a number of officers and citizens; but the crowd was so immense that it was difficult to keep the order of procession. The band of music in the balcony of the State Bank, and the music of the New England guards, had a fine effect."[1] Here was a compliment to the British navy!

The surviving officers and crew of the Java, having quitted the Brazils in two cartels, arrived at Portsmouth early in April; and, on the 23rd of the same month a court-martial sat on board the Gladiator in the harbour, to try them for the loss of their ship. The court agreed, that the capture of the late Java was caused by her being totally dismasted in a very spirited action with the United States ship Constitution, of considerably superior force; in which the zeal, ability, and bravery of the late Captain Lambert, her commander, was highly conspicuous and honourable, being constantly the assailant, until the moment of his much-lamented fall; and that, subsequently thereto, the action was continued with equal zeal, ability, and bravery, by Lieutenant Henry Ducie Chads, the first-lieutenant, and the other surviving officers and ship's company, and other officers and persons who were passengers on board her, until she became a perfect wreck, and the continuance of the action would have been a useless sacrifice of lives; and did adjudge the said Lieutenant Henry Ducie Chads, and the other surviving officers and ship's company to be most honourably acquitted. Rear-admiral Graham Moore was the president; who, in returning Lieutenant Chads his sword, addressed him nearly as follows:—" I have much satisfaction in returning you your sword: had you been

[1] Naval Monument, p. 279.

an officer who had served in comparative obscurity all your life, and never before heard of, your conduct on the present occasion has been sufficient to establish your character as a brave, skilful, and attentive officer.''

On the 8th of September, at 3 P.M., the British schooner Laura, of 10 carronades, 18-pounders, and two short nines, with 41, out of a complement of 60, men and boys, commanded by Lieutenant Charles Newton Hunter, while in the act of taking possession of her fourth prize, an American ship bound into the Delaware, then three leagues off in the north-west, discovered about three miles to leeward a large armed brig, with a French ensign and pendant. This was the French privateer Diligent, Captain Grassin, whose regular armament was 16 carronades, French 24-pounders, and two long 12-pounders, with a crew of at least 120 men; but, owing to a recent gale, three of the guns had been shifted to the hold, and, from manning a prize or two, the crew of the brig had been reduced to 97 men. Having recalled her boat and men from the American ship, the Laura, with the wind from the north-east, bore up for the Diligent, whose name and full force in guns and men had been communicated to Lieutenant Hunter by the third prize he had sent away.

At 3 h. 55 m. P.M, being within musket-shot on the starboard and weather quarter of the Diligent, the Laura opened a fire from her bow-guns, and received the broadside of the French brig. At 4 P.M. the two vessels got fairly alongside each other, and, while the Diligent manœuvred occasionally to gain the wind, the Laura tried to prevent it by lulling, as well as she was able, her opponent's sails. At 4 h. 30 m. P.M. the Diligent set her course and tried to tack, and the Laura put her helm down to effect the same object; but, the wind falling light, both vessels missed stays, and, in paying off, became mutually engaged yard-arm and yard-arm. At 4 h. 45 m., having had her peak-halliards shot away, the Laura fell a little off the wind and fore-reached; and the Diligent grazed the schooner's larboard quarter. Shortly afterwards, dropping astern, the brig caught the breeze, and, having the superiority of sailing, drew up on the weather-quarter of the Laura. At this time, owing to the low firing of the two vessels, neither had materially suffered in rigging or sails. The Diligent, now in her turn, took the wind out of the Laura's sails, and ran her bowsprit over the starboard taffrail, with her jib-boom between the topping-lifts and through the mainsail. Here the brig held fast.

The Diligent now, under the fire of her two bow-guns and her numerous musketry, made repeated attempts to board; but the Laura, although, from having 25 American prisoners to guard below, she could muster no more than 34 officers and men on deck, resisted every attempt. At 4 h. 55 m. Lieutenant Hunter, after having been several times slightly grazed, received a musket-ball near the left ear, which, passing obliquely down the lower part of the back of the head, made its way out. He of course fell, and from excess of bleeding was incapable of further efforts. Unfortunately no officer was left to take the command, the principal officers being absent in the three prizes, and Mr. John C. Griffith, a young midshipman who had been but a short time at sea, having been previously wounded. In this situation, there was no possibility of opposing further resistance to the overwhelming crew of the Diligent, who accordingly rushed on board and hauled down the Laura's colours.

The Laura had 15 killed and severely wounded, including, as already stated, her commander and his only remaining officer. The Diligent, as acknowledged by Captain Grassin, had nine killed and 10 badly wounded; a decided proof that the Laura's small crew had made the best possible use of their 18-pounder carronades. Captain Grassin carried his prize to Philadelphia, and behaved to Lieutenant Hunter in the most honourable and attentive manner. Lieutenant Hunter was landed and taken to the hospital; and, on subsequently reaching Halifax, Nova Scotia, was tried for the loss of the Laura and most honourably acquitted. The president, Vice-admiral Sawyer, then returned Lieutenant Hunter his sword with a very handsome eulogium.

BRITISH AND AMERICAN NAVIES.

In the abstract of the British navy for this year will be found, among the "Ordered to be Built" ships, four first-rates. Two of these were similar to the Caledonia and Nelson; the Britannia, building at Plymouth, and the Prince Regent, at Chatham. The other two were of rather a smaller class; the London, building at Plymouth, and the Princess Charlotte at Portsmouth.[1] To the fine class of N or middling 74s, as many as 11 new individuals have been added. By the addition of these and of other large ships, and by the gradual reduction of the O or small-class 74, and of the 64, although the number of cruising line-of-battle ships is three less than are to be found in Nos. 9 and 16 Abstracts, the tonnage of the 124 in No. 21 Abstract exceeds that of the 121 in No 9 by 8564, and in that of the 126 No. 16 by 5585 tons. This makes the average burden of the 124 line-of-battle ships belonging to the British navy at the commencement of the present year, 1830 tons and a fraction; whereas the average, at the commencement of the year 1802, was 1740, and at the commencement of 1793, only 1645 tons; an unequivocal testimony of the improved state of the British navy.[2]

On the 26th of January in this year a small increase took place in the complements of the different classes of frigates; occasioned, in all probability, by the war with America. As far back as October and December, 1804, the large class of 38s had been ordered to have their complements augmented from 284 to 300 men and boys; but on the 24th of June, 1806, the order was rescinded, and the 38s were again established with 284, and the 18-pounder 36s with 274 men and boys. Subsequently, by special orders, most of the large 38s obtained a

[1] See Appendix, Annual Abstract, No. 21. [2] See Appendix, Nos. 11 and 12.

complement of 300; and the order of January, 1813, gave to the whole class 320, including five additional marines; also to the 18-pounder 36s 284, and to the 18-pounder 32s 270, men and boys. The 24-pounder 40-gun class, including the new ships building, were also increased from 340 to 350 men and boys; and the 18-gun quarter-decked ship-sloops, from 121 to 135. Still, the boys were in far too great a proportion in all the classes. In action they are of no use, because of their physical incompetency; and out of action their services are not required, on account of the number of abler hands ready to do the work. Boys would, doubtless, learn more of practical navigation, and become, in the end, better seamen, by passing their teens in a merchant-vessel; for this plain reason, that, instead of spending their time in comparative idleness, they would be employed in assisting the few hands on board to perform the duties of the ship.

A glance at the "Increase" compartment of this and the preceding year's Abstract will show, at once, what a stir the recent successes of the Americans were making in the English dockyards. In our view of the case, nearly the whole of that stir, with the heavy expense consequent upon it, was unnecessary. Paradoxical as it may seem, we boldly make the assertion, that the way to strengthen the British navy was to break up, not to build, ships. The *matériel* and *personnel* were more than ever out of their due proportions. The mode, that should have been adopted, was to break up, lay up, or, at all events, to disarm and put out of commission, 40 or 50 ships; and, after sweeping from the service and lodging in the hospitals or elsewhere, the old, the infirm, and the ineffective, to put on board the remaining ships adequate crews of able-bodied, stout-hearted British seamen. Let these be practised at the guns, and well officered; and then let it be seen what enemy's ship, with a fifth of numerical superiority, could stand against them. Those, however, who possessed the power to direct these matters, acted as if they thought, that an increase of wood and iron would effect more than an increase of flesh and blood; and now let us see whether, proceeding upon that notion, they went the right way to "fashion the means to the end."

But first we will endeavour to show, that the plan of disarming a great many of the higher rates might have been carried into effect without detriment to the general service of the navy. For this a few facts will suffice. The disaffected and ill-manned state of the French fleet in the Scheldt would have admitted of less than half the number of ships that blockaded Flushing, and the almost equally ill-manned, though perhaps not disloyal, condition of the French fleet at Toulon was keeping before that port, for the most part as mere lookers-on, 10,000 or 12,000 of the best seamen in the British navy; three-fourths of whom were on board three-deckers, ships that, under existing circumstances, were useless anywhere but on that station. Allowing, even, that both the Flushing and the Toulon stations required a numerical force of ships outside nearly equal to that within, a dozen or two of large transports, with a double row of painted ports, would keep the enemy in harbour as effectually as the same number of well-appointed 74s. With respect to the Mediterranean fleet, it was particularly to be regretted that, while there was such a dearth of seamen in the home ports and on the North American station, so many thousands of the very best of seamen, who, under the wise regulations of Sir Edward Pellew, had been daily improving themselves in the neglected art of gunnery, should be denied the power of showing their proficiency where it was so much wanted.

We have already given a very full account, not only of the exploits, but of the force in guns, men, and size, of the American 44-gun frigates; and we will now, as far as lies in our power, point out the steps that were taken by the British admiralty, to put a stop to their further successes. The Majestic, Goliath, and Saturn, three of the small class 74s, were cut down, fore-and-aft, to the clamps of the quarter-deck and forecastle. Each ship was allowed to retain her first-deck battery of 28 long 32-pounders, and, in lieu of her 28 long 18-pounders on the second deck, she received an equal number of 42-pounder carronades, besides two long 12-pounders as chase-guns, making 58 guns on two flush decks, with a net complement of 495 men and boys. This, although a reduction in her numerical force of 22 guns (16 on the quarter-deck and forecastle and six on the poop), gave the ship, even if armed with the full establishment of long guns and carronades assigned to her class, a slightly increased weight of metal in broadside. The advantages contemplated from this alteration in the construction were, superiority in sailing, an equal degree of force, and, with the aid of a black hammock-cloth thrown over the waist-barricade, such a disguised appearance, as might induce the large American frigates to come down and engage. The three 64s reduced in the year 1794[1]

[1] See vol. i. p. 454, note W*.

were converted into real frigates; inasmuch as, excepting the portion of bulwark that lay abaft the gangway-entrance, they were cut down level with the upper deck, and were armed precisely as any frigate of similar dimensions would have been. But these rasé 74s were no more frigates, although frequently so called, than the nine 56 and 54 gun ships purchased into the service in 1795.[1] The latter, although much smaller and more lightly armed than the rasés, were never considered as any other than two-decked ships. It is but justice to Captain William Layman, of the navy, to state, that, in a pamphlet entitled "Precursor to an Exposé on Forest Trees and Timber," &c. published in January, 1813, he recommends the small-class 74 to be cut down, precisely as the Majestic and her two companions were; and, among his six profile views of ships, that officer gives one of the 74 rasés, in illustration of his remarks. The only point wherein he appears to differ is, in arming the lower deck with long 24 instead of 32 pounders, and the upper, with 68 instead of 42 pounder carronades.

It is evident, from the description we have given of the cut-down 74, that she was much more than a match for the heaviest of the American 44s. The command of the Majestic was given to Captain John Hayes, and that of the Goliath to Captain Frederick Lewis Maitland. It was intended, we believe, that Captain Lord Cochrane should have commanded the Saturn; but, unfortunately for himself and his country, his lordship was about this time expelled from the service of which he had hitherto been so bright an ornament. The command of the Saturn, after some delay in consequence of this untoward event, was given to Captain James Nash. These three ships were well manned, especially the Majestic and Saturn. The crew of the latter consisted chiefly of west-country volunteers, induced to enter from belief that Lord Cochrane was to be their captain; and we are convinced that, if the Majestic and Saturn had fallen in with the President, Constitution, and United States sailing in company, Captain Hayes would have attacked them, and, we think, with success. As, however, no glory could have accrued from the capture of an American 44-gun frigate by a British cut-down 74, supposing them to have been singly opposed, the utility of reducing the Majestic and her two companions from their former rank in the service has often been questioned.

But some ships were built to answer the same purpose as the three rasés. They, also, claim a few remarks. The Leander

[1] See vol. i., p. 455, note R* and S*

was constructed of pitch-pine, from a draught prepared by Sir William Rule, the ingenious architect of the Caledonia and many other fine ships in the British navy; and the Newcastle was constructed of the same light wood, from the draught of M. Louis-Charles Barrallier, then an assistant surveyor under Sir William, but now the principal naval architect for the French at Toulon. The first of these ships measured 1572, the other 1556 tons; and they were both constructed of very thin and inadequate scantling. The establishment of each ship was 30 long 24-pounders on the first or "upper" deck, and 26 carronades 42-pounders, and two, afterwards increased to four, long 24-pounders on the second or "spar" deck; total, at first 58, then 60 guns, with a net complement of 480 men and boys. The Leander and Newcastle, therefore, in the disposition of their guns, perfectly agreed with the cut-down 74s; and yet they were officially registered as "frigates," but, by way of salvo for their anomalous structure "with spar decks," was superadded. If by "frigate" is meant a ship with a single battery-deck from stem to stern, is it not a sufficient sketch of the term to apply it to a vessel that has two additional short decks, upon which are mounted nearly as many guns as she carries on her whole deck? But must a ship, having two whole decks, upon each of which an equal number of guns is mounted, be called a single-decked vessel? And yet, in official language, the Leander and Newcastle are not two-decked ships, otherwise their lower battery-deck would not be called their upper-deck, nor their upper their spar-deck; neither would their depth of hold be measured from the deck below the first battery-deck, nor the length of the same deck be registered as the "length of gundeck." These are the only points in which these frigates with spar decks differ from the cut-down 74s, and from the 56 and 54 gun ships already mentioned.

The command of the Leander was given to Captain Sir George Ralph Collier, a name of frequent occurrence in these pages; and the command of the Newcastle, to Captain Lord George Stuart. Great difficulty was experienced in getting these two ships manned; and certainly the crew of the Leander, after it was obtained, was a very indifferent one, containing, besides many old and weakly men, an unusually large proportion of boys. This ineffectiveness of the Leander's crew has recently been contradicted; but we allude to the period of the ship's arrival at Halifax, Nova Scotia. We were then on board the Leander several times, and not only witnessed the quality of her crew, but heard the officers complain, as well they might, of their great inferiority in that respect to the ships against which they were expected to succeed. When she quitted Spithead for Halifax, the Leander was so lumbered with stores, that the ship would scarcely have made the voyage, had she not received a refit in Cork; and even then it was fortunate, much as was to be expected from her captain and officers, that the Leander did not encounter one of the American 44s.

Another ship, of the same force in guns, and nearly so in men, as the Leander and Newcastle, was produced by raising upon the Akbar, formerly a teak-built Indiaman, and more recently known as the 44-gun frigate Cornwallis. The Akbar proved a very indifferent cruiser, sailing heavily, and rolling to such a degree that she was constantly carrying away or springing her masts. The ship actually stowed 450 tons of water; while the Caledonia, a ship of double her measurement, could not stow more than 421 tons. The Akbar has since been converted to the only purpose for which, and carrying a cargo, she was ever adapted, a troop-ship.

If it was deemed necessary to build or equip ships to oppose the large American frigates in fair combat, they should have been frigates, not two-decked ships like the Leander, Newcastle, and Akbar. There was a frigate laid down in the year 1813 which would have answered every purpose; but, after the draught of the Java had been prepared as that of a regular frigate, to carry 52 guns, the pen of authority filled up the gangway with a barricade and a row of ports, and hence the Java was built as a 60-gun two-decked ship, similar to the Newcastle and Leander. If the American frigates, of 1533 tons, could not carry, with ease, their gangway guns, and the two last-named British 60-gun ships, averaging 1564 tons, found some inconvenience in carrying theirs, how could it be expected that the Java, of 1458 tons, could bear the eight additional guns ordered for her?

Even as a frigate mounting 50 guns, the Java might have been as effectively armed as if she had mounted 52, simply by carrying, like the Constitution,[1] one of her chase 24-pounders on the forcastle, and the other on the quarter-deck. No ship, no British ship, at all events, is so well manned as to be able, if attacked by two opponents, to fight all her guns at once: hence, there is no real loss of force in subtracting the two guns. Nor would there be any difficulty, that a little practice could not

[1] See p. 380.

soon overcome, in shifting the travelling-gun, during an action, from one side of the deck to the other. The governing principle should be, to possess the greatest real, with the least numerical, force; and this is chiefly attainable by the power to present in broadside a greater proportion than half the number of guns mounted by the ship.

Our objection to the cut-down 74s and the two-decked 50s, the latter especially, is to their denomination as frigates, and not to the manner in which their guns are mounted. Admitting that, in former times, when British, like French ships, fell in so at their topsides, that, after the boats and booms were stowed in the waist, a mere gangway, or passage from the quarter-deck to the forecastle, was all the space which could be spared on each side, now that British ships are built nearly wall-sided, what is to prevent the gangway, or waist deck from receiving as many guns as its length will admit? These four or five guns, from their midship position, would be the most efficient of any in the tier to which they belonged. Nor, if the light and but equivocally useful carronades on the poop were withdrawn, would the numerical gun-force of the ship be greatly augmented. The addition to her force is not all the advantage the ship would acquire: weight would be taken from the extremity, the weakest extremity, unless the ship has a round stern, and be shifted to the centre, where it can best be borne.

Any objection to the plan, because of the new nomenclature it would introduce, meets an answer in the present mode of classifying the British navy. A three-decker, certainly, would be called a four-decker, a two-decker, except of the R and U classes in the Abstract, a three-decker, and a quarter-decked one-decker, or regular frigate, a two-decker; but is not the old 98 now called a 104, the old 38 a 46, and, a much greater advance in figures, the old 24 a 34? If England does not adopt the plan, other nations will. America, indeed, has already begun to build flush three-deckers, or ships, in the disposition of their guns, not unlike the Swedish Chapman's 94-gun ship mentioned at a former page.[1] France has already built a few flush two-deckers, similar to the Leander's class; and, if she follows the advice of a very ingenious writer on naval affairs of her own, she will by-and-by have flush three and flush four decked ships. "We ought, for the future," says M. Dupin, "to construct our line-of-battle ships without a poop, and compensate that reduction by continuing the battery

[1] See vol. iv., p. 297.

from the forecastle to the quarter-deck. We should then have ships of the line with four, and with three, complete batteries." "Nous devrions à l'avenir ne construire que des vaisseaux sans dunette, et compenser cette suppression, en continuant la batterie des gaillards, depuis l'avant jusqu'à l'arrière. Alors nous aurions des vaisseaux à quatre et à trois batteries complètes."[1]

Our remarks on this subject, as well as those we formerly submitted on the equalization of the calibers of guns,[2] are merely thrown out as loose hints, to be taken advantage of, if thought worthy, by the abler heads of those to whom the subject professionally belongs. We are aware of one objection to placing guns in the waist: the inconvenience, while those guns are in use especially, of working the sails. It is a rare innovation that produces good without some alloy of evil; and perhaps a clever rigger could dispose the ropes and halliards in such a manner, that the force of that objection would be considerably weakened.

Resuming our subject, we have to notice that, besides the two anomalous classes of "frigates," the cut-down 74 and the 50, a few ships were constructed, to which the name of frigate properly applied, and which, with a little more care in constructing and equipping them, would have been able to cope with the President or either of her class-mates. The Endymion is already known to us as a remarkably fine frigate; but she mounted only 26 guns on the main deck. Another pair of guns on that deck were deemed indispensable; and as fine a frigate as ever swam, having the ports for that number of 24-pounders, was then lying among the ordinary in Hamoaze. The Egyptienne, of 1430 tons, was this frigate; but, to save expense we suppose, it was determined to build ships from the draught of the Endymion, and to bring the 13 main-deck ports as much closer as would admit a 14th to be added. This was done; and in a short time appeared the Forth, Liffey, Severn, Glasgow, and Liverpool. The three first were built of fir, and the two last of pitch-pine; and the force of the class was 28 long 24-pounders on the main deck, and 20 carronades, 32-pounders, and two long nines, on the quarter-deck and forecastle, total 50 guns; with a complement of 350 men and boys. The chief complaint against these frigates was, as may be conjectured, that their quarters were rather confined. A class like the Egyptienne, mounting the same number and nature of guns as

[1] Dupin, Force Navale, tome ii., p. 156.   [2] See vol. iv., p. 196.

the Forth's class, with a crew of 420 good men, would have been quite as heavy a frigate as the British, with a due regard to their established character on the ocean, ought to have constructed, if they constructed any at all, to meet the large American frigates.

But the rage for frigate-building in this year did not stop at the Endymion's class. As many as 26 of the two principal 18-pounder classes were ordered to be built, chiefly, for expedition-sake and to save expense, of the red and yellow pine. Some of these, too, were to be fitted with medium 24 pounders instead of their long 18s, and were to have a complement of 330 men and boys. The six and a half feet, 33 cwt. 24-pounder, or Gover's gun, not having been found heavy enough to fire two shot, some guns of the same caliber were constructed, from a foot to a foot and a half longer, and weighing from 40 to 43 cwt. One description of these guns was found fully to answer; and we shall by-and-by have more to say of them. As it turned out, no shot fired from a long or a medium 24-pounder, except in the single instance of a British ship which had been in the service since the year 1797, struck or fell on board an American frigate. The promulgated intention, to arm British frigates with such guns, was quite enough to inspire the Americans with caution; and accordingly the Java was the last British frigate they captured or brought to action, but not, as we shall hereafter see, the last they fell in with. After all, therefore, it is a question, whether it would not have been sufficient, without cutting down Majestics and Goliaths, or building Leanders and Newcastles, to have made the Macedonian's fine class as effective as it ought to have been; and, as the chief means of doing so, to have given to each 38-gun frigate, sent cruising to the westward, a well-trained crew of 370 men.

Some of the minor classes of ships-of-war now claim our attention; and we shall soon have a set of cases to record, which will show that the Americans as much out-built the British in their "sloops," as they had out-witted and out-fought them in their "frigates." The two principal classes of sloops-of-war, at this time belonging to the British navy, were the quarter-decked 18-gun ship-sloop, of about 430 tons, mounting 18 carronades, 32-pounders, on the main deck, and on the quarter-deck and forecastle six carronades, 12 or 18 pounders, and two sixes, total 26 guns, with 121 men and boys; and the well-known 18-gun brig-sloop, mounting no more guns than she rated. As a match for the first-class, it was proposed to Congress, in

November, 1812, to build a few sloops-of-war to mount 16 long 12-pounders on the main deck, and 12 carronades, 24-pounders, on the quarter-deck and forecastle, total 28 guns; with a complement of 180 men. The size is not mentioned, but a ship, so armed, could not measure less than 560 or 570 tons. Whether it was decided to vote all the British quarter-decked ship-sloops "small frigates," and consequently superior to any vessels bearing the denomination of "sloops," or whatever else may have been the reason, the American quarter-decked sloop was laid aside, and the preference was given to a flush-decked ship, to mount 20 carronades, 32-pounders, and two long 18-pounders, with a crew of 175 men, and to measure 509 tons American, or 540 tons English. These were to rate of 18 guns, and to be considered as a fair match for the British 18-gun brig-sloop, which, from the concurrent testimony of such men of veracity as Captain David Porter and Captain Jacob Jones,[1] mounted 22 guns.

Three of the new American sloops were soon afloat, the Peacock, Wasp, and Frolic; and, to be ready to meet these upon equal terms, 18 flush ships were ordered to be built of fir, with all possible despatch. Having in their possession the Andromeda (late the American merchant-ship Hannibal), of 24 guns on a flush-deck, an extraordinary fine ship of 812 tons, the late French corvette Bonne-Citoyenne, and the two ships built after her, the Hermes and Myrmidon, the British could be at no loss for a proper model. Well, what did they do? Why, one of the lords of the admiralty recommended a draught to be prepared upon the reduced lines of the Bonne-Citoyenne. To what extent the reduction went, and whether an augmentation of size would not have better answered the intended purpose, will be seen by the following statement:—

	Length of Main deck.		Breadth, extreme.		Tons.	No.	
	Ft.	in.	Ft.	in.		Guns.	Men.
Bonne-Citoyenne	120	1	30	11	511	20	135
Proposed draught	115	6	29	8	455	22	135
American Frolic	119	6	32	0	540	22	175

Where so much deference was officially due, science had to bow the head, and Sir Joseph Yorke soon had the satisfaction of seeing his "improved Bonne-Citoyennes" afloat and fitting in all the principal dépôts of Great Britain. To diminish a vessel's capacity, and at the same time to increase her armament, was

[1] See pp. 366, 393.

an odd way of improving her qualities. Scarcely were the twenty 32-pounder carronades and two long nines brought on board, than two of the carronades were sent on shore again, as having no proper ports fitted to receive them. Already the remaining 20 guns were too close together, to render the quarters sufficiently roomy. With these, however, the ships went to sea; and they were soon found neither to work well, nor to sail well. The utility of their stern-chase ports may be judged when it is stated, that, owing to the narrowness of the ships at the stern, there was no room to work the tiller while the guns were pointed through the ports. Of this discreditable oversight and its evil consequences, we shall hereafter have to give a practical illustration.

Of the relative stoutness of the spars of the British and American sloops-of-war, thus pitted against each other by the order of the board of admiralty, some idea may be formed, when it is stated, that the girth, just above the deck, of the mainmast of one of the latter, the Frolic, was 7 feet 8 inches; whereas the mainmast established upon the former class measured, at the same place, only 5 feet 8 inches. The Cyrus, if not most of the others, was "doubled," so as to increase her beam about 10 inches, and enable the ship to keep the sea in a gale of wind; and we remember seeing the Medina, at the king's dockyard in Halifax, Nova Scotia, having her lower masts fished, to prevent them from snapping in two with the weight of the top-gear above.

While the cutting-down system was pursuing, a mode presented itself of quickly getting ready a few ships, equal in size and force to the large American sloops. The 10 ships of the *M* class in the Abstracts averaged 534 tons, and mounted 22 carronades, 32-pounders, on the main deck. By having their quarter-decks and forecastles cut away, these ships would have been much improved in sailing and seaworthiness; and then, with two long 9 or 12 pounders in lieu of their two foremost carronades, and with their complement increased to 173 men and boys, they would have been far superior vessels to those built under the auspices of the gallant admiral. Even a precedent was not wanted. The Hyæna, of a similar construction to the ships of the above-mentioned class, was, when taken by the French in 1793, cut down to the clamps of her quarter-deck and forecastle, and became a very fast-sailing and successful privateer. On her subsequent recapture by the British in 1797, the Hyæna was allowed to remain as a flush-ship, and was armed precisely in the manner above recommended.[1] The height between the decks of ships-of-war must, for obvious reasons, be nearly the same; consequently the proportion of top-weight increases, as the length, breadth, and below-water depth of the vessel diminishes. This is the reason that frigate-built ships below 580 or 600 tons, carrying eight or ten guns upon the quarter-deck and forecastle, are usually so crank and unsafe; and one cause of their sailing so ill is, that their masts must be shorter, and their sails smaller, to counteract the strong heeling propensity of their hulls.

Fortunately for the honour of the captains appointed to the new 20-gun ships, some newspaper of the day exaggerated their force and size, and extolled them as very formidable vessels. The consequence was, that the Wasp, Frolic, Peacock, and Hornet avoided every three-masted man-of-war they fell in with; confining the exercise of their prowess to the British brig-sloop, the utmost extent of whose force was well known to them. While we are making this assertion, we bear fully in mind the braggadocio that took place between the Hornet and the Bonne-Citoyenne; but we shall very soon establish the fact, that the behaviour of the Americans on the occasion was nothing but braggadocio, and that of the most despicable kind.

The schooner-classes of the two navies will require but a few words. None can compete with the Americans in the size, beauty, swiftness, or seaworthiness of their schooners. They will arm a schooner of 200 tons, with seven guns, including a traversing 18 or 24 pounder, and give her a crew of at least 100 able-bodied men. If this schooner is captured by the British and deemed eligible for the navy, her bulwarks are raised, and pierced with ports fore and aft, 14 carronades, 18 or 12 pounders, are crowded upon her deck, and she is established (there is no crowding here) with a crew of 45 or 50 men and at least six or seven very young boys. The top-hamper necessarily diminishes the vessel's rate of sailing; and another impediment frequently arises from the inexperience of her commander, in the art of working to advantage a schooner-rigged vessel.

To whatever is classed under one head, people are apt, and very naturally, to attach an idea of equality; and the stronger party is sure to triumph in his victory, until the weaker party has shown the disparity of force against which he had to con-

---

[1] See vol. ii., p. 102.

tend. It too frequently happens that this is not done; and, before it can be done with effect, two operations are necessary : the removal of one impression, and the substitution of another. The President and the Southampton[1] are "frigates;" the Peacock and the Childers[2] are "sloops-of-war:" and the following statement will show, that one "man-of-war schooner" may differ in force and size from another, to even a greater extent than in the case of the frigate or the sloop. The American privateer-schooner Harlequin, of Boston, measured 323 tons, and mounted 10 long 12-pounders, with a crew of 115 men. Her mainmast was 84 feet, and her fore yard 64 feet, in length. Her bulwark was of solid timber, and four inches higher, and two inches thicker, than that of the British 18-gun brig-sloop. The Whiting schooner and her class, on the other hand, measured 75 tons, and mounted four 12-pounder carronades, with a crew of 20 men and boys; and her bulwark, if it deserved the name, consisted, with here and there a small timber, of an outside and an inside plank.

We trust that the importance of the subject, into which we have entered at such length, will be received as an excuse for this digression; but, in reality, it is only the concentration of remarks which would otherwise have been scattered over our accounts of the different American actions, and perhaps not so well understood, nor so usefully applied. Previously to quitting the topic of improvements in ship-building, we have one more observation to make. It has already been stated, that the American government is in the habit of appointing an experienced naval captain, to superintend the construction of each of their larger ships-of-war. This, although accomplished with ease in a small navy like that of the United States, would be quite impracticable in a navy like that of England. But, as in most of the higher classes of British ships it is usual to construct many individuals from one draught, might not that draught, with an accompanying exposé, showing the size of the intended scantling, the number and nature of the ordnance, the length and diameter of the masts and yards, and, in short, every other particular calculated to dispense with the actual inspection of a model, be submitted to a committee of experienced naval officers? Had any three captains or commanders been consulted when the Bonne-Citoyenne's beautifully proportioned form was proposed to be shortened and contracted for "improvement,"

[1] See pp. 271 and 273. [2] See vol. iv., p. 315

the British navy would never have owned such ships as the Cyrus and her 17 class-mates.

The number of commissioned officers and masters, belonging to the British navy at the beginning of the year 1813, was:—

Admirals		64
Vice-admirals		69
Rear-admirals		68
,, superannuated	28	
Post-captains		802
,, superannuated	32	
Commanders, or sloop-captains		602
,, superannuated	50	
Lieutenants		3268
Masters		629

And the number of seamen and marines, voted for the service of the year, was 140,000.[1]

[1] See Appendix, No. 13.

(439)

APPENDIX.

No. 1.—See p. 78.

A List of Ships of the Line and Frigates, late belonging to the French Navy, Captured, Destroyed, Wrecked, Foundered, or Accidentally Burnt, during the year 1809.

Gun-ship.	Name.	How, when, and where Lost.
80	.. Varsovie	Destroyed, April 12, by a British fleet under Admiral Lord Gambier, on the Palles shoal near the road of Isle-d'Aix.
	.. Robust	Destroyed, October 26, by their own crews, after having been driven on shore near Frontignan, Gulf of Lyons, by a British fleet under Vice-admiral Lord Collingwood.
74	.. Lion	
	(M) d'Haupoult	Captured, April 17, by the British 74 Pompée, Castor frigate, and Recruit brig, West Indies.
	.. Aquilon	
	.. Tonnerre	Destroyed, April 12, same as Varsovie, except that the Tonnerre and Indienne were set on fire by their own crews.
50	.. Calcutta, *en flûte*	
Gun-frig.	.. Indienne	
	.. Calypso	Destroyed, February 24, by being driven in action upon the rocks off Sable d'Olonne, by a British squadron under Rear-admiral Stopford.
	.. Cybèle	
	.. Italienne	
	(Z) Fidelle	Captured, August 16, at the surrender of Flushing.
	,, Caroline	Captured, September 21, by a British naval and military force, in the bay of St. Paul Isle Bourbon.
40	,, Junon	Captured, February 10, by the British frigate Horatio and consorts, West Indies.
	,, Amphitrite	Destroyed, February 4, at the attack upon the island of Martinique.
	,, Niemen	Captured, April 6, by the British frigate Amethyst, Bay of Biscay.
	,, Topaze	Captured, January 22, by the British frigate Cleopatra and sloop Hazard, West Indies.
	.. Loire, *en flûte*	Destroyed, December 18, by a British force at Anse le Barque, island of Guadaloupe.
	.. Seine, *en flûte*	

No. 1—*continued.*

	Name.	How, when, and where Lost.
Gun-frig. 36	(B) Furieuse, *en flûte*	Captured, July 6, by the British sloop of war Bonne Citoyenne, lat 43° 41' north longitude, 34° west.
	.. Félicité, *en flûte*	Captured, June 18, by the British frigate Latona, West Indies.
28	(r) Var	Captured, February 15, by the British frigate Belle-Poule, off Corfu, Mediterranean.

No Dutch or Danish vessels above a gun-brig captured in the year 1809; and the only Russian ships-of-war captured were two frigates, the Speshnoy and Wilhemia, detained at Plymouth, but not proceeded against as prize.

An Abstract of French Ships of the Line and Frigates, Captured, &c., during the year 1809.

	Lost through the Enemy.		Lost through Accident.			Total lost to the French Navy.	Total added to the British Navy.
	Capt.	Dest.	Wrecked.	Foundered.	Burnt.		
Ships of the line	1	5	..	..	..	6	1
Frigates	8	8	..	..	..	16	7
Total	9	13	..	..	..	22	8

APPENDIX. 441

No. 2.—See p. 78.

A List of Ships and Vessels late belonging to the British Navy, Captured, Destroyed, Wrecked, Foundered, or Accidentally Burnt, during the year 1809.

	Name.	Commander.	How, when, and where Lost.
Gun-ship. 64	(P) Agamemnon,	Jonas Rose	Wrecked, June 20, in the Rio de la Plata: crew saved.
Gun-frig. 38	(Z) *Junon*	John Shortland	Captured, December 13, by the French Frigates Renommée and Clorinde, West Indies.
32	(E) Proserpine	Charles Otter	Captured, February 28, by the French frigates Pénélope and Pauline, off Toulon.
	(F) Alcmène,	Wm. Hy. Brown Tremlett	Wrecked, April 29, on a rock off Nantes: crew saved.
	(H) Greyhound,	Hon. William Pakenham	Wrecked, Oct. 4 (1808), on the coast of Luconia: crew, except one seaman, saved.
	,, Solebay	Edward Hy. Columbine	Wrecked, July 11, on the coast of Africa: crew saved.
Gn.-sh. slp. 18	(R) Lark	Robert Nicholas	Foundered, August 8, off Cape Causada: crew, except two or three, perished.
G.-bg. slp. 18	(Y) Foxhound	James Mackenzie	Foundered, August 31, on her return from Halifax: crew perished.
	,, Harrier	Thomas R. Ridge	Foundered, as is supposed, in the East Indies.
	,, Magnet	George Morris	Wrecked, Jan. 11, on the ice in the Baltic: crew saved.
	,, Primrose	James Mein	Wrecked, January 22, on the Manacle rocks, near Falmouth: crew, except one boy, perished.
	,, *Victor*	Edward Stopford	Captured, November 28, by the French frigate Bellone, bay of Bengal.
16	(a) *Alaart*	James Tillard	Captured, August 10, by two Danish brigs of war and some gun-boats, off Fredericksvaern.
	,, *Curieux*	Hon. Geo. Moysey	Wrecked, November 3, in the West Indies: crew saved.
	,, *Fama*	Charles Tapping	Wrecked, Dec. 23 (1808), in the Baltic: crew, except eight, saved.
	,, *Glommen*	Charles Pickford	Wrecked, in November, in Carlisle bay, Barbadoes: crew saved.

No. 2—*continued*.

	Name.	Commander.	How, when, and where Lost.
Bb.	(d) Proselyte	H. James Lyford	Wrecked, in January, in the Baltic: crew saved.

Gun-brig.

	Name.	Commander.	How, when, and where Lost.
	(g) Bustler	Richard Welsh	Wrecked, Dec. 26 (1808), on the coast of France: crew saved.
	,, Contest	John Gregory	Foundered, as is supposed, on her passage from America.
	,, Defender	John Geo. Nops	Wrecked, December 14, on Cob point, near Folkstone: crew saved.
12	,, Minx	George Le Blanc	Captured, September 2, by six Danish gun-boats, off the Scaw, where she was stationed with a light.
	,, *Morne-Fortunée*,	John Brown	Wrecked, January 9, off Martinique: crew, except nineteen, perished.
	,, Pelter	William Evelyn	Foundered, December, on her passage from Halifax to Leeward-islands.
	,, *Unique*	Thomas Fellowes	Burnt, May 31, at Basse-Terre, Guadaloupe.

Gun-cut.

	Name.	Commander.	How, when, and where Lost.
14	(i) *Dominica*	Charles Welsh	Foundered, in August, near Tortola: crew, except three, perished.
10	(1) Claudia	A. Bliss W. Lord	Wrecked, January 20, off Norway: crew saved.
	,, *Saloman*	Andrew Duncan	Wrecked, December 22, in the Baltic: crew saved.
4	(o) Carrier	William Milner	Wrecked, February 5, on the French coast: crew saved, but made prisoners.
	,, Haddock	Ch. Wm. Selwyn	Captured, January 30, by the French 16-gun brig Génie, Channel.
	,, Pigeon	Richard Cox	Wrecked, January 15, near Margate: crew, except two, saved.
	,, Sealark	James Proctor	Wrecked, June 18, in the North Sea.
T.S.	(q) Mediator	Jas. Wooldridge	Destroyed, April 11, as a fire-ship in Basque-roads.

APPENDIX. 443

No. 2—*continued*.

ABSTRACT.

	Lost through the Enemy.		Lost through Accident.			
	Capt.	Dest.	Wrecked.	Foundered.	Burnt.	Total.
Ships of the Line . .	..	..	1	..	..	1
„ under the Line	6	1	17	6	1	31
Total . . .	6	1	18	6	1	32

No. 3.—See p. 79.

	£.	s.	d.
For the pay and maintenance of 113,600 seamen and 31,400 marines	7,799,187	10	0
„ the wear and tear of ships, &c.	3,295,500	0	0
„ the ordinary expenses of the navy, including half-pay to sea and marine officers	1,511,075	15	11
„ the expense of sea-ordnance	591,500	0	0
„ the extraordinaries, including the building and repairing of ships, and other extra work . . .	1,841,107	0	0
„ the hire of transports	2,760,000	0	0
„ the maintenance of prisoners of war, in health and sickness	806,000	0	0
„ the same of sick and wounded seamen	370,750	0	0
Total supplies granted for the sea-service .	£18,975,120	5	11

No. 4.—See p. 188.

Extract of Letter from Captain Morice.

"Dans ce même moment, je m'apperçus que ces deux bâtimens étaient démâtés de leurs mâts d'hunes et un de son mât d'artimon; chacun était à son poste et prêt à combattre; le feu cessa alors et je reconnus la Vénus; je passai à portée de pistolet de l'ennemi sans qu'il tirât sur moi, je laissai arriver lof pour lof, et lui passai encore à la même distance sans qu'il tirât; je vins auprès du commandant, qui m'ordonna de demander à ce bâtiment s'il était amené j'exécutai l'ordre sur-le-champ, et vins lui rendre compte que l'ennemi s'était rendu: je mis aussitôt en panne, et j'envoyai un canot commandé par M. Ménager, enseigne de vaisseau, pour prendre les officiers de ce bâtiment et les transporter à bord de la Vénus: cet ordre fut exécuté. Le jour se fit, et je m'apperçus que ces bâtimens avaient combattu sous toutes voiles, en voyant encore une bonnette de hune en pendant à la vergue de misaine de l'ennemi."—*Mon.* December 18, 1810.

APPENDIX.

No. 5.—See p. 206.

A List of Frigates late belonging to the French Navy, Captured, Destroyed, Wrecked, Foundered, or Accidentally Burnt, during the year 1810.

Gun-frig.	Name.	How, when, and where Lost.
	(Z) Venus	Captured, September 18, by the British frigate Boadicea, off Isle-Bourbon.
40	,, Astrée ,, Bellone .. Manche .. Minerve	Captured, December 6, in Port-Louis (with two frigates named below, three armed brigs, prize Indiamen, merchant-vessels, &c.), by the British forces employed in reducing the Isle of France.
	.. Eliza	Wrecked, December 25, between Tatihou and Lahougue, coast of France, and burnt by the boats of the British frigate Diana.
	.. *Canonnière, en flûte*	Captured, February 3, by the British 74, Valiant, off Belle-Isle.
36	(C) *Iphigénie* ,, *Néreide*	Captured with Astrée, &c.
28	.. *Nécessité*	Captured, March 21, by the British frigate Horatio, latitude 33° 10 north, longitude 29° 30' west.

No Russian, Dutch, or Danish vessel of war higher than a sloop captured, &c., this year.

An Abstract of French Frigates Captured, &c., during the year 1810.

Lost through the Enemy.		Lost through Accident.			Total lost to the French Navy.	Total added to the British Navy.
Capt.	Dest.	Wrecked.	Foundered.	Burnt.		
1	..	1	..	..	10	4

No. 6.—See p. 206.

A List of Ships and Vessels late belonging to the British Navy, Captured, Destroyed, Wrecked, Foundered, or Accidentally Burnt, during the year 1810.

	Name.	Commander.	How, when, and where Lost.
Gun-ship. 74	(N) Minotaur	John Barrett	Wrecked, December 22, on the Haak sands, at the mouth of the Texel: 360 of her crew perished.
Gun-frig. 38	(Z) Lively	George M'Kinley	Wrecked, August 26, on some rocks near Malta: crew saved.

No. 6—continued.

	Name.	Commander.	How, when, and where Lost.
36	(B) Sirius	Samuel Pym	Wrecked, August 23, in the harbour of Grand Port, Isle-de-France, when advancing to the attack of a French squadron.
	(C) Iphigenia	Henry Lambert	Captured, August 28, by a French squadron at Isle-de-la-Passe, off Grand Port.
	(D) Magicienne	Lucius Curtis	Wrecked along with Sirius.
	,, Néréide	N. J. Willoughby	Captured, by the French squadron on the same occasion.
	,, Nymphe	Edw. Sneyd Clay	Wrecked, December 18, at the entrance of the Frith of Forth: the crews of both, except one or two men, saved.
32	(H) Pallas	Geo. Paris Monke	
G.-sh. slp. 16	(V) Flèche	George Hewson	Wrecked, May 24, off the river Elbe: crew saved.
G.-b. slp. 16	(a) Satellite	Willoughby Bertie	Foundered, in December, in the Channel.
G.-b. slp. 10	(c) Achates	Thomas Pinto	Wrecked, date unknown, in the West Indies: crew saved.
	,, Wildboar	Thomas Burton	Wrecked, in February, on a rock between Scilly Islands and the main.
G.-brig. 12	(g) Conflict	Joseph B. Batt	Foundered, November 9, in the Bay of Biscay.
G.-cut. 12	(k) Racer	Daniel Miller	Wrecked, May 24, on the coast of France: crew saved, but made prisoners.
10	(1) Alban	Samuel Thomas	Captured, May 24, by several Danish gun-boats.
	,, Diana	Wm. Kempthorne	Wrecked, in May, at the island of Rodrigue, East Indies: crew saved.
4	(o) Cuckoo	S. Hiscutt Paddon	Wrecked, April 4, at Calantzoog, near Haerlem: crew saved, but made prisoners.

ABSTRACT.

	Lost through the Enemy.		Lost through Accident.			
	Capt.	Dest.	Wrecked.	Foundered.	Burnt.	Total.
Ships of the line	..	..	1	..	..	1
,, under the line	3	..	11	2	..	16
Total	3	..	12	2	..	17

446   APPENDIX.

No. 7.—See p. 206.

	£	s.	d.
For the pay and maintenance of 113,600 seamen and 31,400 marines	7,799,187	10	0
,, the wear and tear of ships, &c.	3,675,750	0	0
,, the ordinary expenses of the navy, including half-pay to sea and marine officers	1,578,113	0	0
,, the expense of sea-ordnance	659,750	0	0
,, the extraordinaries, including the building and repairing of ships and other extra work	2,046,200	0	0
,, the hire of transports	2,752,662	6	0
,, the maintenance of prisoners of war in health and sickness	924,336	19	8
,, the same of sick and wounded seamen	352,462	6	0
,, the salaries, contingencies, &c. in the transport-office	32,388	8	4
,, superannuations in ditto	1,150	0	0
Total supplies granted for the sea-service	£19,822,000	10	0

No. 8.—See p. 311.

A List of Frigates late belonging to the French Navy, Captured, Destroyed, Wrecked, Foundered, or Accidentally Burnt, during the year 1811.

	Name.	How, when, and where Lost.
Gun-frig.		
	.. Amazone	Destroyed, March 25, by her own crew, after having been driven on shore near Cape Barfleur, by the Berwick 74 and others.
	(Z) Renommée	Captured, May 20, off Madagascar, by a British squadron under Captain Schomberg.
	,, Néréide	Captured, May 26, at Tamatave, by the same.
40	.. Pomone	Captured, November 29, in the Adriatic, by the British frigates Alceste and Active.
	.. Flore	Wrecked, date unknown, in the Adriatic.
	.. Favourite	Destroyed, March 13, after having been driven on the rocks of Lissa by a British squadron under Capt. Hoste.
	(Z) Corona, ven.	Captured on the same occasion.
32	(H) Bellona, ven.	

No Dutch, Danish, or Swedish vessel of war, above a sloop, captured, &c., during the year 1811.

An Abstract of French Frigates Captured, &c., during the year 1811

Lost through the Enemy.		Lost through Accident.			Total Lost to the French Navy.	Total added to the British Navy.
Capt.	Dest.	Wrecked.	Foundered.	Burnt.		
5	2	1	..	..	8	4

APPENDIX. 447

No. 9.—See p. 311.

A List of Ships and Vessels, late belonging to the British Navy, Captured, Destroyed, Wrecked, Foundered, or Accidentally Burnt, during the year 1811.

Name.	Commander.	How, when, and where Lost.
Gun-ship.		
98 (H) St. George	R. Car. Reynolds, r.-adm. Daniel O. Guion, captain.	Wrecked, December 24; St. George and Defence off the coast of Jutland, on passage from Baltic, Hero on the Haak sand, Texel: crew of latter perished, and both crews of former, except about eighteen men.
74 { (N) Hero	James Newman Newman	
{ (O) Defence	David Atkins	
Gun-frig.		
38 { (Z) Pomone	Robert Barrie	Wrecked, October 14, on the Needle rocks: crew saved.
{ (A) Dover	Edward Tucker	Wrecked, May 2, in Madras roads: crew, except two, saved.
36 { (B) Amethyst	Jacob Walton	Wrecked, February 16, in Plymouth sound: crew, except about thirty, saved.
{ (C) Saldanha	Hon. William Pakenham	Wrecked, December 4, off Loughswilly, on the coast of Ireland: crew mostly perished.
32 (E) Tartar	Joseph Baker	Wrecked, August 18, on a sand in the Baltic: crew saved.
G.-b. slp.		
18 { (Y) Alacrity	Nisbet Palme	Captured, May 26, by the French brig of war Abeille, off Corsica.
{ ,, Grasshopper	Henry Fanshawe	Captured, December 24, at Nieuve-Diep, Texel, whither she had been driven by stress of weather.
{ ,, Pandora	John Ferguson	Wrecked, February 13, on the Scaw reef, Kattegat: crew saved, but made prisoners.
16 (a) Challenger	Goddard Blennerhasset	Captured, March 12, by a frigate and an armed store-ship, off Isle-de-France.
G.-brig.		
12 { (g) Fancy	Alexander Sinclair	Foundered, December 24, in the Baltic: crew perished.
{ ,, Firm	John Little	Wrecked, June 28, on a bank off the coast of France: crew saved.

448   APPENDIX.

No. 9—*continued.*

	Name.	Commander.	How, when, and where Lost.
12	(g) Manly	Richard Wm. Simmonds	Captured, September 2, by three Danish 18-g. brigs, in the Baltic.
	,, Monkey	Thomas Fitzgerald	Wrecked, Dec. 25, (1810), between two rocks at Belle Isle, coast of France.
	,, Safeguard	Thomas England	Captured, June 29, by the Danes in the Baltic.
10	(h) *Guachapin*,	Michael Jenkins	Wrecked, July 29, at Antigua: crew saved.
	,, *Fleur-de-la-mer*	John Alexander	Foundered at sea, January 8: crew saved by an American vessel under her convoy.
G.-cut.	(1) Olympia	Henry Taylor	Captured, March 2, by several French privateers off Dieppe.
10	,, Shamrock	Wentworth P. Croke	Wrecked, February 25, on Cape Sta. Maria.
	,, Thistle	George M'Pherson	Wrecked, March 6, near New York.
4	(o) Grouper	James Atkins	Wrecked, October 21, off Guadaloupe: crew saved.
	,, Snapper	Henry Thrakstone	Captured, July 15, by French national lugger Rapace, off Brest.
S.S.	(r) *Chichester*,	William Kirby	Wrecked, May 2, in Madras roads: crew except two, saved.

ABSTRACT.

	Lost through the Enemy.		Lost through Accident.			
	Capt.	Dest.	Wrecked.	Foundered.	Burnt.	Total.
Ships of the line	..	..	3	..	..	3
,, under the line	7	..	13	2	..	22
Total	7	..	16	2	..	25

APPENDIX.   449

No. 10.—See p. 311.

	£.	s.	d
For the pay and maintenance of 113,600 seamen and 31,400 marines.	7,799,187	10	0
,, the wear and tear of ships, &c.	3,675,750	0	0
,, the ordinary expenses of the navy, including half-pay to sea and marine officers, superannuations, pensions, &c.	1,447,125	12	0
,, the expense of sea-ordnance	659,750	0	0
,, the superannuation allowances to commissioners, clerks, &c.	61,975	0	3
,, the extraordinaries; including the building and repairing of ships, and other extra work	1,696,621	0	0
,, the hire of transports.	2,678,092	12	0
,, the maintenance of prisoners of war, in health and sickness.	968,742	0	0
,, the same of sick and wounded seamen	280,316	4	0
,, the salaries, contingencies, &c. in the transport-office.	38,199	4	0
Total supplies granted for the sea-service	£19,305,759	2	3

No. 11.—See p. 425.

A List of French and Danish Line-of-Battle Ships and Frigates, Captured, Destroyed, Wrecked, Foundered, or Accidentally Burnt, during the year 1812.

	Name.	How, when, and where Lost.
Gun-ship. 74 (M)	Rivoli, F.	Captured, February 22, by the British 74 Victorious, in the Gulf of Venice.
Gun-frig. 40	Arienne, F.	Destroyed, May 22, by the British 74 Northumberland, off Lorient.
	Andromaque, F.	
	Danaé, F.	Burnt by accident, at midnight, September 9, in the harbour of Triest: crew perished.
	Nayaden, D.	Destroyed, along with four brigs, July 7, by the British 64 Dictator and three brigs in the creek o Lyngoe, coast of Norway.

No Dutch vessel-of-war, above a sloop, captured, &c. during the year 1812.

An Abstract of French and Danish Ships of the Line and Frigates, Captured, &c., during the year 1812.

		Lost through the Enemy.		Lost through Accident.			Total loss to the F. & D. Navies.	Total added to the British Navy.
		Capt.	Dest.	Wrecked.	Foundered.	Burnt.		
Ships of the Line	Fr.	1	..	..	..	..	1	1
Frigates	,,	..	2	..	..	1	3	..
	Da.	..	1	..	..	..	1	..
Total		1	3	..	..	1	5	1

VOL. V.   2 G

450   APPENDIX.

No. 12.—See p. 425.

A List of Ships and Vessels, late belonging to the British Navy, Captured, Destroyed, Wrecked, Foundered, or Accidentally Burnt, during the year 1812.

Name.	Commander.	How, when, and where Lost.
Gun-frig.		
(Z) *Guerrière*	Jas. Richard Dacres	Captured, August 19, by the American 44-gun frigate Constitution, lat. 41° north, long. 55° west.
38 ,, *Java*	Henry Lambert	Captured, December 29, by the same frigate off St. Salvador.
,, *Laurel*	S. Campbell Rowley	Wrecked, January 31, on the Govivas rock in the Teigneuse passage: crew saved, except 96 made prisoners.
,, *Macedonian*	John Surman Cardan	Captured, October 25, by the American 44-gun frigate United States, lat. 29° north, long. 29° 30' west.
36 (*C*) *Manilla*	John Joyce	Wrecked, January 28, on the Haak sand, Texel: crew, except twelve, saved, but made prisoners.
28 (*I*) *Barbadoes*	Thomas Huskisson	Wrecked, September 28, on the north-west bar of Sable island: crew, except one, saved.
G.-sh. slp.		
16 (*V*) *Alert*	T. L. P. Laugharne	Captured, August 13, by the American 32-gun frigate Essex, off the coast of North America.
,, *Avenger*	Urry Johnson	Wrecked, October 8, going into Newfoundland: crew saved.
G.-bg. slp.		
(*Y*) *Belette*	David Sloane	Wrecked, November 24, on the rocks, off the island of Lessoe in the Kattegat: crew, except five, perished.
18 ,, *Emulous*	W. Howe Mulcaster	Wrecked, August 3, on Sable island: crew saved.
,, *Frolic*	**Thomas** Whinyates	Captured, October 18, by the American ship-sloop Wasp, lat. 36° north, long 64° west, but recaptured same day by **Poictiers 74.**

APPENDIX. 451

No. 12—*continued.*

	Name.	Commander.	How, when, and where Lost.
G.-b.-slp.			
16 {	(a) Fly	Henry Higman	Wrecked, February 29, on the Knobber reef, on the east point of the island of Anholt: crew saved.
	,, *Magnet*	F. Moore Maurice	Foundered, as is supposed, on her passage to Halifax.
	,, Skylark	James Boxer	Wrecked, May 3, near Boulogne: crew saved.
F.S. (e)	Ephera	Thomas Everard	Wrecked, December 26 (1811), near Cadiz: crew saved.
Gun-brig.			
12 {	(g) Attack	R. W. Simmonds	Captured, August 19, by a squadron of 14 Danish gun-boats, off Foreness.
	,, Encounter	Jas. Hugh Talbot	Wrecked, July 11, in an attempt to cut out some vessels at San-Lucar, coast of Spain.
	,, Exertion	James Murray	Wrecked, July 8, in the river Elbe, and afterwards destroyed by the boats of that ship.
	,, Plumper	James Bray	Wrecked, December 5, in the bay of Fundy: crew part saved.
	,, Sentinel	W. Elletson King	Wrecked, October 10, on the shoals off the island of Rugen: crew saved.
Gun-cut.			
10 {	(1) Alban	W. Sturg. Key	Wrecked, December 18, near Aldborough: crew, except two, perished.
	,, Laura	C. Newton Hunter	Captured, September 8, by the Diligent, French privateer, coast of North America.
	,, Nimble	John Reynolds	Foundered, November 6, in a gale in the Kattegat: crew saved.
4 {	(o) Chubb	Samuel Nisbett	Foundered, August 14, near Halifax: crew perished.
	,, Porgey	(name unknown)	Foundered, date unknown, in the West Indies.
	,, Whiting	Lewis Maxey	Captured, August 22, by the Diligent, French privateer coast of North America.

No. 12—*continued.*

ABSTRACT.

	Lost through the Enemy.		Lost through Accident.			Total.
	Capt.	Dest.	Wrecked.	Foundered.	Burnt.	
Ships of the line	..	..	..	..	..	..
,, under the line	8	..	14	4	..	26
Total	8	..	14	4	..	26

No. 13.—See p. 438.

	£	s.	d.
For the pay and maintenance of 108,600 seamen and 31,400 marines	7,530,250	0	0
,, the wear and tear of ships, &c.	3,549,000	0	0
,, the ordinary expenses of the navy, including the salaries and contingent expense of the admiralty, navy-pay, navy, and victualling-offices, and dock-yards; also half-pay and superannuations to officers of the navy and royal marines, their widows, &c.	1,700,135	11	0
,, the expense of sea-ordnance	637,000	0	0
,, the superannuation allowances to commissioners, clerks, &c.	57,793	0	7
,, the extraordinaries; including the building and repairing of ships, and other extra work	2,822,031	0	0
,, the hire of transports	2,330,943	0	0
,, the maintenance of prisoners of war in health and sickness	1,150,000	0	0
,, the same of sick and wounded seamen	277,754	10	8
,, the salaries, contingencies, &c., in the transport-office	40,510	16	0
,, superannuations in ditto	1,291	13	4
Total supplies granted for the sea-service	£20,096,709	11	7

An ABSTRACT of the Ships and Vessels belonging to the British Navy at the commencement of the Year 1810.

Letters of Reference.	RATE.	CLASS.	For Sea-service.						No.		For Harbour-service, &c.				No.		Built or Ordered to be B...	
			In Commission.		In Ordinary.		TOTAL.		British Built.	Foreign Built.	In Commission.		In Ordinary.		British Built.	Foreign Built.	No.	
			No.	Tons.	No.	Tons.	No.	Tons.			No.	Tons.	No.	Tons.				
A	Three-deckers. First.	120-gun ship	2	5124	—	—	2	5124	2	—	—	—	—	—	—	—	3	
B	,,	112 ,,	1	2351	—	—	1	2351	1	—	—	—	—	—	—	—	—	
C	,,	112 ,, 18-pounder	1	2457	—	—	1	2457	—	1	1	2398	—	—	—	1	2	
D	,,	100 ,, 12 ,,	—	—	1	2286	1	2286	1	—	—	—	1	2091	1	—	—	
E	,,	98 ,, 18 ,,	1	2175	—	—	1	2175	1	—	—	—	—	—	—	—	1	
F	Second.	98 ,, 12 ,,	—	—	1	2276	1	2276	1	—	—	—	—	—	—	—	1	
H		18 ,, 12 ,,	7	14367	3	5774	10	20141	10	—	1	1944	3	5937	4	—	2	
K	Two-deckers. Third.	80 ,,	6	12919	1	2265	7	15184	2	5	2	4191	5	10849	—	7	2	
L	,,	74 ,, 24-pounder	11	20971	1	1927	12	22898	10	2	—	—	1	1889	—	1	—	
M	,,	,, 18 ,, large	14	26259	3	5681	17	31940	10	7	5	9286	4	7497	2	7	—	
N	,,	,, ,, middl.	28	48653	1	1743	29	50396	29	—	6	10504	8	13976	1	13	32	
O	,,	,, ,, small	26	42388	4	6578	30	48966	28	2	3	4766	13	21166	13	3	—	
P	,,	64 ,,	11	15350	1	1376	12	16726	12	—	16	22063	7	9696	11	12	—	
Q	Fourth.	60 ,,	—	—	—	—	—	—	—	—	1	1285	—	—	1	—	—	
		Line	108	193014	16	29906	124	222920	107	17	35	56437	42	73101	33	44	42	
R	,,	56 ,, flush	—	—	—	—	—	—	—	—	1	1256	—	—	1	—	—	
T	,,	50 ,, com. or quarter-decked	7	7599	—	—	7	7599	7	—	3	3137	5	5314	5	3	—	
V	Fifth.	44 ,,	2	1779	—	—	2	1779	2	—	1	882	—	—	1	—	—	
W	One-deckers.	44-gun frigate	2	2772	—	—	2	2772	2	—	1	1370	2	2787	1	2	—	
.	,,	40 ,, 24-pounder	1	1277	—	—	1	1277	1	—	—	—	—	—	—	—	—	
Y	,,	,, 18 ,,	2	2332	1	1142	3	3474	3	—	—	—	3	3242	—	3	11	
Z	,,	38 ,, large	36	39449	5	5631	41	45080	13	28	—	—	2	1975	1	1	—	
A	,,	,, small	12	11915	1	994	13	12909	11	2	—	—	3	3052	—	3	—	
B	,,	36 ,, 18-pounder large	10	10387	1	1028	11	11415	3	8	—	—	2	1808	3	—	9	
C	,,	,, small	29	26985	—	—	29	26985	26	3	1	926	2	1808	3	—	9	
D	,,	,, 12 ,,	10	9154	1	966	11	10120	—	11	—	—	10	9243	—	10	—	
E	,,	32 ,, 18 ,, large	7	6369	—	—	7	6369	7	—	—	—	—	—	—	—	—	
F	,,	,, small	2	1607	—	—	2	1607	2	—	—	—	3	2546	2	1	—	
G	,,	,, 12 ,, large	4	3008	—	—	4	3008	1	3	1	856	3	2546	2	1	—	
H	,,	,, small	18	12242	2	1395	20	13637	—	1	1	683	9	6234	9	1	—	
I	Sixth.	28 ,,	7	4314	1	775	8	5089	6	2	—	—	4	2378	4	—	—	
K		24-gun post-ship, quarter-decked	4	2231	—	—	4	2231	1	3	—	—	3	1686	2	1	—	
M	,,	22 ,, ,,	8	4277	—	—	8	4277	8	—	—	—	6	2726	4	2	—	
O	,,	20 ,, flush ,,	4	1922	—	—	4	1922	—	4	—	—	3	1575	—	3	—	
	Sloops.	Dart, mounting 28 32-pounder carrons.																
Q		18-gun ship-sloop, quarter-decked	37	15879	1	423	38	16302	38	—	—	—	—	—	—	—	2	
R	,,	,, flush	9	3430	—	—	9	3430	6	3	—	—	7	2763	2	5	—	
S	,,	16 ,, quarter-decked, large	16	5957	—	—	16	5957	16	—	1	425	2	791	3	—	—	
T	,,	,, small	1	326	1	327	2	653	2	—	—	—	—	—	—	—	—	
U	,,	,, flush ,,	9	3168	—	—	9	3168	5	4	—	—	7	2524	7	—	—	
V	,,	14 ,, quarter-decked	—	—	—	—	—	—	—	—	—	—	3	905	3	—	—	
W	,,	,, flush	1	305	2	674	3	979	3	—	—	—	6	1615	6	—	—	
X	,,	18-gun brig-sloop large	69	26535	—	—	69	26535	67	2	—	—	2	773	1	1	1	
Y	,,	,, small	1	316	—	—	1	316	1	—	—	—	1	319	1	—	—	
Z	,,	16 ,,	49	15150	—	—	49	15150	19	30	1	234	6	1886	1	7	—	
a	,,	14 ,,	17	4129	—	—	17	4129	12	5	—	—	3	619	1	2	—	
b	,,	10 ,,	33	7842	—	—	33	7842	33	—	—	—	—	—	—	—	—	
c	Bombs, of Fireships,	8 guns and 2 mortars	8	2851	—	—	8	2851	8	—	1	307	6	2000	7	—	—	
d		14 guns	—	—	—	—	—	—	—	—	—	—	1	425	1	—	—	
e	Gun-brigs,	12 ,,	8	1659	1	258	9	1917	2	7	—	—	4	591	4	—	—	
f		12 ,,	69	12407	1	169	70	12576	69	1	—	—	—	—	—	—	—	
g		10 ,,	1	176	—	—	1	176	—	1	—	—	1	152	—	1	—	
h	Cutters, &c.	14 ,,	6	1132	—	—	6	1132	1	5	—	—	—	—	—	—	—	
i		12 ,,	4	600	—	—	4	600	1	3	—	—	4	581	3	1	—	
k		10 ,,	30	3780	—	—	30	3780	17	13	—	—	—	—	—	—	6	
l		8 ,,	1	100	—	—	1	100	1	—	—	—	—	—	—	—	—	
m		6 ,,	5	427	—	—	5	427	4	1	—	—	—	—	—	—	—	
n		4 ,,	17	1312	1	75	18	1387	18	—	—	—	—	—	—	—	—	
		Cruisers	664	450114	35	43763	699	493877	542	157	47	66513	150	133611	106	91	72	
q	Troop-ships		7	6016	2	1768	9	7784	6	3	4	2860	12	11260	11	5	—	
r	Storeships		16	11539	—	—	16	11539	14	2	1	176	3	1759	4	—	—	
w	Surveying-vessel		1	314	—	—	1	314	1	—	—	—	—	—	—	—	—	
x	Advice-boats and Tenders		4	582	—	—	4	582	4	—	—	—	—	—	—	—	—	
a	Hospital, Prison, Receiving-ships, &c.		—	—	—	—	—	—	—	—	13	16230	10	10276	12	11	—	
b	Royal Yachts		—	—	—	—	—	—	—	—	7	1288	—	—	7	—	—	
		Troop-ships, &c	28	18451	2	1768	30	20219	25	5	25	20554	25	23295	34	16	—	
		GRAND TOTAL (a)	692	468565	37	45531	729	514096	567	162	72	87067	175	156906	140	107	72	

VOL. V

453

		Increase and Decrease in the Classes since the date of the last Year's Abstract.																		
GRAND TOTAL.	Built.				Purchased.				Converted from other Classes.		Ordered to be Built.		TOTAL of Increase.		Captured. Destroyed, Wrecked, &c.		Converted to other Classes.		Sold, or taken to Pieces.		TOTAL of Decrease.
	King's Yards.		Merchants' Yards.		British Vessels or Enemy's Privateers.		Enemy's National Vessels.														
Tons.	No.	Tons.	No.	Tons.	No.	Tons.	No.	Tons.	No.	Tons.	No.	Tons.	No.	Tons.	No.	Tons.	No.	Tons.	No.	Tons.	No.	Tons.
12972																						
2351																						
4855																						
6979																						
4266																						
4554																						
32326																						
34362	–	–	–	–	–	–	–	–	2	4138	2	4138										
24787	–	–	1	1919	–	–	–	–	–	–	–	–	1	1919								
48723	1	1819	–	–	–	–	1	1871	–	–	1	–	3	1871								
131134	–	–	6	10557	–	–	–	–	–	–	1	1754	1	1754								
74898																						
48485	–	–	–	–	–	–	–	–	–	–	–	–	–	–	1	1384	–	–	1	1386	2	2770
1285	–	–	–	–	–	–	–	–	–	–	–	–	–	–	–	–	–	–	1	1226	1	1226
431977	1	1819	7	12476	–	–	1	1871	–	–	3	5892	4	7763	1	1384	–	–	2	2612	3	3996
1256																						
16050																						
2661																						
6929																						
1277																						
3474																						
60258	–	–	–	–	–	–	5	5507	–	–	2	2149	7	7656	1	1100	–	–	–	–	1	1100
14884	–	–	–	–	–	–	1	1083	–	–	–	–	1	1083	–	–	–	–	1	999	1	999
14467																						
28204	3	2841	4	3809	–	–	–	–	1	890	1	945	2	1835								
19363																						
6369	–	–	1	918	–	–	–	–	–	–	–	–	–	–	1	922	1	890	–	–	1	890
1607																					1	922
6410	–	–	–	–	–	–	–	–	–	–	–	–	–	–	1	803	–	–	1	808	2	1611
20554	–	–	–	–	–	–	–	–	–	–	–	–	–	–	2	1365	–	–	1	700	3	2065
7467	–	–	–	–	–	–	–	–	–	–	–	–	–	–	–	–	–	–	1	573	1	573
3917	–	–	–	–	–	–	2	1168	–	–	–	–	2	1188								
4815																						
2726																						
3497	–	–	–	–	–	–	–	–	–	–	–	–	–	–	–	–	–	–	2	1132	2	1132
17162	–	–	1	425	–	–	–	–	–	–	–	–	–	–	1	429	–	–	1	386	1	386
6193																				1	423	2	852
7173	–	–	–	–	–	–	1	371	–	–	–	–	1	371	–	–	1	386	2	754	3	1140
653																				1	410	1	410
5692																						
905																						
2594																						
27691	–	–	2	774	–	–	2	749	1	386	1	383	4	1518	5	1933	1	328	–	–	1	328
635																				–	–	5	1933
17270	–	–	–	–	–	–	8	2613	–	–	–	–	8	2613	4	1259	–	–	1	309	5	1595
4748	–	–	4	1008	–	–	–	–	–	–	–	–	–	–					1	336		
7842																						
5158	–	–	–	–	–	–	–	–	–	–	–	–	–	–	1	404	–	–	1	336	2	740
425																						
1917	–	–	–	–	1	210	–	–	–	–	1	–	1	210								
13167	–	–	–	–	–	–	1	178	–	–	–	–	–	178	7	1280	–	–	1	161	8	1441
328																				1	152	1	152
1132																	1	153	–	–	–	–	1	153
1181																				2	305	2	305
4980	–	–	–	–	1	104	–	–	–	–	6	1200	7	1304	2	231	–	–	1	111	3	342
100	–	–	–	–	1	100	–	–	–	–	–	–	–	100								
427	–	–	–	–	1	92	–	–	–	–	1	–	1	92								
1387															4	283	–	–	1	61	5	344
796922	4	4660	19	19410	4	506	21	13560	2	1276	13	10569	40	25911	31	11546	3	1604	22	10568	56	23718
21904	–	–	–	–	–	–	–	–	–	–	2	1105	2	1105	1	689	–	–	–	–	1	689
13474	–	–	1	314	–	–	1	777	1	328	1	314	1	314								
314																						
582	–	–	–	–	1	145	–	–	–	–	1	–	1	145								
26506																						
1288																						
64068	–	–	1	314	1	145	1	777	1	328	1	314	4	1564	1	689	–	–	–	–	1	689
860990	4	4660	20	19724	5	651	22	14337	3	1604	14	10983	44	27475	32	12235	3	1604	22	10568	57	24407

2 H

An ABSTRACT of the Ships and Vessels belonging to the British Navy at the commencement of the Year 1811

Letters of Reference.	RATE.	CLASS.			For Sea-service.						No.		For Harbour-service, &c.				
					In Commission.		In Ordinary.		TOTAL.		British Built.	Foreign Built.	In Commission.		In Ordinary.		British Built.
					No.	Tons.	No.	Tons.	No.	Tons.			No.	Tons.	No.	Tons.	
A	Three-deckers. First.	120-gun ship			2	5124	–	–	2	5124	2	–	–	–	–	–	–
B	,,	112 ,,			1	2351	–	–	1	2351	1	–	–	–	–	–	–
C	,,	,, ,, 18-pounder			1	2457	–	–	1	2457	–	1	1	2398	–	–	–
D	,,	100 ,, 12 ,,			–	–	2	4575	2	4575	2	–	–	–	–	–	–
E	,,	,, ,, 18 ,,			1	2175	–	–	1	2175	1	–	–	–	1	2091	1
F	Second.	98 ,, 12 ,,			1	2278	1	2276	2	4554	2	–	–	–	–	–	–
H	,,	,, ,, 18 ,,			1	2278	1	2276	2	4554	2	–	–	–	–	–	–
	Two-deckers.	,, ,, 12 ,,			7	14403	3	5774	10	20177	10	–	1	1944	4	8056	5
K	Third.	80 ,,			6	12919	1	2265	7	15184	2	5	2	4191	3	6477	–
L	,,	74 ,,			11	20971	1	1927	12	22898	10	2	–	–	1	1889	–
M	,,	,, ,, 18 ,, large			12	22400	3	5765	15	28165	8	7	5	9286	5	9396	4
N	,,	,, ,, ,, ,, middl.			35	61002	1	1743	36	62745	36	–	6	10504	8	13976	1
O	,,	,, ,, ,, ,, small			21	34331	5	8155	26	42486	25	1	4	6478	14	22739	14
P	,,	64 ,,			9	12550	–	–	9	12530	9	–	18	24844	6	8301	12
Q	Fourth.	60 ,,			–	–	–	–	–	–	–	–	1	1285	–	–	1
		Line			107	192941	17	32480	124	225421	108	16	38	60930	42	72925	38
R	,,	56 ,, flush			–	–	–	–	–	–	–	–	1	1256	–	–	–
T	,,	50 ,, common or quarter-decked			5	5492	1	1056	6	6548	6	–	3	3136	4	4266	4
V	Fifth.	44 ,,			2	1779	–	–	2	1779	2	–	1	882	–	–	1
	One-deckers.																
W	,,	44-gun frigate			2	2772	–	–	2	2772	2	–	–	–	3	4157	1
X	,,	40 ,, 24-pounder			1	1277	–	–	1	1277	1	–	–	–	–	–	–
Y	,,	,, ,, 18 ,,			2	2332	1	1142	3	3474	3	–	–	–	5	5395	–
Z	,,	38 ,, ,, ,, large			40	43912	3	3384	43	47296	16	27	–	–	5	5395	–
A	,,	,, ,, ,, ,, small			9	8936	1	1024	10	9960	9	1	–	–	3	2966	2
B	,,	36 ,, 18-pounder large			7	7284	1	1028	8	8312	2	6	–	–	3	3052	–
C	,,	,, ,, ,, ,, small			35	32693	–	–	35	32693	32	3	1	926	2	1808	3
D	,,	,, ,, 12 ,,			7	6425	–	–	7	6425	–	7	–	–	10	9217	–
E	,,	32 ,, 18 ,, large			7	6369	–	–	7	6369	7	–	–	–	–	–	–
F	,,	,, ,, ,, ,, small			2	1607	–	–	2	1607	2	–	–	–	–	–	–
G	,,	,, ,, 12 ,, large			3	2426	–	–	3	2426	–	3	–	–	4	3180	2
H	,,	,, ,, ,, ,, small			15	10203	1	683	16	10886	15	1	–	–	10	6921	–
I	Sixth.	28 ,,			5	3300	–	–	5	3300	3	2	–	–	6	3566	6
K	,,	24-gun post-ship, quarter-decked			3	1709	–	–	3	1709	1	2	–	–	4	2208	1
L	,,	22 ,, ,, ,,			8	4277	–	526	9	4803	9	–	–	–	–	–	–
M	,,	20 ,,			3	1432	–	–	3	1432	–	3	–	–	6	2726	4
O	Sloops.	18-gun ship-sloop, quarter-decked			37	15883	1	43	38	16306	38	–	–	–	2	1070	–
P	,,	,, ,, flush			8	3059	–	–	8	3059	6	2	–	–	1	429	1
R	,,	16 ,, quarter-decked, large			15	5586	–	–	15	5586	15	–	1	425	3	3134	2
S	,,	,, ,, ,, ,, small			–	–	–	–	–	–	–	–	–	–	1	1162	1
T	,,	,, ,, flush			5	1919	–	–	5	1919	5	–	–	–	1	326	–
U	,,	14 ,, quarter-decked			–	–	–	–	–	–	–	–	–	–	8	2805	5
W	,,	,, ,, flush			–	–	2	674	2	674	2	–	–	–	3	905	3
X	,,	18-gun brig-sloop large			67	25785	2	771	69	26536	67	2	–	–	2	645	–
Y	,,	,, ,, small			1	316	–	–	1	316	1	–	–	–	2	773	1
Z	,,	16 ,,			39	11840	2	683	41	12523	18	23	1	234	1	319	–
a	,,	14 ,,			15	3691	–	–	15	3691	11	4	–	–	13	4202	–
b	,,	10 ,,			31	7367	–	–	31	7367	31	–	–	–	3	665	1
c	Bombs, of	8 guns and 2 mortars			5	1788	–	–	5	1788	5	–	–	–	9	2999	9
d	Fireships,	14 guns			6	1224	1	258	7	1482	2	5	–	–	1	425	–
e	Gun-brigs	,, ,,			65	11686	1	179	66	11865	65	1	–	–	2	435	–
f	,,	12 ,,			1	176	–	–	1	176	1	–	–	–	5	803	5
g	Cutters, &c.	14 ,,			7	1336	1	203	8	1539	1	7	–	–	–	–	–
h	,,	12 ,,			4	600	–	–	4	600	1	3	–	–	3	415	–
i	,,	10 ,,			33	4548	–	–	33	4548	21	12	–	–	–	–	–
k	,,	8 ,,			1	100	–	–	1	100	1	–	–	–	–	–	–
l	,,	6 ,,			3	264	–	–	3	264	2	1	–	–	–	–	–
m	,,	4 ,,			14	1083	1	75	15	1158	15	–	–	–	–	–	–
		Cruisers			620	435397	37	44589	657	479986	525	132	46	67789	169	143899	110
q	Troop-ships				18	16844	1	849	19	17693	12	7	3	2181	13	11939	1
r	Storeships				14	10280	–	–	14	10280	12	2	1	176	3	1181	–
w	Surveying-vessel				1	314	–	–	1	314	1	–	–	–	–	–	–
x	Advice-boats and Tenders				5	751	–	–	5	751	5	–	–	–	–	–	–
a	Hospital, Prison, Receiving-ships, &c.				–	–	–	–	–	–	–	–	12	15190	10	10734	1
b	Royal Yachts				–	–	–	–	–	–	–	–	7	1288	–	–	–
		Troop-ships, &c.			38	28189	1	849	39	29038	30	9	23	18835	26	23854	3
		GRAND TOTAL (b)			658	463586	38	45438	696	509024	555	141	69	86624	195	167753	143

VOL. V.

454

. 19.

Increase and Decrease in the Classes since the date of the last Year's Abstract.

ding, r ered o uilt.		Grand Total.		Built.			Purchased.				Converted from other Classes.		Ordered to be Built.		Total of Increase.		Captured, Destroyed, Wrecked, &c.		Converted to other Classes.		Sold, or taken to Pieces.		Total of Decrease.	
				King's Yards.		Mer- chants' Yards.		British Vessels or Enemy's Privateers.		Enemy's National Vessels.																
Tons.	No.	Tons.	No.	Tons.	No.	Tons.	No.	Tons.	No.	Tons.	No.	Tons.	No.	Tons.	No.	Tons.	No.	Tons.	No.	Tons.	No.	Tons.	No.	Tons.
7848	5	12972																						
– –	1	2351																						
– –	2	4855																						
2404	3	6979	1	22890																				
– –	2	4266																						
– –	2	4554	1	2278																				
2149	16	32326	1	2155																				
6217	15	32129	–	–	–	–	–	–	–	–	1	2139	1	2139	–	–	–	–	2	4372	2	4372
– –	13	24787																						
3669	27	50516	–	–	–	–	–	–	–	–	2	3669	2	3669	–	–	–	–	1	1876	1	1876
45732	76	132957	–	–	8	14067	–	–	–	–	2	3541	2	3541	1	1718	–	–	–	–	1	1718
– –	44	71703	–	–	–	–	–	–	–	–	–	–	–	–	–	–	1	1621	1	1574	2	3195
– –	33	45675	–	–	–	–	–	–	–	–	–	–	–	–	–	–	2	2810	–	–	2	2810
– –	1	1285																						
68079	240	427355	3	6722	8	14067	–	–	–	–	5	9349	5	9349	1	1718	3	4431	4	7822	8	13971
– –	1	1256																						
2372	15	16322																						
– –	3	2661	–	–	–	–	–	–	–	–	2	2372	2	2372	–	–	–	–	2	2100	2	2100
– –	5	6929																						
– –	1	1277																						
– –	3	3474																						
9797	57	62488	1	1081	3	3235	–	–	3	3292	–	–	2	2177	5	5469	1	1076	1	1090	1	1673	3	3239
– –	13	12926	–	–	–	–	–	–	–	–	–	–	–	–	–	–	–	–	2	1958	–	–	2	1958
– –	11	11364	–	–	–	–	–	–	–	–	–	–	–	–	–	–	1	1049	2	2054	–	–	3	3103
7520	46	42947	3	2811	3	2897	–	–	–	–	5	4743	5	4743	–	–	–	–	–	–	–	–
– –	17	15642	–	–	–	–	–	–	–	–	–	–	–	–	3	2798	–	–	1	923	4	3721
– –	7	6369																						
– –	2	1607																						
– –	7	5606	–	–	–	–	–	–	–	–	–	–	–	–	–	–	–	–	1	804	–	–	1	804
– –	26	17807	–	–	–	–	–	–	–	–	–	–	–	–	1	667	2	1396	1	684	4	2747
– –	11	6866	–	–	–	–	–	–	–	–	–	–	–	–	–	–	1	601	–	–	1	601
– –	7	3917																						
538	10	5341	–	–	–	–	–	–	1	526	–	–	–	–	1	526								
– –	6	2726																						
512	6	3014	–	–	–	–	–	–	–	–	–	–	1	512	1	512	–	–	–	–	2	995	2	995
427	40	17162	–	–	1	433	–	–	–	–	–	–	–	–	–	–	–	–	–	–	–	–
– –	16	6193																						
– –	19	7173																						
– –	1	326	–	–	–	–	–	–	–	–	–	–	–	–	–	–	1	327	–	–	1	327
– –	13	4724	–	–	–	–	–	–	–	–	–	–	–	–	1	279	–	–	2	689	3	968
– –	3	905																						
– –	4	1319	–	–	–	–	–	–	–	–	–	–	–	–	–	–	–	–	5	1275	5	1275
– –	71	27309	–	–	1	383	–	–	–	–	–	–	–	–	–	–	–	–	1	382	1	382
– –	2	635																						
– –	55	16959	–	–	–	–	–	–	1	312	–	–	1	312	1	289	–	–	1	334	2	623
253	19	4609	–	–	–	–	–	–	–	–	–	–	1	253	1	253	–	–	–	–	2	392	2	392
– –	31	7367	–	–	–	–	–	–	–	–	–	–	–	–	–	–	2	475	–	–	–	–	2	475
– –	14	4787	–	–	–	–	–	–	–	–	–	–	–	–	–	–	–	–	1	371	1	371
– –	1	425																						
– –	9	1917																						
– –	71	12668	–	–	–	–	–	–	–	–	–	–	–	–	1	182	1	169	1	148	3	499
– –	1	176	–	–	–	–	–	–	–	–	–	–	–	–	–	–	–	–	1	152	1	152
– –	8	1539	–	–	–	–	2	407	–	–	–	–	–	–	2	407	–	–	–	–	–	–
– –	7	1015	–	–	–	–	–	–	–	–	–	–	–	–	–	–	–	–	1	166	1	166
– –	33	4548	–	–	6	1200	1	127	–	–	–	–	–	–	1	127	3	444	–	–	1	115	4	559
– –	1	100																						
– –	3	264	–	–	–	–	–	–	–	–	–	–	–	–	–	–	–	–	–	–	2	163	2	163
– –	15	1158	–	–	–	–	–	–	–	–	–	–	–	–	1	75	–	–	2	154	3	229
89498	931	781172	7	10614	22	22215	3	534	5	4130	–	–	16	19406	24	24070	16	9052	13	12026	32	18742	61	39820
– –	35	31813	–	–	–	–	–	–	–	–	10	9909	–	–	10	9909	–	–	–	–	3	2164	3	2164
– –	18	11637	–	–	–	–	–	–	–	–	1	327	–	–	1	327	–	–	–	–	–	–	–	–
– –	1	314																						
– –	5	751	–	–	–	–	–	–	–	–	1	169	–	–	1	169	–	–	–	–	2	2203	2	2203
– –	22	25924	–	–	–	–	–	–	–	–	1	1621	–	–	1	1621	..	–	–	–	–	–	–	–
– –	7	1288																						
– –	88	71727	–	–	–	–	–	–	–	–	13	12026	–	–	13	12026	–	–	–	–	5	4367	5	4367
89498	1019	852899	7	10614	22	22215	3	534	5	4130	13	12026	16	19406	37	36096	16	9052	13	12026	37	23109	66	44187

2 I

An ABSTRACT of the Ships and Vessels belonging to the British Navy at the commencement of the Year 18—

Letters of Reference.	RATE.	CLASS.				For Sea-service.						No.		For Harbour-service, &c.				British
						In Commission.		In Ordinary.		TOTAL.		British Built.	Foreign Built.	In Commission.		In Ordinary.		
						No.	Tons.	No.	Tons.	No.	Tons.			No.	Tons.	No.	Tons.	
		Three-deckers.																
A	First.	120-gun ship	—	—	—	2	5124	—	—	2	5124	2	—	—	—	—	—	
B	,,	112 ,,	18-pounder	—	—	1	2351	—	—	1	2351	1	—	—	—	—	—	
C	,,	,, ,,	12 ,,	—	—	1	2457	—	—	1	2457	—	1	1	2398	—	—	
D	,,	100 ,,	18 ,,	—	—	1	2286	1	2289	2	4575	2	—	—	—	—	—	
E	,,	,, ,,	12 ,,	—	—	1	2175	—	—	1	2175	1	—	—	—	1	2091	
F	Second.	98 ,,	18 ,,	—	—	1	2278	1	2276	2	4554	2	—	—	—	—	—	
H		,, ,,	12 ,,	—	—	5	10409	3	6146	8	16555	8	—	1	1944	4	8107	
		Two-deckers.																
I	Third.	80 ,,	—	—	—	5	10924	1	2257	6	13181	1	5	3	6294	2	4234	
K	,,	74 ,,	24-pounder	—	—	11	20971	1	1927	12	22898	10	2	—	—	1	1889	
L	,,	,, ,,	18 ,,	—	large	12	22375	4	7666	16	30041	8	8	5	9286	5	9396	
M	,,	,, ,,	,, ,,	—	middl.	41	71599	1	1743	42	73342	42	—	6	10504	8	13976	
N	,,	,, ,,	,, ,,	—	small	14	22962	6	9785	20	32747	20	—	6	9716	16	26075	
O	,,	64 ,,	—	—	—	7	9729	—	—	7	9729	7	—	17	23539	9	12407	
P	Fourth.	60 ,,	—	—	—	—	—	—	—	—	—	—	—	1	1285	—	—	
Q					Line	102	185640	18	34089	120	219729	104	16	40	64996	46	78175	
R		56 ,,	flush	—	—	—	—	—	—	—	—	—	—	1	1256	—	—	
T		50 ,,	com. or quarter-decked			4	4369	1	1123	5	5492	5	—	3	3136	4	4266	
U	Fifth.	44 ,,	—	—	—	2	1779	—	—	2	1779	2	—	1	882	—	—	
V		One-deckers.																
W	,,	44-gun frigate	—	—	—	2	2772	—	—	2	2772	2	—	—	—	3	4157	
X	,,	40 ,,	24-pounder	—	—	1	1277	—	—	1	1277	1	—	—	—	—	—	
Y	,,	,, ,,	18 ,,	—	—	2	2314	1	1160	3	3474	3	—	—	—	—	—	
Z	,,	38 ,,	,, ,,	—	large	41	45094	4	4379	45	49473	16	29	—	—	4	4346	
A	,,	,, ,,	,, ,,	—	small	7	6948	2	2022	9	8970	8	1	—	—	3	2966	
B	,,	36 ,,	18-pounder	—	large	6	6215	1	1051	7	7266	1	6	—	—	2	2041	
C	,,	,, ,,	,, ,,	—	small	35	32656	—	—	35	32656	32	3	1	926	4	3666	
D	,,	,, ,,	12 ,,	—	—	5	4564	—	—	5	4564	—	5	—	—	10	9274	
E	,,	32 ,,	18 ,,	—	large	5	4560	1	914	6	5474	6	—	—	—	—	—	
F	,,	,, ,,	,, ,,	—	small	2	1607	—	—	2	1607	2	—	—	—	—	—	
G	,,	,, ,,	12 ,,	—	large	3	2426	—	—	3	2426	—	3	—	—	3	2414	
H	,,	,, ,,	,, ,,	—	small	12	8176	5	3402	17	11578	15	2	1	688	4	2770	
I	Sixth.	28 ,,	—	—	—	3	2059	—	—	3	2059	2	1	—	—	4	2378	
K	,,	24-gun post-ship, quarter-decked				2	1188	1	521	3	1709	1	2	—	—	3	1604	
L	,,	22 ,,	—	—	—	9	4803	—	—	9	4803	9	—	—	—	4	1814	
M	,,	20 ,,	—	—	—	—	—	—	—	—	—	—	—	—	—	1	513	
O	,,	,, ,,	flush	—	—	3	1484	—	—	3	1484	1	2	—	—	1	513	
P	Sloops.	18-gun ship-sloop, quarter decked				36	15458	1	423	37	15881	37	—	—	—	2	854	
Q	,,	,, ,,	flush	—	—	7	2660	1	399	8	3059	6	2	—	—	4	1619	
R	,,	16 ,,	quarter-decked, large			14	5215	—	—	14	5215	14	—	1	425	2	791	
S	,,	,, ,,	,, ,,	—	small	—	—	—	—	—	—	—	—	—	—	1	326	
T	,,	,, ,,	flush	—	—	5	1919	—	—	5	1919	5	—	—	—	7	2479	
U	,,	14 ,,	quarter-decked	—	—	—	—	—	—	—	—	—	—	—	—	2	604	
W	,,	,, ,,	flush	—	—	—	—	—	—	—	—	—	—	—	—	1	340	
X	,,	18-gun brig-sloop	—	—	large	65	24936	—	—	65	24936	63	2	—	—	2	768	
Y	,,	,, ,,	—	—	small	—	—	—	—	—	—	—	—	—	—	—	—	
Z	,,	16 ,,	—	—	—	36	10987	1	315	37	11302	17	20	1	234	11	3594	
a	,,	14 ,,	—	—	—	12	3020	—	—	12	3020	11	1	—	—	1	239	
b	,,	10 ,,	—	—	—	31	7367	—	—	31	7367	31	—	—	—	—	—	
c		8 guns and 2 mortars				7	2510	—	—	7	2510	7	—	—	—	7	2238	
d	Bombs, of															1	425	
e	Fireships,	14 guns	—	—	—	7	1482	—	—	7	1482	2	5	—	—	1	215	
f	Gun-brigs,	12 ,,	—	—	—	60	10775	2	362	62	11137	61	1	1	160	2	313	
g	,,	10 ,,	—	—	—	—	—	—	—	—	—	—	—	—	—	—	—	
h	Cutters, &c.	14 ,,	—	—	—	8	1539	—	—	8	1539	1	7	—	—	—	—	
i	,,	12 ,,	—	—	—	4	600	—	—	4	600	1	3	—	—	3	415	
k	,,	10 ,,	—	—	—	29	4017	—	—	29	4017	21	8	—	—	—	—	
l	,,	8 ,,	—	—	—	1	100	—	—	1	100	1	—	—	—	—	—	
m	,,	6 ,,	—	—	—	3	264	—	—	3	264	2	1	—	—	—	—	
o	,,	4 ,,	—	—	—	13	1002	—	—	13	1002	13	—	—	—	—	—	
				Cruisers		584	413782	39	50160	623	463942	503	120	50	72673	142	135604	
q	Troop-ships	—	—	—	—	18	17197	1	849	19	18046	12	7	2	1295	13	11939	
r	Storeships	—	—	—	—	13	9503	—	—	13	9503	12	1	1	176	3	1181	
w	Surveying-vessels	—	—	—	—	2	435	—	—	2	435	2	—	—	—	—	—	
x	Advice-boats and Tenders					4	603	—	—	4	603	4	—	—	—	—	—	
a	Hospital, Prison, Receiving-ships, &c.					—	—	—	—	—	—	—	—	11	14203	8	8709	
b	Royal Yachts	—	—	—	—	—	—	—	—	—	—	—	—	7	1288	—	—	
			Troop-ships, &c.			37	27738	1	849	38	28587	30	8	21	16962	24	21829	
			GRAND TOTAL (b)			621	441520	40	51009	661	492529	533	128	71	89635	166	157433	

VOL. V.

455

No. 20.

	Grand Total		Built.				Purchased.				Converted from other Classes.		Ordered to be Built.		Total of Increase.		Captured, Destroyed, Wrecked, &c.		Converted to other Classes.		Sold, or taken to Pieces.		Total of Decrease.	
			King's Yards.		Merchants' Yards.		British Vessels or Enemy's Privateers.		Enemy's National Vessels.															
Tons.	No.	Tons.	No.	Tons.	No.	Tons	No.	Tons.	No.	Tons.	No.	Tons.	No.	Tons.	No.	Tons.	No.	Tons.	No.	Tons.	No.	Tons.	No.	Tons.
7848	5	12972																						
	1	2351																						
	2	4855																						
2404	3	6979																						
	2	4266																						
	2	4554																						
	13	26606	1	2149													1	1950	1	1876	1	1894	3	5720
6277	14	29986																				1	2143	1	2143
	13	24787																							
3669	28	52392									1	1876			1	1876									
36865	77	134687	1	1750	6	10593							2	3476	2	3476	1	1746			1	1562	1	1746
	42	68538															1	1603					2	3165
	33	45675																							
	1	1285																							
57063	236	419933	2	3899	6	10593					1	1876	2	3476	3	5352	3	5299	1	1876	3	5599	7	12774
	1	1256																							
3599	15	16493											1	1227	1	1227			1	1056			1	1056
1221	1	1321											1	1321	1	1321								
	3	2661																							
	5	6929																							
	1	1277																							
	3	3474																							
8720	57	62539	1	1077					3	3281					3	3281	1	1076			2	2154	3	3230
	12	11936															1	990			1	1011	1	990
	9	9307															1	1046					2	2057
5695	46	42943	2	1823	1	949							1	947	1	947	1	951			2	1804	1	951
	15	13838																					2	1804
	6	5474															1	895					1	895
	2	1607																							
	6	4840																			1	766	1	766
	22	15036							1	692					1	692					5	3463	5	3463
	7	4437																			4	2429	4	2429
	6	3313																			1	604	1	604
538	10	5341																							
	4	1814																			2	912	2	912
509	5	2506	1	512									1	509	1	509					2	1017	2	1017
427	40	17162																							
798	14	5476											2	798	2	798					4	1515	4	1515
	17	6431															1	371			1	371	2	742
	1	326																			1	326	1	326
	12	4398																			1	301	1	301
	2	604																	2	674	1	305	3	979
	1	340																							
5402	81	31106									1	316	14	5402	15	5718	3	1148			2	773	5	1921
	49	15130																	1	316	1	319	2	635
253	14	3512															1	285			5	1544	6	1829
	31	7367																			5	1097	5	1097
	14	4748									3	1045			3	1045					3	1084	3	1084
	1	425																							
2178	8	1697																			1	220	1	220
	77	13788							2	355			12	2178	14	2533	5	904			3	509	8	1413
	8	1539															1	176					1	176
	7	1015																							
	29	4017			2	288	1	111					2	288	3	399	4	528			3	402	7	930
	1	100																							
	3	264																							
	13	1002															2	156					2	156
86503	895	758722	6	7311	9	11830	1	111	6	4328	5	3237	36	16146	48	23822	24	13454	6	4293	54	28525	84	46272
	34	31280									1	1056			1	1056					2	1589	2	1589
	17	10860	1	121									1	121	1	121	1	777					1	777
	4	603																			1	148	1	148
	19	22912																			3	3012	3	3012
	7	1288																							
	83	67378	1	121							1	1056	1	121	2	1177	1	777			6	4749	7	5526
86503	978	826100	7	7432	9	11830	1	111	6	4328	6	4293	37	16267	50	24999	25	14231	6	4293	60	33274	91	51798

2 K

An ABSTRACT of the Ships and Vessels belonging to the British Navy at the commencement of the Year

Letters of Reference.	RATE.	CLASS.	For Sea-service.						No.		For Harbour-service, &c				British
			In Commission.		In Ordinary.		TOTAL.		British Built.	Foreign Built.	In Commission.		In Ordinary		
			No.	Tons.	No.	Tons.	No.	Tons.			No.	Tons.	No.	Tons.	
	Three-deckers.														
A	First.	120-gun ship — — — — — —	2	5124	—	—	2	5124	2	—	—	—	—	—	
B	,,	112 ,, — — — — — —	1	2351	—	—	1	2351	1	—	—	—	—	—	
C	,,	100 ,, 18-pounder — — —	1	2457	—	—	1	2457	—	1	1	2398	—	—	
D	,,	,, ,, 12 ,, — — —	2	4575	—	—	2	4575	2	—	—	—	—	—	
E	,,	,, ,, 18 ,, — — —	1	2175	—	—	1	2175	1	—	—	—	1	2091	
F	Second.	98 ,, 12 ,, — — —	1	2278	1	2276	2	4554	2	—	—	—	—	—	
G	,,	,, ,, 18 ,, — — —	4	8275	3	6159	7	14434	7	—	1	1944	5	10228	
H		,, ,, 12 ,, — — —													
	Two-deckers.														
K	Third.	80 ,, — — — — — —	2	4396	4	8785	6	13181	1	5	3	4294	2	4234	
L	,,	74 ,, 24-pounder — — —	10	19191	1	1854	11	21045	9	2	—	—	2	3742	
M	,,	,, ,, 18 ,, — large	10	18362	7	13259	17	91821	9	8	5	9286	5	9396	
N	,,	,, ,, ,, ,, — middl.	52	90917	1	1742	53	92659	53	—	8	14011	6	10469	
O	,,	,, ,, ,, ,, — small	14	22990	4	6477	18	29467	18	—	6	9716	16	26086	19
P	,,	64 ,, ,, ,, — —	2	2793	1	1388	3	4181	3	—	16	22232	13	17890	17
Q	Fourth.	60 ,, — — — — —	—	—	—	—	—	—	—	—	1	285	—	—	
		Line — —	102	186084	22	41940	124	228024	108	16	41	67166	50	84136	5
R	,,	56 ,, flush — — — —	—	—	—	—	—	—	—	—	1	1256	—	—	
S	,,	50 ,, common or quar.-decked	2	2136	1	1173	3	3309	3	—	3	3136	5	5326	
T	,,	,, ,, flush — — — —	—	—	—	—	—	—	—	—	—	—	—	—	
U	Fifth.	44 ,, — — — — — —	2	1779	—	—	2	1779	2	—	1	882	—	—	
	One-deckers.														
W	,,	44-gun frigate — — — —	2	2772	—	—	2	2772	2	—	—	—	2	2787	
X	,,	40 ,, 24-pounder — — —	1	1251	2	2528	2	2528	2	—	—	—	—	—	
Y	,,	,, ,, 18 ,, — — —	2	2314	1	1160	3	3474	3	—	—	—	—	—	
Z	,,	38 ,, — — — — large	40	43678	3	3211	43	46979	20	23	—	—	6	6732	
A	,,	,, ,, — — — — small	3	2992	3	2988	6	5980	5	1	—	—	4	3981	
B	,,	36 ,, 18-pounder — large	6	6215	1	1051	7	7266	1	6	—	—	2	2041	
C	,,	,, ,, ,, — small	34	31815	—	—	34	31815	32	2	1	926	6	5494	
D	,,	,, ,, 12 ,, — —	3	2806	—	—	3	2806	—	3	—	—	12	11032	
E	,,	32 ,, 18 ,, — large	5	4560	—	—	5	4560	5	—	—	—	—	—	
F	,,	,, ,, ,, ,, — small	2	1607	—	—	2	1607	2	—	—	—	3	2414	
G	,,	,, ,, 12 ,, — large	2	1578	—	—	2	1578	—	2	1	688	4	2767	
H	,,	28 ,, ,, ,, — small	11	7496	1	672	12	8168	12	—	—	—	4	2378	
I	Sixth.	,, ,, — — — — —	1	679	—	...	1	679	1	—	—	—	3	1604	
K	,,	24-gun post-ship, quarter-decked	2	1188	1	521	3	1709	1	2	—	—	—	—	
L	,,	,, ,, flush — —	1	812	—	—	1	812	—	1	—	—	—	—	
M	,,	22 ,, quarter-decked —	10	5341	—	—	10	5341	10	—	—	—	4	1814	
O	,,	20 ,, ,, ,, —	—	—	—	—	—	—	—	—	—	—	1	513	
P	,,	flush	4	1993	—	—	4	1993	2	2	—	—	2	854	
R	Sloops.	18-gun ship-sloop, quarter-decked	35	15027	2	554	37	15581	37	—	—	—	4	1619	
S	,,	,, ,, flush —	19	3892	1	399	11	4291	8	3	—	—	4	1534	
T	,,	16 ,, quarter-decked, large	12	4472	—	—	12	4472	12	—	1	425	1	326	
U	,,	,, ,, ,, small	—	—	—	—	—	—	—	—	—	—	7	2479	
V	,,	,, ,, flush ,,	2	775	—	—	2	775	2	—	—	—	2	604	
W	,,	14 ,, quarter-decked —	—	—	—	—	—	—	—	—	—	—	1	340	
X	,,	,, ,, flush — —	—	—	—	—	—	—	—	—	—	—	—	—	
Y	,,	18-gun brig-sloop — — large	76	29182	1	385	77	29567	75	2	—	—	—	—	
Z	,,	,, ,, — — small	—	—	—	—	—	—	—	—	—	—	—	—	
a	,,	16 ,, — — — —	31	9576	1	284	32	9860	13	19	1	234	10	3242	
b	,,	14 ,, — — — —	13	3233	—	—	13	3233	11	2	—	—	1	239	
c	,,	10 ,, — — — —	30	7130	—	—	30	7130	30	—	—	—	—	—	
d	Bombs, of	8 guns and 2 mortars — —	6	2177	—	—	6	2177	6	—	—	—	4	1309	
e	Fireships,	14 guns — — — —	—	—	—	—	—	—	—	—	—	—	1	425	
f	Gun-brigs.	,, ,, — — — —	6	1272	—	—	6	1272	2	4	—	—	1	215	
g	,,	12 ,, — — — —	65	11680	1	178	66	11858	65	1	1	160	—	—	
h	Cutters, &c.	14 ,, — — — —	8	1609	—	—	8	1609	2	6	—	—	1	197	
i	,,	12 ,, — — — —	3	459	—	—	3	459	1	2	—	—	3	445	
k	,,	10 ,, — — — —	25	3577	—	—	25	3577	19	6	—	—	—	—	
l	,,	8 ,, — — — —	1	100	—	—	1	100	1	—	—	—	—	—	
m	,,	6 ,, — — — —	2	182	—	—	2	182	1	1	—	—	—	—	
n	,,	4 ,, — — — —	10	774	—	—	10	774	10	—	—	—	—	—	
		Cruisers —	570	404303	40	56093	610	460396	506	104	51	74873	148	146817	116
q	Troop-ships — — — — — —		24	21537	—	—	24	21537	18	6	2	1295	14	12971	10
r	Storeships — — — — — —		13	9503	—	—	13	9513	12	1	1	176	3	1181	
w	Surveying-vessels — — — — —		2	435	—	—	2	435	2	—	—	—	—	—	
x	Advice-boats — — — — —		4	603	—	—	4	603	4	—	—	—	—	—	
a	Hospital, Prison, Receiving-ships, &c.		—	—	—	—	—	—	—	—	11	14203	9	9558	10
b	Royal Yachts — — — —		—	—	—	—	—	—	—	—	7	1298	—	—	
		Troop-ships, &c. —	43	32078	—	—	43	32078	36	7	21	16962	26	23710	3
		GRAND TOTAL (e) — —	613	436381	40	56093	653	492474	542	111	72	91835	174	170527	14

VOL. V.

No. 21.

		Increase and Decrease in the Classes since the date of the last Year's Abstract.																		
Building, or ordered to Built.		Grand Total.		Built				Purchased.				Converted from other Classes.		Ordered to be Built.		Total of Increase.		Captured, Destroyed, Wrecked, &c.		Converted to other Classes.		Sold, or taken to Pieces.		Total of Decrease.	
				King's Yards.		Merchants' Yards.		British Vessels or Enemy's Privateers.		Enemy's National Vessels.															
Tons.	No	Tons.	No.	Tons.	No.	Tons.	No.	Tons.	No.	Tons.	No.	Tons.	No.	Tons.	No.	Tons.	No.	Tons.	No.	Tons.	No.	Tons.	No.	Tons.
13066	7	18190	–	–	–	–	–	–	–	–	–	–	2	5218	2	5218								
4834	3	7185	–	–	–	–	–	–	–	–	–	–	2	4834	2	4834								
–	2	4855																						
2404	3	6979																						
–	2	4266																						
–	3	4554																						
–	13	26606																						
8325	13	32034	–	–	–	–	–	–	–	–	1	2048	1	2048										
–	13	24787																						
1809	28	52312	1	1860	–	–	–	–	1	1804	–	–	1	1804	–	–	–	–	1	1884	1	1884
28002	83	145141	–	–	11	19317	–	–	–	–	6	10454	6	10454								
–	40	65269	–	–	–	–	–	–	–	–	–	–	–	–	–	–	–	–	2	3269	2	3269
–	32	44303	–	–	–	–	–	–	–	–	–	–	–	–	–	–	–	–	1	1372	1	1372
–	1	1285																						
58440	244	437766	1	1860	11	19317	–	–	1	1804	–	–	11	22554	12	24358	–	–	–	–	4	6525	4	6525
–	1	1256																						
3599	14	15370	–	–	–	–	–	–	–	–	–	–	–	–	–	–	1	1123	–	–	1	1123
1321	1	1321																						
–	3	2661																						
–	4	5559	–	–	–	–	–	–	–	–	–	–	–	–	–	–	–	–	1	1370	1	1370
5021	6	7549	–	–	1	1251	–	–	–	–	5	6272	5	6272								
–	3	3474																						
18401	66	72112	4	4312	1	1083	–	–	–	–	14	15076	14	15076	4	4350	–	–	1	1153	5	5503
–	10	9961	–	–	–	–	–	–	–	–	–	–	–	–	–	–	–	–	2	1975	2	1975
–	9	9307																						
14221	56	52456	2	1894	1	949	–	–	–	–	12	11369	12	11369	1	947	–	–	1	909	2	1856
–	15	13838																						
–	5	4560	–	–	–	–	–	–	–	–	–	–	–	–	1	914	–	–	–	–	1	914
–	2	1607																						
–	5	3992	–	–	–	–	–	–	–	–	–	–	–	–	–	–	–	–	1	848	1	848
–	17	11623	–	–	–	–	–	–	–	–	–	–	–	–	4	2730	1	683	–	–	5	3413
–	5	3057	–	–	–	–	–	–	–	–	–	–	–	–	1	775	1	605	–	–	2	1380
–	6	3313																						
–	1	812	–	–	–	–	1	812d	–	–	–	–	–	–	1	812						
–	10	5341	–	–	1	538	–	–	–	–	–	–	–	–								
447	5	2261	–	–	–	–	–	–	–	–	1	447	1	447								
3274	12	5780	1	509	–	–	–	–	–	–	7	3274	7	3274								
427	40	17162																						
–	15	5910	–	–	2	798	–	–	1	434	–	–	1	434								
–	17	6431																						
–	1	326																						
–	9	3254	–	–	–	–	–	–	–	–	–	–	–	–	2	783	–	–	1	361	3	1144
–	2	604																						
–	1	340																						
6177	93	35744	–	–	15	5784	–	–	1	384	17	6559	18	6943	3	1151	–	–	3	1154	6	2305
–	43	13336	–	–	–	–	–	–	–	–	–	–	–	–	3	855	–	–	3	939	6	1794
253	15	3725	–	–	–	–	–	–	1	213	–	–	1	213								
713	33	7843	–	–	–	–	–	–	–	–	3	713	3	713	1	237	–	–	–	–	1	237
1363	14	4849	–	–	–	–	–	–	–	–	4	1363	4	1363	–	–	–	–	4	1262	4	1262
–	1	425																						
–	7	1487	–	–	–	–	–	–	–	–	–	–	–	–	–	–	–	–	1	210	1	210
1461	75	13479	–	–	10	1817	–	–	–	–	6	1100	6	1100	5	918	–	–	3	491	8	1409
–	9	1806	–	–	1	214	1	225	–	–	1	214	2	439	–	–	–	–	1	172	1	172
–	6	874																		1	141	1	141
–	25	3577	–	–	–	–	2	289	–	–	–	–	2	289	3	366	–	–	3	363	6	729
–	1	100																						
–	2	182	–	–	–	–	–	–	–	–	–	–	–	–	3	228	–	–	1	82	1	82
–	10	774																				2	228
115118	919	797204	8	8575	43	31751	4	1326	4	2835	–	–	81	68941	89	73102	26	10610	7	5372	32	18638	65	34620
–	40	35803	–	–	–	–	–	–	–	–	7	5572	–	–	7	5572	–	–	1	849	–	–	1	849
–	17	10860																						
–	2	435																						
–	4	603																						
–	20	23761	–	–	–	–	–	–	1	849	–	–	–	–	1	849						
–	7	1288																						
–	90	72750	–	–	–	–	–	–	–	–	8	6221	–	–	8	6221	–	–	1	849	–	–	1	849
115118	1009	869954	8	8575	43	31751	4	1326	4	2835	8	6221	81	68941	97	79323	26	10610	8	6221	32	18638	66	35469

NOTES TO ANNUAL ABSTRACTS.

NOTES TO ABSTRACT No. 18.

(*a*) Number of hired vessels about 64.

NOTES TO ABSTRACT No. 19.

(*a*) The Queen Charlotte, built from the draught of a ship of the same name, accidentally burnt in the year 1800. See vol. ii., p. 429. Hence a British first-rate is launched in 1810, which was designed in 1779 or 1780. Surely it is sufficient to perpetuate the name without the faults of an old ship. The first Queen Charlotte was never an extraordinary sailer, and her lower-deck ports were only four feet and a half from the water: the inconvenience she suffered on that account, in the action on the 29th of May 1794, may be seen stated at vol. i., p. 154.

(*b*) Number of hired vessels about 60

NOTES TO ABSTRACT No. 20.

(*a*) The Hogue, commonly called the *La* Hogue; an appellation sanctioned not only by Steel's, but, until very recently, by the Admiralty Navy List.

(*b*) Number of hired vessels about 52.

NOTES TO ABSTRACT No. 21.

(*a*) The Forth, built of fir. The remaining four in the "Building" column are the Liffey and Severn, also of fir, and the Glasgow and Liverpool of pitch-pine.

(*b*) Of these 14 frigates, two were ordered to be built of teak, four of oak, and the remainder of red pine.

(*c*) Of these 12 frigates, two were ordered to be built of oak, three of yellow and the remainder of red pine.

(*d*) Late the Hannibal, American merchantman; an extraordinarily fine ship, mounting 24 guns on a flush deck.

(*e*) Number of hired vessels about 52.

END OF VOL. V.

www.ingramcontent.com/pod-product-compliance
Lightning Source LLC
Chambersburg PA
CBHW070949160426
43193CB00012B/1811